CONSUMER BEHAVIOR

Consumer

PRENTICE-HALL, INC., ENGLEWOOD CLIFFS, N.J. 07632

Behavior

LEON G. SCHIFFMAN

Baruch College
City University of New York

LESLIE LAZAR KANUK

Baruch College
City University of New York

Library of Congress Cataloging in Publication Data

Schiffman, Leon G
   Consumer behavior.

   Includes bibliographical references and index.
     1. Consumers.   2. Motivation research (Marketing)
3. Diffusion of innovations.   I. Kanuk, Leslie Lazar,
joint author.   II. Title.
HF541 5.3.S29   658.8'34   77-25032
ISBN   0-1 3-1 69201-1

CONSUMER BEHAVIOR
Leon G. Shiffman and Leslie Lazar Kanuk

Printed in the United States of America

10 9 8 7 6 5 4 3 2 1

Prentice-Hall International, Inc., *London*
Prentice-Hall of Australia Pty. Limited, *Sydney*
Prentice-Hall of Canada, Ltd., *Toronto*
Prentice-Hall of India Private Limited, *New Delhi*
Prentice-Hall of Japan, Inc., *Tokyo*
Prentice-Hall of Southeast Asia Pte. Ltd., *Singapore*
Whitehall Books Limited, *Wellington, New Zealand*

To Arlene Schiffman and Jack L. Kanuk

contents

part **II**

THE CONSUMER AS AN INDIVIDUAL   *21*

2 consumer needs and motivation   23

7 communication and consumer behavior   170

part **III**

SOCIAL AND CULTURAL DIMENSIONS OF CONSUMER BEHAVIOR   *201*

10 personal influence and the opinion leadership process   262

11 social class and consumer behavior   293

12 the influence of culture on consumer behavior   329

15 consumer decision making   432

preface

All of us like to think we practice what we preach. As professors of marketing, we long have "preached" the marketing concept; that is, that marketers should develop products which meet the needs of the consumer.

This book is based on the very same premise. Its entire focus has been to meet the needs of *our* consumers—the students who for years have individually and collectively asked for a text that is highly readable and that clearly and simply explains the relevant concepts and theories upon which the discipline of consumer behavior is based. Furthermore, our book is designed to answer the perennial student question, "So what?" by showing how these concepts can help a marketing practitioner develop more effective marketing strategies.

We have attempted to write a book that is comprehensive without being encyclopedic. We have tried to prepare an inviting and provocative textbook, one which would capture the imagination and the interest of both undergraduate and graduate students alike. We strongly believe that we have achieved a good balance among three specific content areas: selected behavioral science concepts, relevant consumer research and practical marketing applications.

We are convinced that the major contribution of consumer behavior studies to the practice of marketing is the provision of structure and direction for effective market segmentation. Consumer behavior provides the framework which enables the marketer to identify the specific market which he best can serve. We have attempted to illustrate the application of consumer behavior concepts to a wide range of market segmentation problems. It is our hope that this book will provide the future marketer with relevant insights into consumer behavior which will enable him to make informed marketing decisions.

The book is divided into four parts: Part I introduces the reader to the study of consumer behavior. It discusses what consumer behavior is, how and why it developed, and how consumer behavior findings are used by marketing practitioners. In addition, it discusses the theory and practice of market segmentation, and shows how consumer behavior provides the conceptual framework and strategic direction for the practical segmentation of markets.

Part II discusses the consumer as an individual. It examines the underlying concepts of consumer motivation, perception, learning, personality, and attitude formation and change. This section concludes with a discussion of communication, and relates the consumer as an individual to the world and the people around him. Thus, it serves as a "bridge" between Parts II and III.

Part III deals with the social and cultural dimensions of consumer behavior. It discusses group dynamics and consumer reference groups, the influence of the family, the influence of other individuals and opinion leaders, and the influence of social class on consumer behavior. It examines the consumer in his cultural milieu, and investigates the influence of societal values, beliefs, and customs on consumer behavior. Then it discusses the consumer as a member of various subcultures, with their own special values, beliefs, and customs. This part concludes with a discussion of consumer behavior in other countries, and indicates the need for careful cross-cultural analyses in this period of increasing multinational marketing.

Part IV discusses the diffusion of innovations: how new products get accepted and adopted throughout a market. It concludes with a chapter that describes how consumers make product decisions, and offers the reader a simple theoretical model of consumer decision making which ties together all of the concepts discussed throughout the book.

Of the many people we wish to thank for their help in the preparation of this book, we would especially like to thank our own consumers, the students who have encouraged us to write it, and the graduate and undergraduate students who have given us their critical comments during its development. Our special thanks go, too, to Professor Michael L. Ray of Stanford University, for writing Chapters 4 and 6.

We would like to thank Professor Conrad Berenson, Chairman of the Marketing Department at Baruch College, for his encouragement, his advice, and his continued support, our colleagues at Baruch for their invaluable suggestions, and Professor William R. Dillon of the University of Massachusetts for reviewing the manuscript and for his constructive suggestions throughout. Other people who have provided valuable assistance include Maureen Coughlin, Joe Wisenblit, Bennie

Barak, Amy Fong, and our typist, Diane Merritts, who labored long and hard in helping us meet our deadlines.

Finally, our families have been exceedingly patient and understanding during the long months that this book was in work. We acknowledge their love and their support by dedicating this book to them: to Arlene, Janet, and David Schiffman, and to Jack, Randi, and Alan Kanuk.

LEON G. SCHIFFMAN
LESLIE LAZAR KANUK

INTRODUCTION

1

Part I is designed to introduce the reader to the study of consumer behavior. It sets the stage for the remainder of the book by focusing on (1) what consumer behavior is, (2) why we study consumer behavior, (3) how firms apply consumer behavior findings, and (4) how and why consumer behavior has developed as a theoretical and applied discipline. In addition, Part I discusses the theory and practice of market segmentation and demonstrates how consumer behavior provides both the conceptual framework and the strategic direction for the practical segmentation of markets.

consumer behavior: introduction

1

Introduction

One of the few common denominators among all of us — no matter what our education, our politics, or our commitments — is that, above all, we are consumers. That is, we use or consume — on a regular basis — food, clothing, shelter, transportation, education, brooms, dishes, vacations, necessities, luxuries, services, even ideas. As consumers, we play a vital role in the health of the economy — local, national, and international. The decisions we make concerning our consumption behavior affect the demand for basic raw materials, for transportation, for production, for banking; they affect the employment of workers and the deployment of resources, the success of some industries and the failure of others. Thus, consumer behavior is an integral factor in the ebbs and flows of *all* business in a consumer-oriented society such as our own.

This book is designed to give the reader a strong understanding of the basic principles of consumer behavior, an insight into the scientific investigations on which our knowledge of consumer behavior is based, and an awareness of how these consumer behavior findings can be practically applied to the professional practice of marketing.

This chapter introduces the reader to the notion of consumer behavior as an interdisciplinary science designed to investigate the decision-making activities of the individual in his consumption role. It describes the reasons for the development of consumer behavior as an academic discipline and an applied science. The role and scope of the research process in the study of consumer behavior is considered. The chapter discusses the evolution of marketing in this country from a production orientation to a selling orientation to a consumer orientation, and examines the importance of market segmentation strategies in a consumer-oriented economy. Finally, it demonstrates how market segmentation as a strategy is dependent upon the insights and revelations provided by a knowledge of consumer behavior.

WHAT IS CONSUMER BEHAVIOR?

The term *consumer behavior* can be defined as *the behavior that consumers display in searching for, purchasing, using and evaluating products, services and ideas which they expect will satisfy their needs*. The study of consumer behavior is the study of how individuals make decisions to spend their available resources (money, time, effort) on consumption-related items. It includes the study of *what* they buy, *why* they buy it, *how* they buy it, *when* they buy it, *where* they buy it, and *how often* they buy it. Thus, the study of an individual's consumption behavior in the area of toothpaste products might include a study of which brand of toothpaste he buys (e.g., Close-Up), why he buys it (because he believes that it will whiten his teeth better than competing brands), how he buys it (for cash and coupon), when he buys it (when he does the food shopping), where he buys it (in a supermarket) and how often he buys it (approximately every three weeks).

A study of another individual's consumption behavior regarding a more durable item, such as a rug, might include a study of what kind of rug she buys (e.g., a handloomed six-by-nine-foot rug), why she buys it (to give physical and visual warmth to her living room and to impress her friends), how she buys it (on credit), when she buys it (on home-furnishings sale days), where she buys it (at a well-known department store), and how often she buys or replaces it (when it is worn or when she refurnishes her living room).

In many cases, the study of consumer behavior goes even further and examines the feelings and the actions of the consumer *after* she makes her purchase. For example, it seeks to discover if she suffers feelings of remorse or dissatisfaction about her decision, and how such feelings affect her communications to her friends and her future purchase decisions.

types of consumers

The term *consumer* is often used to describe two different kinds of consuming entities: (1) the personal consumer, and (2) the organizational consumer. The *personal consumer* is the individual who buys goods and services for her own use (e.g., lipstick), for the use of her household (a cake mix) or for just one member of her household (a shirt), or even as a gift for a friend (a book). In all of these contexts, the goods are bought for final or "end" use by individuals, who are referred to as "end users" or "ultimate consumers."

The second category of consumer, the *organizational consumer*, encompasses private businesses, government agencies (local, state, and national), and institutions (schools, churches, prisons), all of which must buy products, equipment, and services in order to run their organizations—whether for profit or nonprofit. Manufacturing companies must buy the raw materials and other components to manufacture and sell their own products; service companies must buy the equipment necessary to render the services they sell; government agencies must buy the variety of products they need to operate their departments; and institutions must buy the materials they need to maintain themselves and their populations.

Despite the importance of both categories of consumers—individuals and organizations—this book will focus on the individual consumer, who purchases for his or her own personal use or for household use. End-use consumption is perhaps the most pervasive of all types of consumer behavior, since it involves every individual, of every age and every background, in the role of either buyer, or user, or both.

buyers versus users

Inherent in the notion that individuals buy products for themselves and their families is the distinction that exists between buyers and users. The person who makes the actual purchase is not always the user, or the only user, of the product in question. Nor is she necessarily the person who makes the product decision. A mother may buy toys for her children (who are the users); she may buy food for dinner (and be one of the users); she may buy a handbag (and be the only user). She may buy a record that one of her teenagers requested, or a magazine that her husband requested, or she and her husband together may buy a car they both selected. The various influences on family product-related decisions are discussed in detail in Chapter 9; suffice it here to stress the fact that buyers are not always the users, or the only users, of the products they buy, nor are they necessarily the persons who make the product selection decisions.

prospects

Marketers must decide at whom to direct their promotional efforts; in so doing, they must identify the best *prospect* for the product they want to sell. Some marketers believe that the buyer of the product is the best prospect, others believe it is the user of the product, while still others play it safe by directing their promotional efforts to both buyers and users. For example, some toy manufacturers advertise their products on children's television shows to reach the users, others advertise in *Parents' Magazine* to reach the buyers, while still others run dual campaigns designed to reach both children and their mothers. Because such toy marketers are uncertain as to how much influence the child exerts on his mother, they try to favorably influence her so that she will be receptive to her child's request to buy the toy in question.

WHY WE STUDY CONSUMER BEHAVIOR

The study of consumer behavior is concerned not only with *how* consumers behave, but with *why* they behave as they do. As consumers, it is important for us to study consumer behavior so that we may gain greater insight into our own consumer-related decisions: what we buy, why we buy, and how we buy. The study of consumer behavior enables us to analyze our own consumption decisions and makes us aware of the subtle influences that persuade us to make the product choices we do.

As students of human behavior, it is important for us to understand the internal and external influences that impel individuals to act in certain consumption-related ways. Consumer behavior is simply a subset of the larger field of human behavior. As scientists, we are interested in understanding every aspect of human behavior. Certainly, as scientists, we should also want to understand the special aspect of human behavior known as consumer behavior.

As future marketers, it is important for us to be sufficiently well versed in the field of consumer behavior so that we may make meaningful contributions to the development of marketing strategy when we enter our chosen profession. Without doubt, marketers who do understand consumer behavior have a great competitive advantage in the marketplace.

HOW MARKETING FIRMS USE CONSUMER BEHAVIOR

To operate successfully, marketing firms must have a thorough understanding—explicit rather than implicit—of what makes consumers buy. They have to know *why* they buy, what *needs* they are trying to fulfill, and what outside *influences* affect their product choices in order to design marketing strategies that will favorably influence related consumer decisions.

designing marketing strategies

Marketers use an understanding of consumer behavior to anticipate future behavior based on the implementation of specific marketing strategies. For example, an awareness of the consumer's predispositions and needs and present attitudes toward the product enables the marketer to design an effective marketing mix, using variables over which he has control (such as advertising messages, packaging, pricing, retail outlets) to favorably influence the consumer to buy his product. As depicted in Figure 1–1, *understanding* (and this is true of any human phenom-

FIGURE 1–1

Knowledge of Consumer Behavior Facilitates Development of Successful Marketing Strategies

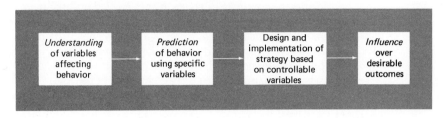

enon) permits *prediction,* which in turn permits the development of strategies designed to achieve favorable results.

measuring marketing performance

Clearly, a knowledge of consumer behavior serves as a strong basis for the development of marketing strategies. However, not only does consumer behavior *affect* marketing strategy, it also serves to *reflect* marketing strategy. A careful monitoring of consumer behavior in the marketplace enables the marketer to measure the success or failure of a specific marketing strategy. For example, if an advertising campaign that stresses a product's convenience does not produce the anticipated sales volume, the marketer may conclude that convenience is not a major factor in the decision to buy his product, and endeavor to find a more effective marketing strategy.

segmenting markets

Marketers also use a knowledge of consumer behavior to segment their markets. The American consumer market is made up of some 210 million consumers who consume over $1.3 trillion worth of products and services each year. With such a vast market, made up of individuals who vary significantly in terms of their education, ages, interests, incomes, occupations, tastes, attitudes, residences, and so forth, it would be close to impossible for the average marketer to design a marketing mix (product, price, promotion, and distribution strategy) with sufficiently universal appeal to influence the purchase decisions of all.

The strategy that most marketers have developed to handle their vast potential market is to divide it up into smaller subgroups—or segments—each of which is similar (i.e., homogeneous) regarding some characteristic that is relevant to the purchase or the usage of the product or product category. This process is called market segmentation. One of the major contributions of consumer behavior to marketers is the identification of meaningful variables upon which to segment markets. (Market segmentation will be discussed in greater detail later in this chapter and is a basic theme throughout the book.)

The field of consumer behavior is based upon concepts and theories about people, which have been developed by scientists in disciplines and fields of inquiry other than marketing. This "interdisciplinary" nature of consumer behavior is perhaps its greatest strength: it serves to integrate existing knowledge from other fields into a comprehensive body of information about the consumer. Although the study of consumer behavior is of relatively recent origin, its underpinnings are rooted in strong scientific evidence that has emerged from many years of research by scientists specializing in the study of human behavior.

The major disciplines on which consumer behavior is based (i.e., from which it "borrows") include psychology, sociology, social psychology, cultural anthropology, and economics.

PSYCHOLOGY

Psychology is the study of the individual. It includes the study of his motivations, his perceptions, his attitudes, his personality, and how he learns. All of these factors are integral to an understanding of consumer behavior. They enable us to understand the various consumption needs of the individual, his actions and reactions in response to different products and product messages, and the way his personality and previous experiences affect his product choices.

SOCIOLOGY

Sociology is the study of groups. Group behavior — the actions of individuals in groups — often differs from the actions of individuals operating alone. The influence of group memberships, family structure, and social class on consumer behavior are all relevant to the study of consumer segments in the marketplace.

SOCIAL PSYCHOLOGY

Social psychology is an amalgam of sociology and psychology. It is the study of how an individual operates in a group. The study of consumer behavior is not only the study of how groups operate in terms of market behavior; it is also the study of how individuals are influenced in their personal consumption behavior by those whose opinions they respect: their peers, their reference groups, their families, and opinion leaders.

CULTURAL ANTHROPOLOGY

The study of man in society is the study of cultural anthropology. It traces the development of the core beliefs, values, and customs that are passed down to the individual from his parents and grandparents and which influence much of his purchase and consumption behavior. It also includes the study of subcultures (subgroups within the larger society) and lends itself to a comparison of consumers of different nationalities with diverse cultures and customs.

ECONOMICS

An important component of the study of economics is the study of the consumer: how he spends his funds, how he evaluates alternatives, and how he makes decisions to maximize his satisfactions. Many of the early theories concerning consumer behavior were based on economic theory. For example, the "economic man" theory postulates that individuals act rationally to maximize their utilities (i.e., their benefits) in the purchase of goods and services. More recent consumer studies have indicated that man often acts less than rationally (i.e., emotionally) to fulfill his psychological needs.

Research in consumer behavior

To gain a greater understanding of consumers and their life-styles, consumer researchers engage in extensive behavioral research into consumers and their consumption practices. As in any science, consumer behavior theories must be tested and either supported or rejected before conclusions can be generalized and applied to marketing practice. Some consumer behavior research is conducted on the basis of observations of actual behavior in the marketplace, other research is conducted under controlled conditions in the laboratory, and still other research is based on the manipulation of marketing variables within a simulated marketing context. Only through the constant testing, evaluation, rejection, and support of related hypotheses can a conceptual framework be developed that permits us to understand consumer behavior in depth. Consumer behavior research also enables marketers to carve out new market segments based on variables that emerge as important discriminators among consumers for a specific product or product category.

SCOPE OF CONSUMER BEHAVIOR RESEARCH

Consumer behavior research takes place at every phase of the consumption process: from *before the purchase* takes place (when the consumer first becomes aware of her needs, searches for information on how best to fulfill them, and evaluates various product alternatives), to the *actual purchase decision* (including product and brand choice, store choice, method of payment), to *after the purchase* takes place (through any periods of uncertainty, satisfaction, dissatisfaction, repurchase, or further search in the marketplace).

Development of consumer behavior as a discipline

There are a number of reasons why consumer behavior has developed as a separate discipline. Marketing scientists had long noted that consumers did not always act or react as economic theory would suggest. The size of the consumer market in this country was vast and still growing. Billions of dollars were being spent on goods and services by millions of people. The development of consumer behavior studies was in fact an outgrowth of the evolution of marketing philosophy and practice.

IMPACT OF THE MARKETING CONCEPT

At the end of World War II, marketers found that they could sell almost any goods they could produce to consumers who had long done without because the nation's manufacturing facilities had been mobilized for the production of war materials. After consumer production had been resumed for a number of years, the public's appetite for consumer goods was somewhat sated and people began to exercise discrimination in their selection of products.

At this point, many companies went from a production orientation to a selling orientation; that is, they switched their primary focus from production to selling. During this period, companies exerted a tremendous "hard sell" on consumers in order to move the goods that they had decided to produce.

Finally, in the early 1950s, many marketers began to realize that they could sell more goods, more easily, if they produced only those goods that they had already determined consumers would buy. Instead of trying to get customers to buy what the firm has produced, a marketing-oriented firm tries to sell only what the customers want. Thus, consumers' needs become the firm's primary focus. This consumer-oriented marketing philosophy has come to be known as the "marketing concept."

The widespread adoption of the marketing concept by American business provided the impetus for the study of consumer behavior. To identify unsatisfied needs of consumers, companies had to engage in extensive marketing and consumer research. In so doing, they discovered that consumers were highly complex individuals, subject to a variety of psychological and social needs quite apart from their survival needs. They discovered that individuals' needs and their priorities differed dramatically. And they discovered that in order to design new products and marketing strategies that would fulfill the needs of consumers, they had to study consumers and their consumption behavior in depth. Thus the stage was set for the development of a new discipline called consumer behavior.

FAST PACE OF NEW-PRODUCT INTRODUCTION

The technological explosion that hit this country soon after World War II has resulted in the introduction of new products at an ever-increasing rate. Many of these new products—some experts estimate over 80 per-cent—fail badly. To increase the likelihood of success, marketers realize they need better information about what consumers are willing to buy. Thus many marketers are carefully researching their consumer markets to try to discover new consumer needs. To find out what consumers want in the way of new products, how acceptable the new-product idea is, and how best to introduce it so that it will receive wide consumer acceptance, marketers realize that they have to learn as much as they can about the consumer and what makes her "tick." Thus they have increased their interest in and study of consumer behavior as a way to reduce new-product failures.

SHORTER PRODUCT LIFE CYCLES

Because of the fast pace of new-product introductions, products tend to have a shorter life, since they are constantly subjected to modification, improvement, and replacement by new and substitute products. Faced with a much shorter product life cycle, companies constantly seek new-product ideas and concepts that will satisfy consumer needs. They also try to anticipate consumer life-styles in an effort to develop products that will satisfy future needs. To do so, they must engage in considerable research to try to discover consumer wants, needs, wishes, and life-styles—both present and anticipated. Furthermore, they must engage in research designed to reveal how best to reach the consumer in order to influence her purchase behavior. For all of these reasons, successful marketers have ongoing programs designed to study the consumer and her consumption behavior.

GROWTH OF SEGMENTATION AS A MARKETING STRATEGY

As marketers began to study the behavior of consumers, they soon real-ized that despite overriding similarities, consumers were not all alike; nor did they wish to use the identical products that everyone else used. Rather, many consumers preferred differentiated products, which they felt closely reflected their own personal needs, wishes, personalities, life-styles, and so forth. To better cater to the specialized needs of selected groups of consumers, marketers adopted a policy of market segmenta-tion, in which they divided their total potential market into smaller, homogeneous segments for which they could design a specific marketing mix. A market segmentation strategy is based on satisfying the needs and wants of specific groups of consumers; thus it requires a great deal of insight into the consumption habits of selected market segments. The collection and analysis of such information is the province of the field of consumer behavior.

INCREASED INTEREST IN CONSUMER PROTECTION

The increased interest in consumerism and the growth of private consumer groups concerned with protecting the rights of the consuming public have created a much greater need to understand consumer behavior in depth. For example, it is important to discover how consumers perceive various marketing and promotional appeals in order to identify potential sources of consumer confusion and deception. A large, half-filled package of noodles may be preferred by consumers who are deceived into thinking that it contains a greater quantity than more tightly packaged competitive brands. Consumer research that reveals such erroneous consumer perceptions provides the basis for recommendations concerning new consumer protection legislation.

SETTING OF PUBLIC POLICY

Parallel with the growth of the consumer protection movement, public policy makers at the local, state, and federal levels became more aware of their responsibility to sponsor legislation designed to protect the interests and the well-being of their consumer constituents. At the federal level, such agencies as the Federal Trade Commission, Federal Communications Commission, and Food and Drug Administration are increasingly undertaking research to discover the impact of products and promotional campaigns on the consuming public. As the surge of interest in consumer protection increases, these agencies are likely to undertake increasing numbers of consumer-oriented studies in order to determine the public's reaction to proposed social legislation.

ENVIRONMENTAL CONCERNS

Increasing public concern over dangers to the environment have made both marketers and public policy makers aware of the potentially negative impact of a number of consumer products, such as high-suds detergents, aerosol sprays, disposable bottles, and nonbiodegradable packages. Research into consumer needs and practices has enabled marketers to develop and effectively promote environmentally sound product substitutes for the socially concerned consumer.

GROWTH OF NONPROFIT MARKETING

Organizations in the public and the nonprofit sectors have begun to realize the importance of adopting marketing practices in order to bring their services to the attention of their relevant publics. For example, organizations such as private and public colleges, welfare agencies, hospitals, and museums have found that to successfully identify their appropriate markets and to adequately satisfy the needs of these markets, they have to undertake in-depth consumer behavior research.

COMPUTER AND STATISTICAL TECHNIQUES

The development of appropriate tools and techniques has encouraged and facilitated research into consumer behavior. For example, the computer enables scientists to process and store vast amounts of data concerning consumer activities, and the use of sophisticated statistical techniques enables researchers to analyze a mass of information concerning consumers.

Market segmentation

We briefly introduced the concept of market segmentation earlier in this chapter. Because of the strong interrelationship that exists between consumer behavior and market segmentation, it is important that the student understand why this strategy is an essential marketing tool.

Market segmentation, in brief, is *the process of dividing a potential market into distinct subsets of consumers and selecting one or more segments as a market target to be reached with a distinct marketing mix.*

REQUIREMENTS FOR EFFECTIVE MARKET SEGMENTATION

If a company is to effectively practice a policy of market segmentation, it must be able to identify, measure, and reach significant subgroups of its total potential market.

identification

Segments must be identifiable; that is, a significant proportion of a firm's potential market must have a common need or characteristic that can be identified by the marketer. For example, if a sufficient number of people in the household detergent market have newborn infants, then mothers of newborn infants can become a feasible market segment for a specifically differentiated product promoted through a campaign carefully tailored to appeal to their special needs and interests. If a substantial number of families own homes that are valued between $35,000 and $50,000, then middle-income homeowners can become a feasible market segment for a home maintenance service.

Some segmentation characteristics are easily identifiable, such as age group, occupation, race, or geographic location. Other characteristics can be determined through questioning, such as education, income, or marital status. Still other characteristics are much more difficult to identify, such as attitudes or personality or life-styles. A knowledge of consumer behavior is especially useful to the marketer who wishes to segment his markets on the basis of such elusive or intangible consumer characteristics.

sufficiency

There must be a sufficient number of people with the same characteristic to make it profitable for a marketer to adopt a policy of market segmentation. For example, few shoe manufacturers have found it worthwhile to market shoes for people who have two different-sized feet because the number of people who require two different sized shoes is not great enough to warrant special treatment. On the other hand, it has been worthwhile for some manufacturers to market shoes for men with very large or very wide feet, because the number of men who have outsized feet is sufficiently large to make it a profitable market segment.

accessibility

Another requirement for effective market segmentation is that the segment be accessible; that is, the marketer must be able to reach the market segment efficiently through appropriate media with a minimum of waste coverage. For example, a manufacturer of expensive lawn furniture may reach owners of luxury homes efficiently through *House Beautiful;* however, he would incur a great deal of waste circulation if he advertised in *TV Guide.*

BENEFITS OF MARKET SEGMENTATION

The marketer who is able to subdivide his market into distinct segments of consumers with different needs and interests is in the position to develop marketing mixes that specifically appeal to the needs of each segment. Prospects are more likely to identify with messages specifically tailored to their needs. Because it is carefully targeted at a specific group of consumers, a market segmentation strategy is sometimes called the "rifle" approach to marketing. On the other hand, an undifferentiated marketing strategy, which tries to be all things to all people, is usually referred to as a "shotgun" approach, because it scatters its appeal to a mass audience made up of diverse types of people. As such, it usually ends up meaning very little to anybody.

A market segmentation strategy enables the marketer to focus his efforts on one or more distinct segments of homogeneous consumers, and to achieve a strong market position in the particular segments he serves. The study of consumer behavior provides the basis for much of what is known about consumers, their needs, and their interests. It provides the basic foundation for the development of a market segmentation strategy.

BASES FOR SEGMENTATION

Marketers use several different categories of consumer characteristics as bases for the segmentation of their markets. These categories provide the foundations for geographic segmentation, demographic segmentation, psychographic segmentation, social-cultural segmentation, and user behavior segmentation.

geographic segmentation

In geographic segmentation, the market is divided into different locations. Consumers have been found to differ in their consumption preferences according to the regions in which they live. For example, people who live in the northeast region of the United States have been found to favor a different blend of coffee than people who live in the southwest. Clothing styles tend to be much more informal in the west than in the east. More furs and expensive jewelry are sold in major cities than in small cities throughout the country. Differences in climate, an offshoot of region, also affect consumer preferences. For example, swimming pools have greater acceptability in warm climates where they can be used year-round. Even in the same metropolitan area, city dwellers tend to buy different types of clothing, household furnishings, and leisure products than suburban or exurban dwellers.

Thus, geographic location is a valid basis for the segmentation of markets. Similarly, it is a valid basis on which to study differences in consumer behavior. (The study of geographic differences in consumer behavior is discussed in greater detail in Chapter 13, "Subcultural and Cross-Cultural Aspects of Consumer Behavior.")

demographic segmentation

Demographic characteristics, such as age, income, occupation, sex, and education, are most often used as the basis for market segmentation. *Demography* refers to the vital and measurable statistics of a population. Demographic characteristics are generally easy to identify and to measure; furthermore, they can often be associated with the usage of specific products. For example, age is a demographic variable that can be associated with very distinct product usage. Preschool children, teenagers, college youth, the middle-aged, and the elderly—all can be associated with specific product needs and interests and usage. To take just one age grouping, college youth provide an important market for books, records, camping equipment, and travel.

Sex has always been a distinct segmentation variable, though in recent years it has become less clear in discriminating product usage. However, women are still the prime users of such products as hair coloring and cosmetics, and men of cigars and shaving preparations. Income is an important segmentation characteristic in terms of luxury goods and in terms of product appeals. Education is also an important segmentation variable. Individuals who have achieved high educational levels often have different product needs and are susceptible to different communication styles than individuals with little education. Thus they require a separate marketing treatment.

Many demographic characteristics have become the basis for the identification of distinct subcultural groups in our society—race, age, occupation, and so forth. (The differing consumption needs and choices of subcultural groups are discussed in Chapter 13.)

psychographic segmentation

Psychographic characteristics are the intrinsic qualities of the individual, such as his personality, his buying motives, his life-style, his attitudes, and his interests. Individual psychological differences are important bases for segmentation because people within the same demographic group can differ widely in terms of their consumption behavior. For example, two thirty-year-old unmarried lawyers residing in New York City who each earn $25,000 annually may prove to be vastly different marketing prospects because of their differing life-styles. One may be a free-swinging, high-spending hedonist, while the other may be an introvert who carefully invests all of his disposable income in blue chip bonds. With such widely differing consumption styles, it would be pointless for some marketers to include them in the same market segment, despite the similarity of their demographic characteristics.

For some products, consumer personality traits and consumer self images are good bases upon which to segment markets. Since consumers are more likely to buy products with brand images that they perceive are similar to their own self-images, marketers often try to endow their products with distinctive "personalities" which are consistent with the personalities of their target segments. (Brand personalities and consumer personalities are examined in Chapter 3, "The Consumer as a Perceiver," and Chapter 5, "Personality and Consumer Behavior.")

Some marketers prefer to segment their markets on the basis of the benefits sought by consumers. For example, the automobile market is often segmented on the basis of such consumer benefits (i.e., needs) as transportation, safety, prestige, or social fulfillment. Some marketers have attempted to identify specific personality characteristics for each benefit segment. Marketers have also tried to associate specific demographic characteristics with each benefit segment (e.g., consumers who buy station wagons have large families and those who buy subcompacts are under thirty). If distinctive media patterns can also be determined for each segment, marketers can target specific marketing programs directly to each segment.

social-cultural segmentation

Sociological (i.e., group) and anthropological (i.e., cultural) variables provide further bases for market segmentation. For example, target populations have been successfully subdivided into market segments on the basis of social class membership, reference group membership, cultural (and subcultural) memberships, and stage in the family life cycle.

Social class has been particularly amenable to market segmentation. Studies have shown that consumers in different social classes vary in terms of their product choices, their life-styles, their buying habits, and their values. Marketers have used this knowledge to design marketing mixes that specifically appeal to individuals in a particular social class.

Social class is usually measured by an index comprised of several demographic variables: education, income, occupation, residence. The concept of social class implies that there are people higher or lower on the social scale. Individuals tend to behave in a manner consistent with the class to which they belong or to the one just above them. Thus they may buy a certain make of car because people in their social class or in their "circle" own the same make. (The influence of social class on consumer behavior is discussed more fully in Chapter 11, "Social Class and Consumer Behavior.")

In addition to their social class membership, most individuals belong to some groups, aspire to belong to other groups, and try to avoid still others. Because group memberships profoundly affect consumer behavior, they are useful segmentation variables. For example, a hotel operator may wish to target his promotional messages to members of ski clubs or special-interest organizations. Or, a marketer may use a sports celebrity to endorse his breakfast cereal, knowing that young boys often aspire to membership in the sports celebrity "fraternity." (Chapter 8, "Group Dynamics and Consumer Reference Groups," discusses the influence of group memberships on consumer behavior.)

Some marketers have found it useful to segment their markets on the basis of cultural heritage, since members of the same society tend to have the same values, beliefs, and customs. For example, such products as pasta or soul food have been promoted on the basis of cultural identification. (The influence of culture and subculture on consumer behavior is discussed more fully in Chapters 12 and 13.)

Many marketers have segmented their populations on the basis of stage in the family life cycle. Young marrieds, for example, tend to be interested in furnishings for the home; with the birth of a child, their interests change to baby-rearing equipment; as their family progresses, products and product usage change until, finally, when their children set up their own homes, they are free to once again follow their own interests. (Family life cycle influence on consumer behavior is discussed in Chapter 9, "The Family.")

user behavior segmentation

Other important bases for segmenting markets are the rate of usage of the product category and the degree of brand loyalty exhibited by the consumer. Marketers may want to segment their markets on the basis of rate of product usage; for example, into low, medium, and heavy users, and nonusers. By segmenting markets in this way, a tea manufacturer, for example, may decide to direct his advertising to heavy tea drinkers (in an effort to win market shares from his competitors), to light drinkers (in order to expand the total tea-drinking market), or to coffee drinkers (to try to switch them to tea). Sometimes research shows that a very small percentage of the total market accounts for the major sales of the product; in such cases, it might be more useful to target a campaign to the heavy users rather than to spend considerably more money trying to attract the light users.

Sometimes brand loyalty is a useful basis for segmentation. Mar-

---

TABLE 1–1

Market Segmentation Categories and Selected Segmentation Variables

Variables	*Examples*
Geographic Characteristics	
Region	Northerners, southerners, easterners, westerners
City size	Major metropolitan areas, small cities, towns
Density of area	Urban, suburban, exurban, rural
Climate	Temperate, hot, humid
Demographic Characteristics	
Age	Under 11, 12–17, 18–34, 35–49, 50+
Sex	Male, female
Marital status	Singles, marrieds
Family size	1 child, 2–4 children, 5 or more children
Income	Under $10,000, $10,000–$14,999, $15,000 and over
Occupation	Professional, blue-collar, white-collar, agricultural
Education	Some high school, high school graduate, some college, college graduate
Psychographic Characteristics	
Life-style	Swingers, straights, conservatives, status seekers
Personality	Extroverts, introverts, dogmatics
Attitudes	Positive, negative, indifferent
Benefits sought	Convenience, prestige, economy
Social-Cultural Characteristics	
Religion	Jewish, Catholic, Protestant, other
Race	Black, Caucasian, Oriental
Nationality	American, Italian, British, Chinese, Mexican
Social class	Lower, middle, upper
Family life cycle	Bachelors, young marrieds, empty nesters
User Behavior Characteristics	
Usage rate	Heavy, medium, light users, non-users
Brand loyalty status	None, medium, strong

keters may try to identify the characteristics of their brand-loyal consumers so that they can direct their promotional efforts to people with similar characteristics in the larger population. Or they may decide to go after consumers who are not brand loyal; such people may represent greater market potential than consumers who are loyal to competing brands. Non-brand-loyal consumers also suggest a different type of marketing mix to the marketing practitioner (low price, consumer "deals," point-of-purchase displays, etc.).

Table 1–1 lists the major variables used to segment markets and their typical breakdowns.

Summary

Consumer behavior can be defined as *the behavior that consumers display in searching for, purchasing, using, and evaluating products, services, and ideas which they expect will satisfy their needs.* The study of consumer behavior is concerned not only with *what* consumers buy, but with *why* they buy it, *when, where* and *how* they buy it, and *how often* they buy it. Consumer behavior research takes place at every phase of the consumption process: before the purchase, during the purchase, and after the purchase.

There are two kinds of consumers: the *personal* (or *ultimate) consumer,* who buys goods and services for his own use or for household use, and the *organizational consumer,* who buys products, equipment, and services in order to operate his organization (which may be profit, nonprofit, or governmental).

Consumer behavior is interdisciplinary; that is, it is based upon concepts and theories about people which have been developed by scientists in such diverse disciplines as psychology, sociology, social psychology, cultural anthropology, and economics.

Marketing firms use their knowledge of consumer behavior to design marketing strategies, to measure marketing performance, and to segment markets. The development of consumer behavior studies was an outgrowth of the evolution of marketing philosophy from a production orientation to a selling orientation to a marketing orientation (the so-called "marketing concept.") Other factors that have contributed to the development of consumer behavior studies include the fast pace of new-product introduction, shorter product life cycles, the high rate of new-product failures, increased interest in consumer protection by private groups and public policy decision makers, concern over the environment, the adoption of marketing practices by nonprofit organizations, the availability of computers and sophisticated statistical techniques, and the growth of segmentation as a marketing strategy.

Market segmentation is the process of dividing a vast potential market into smaller groups, or segments, each of which is similar regarding some characteristic that is relevant to the purchase or the usage of the product or product category. A market segmentation strategy is based on designing a specific marketing mix to satisfy the needs and wants of one or more distinct segments selected for market targets. If a company is to effectively practice a policy of market segmentation, it must be able to identify, measure, and reach significant subgroups of its total potential market. The various categories used as bases for segmenting markets include geographic, demographic, psychographic, sociological, cultural, and user behavior variables.

Discussion questions

1. Mrs. Jones, a housewife, is buying a can of Campbell's soup. Mr. Jones, her husband, a buyer for a quality men's store, is ordering a new line of men's leisure suits. Describe the consumer behavior aspects of each purchase in terms of:
   a. what, why, how, when, how often
   b. personal versus organizational buying
   c. buyer versus user.

2. In the 1920s, Henry Ford is known to have remarked that his customers can have any color car they want, so long as it's black. Why won't the president of Ford Motor Company make the same statement today? In your answer, discuss the changes in marketing philosophy which have occurred since the 1920s.

3. You are the product manager of a line of toys for pre-school children. Describe how an understanding of consumer behavior can be useful to you in terms of:
   a. market segmentation strategy
   b. new product introduction
   c. product life cycle
   d. consumer protection and public policy issues.

4. Suggest a useful way (or ways) to segment the market for each of the following: (a) umbrellas (b) household detergents (c) household coffee (d) suntan lotion.

5. Name three ways in which an understanding of consumer behavior can help the marketer design effective marketing strategies.

6. Consumer behavior has been said to both *affect* and *reflect* marketing strategy. Discuss.

7. Consumer behavior is based on principles "borrowed" from other disciplines. Name five such disciplines and explain how they contribute to the study of consumer behavior.

8. Why is the study of consumer behavior basic to the development of a market segmentation strategy? (In your answer include a discussion of the five broad categories of variables used for market segmentation.)

THE CONSUMER AS AN INDIVIDUAL

II

Chapters 2 through 6 are designed to provide the reader with a comprehensive picture of consumer psychology. The objectives of these chapters are (1) to explain the basic psychological concepts that account for individual behavior, and (2) to show how these concepts influence the individual's consumption-related behavior. Chapter 7, "Communication and Consumer Behavior," provides the bridge between the individual and his connection with the outside world.

consumer needs and motivation

2

We have all grown up "knowing" that people are different. They seek different pleasures, spend their money in different ways. A woman may save her household money to carpet her bedrooms; her neighbor may save hers to buy a second car. A couple may spend their vacation traveling to Europe; their friends are content with two weeks in a cottage by the sea. A doting father may buy his son a set of encyclopedias; another may buy his son a set of electric trains. Different modes of consumer behavior — different ways of spending money — do not surprise us. We have been brought up to believe that the differences in people are what makes life interesting.

However, this apparent diversity in human behavior often causes us to overlook the fact that people are really very much alike. There are underlying similarities — constants that tend to operate across many types of people — which serve to explain and to clarify their consumption behavior. Psychologists and consumer behaviorists agree that basically most people experience the same kinds of needs and motives; they simply express these motives in different ways. For this reason, an understanding of human motives is very important to marketers: it enables them to understand, and even anticipate, human behavior in the marketplace.

This chapter will discuss the basic needs that operate in most people to motivate behavior. It explores the influence such needs have on consumption behavior. Later chapters in this section ex-

Understanding human needs is half the job of meeting them.

ADLAI STEVENSON:
*Speech,
Columbus, Ohio
(October 3, 1952)*

plain why and how these basic human motives are expressed in so many diverse ways.

WHAT IS MOTIVATION?

There are several basic concepts which are integral to an understanding of human motivation. Before we discuss these, it is necessary to agree on some basic definitions.

motivation

Motivation can be described as *the driving force within an individual that impels him to action.* This driving force is produced by a state of tension, which exists as the result of an unfilled need. Individuals strive—both consciously and subconsciously—to reduce this tension through behavior that they anticipate will fulfill their needs and thus relieve them of the stress they feel. The specific goals they select and the patterns of action they undertake to achieve their goals are the results of individual thinking and learning. Figure 2–1 presents a model of the motivational process. It portrays motivation as a state of need-induced tension, which exerts a "push" on the individual (i.e., drives him) to engage in behavior that he expects will gratify his needs and thus reduce his tension. Whether gratification is actually achieved depends on the course of action pursued. (If a high school girl pins her hopes of being asked to the senior prom on her switch to a highly advertised "sexy" toothpaste, she may be disappointed.)

The specific course of action undertaken by a consumer and the specific goal she chooses are selected on the basis of her thinking

FIGURE 2–1

A Model of the Motivation Process

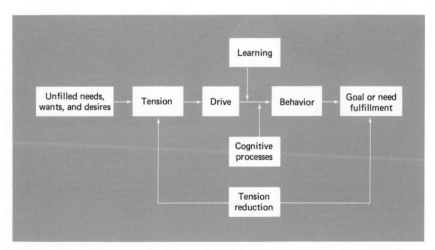

processes (i.e., cognition) and her previous learning. Thus, marketers who understand motivational theory attempt to influence the consumer's thinking or cognitive processes.

needs

Every individual has needs; some are innate, others are acquired. Innate needs are physiological (i.e., biogenic); they include the needs for food, for water, for air, for clothing, for shelter, and for sex. Because all of these factors are needed to sustain biological life, the biogenic needs are considered *primary* needs or motives.

Acquired needs are needs that we learn in response to our culture or environment. These may include needs for esteem, for prestige, for affection, for power, and for learning. Because acquired needs are generally psychological (i.e., psychogenic), they are considered *secondary* needs or motives. They result from the individual's subjective psychological state and from his relations with others. For example, all individuals need shelter from the elements; thus, finding a place to live fulfills an important primary need for a newly transferred executive. However, the kind of house he buys may be the result of secondary needs. He may seek a place to live where he can entertain large groups of people (and fulfill his social needs); furthermore, he may want to buy a house in an exclusive community in order to impress his friends and family (and fulfill his ego needs). The house that he ultimately purchases thus may serve to fulfill both primary and secondary needs.

goals

Goals are the sought-after results of motivated behavior. As Figure 2 – 1 indicates, all behavior is goal-oriented. Our discussion of motivation in this chapter is in part concerned with consumers' *generic* goals; that is, the general classes or categories of goals they select to fulfill their needs. Marketers are even more concerned with consumers' *product-specific* goals; that is, the specifically branded or labeled products they select to fulfill their needs. For example, the Thomas J. Lipton Company wants consumers to view iced tea as a good way to quench summer thirst (i.e., as a generic goal). However, it is even more interested in having consumers view *Lipton's* iced tea as the *best* way to quench summer thirst (i.e., as a product-specific goal). As trade association advertising indicates, marketers recognize the importance of promoting both types of goals. The American Dairy Association advertises that "milk is a natural," while Borden's, a member of the association, stresses its own brand of milk in its advertising.

POSITIVE AND NEGATIVE MOTIVATION

Motivation can be either positive or negative in direction. We may feel a driving force *toward* some object or condition or a driving force *away* from some object or condition. For example, a person may be impelled toward a restaurant to fulfill his hunger need and away from airplane transportation to fulfill his safety need. Some psychologists refer to positive drives as needs, wants, or desires, and negative drives as fears or aversions. However, though negative and positive motivational forces seem to differ dramatically in terms of physical (and sometimes emotional) activity, they are basically similar in that they both serve to initiate and sustain human behavior. For this reason, researchers often refer to both kinds of drives or motives as needs, wants, and desires.[1]

Goals, too, can be either positive or negative. A positive goal is one toward which behavior is directed, and thus it is often referred to as an *approach* object. A negative goal is one from which behavior is directed away, and thus it is sometimes referred to as an *avoidance* object. Since both approach and avoidance goals can be considered objectives of motivated behavior, most researchers refer to both types simply as goals. Consider this example. A middle-aged woman may wish to remain as attractive as possible to her husband. Her positive goal is to appear desirable, and therefore she may use a perfume advertised to make her "irresistible." A negative goal may be to prevent her skin from drying and aging, and therefore she may buy and use face creams advertised to prevent wrinkles. In the former case, she uses perfume to help her achieve her positive goal—sexual attractiveness; in the latter case, she uses face creams to help her avoid her negative goal—wrinkled skin.

THE SELECTION OF GOALS

For any given need, there are many different and appropriate goals. The goal selected by an individual depends on his personal experiences, his physical capacity, prevailing cultural norms and values, and the goal's accessibility in the physical and social environment.[2] For example, an individual may have a strong hunger need. If he is a young American athlete, he may envision a rare sirloin steak as his goal-object; however, if he is also an orthodox Jew, he may require that the steak be kosher to conform to Jewish dietary laws. If the individual is old or infirm, he may not have the physical capacity to chew or digest a steak; therefore, he may select hamburger instead. If he has never tasted steak, if it is out of his realm of personal experience, he will probably not even think of steak as a goal-object, but instead will select a food that has satisfied his hunger before, perhaps fish or chicken.

Finally, the goal-object has to be both physically and socially accessible. If the individual were shipwrecked on an island with no food provisions or living animals, he could not realistically select steak as his goal-object, though he might fantasize about it. If he were in India where cows are considered sacred deities, he could not realistically hope to consume steak because to do so would be considered sacrilegious. Therefore, he would have to select a substitute goal more appropriate to the social environment.

The individual's own conception of himself also serves to influence the specific goals he selects. The products that a person owns, would like to own, or would not like to own are often perceived in terms of how closely they reflect (are congruent with) his self-image. A product that is perceived as fitting to an individual's self-image has a greater probability of being selected than one that is not.[3] Thus, a person who perceives himself as young and "swinging" may drive a Corvette; if he perceives himself as rich and conservative, he may drive a Mercedes. The types of houses people live in, the cars they drive, the clothes they wear, the very foods they eat—these specific goal-objects are often chosen because symbolically they reflect the individual's own self-image while they satisfy his specific needs.[4] (The relationship of self concept to product choice is explained more fully in Chapter 3.)

RATIONAL VERSUS EMOTIONAL MOTIVES

Some consumer researchers distinguish between so-called rational motives and emotional (or nonrational) motives. They use the term *rationality* in the traditional economic sense that assumes that the consumer behaves rationally when she carefully considers all alternatives and chooses the one that gives her the greatest utility (i.e., satisfaction).[5] In a marketing context, the term *rationality* implies that the consumer selects goals based on totally objective criteria, such as size, weight, price, or miles per gallon. *Emotional* motives imply the selection of goals according to personal or subjective criteria (the desire for individuality, pride, fear, affection, status). The assumption underlying this distinction is that subjective or emotional criteria do not maximize utility or satisfaction. However, it is reasonable to assume that the consumer always attempts to select alternatives that, *in her view,* serve to maximize her satisfaction. Obviously, the assessment of satisfaction is a very personal process, based upon the individual's own need structure as well as on her behavioral, social, and learning experiences. What may appear as irrational to an outside observer may be perfectly rational within the context of the consumer's own psychological field. For example, a product purchased to enhance one's self-image (such as perfume) is a perfectly rational form of consumer behavior. If behavior did not appear rational to the person who undertakes it at the time that he undertakes it, obviously he would not do it. Therefore, the distinction between rational and emotional motives does not appear to be warranted.

INTERDEPENDENCY OF NEEDS AND GOALS

Needs and goals are interdependent. One does not exist without the other.[6] However, people are often not as aware of their needs as they are of their goals. For example, a teenager may not be aware of her social needs, but she may join many clubs to meet new friends. A local politician may not be consciously aware of his power need, but he may regularly run for public office. A woman may not recognize her ego needs, but she may strive to have the most elaborate house in town.

Individuals are usually somewhat more aware of their physiological needs than they are of their psychological needs. Most people know when they are hungry or thirsty or cold, and they take appropriate steps to satisfy these needs. Sometimes they may subconsciously engage in behavior designed to fulfill their bodily needs, even though they are not consciously aware of such needs. For example, medical researchers have reported the case of a young child who had an overwhelming craving for salt almost from the time of his birth. All the foods he liked were salty; in addition, he ate about a teaspoonful of salt daily. When he was about three and one-half years old, he was placed in a hospital for observation, and was restricted to a routine hospital diet. Within seven days he was dead. A postmortem examination revealed a glandular deficiency, which had caused excessive loss of salt from his body through urination. The boy had literally kept himself alive for three and one-half years by eating great quantities of salt to compensate for his salt deficiency. When he no longer had free access to salt, he died.[7]

The dynamic nature of motivation

NEEDS AND GOALS ARE CONSTANTLY CHANGING

Needs and goals are constantly growing and changing in response to an individual's physical condition, his environment, his interactions with others, and his experiences. As individuals attain their goals, they develop new goals. If they do not attain their goals, they continue to strive for old goals or they develop substitute goals. Some of the reasons why human activity never ceases are: (1) Existing needs are never completely satisfied and thus constantly require activity designed to attain and maintain fulfillment. (2) As needs become satisfied, new, higher-order needs emerge, which must be fulfilled. (3) People who achieve their goals set new and higher goals for themselves.

needs are never fully satisfied

Most human needs are never completely, or finally, satisfied. For example, people experience hunger needs at regular intervals that must be satisfied by eating. Most people regularly seek companionship and approval from others in order to satisfy their social needs. Even more complex psychological needs are rarely sated. For example, a person may partially or temporarily satisfy her power need by serving on the PTA, but this small taste of power may not sufficiently satisfy her need, so she may run successively for higher public office. In this instance, temporary goal achievement does not fully satisfy her need for power, and so she keeps striving to more fully satisfy her need.

new needs emerge as old needs are satisfied

Some motivational theorists believe that a hierarchy of needs exists and that new, higher-order needs emerge as lower-order needs are fulfilled.[8] For example, a man who has largely satisfied all his basic physiological needs may turn his efforts to achieving acceptance among his new neighbors by joining their clubs and supporting their candidates. Having achieved such acceptance, he may then seek recognition by driving a luxury car, by winning tennis trophies, or by giving lavish parties.

success and failure influence goals

A number of researchers have explored the nature of the goals that individuals set for themselves.[9] In general, they have concluded that individuals who successfully achieve their goals usually set new and higher goals for themselves; that is, they raise their levels of aspiration. This is probably due to the fact that they become more confident of their ability to reach their goals. Conversely, those who do not reach their goals sometimes lower their levels of aspiration. Thus a person's goal selection is often a function of his success and failure experiences. For example, a college senior who is not accepted into medical school may try, instead, to go to dental school; failing that, he may train to be a laboratory technician.

The nature and persistence of an individual's behavior are often influenced by his expectations of success or failure in reaching his goals. His expectations, in turn, are often based upon his past experiences in attaining goals. A man who takes good snapshots with an inexpensive camera may be motivated to buy a more expensive camera in the belief that he will be able to take even better photographs. In this way, he may eventually upgrade his camera by several hundred dollars. On the other hand, a person who cannot take good pictures is just as likely to keep the same camera or may even lose all interest in photography.

These effects of success and failure on goal selection have strategy implications for the marketer. Goals should be reasonably attainable. Advertisements should not promise more than the product will deliver. Even a good product will not be repurchased if it does not live up to the consumer's expectations. Research shows that a disappointed consumer will regard a product that has not lived up to her expectations with even less satisfaction than its objective performance warrants.[10] Thus, advertisers who create unrealistic expectations for their products are likely to cause dissatisfaction among consumers. It has been suggested that the frustration and disappointment that result from just such consumer dissatisfaction have been the driving force behind consumerism.[11]

substitute goals

When, for one reason or another, an individual cannot attain a particular goal or type of goal that she anticipates will satisfy her needs, she may direct her behavior to a substitute goal. Although the substitute goal may not be as satisfactory as her primary goal, it may serve her needs sufficiently to dispel uncomfortable tension. Continued deprivation of a primary goal may result in the substitute goal's assuming primary-goal status. A woman who has stopped drinking whole milk because she is dieting may actually begin to prefer skimmed milk. A person who cannot afford a Cadillac may convince himself that an Oldsmobile has an image he clearly prefers. Of course, in this instance, the substitute goal may be a defensive reaction to frustration.

FRUSTRATION

Failure to achieve a goal often results in feelings of frustration. Everyone has at one time or another experienced the frustration that comes from an inability to attain one's goal. The barrier that prevents attainment of a goal may be personal to the individual (i.e., it can be a physical or financial limitation, or a psychological barrier such as conflicting goals), or it can be an obstacle in the physical or social environment. Regardless of the cause, individuals react differently to frustrating situations. Some people are adaptive and manage to cope by finding their way around the obstacle or, if that fails, by selecting a substitute goal. Others are less adaptive and may regard their inability to achieve their goals as a personal failure and may experience feelings of anxiety. An example of adaptive behavior would be the college student who would prefer a sports car but settles for a secondhand jalopy. If he cannot afford the insurance for a used car, he may settle for a bike on which to ride around campus.

A person who cannot cope with frustration often mentally redefines the frustrating situation in order to protect his self-image and defend his self-esteem. For example, a newly married woman may yearn for a genuine leather sofa which she cannot afford. The coping individual may have the same sofa copied by a local upholsterer for less money, or have it made up in a synthetic leather fabric, or settle for a different model completely. The woman who cannot cope may react with anger toward her husband for not making enough money to afford it, or she may ask her parents to buy it for her. These last two possibilities are examples, respectively, of aggression and regression, defense mechanisms that people sometimes adopt to protect their egos from feelings of failure when they cannot attain their goals. Other defense mechanisms include rationalization, withdrawal, projection, autism, identification, and repression.[12]

rationalization

Sometimes the individual redefines the frustrating situation by inventing plausible reasons for not being able to attain her goal. Or, she may decide she really did not want that goal anyway. Rationalizations are not deliberate lies, since the individual is not fully aware of the cognitive distortion she undergoes as a result of the frustrating situation. Thus a consumer who cannot give up smoking may convince herself that she is smoking less if she smokes fewer (though longer) cigarettes.

withdrawal

Frustration is often resolved by simply withdrawing from the frustrating situation. A woman who has difficulty using a sewing machine properly may simply stop sewing. Furthermore, she may rationalize her withdrawal by deciding that it really is cheaper to buy ready-made clothing; in addition, she may decide she can use her time more constructively in other activities.

projection

The individual may redefine the frustrating situation by assigning (or "projecting") blame for his own failures and inabilities on other objects or persons. Thus the golfer who misses a stroke may blame his caddy or his ball; the driver who has an automobile accident may blame the other driver or the condition of the road.

autism

Autism, or autistic thinking, refers to thinking that is almost completely dominated by needs and by emotions, with no effort made to relate to reality. Such daydreaming, or fantasizing, enables the individual to attain imaginary gratification of his unfulfilled needs. Thus a man who is dieting may daydream about gorging himself with ice cream and candy bars, or a poor office clerk may dream of marrying a millionairess. Figure 2–2 illustrates an autism appeal which suggests that ownership of a tuxedo will enable the reader to marry an heiress.

identification

Sometimes people resolve their feelings of frustration by subconsciously identifying with other persons or situations that they consider relevant. Marketers have long recognized the importance of this defense mechanism and often use it as the basis for advertising appeals. That is why "slice-of-life" commercials or advertisements are so popular. Such advertisements usually portray a stereotypical situation in which an individual experiences a frustration and then overcomes her problem (i.e., her frustration) by using the advertised product (see Figure 2–3). If the viewer can identify with the frustrating situation, she may very likely adopt the proposed solution and buy the product advertised. For example, a girl who has difficulty attracting a boy she likes may decide to use the same mouthwash or shampoo or deodorant that "worked" for the girl in the commercial. Interestingly enough, use of the product may increase her self-confidence sufficiently to enable her to achieve her goal.

FIGURE 2-2

Autism Appeal

HOW TO MARRY AN HEIRESS ON A $129.50 INVESTMENT.

Your own tux.

It'll take you anywhere.

Make you feel relaxed in any surroundings.

Help you look as if you belong.

And once you're on the scene, you're on your own.

After all, it's just as easy to develop a meaningful relationship with a rich girl.

To be certain that no man is deprived of his chance to be in the right place at the right time in the right clothes, After Six is making a very special offer: the $129.50 investment. It includes this trim, classic tuxedo, the graceful bowtie in the latest shape and elegant flyfront shirt with ruffles and matching link cuffs.

If you have accessories, you can buy the tux alone for about $110. Or you can buy the shirt and tie separately.

At the fine stores listed opposite, or write After Six Inc., 1290 Avenue of the Americas, N.Y. 10019.

The After Six $129.50 investment. Even if you're happily married, it's worth it for celebrating your good fortune.

FIGURE 2–3

Identification Appeal

"You know the feeling. I thought everyone was staring at my hands."

"Those horrid weathered age spots made me so self-conscious I hated to play cards. Then the girls told me about this cream Esoterica. What a blessing. It's just made to fade age spots. And it creams your hands beautiful besides. You'll see."

Esoterica.
It's made to fade age spots
(and it creams your hands beautiful besides).

Cream and Lotion

aggression

An individual who experiences frustration may resort to aggressive behavior in an attempt to protect his self-esteem. This was aptly illustrated during the 1976 Olympics by two British yachtsmen who, disappointed at their poor showing in the sailing competition, burned their boat and swam ashore. Frustrated consumers have boycotted manufacturers in their efforts to improve product quality and boycotted retailers in their efforts to have prices lowered.

repression

Another way that the individual avoids the tension arising from frustration is by repressing the unsatisfied need. Thus the individual "forgets" his need; that is, he forces the need out of his conscious awareness. Sometimes repressed needs manifest themselves indirectly. A woman who cannot have children may surround herself with plants or pets, which she nurtures to growth. Or, she may teach school, or work in a library, or do volunteer work in an orphan asylum. The manifestation of repressed needs in a socially acceptable form of behavior is called *sublimation,* another type of defense mechanism.

regression

Sometimes people react to frustrating situations by adopting childish or immature behavior. A woman attending a bargain sale, for example, may fight over merchandise and resort to tearing a garment that another woman will not relinquish, rather than allow her to have it.

This listing of defense mechanisms is far from exhaustive. People have virtually limitless ways of redefining frustrating situations so that they can protect their self-esteem from the anxieties that result from experiencing failure. Based on their early experiences, individuals tend to develop their own characteristic ways of handling frustration.

Marketers often consider this fact in their selection of advertising appeals. For example, a flour manufacturer may convince consumers that their baking failures were caused by the ingredients they used rather than the ineptness of their efforts.

MULTIPLICITY OF NEEDS

Consumer behavior is often designed to fulfill more than one need. In fact, it is more likely that specific goals are selected because they fulfill several needs. We buy clothing for protection and for modesty; in addition, our clothing fulfills an enormous range of both personal and social needs. Usually, however, there is one overriding (i.e., prepotent) need that initiates behavior. For example, a man may stop smoking because he wants to rid himself of a chronic cough; he may also be concerned about the cigarette-cancer controversy; in addition, his current girlfriend is "turned off" by the smell of cigarette smoke. If the cumulative amount of tension produced by each of these three reasons is sufficiently strong, he will stop smoking; however, just one of the reasons (e.g., his girlfriend's influence) may serve as the triggering mechanism. That one would be called the prepotent need.

NEEDS AND GOALS VARY AMONG INDIVIDUALS

One cannot accurately infer motives from behavior. People with different needs may seek fulfillment through selection of the same goals, while people with the same needs may seek fulfillment through different goals. Consider the following examples. Five women who are active in a consumer organization may each belong for a different reason. The first woman may be genuinely concerned with protecting consumer interests, the second may be personally concerned with rising prices, the third may seek the social contacts that derive from organizational meetings, the fourth may enjoy the power inherent in directing a large group, and the fifth may enjoy the status provided by membership in a powerful organization.

Similarly, five women may be driven by the same need (e.g., an ego need) to seek fulfillment in different ways. The first may seek advancement and recognition through a professional career, the second may become a director of the League of Women Voters, the third may attend beauty spas in an effort to maintain her figure, the fourth may take great pride in her sparkling kitchen floor (as so many television commercials suggest), and the fifth may seek attention by wearing elaborate clothes to church.

AROUSAL OF MOTIVES

Most of the specific needs of an individual are dormant much of the time. The arousal of any particular set of needs at a specific point in time may be caused by internal stimuli found in the individual's physiological condition or his thinking processes, or by external stimuli in his outside environment.

physiological arousal

A person's bodily needs at any one specific moment are rooted in his physiological condition at that moment. A drop in his blood-sugar level or stomach contractions will trigger his awareness of a hunger need. Secretion of sex hormones will awaken his sex need. A drop in body temperature will induce shivering, which makes him aware of his need for warmth. Most of these physiological cues are involuntary; however, they arouse related needs which cause uncomfortable tensions until they are satisfied. For example, a shivering man may turn up the heat in his home to relieve his discomfort; he may also make a mental note to buy a new overcoat.

cognitive arousal

Sometimes thinking or daydreaming results in the arousal or stimulation of latent needs. People who are bored or frustrated in their attempts to achieve their goals often engage in daydreaming (autistic thinking), in which they imagine themselves in all sorts of desirable situations. These thoughts tend to arouse dormant needs, which may produce uncomfortable tensions that "push" them into goal-oriented behavior. A young girl who dreams of becoming a movie actress may identify with a star of her choice by imitating her walk and using the beauty products she endorses. Similarly, a young man who wants to play football professionally may identify with a major league player and use the products he recommends commercially.

environmental stimuli

The set of needs that are activated at a particular time are often determined by specific cues in the environment. Without these cues, the needs would remain dormant. Thus, the six o'clock news, the vision or smell of food, food commercials on television, the children's return from school—all of these may arouse the "need" for food. In such cases, modification of the environment may be necessary in order to reduce the arousal of hunger.

A most potent form of situational cue is the goal-object itself. A woman may experience an overwhelming need for a new dishwasher when she sees her neighbor's new dishwasher; a man may suddenly experience a need for a new car when he passes a dealer's display window. Sometimes an advertisement or other environmental cue produces a psychological imbalance in the mind of the viewer. For example, a man who prides himself on his gardening may see an advertisement for a tractor mower that apparently works more efficiently than his own rotary mower. The ad may make him so unhappy with his old mower that he experiences severe tension until he buys himself a new tractor model.

When people live in a complex and highly varied environment, they experience many opportunities for need arousal. Conversely, when their environment is poor or deprived, fewer needs are activated. This explains why television has had such a mixed effect on the lives of the ghetto poor. It exposes them to various life-styles and expensive products that they would not otherwise see, and it awakens wants and desires that they have little opportunity or even hope of attaining. Thus, while it enriches their lives, television may also serve to frustrate their lives, and it sometimes results in the adoption of antisocial defense mechanisms such as aggression.

Types and systems of needs

DIVERSITY OF NEEDS

For many years, psychologists and others interested in human behavior have attempted to develop exhaustive lists of human needs or motives. These lists have proved to be as diverse in content as they have been in length. Although there is little disagreement about specific *physiological* needs, there is considerable disagreement about specific *psychogenic* needs. For example, in 1923 a professor of business psychology at the Harvard Business School compiled a list of forty-four human motives for use as copy appeals (see Table 2 – 1).[13]

In 1938, psychologist Henry Murray prepared a detailed list of twenty-eight psychogenic needs, which has served as the basic construct for a number of widely used personality tests (for example, the Thematic Apperception Technique and Edward's Personal Preference Schedule).[14] Murray believed that everyone has the same basic set of needs, but that individuals differ in their priority ranking of these needs. Murray's basic needs include many motives that are assumed to play an

TABLE 2–1

Motives in Male and Female Adults

Appetite – Hunger	Respect for Deity
Love of Offspring	Sympathy for Others
Health	Protection of Others
Sex Attraction	Domesticity
Parental Affection	Social Distinction
Ambition	Devotion to Others
Pleasure	Hospitality
Bodily Comfort	Warmth
Possession	Imitation
Approval of Others	Courtesy
Gregariousness	Play – Sport
Taste	Managing Others
Personal Appearance	Coolness
Safety	Fear – Caution
Cleanliness	Physical Activity
Rest – Sleep	Manipulation
Home Comfort	Construction
Economy	Style
Curiosity	Humor
Efficiency	Amusement
Competition	Shyness
Cooperation	Teasing

Source: Daniel Starch, Principles of Advertising
(Chicago: A. W. Shaw & Co., 1923), p. 273.

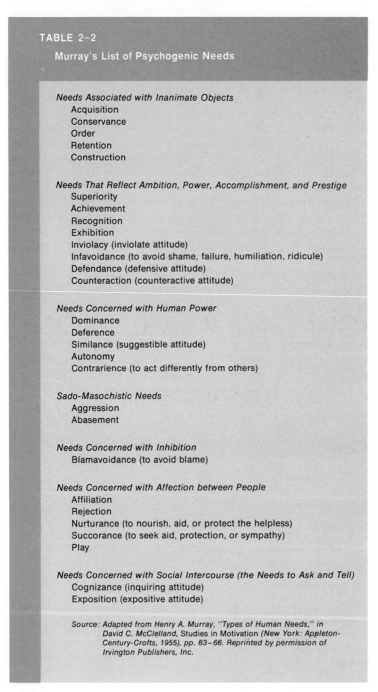

TABLE 2–2

Murray's List of Psychogenic Needs

Needs Associated with Inanimate Objects
    Acquisition
    Conservance
    Order
    Retention
    Construction

Needs That Reflect Ambition, Power, Accomplishment, and Prestige
    Superiority
    Achievement
    Recognition
    Exhibition
    Inviolacy (inviolate attitude)
    Infavoidance (to avoid shame, failure, humiliation, ridicule)
    Defendance (defensive attitude)
    Counteraction (counteractive attitude)

Needs Concerned with Human Power
    Dominance
    Deference
    Similance (suggestible attitude)
    Autonomy
    Contrarience (to act differently from others)

Sado-Masochistic Needs
    Aggression
    Abasement

Needs Concerned with Inhibition
    Blamavoidance (to avoid blame)

Needs Concerned with Affection between People
    Affiliation
    Rejection
    Nurturance (to nourish, aid, or protect the helpless)
    Succorance (to seek aid, protection, or sympathy)
    Play

Needs Concerned with Social Intercourse (the Needs to Ask and Tell)
    Cognizance (inquiring attitude)
    Exposition (expositive attitude)

Source: Adapted from Henry A. Murray, "Types of Human Needs," in David C. McClelland, Studies in Motivation (New York: Appleton-Century-Crofts, 1955), pp. 63–66. Reprinted by permission of Irvington Publishers, Inc.

important role in consumer behavior, such as acquisition, achievement, recognition, and exhibition (see Table 2 – 2).

Lists of human motives are often too long to be of practical use to marketers. The most useful kind of list is a limited one in which needs are sufficiently generic in title to subsume more detailed human needs. For example, one consumer behaviorist grouped the various lists of psychogenic needs into just three broad categories: affectional needs, ego-bolstering needs, and ego-defensive needs.[15]

Affectional needs are described as the needs to form and maintain warm, harmonious, and emotionally satisfying relations with others.

Ego-bolstering needs are the needs to enhance or promote the personality (to achieve, to gain prestige and recognition, and to satisfy the ego through domination of others).

Ego-defensive needs are the needs to protect the personality (to avoid physical and psychological harm, to avoid ridicule and "loss of face," to prevent loss of prestige, and to avoid or obtain relief from anxiety).[16]

While some psychologists have suggested that people have different need priorities based on their personalities, their experiences, their environments, and so forth, others believe that most human beings assign a similar priority ranking to their basic needs.

HIERARCHY OF NEEDS

The first proponent of the theory of a universal hierarchy of human needs was Dr. Abraham Maslow, a psychologist who formulated this widely accepted theory of human motivation after some twenty years of clinical practice.[17] Maslow's theory postulates five basic levels of human needs, which rank in order of importance from low-level (biogenic) needs to higher-level (psychogenic) needs. It suggests that individuals seek to satisfy lower-level needs before higher-level needs emerge. The lowest level of chronically unsatisfied need which an individual experiences serves to motivate his behavior; when that need is fairly well satisfied, a new (and higher) need emerges which the individual is motivated to fulfill. When this need is satisfied, a new (and still higher) need emerges, and so on. Of course, if a lower-level need experiences some renewed deprivation, it may temporarily become dominant again. Figure 2 – 4 presents Maslow's *Hierarchy of Needs* in diagrammatic form. For clarity, each level of need is depicted as mutually exclusive; however, according to the theory, there is some overlap between each level, since no need is ever completely satisfied. For this reason, though all levels of need below the dominant level continue to motivate behavior to some extent, the *prime* motivator – the major driving force within the individual – is the lowest level of need that remains largely unsatisfied.

physiological needs

In the hierarchy of needs theory, the first and most basic level of needs is physiological. These needs, which are required to sustain biologi-

FIGURE 2-4

Maslow's Hierarchy of Human Needs

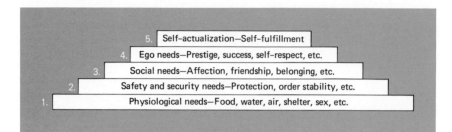

5. Self-actualization—Self-fulfillment
4. Ego needs—Prestige, success, self-respect, etc.
3. Social needs—Affection, friendship, belonging, etc.
2. Safety and security needs—Protection, order stability, etc.
1. Physiological needs—Food, water, air, shelter, sex, etc.

cal life, include food, water, air, shelter, clothing, sex—all of the biogenic needs, in fact, that were listed as primary needs earlier. According to Maslow, physiological needs are dominant when they are chronically unsatisfied: "For the man who is extremely and dangerously hungry, no other interest exists but food. He dreams food, he remembers food, he thinks about food, he emotes only about food, he perceives only food and he wants only food."[18] In this country, for most citizens most of the time, the biogenic needs are regularly and easily satisfied. Thus the higher-level needs are usually dominant.

safety needs

After the first level of needs is satisfied, safety and security needs become the driving force behind an individual's behavior. These needs are concerned with much more than physical safety. They include order, stability, routine, familiarity, and certainty—the knowledge, for example, that the individual will eat dinner not only that day and the following day but also far into the future. The impetus for the growth of labor unions in the United States derives from the safety need, since unions provide members with the security of knowing that their employment does not depend on the day-to-day whims of their employers. The social welfare programs enacted by this country (e.g., social security, unemployment insurance, medicare) tend to provide some degree of security to American citizens. Savings accounts, insurance policies, education, and vocational training are all ways in which the need for security is fulfilled. Like the physiological need level, the safety level tends to be fairly well satisfied for many American citizens, and thus it rarely dominates behavior except in severe emergencies such as war, epidemics, and crime waves. Advertisers tend to use this appeal sparingly, because they are unsure of its ultimate effect on the consumer (see Chapter 7).

social needs

The third level of Maslow's hierarchy includes such needs as love, affection, belonging, and acceptance. People seek warm and satisfying human relationships with other people. (The importance of group acceptance and group influence on consumer behavior is examined more fully in Chapter 8.) Because of the importance of social motives in our society, most advertisers of personal-care products emphasize this appeal in their advertisements (see Figure 2–5).

egoistic needs

When the social needs are more or less satisfied, the fourth level of Maslow's hierarchy becomes operative. This level is concerned with egoistic needs. These needs can take either an inward or an outward orientation, or both. Inwardly directed ego needs reflect an individual's need for self-acceptance, for self-esteem, for achievement, for success, for independence, for personal satisfaction with a job well done. Outwardly directed ego needs include the need for prestige, for reputation, for status, for recognition from others. The desire to "keep up with the Joneses" is a reflection of an outwardly oriented ego need. Figure 2–6 presents an advertisement designed to appeal to the ego need.

need for self-actualization

According to Maslow, most people do not satisfy their ego needs sufficiently to ever move to the fifth level—the need for self-actualization or self-fulfillment. This need refers to an individual's desire to fulfill his own potential—to become everything he is capable of becoming. "What a man *can* be, he must be."[19] This need is expressed in different ways by different people. A young man may desire to be the best athlete he possibly can be (e.g., Bruce Jenner, who won the Decathlon Competition in the 1976 Olympics, worked single-mindedly for four years to become "the world's best athlete"). An artist may need to express himself on canvas; a businessman may try to build an empire. Maslow noted that this need is not necessarily a creative urge, but that in people with some capacity for creativity, it is likely to take that form. Advertisements for art lessons, for luxury cars, and even for diamond watches often try to appeal to the self-actualization need. Figure 2–7 presents an advertisement designed to appeal to the need for self-actualization.

In summary, the hierarchy of needs theory postulates that there is a five-level hierarchy of prepotent human needs. Higher-order needs become the driving force behind human behavior as lower-level needs are satisfied. The theory says, in effect, that satisfaction does not motivate behavior; only dissatisfaction does.

AN EVALUATION OF THE NEED HIERARCHY

The need hierarchy has received wide acceptance in many social disciplines because it appears to reflect the assumed or inferred motivations of many people in our society. The five levels of need postulated by the need hierarchy are generic enough to encompass most lists of individual

FIGURE 2–5

Social Appeal

Courtesy of Chanel, Inc.

FIGURE 2–6

Egoistic Appeal

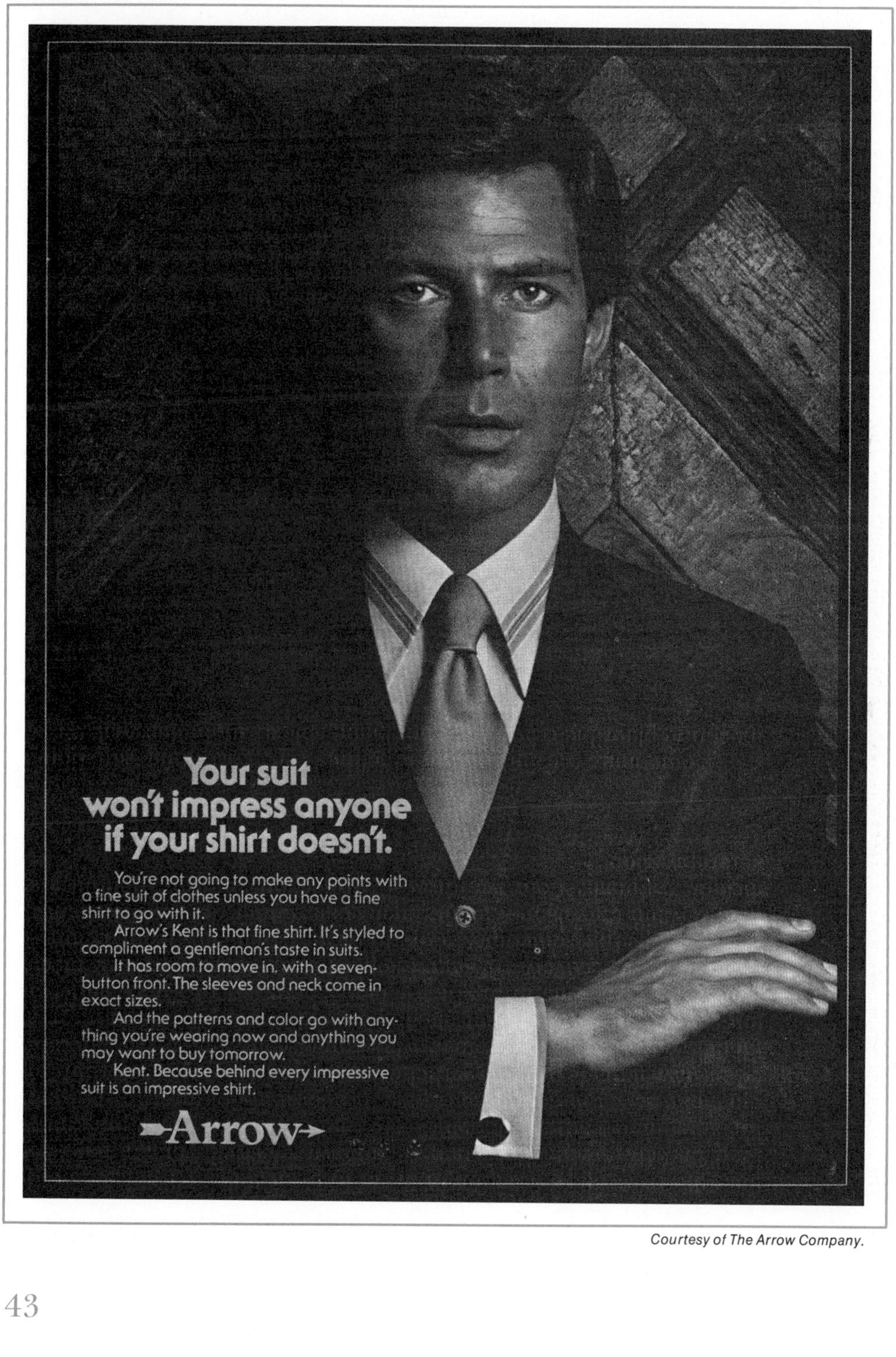

Courtesy of The Arrow Company.

FIGURE 2–7

Self-actualization Appeal

The Dale Carnegie Course brought them new confidence and a fresh outlook on life.

James Violette, Department Supervisor
Advest Company, Hartford, Connecticut

LaVerne Church, Auditor, U.S. Government, St. Louis, Missouri

■ Before she took the Dale Carnegie Course, LaVerne Church felt that she tended to underrate her own abilities. "The best thing I got from the Course," says LaVerne, "was the confidence that I can do just about anything I make up my mind to.

"Using Dale Carnegie principles, I developed new ideas for handling problem situations. Through learning how to better understand why people act and say the things they do, I get along much better with them. I find I can express my ideas better, and have them accepted by others.

"At home, too, I have more energy to plan what I want to do, and then do it instead of just drifting. The Course was an outstanding experience in my life."

■ "I took the Dale Carnegie Course because I wanted to improve the way I organize my thinking," says Jim Violette. "As a result, I'm better able to express myself and get my ideas across to people.

"In the Course, I developed more confidence. I also learned to get along better with people, especially at work.

Now I'm better able to get their cooperation and we accomplish a lot more, working together.

"The Course has helped me to advance in my career. My boss said he noticed the positive change in my attitude, and it's true. I have a brighter outlook toward my job and my family. Taking the Course was for me a unique experience."

The strong inner confidence you develop in the Dale Carnegie Course helps you make full use of your capabilities. It adds new interest and satisfaction to everyday living, new appreciation of the relationships you have with others. Dale Carnegie training is offered in more than 1,000 U.S. communities, including all major cities—also in more than 50 other countries. For information, call toll-free (800) 645-3466. In New York state, (800) 342-9833. Or write us.

DALE CARNEGIE COURSE

SUITE 556N · 1475 FRANKLIN AVENUE · GARDEN CITY · NEW YORK 11530

Courtesy of Dale Carnegie & Associates, Inc.

44

needs. The major problem with the theory is that it cannot be empirically tested—there is no way to measure precisely how well satisfied one need is before the next higher need becomes operative. It also appears to be very closely bound to our contemporary American culture (i.e., it appears to be culture and time bound). Nevertheless, the hierarchy is a useful tool for understanding consumer motivations, and is readily adaptable to marketing strategy, primarily because consumer goods can be used to fulfill each of the need levels. For example, individuals buy houses, food, and clothing to fulfill their physiological needs; they buy insurance and radial tires and vocational training to fulfill their safety and security needs. Almost all personal-care products (cosmetics, toothpaste, shaving cream) are bought to fulfill social needs. Luxury products such as furs or jewels or big cars are usually bought to fulfill ego needs, and college training and art lessons are sold as ways to achieve self-fulfillment.

The hierarchy also provides a useful, comprehensive framework for marketers trying to establish appropriate advertising appeals for their products. It is adaptable in two ways: first, an analysis of consumer characteristics may lead the marketer to focus his advertising appeals on a need level that is likely to be shared by a large segment of the prospective audience; second, it facilitates product positioning.

segmentation applications

The need hierarchy is often used as the basis for market segmentation, as specific advertising appeals are directed to individuals on one or more need levels. For example, soft drink ads directed to teenagers may stress a social appeal by showing a group of young people mutually sharing good times as well as the advertised product.

positioning applications

Another way to utilize the hierarchy is for "positioning" products; that is, deciding how the product is to be perceived by prospective consumers. The key to positioning is to find a position that is not occupied by any competing brand. This use of the need hierarchy for positioning utilizes the notion that no need is ever fully satisfied, that it always continues to be somewhat motivating. A recent advertising campaign by Mercedes Benz positioned its car uniquely in relation to other leading competitive luxury automobiles. Most luxury cars used status appeals ("Impress your friends"), or self-actualizing appeals ("You deserve the very best"), or even social appeals ("The whole family can ride in luxurious comfort"). However, no luxury car was currently using safety appeals. The Mercedes campaign combined both the safety need and the social need in advertisements to well-to-do executives ("When your wife is driving the two children home on a dark and stormy night, you can relax if she's driving the Mercedes").

It is interesting, in light of the cigarette-cancer controversy, to recall that in the late 1940s, most cigarette commercials stressed medical endorsements ("Two out of three doctors interviewed smoke Camels"). Cigarette smoking was advertised as relaxing, soothing, and good for the nervous system; in effect, as a means of fulfilling physiological needs. Then a new competitive campaign broke upon the scene which repositioned a cigarette brand by suggesting social fulfillment. The advertisement showed a young man surrounded by a bevy of beautiful girls and a headline that read, "For a treat instead of a treatment, smoke Old Golds."

versatility of the need hierarchy

One way to illustrate the usefulness of the need hierarchy in designing promotional programs is to show how workable appeals for a single product can be developed from each level. Consider, for example, the following potential promotional appeals for a microwave oven. An appeal to *physiological* needs would show how quickly food can be prepared (i.e., satisfy hunger needs) in a microwave oven. A *safety* appeal can demonstrate how safe the microwave oven is in comparison with other cooking appliances (e.g., no burned fingers). *Social* appeals can be invoked by illustrations of party and holiday dinners prepared in a microwave oven. *Status* is easily demonstrated through such standard appeals as "Impress your friends," or "Be the first of your friends to own one," or "For a truly luxurious kitchen, you need a microwave oven." Finally, appeals to *self-actualization* may stress that the "ultimate" kitchen appliance for gourmet cooking is a microwave oven because it enables the cook to produce superb meals that could not possibly be produced by any other kind of oven.

A TRIO OF NEEDS

Several psychologists have written extensively on the existence of a trio of basic needs: the needs for power, for affiliation, and for achievement.[20] These needs can each be subsumed in Maslow's need hierarchy; however, considered individually, they each have a unique relevance to consumer motivation.

power needs

The power need relates to an individual's desire to control his environment. It includes the need to control other persons and various objects. This need appears to be closely related to the ego need, in that many individuals experience increased self-enhancement when they exercise power over objects or people. A number of products lend themselves to promises of power or superiority for their users. An automobile advertisement might stress enormous speed capability even though this capability can rarely be exercised because of legal or practical limits. Nevertheless, the implied promise of power will attract individuals with strong power needs.

affiliation needs

Affiliation is a well-known and well-researched social motive which has far-reaching influence on consumer behavior. The affiliation need suggests that an individual's behavior is highly influenced by his desire for friendship, for acceptance, for belonging. People with high affiliation needs tend to have a strong social dependency on others. They often select goods that they feel will meet with the approval of friends. They may shop with others as a social activity — more as an end in itself rather than as a means to an end.[21] They appreciate the assistance and the opinions of friendly salespeople and may purchase clothing or even household goods in order to merit the approval of an encouraging salesperson. People with high affiliation needs often adapt their purchase behavior to the norms and standards of their reference groups (see Chapter 8).

achievement needs

A number of research studies have focused on the achievement need.[22] Individuals with a strong need for achievement regard personal accomplishment as an end in itself. The achievement need is closely related to the egoistic need, in that satisfaction with a job well done serves to enhance the individual's self-esteem. A person with a high need for achievement has certain traits that may make him vulnerable to relevant appeals. He is more self-confident, enjoys taking calculated risks, researches his environment actively, and is very much interested in feedback. (His interest in money rewards or profits is primarily due to the feedback money provides as to how well he is doing.) He likes situations in which he can take personal responsibility for finding problem solutions.[23]

High-achievement people are often good prospects for cleverly presented innovative products, for do-it-yourself projects, for older houses, and even for moderately speculative stock issues. They are also likely to be receptive to appeals from advertisers in whom they recognize similar needs (i.e., with whom they can identify). For example, the Avis Car Rental slogan "We try harder" might strike a responsive note in individuals with high achievement needs.

Several research studies indicate that individuals with a high need for achievement may constitute a special market segment for certain products. For example, one study found that men with a high need for achievement tend to favor products considered virile and masculine, such as boating equipment, straight razors, and skis. Men with low-need achievement scores preferred to buy products characterized as meticulous or fastidious, such as mouthwash, deodorant, and automatic dishwashers.[24] Another study suggested that many of the people who engage in active outdoor sports have a high need for achievement.[25] People with a high need for achievement are also more likely to patronize stores that not only use appeals of excellence but liberally use positive achievement words.[26]

In summary, then, individuals with specific psychological needs seem to be receptive to advertising appeals directed to those needs. They also seem to be receptive to certain kinds of products. Thus, such needs provide marketers with additional bases on which to separate their markets into smaller, homogeneous market segments.

The measurement of motives

How are motives identified? How are they measured? How do researchers know which motives are responsible for certain kinds of behavior? These are difficult questions to answer because motives are hypothetical constructs; that is, they cannot be seen or touched, handled, smelled, or otherwise tangibly observed. For this reason, no one measurement method can be considered a reliable index of motivation. Instead, researchers usually rely on a combination of methods used in tandem to try to establish the presence or the strength of various motives. These methods are complementary and include observation and inference, self-reports, and projective techniques.

OBSERVATION AND INFERENCE

Motivations are often inferred from the actions and statements of individuals.[27] If a person undertakes extensive search behavior for a specific kind of product and continues such activity until he makes a purchase selection, then inferences are often made as to the need that motivated his behavior.[28] For example, prior to buying a washing machine, if a woman visits appliance stores to examine and to price washing machines, and if she studies appliance advertisements and seeks relevant information from *Consumer Reports*, the logical inference is that she has a need for an efficient, practical way to wash clothes. Of course, motive identification through inference can be somewhat circular in reasoning; that is, a motive may be attributed to observed behavior and then be used to explain the behavior from which it was inferred. For example, observers may assume that a woman's purchase of a mink coat is motivated by her need for prestige, and then they "explain" her wearing of mink as a reflection of her need for prestige. Mink, however, is actually an extremely warm, durable, and lightweight fur. For someone who can afford it, a mink coat may simply be the most practical way to keep warm in the winter.

Although we may feel that we can plausibly infer a motive from certain kinds of behavior, we cannot validly claim to do so. For example, it may seem reasonable to assume that a woman who devotes her time and effort to school board activities is doing so out of esteem or self-actualization needs; however, in reality she may find such activities a way of fulfilling social needs. Similarly, it may seem reasonable to assume that a man who works long hours in business has a strong achievement motive, but in reality he may have an overwhelming need for security which he satisfies through the accumulation of money. Or, he may simply be setting aside a nest egg in order to fulfill a secret wish to buy a cabin cruiser.

In addition to observation, another source of inference about the motives of individuals is the nonstructured, or "depth," interview. In this type of interview, respondents are questioned singly or in small groups for several hours by an interviewer who is trained to establish rapport but not to guide the discussion excessively. Respondents are encouraged to talk freely about their activities or interests, or about a specific subject or brand under study (in which case the interview is termed a "focus" interview). A verbatim account of the interview is then carefully studied in an attempt to infer respondents' attitudes or motivations concerning brands or types of products. Obviously, analysis of the responses in a depth interview requires a great deal of skill on the part of the researcher.

To avoid errors of inference, a motivational analysis that is based on observation or in-depth interviews is often supplemented with other methods, such as subjective or self reports.

SELF REPORTS

Some researchers claim that the best way to find out about the needs and goals of individuals is simply to ask them. A number of pencil-and-paper "tests" given to consumers inquire directly about their wants, desires, fears, goals, successes, failures. The information so obtained is then quantified (assigned a numerical score) to yield a measure of the strength of a specific need or motive.

There are two potential problems with self reports of this nature. First, individuals may not themselves be aware of the actual reasons or motives underlying their behavior and they may unconsciously rationalize their actions; that is, they may assign reasons or motives that are acceptable to their personalities but which are not, in fact, accurate. They do this with no awareness that they are rationalizing. A woman may believe that she sends her children to summer camp because the fresh air and organized activities are "good for them," but she may not consciously realize that she does so primarily to free herself from oppressive child-care responsibilities for two months. Or, a housewife may devote herself to cooking and canning and other domestic activities in the belief that she does so out of love for her family, while actually she does so because these activities fulfill her esteem needs or her needs for creativity.

Aside from unconsciously rationalizing her own motives, a person may also deliberately falsify self-report inventories to impress the researcher, or to please the researcher, or to avoid personal embarrassment. It is difficult for a researcher to distinguish among true reports, rationalized reports, or deliberately falsified reports. For this reason, psychologists and other researchers interested in motivation have developed techniques designed to delve below the consumer's level of conscious awareness, to tap the underlying motives of individuals despite their unconscious rationalizations or conscious concealment. These methods are called projective techniques.

PROJECTIVE TECHNIQUES

Projective techniques are designed to reveal a person's true feelings and motivations. They consist of a variety of disguised tests that contain ambiguous stimuli, such as incomplete sentences, untitled pictures or cartoons, inkblots, word-association tests, and other-person characterizations. (See Figures 2–8 and 2–9 for examples of projective tests.) The respondent is asked to complete, describe, or explain what meaning each stimulus has for him. The theory behind projective tests is that the individual's own needs and motives will influence how he perceives ambiguous stimuli. Thus the story he tells or the sentence he completes is actually a projection of his own feelings, though he attributes his responses to something or someone else. In this way, the re-

FIGURE 2–8

Example of Thematic Apperception Test

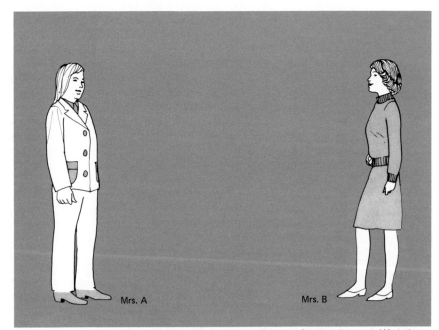

Mrs. A   Mrs. B

Source: Howard L. Steck, "On the Validity of Projective Questions," Journal of Marketing Research, August 1964, p. 46.

FIGURE 2-9

Example of Sentence-Completion Projective Test

Instruction: I'm going to read off to you some sentences which I want you to finish. Say the first words that come into your mind.

1. "Land of the Sky Blue Waters" means _____

2. My friends say that Budweiser is _____

3. I think the girl in the Riester beer commercial is the kind of girl who _____

4. The kind of tavern that sells Budweiser is _____

5. The last time I saw Schlitz in a store _____

6. Riester beer is _____

7. My wife thinks the Riester beer girl is _____

8. Bartenders say Falstaff is _____

Source: Harper W. Boyd, Jr., and Ralph Westfall, Marketing Research Text and Cases, *3rd ed. (Homewood, Ill.: Richard D. Irwin, 1972), p. 642. Reprinted with permission.*

spondent is expected to reveal his underlying needs, wants, fears, aspirations, and motives, whether or not he himself is fully aware of them. For example, if a subject looks at a picture of a woman wearing stylish clothes and describes her as a "show-off," one may infer that the subject is concerned with ego needs.

The basic assumption underlying projective techniques is that the individual is unaware that he is exposing his own feelings. This is sometimes illustrated by the old joke about a psychologist who shows a subject a series of geometric figures and asks him to describe what he sees. In each case, the subject reports seeing a lewd or lascivious scene. When the psychologist comments that the subject has an obvious sexual fixation, the latter retorts, "It's not *my* fixation; after all, it's *you* who are showing me the dirty pictures."

Obviously, the identification and measurement of human motives is still a very inexact process. Some psychologists point out that most measurement techniques do not meet the crucial test criteria of validity and reliability.[29] *Validity* ensures that the test measures what it purports to measure; *reliability* refers to the consistency with which the test measures what it does measure. By using a combination of assessments based on behavioral data (e.g., observation), subjective data (e.g., self reports).

and projective techniques, many consumer researchers feel confident that they gain valuable insights into the consumer's motivations. However, there is clearly a need for improved methodological procedures for measuring human motives.

Motivational research

The term *motivational research*, which should include all types of research into human motives, is generally used to refer to qualitative research designed to uncover the consumer's subconscious or hidden motivations.[30] Operating on the premise that the consumer is not always fully aware of the basic reasons for his actions, motivational research attempts to discover underlying feelings, attitudes, and emotions concerning product, service, or brand usage.

METHODOLOGY AND ANALYSIS

Because emotional feelings are not easily or accurately revealed by consumers upon direct questioning, motivational researchers utilize clinical psychological methods such as the nondirective (depth) interview and projective techniques (word-association tests, sentence completion tests, inkblot and cartoon tests, other-person characterizations). Careful analysis of the data generated by these techniques provides the researchers with varying degrees of insight into the underlying reasons why consumers buy or do not buy products or product categories under study.

Motivational research analyses often suggest new ways for marketers to present their products to the public. For example, a study prepared for a hair-coloring manufacturer revealed that women regarded becoming blond as a way of changing their images and personality. Respondents considered blonds to be attractive and sexy women, leading "fun" and "swinging" lives. These and other findings provided the company with substantial material on which to base a new advertising campaign.

DEVELOPMENT OF MOTIVATIONAL RESEARCH

Motivational research came into great popularity in the early 1950's when Dr. Ernest Dichter, formerly a psychoanalyst in Vienna, adapted his psychoanalytic techniques to the study of consumer buying habits. Marketing research up to this time had focused on *what* consumers did (it tended toward quantitative, descriptive studies) rather than on *why* they did it. Marketers were quickly fascinated by the glib, entertaining, and usually surprising explanations offered for consumer behavior, especially since many of these explanations were rooted in sex. (Most early motivational researchers were Freudian in their thinking and took the approach that all behavior is sexually motivated [see Chapter 5].) Thus, marketers were told that cigarettes and lifesaver candies were bought because of their sexual symbolism, that men regarded convertible cars as surrogate mistresses, that women baked cakes to fulfill their reproductive yearnings.[31] Before long, almost every advertising agency on Madison Avenue had a psychologist on its staff payroll in charge of motivational research studies.

SHORTCOMINGS OF MOTIVATIONAL RESEARCH

By the early 1960s, marketers realized that motivational research had some drawbacks. Because of the intensive nature of qualitative research, samples were necessarily small; thus, there was concern about the generalizability of the findings to the total market. Also, marketers soon realized that the analysis of projective tests and depth interviews was highly subjective. The same data given to three different analysts could produce three different reports, each offering its own explanation of the consumer behavior examined. Critics noted that many of the projective tests that were used had originally been developed for clinical purposes, rather than for studies of marketing or consumption behavior. (One of the basic criteria for test development is that tests be developed and validated for the specific purpose and on the specific audience from which information is desired.)

Finally, too many motivational researchers imputed highly exotic reasons to rather prosaic consumer purchases, and marketers began to question their recommendations (e.g., Is it better to sell a man a pair of suspenders as a means of holding up his pants or as a "reaction to castration anxiety"?[32] Is it easier to persuade a woman to buy a garden hose to water her lawn or as a symbol of the "futility of genital competition for the female"?[33]) Often, motivational researchers came up with sexual explanations for the most mundane activities. For example, an ad showing a hostess behind a beverage table filled with large bottles of soft drinks was commended by a leading motivational researcher for its "clever use of phallic symbolism."[34]

MOTIVATIONAL RESEARCH TODAY

Despite these criticisms, motivational research is still being extensively used by marketers who are concerned with gaining deeper insights into the whys of consumer behavior than conventional marketing research techniques can yield. As one agency professional pointed out, motivational research is a "chance to experience a 'flesh and blood' customer . . . to experience the emotional framework in which the product is being used."[35]

Since motivational research often reveals unsuspected motivations of consumers concerning product or brand usage, its principal use is in the development of new ideas for promotion campaigns, ideas that can penetrate the consumer's conscious awareness by appealing to her unrecognized needs. It also provides marketers with a basic orientation for new-product categories, and it enables them to explore consumer reactions to ideas and copy at an early stage so that costly errors can be avoided. Furthermore, motivational research provides the basic cues for more structured marketing research studies—studies that can be conducted on larger, more representative samples of consumers.

Motivational research continues to be a useful tool to many marketers who are concerned with knowing the actual reasons underlying consumer behavior. However, it is no longer considered the *only* method for uncovering human motivation, but rather one of a variety of research techniques available to the consumer researcher.

Summary

Motivation is *the driving force within an individual that impels him to action.* This driving force is produced by a state of uncomfortable tension, which exists as the result of an unfilled need. All individuals have needs, wants, and desires. The individual's subconscious drive to reduce his need-induced tension results in behavior that he anticipates will satisfy his needs and thus restore him to a more comfortable state.

All behavior is goal oriented. Goals are the sought-after results of motivated behavior. The form or direction that behavior takes—the goal that is selected—is a result of thinking processes (cognition) and previous learning. Marketers talk of two types of goals: generic goals and product-specific goals. A *generic* goal is a general goal or category of goal that may fulfill a certain need; a *product-specific* goal is a specifically branded or labeled product that the individual sees as a way to fulfill his need.

Innate needs—those an individual is born with—are primarily physiological (biogenic); they include all the factors required to sustain physical life (e.g., food, water, clothing, shelter, sex). Acquired needs— those an individual develops after birth—are primarily psychological (psychogenic); they include esteem, fear, love, and acceptance. For any given need, there are many different and appropriate goals. The specific goal selected depends on the individual's experiences, his physical capacity, prevailing cultural norms and values, and accessibility in the physical and social environment.

Needs and goals are interdependent, and change in response to the individual's physical condition, his environment, his interaction with other people, and his experiences. As needs become satisfied, new, higher-order needs emerge which must be fulfilled.

Failure to achieve a goal often results in feelings of frustration. Individuals react to frustration in two ways: they may cope by finding a way around the obstacle that prohibits goal attainment or by finding a substitute goal, or they may adopt a defense mechanism that enables them to protect their self-esteem. The defense mechanisms include aggression, regression, rationalization, withdrawal, projection, autism, identification, and repression.

Motives cannot be easily inferred from consumer behavior. People with different needs may seek fulfillment through selection of the same goals; people with the same needs may seek fulfillment through different goals.

While some psychologists have suggested that people have different need priorities, others believe that most human beings experience the same basic needs, to which they assign a similar priority ranking. Maslow's Hierarchy of Needs theory proposes five levels of prepotent human needs: physiological needs, safety needs, social needs, egoistic needs, and self-actualization needs. A trio of other needs widely used in consumer appeals are the needs for power, for affiliation, and for achievement.

There are three commonly used methods for identifying and "measuring" human motives: observation and inference, subjective reports, and projective techniques. None of these methods is completely reliable by itself; therefore, researchers often use a combination of two or three techniques in tandem to assess the presence or strength of consumer motives.

Motivational research is qualitative research designed to delve below the consumer's level of conscious awareness. Despite some shortcomings, motivational research has proved to be of great value to marketers concerned with developing new ideas and new copy appeals.

Endnotes

1. David Krech, Richard S. Crutchfield, and Egerton L. Ballachey, Individual in Society (New York: McGraw-Hill, 1962), 69.

2. Ibid., 76–77.

3. Harold H. Kassarjian, "Personality and Consumer Behavior: A Review," Journal of Marketing Research, 8 (November 1971), 413; and Landon E. Laird, Jr., "Self Concept, Ideal Self Concepts and Consumer Purchase Intentions," Journal of Consumer Research, 1 (September 1974), 44–51.

4. Edward L. Grubb and Bruce L. Stern, "Self-Concept and Significant Others," Journal of Marketing Research, 8 (August 1971), 382.

5. George Katona, "Rational Behavior and Economic Behavior," Psychological Review, 60 (September 1953), 307–18.

6. Krech et al., Individual in Society, 69.

7. L. Wilkens and C. P. Richter, "A Great Craving for Salt by a Child with Cortico-Adrenal Insufficiency," Journal of the American Medical Association, 14 (1940), 866–68.

8. See Abraham H. Maslow, "A Theory of Human Motivation," Psychological Review, 50 (1943), 370–96; Abraham H. Maslow, Motivation and Personality (New York: Harper & Row, 1954); and Abraham H. Maslow, Toward a Psychology of Being (New York: Van Nostrand Reinhold, 1968), 189–215.

9. *A number of studies have focused on human levels of aspiration. See, for example,* Kurt Lewin et al., "Level of Aspiration," *in* J. McV. Hunt, Personality and Behavior Disorders *(New York: Ronald Press, 1944); and* I. L. Child and J. William Whiting, "Determinants of Level of Aspiration: Evidence from Everyday Life," Journal of Abnormal Social Psychology, *44 (1949), 303–14.*

10. *Rolph E. Anderson, "Consumer Dissatisfaction: The Effect of Disconfirmed Expectancy on Perceived Product Performance,"* Journal of Marketing Research, *10 (February 1973), 38–44.*

11. *Richard H. Buskirk and James T. Rothe, "Consumerism—An Interpretation,"* Journal of Marketing, *34 (October 1970), 61–62, 65. See also George S. Day and David A. Aaker, "A Guide to Consumerism,"* Journal of Marketing, *34 (July 1970), 12–19.*

12. *Krech et al.,* Individual in Society, *119–23.*

13. *Daniel Starch,* Principles of Advertising *(Chicago: A. W. Shaw, 1923), 273.*

14. *Henry A. Murray et al.,* Explorations in Personality *(New York: Oxford University Press, 1938), 80–85, 109–15.*

15. *James A. Bayton, "Motivation, Cognition, Learning—Basic Factors in Consumer Behavior,"* Journal of Marketing, *23 (January 1958), 282–89.*

16. *Ibid.*

17. *Maslow, "Theory of Human Motivation," 380.*

18. *Ibid.*

19. *Ibid.*

20. *See, for example, David C. McClelland,* The Achieving Society *(Princeton, N.J.: Van Nostrand, 1961); and* John Atkinson and N. T. Feather, eds., A Theory of Achievement Motivation *(New York: John Wiley, 1966).*

21. *See, for example, Edward M. Tauber, "Why Do People Shop,"* Journal of Marketing, *36 (October 1972), 46–59.*

22. *David C. McClelland,* Studies in Motivation *(New York: Appleton-Century-Crofts, 1955).*

23. *David C. McClelland, "Business Drive and National Achievement,"* Harvard Business Review, *July-August 1962, 99; "Achievement Motivation Can Be Developed,"* Harvard Business Review, *November-December 1965, 5–24, 178; and* Abraham K. Korman, The Psychology of Motivation *(Englewood Cliffs, N.J.: Prentice-Hall, 1974), 190.*

24. *E. Laird Landon, Jr., "A Sex Role Explanation of Purchase Intention Differences of Consumers Who Are High and Low in Need for Achievement," in* M. Venkatesan, ed., Proceedings of the Third Annual Conference *(Association for Consumer Research, 1972), 1–8.*

25. *David M. Gardner, "An Exploratory Investigation of Achievement Motivation Effects on Consumer Behavior," in* M. Venkatesan, ed., Proceedings of the Third Annual Conference *(Association for Consumer Research, 1972), 20–33.*

26. *Charles D. Schewe, "Selected Social Psychological Models for Analyzing Buyers,"* Journal of Marketing, *37 (July 1973), 31–39; and David C. McClelland and Alvin M. Liberman, "The Effect of Need for Achievement on Recognition of Need-Related Words,"* Journal of Personality, *18 (December 1949), 236–51.*

27. *The use of observation as a way of measuring or determining motivation has been called an unobtrusive measure by some psychologists, since the subjects do not know they are being measured. See, for example,* E. J. Webb, D. T. Campbell, R. D. Schwartz, and L. Sechrest, Unobtrusive Measures: Nonreactive Research in the Social Sciences *(Chicago: Rand McNally, 1966).*

28. *Krech et al.,* Individual in Society, *87.*

29. *Korman*, Psychology of Motivation, *124–51.*

30. *Ernest Dichter,* A Strategy of Desire *(Garden City, N. Y.: Doubleday, 1960).*

31. *For additional reports of motivational research findings, see Dichter,* Strategy of Desire; *Vance Packard,* The Hidden Persuaders *(New York: Pocket Book, Inc., 1957); Pierre Martineau,* Motivation in Advertising *(New York: McGraw-Hill, 1957).*

32. *R. Ferber and H. G. Wales, eds.,* Motivation and Market Behavior *(Homewood, Ill.: Richard D. Irwin, 1958), 20*

33. *Ibid.*

34. *Leslie Kanuk, "Emotional Persuasion in Print Advertising" (Master's thesis, City College of New York, 1964).*

35. *"Qualitative Is Most Vulnerable Research: Axelrod,"* Advertising Age, *May 13, 1974, 82.*

Discussion questions

1. What is motivational research? What are its strengths and its weaknesses? How can it best be utilized in the development of marketing strategy?

2. How can a marketer attempt to reduce consumer frustration through his promotional strategy? Find an advertisement that illustrates this attempt.

3. Choose five magazine advertisements for different consumer goods. Carefully review Murray's list of human needs. Identify, through advertising appeal, which need(s) each product is presumed to satisfy.

4. Briefly explain how marketers can employ Maslow's Need Hierarchy in their marketing strategies. Give at least two examples.

5. Explain briefly the needs for power, affiliation, and achievement. Find three advertisements, each aimed at satisfying one of these needs through the purchase of the advertised product.

6. Suppose you are vice president of consumer research for a large U.S. liquor distributor. A new project assigned to you requires you to determine *why* people drink alcoholic beverages. Discuss the measurement techniques you would employ.

7. Develop five different advertising appeals—one for each level of Maslow's Need Hierarchy—that the General Motors marketing staff might employ for its new fall line of automobiles.

8. Consumers have both innate needs and acquired needs. Give examples of each kind of need and show how the same purchase can serve to fulfill either or both kinds of needs.

3

the consumer as a perceiver

Introduction

As individuals, we tend to see the world and all its varied happenings in our own special ways. Four people can view the same event at the same time, and each will report in total honesty a story different from all the others. For example, the classic Japanese film *Rashomon*—shown frequently on late night television—tells the story of the abduction and rape of a woodcutter's wife and the murder of her husband, first from the point of view of the bandit, then the wife, then the husband, and finally a hidden bystander. Each story varied because each participant perceived the events that occurred in a different way. Hard to believe? Not really. For each individual, reality is a totally personal phenomenon, based on that person's needs, wants, values, and personal experiences.

Reality to an individual is merely his perception of what is "out there"—of what has taken place. He acts and reacts on the basis of his perceptions, not on the basis of objective reality (i.e., reality as recorded by a camera). Thus, the consumer's perceptions are much more important to the marketer than his knowledge of objective reality. For, if one thinks about it, it's not what actually is so, but what the consumer *thinks* is so, that affects his actions, his buying habits, his leisure habits, and so forth. And, because individuals make decisions and take actions based on what they *perceive* to be reality, it is important that marketers understand the whole notion of perception and its related concepts so that they can more readily determine what influences consumers to buy.

Every man takes the limits of his own field of vision for the limits of the world.
SCHOPENHAUER: *"Further Psychological Observation," Parerga and Paralipomena* (1851)

This chapter examines the psychological and physical bases of human perception and discusses the principles that control our reception and interpretation of the world we see. Knowledge of these principles of perception enables astute marketers to develop strategies that have a good chance of being seen and remembered by their target consumers.

WHAT IS PERCEPTION?

Perception can be described as "how we see the world around us." Two individuals may be subjected to the same stimuli under apparently the same conditions, but how they recognize them, select them, organize them, and interpret them is a highly individual process, based on each person's own needs, values, expectations, and the like. The influence that each of these variables plays in the perceptual process, and its relevance to marketing, will be examined in some detail. First, however, we will examine some of the basic concepts that underlie the perceptual process. These will be discussed within the framework of consumer behavior.

Perception can be defined as *the process by which an individual selects, organizes, and interprets stimuli into a meaningful and coherent picture of the world.* A *stimulus* is any unit of input to any of the senses. Examples of stimuli (i.e., *sensory inputs*) include products, packages, brand names, advertisements, and commercials. *Sensory receptors* are the human organs (the eyes, ears, nose, mouth, and skin) that receive sensory inputs. Their sensory functions are to see, hear, smell, taste, and feel. All of these functions are called into play—either singly or in combination— in the evaluation and use of most consumer products. The study of perception is largely the study of what we subconsciously add to or subtract from our raw sensory inputs to produce our private picture of the world.

SENSATION

Sensation is the immediate and direct response of the sensory organs to simple stimuli (an illustration, a package, a brand name). Human sensitivity refers to the experience of sensation. An individual's sensitivity to stimuli varies both as a function of the quality of his *sensory receptors* (e.g., his eyesight or his hearing) and the amount or intensity of the stimuli to which he is exposed. For example, a blind person may have a more highly developed sense of hearing than the average sighted person, and may be able to hear sounds that the average person cannot.

Sensation itself depends on energy change or differentiation of input. A perfectly bland or unchanging environment—regardless of the strength of the sensory input—provides little or no sensation at all. Thus a person who lives on a busy street in midtown Manhattan would probably receive little or no sensation from the inputs of such noisy stimuli as horns honking, tires screeching, or fire engines clanging, since such sounds tend to be the rule in New York City. One more horn or one less horn honking would never be noticed. In situations where there is a great deal of sensory input, the senses do not detect small intensities or differences in input.

As the sensory input *decreases,* however, the ability to detect changes in input or intensity *increases,* to the point where we attain our maximum sensitivity under conditions of minimal stimulation. This accounts for the statement "It was so quiet I could hear a pin drop." It also accounts for the increased attention given to a commercial that appears alone during a program break, or the attention given to a black and white advertisement in a magazine full of four-color advertisements. This ability of the human organism to accommodate itself to varying levels of sensitivity as external conditions vary not only provides more sensitivity when it is needed but also serves to protect us from damaging, disruptive, or irrelevant bombardment when the input level is high.

THE ABSOLUTE THRESHOLD

The lowest level at which an individual can experience a sensation is called the *absolute threshold.* The point at which a person can detect a difference between "something" and "nothing" is that person's absolute threshold for that stimulus. To illustrate, the distance at which a driver can note a specific billboard on the highway is his absolute threshold. Two people riding together may first spot the billboard at different times (i.e., at different distances); thus they appear to have different absolute thresholds.

Under conditions of constant stimulation, such as driving through a "corridor" of billboards, the absolute threshold increases (that is, the senses tend to become increasingly dulled). After an hour of driving through billboards, it is doubtful that any one billboard will make an impression. Hence, we often speak of "getting used to" a hot bath, a cold shower, the bright sun, or even the odor in a locker room. In the field of perception, the term *adaptation* refers specifically to "getting used to" certain sensations, becoming accommodated to a certain level of stimulation. It is because of adaptation that advertisers tend to change their advertising campaigns seasonally. They are concerned that consumers will get so used to their current print ads and commercials that they will no longer "see" them; that is, the ads will no longer provide a sufficient sensory input to be noted.

Package designers try to determine consumers' absolute thresholds to make sure that their new product designs exceed this level, so that new products will stand out from the competition on retailers' shelves.

THE DIFFERENTIAL THRESHOLD

The minimal difference that can be detected between two stimuli is called the *differential threshold,* or the *j.n.d.* (for *just noticeable difference*). A nineteenth-century German scientist named Ernst Weber discovered that the just noticeable difference between two stimuli was not an absolute amount, but an amount relative to the intensity of the first stimulus.

Weber's law, as it has come to be known, states that the stronger the initial stimulus, the greater the additional intensity needed for the second stimulus to be perceived as different. For example, if the price of an automobile were increased by five dollars, it would probably not be noticed (that is, the increment would fall below the j.n.d.); it would probably take an increase of fifty dollars or more before a differential in price would be noticed. However, a ten-cent increase in the price of gasoline would be very quickly noticed by consumers, because of the relatively low price of gasoline.

According to Weber's law, an additional level of stimulus equivalent to a j.n.d. must be added for the majority of people to perceive a difference between the resulting stimulus and the initial stimulus.

Let us say that a manufacturer of silver polish wishes to improve his product sufficiently to claim that it retards tarnish longer than the leading competitor's. In a series of experiments, he has determined that the j.n.d. for his present polish, which now gives a shine that lasts about twenty days, is five days. According to Weber's law, the j.n.d. is

$$\frac{dI}{I} = k,$$

where k is the constant ratio, I is the initial stimulus, and dI is the just noticeable difference. In this case,

$$\frac{dI}{I} = \frac{5}{20} = \frac{1}{4}$$

That is, the shine given by the improved silver polish must last at least one-fourth longer than that of the present polish for it to be perceived by the majority of users as improved. By finding this j.n.d. of five days, the company has isolated the minimum amount of time necessary to make its claim of "lasts longer" believable to the majority of consumers.

If the company had decided to make the silver polish effective for forty days, it would have sacrificed a good deal of purchase frequency. If it had decided to make the polish effective for twenty-three days (just three extra days of product life), the improvement claim of "lasts longer" would not be perceived as true by most consumers. Making the product improvement just equal to the j.n.d. thus becomes the most efficient decision that management could make.

The j.n.d. has other uses as well. For example, retailers have long made use of a general rule of thumb that markdowns of merchandise must amount to at least 20 percent of the old price, since a smaller amount is often not noted by consumers.[1] Even the consent orders signed by the tobacco industry in 1972 took note of the j.n.d. They stipulated that the Surgeon General's warning concerning the hazards of cigarette smoking to health must appear in at least 10-point type in small-space advertisements, 12-point type in one-third-page ads, 14-point type in half-page ads, and 16-point type in full-page ads in standard-sized newspapers. These requirements recognize that the just noticeable difference is not an absolute size, but rather a relative size contingent upon the size of the total advertisement. The Federal Trade Commission monitors the size of the printed warnings in cigarette advertisements to ensure that people do have the opportunity to perceive them when reading cigarette advertisements.[2]

Weber's law is concerned with comparisons between two stimuli. It holds for all the senses and for almost all intensities. In the case of vision and hearing, it is operable in more than 99.9 percent of the useable stimulus range (the broad normal range of intensities).[3]

marketing applications of the j.n.d.

Weber's law has important applications to marketing. Manufacturers and marketers should endeavor to determine the relevant j.n.d. for their products for two very different reasons: (1) so that reductions in product size, increases in product price, and changes in packaging *are not* readily discernible to the public; and (2) so that product improvements *are* readily discernible to the public without being wastefully extravagant. For example, because of rising costs, many manufacturers are faced with the choice of increasing their prices or reducing the quantity or the quality of the product offered at the existing price. Manufacturers who choose the former alternative prefer to increase their prices to just under the j.n.d. so that the majority of consumers do not detect that the price has risen.

Manufacturers who choose to reduce the size or quality of their product try to ensure that product changes remain just under the point of noticeable difference. For example, when the price of coffee beans goes up, coffee processors often downgrade their quality by using inferior beans, up to but not including the j.n.d.—the point at which the consumer will notice a difference in taste.

Another type of problem faced by many marketers is the need to update their existing packaging without losing the ready recognition of consumers who have been exposed to years of cumulative advertising impact. In such cases, marketers usually make a number of imperceptible changes, each one carefully designed to fall below the j.n.d. so that consumers will not perceive the difference. For example, the familiar Crackerjack package which we have all known as children has undergone some fifteen to twenty changes in small increments over the years without alerting consumers that changes have been made.

The Campbell Soup Company has been one of the most subtle of all marketers in changing its package. An alteration here, a slight typographic change there, refinement of its logotype, have all combined to keep the product looking up-to-date without losing any of the valuable Campbell image. Campbell is still one of the most widely recognized packages in the world today.[4]

Another interesting example is Ivory soap, which was first introduced in 1879. The subtle packaging changes Ivory experienced over the years were each small enough to avoid notice, but in sum they contributed to a more contemporary look. The latest Ivory package is considerably different from the original (see Figure 3–1), but the changes

FIGURE 3–1

Sequential Changes in Packaging That Fall Below the J.N.D.

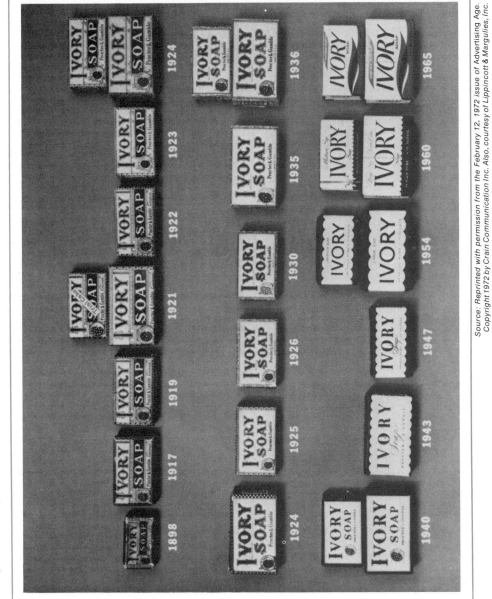

Source: Reprinted with permission from the February 12, 1972 issue of Advertising Age. Copyright 1972 by Crain Communication Inc. Also, courtesy of Lippincott & Margulies, Inc.

made each step of the way were so skillfully designed that the transition has been hardly noticeable to the consumer.

The examples given above are concerned with changes that marketers do not want consumers to perceive. When it comes to product improvements, however, marketers very much want to meet or exceed the consumer's differential threshold; that is, they want consumers to readily perceive the improvement made to the original product. One well-known marketing authority has suggested that marketers use the j.n.d. to determine the amount of improvement they should plan to make in their products.[5] Less than the j.n.d. is wasted because it will not be perceived; more than that may be wasteful because it will cut into repeat sales.

LEVELS OF AWARENESS

In the preceding chapter, we spoke of people being motivated "below their level of conscious awareness." People are also *stimulated* below their level of conscious awareness; that is, they can perceive stimuli without being consciously aware of the stimuli in question. The threshold for conscious awareness or conscious recognition appears to be higher than the absolute threshold for effective perception. Thus, stimuli that are too weak or too brief to be consciously seen or heard may nevertheless be strong enough to be perceived by one or more receptor cells. This process is called "subliminal perception" because the stimulus is *beneath* the threshold, or "limen," of awareness, though obviously not beneath the absolute thresholds of the receptors involved. (Perception of stimuli that are *above* the level of conscious awareness is called "supraliminal perception.")

Subliminal perception created a great furor in the 1950s when it was reported that advertisers could expose consumers to subliminal advertising messages that they were not aware of receiving. Supposedly, these messages could persuade people to buy goods or act in ways that would benefit the advertiser without being aware of why they did so. The effectiveness of such subliminal advertising was reportedly tested in a drive-in movie in New Jersey, where popcorn and Coca-Cola ads were flashed on the screen during the showing of the movie so rapidly that viewers were not consciously aware of having seen them. It was reported that during the six-week period of the test, popcorn sales increased 58 percent and Coca-Cola sales increased 18 percent.[6] However, since apparently no scientific controls were used in the so-called experiment, the results are somewhat dubious. What is more interesting, no one has been able to replicate the results. Although laboratory experiments have supported the notion that individuals can perceive subliminally, there is no scientific evidence that subliminal stimulation will cause subsequent action.[7] Therefore, it seems highly implausible that consumers can be persuaded to buy goods or to vote for candidates against their will. As the following section points out, stimuli are only one of a number of influences on perception; thus it is unlikely that they would have such an overriding influence on consumer behavior.

One researcher who conducted several experiments designed to test the effectiveness of subliminal stimulation found that while the simple subliminal stimulus COKE did serve to arouse thirst in subjects, the subliminal command to DRINK COKE did not have any greater effect nor did it have any behavioral consequences.[8] In another experiment, he found that subliminal stimuli associating a brand name with a sexy girl did not significantly affect recall or choice of the product by either sex.[9] It is clear that these experiments failed to demonstrate that subliminal stimuli can be used effectively to persuade consumers to buy. In summary, it appears that effective consumer persuasion still depends on supraliminal stimuli; that is, stimuli that are presented above the level of conscious awareness.

The dynamics of perception

The preceding section on sensation set the stage, so to speak, for our discussion of the dynamics of perception. It explained how the individual receives sensations from stimuli in the outside environment, and how the human organism adapts to the level and intensity of sensory input. We now come to one of the major principles of perception: raw sensory input by itself does not produce or explain the coherent picture of the world that most adults possess.

The human being is constantly being bombarded with stimuli of every type during every minute and every hour of every day. The sensory world is made up of an almost infinite number of discrete sensations, which are constantly, though perhaps minutely, changing. According to the principles of sensation, such heavy intensity of stimuli should serve to "turn off" most individuals, as the body protects itself from the heavy bombardment to which it is subjected. Otherwise, the billions of different stimuli to which we are constantly exposed might serve to totally confuse us and keep us perpetually disoriented in a constantly changing environment. However, neither of these alternatives tends to occur, because perception is not a function of sensory input alone; rather, it is the result of two different kinds of inputs which interact to form the personal pictures, the perceptions, that each individual experiences.

One type of input is the physical stimuli from the outside environment; the other type of input is provided by the individual himself in the form of certain predispositions, such as expectations, motives, and learning based on previous experience. The combination of these two very different kinds of inputs produces for each of us a very private, very personal picture of the world. Because each individual is a unique entity, with unique experiences, wants, needs, wishes, and expectations, it follows that each individual's perceptions are also unique. This explains why no two people see the world in precisely the same way.

Individuals are very selective in terms of which stimuli they "recognize;" they organize the stimuli they do recognize according to some widely-held subconscious, though innate, principles; and they give meaning to such stimuli (i.e., they interpret them) very subjectively in accordance with their own needs, expectations, and experiences. Let us examine in more detail each of these three aspects of perception: selection, organization, and interpretation.

PERCEPTUAL SELECTION

The consumer subconsciously exercises a great deal of selectivity regarding what aspects of the environment—what stimuli—she will perceive. She may look at some things, ignore others, and turn away from still others. In total she actually receives—or perceives—only a small fraction of the stimuli to which she is exposed. Consider, for example, the consumer in a supermarket. She is exposed to literally thousands of products of different colors, sizes, and shapes; to perhaps a hundred people (looking, walking, searching, talking); to smells (from fruit, from meat, from disinfectant, from people); to sounds within the store (cash registers ringing, shopping carts rolling, air conditioners humming, and clerks sweeping, mopping aisles, stocking shelves); and to sounds from outside the store (planes passing, cars honking, tires screeching, children shouting, car doors slamming). Yet she manages on a regular basis to visit her local supermarket, select the items she needs, pay for them, and leave, all within a relatively brief time, without losing her sanity or her personal orientation to the world around her. This is because she exercises selectivity in perception. Which stimuli get selected depends on two major factors in addition to the nature of the stimulus itself: the consumer's previous experience as it affects her expectations (what she is prepared or "set" to see) and her motives at the time (her needs, desires, interests, and so on). Each of these factors can serve to increase or decrease the probability that the stimulus will be perceived, and each can affect the consumer's selective exposure to and selective awareness of the stimulus itself.

nature of the stimulus

Marketing stimuli include an enormous number of variables, all of which affect the consumer's perception, such as the nature of the product, its physical attributes, the package design, the brand name, the advertisements and commercials (including copy claims, choice and sex of model, positioning of model, size of ad, and typography); the position of the ad or time of the commercial, and the editorial environment.

In general, contrast is one of the most attention-compelling attributes of a stimulus.[10] Advertisers often use extreme attention-getting devices to achieve maximum contrast and thus penetrate the consumer's perceptual screen. The chairman of the board of a major advertising agency once complained that his competitors were using "exotic locales, bizarre plots and overstated characterizations to a degree that is reducing the airwaves to an absolute babble."[11] Actually, advertising does not have to be "way out" to achieve a high degree of differentiation; it must simply contrast with the environment in which it is run. The use of lots of white space in an advertisement, the absence of sound in a commercial's opening scene, a sixty-second commercial in a string of twenty-second spots—all of these offer sufficient contrast from their environment to achieve differentiation and merit the consumer's attention.

Astute marketers usually try to differentiate their packaging sufficiently to ensure rapid consumer perception. Since the average package on the supermarket shelf has about one-tenth of a second to make an impression on the consumer, it is important that every aspect of the package—its name, shape, color, label, and copy—provide sufficient sensory stimulation to be noted and remembered. A survey designed to test whether consumers could recognize a number of well-known packages with their brand names concealed found that many packages do not achieve the recognition their marketers assume.[12] Figure 3–2 presents the packages tested in the study; Table 3–1 lists the recognition scores received. The packages with low recognition scores obviously do not provide sufficient sensory input to the consumer to be readily perceived and remembered.

expectations

People usually see what they expect to see, and what they expect to see is usually based on familiarity, on previous experience, or on preconditioned "set." A number of interesting experiments have supported this notion. For example, one researcher had a "guest speaker" give the same prepared lecture to two different college classes. He preconditioned the students in the first class by telling them in advance of the lecture that the speaker was an expert in his field but "cold" in nature; the second class was told that the speaker was an expert and "warm" in nature. Questionnaires completed after each lecture showed that the students who were "set" to hear a cold lecturer did indeed find him cold; those who anticipated a warm lecturer found him to be warm. Furthermore, there was more interaction and participation in the classroom discussion from those students who expected the lecturer to be warm than from those who expected him to be cold.[13]

In a marketing context, people tend to perceive products and product attributes according to their own expectations. A housewife who has been told by her friends that a new brand of coffee has a bitter taste will probably perceive the taste to be bitter; a teenager who attends a horror movie that has been billed as terrifying will probably find it so.

On the other hand, stimuli that conflict sharply with expectations often receive more attention than those that conform to expectations. In other words, novelty tends to promote perception. An advertisement for bathing suits by Cole of California showed a lineup of pretty girls on a beach wearing a variety of bathing suit styles. However, the girl on the end wore no suit at all. Research showed that many readers simply glanced at the advertisement and started to turn the page; they then did a double take when they realized what they had seen and turned back to

FIGURE 3–2

Well-Known Packaged Goods Tested for Recognition

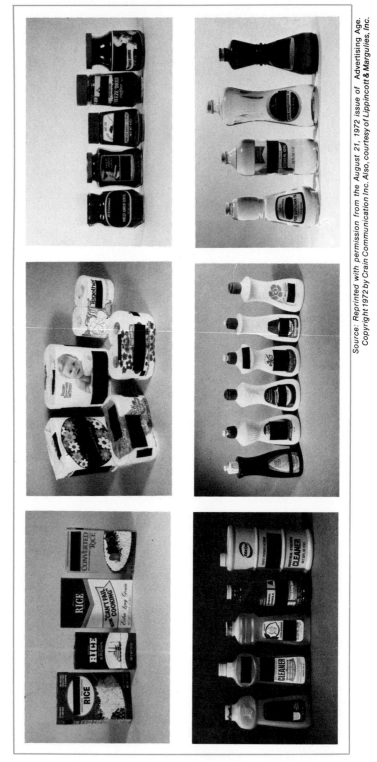

Source: Reprinted with permission from the August 21, 1972 issue of Advertising Age. Copyright 1972 by Crain Communication Inc. Also, courtesy of Lippincott & Margulies, Inc.

TABLE 3–1
Recognition Scores of Well-Known Packaged Goods

Product	Recognition
Rice	
Minute Rice	62%
River	–
Carolina	63%
Uncle Ben's	72%
Bathroom Tissue	
Waldorf (top row)	20%
Charmin (top row)	97%
Hudson (top row)	20%
Lady Scott (bottom row)	42%
Soft-Weve (bottom row)	–
Freeze-Dried Coffee	
Brown Gold	11%
Taster's Choice	92%
Maxim	51%
Martinson's	9%
Yuban	72%
Liquid Cleaners	
Top Job	29%
Lysol	18%
Mr. Clean	68%
Lestoil	30%
Janitor in a Drum	87%
Liquid Dishwashers	
Palmolive	52%
Joy	51%
Dove	50%
Ivory	39%
Ajax	–
Lux	31%
Salad Oils	
Kraft	–
Mazola	63%
Wesson	55%
Crisco	64%

Source: Reprinted with permission from the August 21, 1972 issue of Advertising Age.
Copyright 1972 by Crain Communication Inc. Also, courtesy of Lippincott & Margulies, Inc.

look at the ad more closely. Thus the ad ended up receiving much more attention than it otherwise would have, simply because of the inclusion of an element that surprised readers.

Advertisers of sheets and blankets are beginning to discover that showing a male model in bed instead of the traditional female model improves readership. After running a series of ads for its sheets which featured a male model, J. P. Stevens reported receiving a number of approving letters from consumers, one of which said: "For ten years as a housewife, I have never noticed an ad for sheets that particularly caught my attention—until this one."[14]

For years certain advertisers have used blatant sexuality in advertisements for products to which sex was not relevant because they knew such advertisements attracted a high degree of attention; however, such ads often defeated their own purpose because readers tended to remember the sex (e.g., the girl), but not the product. Today sexuality in advertising has become so commonplace that it has ceased to shock; since it no longer stands out as "different" from other advertisements, it is not as readily perceived as it was in an earlier day.

motives

People tend to perceive things they need or want; the stronger the need, the greater the tendency to ignore unrelated stimuli in the environment. A housewife who wants to replace her bed will carefully note every mattress advertisement in her local newspaper; one who has no need of a new bed will rarely notice such advertisements. In general, there is a heightened awareness of stimuli that are relevant to one's needs and interests, and a decreased awareness of stimuli that are irrelevant to those needs.

An individual's perceptual process simply attunes itself more closely to those elements of the environment that are important to her. A hungry man looks for, and more readily perceives, signs of food; a sexually repressed person perceives sexual symbolism where none may exist.

Marketing managers recognize the efficiency of targeting their products to the perceived needs of consumers. In this way, they help to ensure that their products will be perceived by potential prospects. The identification of perceived consumer needs has a number of different applications. For example, marketers can determine through marketing research what consumers consider to be the ideal attributes of the product category, or what consumers perceive their needs to be in relation to the product category. The marketer can then segment his market on the basis of these needs into a number of smaller market segments, each composed of individuals with similar perceived needs in connection with the product category. The marketer is now able to develop different marketing strategies for each segment which stress how his product can fulfill the perceived needs of that segment. In this way, the marketer can vary his advertising to specific market segments so that consumers in each segment will perceive the product as meeting their own specific needs, wants, and interests.

related concepts

As the preceding discussion illustrates, the consumer's "selection" of stimuli from the environment is based on the interaction of her expectations and her motives with the stimulus itself. These factors give rise to a number of important concepts concerning perception.

SELECTIVE EXPOSURE. Consumers actively seek out messages that are pleasant or with which they are sympathetic, and they actively avoid painful or threatening ones. Thus, heavy smokers avoid articles that link cigarette smoking to cancer and note (and quote) the relatively few that deny the relationship. Consumers also selectively expose themselves to advertisements that reassure them of the wisdom of their purchase decisions.

SELECTIVE ATTENTION. Consumers have a heightened awareness of stimuli that meet their needs or their interests and a depressed awareness of stimuli irrelevant to their needs. Thus they are likely to note ads for products that meet their needs and disregard those in which they have no interest. While estimates of the number of advertisements the average consumer is exposed to each day vary widely (from about three hundred to fifteen hundred exposures per day), daily exposure to magazines, newspapers, television, radio, billboards, direct mail, transit advertising, and the like is undoubtedly far above the five hundred mark.[15] *Exposure* however, is not equivalent to *perception.*

People also vary in the kind of information in which they are interested and in the form of message and type of medium they prefer. Some people are more interested in price, some in appearance, and some in social acceptability.[16] Some people like complex, sophisticated messages; others like simple graphics. Consumers, therefore, exercise a great deal of selectivity in terms of the attention they give to commercial stimuli.

PERCEPTUAL DEFENSE. Consumers subconsciously screen out stimuli that for them are important *not* to see, even though exposure has already taken place. Thus, threatening or otherwise damaging stimuli are less apt to reach awareness than neutral stimuli at the same level of exposure.[17] Furthermore, individuals may distort information that is not consistent with their needs, values, beliefs, and so forth.[18] For example, a consumer may "hear" that a set of dishes she loves is dishwasher safe (even though the salesclerk has clearly warned her it is not), because the dishes match her dining-room rug so perfectly. This is another example of people hearing what they want to hear rather than what has actually been said.

PERCEPTUAL BLOCKING. Consumers protect themselves from bombardment of stimuli by simply "tuning out"—blocking such stimuli from achieving conscious awareness. For example, tests have shown that enormous amounts of advertising are being screened out by consumers, though there are suggestions that this problem may be more severe for television than for print.[19] Various hypotheses have been offered to explain why television advertising recall scores are falling, such as the greater amount of time allotted for commercials, the use of shorter commercials (and thus the greater number of advertising messages aired within the same period of time), the greater number of commercials that are strung together back to back, the greater number of advertisers, and the greater number of products being advertised.

In 1969, the American Association of Advertising Agencies conducted a joint study with Harvard University in which a large national sample of consumers were asked to register every advertisement they saw in a half-day period on a mechanical counter.[20] Most of the respondents noted from 11 to 20 advertising exposures during this period, yet the most recently cited figure at the time the study was conducted indicated that the average adult was exposed to about 150 advertisements in the same period (or 300 in a full day.) A leading advertising agency head said: "People are tired. They see lots of ads. They have seen lots of ads."[21] Obviously, seeing these ads and perceiving them are far from the same thing.

PERCEPTUAL ORGANIZATION

People do not experience the numerous stimuli that they select from the environment as separate and discrete sensations; rather, they tend to organize them into groups and perceive them as unified wholes. Thus the perceived characteristics of even the simplest stimulus are viewed as a function of the whole to which the stimulus appears to belong. This method of organization simplifies life considerably for the consumer.

The specific principles underlying perceptual organization are often referred to by the name given the school of psychologists who first developed and stressed "Gestalt" psychology. (*Gestalt* in German means "pattern" or "configuration".) Three of the most basic principles of organization center on figure and ground relationships, grouping, and closure.

figure and ground

We noted earlier that to be noticed, stimuli must contrast with their environment. A sound must be louder or softer, a color brighter or paler. The simplest visual illustration consists of a figure on a ground (i.e., background). The figure is usually perceived clearly because, in contrast to its ground, it appears to be well defined, solid, and in the forefront. The ground, however, is usually perceived as indefinite, hazy, and continuous. The common line that separates the figure and the ground is perceived as belonging to the figure rather than to the ground, which helps give the figure greater definition. Consider the stimulus of music. People can either "bathe" in music or listen to music. In the first case, music is simply ground to other activities; in the second, it is figure. Figure is more clearly perceived because it appears to be dominant; by contrast, ground appears to be subordinate and therefore unimportant.

People have a tendency to organize their perceptions into figure and ground relationships. However, learning affects which stimuli will be perceived as figure and which as ground. We are all familiar with reversible figure-ground patterns, such as the picture of the woman in Figure 3–3. How old would you say she was? Look again, very carefully. Depending on how you perceived figure and how you perceived ground, she can be either in her twenties or her late seventies.

Like perceptual selection, perceptual organization is affected by motives and by expectations based on experience. For example, how a reversible figure-ground pattern will be seen can be influenced by prior pleasant or painful associations with one or the other element in isolation.

The consumer's own physical state can also affect how she per-

Figure 3–3

Figure-Ground Reversal

ceives reversible figure-ground illustrations. For example, after a particularly strenuous week, the thirty-five-year-old secretary of one of the
authors happened to note with surprise the picture of the old woman
shown in Figure 3–3. It took a great deal of concentrated effort for her
to recognize it as the reversal of the picture of the smartly dressed young
woman that she had been used to seeing on the author's desk.

Advertisers have to plan their advertisements carefully to make
sure that the stimulus they want noted is seen as figure and not as
ground. The musical background must not overwhelm the jingle; the
background of an advertisement must not detract from the product.
Some print advertisers often silhouette their products against a white
background to make sure that the features they want noted are clearly
perceived. Others use reverse lettering (white letters on a black background) to achieve contrast; however, they must be careful to avoid the
problem of figure-ground reversal.

Marketers sometimes make the mistake of running advertisements
that confuse the consumer because there is no clear indication of what is
figure and what is ground. A steel company that produces the steel for a
variety of products, including bedsprings, once ran an ad that showed a
sexy-looking girl bouncing up and down on a bed. Many critics won-
dered aloud just which product the sponsor was selling, i.e., which was
figure and which was ground.

We also tend to structure the social environment into figure and
ground, much as we do the impersonal environment. We see the world
clearly as "us" and "them," as "good guys" and "bad guys," as friends and
enemies. Politicians and reporters have often structured the world into
the "free world" and the "Communist world," ignoring many of the
other differences between nations and governments and people.[22]

grouping

Individuals tend to automatically group stimuli so that they form a
unified picture or impression. Experiments have shown that the perception of stimuli as groups or "chunks" of information, rather than as discrete bits of information, facilitates their memory and recall.[23] For example, most of us can remember and repeat our social security numbers
because we automatically group them into three chunks rather than nine
separate numbers. When the telephone company introduced the idea of
all-digit telephone numbers, consumers objected strenuously on the
grounds that they would not be able to recall or repeat so many numbers. However, because we automatically group telephone numbers into
just two chunks (or three, with the area code), the problems that were
anticipated never occurred.

Grouping can be used advantageously by marketers to imply certain desired meanings in connection with their products. For example,
an advertisement for tea may show a young man and woman sipping tea
in a well-furnished room before a blazing hearth. The grouping of

stimuli by proximity leads the consumer to associate the drinking of tea with romance, fine living, and winter warmth.

closure

Individuals have a need for closure. They express this need by organizing their perceptions so that they form a complete picture. If the pattern of stimuli to which they are exposed is incomplete, they tend to perceive it, nevertheless, as complete; that is, they consciously or subconsciously fill in the missing pieces. Thus a circle that has a section of its periphery missing will usually be perceived as whole. The need for closure is also seen in the tension that an individual experiences when a task is incomplete, and the satisfaction and relief that come upon its completion. A classic study reported in 1927 found that incomplete tasks are better remembered than complete tasks.[24] One explanation for this phenomenon is that the person who begins a task develops a need to complete it. If he is prevented from doing so, he is left in a state of tension, which manifests itself in improved memory for the uncompleted task. One researcher extended this theory to advertising messages and suggested that hearing the beginning of a message leads to the development of a need to hear the rest of it—"rather like waiting for the second shoe to drop."[25] The resulting tension leads to improvement in memory for that part of the message that has already been heard.

The need for closure has some interesting implications for marketers. The presentation of an incomplete advertising message "begs" for completion by the consumer, and the very act of completion serves to involve her more deeply in the message itself. Thus an incomplete ad tends to be perceived more readily than a complete one. Clever marketers have tried to exploit this phenomenon by constructing commercials that are deliberately "interrupted" before their expected finish. For example, Salem cigarettes very successfully ran a commercial that featured a catchy musical jingle that went: "You can take Salem out of the country, *but,* you can't take the country out of Salem." After repeating the jingle a number of times, the commercial ceased abruptly on a high note after the "*but.*" Due to the individual's need for closure, for completion, listeners invariably completed the jingle themselves, either aloud or silently: ". . . you can't take the country out of Salem." Such close involvement with the commercial served to increase its overall impact on the consumer.

In a related vein, advertisers have discovered that they can use the soundtrack of a frequently shown television commercial on radio with excellent results. Consumers who are familiar with the TV commercial perceive the audio part alone as incomplete; in their need for completion, they mentally play back the visual content as well.

In summary, it is clear that perceptions are not equivalent to the raw sensory input of discrete stimuli or the sum total of discrete stimuli. Rather, people tend to add to or subtract from the stimuli to which they are exposed according to their own expectations and motives, using generalized principals of organization based on Gestalt theory.

PERCEPTUAL INTERPRETATION

The preceding discussion has emphasized that perception is a personal phenomenon. People exercise selectivity in terms of which stimuli they perceive, and they organize these stimuli on the basis of certain psychological principles. The interpretation of stimuli is also uniquely individual, since it is based upon what the consumer expects to see in light of her previous experience, on the number of plausible explanations she can envision, and on her motives and interests at the time of perception.

Stimuli are often highly ambiguous. Some stimuli are weak because of such factors as poor visibility, brief exposure, high noise level, and constant fluctuation. Even stimuli that are strong tend to fluctuate dramatically because of such factors as different angles of viewing, varying distances, and changing levels of illumination.

The consumer usually attributes the sensory input she receives to sources that she considers most likely to have caused the specific pattern of stimuli. Past experience and social interaction with other people may help to form certain expectations which provide categories or alternatives that the individual can use in interpreting stimuli.[26] The narrower the individual's experience, the more limited her access to alternative categories.

When stimuli are highly ambiguous, an individual will usually interpret them in such a way that they serve to fulfill her own needs, wishes, interests, and so on. It is this principle that provides the rationale for the projective tests discussed in Chapter 2. Such tests provide ambiguous stimuli (such as incomplete sentences, unclear pictures, untitled cartoons, and inkblots) to respondents who are asked to interpret them. How a person describes a vague illustration, what meaning he ascribes to an inkblot, is a reflection not of the stimulus itself, but of his own needs, wants, and desires. Thus, through the interpretation of ambiguous stimuli, the respondent reveals a great deal about himself.

How close a person's interpretations are to reality, then, depends on the clarity of the stimulus, the past experiences of the perceiver, and his motives and interests at the time of perception.

distorting influences on perception

The individual is also subject to a number of influences that tend to distort perception, some of which are discussed below.

PHYSICAL APPEARANCES. People tend to attribute the qualities they associate with certain people to others who may resemble them whether or not they consciously recognize the similarity. For this reason, the selection of models for advertisements and for television commercials can be a key element in their ultimate persuasibility. For example, baking advice given by a woman who looks like somebody's kindly old grandmother is likely to be perceived as very helpful.

STEREOTYPES. Individuals tend to carry "pictures in their minds" of the meaning of various kinds of stimuli. These stereotypes serve as expectations of what specific situations or people or events will be like and are important determinants of how such stimuli are subsequently perceived. For example, an ad headlined "First Date" which shows a young man ringing a front doorbell will set up a whole chain of expectations and interpretations based on stereotypical movies, TV shows, and books.

HALO EFFECT. A generalized impression that may be favorable or unfavorable is extended to the interpretation of nonrelevant stimuli. This effect tends to be more pronounced when the perceiver is interpreting stimuli with which he has had little experience. Thus a consumer who is very satisfied with her Sears vacuum cleaner may decide that Sears is the best place to shop for all her appliances.

RESPECTED SOURCES. We tend to give added perceptual weight to advice coming from sources we respect. Marketers often use celebrities or known experts to give testimonials for their products or to act as company spokesmen to ensure that their products will be perceived well.

IRRELEVANT CUES. When required to form a difficult perceptual judgment, consumers often respond to irrelevant stimuli. For example, many high-priced automobiles are sold on the basis of color, or an illuminated vanity mirror, or type of upholstery, rather than on the basis of mechanical or technical superiority.

FIRST IMPRESSIONS. First impressions tend to be lasting, yet in forming such impressions the perceiver does not yet know which stimuli are relevant, important, or predictive of later behavior. For this reason, introducing a new product before all its "bugs" have been worked out may prove fatal to the product because subsequent information about its superiority, though true, will often be negated by memory of its early failure.

JUMPING TO CONCLUSIONS. Many people tend to jump to conclusions before examining all the relevant evidence. For example, the consumer often perceives just the beginning of a commercial message and draws her conclusions regarding the product or service being advertised on the basis of such limited information. For this reason, the advertising copywriter should be careful not to save his best "shots" for last.

The reader may well ask how "realistic" perception can be, given the many subjective influences of the consumer on her perceptual interpretations. It is therefore somewhat reassuring to remember that previous experience usually serves to resolve stimulus ambiguity in a realistic way and helps in its interpretation. It is only in situations of unusual or changing stimuli conditions that learned expectations lead to wrong interpretations.

Consumer imagery

Consumers have a number of enduring perceptions, or images, which are particularly relevant to the study of consumer behavior. These include the image they hold of themselves and their perceived image of products and product categories, of retail stores, and of producers.

SELF-IMAGE

Each person has a perceived image of himself as a certain kind of person, with certain traits, habits, possessions, relationships, and ways of behaving. As with other types of perceptions, each individual's self-image is unique, a product of his own background and experience. The individual develops his perceived self-image through interactions with other people: his parents to begin with, then other individuals or groups with whom he relates over the years.

Products and other objects have symbolic value for the individual, who evaluates them on the basis of their consistency (i.e., congruence) with his personal picture of himself. Some products seem to agree with the individual's self-image; others seem totally alien to the kind of person he perceives himself to be. The consumer attempts to preserve or enhance his self-image by buying products that he believes are congruent with his self-image and avoiding products that are not. These strategies have been the subject of a number of consumer studies.[27]

Several researchers have explored the notion that an individual's ideal self-concept (that is, how an individual would like to perceive himself) is more relevant to consumption behavior than his actual self-concept (how he does perceive himself). However, there is no evidence as yet that the distinction is relevant to product choice.[28]

The concept of self-image has strategy implications for marketers. For example, marketers can segment their markets on the basis of relevant consumer self-images and position their products as symbols of such self-images. Such a marketing strategy is in complete agreement with the classical marketing concept, in that the marketer first determines what the consumer's needs are (both in respect to the product category and in respect to an appropriate symbol of her self-image) and proceeds to develop and market a product that meets both criteria.

PRODUCT IMAGE

The way the product is perceived is probably more important to its ultimate marketing success than are its actual product characteristics. For example, taste tests reveal that most beer drinkers cannot discriminate between beer tastes, but many brand-loyal beer drinkers insist that their brand of beer has a superior taste.[29] In such cases, it is clear that the *image* of the product prevails, since taste tests do not support any other conclusion.

product positioning

Marketers try to "position" their brands so that they are perceived by specific market segments as fulfilling certain needs or possessing certain attributes. The product's positioning is especially important in relation to other brands in the same product category. For example, a toothpaste manufacturer may position his product as a mouth deodorant because research reveals that this niche is not being occupied by competing brands. In effect, he seeks to carve out a market segment of toothpaste users who are more interested in the mouthwash characteristics of toothpaste than they are, for example, in decay prevention, teeth whiteners, or sex appeal.

The technique of perceptual mapping helps marketers to determine just how their products appear to consumers in relation to competitive brands on one or more product characteristics. It enables them to see gaps in the positioning of all brands in the product class, and to identify areas in which consumer needs are not being adequately met. The manufacturer of luxury car *A* (see Figure 3–4) may discover that consumers now perceive his car to be very similar to luxury cars *B* and *C;* at the same time, he may note that consumers do not perceive any luxury car to have good gas mileage. To carve out a new market segment con-

Figure 3–4

A Consumer's Perceptual Map of Automobile Characteristics Facilitates Product Positioning

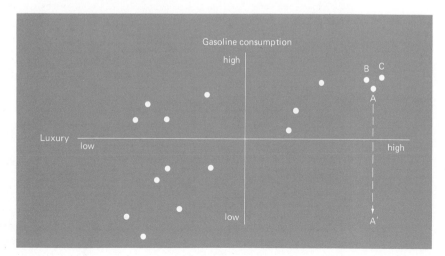

sisting of luxury owners who are interested in low gas consumption, he may decide to reposition his car's image from point A to point A' (i.e., as a low-gas-consumption luxury car). This could be accomplished through a promotional campaign directed to the luxury car market which stresses both luxury and good gas mileage. Of course, such a campaign could not succeed unless the car actually does have low gas consumption

unfavorable product images

Sometimes product categories develop unfavorable images that inhibit their success in the marketplace. These images may result from early unfavorable trial of a product, or simply from human resistance to change. Unfortunately, many unfavorable product images tend to persist. For this reason, marketers should resist the temptation of introducing a new product prematurely; that is, before it has been totally perfected. (Remember, first impressions tend to be lasting.)

Sometimes unfavorable product images may be totally unwarranted. For example, some people claim that decaffeinated coffee is inferior in taste to regular coffee. In blind taste tests, however, consumers have not been able to differentiate between the two.[30]

evoked set

The specific brands that a consumer will consider in making a purchase choice in a particular product category are known as her "evoked

FIGURE 3-5

The Evoked Set as a Subset of All Brands in a Product Class

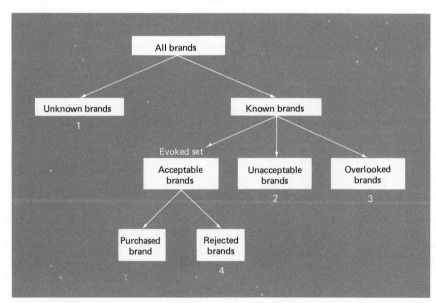

set." Regardless of the total number of brands in a product category, the consumer's evoked set tends to be quite small. A study concerning such large product categories as toothpaste and laundry detergent revealed an average evoked set of only three brands and five brands respectively.[31] This is not surprising, since research indicates that most people have a span of recall limited to approximately seven items.[32]

Among those brands with which the consumer is familiar, there are acceptable brands, unacceptable brands, and overlooked (or forgotten) brands. The evoked set consists of the small number of brands that the consumer is familiar with, remembers, and finds acceptable. Figure 3–5 presents a simple model of the evoked set as a subset of all available brands in a product category. As the figure indicates, it is essential that a product be part of a consumer's evoked set if it is to be considered at all. The four terminal positions in the model which do *not* end in purchase (labeled 1, 2, 3, and 4) would appear to have perceptual problems. For example: (1) Brands may be *unknown* because of the consumer's selective exposure to advertising media and her selective perception of advertising stimuli. (2) Brands may be *unacceptable* because of poor or inappropriate positioning in either advertising or product characteristics or both. (3) Brands may be *overlooked* because they have not been clearly positioned or sharply targeted at the consumer market segment under study. (4) Brands may be *rejected* because they are perceived by the consumer as unable to satisfy her perceived needs as completely as the brand she selects.

In each of these instances, the implication for marketers is that promotional techniques should be designed to impart a more favorable, perhaps more relevant, product image to the target consumer. This may sometimes require a change in product attributes as well.

perceived quality

Consumers often judge the quality of a product on the basis of a variety of informational cues which they associate with the product. Some of these cues are intrinsic to (inherent in) the product, such as specific product characteristics; others are extrinsic to (external to) the product, such as price, store image, brand image, and promotional message.[33] Either singly or in composite, such cues provide the basis for perceptions concerning product quality.

INTRINSIC CUES. Cues that are intrinsic concern physical characteristics of the product itself, such as size, color, flavor, or aroma. Consumers like to believe that they base their product quality evaluations on intrinsic cues, because they can justify resulting product decisions (either positive or negative) on the basis of "rational" or "objective" product choice. However, research studies rarely support this thesis. Many brand-loyal customers cannot identify their own brands in blind taste tests despite their claims of taste superiority. Other tests have also indicated that intrinsic product cues are not easily discerned by consumers; thus they are not likely to be the basis for product quality perceptions.

In one study, Budweiser-loyal beer drinkers were asked to sample two beers: first Budweiser and then a second brand of beer which they had professed to dislike. The subjects could not bring themselves to finish the second beer because of its "skunky" and "terrible" taste. In actuality, both samples of beer were Budweiser. In this situation, perception of taste was clearly based on the product images, not on actual taste differences.[34] In another study, housewives were asked to evaluate the tastes of two different beverages successively, which were identified as Coke and Diet Coke.[35] The housewives were enthusiastic about the Coke but complained about the bitter aftertaste of Diet Coke. Both samples, however, actually contained the same beverage—regular Coke. Because some of the early diet beverages did have a bitter aftertaste, many consumers simply attributed that characteristic to all diet sodas and thus "tasted" (perceived) what they expected to taste. Other consumers may not have wished to identify with a product designed for overweight people because of its lack of congruence with their self-images.

The inability of most consumers to discriminate cola beverages in blind taste tests became the basis for a major marketing campaign in the mid-1970s, in which Pepsi Cola invited consumers to "Take the Pepsi Challenge" and compare the tastes of Pepsi and its arch rival, Coke. This campaign played up the fact that a major number of self-professed Coke drinkers actually chose Pepsi as their preferred drink in blind taste test comparisons. Figure 3–6 presents a print advertisement from this campaign.

EXTRINSIC CUES. In the absence of actual experience with a product, consumers often "evaluate" quality on the basis of factors quite external to the product itself, such as its price, the image of the store(s) that carries it, or the image (that is, the reputation) of the manufacturer who produces it.

1. *Price-Quality Relationship.* A number of research studies support the view that consumers rely on price as an indicator of product quality. Several studies have shown that consumers attribute differential qualities to identical products that carry different price labels. For example, one study reported that subjects ranked the quality of three samples of unlabeled beer in a direct relationship to the prices they carried: the high-priced beer was ranked first in quality, the medium-priced beer second, and the low-priced beer as lowest in quality, despite the fact that all three beer samples were actually the same brand.[36] Another study found that housewives rated high-priced panty hose as better in quality than medium-priced or low-priced panty hose, even though the three samples were of identical quality.[37] Some marketers have successfully used the price-quality relationship to position their products as the top quality offering in their product category. For example, Chock Full O' Nuts coffee was introduced as a high-priced coffee that was "worth the difference" in cost because of "superior" flavor and taste.

FIGURE 3–6

Pepsi Challenges Coke Drinkers in Blind Taste Test Comparisons

A message to consumers from the Pepsi-Cola Company.

We have believed for a long time that we produce a better-tasting product than our leading competitor. But we wanted to be sure of that fact. We did not want to advertise it until we had it documented by careful, objective, independent research. We now have that documentation.

Truth in advertising is very important to us. And the truth is:

NATIONWIDE, MORE COCA-COLA DRINKERS PREFER PEPSI THAN COKE.

The better taste we always thought we had has now been confirmed by blind taste tests conducted among thousands of people in over a hundred cities and towns throughout this country. This concrete fact may explain some of the strange advertising sponsored by the Coca-Cola Company lately. Advertising like the silly blindfold commercials comparing Fresca (a sugar-free, citrus flavored drink) with Pepsi. These commercials announce that one third of the participants chose Fresca. They fail to point out that what this actually means is that *two thirds* preferred Pepsi.

Now they've come out with a series of comparative commercials in which both Pepsi and Coke are tasted side-by-side. In these, they claim that New Yorkers prefer Coke to Pepsi 2 to 1. But each product in these commercial tests is clearly identified. How can the results be valid when the only fair test must be a *blind* test, eliminating the bias of habit, which may have nothing to do with taste.

All this is Coca-Cola's attempt to answer what we call, "The Pepsi Challenge." The fact that none of these efforts constitute a real answer is not surprising. After all, how can there be a real answer when there is no real question, no question whatsoever that NATIONWIDE, MORE COCA-COLA DRINKERS PREFER PEPSI THAN COKE. (And, of course, Pepsi-Cola drinkers overwhelmingly prefer Pepsi.)

But don't take our word for it. Don't take anybody's word for it—

Let your taste decide. Take the Pepsi Challenge.

For a summary of these research findings, please write to P.O. Box 102, Purchase, New York 10577

Courtesy of the Pepsi-Cola Company.

2. *Store image.* Retail stores have images of their own, which serve to influence the perceived quality of products they carry as well as the decisions of consumers as to where to shop. For example, retail stores may have a high-fashion image, a low-price image, a wide-selection image, or a good-service image. The type of product the consumer wishes to buy will influence her selection of retail outlet; conversely, her evaluation of a product will be influenced by her knowledge of where it was bought. A consumer wishing to buy an elegant dress for a special occasion may go to a store with an elegant, high-fashion image, such as Bergdorf Goodman in New York. Regardless of what she actually pays for the dress she selects (regular price or marked-down price), she will probably perceive its quality to be high. However, she may perceive the quality of the same dress to be much lower if she buys it in a discount store with a low-price image.

Most studies of the effects of extrinsic cues on perceived product quality have focused on just one variable—price or store image. However, where another extrinsic cue is available, it is likely that perceived quality will be a function of the interaction of both cues on the consumer. To test this hypothesis, four identical samples of carpet—cut from the same bolt—were given to female subjects, who were asked to rate their quality on a scale from very low to very high.[38] Each carpet sample was labeled with a price and the name of a store, as follows: (1) high-image store, high price; (2) high-image store, low price; (3) low-image store, high price; and (4) low-image store, low price. The researchers discovered that the samples with the high price were perceived as having significantly better quality than the samples with the low price; similarly, the samples from the prestige store had a somewhat better perceived image than the samples from the low-prestige store. In addition, the researchers found that the interactive effects of both price and store image significantly altered the subjects' perceptions of the product's quality from the perceptions achieved by either cue alone.

3. *Manufacturer's image.* Consumer imagery extends beyond perceived price and store image to the producers themselves. Manufacturers who enjoy a favorable image generally find that their new products are accepted more readily than those of manufacturers who have a less favorable or "neutral" image. Obviously, consumers have greater confidence that they will not be disappointed in a major name-brand product. Buying well-known brands is a consumer purchasing strategy that will be discussed later in the chapter.

PERCEIVED RISK

Consumers must constantly make decisions regarding what products or services to buy and where to buy them. Because the outcomes (or consequences) of such decisions are often uncertain, the consumer faces some degree of "risk" in making a purchase decision. The concept of *perceived risk* has been defined as follows: "Consumer behavior involves risk in the sense that any action of a consumer will produce consequences which he cannot anticipate with anything approximating certainty."[39] This definition highlights two relevant dimensions of perceived risk: *uncertainty* and *consequences.*

The degree of risk that the consumer perceives and her own tolerance for risk-taking serve to influence her purchase strategies. It should be stressed that the consumer is influenced only by risk that she *perceives,* whether or not such risk actually exists. Risk that is not perceived — no matter how real or how dangerous — will not influence consumer behavior. Furthermore, the amount of money involved in the purchase is not directly related to the amount of risk perceived. Selecting the right mouthwash may present as great a risk to the consumer as selecting a new television set.

why consumers perceive risk

In making product decisions, the consumer perceives risk because she may have had little or no experience with the product or product category she is considering — either because she has never used it or because it is new on the market. Or, she may have had an unsatisfactory experience with another brand and is somewhat concerned about making a similar mistake. Her financial resources may be very limited, so that she may recognize that her selection of one product requires her to forgo purchase of another. Finally, she may feel that she has very limited knowledge on which to base a decision or she may lack self-confidence in her ability to make the "right" decision.

types of risk

The major types of risk that a consumer perceives in making product decisions include the following: functional risk, physical risk, financial risk, social risk, and psychological risk. They are defined as follows:

1. *Functional risk*—the risk that the product will not perform as expected. ("Will the dishwasher really clean my dishes *and* my pots?")
2. *Physical risk*—the risk to self and to others which the product may pose. ("Is a microwave oven really safe or does it emit harmful radiation?")
3. *Financial risk*—the risk that the product will not be worth its cost either in time or in money. ("Will graduate school really help me get a better job?")
4. *Social risk*—the risk that a poor product choice may result in embarrassment before others. ("Will that new deodorant really suppress perspiration odor?")
5. *Psychological risk*—the risk that a poor product choice will bruise the consumer's ego. ("Will I really be happy in this house?")

Table 3–2 lists the specific types of uncertainty that the consumer faces in making product choices. These are categorized by the types of perceived risk listed above.

TABLE 3-2

Types of Uncertainty Faced by Consumers Making Product Decisions

Type of Risk	Type of Uncertainty
Functional	1. Will it do what it's supposed to do? 2. Will it last? 3. Will it work as well as or better than competitive products?
Physical	1. Is it safe to use? 2. Does it pose any physical threat to others? 3. Does it pose any danger to the environment?
Financial	1. Is it the best use of my limited funds? 2. Is it worth the money (or time or effort) it costs?
Social	1. Will my family and friends *approve*? 2. Will it *please* others whose opinions are important to me? 3. Is it similar to products used by groups with whom I identify?
Psychological	1. Will I feel good using it? 2. Will it impress others? 3. Do I deserve it? 4. Will I make the right decision?

the perception of risk varies

Studies show that the perception of risk by the consumer varies, depending on the person, the product, and the situation.

RISK PERCEPTION VARIES BY CONSUMER. The *amount* of risk perceived depends on the consumer. Some consumers tend to perceive high degrees of risk in various consumption situations; others tend to perceive little risk.[40] High-risk perceivers have been described as "narrow categorizers," since they limit their product choices to a few safe alternatives.[41] They would rather exclude some perfectly good alternatives than chance a poor selection. Low-risk perceivers have been described as "broad categorizers," since they tend to make their choices from a much wider range of alternatives.[42] They would rather risk a poor selection than limit the number of alternatives from which they can choose.

The *kind* of risk perceived also depends on the consumer. For example, a study of the acceptance of a new product found that low-risk perceivers reported perceiving only one risk in buying the new product (inconvenience—a functional risk), while high-risk perceivers perceived two major risks (wasting money—a financial risk, and their husbands' reactions—a social risk).[43] Along these lines, other consumer researchers have suggested that the importance of possible negative consequences of a specific purchase decision may vary by individual and thus may be a relevant variable upon which to segment markets.[44]

RISK PERCEPTION VARIES BY PRODUCT CATEGORY. An individual's perception of risk varies with product categories. For example, purchasers of headache remedies were found to perceive a higher degree of risk than did purchasers of dry spaghetti.[45] Similarly, consumers were found to perceive a higher degree of risk in the purchase of color television sets than in the purchase of golf clubs.[46]

RISK PERCEPTION VARIES WITH THE SHOPPING SITUATION. Researchers have found that the degree of risk perceived by the consumer is affected by the shopping situation. For example, consumers were found to perceive a higher degree of risk in shopping by telephone than in shopping in person.[47] Similarly, consumers were found to perceive a significantly greater risk in ordering products by mail than in buying the same products in person.[48]

how consumers handle risk

Consumers characteristically develop their own unique strategies for reducing perceived risk. These risk-reduction strategies enable them to act with increased confidence in making product decisions, even though the consequences of such decisions are still somewhat uncertain. Some of the more common risk-reduction strategies are listed in Table 3–3 and discussed below.

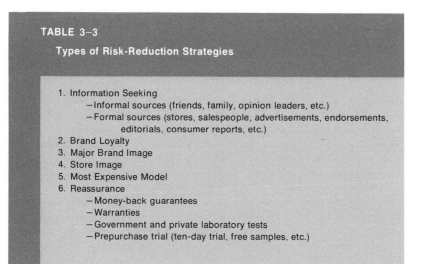

TABLE 3–3

Types of Risk-Reduction Strategies

1. Information Seeking
    —Informal sources (friends, family, opinion leaders, etc.)
    —Formal sources (stores, salespeople, advertisements, endorsements, editorials, consumer reports, etc.)
2. Brand Loyalty
3. Major Brand Image
4. Store Image
5. Most Expensive Model
6. Reassurance
    —Money-back guarantees
    —Warranties
    —Government and private laboratory tests
    —Prepurchase trial (ten-day trial, free samples, etc.)

CONSUMERS SEEK INFORMATION. Consumers seek information about the product and the product class through word-of-mouth communication from friends and family, from people whose opinions are valued, from stores and from salespeople, and from mass-media communications (such as newspapers and magazines, consumer reports, testimonials, and endorsements).

This strategy is straightforward and logical, since the more information the consumer has regarding the product and the product category, the less uncertain the probable consequences, and thus the lower the perceived risk. One researcher reported that high-risk perceivers were more likely than low-risk perceivers to have engaged in product-related conversations during the past six months for two out of three products studied.[49] Furthermore, high- and medium-risk perceivers were found to be about one and one-half times more likely than low-risk perceivers to seek information when they initiated a product-related conversation.

High-risk perceivers are also more likely to act upon the advice they seek than low-risk perceivers. Research has found, for example, that high-risk perceivers are more affected by both favorable and unfavorable information than low-risk perceivers.[50]

CONSUMERS ARE BRAND LOYAL. Consumers can avoid risk by remaining loyal to a brand with which they have been satisfied instead of purchasing new or untried products. A study of the acceptance of a new food product revealed that high-risk perceivers were more likely to be loyal to their old brands and less likely to purchase the new product.[51] A study of consumers of headache remedies found that a significantly greater number of high-risk perceivers were brand loyal as compared with low-risk perceivers.[52]

CONSUMERS SELECT BY BRAND IMAGE. If consumers have no experience with a product, they tend to "trust" a favored or well-known brand name. Consumers often think well-known brands are better and are worth buying for the assurance offered of quality, dependability, performance, and service. The marketer's promotional efforts supplement the quality of his products in helping to build and sustain a favorable brand image.

CONSUMERS RELY ON STORE IMAGE. If consumers have no other information about a product, they will trust the judgment of the buyer of a reputable store and will depend on him to have made a carefully weighed decision in selecting the product for that store. Store image also imparts the implication of product testing and the assurance of service, return privileges, and adjustments in case of dissatisfaction.

CONSUMERS BUY THE MOST EXPENSIVE MODEL. When in doubt, consumers may feel that the most expensive model is probably the best in terms of quality; i.e., they equate price with quality (The price-quality relationship was discussed in some detail earlier in this chapter.)

CONSUMERS SEEK REASSURANCE. Consumers who are uncertain about the wisdom of a product choice seek reassurance through money-back guarantees, government and private laboratory test results, warranties, and prepurchase trial (such as free samples or limited free trials).

Of the risk-reduction strategies listed above, one researcher found that the most favored strategies were brand loyalty and brand image.[53] The least favored strategies were buying the most expensive model, private laboratory tests, money-back guarantees, and endorsements. These findings suggest that a marketer should first determine the kind of risk perceived by customers and then create a mix of "risk relievers" tailored to target consumer and the type of risk she perceives.

The concept of perceived risk has major implications for the introduction of new products. Since high-risk perceivers are less likely to purchase new products than low-risk perceivers, it is important to provide them with acceptable risk-reduction strategies, such as distribution through reputable retail outlets, informative advertising, publicity stories in the media, impartial test results, free samples, and money-back guarantees. And, of course, as will be discussed in Chapter 10, it is most important to reach the influentials—the opinion leaders—from whom product advice and information are actively sought and acted upon.

Summary

Perception is *the process by which individuals select, organize, and interpret stimuli into a meaningful and coherent picture of the world.* It has strategy implications for marketers because consumers make decisions based upon what they perceive, rather than on the basis of objective reality.

The lowest level at which an individual can perceive a specific stimulus is called the *absolute threshold.* The minimal difference that he can perceive between two stimuli is called the *differential threshold,* or *just noticeable difference* (j.n.d.).

Most stimuli are perceived *above* the level of the consumer's conscious awareness; however, weak stimuli can be perceived *below* the level of conscious awareness (i.e., subliminally). There is no scientific evidence that subliminal perception can be used to influence the consumer's behavior.

The consumer's selection of stimuli from the environment is based on the interaction of her expectations and her motives with the stimulus itself. The principle of selective perception includes the following concepts: selective exposure, selective attention, perceptual defense, and perceptual blocking. People usually perceive things they need or want, and they block the perception of unfavorable or painful stimuli.

The interpretation of stimuli is highly subjective, since it is based upon what the consumer expects to see in light of her previous experience, on the number of plausible explanations she can envision, on her motives and interests at the time of perception, and on the clarity of the stimulus itself. Influences that tend to distort objective interpretation include physical appearances, stereotypes, halo effects, respected sources, irrelevant cues, first impressions, and the tendency to jump to conclusions.

Each individual has a perceived image of himself as a certain kind of person, with certain traits, habits, possessions, relationships, and ways of behaving. The consumer attempts to preserve or enhance his self-image by buying products that he believes are consistent with his self-image and by avoiding products that are not.

Products also have images (i.e., symbolic meanings) for the consumer. The way the product is perceived is probably more important to its ultimate success than are its actual product characteristics. Products that are perceived favorably obviously have a better chance of being purchased than those that are not. The brands that a consumer considers in making a purchase choice in a particular product category, are known as her *evoked set.*

In the absence of more objective information, consumers often judge the quality of a product on the basis of cues that are *intrinsic* to the product (e.g., flavor) or *extrinsic* to the product (e.g., price, store image, or brand image).

Consumers often perceive risk in making product selections because of uncertainty as to the consequences of their product decisions. The most frequent types of risk that consumers perceive are functional risk, physical risk, financial risk, social risk, and psychological risk. Studies show that the perception of risk by the consumer varies with the individual, the product, and the shopping situation.

People characteristically develop their own strategies for reducing or handling risk. Some of these strategies include seeking added information through word-of-mouth and through the media, loyalty to brands with which they have previously been satisfied, buying products that carry major brand names, buying from stores that have a favorable image, buying the most expensive model, and seeking reassurances in the form of money-back guarantees, warranties, laboratory test results, and prepurchase trial.

The concept of perceived risk has important implications for marketers, who can facilitate the introduction and acceptance of new products by providing consumers with an optimal number of acceptable risk-reduction strategies.

Endnotes

1. *Richard Lee Miller, "Dr. Weber and the Consumer,"* Journal of Marketing, *26 (January 1962), 57 – 61.*

2. *John Revett, "FTC Threatens Big Fines for Undersized Cigarette Warnings,"* Advertising Age, *March 17, 1975, 1 and 74.*

3. *Bernard Berelson and Gary A. Steiner,* Human Behavior: An Inventory of Scientific Findings *(New York: Harcourt, Brace & World, 1964), 87–130.*

4. *Walter P. Margulies, "Design Changes Reflect Switches in Consumer Retail Graphics,"* Advertising Age, *February 14, 1972, 41.*

5. *Stewart Henderson Britt and Victoria M. Nelson, "The Marketing Importance of the 'Just Noticeable Difference,'"* Business Horizons, *14 (August 1976), 38–40.*

6. *H. Brean, "What Hidden Sell Is All About,"* Life, *March 31, 1958, 104–14.*

7. *J. K. Adams, "Laboratory Studies of Behavior without Awareness,"* Psychological Bulletin, *54 (1957), 383–405.*

8. *Del Hawkins, "The Effects of Subliminal Stimulation on Drive Level and Brand Preference,"* Journal of Marketing Research, *7 (August 1970), 322–26.*

9. *Ibid.*

10. *Berelson and Steiner,* Human Behavior, *95.*

11. *Russell I. Haley, "Beyond Benefit Segmentation,"* Journal of Advertising Research, *11 (August 1971), 5.*

12. *Walter P. Margulies, "How Many Brands Can You Spot with Names off Packages?"* Advertising Age, *August 21, 1972, 37.*

13. *H. H. Kelley, "The Warm-Cold Variable in First Impressions of Persons,"* Journal of Personality, *18 (1950), 431–39.*

14. *"Man-in-Bed Ads Score Well with Women, Stevenson Says,"* Advertising Age, *February 26, 1973, 136.*

15. *Stewart Henderson Britt, Stephen C. Adams, and Allan S. Miller, "How Many Advertising Exposures per Day?"* Journal of Advertising Research, *12 (December 1972), 3–9.*

16. *Raymond Bauer and Stephen Greyser,* What Americans Think of Advertising *(New York: Dow Jones-Irwin 1969).*

17. *Berelson and Steiner,* Human Behavior, *102–3.*

18. *Ibid.*

19. *Haley, "Beyond Benefit Segmentation," 5.*

20. *Bauer and Greyser,* What Americans Think.

21. *Haley, "Beyond Benefit Segmentation," 5.*

22. *Ernest R. Hilgard,* Introduction to Psychology, *3rd ed. (New York: Harcourt, Brace & World, 1962), 552–53.*

23. *George A. Miller, "The Magical Number Seven, Plus or Minus Two: Some Limits on Our Capacity for Processing Information,"* Psychological Review, *63 (March 1956), 81–97.*

24. *James T. Heimbach and Jacob Jacoby, "The Zeigarnik Effect in Advertising,"* in M. Venkatesan, Ed., Proceedings of the Third Annual Conference *(Association for Consumer Research, 1972), 746–58.*

25. *Ibid.*

26. *Jerome Bruner, "Social Psychology and Perception,"* in E. Maccoby, T. Newcomb, and E. Hartley, eds., Readings in Social Psychology, *3rd ed. (New York: Holt, Rinehart & Winston, 1958), 85–94.*

27. *For example, see Ira J. Dolich, "Congruence Relationships between Self Images and Product Brands,"* Journal of Marketing Research, *6 (February 1969), 80–84; B. Curtis Hamm and Edward W. Cundiff, "Self-Actualization and Product Perception,"* Journal of Marketing Research, *6 (November 1969), 470–73; and Edward L. Grubb and Gregg Hupp, "Perception of Self, Generalized Stereotypes and Brand Selection,"* Journal of Marketing Research, *5 (February 1968), 58–61.*

28. *Ivan Ross, "Self-Concept and Brand Preference,"* Journal of Business, *44 (January 1971), 38–50.*

29. *For example, see Ralph L. Allison and Kenneth P. Uhl, "Influence of Beer Brand Identification on Taste Perception,"* Journal of Marketing Research, *August 1964, 36–39.*

30. *Charles E. Overholser and John M. Kline, "Advertising Strategy from Consumer Research,"* Journal of Advertising Research, *11 (October 1971), 3–10.*

31. *Lance P. Jarvis and James B. Wilcox, "Evoked Set Size—Some Theoretical Foundations and Empirical Evidence," in Thomas V. Greer, ed., 1973 Combined Proceedings (Chicago: American Marketing Association, 1974), 326–40.*

32. *Miller, "Magical Number Seven," 82.*

33. *George J. Szybillo and Jacob Jacoby, "Intrinsic versus Extrinsic Cues as Determinants of Perceived Product Quality,"* Journal of Applied Psychology, *59 (February 1974), 74–77.*

34. *David M. Stander, "Testing New Product Ideas in an 'Archie Bunker' World,"* Marketing News, *November 15, 1973, 1, 4, 5, and 10.*

35. *Ibid.*

36. *J. Douglas McConnell, "Effect of Pricing on Perception of Product Quality,"* Journal of Applied Psychology, *52 (1968), 331–34.*

37. *Barry Berman, "The Influence of Socioeconomic and Attitudinal Variables on the Price-Quality Relationship" (Doctoral dissertation, University of New York, 1973).*

38. *Ben M. Enis and James E. Stafford, "Consumers' Perception of Product Quality as a Function of Various Informational Inputs," in Philip R. McDonald, ed.,* Marketing Involvement in Society and the Economy *(Chicago: American Marketing Association, (1969), 340–44.*

39. *Raymond A. Bauer, "Consumer Behavior as Risk Taking," in Robert S. Hancock, ed.,* Dynamic Marketing for a Changing World *(Chicago: American Marketing Association, 1960), 87.*

40. *For example, see Johan Arndt, "Role of Product-Related Conversations in the Diffusion of a New Product,"* Journal of Marketing Research, *4 (August 1967), 291–95; Leon G. Schiffman, "Perceived Risk in New Product Trial by Elderly Consumers,"* Journal of Marketing Research, *9 (February 1972), 106–8; and James R. Bettman, "Perceived Risk and Its Components: A Model and Empirical Test,"* Journal of Marketing Research, *10 (May 1973), 184–90.*

41. *Thomas F. Pettigrew, "The Measurement and Correlates of Category Width as a Cognitive Variable,"* Journal of Personality, *26 (December 1968), 532.*

42. *Ibid.*

43. *Johan Arndt, "Perceived Risk, Sociometric Integration and Word of Mouth in the Adoption of a New Food Product," in Donald F. Cox, ed.,* Risk Taking and Information Handling in Consumer Behavior *(Boston: Division of Research, Graduate School of Business, Harvard University, 1967), 303.*

44. *J. Paul Peter and Michael J. Ryan, "An Investigation of Perceived Risk at the Brand Level,"* Journal of Marketing Research, *13 (May 1976), 184–88.*

45. *Scott Cunningham, "Major Dimensions of Perceived Risk," in Cox,* Risk Taking and Information Handling, *87.*

46. *Michael Perry and B. Curtis Hamm, "Canonical Analysis of Relations between Socioeconomic Risk and Personal Influence in Purchase Decisions,"* Journal of Marketing Research, *6 (August 1969), 352.*

47. *Donald F. Cox and Stuart V. Rich, "Perceived Risk and Consumer Decision Making: The Case of Telephone Shopping," in Cox,* Risk Taking and Information Handling, *504.*

48. *Homer E. Spence, James F. Engel, and Roger D. Blackwell, "Perceived Risk in Mail-Order and Retail Store Buying,"* Journal of Marketing Research, 7 *(August 1970), 364–69.*

49. *Scott M. Cunningham, "Perceived Risk as a Factor in Informal Consumer Communication," in Cox,* Risk Taking and Information Handling, 274.

50. *Arndt, "Perceived Risk, Sociometric Integration," 315.*

51. *Arndt, "Role of Product-Related Conversations," 294.*

52. *Scott M. Cunningham, "Perceived Risk and Brand Loyalty," in Cox,* Risk Taking and Information Handling, 513.

53. *Ted Roselius, "Consumer Rankings of Risk Reduction Methods,"* Journal of Marketing, 35 *(January 1971), 61.*

Discussion questions

1. Give two examples of how a marketer of consumer detergents can apply his knowledge of differential threshold in a period of rising prices and increasing competition.

2. An advertising agency has submitted a proposed promotional campaign based on subliminal advertising to the marketer of an established line of male fragrances. As vice president of marketing of this company, how would you evaluate the prospects of this new campaign?

3. As a market researcher for an automobile manufacturer, you are attempting to segment the market in terms of consumer self-images. Would you want to determine actual or ideal self-image? Discuss.

4. Find three different wine advertisements that you believe are directed to different market segments. In each case, has the marketer effectively positioned his product to communicate a specific image? Discuss.

5. Choose two product advertisements from different product categories. List the possible risks the consumer may perceive in purchasing these products. Has each marketer incorporated any risk reduction strategies in his advertisement? Discuss.

6. Recently, the management of a well known quality cosmetic company decided to add shampoo to its product line. From your knowledge of perceived risk, outline a strategy to reduce consumers' perceived risk in the new shampoo introduction.

7. Discuss the relationship of (a) extrinsic cues and (b) intrinsic cues in the perception of product quality of a line of readymade draperies.

8. Mrs. Brown spent the hour from 1 to 2 PM ironing while she watched her favorite soap operas. Yet, when questioned by a television researcher two hours later, she could not recall even one commercial that she had seen, though she could repeat the story line of both TV shows in detail. How can you explain her apparent forgetfulness?

4

the consumer as a learner*

Introduction

As consumers, we show amazing differences, from situation to situation, in our ability to learn. For instance, we can remember word for word and note for note the radio jingles of ten or twenty years ago, but forget the name of the sponsor of a particularly appealing television commercial we saw yesterday.

As students, we will, almost without thought, sit in exactly the same place in a three-hundred-seat lecture hall, but will fail to make the proper response on a multiple-choice question based on reading and lecture material discussed many times.

As citizens, many of us know the names of obscure character actors on a television program, but are totally unaware of the names of congressmen or senators who may have spent millions of dollars and received literally hundreds of hours and many pages of free media time and space during campaigns for office.

When a new product hits the market, it often becomes a household word very quickly, enjoys strong initial sales, and then recedes into oblivion as the old standards in the market take over.

Marketers are fascinated with these seemingly irrational differences in the ability and tendency of consumers to learn and apply what they learn. For if it is possible to understand how people acquire information, beliefs, and behavioral tendencies and why

I am always ready to learn, although I do not always like being taught.
WINSTON CHURCHILL

*Written by Michael L. Ray, Stanford University.

94

they then forget them, consumers could do a better job of consuming, and marketers could plan strategies much more efficiently.

In the preceding two chapters we developed the basis for this sort of understanding. Consumer learning is affected by needs and motivations (Chapter 2), as well as by the way the consumer perceives the situation (Chapter 3). We will now examine the way these motivations and perceptions, along with a variety of consumer experiences, can lead to *learning* that will affect consumer behavior in important ways. Understanding of learning is basic to the development of efficient marketing strategies.

WHAT IS LEARNING?

Learning is *the result of a combination of motivation, strongly perceived experience, and repetition upon behavioral tendencies in response to particular stimuli or situations.* In consumer behavior, learning is the change, brought about by experience, in tendencies to perceive, think, or act in certain ways, with regard to brands, products, or services. If the experience is strong enough, is repeated often enough, and the consumer is motivated, it will lead to learning.

Take, for instance, the kind of learning that occurred from old radio jingles as opposed to yesterday's television commercial. Learning of the jingle occurred because we heard it repeatedly when we were young and when it made a strong impression. If learning of the brand name from yesterday's commercial did not occur, it is probably because the name was not strong enough in relation to the appealing aspects of the commercial and the commercial has not been repeated so frequently. After repetition, the brand name may "get through;" that is, we will learn the brand name or associate it more quickly with the product.

All of consumer behavior is the result of learning, relearning, or maintenance of learning. The main job of consumers consists of learning which consumption practices are best for them. The main job of marketers consists of competing successfully for consumer learning by consistently providing strong positive experiences to market segments of well-motivated consumers. This is by no means an easy job. But there are several clear principles of learning that make it possible.

How learning works

The three basic mechanisms of learning have already been stated. First, the consumer must be appropriately motivated. Second, there must be a strong experience. Third, there must be some repetition. Although this chapter does not discuss the complex and esoteric field of learning theory in detail, it should be noted that the many learning theories available can be classified into those that emphasize motivation, experience, or repetition.[1] We have seen how the proper combination of these three elements has led to our learning an old radio jingle, while the wrong combination has led to our not learning or our forgetting the name of the sponsor of a commercial. Let us look now at how these three variables—motivation, experience, and repetition—work in general.

MOTIVATION, REINFORCEMENT, AND LEARNING

As we saw in Chapter 2, motivation is the basis for behavior, including learning. *Reinforcement theory,* probably the most popular type of learning theory, is based on the idea that learning occurs when a motivated individual receives a reward (i.e., reinforcement) related to his or her actions.[2] A woman is hungry, she eats a Big Mac hamburger; her hunger is satisfied. On the basis of this reinforcement, she may learn to like this type of hamburger. Her learning depends, of course, on the other two mechanisms: specifically, how she perceived the experience and whether it is repeated.

Appropriate motivation is important. In some cases, however, lack of motivation can facilitate learning. Some marketers believe that the reason for television advertising's success in getting certain ideas across—such as general positive ideas about brands—is that people are not highly motivated or actively involved in learning the messages.[3] When consumers are highly motivated or involved, they may be more likely to show skepticism toward commercials. If they are unmotivated, they may learn general ideas from the TV messages without thinking about them. This may therefore be an *appropriate* level of motivation for learning general ideas from TV commercial messages.

EXPERIENCE AND LEARNING

Appropriate motivation is the first requirement, but a strongly perceived experience is necessary before the motivation can be turned into learning. Perceptions of similar experiences differ from person to person (see Chapter 3). Just having an experience does not guarantee learning. The experience must be strong enough to effect a change in tendencies to behave in the same situation in the future. Enjoying a hamburger or a pizza *when hungry* is a strong experience that may lead to learning. Seeing a typical commercial on television just once is seldom strong enough. That is why repetition of commercials is usually necessary if learning is to occur.

Marketers must be quite certain that the learning experience related to their products and services is consistently strong and positive. There is evidence, for instance, that reformulations of beers have led to sales declines over time, due to the variations in quality or flavor—an example of inconsistent experience. Consumers are said to be able to detect supermarket price increases quite quickly, although some chains, by featuring bargain prices, distract and thereby deter consumers from recognizing price increases.

REPETITION AND LEARNING

Learning occurs through strong motivation, a strongly perceived experience, and *repetition*. Although it is possible for certain single traumatic events to be etched in our memories and affect our behavior forever, in most instances, if there is no repetition, there is no learning.

Repetition works at different rates in different situations. If the motivation is high and the experience is strong, fewer repetitions are needed to produce learning. But there is a limit to the effects of repetition. Each repetition beyond a certain point produces less learning, and finally leads to *fatigue, habituation,* or *wear-out,* which may cause forgetting or, worse yet, disliking. Although strong motivation and experience situations may lead to learning with need of fewer repetitions than do weak motivation and experience situations, they also reach a point of fatigue sooner. The motivation of hunger and the experience of eating a Big Mac may lead to a consumer's learning to like the hamburger very quickly. But how long could you last with a diet of just hamburgers before your liking turned into distaste?

Marketers must be careful to balance the three mechanisms of learning. Repetition can quickly turn learning into forgetting, or even hating, if the stimulus is too strong. In product policy, one guard against this is variety. All fast-food chains soon learn that they must add variety to their menus. If a consumer gets tired of Big Macs, for instance, there are other items to choose from at McDonald's.

The same kind of variety is utilized in other product categories so that repetition will not become overwhelming. For instance, it has long been recognized that washing clothes can be a dreary task that the homemaker tries to enliven by changing brands of detergents from time to time. To deal with this habituation response, a company will market a wide variety of brands of detergent and continually offer "new improved" versions. Procter and Gamble, for instance, markets Tide, Cheer, Gain, Bold, Dash, Oxydol, Dreft, Duz, Bonus, Salvo, Ivory Flakes, and Ivory Snow for clothes washing.[4] Some of this variety is meant to appeal to different market segments. New brands may appeal to particular motivations and provide satisfying experiences. But the reason for much of the success of such a varied product line is that it allows homemakers to switch brands and take some of the over-repetition and fatigue out of a dreary task.

Conditioning

We have seen that learning occurs with the proper combination of motivation, strongly perceived experiences, and repetition. Let us now look at the two principal ways in which these combinations can occur: classical conditioning and instrumental conditioning.

CLASSICAL CONDITIONING

The kind of learning known as *classical conditioning* was discovered by the Russian physiologist Ivan Pavlov in his studies with dogs. The dogs were hungry and highly motivated. In his experiments, Pavlov sounded a tone, and immediately followed it by applying a meat paste to the dogs' tongues, which caused salivation. Learning or conditioning occurred when, after a sufficient number of repetitions of the tone followed by the food, the tone *alone* caused salivation. The tone had been *learned* to be an indicator of the rewards of the meat paste.

Learning researchers believe we learn much about consuming in the same way. That is, every time an originally neutral stimulus is followed by a reward, we build a positive feeling toward it. In some cases, food odors from bakeries, pizza restaurants, or the kitchen on Thanksgiving Day may literally start us salivating. In other cases, we have learned that certain brand names are connected with rewarding products. That is why we sometimes positively evaluate a new product without trying it because it has the same name as an old one or is made by a company that we know has manufactured good products in the past.

Classical conditioning often occurs in consumer behavior, when a brand name, idea, or product is associated by consumers with another stimulus they already see as rewarding. The most effective marketing applications are in branding, packaging, promotions, and advertising. When we want consumers to learn to repeat a specific behavior, however, we must turn to a second major type of conditioning.

INSTRUMENTAL CONDITIONING

In *instrumental conditioning,* when we make a response (e.g., a purchase), it may or may not be rewarded (i.e., we may or may not be satisfied). If it is rewarded, the response is more likely to be repeated in the future. The response is "instrumental" in causing the reward.

The leading exponent of instrumental conditioning in the laboratory is B. F. Skinner.[5] Such animals as rats or pigeons receive rewards in his "Skinner box" if they make appropriate movements and depress levers or peck keys to receive the food reinforcement. Skinner and his many followers have been able to do amazing things with this simple apparatus, including teaching pigeons to play Ping-Pong, to cha-cha, and even to act as the guiding system in a missile!

More important for consumer behavior, however, is the fact that of the two kinds of conditioning, instrumental conditioning is likely to be the more typical, especially in terms of learning to act and make decisions. Sellers hope that their products will provide rewards for the consumers who buy them. If this is true and if these rewards can be reinforced by advertising, the consumer is much more likely to continue buying the product.

A consumer looking for an effective dandruff-removing shampoo may try a product that is advertised by the slogan "It really works." If it does indeed work and the consumer is pleased with the results, his positive attitude toward the product will be reinforced by later commercials that repeat the slogan "It really works."

Detailed learning characteristics

Almost any consumer learning situation can be analyzed by looking for its relevant motivations, experience perceptions, and repetitions and by considering whether classical or instrumental conditioning is likely to occur. Learning research has provided much more information for consumer analysis, however. In the following sections, we will consider seven specific aspects of learning:

1. Extinction and forgetting
2. Stimulus generalization
3. Stimulus discrimination
4. Schedules of reinforcement
5. Habits
6. Individuals' learning differences
7. Measurement of learning

EXTINCTION AND FORGETTING

Theoretically, extinction of a learning response occurs when the response is no longer connected to a reward or, in the case of a thought or cognition, when it is no longer rehearsed. In popular terminology, this is called forgetting. The explanations as to why a response is extinguished or why we forget are the basis for understanding both learning and memory.

Learning takes work. Without this work and subsequent repetition, responses and memories atrophy. At least three aspects of learning seem to be directly related to extinction and forgetting: the meaningfulness of the material, the opportunity for rehearsal, and the learning activities before and after the key learning situation.

meaningfulness

Materials of low meaningfulness, such as nonsense syllables or even some advertising, are forgotten quite rapidly if there is no reinforcement or reexposure. Research indicates, however, that if material is *meaningful* — if it can be related in some way to the consumer's purposes or has "image-producing" properties — forgetting is slower, is incomplete, or, in some cases, eliminated. If, for instance, we see an ad that describes a revolutionary product for solving a problem that we are particularly concerned with, we are not going to forget that ad even if it takes us several days to act on it. Or, if the ad shows scenes or evokes ideas of our family and friends, we are again more likely to remember it.

rehearsal

If an individual can mentally rehearse an idea and get it into memory, the chances of learning it are increased tremendously, for rehearsal is a form of repetition. Thus the quality of recall is very much influenced by whether people can rehearse responses and ideas during and directly after exposure to a message, an idea, or an object. Even simple ideas that are carried from an advertisement, such as a brand name or a jingle, are likely to be forgotten rapidly unless the message is repeated often. Fortunately for advertisers, some messages, such as the radio jingles discussed above, are repeated quite often — to the point of over-learning. If there is no repetition, however, and the material is not especially meaningful, the material is likely to be forgotten quickly.

the surrounding situation

Finally, forgetting is affected by the activities before and after the learning experience itself. For instance, a television commercial in the middle of a string of commercials is recalled less well, probably because it is affected by the learning process for the early and the late commercials in the break. (Chapter 7 discusses the effects of "primacy" and "recency" in greater detail.)

But there is more to this aspect of learning and forgetting than the simple presence of the learning materials before and after the key materials are learned. The *quality* of the preceding and following material must be considered also. Some surrounding materials can be very inhibiting, while others are not. If they are very different from the commercial of interest, forgetting can be reduced substantially. We know that a single commercial surrounded by a program does better than a commercial surrounded by other commercials. If the surrounding commercials are boring or uninteresting, the learning of an interesting middle commercial is enhanced and forgetting of that commercial is sharply reduced.[6] If the surrounding commercials are for the same or similar products, the consumer is likely to recall commercials for the product category but confuse the brand names and appeals with those of the market leader.[7]

It seems, therefore, that we should assume a rapid rate of forgetting in any situation. In addition, the meaningfulness, rehearsal, and situational factors can also affect forgetting in one way or the other.

In the situation mentioned earlier in this chapter, in which a new product in the market takes over, we could assume that both the new brand and the old brand produce similar forgetting patterns. However, it would probably be more realistic to acknowledge that since the old brand has been around for a much longer time, it probably has already reached the low point in consumers' promotional awareness, therefore suffering little from lack-of-rehearsal forgetting. When the new brand's heavy introductory promotion stops, however, forgetting of the new brand proceeds much faster, plummeting below the now relatively stable consumer-awareness level of the older brand. This effect alone could explain why the new brand loses out in the market. Of course, results can differ if the new brand takes advantage of meaningfulness to make the learning process take a longer-lasting hold on the consumer.

STIMULUS GENERALIZATION

Stimulus generalization was discovered by Pavlov during classical conditioning when his dogs started salivating to such sounds as the jangling of keys, which sounded like the learned tone. This was called stimulus *generalization* because the dogs *generalized* their learning from the originally learned tone to one which was similar.

The same sort of phenomenon is used in consumer behavior by marketers' product, packaging, or branding practices. Many new products are similar enough to old, successful products to ensure success. To take advantage of positive stimulus generalization, private or store brands of food items often copy the packaging of the leading national brands.

The idea of *family branding* is based on stimulus generalization. Marketers will have a whole "family" of brands with the same or similar names. The idea is that if one product has been successful, another product with the same or a similar brand name will be more rapidly accepted because people will have accumulated positive experiences and learning with the name. The danger in the family-branding strategy is, of course, that the brand name may be associated with a product that is a failure. This could create a negative attitude toward the whole family of brands. It is because of this danger that some marketers avoid the family-branding idea. Procter and Gamble, for instance, studiously avoids mention that such brands as Duncan Hines, Tide, Crest, Folgers, Ivory, and Gleem are all made by the same company. The Kraft name, on the other hand, is directly associated with virtually all of that firm's products.

Stimulus generalization can also be used in advertising. Figure 4-1 shows how Volkswagen sought positive stimulus generalization from the highly successful "Beetle" to the newer "Rabbit."

STIMULUS DISCRIMINATION

Stimulus discrimination is the ability to select the correct stimulus from others similar to it. It is the key to the marketing concept of *positioning*.[8] Because there are so many brands of so many products and services available to consumers today, the marketing problem is not to create stimulus generalization but rather to lead consumers to discriminate one brand from its competitors. This is an extremely difficult job for

FIGURE 4–1

An Attempt to Develop Stimulus Generalization

Courtesy of Volkswagen of America Inc.

those brands that are not leaders in a product category. Marketers deal with this problem by *positioning*, or establishing a clear discriminative position for their specific brand in the consumer's mind.

Such stimulus discrimination attempts have been made in the past by Avis when the company advertised itself as being "No. 2" in rental cars and by B. F. Goodrich in its attempts to differentiate itself from Goodyear tires.

Avis, along with National, was a distant second to Hertz in rental cars at the beginning of the Avis "We're No. 2, We try Harder" campaign. Not only did the campaign dramatically increase business for Avis, but it also created a unique position in the consumer's mind. On one hand, stimulus generalization occurred: Avis was seen as a company battling it out in the same league as the giant, Hertz. On the other hand, clear stimulus discrimination was achieved: National was suddenly relegated to the position of also-ran although initially it had been tied with Avis.[9]

A more difficult positioning and stimulus discrimination task was attempted by B. F. Goodrich. The difficulty occurred because the name is so similar to Goodyear, the leader in tires. The campaign attacked the problem directly by referring specifically to the similarity in names, with an innovativeness and care for the consumer that distinguished Goodrich. One of the early ads had the headline "The Curse of Our Founder's Name" (it was *Benjamin Franklin* Goodrich). The television commercials concentrated on the well-known Goodyear blimp, very often seen at televised football games. Characters would confuse the names, talking about the Good*rich* blimp. One particularly clever scheduling was Goodrich sponsorship of the pre-game show for the eleventh Super Bowl. A number of commercials referring to the blimp were exposed. Then, during the Super Bowl telecast itself, the Goodyear blimp was exposed, possibly engendering further stimulus discrimination among the tens of millions who watched both telecasts.

Stimulus discrimination and its counterpart, stimulus generalization, occur in all areas of marketing and consumer behavior. A distinctive, individualized position is usually developed on the basis of some combination of product naming and package, price, distribution, and promotion to reinforce stimulus discrimination.[10]

SCHEDULES OF REINFORCEMENT

Different *schedules* of repetition and reinforcement can lead to different patterns of learning. In general, it seems to be better to spread the repetitions over a period of time rather than to bunch them all up at once. But in marketing, this depends on the campaign situation. It may be necessary to bunch up exposures in a particular period of time in order to get any meaningful response from the market at all. Advertisers with limited budgets often do this.

In learning research, *partial reinforcement* occurs when the experimental subject is rewarded "partially;" that is, only on some trials, even if he has made the "correct" response on all trials. An experimental subject who is not rewarded on every trial will usually continue to perform much longer and harder than one who is rewarded continuously.

Advertising with many different advertisements in a campaign can be more effective over the long run than a single-ad campaign. Benson and Hedges used this method in its cigarette commercials, using the same theme—the breaking cigarette—in a variety of situations. Excedrin applied it in its numbered-headache campaign. This method allows the consumer to identify with any of a number of situations that make the same point, while varying the actual commercial to encourage continued interest and attention. A black-and-white ad will stand out from four-color ads through contrast; two-sided messages (with some mildly negative points) are often effective because they give an impression of openness and honesty. Partial or inconsistent reinforcement from the product itself should, of course, be avoided; the product should work well with every exposure.

HABITS

A *habit* is some consistent pattern of behavior that is performed without considered thought. Although there may have originally been strong motivation and perceived experiences, consistent repetition is indicative of habit. Many types of purchasing fit into the category of habit. This is especially true of frequently purchased, low-priced items that have been on the market for a long time and for which there is almost no difference between brands. For such situations, purchasing behavior is habitual. As with other habits, a change will occur only after a great deal of effort — such as introduction of a startlingly new product, an intensive advertising campaign, or dramatic changes in distribution or at the point of purchase. Changes are so difficult to effect in a mature market that strategists are well advised to introduce new products before habitual behavior begins.

INDIVIDUAL DIFFERENCES

Market segments span a wide range of learning tendencies and consumer behavior. First, people differ widely in native intelligence. Then, their experience in relation to any particular product or service class varies extensively. A mechanic, for instance, might have a lower IQ than a college professor but might do a better job of choosing a car. Finally, people differ in their involvement and interests in learning. If a man needs money, he will do a very good job of learning about alternative loan sources, even if he is not as intelligent as someone else who is not particularly interested in borrowing money.

There is a limit, however, to the effect that such variables as intelligence, past experience, and involvement have on learning. Research has shown that these variables have increased learning only up to a point, after which there may be a retardation of the learning process.

The highly intelligent segment may be turned off by an overly simplistic or hard-sell television commercial. The mechanic who has extensive experience with automobiles may see through claims that are made in what would be considered (for any other consumer) a technical manner. And the highly involved consumer can also be highly vigilant, guarding against certain messages or buying one product repeatedly. We should look for differences between consumer segments in intelligence, experience, and involvement — recognizing that the learning process will be quite different for people who differ on these variables.

MEASUREMENT OF LEARNING

A picture of consumer learning can vary considerably according to how learning is measured and by what criteria it is judged.

If we consider just cognition (knowledge), attitude, and behavior learning, we can see that a person who may do well on a measure of cognitive learning may in fact do quite poorly on a measure of attitude or behavior learning. Someone might, for instance, learn a brand name or even be able to recite an advertising message (cognition) but not learn to either like the brand (attitude) or take any action with regard to it (behavior). Conversely, someone could purchase a product repeatedly without really thinking about it, so that the results of a behavioral measure of his learning would look good although the results of a detailed cognitive measure would indicate inadequate learning.

Even within one type of learning, there are many different measures. For instance, in cognitive learning there are *unaided recall* measures in which the respondent is given no cues, for example, as to the type of advertisement he is asked to recall. In contrast, there are *aided recall* measures in which a respondent may be told the product class of the advertisement to be recalled or, even easier, *recognition* measures in which the consumer is shown a specific advertisement and is asked whether he or she has seen it. Each of the aided or unaided recall tasks can vary a great deal in terms of what the researchers' criteria are for a "correct" response.

Four types of learning

Learning can vary from that of an infant developing the tendency to push air up through its larynx to make sounds, to the complex series of movements it takes to make a tennis shot, to the even more complex thoughts, evaluations, intentions, and actions that make up a major consumer purchase. In some cases, the learning is so early and so thorough that the marketer cannot avoid taking it into account. In other cases, it is so unimportant that the marketer can easily ignore it. In still other cases, it can be affected and is important enough to become the main goal of marketing strategy.

Basically four kinds of learning are involved in the development of consumer learning: (1) early basic learning, (2) cognitive (information) learning, (3) attitude learning, and (4) behavior learning. Each of these types is discussed in the following pages.

EARLY BASIC LEARNING

The complex acts of human behavior are made up of thousands of simpler behaviors: muscle twitches, thoughts, simple understandings, and so forth, that are taken for granted by most people. As children we learn to speak, to walk, to differentiate people from things, and a host of other responses to simple stimuli. This early basic learning is so fundamental and complete that our responses are made almost unconsciously. We are aware that we are making them only when they are somehow hampered, someone brings them to our attention, or someone tries to change them.

Early basic learning is so fundamental that marketers can seldom affect it. It is a basic principle of psychology that the earlier a response to a particular situation is learned, the more embedded or central that response will be. In other words, a person is most likely to do what he or she has done in the past. This idea is the basic assumption behind Freudian psychology, which holds that the learning experiences of the first few years of life are critical to the behaviors of adulthood.

basic learning in consumer behavior

Early basic learning is *not* over after the first few years of life. People can learn to participate in a variety of sports for the first time later in life, just as they can learn about new products and new purchasing situations. Of course, such learning is not *as* basic and wide-ranging in effect. It does, however, have many of the same characteristics of early-life learning since it influences all subsequent learning on that subject.

It is difficult to observe the effects of early learning in a pure sense in the marketplace. The brand that gets into the market first often develops a greater market share right away and therefore has greater impact than competing brands in the later stages of the product's life. Also, the early learning of consumers is generally more complex than the early basic learning in the first few years of life. But many specific brands have continued to do well over generations of buyers. The "habit" of buying a particular brand is passed on from parent to child for such brands as Hershey (chocolate bars), Campbell (canned soups), Morton (salt), and, more recently, Crest (toothpaste).

Even without advertising its chocolate bars, Hershey remained a leader for over fifty years. No one has been able to challenge Campbell in the canned soup field, and thus Lipton could succeed only by concentrating on the powdered soup market. It is difficult to imagine a less differentiated commodity than salt, but Morton has managed to maintain a dominant share of the market by continually matching competitors' package innovations and taking advantage of the early basic learning in the field. Crest has been attacked by formidable advertising campaigns and excellent competitive products, some of which have also received the American Dental Association's seal of approval. Again, however, the advantage of being there first with early-learning influence has triumphed.

COGNITIVE LEARNING

Much of what we learn as consumers is simply information: brand names, product characteristics, where to buy products, appropriate product uses, and so forth. This is cognitive (knowledge) learning, and it is often basic to all other types of learning.

consumers' limited ability

Although people are very unusual among animals in regard to their ability to use language or symbols, the most important principle from cognitive learning research is that people actually have a very limited ability to learn information. This should be especially noted by marketers who are trying to get consumers to learn advertising appeals, brand names, and package information.

Our limited cognitive learning ability can be illustrated by a common example. Assume that a consumer is trying to learn something about a new food product from an advertisement. To use even one of the bits of information in the ad, the consumer must first be aware of it and hold it in mind long enough so that it can somehow be rehearsed and memorized.[11] A person can attend to only a limited amount of information at any given time. The information selected usually has to have some novelty in order to be noticed. Or the person may be looking for certain information—attention is selective. In any case, if the information is too strange or very ordinary it may be avoided or simply learned incorrectly as fitting with expectations.[12]

Once information is noticed, it still faces a somewhat limited mental capacity. Apparently, people can only hold about seven relevant bits of information or ideas in their minds at any given time.[13] This limit is evident every time you use a new telephone number. It consists of exactly seven numbers. You find it in the telephone book, hold it in your mind, and turn to make the call. But if someone interrupts you, you forget the number. This is just too much information, and the memory process is not complete.

It is possible, of course, for each of these seven bits of information to be summary ideas representing a whole class of ideas. But research indicates—just as when we are trying to learn a telephone number—that from five to ten seconds are required to mentally rehearse and fix *one* bit of information.[14] If material is not rehearsed in this way, it is lost and forgotten within roughly thirty seconds.[15] It is no wonder we have difficulty remembering even brand names from the cluttered and fast-moving world of television!

slow learning, fast forgetting

Because cognitive learning is faced with limited consumer capabilities as well as low motivation (especially in the case of advertising) and weak perceptual experiences, the most important single variable tends to be *repetition*. Cognitive learning tends to depend on many repetitions, and unless it is supported by the other two types of learning (attitude and behavior), forgetting takes place very fast.

This is why the scheduling of advertising over the year and within certain time periods is so important. If there are not enough repetitions within a period, names and appeals will not be learned. If there is too much bunching up in a specific period, then there will be nonadvertising periods when consumers will forget.

It is possible, of course, that scheduling at certain times of the year (such as new-car introduction time, watches at graduation time, small electrical gadgets and toys at Christmas time, and beer advertising in the summer) could tap strong motivation and heighten the learning experience.

Still, it is not easy for the consumer to learn information relevant to purchasing decisions. Clutter abounds in the advertising media and in retail stores. Even if it is possible for the advertiser to get through all of the "noise" in the environment, the forgetting process is rapid. The learning of any new piece of information is affected by the material already known by the consumer. It appears that the best approach for the marketer is to attempt to put the product in as uncluttered an environment as possible. Certainly it is best to be in first position, but one should not stake all hope on single, strong exposures. For one thing, learning research indicates that spread-out schedules (distributed practice) work and that reminder messages during purchasing decision times are quite important. Messages that fit the audience's past experience and can be classified with other information can help the consumer in his cognitive-learning chores. And cognitive-learning research indicates that novel information and information that involves the consumer can cut through the noise in the environment to register on the consumer's mind.

LEARNING OF ATTITUDES AND TASTES

Attitudes and tastes involve evaluations. We know we have an attitude when we feel good or bad about something. Although some writers talk about the "learning of tastes" without reference to attitude, the two concepts — attitudes and tastes — are virtually equivalent.

Attitudes comprise a vast subject in themselves. Some theorists consider them the entire subject of social psychology. Attitudes are certainly important in consumer behavior and will be discussed more fully in Chapter 6. For our present purposes, however, *attitude* can be defined as a learned tendency to respond in a consistently favorable or unfavorable manner with respect to a given social object or concept, such as a product, service, brand, company, store, or spokesperson.[16]

Note that attitudes have to do with evaluations or feelings, which can lead to certain kinds of behaviors and other evaluations. And, most important for our present purposes, attitudes arise from our experience; that is, they are *learned*. Chapter 6 discusses attitude learning in terms of attitude development and change. Here it is important to understand in general where attitudes come from and how the learning process might be used to change them in the consumer behavior setting.

Why is it that we may have a more positive attitude toward one brand of soft drink than toward another, toward one type of meat than toward another, toward faster cars than toward economical ones, or toward bicycle riding than toward driving? Such attitudes can develop in at least six ways, as follows:

EXPOSURE OR REPETITION. Development of attitudes can be related partly to repetition or familiarity, as shown in studies in which classical music lovers were repeatedly exposed to pop music and eventually increased their positive evaluations of such music.[17] We find comfort in familiarity.

EARLY BASIC LEARNING. Early exposures are also extremely important in forming long-term attitudes. A large amount of sugar in a child's diet, for instance, may lead to a taste for, or a positive attitude toward, sweet foods in adulthood.

COGNITIVE LEARNING. Cognitive learning is also basic to the development and change of attitudes and tastes. Information or knowledge is necessary for the development of certain attitudes. Beliefs, too, are part of cognition. If, for instance, a person has learned to *believe* that fiber content and lack of sugar is essential in a good bread, and also *believes* that a certain bread has both high fiber content and lack of sugar, then these two learned beliefs should lead to a positive attitude toward that brand of bread.

CLASSICAL CONDITIONING. People can develop attitudes toward an originally neutral item through classical conditioning. If a brand name is repeatedly followed by (or associated with) a reward, a positive attitude will result.

ASSOCIATION. Association is closely tied to the cognitive learning and classical conditioning forms of attitude development, and is frequently used by advertisers forming an *association* between the product and favorable attributes or celebrities. Outside of advertising, association can take the form of stimulus generalization.

INSTRUMENTAL CONDITIONING. Behavior can be initiated by circumstances before attitudes have had an opportunity to develop. As this type of behavior habitually continues, the consistent buying may be rewarded and thereby influence favorable evaluations (attitudes) toward the brand.

positive attitudes encourage patronage

Let us now examine how some of these forms of attitude learning can lead to a positive attitude toward a particular company or brand. The first method of attitude learning mentioned above was that of mere *exposure* or *repetition*. If a service station chain has numerous service stations in a city, then a typical consumer would be repeatedly exposed to the brand name and the sight of many cars entering the stations. It is also likely that such a chain would do a large amount of advertising throughout the city to which the typical consumer would be repeatedly exposed.

Second, attitudes are said to be developed by *classical conditioning*. Again, advertising could associate some positive ideas or credible personalities with the brand name. This too could contribute to a positive attitude toward the chain of service stations.

Third, attitudes are said to be developed by *instrumental conditioning*. Let us assume that a typical consumer has two service stations near her home. Since she is frequently short of gas in the morning, she must often stop in one of the two stations on her way to work. If our chain's station is on the right side of the street as she goes to work, then she is more likely to stop in that station for gas in the morning. This will lead to a whole new round of rewards in the form of getting gas, more reinforcement in terms of knowing the attendants who service her car, possibly further good experiences in terms of having the car serviced, and, eventually, a use of the company's credit card, which will lead to further repetitive exposures to the chain at other service station locations. Studies have supported this view of attitude learning and influence in the service station field. It has been found that a company must have a certain number or proportion of service stations in any given city before that company can achieve a respectable market share. Apparently, such a distribution must exist before attitudes can be learned and can affect predispositions to respond.

LEARNING TO ACT AND MAKE DECISIONS

In some sense, learning to act and make decisions involves just a combination of the simple early learning, cognitions, and attitudes already discussed. On the other hand, we learn how to make decisions and purchases in each situation in a specific way.

We have all experienced the kind of learning involved in acting and making decisions in consumer behavior. As children, such decision-making may have come quite easily because of influence from advertising or from our parents.[18] As young adults, when we are no longer living at home and have to make many consumption decisions for the first time, they do not come quite so easily. There is still some influence from advertising and from parents. But money is short, and we want to make decisions correctly on our own. It is difficult to make these decisions for the first time. But with each subsequent shopping trip they become easier until some of them become almost automatic (that is, habitual).

The same sort of thing happens at each stage of the family life cycle (see Chapter 9) — at marriage, when the first baby comes, when it is time to send the children to college, when planning retirement, and so forth.

There are six ways in which people learn to act and make decisions:[19]

BLIND TRIAL AND ERROR. Like the rat in a psychologist's learning experiment, we sometimes bring no early learning, cognition, or attitude to a decision situation. We may not even know what decision we are trying to make. Thus there is a tendancy to try various approaches and stay with the one that seems to work.

PERCEPTION. Sometimes we can "see" the right decision from a number of possible alternatives. This might happen, for instance, when buying a headache remedy where the package information may show a decided advantage for one brand. The same sort of thing happens in stores where there is a unit-pricing policy and one brand has an advantage.

OBSERVATION OF OTHERS' RESPONSES. If a child observes her mother buying frozen orange juice instead of fresh oranges on one shopping trip, the child might run to the frozen-food counter and pull out a can on the next shopping trip. The mother might then reward the child with a kind word or an affectionate squeeze. That reward would lead to an expectancy that buying frozen orange juice would always have a reward connected with it.

OBSERVATION OF OTHERS' REWARDS AND PUNISHMENTS DURING LEARNING. This often occurs as a result of television. One could imagine, for instance, one child developing a preference for frozen orange juice on the basis of observing another child enjoying it on television. These forms of observation can then be generalized. For instance, the child watching television might be more likely to buy frozen forms of other juices rather than fresh fruit.

VERBAL INSTRUCTIONS ABOUT RESPONSES. Parents, friends, and teachers all teach us how to make purchasing decisions. In this way we are already somewhat prepared to make them on our own, even the first time we make a particular kind of purchase.

VERBAL INSTRUCTIONS ABOUT REWARDS AND PUNISHMENTS. In the same way that we can be told about the acts or decisions to make, we can be told about the rewards we might receive for doing certain things or punishments for doing others ("Go to Joe's Grill. You'll get a great hamburger there;" "That suntan lotion will make your skin break out.") An infinite number of verbal instructions about consuming come to us throughout our lives. They are a very powerful method by which we learn to act and make purchasing decisions.

But what in general do we learn about acting and making purchasing decisions throughout our lives as consumers? One thing we learn is that some decisions are more important than others and require more time and detailed consideration. Another thing we learn is that some acts and decisions are more obvious to others, so we must take their opinions and attitudes into account.

But probably the most important consumer learning is the development of regular purchasing patterns that, because of their regularity, take much of the confusion and bother out of making consumption decisions. Consider, for example, the practice of issuing a free sample of a product with a coupon enclosed in the package to stimulate future buying of the product. This may begin a usage habit of that particular product, or, more specifically, of that particular brand. From a marketing standpoint, these regular patterns get translated into *brand loyalty.*

Brand loyalty

Brand loyalty can be considered the ultimate goal of any marketing program. For if loyalty can be established, a segment of consumers will almost certainly buy not only now but in the future. A healthy brand is one that has a large segment of loyal buyers. A sick brand is one that has a small and diminishing segment of loyal buyers. Learning processes are critical to the development of brand loyalty.

WHAT IS BRAND LOYALTY?

At the simplest level, brand loyalty means consistent purchasing of one brand or service in a category. It is most commonly measured by research that checks the number of consecutive times or the proportion of times a brand is bought by a consumer.[20] If a brand is bought consistently, it is assumed that learning has occurred and that no matter what happens in the market (such as price changes, out-of-stock conditions, competitive activity), the consumer will continue to buy the same brand.

At a more complex level, it is important to realize that people are often loyal to a *set* of brands (that is, the evoked set) rather than just a single one. Brand loyalty can be diffuse. People may be willing to forgo their favorite brand if it is not available or if there is a sale on another brand in the same general category. This type of "satisficing" behavior (i.e., being satisfied with a brand that is acceptable instead of seeking the best brand) often confuses marketing researchers, who expect buyers to be loyal to only one brand.[21] But some purchasing decisions are not really important enough to require a search for the ideal (see Chapter 15). In some markets, therefore, it is enough for the company to get its brand into the evoked set for consumer consideration.

Instead of searching for the "brand loyal buyer," therefore, marketers tend to look for positive *brand perceptions* and *brand attitudes.*[22] Good marketers are aware of the cognitive and attitudinal underpinnings of loyalty. If consumers can learn the desired perceptions and attitudes, then loyalty—in the sense of a brand's having a high position in the evoked set—will follow.

HOW WE LEARN BRAND LOYALTY

Loyalty is a convenience that allows us to make purchases without thinking them through each time. We see it developing, therefore, only when consumers are just beginning to purchase in a product category or when a new product enters the market.

The most important type of learning related to loyalty is the early basic form. As new consumers or consumers purchasing in a new category, we find that first impressions can be critical. As mentioned earlier, this is part of the reason for the strong brand loyalty associated with Campbell soup, Morton salt, Hershey chocolate, and Crest toothpaste.

The three other types of learning—cognitive, attitude, and behavioral learning—depend on much more than a brand's just being first. Research on new-product adoption indicates that we tend to go through a process of awareness, interest, evaluation, trial, and adoption (see Chapter 14). In marketing, brand-learning research emphasizes the awareness, trial, and repeat use-reinforcement stages.[23] Simply stated, we develop brand loyalty by first learning something about the brand (cognition), forming an initial evaluation (attitude), trying it (behavior), having a satisfying experience with it (attitude), and then repeatedly buying and using it with further reinforcement.

STRATEGIES FOR BRAND LOYALTY DEVELOPMENT

Given this picture of the way brand loyalty develops, what strategies can be used to increase loyalty for a specific brand? By definition, loyalty is something quite strong, even when it is defined in terms of an entire evoked set. Thus, strong actions related to the three parts of the learning process—motivation, perception of experiences, and repetition—are required.

motivation

Most buyers in a product class are not highly motivated to change their loyalties. Perhaps the first strategic suggestion for evoking loyalty that might be made is related to segmentation. The easiest targets are those segments that are not presently loyal, especially if they are new consumers in the market.

If new segments are not available, then it might be possible to tap new motivations. This can be done by determining whether there is some problem or need that is not currently being satisfied by the brands on the market. Such a strategy was used in the hair rinse and conditioner market when the Tame creme rinse marketers pointed out that their product eliminated the problem of oily buildup that plagued balsam conditioners even though they were perfectly good for conditioning.

All new products, many pricing changes, and some distribution changes, in fact, tend to change the motivation basis for brand loyalty and to start new learning processes in favor of the product or brand involved.

perception of experiences

Probably the most important experience in the development of brand loyalty is product trial. Each trial and repeat use can be a learning experience. Applying this to marketing strategy, we can see that the best competitive moves are those that allow the consumer to try the product, especially if it is a good one. This is why product sampling is such a frequent strategy in the marketing of new products.

If sampling is not feasible—either financially or otherwise—then very strong advertising is necessary. The messages must change the basis on which consumers judge the brands in the category. The positioning, stimulus-discrimination type of message is best.

repetition

Developing brand loyalty takes consistent and strong experiences. While it may be difficult to develop loyalty by providing consumers with advertising messages alone, an extensive campaign that includes a great deal of repetition can do the trick. The difficulty in developing brand loyalty is representative of the consistent, coordinated effort necessary for effective learning throughout the study of consumer behavior.

Summary

Learning is *the effect of a combination of motivation, strongly perceived experiences, and repetition upon behavioral tendencies in response to particular stimuli or situations.* It comes about primarily through one of two processes: classical conditioning or instrumental conditioning. *Classical conditioning* is implemented by consistently associating the product or brand name to be learned with a reward. Conversely, *instrumental conditioning* occurs when the desired purchasing behavior is consistently rewarded and thereby reinforced.

Learning characteristics that are relevant to the planning of marketing strategy include the tendency for consumers to *forget* recent learning, *stimulus generalization* to family brands, and *stimulus discrimination* through product positioning. Advertising schedules should be planned to reinforce the promotional message without risking consumer fatigue. The marketer should try to encourage the formation of favorable consumer *habits* through sampling and couponing campaigns. Individual differences in learning can be identified through such measurement tools as recognition and aided and unaided recall techniques.

There are four basic types of learning involved in the development of consumer behavior: (1) basic childhood learning, which is usually firmly rooted in the consumer and which the marketer can seldom affect; (2) cognitive learning, which is simply the acquisition of information; (3) attitudinal learning, which involves making value judgements; and (4) behavioral learning.

A marketer can use the knowledge of how consumers learn attitudes, discriminate between brands, and develop consumption patterns to design marketing programs that influence the development of favorable consumer behavior patterns.

In the long run, the most important goal of a marketing program is the development of brand loyalty among consumers. This can be accomplished by motivating consumers, by facilitating product trial, and by repetition of promotional appeals.

Endnotes

1. *Michael L. Ray, "Psychological Theories and Interpretations of Learning," in* Consumer Behavior: Theoretical Sources, *ed. Scott Ward and Thomas S. Robertson (Englewood Cliffs, N.J.: Prentice-Hall, Inc. 1973), 45–117.*

2. *Ray, "Psychological Theories."*

3. *Herbert E. Krugman, "The Impact of Television Advertising: Learning without Involvement,"* Public Opinion Quarterly, 29 *(Autumn 1965), 349–56; Michael L. Ray, "Marketing Communication and the Hierarchy of Effects," in* New Models for Communication Research, ed. *Peter Clark (Beverly Hills, Calif.: Sage Publishing, 1973), 147–76; and Thomas S. Robertson, "Low Commitment Consumer Behavior,"* Journal of Advertising Research, 16 *(April 1976), 19–24.*

4. *"Procter & Gamble Co.,"* Advertising Age, 47 *(August 23, 1976), 138–40.*

5. *B. F. Skinner,* The Behavior of Organisms *(New York: Appleton-Century-Crofts, 1938); B. F. Skinner, "Teaching Machines,"* Scientific American, 205 *(1965), 90–102; and Ray, "Psychological Theories."*

6. *Burke Marketing Research Inc., "Viewer Attitudes toward Commercial Clutter on Television and Media Buying Implications" (Presentation to 18th ARF Conference, November 14, 1972); and Michael L. Ray and Peter Webb, "Experimental Research on the Effects of TV Clutter: Dealing with a Difficult Media Environment,"* Marketing Science Institute Report No. 76–102 *(April 1976).*

7. *Roger M. Heeler, "The Effects of Mixed Media, Multiple Copy, Repetition, and Competition in Advertising: A Laboratory Investigation" (Doctoral dissertation, Graduate School of Business, Stanford University, 1972).*

8. *Harper W. Boyd, Jr. Michael L. Ray and Edward C. Strong, "An Attitudinal Framework for Advertising Strategy,"* Journal of Marketing, 36 *(1972), 27–33; and Jack Trout and Al Ries, "The Positioning Era,"* Advertising Age, *April 24, May 1, and May 8, 1972.*

9. *Jerry Della Femina, with Charles Sopkin, ed.,* From Those Wonderful Folks Who Gave You Pearl Harbor *(New York: Simon & Schuster, 1970).*

10. *Stuart Henderson Britt, "Applying Learning Principles to Marketing,"* MSU Business Topics, 23 *(Spring, 1975), 5–12; Joseph N. Fry, "Family Branding and Consumer Brand Choice,"* Journal of Marketing Research, 4 *(August 1967), 237–47; Joe Kent Kerby, "The Role of Generalization in the Marketing of Consumer Goods,"* California Management Review, 11 *(Winter 1968), 65–71; Henry Bernstein, "Carte Blanche to Start TV Drive Aimed at No. 1,"* Advertising Age, *February 19, 1973, pp. 1 and 8; and Colin F. Neuhaus and James R. Taylor, "Variables Affecting Sales of Family-Branded Products,"* Journal of Marketing Research, 9 *(November 1972), 419–22.*

11. *James G. Greeno and Robert A. Bjork, "Mathematical Learning Theory and the New 'Mental Forestry,'"* Annual Review of Psychology, 24 *(1973), 81–116.*

12. *John C. Maloney, "Is Advertising Believability Really Important?"* Journal of Marketing, 27 *(October 1963), 1–8; and M. Venkatesan, "Cognitive Consistency and Novelty Seeking," in* Consumer Behavior: Theoretical Sources, *ed. Scott Ward and Thomas S. Robertson (Englewood Cliffs, N.J.: Prentice-Hall, Inc. 1973), 354–84.*

13. *George A. Miller, "The Magical Number Seven, Plus or Minus Two: Some Limits on Our Capacity for Processing Information,"* Psychological Review, 63 *(1956), 81–97; Herbert A. Simon,* The Sciences of the Artificial *(Cambridge, Mass.: M.I.T. Press, 1969); and Herbert A. Simon, "How Big Is a Chunk?"* Science, 183 *(February 8, 1974), 44–88.*

14. *Allan Newell and Herbert A. Simon,* Human Problem Solving *(Englewood Cliffs, N.J.: Prentice-Hall, Inc., 1972), 793–96; Simon,* Sciences of the Artificial, 35–42: *and B. R. Bugelski, "Presentation-Time, Total Time in Mediation of Paired, Associate Learning,"* Journal of Experimental Psychology, 63 *(1962), 409–12.*

15. *Richard C. Atkinson and Richard N. Shiffrin, "Human Memory: A Proposed System and Its Control Processes," in* The Psychology of Learning and Motivation, *ed. Kenneth W. Spence and Janet P. Spence (New York: Academic Press, 1968), 89–195; and Nancy C. Waugh and Donald A. Norman, "Primary Memory,"* Psychological Review, 72 *(1965), 89–104.*

16. *Martin Fishbein and Icek Ajzen,* Belief, Attitude, Intention and Behavior: An Introduction to Theory and Research *(Reading, Mass.: Addison-Wesley, 1975), 6.*

17. *Herbert E. Krugman, "Affective Response to Music as a Function of Familiarity,"* Journal of Abnormal and Social Psychology, 3 *(1943), 388–92.*

18. *Scott Ward, "Consumer Socialization,"* Journal of Consumer Research, 1 *(September 1974), 1–15.*

19. *Donald P. Campbell, "Social Attitudes and Other Acquired Behavioral Dispositions," in* Psychology, A Study of the Science, ed. *Sigmund Koch, 6 (New York: McGraw-Hill, 1973), 94–1972; and Ray, "Psychological Theories."*

20. *William F. Massy, "Brand and Store Loyalty as Bases for Market Segmentation," in* On Knowing the Consumer, *ed. Joseph W. Newman (New York: John Wiley, 1969).*

21. *Herbert A. Simon,* Models of Man *(New York: John Wiley, 1957), pp. 204–5; and John A. Howard and Jagdish N. Sheth,* The Theory of Buyer Behavior *(New York: John Wiley, 1969).*

22. *George S. Day, "A Two-Dimensional Concept of Brand Loyalty,"* Journal of Advertising Research, 9 *(September 1969), 29–35; Jerry C. Olson and Jacob Jacoby, "Measuring Multi-Brand Loyalty," in* Scott Ward and Peter Wright, eds., Advances in Consumer Research, 1 *(Association for Consumer Research, 1973), 447–48; Jagdish N. Sheth and C. Whan Park, "A Theory of Multi-Dimensional Brand Loyalty," in* Scott Ward and Peter Wright, eds., Advances in Consumer Research, 1 *(Association for Consumer Research, 1973), 449–59; and Maureen Kallick, Joseph Nearby, and Jay Shaffer, "The Dimensions of Brand Consistent Behavior," in* Scott Ward and Peter Wright, eds., Advances in Consumer Research, 1 *(Association for Consumer Research, 1973), 460–62.*

23. *Henry J. Claycamp and Lucien E. Liddy, "Prediction of New Product Performance: An Analytical Approach,"* Journal of Marketing Research, 6 *(1969), 414–20; and Andrew S. C. Ehrenberg, "Repetitive Advertising and the Consumer,"* Journal of Advertising Research, 14 *(April 1974), 25–34.*

Discussion questions

1. Which of the following consumer behaviors demonstrate real learning as opposed to mere behavior? Why or why not?
   a. Buying the "store brand" of canned peas when it is the only one available.
   b. Recommending a brand you have used for years.
   c. Telling a friend about a funny television commercial but forgetting the brand name.

2. When a person is in a supermarket, his ultimate actions are affected by the four types of learning discussed in this chapter. Give an example of how each of the four may have affected your shopping behavior during your last trip to a supermarket.

3. How might classical conditioning affect our responses to certain kinds of food?

4. In what ways can brand-purchasing behavior be affected by *both* stimulus generalization and stimulus discrimination?

5. Kraft Foods uses family branding, but Procter and Gamble (Crest, Duncan Hines, Charmin, Tide) does not. Yet both companies are successful. Describe in learning terms the conditions under which family branding is a good policy and those under which it is not. What do you think are the reasons for the difference in family-branding policy for Kraft and P&G?

6. List all the learning factors that affect the rate at which we will forget a brand name. (Hint: there are many more than three.)

7. Assume that you are advising the brand manager of Royal Crown Cola. Using your knowledge of brand loyalty, outline the strategies he might use for capturing a greater market share from the leaders, Pepsi and Coke.

8. Of the six ways in which consumers learn to act and make decisions, which one can most easily be affected by marketing strategy? How? Why is this the most amenable to marketing effort?

9. Why is it important to reach consumers when they are young or when they are making their first purchases in a product category?

10. Explain each of the four examples given in the introduction of this chapter. Why are there such big differences in learning in these situations? Try to determine how motivation, strength of experience, and repetition affect learning in each situation.

5 personality and consumer behavior

Introduction

For several decades marketers have been interested in identifying specific market segments in terms of how they differ in personality characteristics. Their objective has been to isolate the personality traits of market segments they would like to reach, so that they can develop marketing strategies that will attract their desired target market. Interest in segmenting consumers on the basis of personality is founded upon the belief that a consumer's purchase behavior is in part a reflection of his personality.

This chapter examines what personality is, and how personality interrelates with other consumer behavior concepts. It reviews several major personality theories and describes how they have stimulated marketers' interest in the study of consumer personality.

Particular attention is given to how a knowledge of consumer personality characteristics can be employed by marketers to segment markets. The chapter concludes with an examination of psychographics, a relatively new and highly promising type of consumer research which is in large measure an outgrowth of personality research.

WHAT IS PERSONALITY?

The examination of personality has been approached by theorists in a variety of ways. Some theorists have emphasized the dual

118

influence of heredity and early childhood experiences on personality development, while others have stressed broader social and environmental influences and the fact that personalities continuously develop over time. Some theorists prefer to view personality as a unified whole, while others focus on specific traits. The wide variation in viewpoints makes it somewhat difficult to arrive at a single definition of personality. However, we propose that *personality* be defined as *those inner psychological characteristics that both determine and reflect how a person responds to his environment.*

The emphasis in this definition is on the person's *inner* characteristics — those specific qualities, attributes, traits, factors, and mannerisms that distinguish one individual from other individuals. As we will discover later in this chapter, the deeply ingrained characteristics that we call personality are likely to influence the individual's product and store choices; they also affect the way she responds to a firm's communication efforts. Therefore, the identification of specific personality characteristics that are associated with consumer behavior may be highly useful in the development of a firm's market segmentation strategies.

THE NATURE OF PERSONALITY

In approaching the study of personality, three distinct properties are of central importance: (1) personality is the essence of individual differences, (2) personality is consistent and enduring, and (3) personality can change.[1]

individual differences

Because the inner characteristics that constitute an individual's personality are a unique combination of factors, no two individuals are exactly alike. Nevertheless, many individuals tend to be similar in terms of a single personality characteristic. For instance, many people can be described as "high" in sociability (the degree of interest they display in social or group activities), while others can be described as "low" in sociability. Personality is a useful consumer behavior concept because it enables us to categorize people into different groups on the basis of a single trait or a small number of traits. If each person were different in *all* respects, it would be impossible to segment people into similar consuming groups; thus there would be little reason to develop standardized products and promotional campaigns.

personality is consistent and enduring

An individual's personality is commonly thought to be both consistent and enduring. Indeed, the mother who comments that her child "has been stubborn from the day he was born" is supporting the contention that personality has both consistency and endurance. Both of these qualities are essential if marketers are to explain or predict consumer behavior in terms of personality.

The stable nature of personality suggests that it is unreasonable for marketers to attempt to change consumers' personalities to conform to certain products. At best, they may learn which personality characteristics influence specific consumer reponses, and attempt to appeal to relevant personality traits inherent in their target group of consumers.

Even though an individual's personality may be very consistent, his consumption behavior may vary considerably because of psychological, social-cultural, and environmental factors that affect his behavior. For instance, even though an individual's personality may be largely stable, his specific needs or motives, his attitudes, his reaction to group pressures, and even his responses to the brands that are now available may cause a change in his behavior. Therefore, personality is only one of a combination of factors that influence how a consumer behaves.

personality can change

Although personality tends to be consistent and enduring, it may still change under various circumstances. For instance, an individual's personality may be altered because of major life events (the birth of a child, the death of a loved one, a divorce, a major career promotion). An individual's personality changes not only in response to abrupt events in his life but also as part of a gradual maturing process.

Theories of personality

In this section we will briefly review three major theories of personality: (1) Freudian theory, (2) neo-Freudian theory, and (3) trait theory. These theories have been chosen for discussion from among many theories of personality because each has played a prominent role in the study of the relationship between consumer behavior and personality.[2]

FREUDIAN THEORY

Sigmund Freud's psychoanalytic theory of personality is the cornerstone of modern psychology. This theory was built on the premise that unconscious needs or drives, especially biological and sexual drives, are at the heart of human motivation and personality. Freud constructed his theory on the basis of patients' recollections of early childhood experiences, analysis of their dreams, and the specific nature of their mental and physical adjustment problems.

id, superego, and ego

Based upon his analyses, Freud proposed that the human personality consists of three interacting systems—the *id*, the *superego*, and the *ego*. The *id* was conceptualized as a "warehouse" of primitive and impulsive drives—basic physiological needs such as thirst, hunger, and sex—for which the individual seeks immediate satisfaction without concern for the specific means of satisfaction.

In contrast, the *superego* is conceptualized as the individual's internal expression of society's moral and ethical codes of conduct. The superego's role is to see that the individual satisfies his needs in a socially acceptable fashion. Thus, the superego is a kind of "break" that restrains or inhibits the impulsive forces of the id.[3]

Finally, the *ego* is the individual's conscious control. It functions as an internal monitor which attempts to balance the impulsive demands of the id and the social-cultural constraints of the superego.

stages of personality development

In addition to specifying a structure for personality, Freud emphasized that an individual's personality is formed as he passes through a number of distinct stages of infant and childhood development. Freud labeled these stages of development to conform to the area of the body on which he believed the child's sexual instincts are focused at the time. They include the oral, anal, phallic, latent and genital stages. (1) *Oral stage*—The infant first experiences social contact with the outside world through his mouth (e.g., eating, drinking, and sucking). A crisis develops at the end of this stage as the child is weaned from his mother's breast or from the bottle. (2) *Anal stage*—During this stage, the child's primary source of pleasure is the process of elimination. A second crisis develops at the end of this stage as the parents try to toilet train the child. (3) *Phallic stage*—The child experiences self-oriented sexual pleasure during this phase as he discovers his sexual organs. A third crisis occurs as the child experiences sexual desire for the parent of the opposite sex. How he resolves this crisis affects later relationships with persons of the opposite sex and with authority figures. (4) *Latency stage*—Freud believed that the sexual instincts of the child lie dormant from about the age of five till the beginning of adolescence and that no important personality changes occur during this dormant stage. (5) *Genital stage*—At the age of adolescence, the individual develops a sexual interest in persons of the opposite sex, beyond his self-oriented love and his love for his parents. If this crisis is adequately resolved, the individual's personality enters into the genital stage.

According to Freud, an adult's personality is determined by how well he deals with the crises that he experiences as he passes through each of these childhood stages (particularly the first three). For instance, if a child's oral needs are not adequately satisfied at the first stage of development, he may become fixated at this stage and display an adult personality which includes such "oral" traits as ". . . dependence, passivity, greediness, and excessive tendencies toward oral activities, as in smoking, chewing, or garrulous speech."[4] If an individual is fixated at the anal stage, his adult personality may display traits of stinginess, obstinacy, excessive need for neatness, and problems in relating to other people.[5]

applications of freudian theory to consumer behavior

Motivational researchers have applied Freud's psychoanalytic theory to the study of consumer behavior by underscoring the belief that human drives are largely *unconscious*, and that consumers are not consciously aware of their true motives. Thus, the emphasis of motivational research studies has been on discovering the underlying motivations for specific consumer behavior. To discover consumer's basic motivations, researchers use a variety of clinical measurement procedures, such as observation and inference, self-reports, projective techniques, and depth interviews (discussed in Chapter 2). The same basic measurement procedures are used to study motivations and personality, since both areas are usually treated as unified or complementary psychological concepts.

In applying the psychoanalytic theory of personality, the motivational researcher tends to focus on the consumer's purchases, treating them as a reflection and an extension of the consumer's own personality. In essence, the motivational researcher tries to determine the product's personality and then works backwards to determine the consumer's personality. The following comment captures this viewpoint: "Indications of a person's personality can be gained not only from the type of food he eats, but also from the way in which he eats it. Food habits are among the first ones we acquire. Any mother of several children knows how early in life these habits are developed and how they vary with different children."[6] Table 5–1 briefly describes the general "personalities" that a

TABLE 5–1

Selective Product Personality Profiles

Product	Description of Product Personality
Prunes	Long identified with its laxative properties, prunes are a symbol of old age; they are like dried-out spinsters, and have none of the soft pleasurableness of plums.
Rice	Rice is viewed as a feminine food. It typically suggests a strong, healthy, fertile female. Throwing rice at newly married couples symbolizes the wish that the marriage be blessed with children.
Power tools	Power tools are a symbol of manliness. They represent masculine skill and competence, and are often bought more for their symbolic value than for active do-it-yourself applications. Ownership of a good power tool or circular saw provides a man with feelings of omnipotence.
Ice cream	Ice cream is often associated with love and affection. It derives particular potency from childhood memories, when it was given to a child for being "good", and withheld as an instrument of punishment. People refer to ice cream as something they "love" to eat.

Adapted from Handbook of Consumer Motivations, *by Ernest Dichter. Copyright 1964, McGraw-Hill Book Company. Used with permission of McGraw-Hill Book Company.*

leading motivational researcher has attributed to several product categories.

NEO-FREUDIAN PERSONALITY THEORY

Several of Freud's colleagaues disagreed with his contention that personality is primarily instinctual and sexual in nature. Instead, these neo-Freudians believed that *social relationships* are fundamental in the formation and development of personality. For instance, Alfred Adler viewed man as seeking to attain various rational goals, which he called *style of life*. He also placed much emphasis on the individual's effort to overcome feelings of inferiority (i.e., to strive for superiority).

Harry Stack Sullivan, another neo-Freudian, stressed that people continuously attempt to establish meaningful and rewarding relationships with others. He was particularly concerned with the individual's efforts to reduce tensions such as anxiety.

Like Sullivan, Karen Horney was also interested in anxiety. She focused on the impact of child-parent relationships, especially the individual's desire to conquer feelings of anxiety. Horney proposed that individuals can be classified into three personality groups: compliant, aggressive and detached.[7] (1) *Compliant* individuals are those who move *toward* others (they desire to be loved, wanted, and appreciated). (2) *Aggressive* individuals are those who move *against* others (they desire to excel and win admiration). (3) *Detached individuals* are those who move *away* from others (they desire independence, self-sufficiency, and freedom from obligations).

Neo-Freudian theories of personality have received suprisingly little attention from consumer researchers, despite their emphasis on the importance of the individual's social-cultural environment as a determinant of personality. However, several researchers have applied Horney's classification system to the study of consumer behavior. For example, one consumer researcher developed a test based on Horney's theory and found some tentative relationships between college students' responses and their product and brand usage patterns.[8] Highly compliant students were found to prefer name brand products, such as Bayer aspirin; students classified as aggressive showed a preference for Old Spice deodorant over other brands (seemingly because of its masculine appeal); and highly detached students were heavy tea drinkers (possibly reflecting their desire not to conform).[9] More recent studies employing the same personality test have also found Horney's scheme to be useful in exploring selective aspects of consumer behavior.[10] However, additional work is necessary to assess the appropriate conditions under which this personality measure can be fruitfully used.

Although neo-Freudian theories of personality have not received wide attention, it is likely that marketers have employed some of these theories intuitively. For example, marketers who position their products as providing "unexcelled" craftsmanship or quality seem to be guided by Adler's theory that individuals constantly strive for superiority.

TRAIT THEORY

Trait theory represents a major departure from the basically *qualitative* or subjective measures that typify the Freudian and neo-Freudian movements (personal observation, self-reported experiences, dream analysis, and projective techniques).

The orientation of trait theory is primarily *quantitative* or empirical; it focuses on the measurement of personality in terms of specific psychological characteristics of the individual called traits. *Trait* is defined as ". . . any distinguishing, relatively enduring way in which one individual differs from another."[11] Accordingly, trait theorists are concerned with the construction of personality tests or inventories that pinpoint individual differences in terms of specific traits.

Viewing personality as a set of enduring traits has a natural appeal because it conforms to many commonly-held practices. For example, many individuals distinguish between friends as "reserved" or "outgoing." In this way, they are intuitively evaluating them in terms of traits.

constructing a personality scale

To more fully understand what is meant by a personality trait, and why the trait approach is considered quantitative rather than qualitative, we will briefly consider how a personality test is developed.

A personality test usually consists of one or more scales, each of which measures a specific personality trait. A *scale* is a series of questions or items that are designed to measure a single personality trait. The scores achieved by an individual on each of the items in the scale are combined to produce a single index, which reflects the degree to which he possesses that trait. Some personality tests consist of a single scale; that is, they are designed to measure only one trait, such as "dogmatism" (how willing a person is to accept a different viewpoint).[12] Other personality tests include more than one scale, with each scale measuring a different trait. An example of a multitrait personality test is the 480-item California Psychological Inventory, which consists of eighteen scales, each measuring a specific trait (e.g., dominance, sociability, self-acceptance, tolerance).[13] Later in this chapter, we will examine how single-trait and multitrait personality inventories have been employed in the study of consumer behavior.

In constructing a scale to measure a specific trait, the test developer starts by observing the behavior of people who he feels typify the personality trait he wishes to measure. He then develops a large number of questions that he believes reflect the actual observed behavior, and he administers these questions to samples of people who might reasonably be expected to score either high or low on the trait under study. For example, if the researcher was developing a scale to measure "outgoingness," he might administer his questions to a sample of salesmen and a sample of laboratory scientists. If he has developed questions that appropriately measure the trait "outgoingness," he should find that salesmen (who might be expected to score "high" on outgoingness) do in fact score "high," and that laboratory scientists (who might be expected to score "low" on outgoingness) do in fact score "low." After repeated testing on different samples with similar results, the researcher can conclude that his series of questions constitute a valid scale for the measurement of outgoingness. He will then try to reduce the number of questions (through factor analyses) without impairing the scale's ability to measure the trait in question.[14]

personality traits and consumer behavior

Because personality scales are easy to combine and administer in the form of a questionnaire, such "paper-and-pencil" personality tests have become the most popular approach for assessing consumer personality.

Although consumer personality research has been conducted for more than two decades, the results from this research have been very uneven.[15] Some studies have found that personality traits have added little to our understanding of consumer behavior, while other studies, more recent ones, have been more encouraging. To demonstrate how personality tests might be effectively used by marketers, we will now review some of these studies.

CONSUMER PERSONALITY RESEARCH. As a group, consumer studies that have *not* been able to identify a relationship between personality and consumption behavior have two factors in common: (1) they were based on multitrait rather than single-trait tests, and (2) they had no *a priori* hypotheses that stipulated a proposed relationship between the traits under study and specific consumer behavior. A number of researchers have used several popular multitrait personality tests simply because they are easy to administer and to score, hoping to find some chance relationship between the traits they measured and specific consumer behavior. They did not select the tests because of a hypothesized relationship between the traits measured and the behavior studied.

The earliest and most controversial application of a standard multitrait personality inventory examined two groups of consumers: those who owned 1955–58 Fords and those who owned comparable year Chevrolets.[16] The objective of the study was to determine the extent to which personality traits could distinguish between the owners of these two makes of cars. The study employed eleven of the fifteen traits measured by the Edwards Personal Preference Schedule (EPPS). Table 5–2 lists and briefly defines these traits, and indicates the ones selected for the Ford-Chevrolet study.

Generally, the results revealed that the personality traits measured did not discriminate between the owners of the two types of cars.[17] How-

TABLE 5–2

**A Summary of Personality Traits Measured by
the Edwards Personal Preference Schedule**

*1. *Achievement:* To do one's best, accomplish tasks of great significance, do things better than others, be successful, be a recognized authority.

*2. *Deference:* To get suggestions, follow instructions, do what is expected, accept leadership of others, conform to custom, let others make decisions.

3. *Order:* To have work neat and organized, make plans before starting, keep files, have things arranged to run smoothly, have things organized.

*4. *Exhibition:* To say clever things, tell amusing jokes and stories, talk about personal achievements, have others notice and comment on one's appearance, be the center of attention.

*5. *Autonomy:* To be able to come and go as desired, say what one thinks, be independent in making decisions, feel free to do what one wants, avoid conformity, avoid responsibilities and obligations.

*6. *Affiliation:* To be loyal to friends, do things for friends, form new friendships, make many friends, form strong attachments, participate in friendly groups.

*7. *Intraception:* To analyze one's motives and feelings, observe and understand others, analyze the motives of others, predict their acts, put one's self in another's place.

8. *Succorance:* To be helped by others, seek encouragement, have others feel sorry when sick, have others be sympathetic about personal problems.

9. *Dominance:* To be a leader, argue for one's point of view, make group decisions, settle arguments, persuade and influence others, supervise others.

*10. *Abasement:* To feel guilty when wrong, accept blame, feel need for punishment, feel timid in presence of superiors, feel inferior, depressed about inability to handle situations.

11. *Nurturance:* To help friends in trouble, treat others with kindness, forgive others, do small favors, be generous, show affection, receive confidence.

*12. *Change:* To do new and different things, travel, meet new people, try new things, eat in new places, live in different places, try new fads and fashions.

13. *Endurance:* To keep at a job until finished, work hard at a task, keep at a problem until solved, finish one job before starting others, stay up late working to get a job done.

*14. *Heterosexuality:* To go out with opposite sex, be in love, kiss, discuss sex, become sexually excited, read books about sex.

*15. *Aggression:* To tell others what one thinks of them, criticize others publicly, make fun of others, tell others off, get revenge, blame others.

*The eleven traits used in the Ford-Chevrolet study.

Reproduced from the Edwards Personal Preference Schedule. Copyright 1954, © 1959 by The Psychological Corporation, New York, N.Y. All rights reserved.

ever, when the data were reanalyzed on the basis of specific hypotheses concerning the relationship of certain personality traits to ownership of one or the other make of car, the results revealed some improvement in the ability of the EPPS to differentiate between Ford and Chevrolet owners.[18] Most importantly, the reanalysis underscored the need to justify the measurement of specific personality traits by hypothesizing how each trait relates to the consumer behavior under investigation.

Other studies have used multitrait personality tests in attempts to explain such consumer-related activites as the ownership of different types of cars (convertibles, standards, and compacts), the purchase and use of various convenience goods, the purchase of store brands versus national brands, and usage of specific types of banking institutions.[19] Like the original Ford-Chevrolet study, the results of these studies have typically been disappointing.[20] In summary, it appears that the inability of much personality research to find significant relationships between personality and consumer behavior is due to the fact that many researchers indiscriminantly employ all of the scales included in the standard multitrait personality test they employ, without specifying how each trait is expected to relate to the specific consumer behavior under study.

PROMISING STUDIES IN CONSUMER PERSONALITY RESEARCH. The persistent efforts of both marketing practitioners and consumer researchers to demonstrate that personality is an inherently useful tool for segmenting consumer markets have recently paid off in some important refinements to consumer personality research.

For instance, evidence suggests that other consumer behavior variables, such as demographic factors (age, sex, education, income) or the type or amount of risk perceived, can be used to crystallize the relationship between personality and consumer behavior.[21] To illustrate, a marketer may find that no meaningful relationship exists between consumers' purchase of his new frozen vegetables and selected personality traits. However, if he were to divide the sample of consumers into "low" and "high" income groups, and then separately examine each income group for a relationship between selected personality traits and the purchase of the new product, he might find that meaningful personality profiles emerge. In such instances, the additional consumer behavior variables would serve as "filters" to purify the relationship between personality and consumer behavior.

Another promising approach to consumer personality research involves the use of carefully selected single-trait personality tests (tests that measure just one trait, such as self-confidence) rather than multitrait inventories. In addition, there has recently been some effort to develop personality scales specifically designed for the study of consumer behavior. Two examples of such tailor-made personality tests are a test that measures *self-actualization* (derived from Maslow's need hierarchy described in Chapter 2), and a test that measures *innovativeness* (how receptive a person is to new experiences).[22]

Marketers are interested in understanding how consumers' personalities influence their consumption behavior because such knowledge enables them to segment consumers into groups that will respond favorably to their promotional strategies. This section examines a number of specific types of consumer behavior in which the influence of personality characteristics appears to be particularly promising for market segmentation.

PERSONALITY AND BRAND USAGE

Academic consumer researchers have paid little attention to the question of how personality traits influence consumers' brand choices, perhaps because of the poor initial results obtained in earlier studies (e.g., the Ford-Chevrolet research). However, there are indications that a number of marketers of well-known brands do segment their markets on the basis of specific personality traits.[23] Since personality segmentation is obviously of important competitve value, such marketers have been somewhat reluctant to openly discuss what they have discovered concerning the influence of personality on brand choice.

Fortunately, several advertising agencies and consumer goods firms have been willing to disclose certain aspects of their research linking personality traits to consumer brand choice. For example, the director of research for a leading advertising agency has reported the successful development of market segmentation strategies based on personality traits for specific brands in such product categories as women's cosmetic products, cigarettes, insurance, and liquor.[24] Table 5–3 lists the personality traits that were found to be helpful in segmenting the women's cosmetic market. A clinical psychologist employed by the advertising agency selects the initial personality traits that he feels can logically be expected to influence brand choice decisions. Pilot test studies are then undertaken to eliminate those traits that do not appear to contribute to an understanding of consumer differences. In the final phase of the personality segmentation research, personality scales that have been found to be related to product and brand purchase behavior are used to develop profiles of specific brand usage segments.[25]

personality and beer consumption

Anheuser-Busch, the nation's leading marketer of beer, has sponsored consumer behavior research designed to segment beer and other alcoholic beverage drinkers into specific drinker-personality types.[26] This research effort represents a particularly good case history of the successful application of personality theory as a market segmentation tool.

An extensive amount of exploratory research identified four distinct types of alcoholic beverage drinkers with correspondingly unique

TABLE 5–3

Personality Scales Found Useful in the Segmentation of the Women's Cosmetic Market

Scale	Description
Narcissism—	Tendency to be preoccupied with the details of one's personal appearance
Appearance Conscious—	Emphasis on the social importance of looking properly groomed
Exhibitionism—	Tendency toward self-display and attention seeking
Impulsive—	Tendency to act in a carefree, impetuous and unreflective manner
Order—	Tendency to be compulsively neat, and live by rules and schedules
Fantasied Achievement—	Measure of narcissistic aspiration for distinction and personal recognition
Capacity For Status—	Measure of the personal qualities and attributes that underline and lead to status
Dominant—	Need to be superior to others by being in control and in the forefront
Sociable—	Need for informal, friendly, agreeable relationship with others
Active—	Need to be on the go, doing things, achieving goals set out for oneself
Cheerful—	Tendency to feel bright, cheerful and optimistic about life
Deference—	Tendency to submit to opinions and preferences of others perceived as superior
Subjective—	Tendency toward naive, superstitious and generally immature thinking

Source: Shirley Young, "The Dynamics of Measuring Unchange," in Russell I. Haley, ed., Attitude Research in Transition (Chicago: American Marketing Association, 1972), 62.

personality types. Table 5–4 presents a simplified summary of these four drinker-personality types. Employing this classification scheme, university researchers have been able to identify specific advertising messages and media exposure patterns that effectively reach the specific drinker-personality types that constitute the prime market for Budweiser, Michelob, and Busch (the three brands produced by Anheuser-Busch). Applying this information about drinker-personality types and their susceptibility to specific advertising messages, Anheuser-Busch was able to boost the sales of Michelob beer by successfully appealing to the drinkers in a larger drinker-personality segment.

Further research indicated which drinker-personality types were most likely to be brand switchers and which were most likely to be brand loyal. Such insights are invaluable to marketers introducing a new brand, entering a new market, or trying to combat the advances of competitive brands.

TABLE 5–4

Drinker Personality Characteristics

Type of Drinker	Personality Type	Drinking Pattern
Social drinker	Driven by his own needs, particularly to achieve, and attempts to manipulate others to get what he wants. Driven by a desire to get ahead. Usually a younger person.	Controlled drinker who may sometimes become high or drunk but is unlikely to be an alcoholic. Drinks primarily on weekends, holidays, and vacations, usually in a social setting with friends. Drinking is seen as a way to gain social acceptance.
Reparative drinker	Sensitive and responsive to the needs of others and adapts to their needs by sacrificing his own aspirations. Usually middle-aged.	Controlled drinker who infrequently becomes high or drunk. Drinks primarily at the end of the workday, usually with a few close friends. Views drinking as a reward for sacrifices made for others.
Oceanic drinker	Sensitive to the needs of others. Often a failure who blames himself for his nonachievement.	Drinks heavily, especially when under pressure to achieve. At times shows a lack of control over his drinking and is likely to become high, drunk, and even alcoholic. Drinking is a form of escape.
Indulgent drinker	Generally insensitive to others and places the blame for his failures on others' lack of sensitivity to him.	Like the oceanic drinker, he drinks heavily, often becomes high, drunk, or alcoholic. Drinks as a form of escape.

Source: Adapted from Russell L. Ackoff and James R. Emshoff, ''Advertising Research at Anheuser-Busch, Inc. (1968–74),'' Sloan Management Review, Vol. 16, No. 3 (Spring 1975), 1–15.

This research project, which has been ongoing since 1968, exemplifies the fact that a marketer who is willing to expend the funds for creative personality research can reap handsome rewards.

CONSUMER-INNOVATORS

Marketing practitioners must learn all they can about consumers who are willing to try new products or brands, for the market response of such innovators is often crucial to the ultimate success of a new product.

This section discusses several personality traits that have proved useful in differentiating between consumer-innovators and noninnovators. (Chapter 14 examines in detail more of the distinguishing characteristics of these two groups.)

dogmatism

Dogmatism is a personality trait that measures the amount of rigidity a person displays toward the unfamiliar and toward information that is contrary to his own established beliefs.[27] A person who is highly dogmatic approaches the unfamiliar defensively and with considerable discomfort and uncertainty. On the other end of the spectrum, the person who is low in dogmatism will readily consider the unfamiliar or opposing beliefs.

In two closely parallel experiments, subjects who were low in dogmatism (open-minded) were found to be significantly more likely to prefer innovative products to established or traditional alternatives.[28] In contrast, highly dogmatic subjects (closed-minded) were more likely to choose established rather than innovative product alternatives. A third study found that early patrons of self-service gas stations (then highly innovative) were significantly less dogmatic than customers of traditional full-service stations.[29]

However, some seemingly contradictory research suggests that highly dogmatic consumers may be more willing to accept new products than low dogmatic consumers *if* the products are presented in an authoritative manner (e.g., by an admired celebrity, a recognized expert, or in the context of a reassuring and ego-boosting message).[30] The format of the promotional message can significantly affect the reception of a new product by consumers who differ in terms of dogmatism. It has been suggested that low dogmatic consumer-innovators are more receptive to messages that stress factual differences and product benefits.[31] For this reason, a marketer of a new type of electric shaver might be wise to emphasize in his initial promotional campaign the reasons why the shaver will provide a better shave. However, to reach more resistant or highly dogmatic consumers, he might alter his promotional approach and employ celebrities' and experts' testimonials, since highly dogmatic consumers are more likely to respond favorably to such authoritative appeals.

social character

The personality trait known as social character has its origin in sociological research, which focuses on the identification and classification of societies into distinct social-cultural types.[32] However, as it is used in consumer psychology, social character is a personality trait that ranges on a continuum from *inner-directedness* to *other-directedness*. Available evidence indicates that inner-directed consumers tend to rely on their own "inner" values or standards in evaluating new products and are more likely to be consumer-innovators. Conversely, other-directed consumers tend to look to others for direction on what is right or wrong; thus they are less likely to be consumer-innovators.[33]

Research on innovativeness and social character has found that when new food products were ranked in terms of how much they differed from more traditional alternatives, the more novel the product, the more likely it was to be purchased by inner-directed consumers, and the less likely it was to be purchased by other-directed consumers.[34]

A study which compared the first purchasers of the Ford Maverick (when it was introduced in April 1969) with later purchasers of the same car and concurrent purchasers of an already established small car, found that the consumer-innovators who first purchased the Maverick were significantly more inner-directed than later purchasers of Mavericks and concurrent purchasers of the established car.[35] These findings strongly support the notion that innovators tend to have inner-directed personalities, while later adopters have other-directed personalities.

Available evidence also suggests that inner- and other-directed subjects have different preferences in terms of promotional messages.[36] Specifically, inner-directed people seem to prefer ads that stress product features and personal benefits (enabling them to use their own values and standards in evaluating products), while other-directed people seem to prefer ads that feature a social environment or social acceptance (in keeping with their tendency to look to others for direction). For marketing practitioners, this research suggests that consumers respond favorably to promotional themes that are consistent with their personality predispositions.

category width

Another personality trait that has been found to discriminate between innovative and noninnovative consumers is *category width*. This trait seems to tap an important dimension of a person's risk-handling strategy. Research has shown that people handle risky decisions differently.[37] Some people tend to have a tolerance for error; that is, they are willing to accept the possibility of poor or negative outcomes in order to maximize the number of satisfying or positive alternatives from which to choose. Other people handle risk in the opposite way; that is, they have a low tolerance for error, and prefer to forgo satisfying or positive alternatives so that they might minimize exposure to poor or negative alternatives. As measured by the category-width scale, individuals who have a high tolerance for error are called "broad categorizers," while individuals with a low tolerance for error are called "narrow categorizers."[38]

The first use of the category-width scale in consumer behavior research explored its relationship to individuals' perceived willingness to try new products.[39] The results found that student subjects who were broad categorizers were willing to try qualitatively different brands (innovations), while those who were narrow categorizers tended to choose established or familiar alternatives (noninnovations). These findings were substantiated in later research among actual consumers.[40]

Another study found that homemakers who were broad categorizers were more likely to have purchased genuinely new products (e.g., nonrefrigerated main dishes), while those who were narrow categorizers were more likely to have purchased superficially new products (e.g., lime-scented dishwashing detergent).[42] For the marketer, this study indicates that the degree of newness inherent in a product may influence consumers differently, depending upon their personalities. That is, broad categorizers may be more willing to purchase genuinely new or novel products, while narrow categorizers may be more receptive to superficially new products. Thus it would seem that the marketing practitioner should carefully consider the *degree* of newness inherent in his new product when he designs his marketing strategy.

The research on dogmatism, social character, and category width indicates that the consumer-innovator differs from the noninnovator in terms of personality orientation. A knowledge of these personality differences should enable the marketer to segment his market for new products and to design distinct promotional strategies for both consumer-innovators and later adopters.

THE ACCEPTANCE OF FOREIGN-MADE PRODUCTS

Several consumer studies suggest that personality characteristics may be useful in distinguishing between consumer segments that are likely to be receptive to foreign-made products and those that are not.

Specifically, evidence indicates that American consumers who purchase foreign compact automobiles are less conservative and less dogmatic than purchasers of American-made compact cars.[42] Supporting this conclusion, another personality study found that highly dogmatic consumers were significantly more likely to rate favorably products manufactured in countries perceived to be similar to the United States (e.g., England and West Germany) than those manufactured in countries that were rated dissimilar.[43] The opposite was also true: low dogmatic consumers were more accepting of products manufactured in countries judged dissimilar to the United States. This study also found that highly dogmatic consumers have a more favorable image of products manufactured in the United States than low dogmatic consumers.

These studies suggest that the low dogmatic consumer should be the prime market segment for marketers of foreign-made products, and that promotional appeals should stress the distinctive features and benefits of these products over available American alternatives. On the other hand, domestic marketers wishing to impede inroads of foreign products should stress a "nationalistic" theme in their promotional appeals (e.g., "Made in America"), for such appeals are likely to attract the highly dogmatic consumer.

PERSONALITY AND STORE CHOICE

Personality also influences the choice of stores in which the consumer decides to shop. The consumer's self-confidence has been found to be associated with the type of retailer from which he purchases certain kinds of merchandise. For instance, female clothing shoppers who scored high in self-confidence were found to prefer discount stores as a place to buy their clothing, while shoppers with less self-confidence tended to favor the more traditional neighborhood retailer.[44] A recent study reports that consumers who purchased expensive audio equipment (record players, tape players, tuners, and amplifiers) from an audio equipment specialty store were more self-confident than consumers who purchased from a traditional department store.[45]

The findings of these two studies suggest that the newer types of retailing establishments (e.g., the clothing discounter and the audio equipment specialty store) tend to attract a more self-confident type of customer than the older types of retail establishments. Therefore, it would appear that new types of retailers should try to reach a more self-confident market segment by appealing to the consumer's ability to recognize and properly evaluate unlabeled or specialty merchandise. More traditional retailers should attempt to reassure their less confident customers that they will stand behind them and assist them in their shopping tasks.

Evidence indicates that shoppers' personalities may even influence the kind of salesperson they prefer to have serve them. Specifically, "dependent" shoppers seem to prefer an aggressive salesperson who makes suggestions and takes the initiative, while "independent" shoppers prefer a less-aggressive salesperson.[46]

ECOLOGICALLY-CONCERNED CONSUMERS

With increasing recognition that our environment and natural resources are in danger, there has in recent years been a mounting interest among marketers and government policymakers to identify those consumers who are most likely to respond to socially conscious appeals. A market segment of socially conscious consumers would be a prime target for new ecologically oriented products or services and would provide the support needed for public policies designed to protect the environment. The available evidence suggests that certain demographic, psychological, and social characteristics distinguish the socially concerned consumer from the rest of society. Of particular interest to our present discussion, personality traits have been found to be especially useful in the development of a profile of the socially responsive consumer.[47]

In examining consumer social consciousness, researchers have found it fruitful to focus on ecologically-related consumer attitudes and behavior For example, studies have explored the characteristics of consumers who use recycling facilities, those who purchase low-lead or lead-free gasoline, beverages in returnable bottles, recycled paper products, or low-polluting washing machine detergents.[48]

Consumers who used the facilities of a local recycling plant were found to be less dogmatic, less conservative, and less status conscious, and more cosmopolitan (i.e., a broader general outlook), more isolated or alienated from society, and more likely to feel that they have some control over their personal lives and environment (i.e., personal competence) than those consumers who did not use such facilities.[49] While not employing the same personality traits, related research tends to substantiate this personality profile of the ecologically concerned consumer.[50]

Taken as a whole, the ecologically concerned consumer appears to be a *self-actualizer,* one who is able to constructively deal with his feelings of alienation through a belief that his actions can affect change in his personal life and environment.[51] A recent study that employed a tailor-made personality scale to measure self-actualization found that ecologically concerned consumers scored signficantly higher on the self-actualization test than did those who were less ecologically concerned.[52]

The research evidence suggests that ecologically responsible consumers do represent a distinct market segment. In communicating with this market segment, marketers would be wise to stress the environmental benefits of their products, since such promotional appeals would be consistent with the personality characteristics of the ecologically concerned consumer.

Psychographic segmentation

Researchers have broadened the measurement of consumer personality variables to include the measurement of related behavioral concepts such as consumer life-styles, interests, attitudes, and opinions. This broadened area of research is called psychographics. Psychographic research has caught the imagination of many marketers since reports of its applications to segmentation strategy first started appearing in the late 1960s.

Psychographic research is designed to identify consumer differences on a wide range of psychological and social-cultural characteristics. To more fully understand what psychographic characteristics are, it is useful to contrast them with demographic characteristics.

As we noted in Chapter 1, demographic characteristics are objective and somewhat easily measurable characteristics of a population, such as age, income, education, sex, and marital status. Psychographic characteristics, on the other hand, are relatively intangible, elusive variables such as interests, attitudes, and life-styles, but they lend themselves to ready measurement with the use of specially tailored psychographic inventories.

Like motivational research, psychographic research provides the marketer with a comprehensive and rich profile of the consumer. Unlike motivational research, psychographic research produces a quantitative rather than a qualitative measure of the consumer characteristics under study. In this respect, its measurement is somewhat similar to the measurement of personality traits, in that it requires the use of self-administered questionnaires or "inventories" comprised of statements or questions concerning the respondent's needs, perceptions, attitudes, beliefs, values, interests, activities, tastes, and problems. It is this blending of the desirable characteristics of both motivational research and standard paper-and-pencil personality tests that gives psychographic measurement its distinctive appeal as a consumer behavior research tool.

Psychographic variables are often referred to as AIOs, for much psychographic research focuses on the measurement of activities, interests and opinions.[53]

ACTIVITIES: Refers to how the consumer (or his family) spends his time.
INTERESTS: Refers to the consumer's (or his family's) preferences and priorities.
OPINIONS: Refers to how the consumer feels about a wide variety of events or things.

Table 5–5 lists some of the general elements often included within each of these major dimensions of psychographic analysis.

Psychographic or AIO inventories usually require the consumer to evaluate his stand in relation to a wide variety of statements, such as

"I wish I had more good neighbors."
"I budget my money very carefully."
"I avoid joining clubs and other organizations."
"I have a first-aid kit in my car."
"I find that I'm always buying new gadgets."

In responding to a psychographic inventory, consumers are asked to rate the extent of their "agreement" or "disagreement" with such statements. Table 5–6 presents a portion of an actual psychographic

TABLE 5–5

AIO Studies Encompass a Wide Variety of Variables

Activities	Interests	Opinions
Work	Family	Themselves
Hobbies	Home	Social issues
Social events	Job	Politics
Vacation	Community	Business
Entertainment	Recreation	Economics
Club membership	Fashion	Education
Community	Food	Products
Shopping	Media	Future
Sports	Achievement	Culture

Source: Joseph T. Plummer, "The Concept and Application of Life Style Segmentation," Journal of Marketing, 38 (January 1974), 34.

TABLE 5–6

A Portion of an Actual Psychographic Inventory

Understanding what the telephone means to you, how you use it and how it fits into your life is important to us in planning for your telephone needs. Each of the following statements is about telephones or how they fit into your life. Please read each statement and then put an "X" in the box which best indicates how strongly you agree or disagree with the statement in terms of your home phone. For example, if you "strongly agree" with a statement you would put an "X" in the "+3" box ([X]). If you "somewhat disagree" you would put an "X" in the "–2" box ([X]). If you neither agree nor disagree, you would put an "X" in the "0" box ([X]). *Please disregard the small black numbers beside the boxes. They are for office use only.*

	Completely agree		Neither agree nor disagree		Completely disagree		
I spend a lot of time talking on the telephone	+3 ¹	+2 ²	+1 ³	0 ⁴	–1 ⁵	–2 ⁶	–3 ⁷ 31
People who have stylish telephones are lucky because they can afford them	+3 ¹	+2 ²	+1 ³	0 ⁴	–1 ⁵	–2 ⁶	–3 ⁷ 32
We live a long way from our friends and relatives	+3 ¹	+2 ²	+1 ³	0 ⁴	–1 ⁵	–2 ⁶	–3 ⁷ 33
Those who know me would consider me to be thrifty	+3 ¹	+2 ²	+1 ³	0 ⁴	–1 ⁵	–2 ⁶	–3 ⁷ 34
I need several telephones in my home because of my work/business . .	+3 ¹	+2 ²	+1 ³	0 ⁴	–1 ⁵	–2 ⁶	–3 ⁷ 35
I am influential in my neighborhood . .	+3 ¹	+2 ²	+1 ³	0 ⁴	–1 ⁵	–2 ⁶	–3 ⁷ 36
Pushbutton telephones probably break down a lot	+3 ¹	+2 ²	+1 ³	0 ⁴	–1 ⁵	–2 ⁶	–3 ⁷ 37
I prefer to have several telephones in my home as a convenience	+3 ¹	+2 ²	+1 ³	0 ⁴	–1 ⁵	–2 ⁶	–3 ⁷ 38
For me the telephone is a means of avoiding seeing some people	+3 ¹	+2 ²	+1 ³	0 ⁴	–1 ⁵	–2 ⁶	–3 ⁷ 39
I prefer colored appliances	+3 ¹	+2 ²	+1 ³	0 ⁴	–1 ⁵	–2 ⁶	–3 ⁷ 40
My home is an open house, with friends and neighbors always visiting . .	+3 ¹	+2 ²	+1 ³	0 ⁴	–1 ⁵	–2 ⁶	–3 ⁷ 41
I prefer pushbutton phones even though they are more expensive	+3 ¹	+2 ²	+1 ³	0 ⁴	–1 ⁵	–2 ⁶	–3 ⁷ 42
When I must choose between the two, I usually dress for fashion, not comfort	+3 ¹	+2 ²	+1 ³	0 ⁴	–1 ⁵	–2 ⁶	–3 ⁷ 43

Source: Joseph N. Spiers, "Getting More from Market Research," Industry Week, December 1, 1975, 34. Also, courtesy of the American Telephone and Telegraph Company.

inventory used by the American Telephone and Telegraph Company to study various aspects of consumers' telephone behavior.

CONSTRUCTING A PSYCHOGRAPHIC INVENTORY

In constructing an inventory of psychographic items or statements, researchers first review available market research studies that might be of help in isolating psychographic variables. Motivational research studies are a particularly good source, for they tend to include consumers' reflections on their experiences and needs. Based upon such a review, psychographic statements are prepared which reflect the range of activities, interests, and opinions that the researcher wishes to evaluate. Table 5–7 lists several psychographic categories and corresponding statements employed in a study designed to identify consumers with different degrees of commitment to in-home catalog shopping.

general and product-specific statements

In preparing a psychographic inventory designed to study consumer behavior within a specific product category, researchers generally include both general and product-specific statements. For example, a

---

TABLE 5–7

A Sample of Psychographic Categories and Corresponding Statements

Psychographic category	Sample Items
Time consciousness	It takes too much time to shop out of town.
	I always shop where it saves me time.
Gregarious community work	I like to work on community projects.
	I have personally worked on projects to better our town.
Attitudes toward local shopping conditions	Local prices are out of line with other towns.
	Local stores are attractive places to shop.
Shopping center orientation	I enjoy going to big shopping centers.
	I prefer shopping centers over downtown shopping areas.
Price consciousness	I shop a lot for specials.
	A person can save a lot of money by shopping around for bargains.
Venturesomeness	I often buy it just to see what it is like.
	I enjoy doing new things.
Self-confidence	I think I have a lot of personal ability.
	I like to be considered a leader.

Source: Adapted from Fred D. Reynolds, "An Analysis of Catalog Buying Behavior," Journal of Marketing, 38 (July 1974), 49.

study designed to examine women's hair-care behavior and preferences might include a general statement such as "When shopping in a supermarket, I always look for sales." In addition, it might include a product-specific statement such as "My hair is very unmanageable." Both types of statements supply valuable insights regarding consumers' attitudes; however, the product-specific statements pertain directly to the product and its use, while the general statements focus on broader perceptions, preferences, or "style of life."

APPLICATIONS OF PSYCHOGRAPHIC ANALYSIS

Psychographic analysis is particularly useful in three closely related areas of marketing strategy: (1) segmenting markets, (2) positioning and repositioning products, and (3) developing specific promotional campaigns.

market segmentation

Psychographic research is an efficient way of identifying the psychological and social-cultural characteristics of specific target markets. For example, a psychographic study that contrasted "heavy" moviegoers (those who had gone to the movies at least nine times in the preceding year) and nonmoviegoers (those who had not gone to the movies in the preceding year) produced the following behavioral profile of "heavy" moviegoers as contrasted with nonmovie goers:[54]

1. Heavy moviegoers are more ambitious, optimistic and more self-confident.
2. Heavy moviegoers have a richer fantasy life.
3. Heavy moviegoers are more active and more socially oriented.
4. Heavy moviegoers have more "swinging" interests.
5. Heavy moviegoers are more inclined toward new and sporty possessions.
6. Heavy moviegoers have more "contemporary" values.

A portion of the AIO inventory from which this summary characterization was drawn is presented in Table 5–8.

product positioning and repositioning

If a company is not certain which one of a number of alternative customer segments should be the target for a new-product concept, it can use psychographic analysis to identify those consumers who seem to be least satisfied with existing products, and thus more likely to respond to a new product. On the basis of its findings, the company can design a product and marketing strategy that specifically appeals to this market.

For existing products, especially those with declining sales, psychographic research can be employed to identify the psychographic characteristics of the present market and of competitors' markets, so that a campaign can be designed to appeal to the more promising market seg-

TABLE 5–8

A Partial Psychographic Comparison of "Heavy" Moviegoers
and Nonmoviegoers

	Percentage Agreement	
	Non-Moviegoers	"Heavy" Moviegoers
My greatest achievements are still ahead of me.	49	80
Five years from now the family income will probably be a lot higher than it is now.	63	88
I'd like to spend a year in London or Paris.	19	42
I like to be considered a leader.	60	82
I don't like to take a chance.	71	51
I like parties where there is lots of music and talk.	37	65
I always have the car radio on when I drive.	49	82
"Playboy" is one of my favorite magazines.	13	48
I think I'm a bit of a swinger.	13	33
I like sports cars.	29	58
Liquor is a curse on American life.	59	36
A woman should not smoke in public.	62	36
If Americans were more religious, this would be a better country.	83	63

Source: Glen Homan, Robert Cecil, and William Wells, "An Analysis of Moviegoers By Life Style Segments," in Mary Jane Schlinger, ed., Advances in Consumer Research, 2 (Association for Consumer Research, 1975), 219.

ments, even if it means repositioning the product. For instance, an advertising agency was requested by a client who produced a heavy-duty hand soap to reposition the product to appeal to new market segments, since the traditional audience for the product (men who used it after completing dirty jobs around the house or shop) was felt to be too restrictive in size.[55] A psychographic study of female users of heavy-duty hand soap produced the following profile:[56]

1. Her interests and activities are centered on her home and her children.
2. She influences others and sees herself as an expert on products.
3. She needs to live within a limited income.
4. Many of her ideas and values are traditionally blue-collar.
5. She has a strong predisposition for deep-down cleanliness.

The AIO statements from which this profile was drawn are presented in Table 5–9. The findings provided valuable insights for repositioning the product to a female audience.

TABLE 5-9

A Comparison of "Users" and "Non-Users" of Heavy-Duty Hand Soap

	Percentage agreement	
	Non-users	*Users*
Home-Oriented		
I must admit I really don't like household chores.	44	29
I always make my cakes from scratch.	17	48
I try to arrange my home for my children's convenience.	31	44
When making important family decisions, consideration of the children should come first.	40	50
She is a "Gatekeeper" and Knowledgeable Shopper		
I like to go grocery shopping.	44	65
People come to me more often than I go to them for information about brands.	24	35
Budget-Conscious		
I shop a lot for "specials."	41	52
When I think of bad health, I think of doctor bills.	42	53
Traditional Blue-Collar Values		
Women should not use false eyelashes.	20	49
A woman should not chew gum.	37	21
Clothing should be dried in the fresh air and sunshine.	34	49
There should be a gun in every home.	22	38
Compulsive Concern with Cleanliness		
You have to use disinfectants to get your house really clean.	35	58
I am uncomfortable when my house is not completely clean.	51	64
Everyone should use a mouthwash.	44	63

Source: Adapted from Joseph T. Plummer, "Life Style and Advertising: Case Studies," *Combined Proceedings (Chicago: American Marketing Association, 1972), pp. 294–95.*

promotional campaigns

Psychographic analysis has been widely used in the development of advertising campaigns to answer three questions: (1) Whom should we aim our advertising at? (2) What should we say? and (3) Where should we say it? In the past, copywriters tended to rely on their own intuition or on small-scale motivational research studies as a guide for the creation of copy. However, psychographic profiles provide the opportunity to create advertising copy based on more objective, large-scale research studies.

Mass media also develop psychographic (and demographic) profiles of their audiences. (Table 5-10 presents a brief comparison of "heavy" *Playboy* and "heavy" *Reader's Digest* readers.) By offering media buyers psychographic studies of their audiences, mass-media publishers

TABLE 5–10

A Psychographic Comparison of *Playboy* and *Reader's Digest* Readers

	Percent who definitely agreed among	
	Heavy Playboy Readers	*Heavy Reader's Digest Readers*
My greatest achievements are still ahead of me.	50	26
I go to church regularly.	18	40
Movies should be censored.	14	40
Most men would cheat on their wives if the right opportunity came along.	27	12

Source: Douglas J. Tigert, "Life Style Analysis as a Basis for Media Selection," in William D. Wells, ed., Life Style and Psychographics *(Chicago: American Marketing Association, 1974), 179.*

make it possible for advertisers to select media that have audiences most closely resembling their own target audiences.

Psychographic research has served as a foundation for numerous promotional campaigns. For example, the following products have had their advertising themes or media selected with the help of psychographic studies: Schlitz Beer, Lava Soap, Union 76 Gasoline, Kentucky Fried Chicken, Dewar's White Label Scotch, Nescafé and Taster's Choice coffees, Chevrolet Vega, Colgate-Palmolive's Irish Spring bar soap, Sony Betamax videotape player, Jack Daniel's Whisky, Peter Paul's Mounds and Almond Joy, and Tums.

At the present time, the outlook for psychographic segmentation seems to be bright indeed.

Summary

Personality can be described as the psychological characteristics that both determine and reflect how a person will respond to his environment. Although personality tends to be consistent and enduring, it has been known to change abruptly in response to major life events, as well as gradually over time.

Three theories of personality are prominent in the study of consumer behavior: psychoanalytic theory, neo-Freudian theory, and trait theory. Freud's psychoanalytic theory provided the foundation for the study of motivational research, which operates on the premise that human drives are largely unconscious in nature and serve to motivate many consumer actions. Neo-Freudian theory tends to emphasize the fundamental role of social relationships in the formation and development of personality. Alfred Adler viewed man as seeking to overcome feelings of inferiority. Harry Stack Sullivan believed that people attempt to establish meaningful and rewarding relationships with others. Karen Horney saw individuals as trying to overcome feelings of anxiety, and categorized them as compliant, aggressive, or detached personality types. Both Freudian theory and neo-Freudian theory use qualitative measures such as observation, self-report, and projective techniques to identify and measure personality characteristics.

Trait theory is a major departure from the qualitative or subjective approach to personality measurement. It postulates that individuals possess innate psychological traits (e.g., self-confidence, aggression, responsibility, curiosity) to greater or lesser degree, and that these traits can be measured by specially designed questionnaires or inventories. Because they are simple to use and to score and can be self-administered, personality inventories are the preferred method of many researchers for the assessment of consumer personality.

The results of consumer personality research are somewhat uneven. Findings suggest that studies that use single-trait tests based on prior hypotheses concerning the relationship between specific consumer behavior and the trait under study are more likely to be successful than studies that try to find chance relationships through the use of multitrait personality tests.

The identification of personality variables that are linked to product usage behavior enables marketers to segment their markets on the basis of personality characteristics. Thus they can either design specific products to appeal to certain personality types, or design promotional strategies that will appeal to the personality characteristics of their existing target audiences. Personality research that identifies differences in personality characteristics between innovators and non-innovators is useful in the development of strategies for new product introduction.

Psychographic research is designed to identify consumer differences on a wide range of psychological and social-cultural characteristics, including personality, life-style, attitudes, opinions, and interests. It combines the desirable characteristics of both motivational research and standard personality trait measurement, and produces rich and comprehensive consumer profiles. Psychographic analysis is of particular value in three closely related areas of marketing strategy: segmenting markets, positioning and repositioning products, and designing promotional campaigns.

Endnotes

1. *E. Earl Baughman and George Schlager Welsh,* Personality: A Behavioral Science *(Englewood Cliffs, N.J.: Prentice-Hall, 1962), 22.*

2. *For a more-detailed examination of these and other theories of personality, see Calvin S. Hall and Gardner Lindzey,* Theories of Personality *(New York: John Wiley, 1957).*

3. *David Krech, Richard S. Cruchfield and Norman Livson,* Elements of Psychology, *2nd ed. (New York: Knopf, 1969), 745.*

4. *Ibid., 746.*

5. *William D. Wells and Arthur D. Beard, "Personality and Consumer Behavior," in Scott Ward and, Thomas S. Robertson, eds.,* Consumer Behavior: Theoretical Sources *(Englewood Cliffs, N.J.: Prentice-Hall, 1973), 146.*

6. *Ernest Dichter,* Handbook of Consumer Motivations *(New York: McGraw-Hill, 1964), 58.*

7. *For example, see Karen Horney,* The Neurotic Personality of Our Time *(New York: Norton, 1937).*

8. *Joel B. Cohen, "An Interpersonal Orientation to the Study of Consumer Behavior,"* Journal of Marketing Research, *6 (August 1967), 270–78.*

9. *Ibid.*

10. *Arch G. Woodside and Ruth Andress, "CAD Eight Years Later,"* Journal of the Academy of Marketing Science, *3 (Summer-Fall 1975), 309–13.*

11. *J. P. Guilford,* Personality *(New York: McGraw-Hill, 1959), 6.*

12. *Milton Rokeach,* The Open and Closed Mind *(New York: Basic Books, 1960).*

13. *H. G. Gough,* Manual for the California Psychological Inventory *(Palo Alto, Calif.: Consulting Psychological Press, 1964).*

14. *For a more-detailed discussion of personality scale development, see Jum C. Nunnally, Jr.,* Tests and Measurements: Assessment and Prediction *(New York: McGraw-Hill, 1959).*

15. *Harold H. Kassarjian, "Personality and Consumer Behavior: A Review,"* Journal of Marketing Research, *8 (November 1971), 409–18.*

16. *Franklin B. Evans, "Psychological and Objective Factors in the Prediction of Brand Choice: Ford versus Chevrolet,"* Journal of Business, *32 (October 1959), 340–69.*

17. *Ibid.*

18. *Jacob Jacoby, "Personality and Consumer Behavior: How Not to Find Relationships" (Purdue Papers in Consumer Psychology, Paper No. 102, 1969).*

19. *Ralph Westfall, "Psychological Factors in Predicting Product Choice,"* Journal of Marketing, *26 (April 1962), 34–40; Ronald E. Frank, "Market Segmentation Research: Findings and Implications," in F. M. Bass, C. W. King, and Edgar A. Pessemier, eds.,* Applications of the Sciences in Marketing Management *(New York: John Wiley, 1968), 49–61; John G. Myers, "Determination of Private Brand Attitudes,"* Journal of Marketing Research, *4 (February 1967), 73–81; and Henry J. Claycamp, "Characteristics of Owners of Thrift Deposits in Commercial Banks and Savings and Loan Associations,"* Journal of Marketing Research, *2 (May 1965), 163–70.*

20. *For a detailed review, see Wells and Beard, "Personality and Consumer Behavior," 178–90.*

21. *For example, see Robert P. Brody and Scott M. Cunningham, "Personality Variables and the Consumer Decision Process,"* Journal of Marketing Research,

5 (February 1968), 50–57; Joseph N. Fry, "Personality Variables and Cigarette Brand Choice," Journal of Marketing Research, *8 (August 1971), 298–304; and Robert A. Peterson, "Moderating the Personality—Product Usage Relationships," in Ronald C. Curhan, ed.,* 1974 Combined Proceedings *(Chicago: American Marketing Association, 1975), 109–12.*

22. *George Brooker, "An Instrument to Measure Consumer Self-Actualization," in Mary Jane Schlinger, ed.,* Advances in Consumer Research, *2 (Association for Consumer Research, 1975), 563–75; and Clark Leavitt and John Walton, "Development of a Scale for Innovativeness," in Schlinger, ed.,* Advances in Consumer Research, *2 (Association for Consumer Research, 1975), 545–54.*

23. *For example, see Shirley Young, "The Dynamics of Measuring Unchange," in Russell I. Haley, ed.,* Attitude Research in Transition *(Chicago: American Marketing Association, 1972), 61–82.*

24. *Ibid., 63.*

25. *Ibid., 62–63.*

26. *Russell L. Ackoff and James Emshoff, "Advertising Research at Anheuser-Busch, Inc. (1968–74),"* Sloan Management Review, *16 (Spring 1975), 1–15.*

27. *Rokeach,* Open and Closed Mind.

28. *Jacob Jacoby, "Personality and Innovation Proneness,"* Journal of Marketing Research, *8 (May 1971), 244–47; and Kenneth A. Coney, "Dogmatism and Innovation: A Replication,"* Journal of Marketing Research, *9 (November 1972), 453–55.*

29. *J. M. McClurg and I. R. Andrews, "A Consumer Profile Analysis of the Self-Service Gasoline Customer,"* Journal of Applied Psychology, *59 (February 1974), 119–21.*

30. *Brian Blake, Robert Perloff, and Richard Heslin, "Dogmatism and Acceptance of New Products,"* Journal of Marketing Research, *7 (November 1970), 483–86; and Michael B. Mazis and Timothy W. Sweeney, "Novelty and Personality with Risk as a Moderating Variable," in Boris W. Becker and Helmut Becker, eds.,* 1972 Combined Proceedings *(Chicago: American Marketing Association, 1973), 406–11.*

31. *Jacoby, "Personality and Innovation Proneness," 246.*

32. *David Riesman, Nathan Glazer, and Reuel Denny,* The Lonely Crowd *(New Haven, Conn.: Yale University Press, 1950).*

33. *James H. Donnelly, Jr., "Social Character and Acceptance of New Products,"* Journal of Marketing Research, *7 (February 1970), 111–13; James H. Donnelly, Jr., and John M. Ivancevich, "A Methodology for Identifying Innovator Characteristics of New Brand Purchasers,"* Journal of Marketing Research, *11 (August 1974), 331–34; and John Jay Painter and Max L. Pinegar, "Post-High Teens and Fashion Innovation,"* Journal of Marketing Research, *8 (August 1971), 368–69.*

34. *Donnelly, "Social Character," 112.*

35. *Donnelly and Ivancevich, "Methodology for Identifying Innovator Characteristics."*

36. *Harold H. Kassarjian, "Social Character and Differential Preference for Mass Communication,"* Journal of Marketing Research, *11 (May 1965), 146–53; and Robert B. Settle and Richard Mizerski, "Differential Response to Objecttive and Social Information in Advertisements," in Thomas V. Greer, ed.,* 1973 Combined Proceedings *(Chicago: American Marketing Association, 1974), 250–55.*

37. *Thomas F. Pettigrew, "The Measurement and Correlates of Category Width as a Cognitive Variable,"* Journal of Personality, *26 (December 1956), 532–44.*

38. *Ibid.,* 532.

39. *Donald T. Popielarz, "An Exploration of Perceived Risk and Willingness to Try New Products,"* Journal of Marketing Research, 4 (November 1967), 368–72.

40. *James H. Donnelly, Jr., Michael J. Etzel, and Scott Roeth, "The Relationship between Consumers' Category Width and Trial of New Products,"* Journal of Applied Psychology, 57 (May 1973), 335–38; James H. Donnelly, Jr., and Michael J. Etzel, "Degree of Product Newness and Early Trial," Journal of Marketing Research, 10 (August 1973), 295–300; and Leon G. Schiffman, "Perceived Risk in New Product Trial by Elderly Consumers," Journal of Marketing Research, 9 (February 1972), 106–8.

41. *Donnelly and Etzel, "Degree of Product Newness,"* 299.

42. *William H. Cunningham and J. E. Crissy, "Market Segmentation by Motivation and Attitude,"* Journal of Marketing Research, 9 (February 1972), 100–102.

43. *Richard C. Tongberg, "An Empirical Study of the Relationship between Dogmatism and Attitudes toward Foreign Products,"* in Thomas V. Greer, ed., 1973 Combined Proceedings (Chicago: American Marketing Association, 1974), 87–91.

44. *H. Lawrence Issacson, "Store Choice"* (Doctoral dissertation, Graduate School of Business Administration, Harvard University, 1964), 85–89.

45. *Joseph F. Dash, Leon G. Schiffman, and Conrad Berenson, "Risk' and Personality-Related Dimensions of Store Choice,"* Journal of Marketing, 40 (January 1976), 36.

46. *James E. Stafford and Thomas V. Greer, "Consumer Preference for Types of Salesmen: A Study of Independence-Dependence Characteristics,"* Journal of Retailing, 41 (Summer 1965), 27–33.

47. *W. Thomas Anderson, Jr., and William H. Cunningham, "The Socially Conscious Consumer,"* Journal of Marketing, 36 (July 1972), 23–31; and W. Thomas Anderson, Jr., Karl E. Henion, and Eli P. Cox III, "Socially vs. Ecologically Responsible Consumers," in Ronald C. Curhan, ed., 1974 Combined Proceedings (Chicago: American Marketing Association, 1975), 304–10.

48. *Thomas C. Kinnear, James R. Taylor, and Sadrundin A. Ahmed, "Ecologically Concerned Consumers: Who Are They?"* Journal of Marketing, 38 (April 1974), 20–24; Frederick E. Webster, Jr., "Determining the Characteristics of the Socially Conscious Consumer," Journal of Consumer Research, 2 (December 1975), 188–96; and George Brooker, "The Self-Actualizing Socially Conscious Consumer," Journal of Consumer Research, 3 (September 1976), 107–12.

49. *Anderson, Henion, and Cox, "Socially vs. Ecologically,"* 308.

50. *Webster, "Determining the Characteristics."*

51. *Anderson, Henion, and Cox, "Socially vs. Ecologically,"* 310.

52. *Brooker, "The Self-Actualizing,"* 109.

53. *William D. Wells and Douglas J. Tigert, "Activities, Interests and Opinions,"* Journal of Advertising Research, 11 (August 1971), 27–35; and Joseph T. Plummer, "The Concept of Life Style Segmentation," Journal of Marketing, 38 (January 1974), 33–37.

54. *Glen Homan, Robert Cecil, and William Wells, "An Analysis of Moviegoers by Life Style Segments,"* in Mary Jane Schlinger, ed., Advances in Consumer Research, 2 (Association for Consumer Research, 1975), 219.

55. *Joseph T. Plummer, "Life Style and Advertising: Case Studies,"* in Fred C. Allvine, ed., 1971 Combined Proceedings (Chicago: American Marketing Association, 1972), 294–95.

56. *Ibid.*

Discussion questions

1. Contrast the major distinctive characteristics of the following personality theories:
a. Freudian theory
b. Neo-Freudian theory
c. Trait theory

2. How would you explain the fact that no two individuals have identical personalities, yet personality is used in consumer research to identify distinct market segments – each consisting of many consumers?

3. Horney classified individuals into three personality groups: compliant individuals, aggressive individuals, and detached individuals. Choose a separate magazine advertisement that seems to be directed to each of the personality types. For each advertisement indicate why you feel it will appeal to the specific personality type.

4. In terms of the study of consumer behavior, describe several advantages that trait-theory personality tests have over the Freudian personality measurement approach employed by motivational researchers?

5. Find a print advertisement for one of Anheuser-Busch's beers (Budweiser, Busch, or Michelob). Compare the contents of the ad to the drinker and personality profile described in Table 5–4. Which drinker-personality type(s) does the ad appeal to and why?

6. Describe the type of advertising message that would seem most suitable for individuals with the following personality characteristics:
a. low dogmatic consumers
b. high dogmatic consumers
c. inner-directed consumers
d. other-directed consumers

7. A media buyer for a local beverage distributor has relied entirely on demographic profiles to identify magazines and TV shows in which to place her company's advertising. Describe several benefits that her company might receive by using psychographic profiles to identify target audiences.

8. The president of a fast-food chain has asked you to prepare a psychographic profile of families living in a number of communities surrounding a new location he is considering. Construct a 10-question psychographic questionnaire that would seem appropriate for segmenting families in terms of their dining-out preferences.

6

attitudes in consumer behavior*

Introduction

Attitudes and attitude measurement play a major role in both consumer research and marketing attempts to affect consumer behavior. Through studying attitudes, it is easier to understand the character of thoughts and feelings that precede purchase. And if these thoughts and feelings can be understood, then presumably they can be changed in order to change behavior.

The concept of attitude combines many of the ideas from the preceding chapters. Attitudes are affected by *motivations* (Chapter 2). Attitudes affect and are affected by our *perception* of the world (Chapter 3). Attitudes are *learned* (Chapter 4). And it is on the basis of certain combinations of attitudes that we can differentiate between individuals within an entire marketing segment.

These individual aspects of attitude are now brought together for a more comprehensive understanding of how they affect consumer behavior. This chapter (1) defines *attitude* and compares it with other similar concepts in consumer behavior, (2) outlines the methods of attitude measurement, (3) explains the processes of attitude development and change, and (4) discusses various applications of consumer attitude research to marketing strategy.

In your heart
You know he's
right
POLITICAL
BOARD, *(1964)*

*Written by Michael L. Ray, Stanford University.

148

WHAT IS
AN ATTITUDE?

Although attitudes are actually a way of thinking, we know that a person has an attitude only by what he or she says or does. When someone buys a brand consistently and recommends it to friends, we infer that he has a positive attitude toward that brand. If he were to rank the brand among all other brands of the product, he would probably rank it first. And if a market research interviewer asked about this consumer's beliefs, opinions, and intentions, it is likely he would find them to be favorable also.

Evidently, a whole universe of activities—consistent purchasing, recommendations, top rankings, beliefs, opinions, and intentions—are related to attitude. What, then, are attitudes? Attitudes are *learned tendencies to perceive and act in some consistently favorable or unfavorable manner with regard to a given object or idea, such as a product, service, brand, company, store, or spokesperson.*[1] Each part of this definition is critical for understanding the relationship between attitudes, consumer behavior, and marketing.

Attitudes, as noted in Chapter 4, are learned. This means that we are not born with the attitudes relevant for our purchasing behavior. Attitudes are derived from past experience (learned) and they direct future behavior (tendencies). It is important to remember, however, that they are just *tendencies* to behave, and can be affected by the situation. A purchasing agent, for instance, may have an extremely favorable attitude toward Supplier A but may feel compelled to buy from Supplier B because Supplier B's price is markedly lower. In general, the more favorable the attitude a market segment has toward a brand, the more likely the consumers are to buy it. But because attitudes are only tendencies to behave, all aspects of the situation, including attitudes, must be taken into consideration in order to make predictions.

The importance of attitudes in the study of marketing and consumer behavior is due largely to the fact that they are learned tendencies to both perceive *and* act—a linkage of perceptions (beliefs, opinions, images, etc.) and actual consumer behavior. Because perceptions can be measured relatively easily, they are a key to understanding why people behave the way they do.

One study of dog-food buyers found, for instance, that the two most important perceptions related to actual purchase behavior were nutritional value and the speed at which the dog ate.[2] By knowing this attitude linkage and knowing that the food's moisture content was negatively related to purchase, marketers could better plan product development and promotion.

Because attitude research offers rich insights into both perceptions and actions, it is invaluable in the development of marketing strategy.

Consistency is another major reason for the value of attitudes in the study of consumer behavior. If attitudes are consistent, then a measure of a consumer's attitude should relate to the way the consumer can be expected to behave in the future.

It is the consistency of attitude-directed perceptions and acts that distinguishes them from random responses. We can assume that there is some underlying logic to the variety of perceptions and acts related to attitude toward a brand. It is logical, for instance, that a person would *perceive* a brand as having all important attributes, *rate* it as the best brand, and *buy* it whenever it is available (even when it takes a little trouble to find a store that carries it). If the brand should become unavailable, however, the consumer's failure to purchase it does not necessarily indicate inconsistency in his attitudes and behavior.

Attitudes are evaluations. They reflect our *favorable* or *unfavorable* feelings toward something. In consumer behavior, we make choices that are presumably related to an evaluation of alternative choices. If we can understand the evaluation (the attitude) that is related to the choice, then we can better understand consumer behavior and plan strategy more effectively.

Attitude structure and measurement

THE TRI-COMPONENT MODEL

Now that you know what attitudes are, it is important to understand their structure and measurement in order to be able to use attitudes in consumer analysis. Since favorable or unfavorable attitudes (that is, evaluations or feelings) affect action tendencies, it follows that attitudes are made up of three components: perceptions, evaluations, and action tendencies.[3] Attitude measurement, therefore, consists of determining the extent and nature of consumers' relevant perceptions and related evaluations and their action tendencies toward a product, a brand, a store, or whatever the object under study.

The relationship between relevant perceptions, evaluations, and action components can determine the nature of consumer behavior in any given situation. It follows, therefore, that marketers can affect consumer behavior by affecting one or more of the three components, thereby altering the overall attitude.

the perceptual component

The perception of a brand, product, or service can be a part of attitude and can lead to evaluations. If we *perceive* that cigarette smoking poses a danger to our health, we may *dislike* cigarettes. Conversely, evaluations can affect perceptions. If we *like* Honda automobiles, we are likely to *perceive* them as being roomier than they actually are.

The perceptual component is basically a cognitive, or informational, one. To measure the perceptual component, consumers are asked whether they think that certain brands have certain characteristics. The consumer's evaluations of each brand are influenced by his belief of each characteristic's importance.[4] If, for instance, he *believes* that clarity is an important characteristic in a CB radio, and he *perceives* that the General Electric CB has outstanding clarity features, he is likely to give the GE CB radio a high rating and is likely to purchase that brand if he buys a CB radio at all. If he does *not* believe sound quality is important, however, his perception of a given brand's sound quality is not likely to affect his evaluations and his action tendencies toward that brand.

The perceptual-cognitive component of attitude is almost always basic to the other parts of attitude and to purchasing behavior itself. However minimal, there must always be *some* cognitive or informational basis to attitudes. Strong brand awareness alone can be enough, especially where product characteristic differences are slight. For some products, consumers may believe that a host of characteristics are important, and they may perceive differences between brands based on these characteristics. The cognitive component of an attitude is more important for such major purchases as a house, an automobile, or a piece of home entertainment equipment than for small or minor purchases.[5]

Perception-cognition is probably the most important attitude component in the development of marketing strategy. If marketers can change consumers' beliefs about products and their perception of brand characteristics, they have a chance to change evaluations, action tendencies, and subsequent purchasing behavior. In order to effect changes in perceptions, however, marketers must be careful to consider competitive brand characteristics. Promotional efforts should emphasize only important characteristics in which the brand has a competitive advantage. In the example given above, GE should emphasize clarity only if it is an important characteristic or one in which their brand has a competitive advantage.

PERCEPTUAL MAPPING. One particularly effective tool for competitive perceptual (cognitive) measurement is *perceptual mapping*, which was discussed in Chapter 3. With this approach, we can determine how people perceive one brand in comparison to another on important characteristics. In the toothpaste category, it might be found that two attributes perceived to be important are decay prevention and flavor. Crest toothpaste might be perceived as superior on decay prevention but not on taste. This could call for product improvement and interim advertising copy which emphasizes the advantageous attribute (decay prevention) and deemphasizes the less advantageous characteristic (taste).

the evaluation component

The nucleus of attitudes is *evaluation*. Sometimes it is the only component measured. Studies in psycholinguistics indicate that our reactions to words or concepts are primarily in terms of how "good" or "bad" we feel they are.[6] In consumer behavior, the evaluation component is measured by asking consumers how well they feel the product will (or does) perform, especially in comparison with other brands. Consumers are given the task of rating brands on scales such as those shown in Figure 6–1.

In the early stages of product development, *projective techniques,* such as word association, thematic apperception techniques, and sentence completion tests (see Chapter 2), are sometimes used to obtain general evaluations. Projective techniques can provide rich qualitative information but typically cannot be used to indicate the frequency of various attitudes within the population. Ratings, however, can.

Brand ratings provide one of the best indications of how well or how poorly a brand is perceived. They have been used, with great success, to monitor consumer attitudes about established grocery, drug, and toiletry products.[7] Consumers who buy such products repetitively generally have favorable attitudes toward them, and it is not too surprising that brand rating scales can accurately and consistently indicate these attitudes.

The brand manager for a dog-food brand whose rating has gone down may find it advisable to examine the perceptual-cognitive component of consumers' attitudes in his effort to identify the root of the problem. Perhaps potential buyers perceive the product as low in nutrition or as unappealing to their pets.[8] Product reformulation with greater meat content might help. An assurance that dogs will love the product may invoke trial purchases. With this revised strategy, hopefully brand ratings (and sales), will go up.

FIGURE 6–1

Examples of Evaluative Rating Scales.

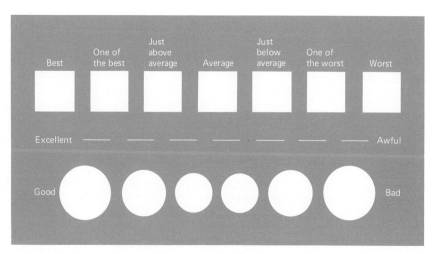

the action-tendency component

The transition from attitudes to actual buying is usually made through the action-tendency component, which can be measured by questions regarding buying intentions or preferences. The typical buying intention question asks consumers to rank brands in terms of likelihood of purchase. Sometimes consumers are asked to indicate the relative probability of their making a certain purchase. For instance, in one study, consumers were asked the probability that they, or a member of their family, would buy a car that year, either new or used.[9] The results revealed a strong direct association between what the respondents said their buying intention was and what their actual automobile purchasing during the year really was. The general finding of buying-intention questionnaires is that the more specific the buying intention question is, the more likely it is to accurately predict subsequent action.[10] For instance, questions such as "Which brand are you most likely to buy the next time you shop for canned peas?" will probably not predict as accurately as the "percent likely" type of question mentioned above. An even better question would pinpoint the conditions of possible purchase. Action-tendency, buying intention, and product preference questions are relatively easy to administer and to use in planning marketing strategy.

summary of the tri-component model

The tri-component attitude model and its relation to buying behavior is depicted in Figure 6-2. Several points should be noted. First, the

FIGURE 6-2

The Tri-Component Attitude Model and Its Relation to Buying Behavior

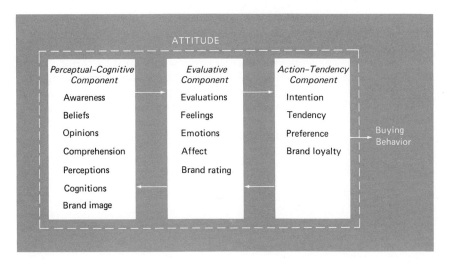

three components build upon each other. Variations in the way people perceive the world affect their evaluations, which in turn, affect their action tendencies.

Second, evaluations (that is, favorable or unfavorable feelings) are the key aspect of attitude. Notice the arrows going in both directions from and to this component. They indicate that while perceptions can lead to evaluations, evaluations can also affect perceptions. Similarly, though evaluations usually lead to action tendencies, the tendencies, as well as the action itself, can also affect evaluations.

Third, attitudes relate in only general ways to buying behavior. The correspondence between attitudes and actual purchasing behavior is closest when the action prediction is made from buying intentions. The more specific the buying intention, the closer the correspondence will be between the prediction and the purchase behavior.

Attitude development and maintenance

Where do attitudes come from? Why do some attitudes remain for long periods of time and others fit just one situation? The answers to such questions are extremely important. We have already discussed what attitudes are, how they might affect consumer behavior, and how they can be measured. But unless we know how they are developed and maintained, we will not be able to use them to either understand or to affect consumer behavior.

The processes of attitude development and maintenance are intimately linked to the methods of attitude change. The more strongly an attitude is developed and maintained, the less easily it can be changed. An adult who has never eaten meat, who has been taught from childhood that it is sinful to eat meat, and who has had this anti-meat attitude reinforced repeatedly, to the point where he finds the very thought of meat sickening, is not a good prospect for an attitude-change campaign to increase the consumption of meat.[11]

Moreover, the general processes that contribute to the development and maintenance of attitudes are the same ones that can be used to change attitudes. This section discusses four general processes involved in the development and maintenance of attitudes: learning, interpersonal influences, personality effects, and consistency. These same four processes are discussed in the following section on attitude change.

LEARNING OF ATTITUDES

Our basic definition of attitudes indicates that they are learned. Chapter 4 described six ways in which this learning can take place. This section discusses how these learning processes apply to the development of attitudes.

exposure and repetition.

Familiarity strengthens attitudes. Some consumer behavior researchers believe that attitudes or tastes can be developed by exposure or repetition alone. For example, when classical music lovers were repeatedly exposed to pop music, they eventually increased their positive evaluations of such music.[12] In another study, people who were repeatedly exposed to unfamiliar Turkish symbols were more likely to choose the most frequently repeated symbols as representing positive things.[13] In such studies, the objects presented were not given any extra value; they were simply repeated. So it seems clear that part of the development of attitudes can be related to repetition or familiarity.

We find comfort in familiar things. That is why a consistent experience leads us to evaluate more highly those things to which we are exposed more frequently, whether or not the exposures are rewarding. This is the assumption of some advertising strategists who emphasize use of high-frequency campaigns. Usually, the only component of attitude that is affected by repetition alone is perception, through an increase in awareness.

early basic learning effects

Not all attitude learning is due to mere exposure or repetition. The timing of initial exposures is extremely important in forming long-term attitudes. Our earliest experiences as children can develop very basic attitudes and values that carry into adulthood.[14] A child who consistently consumes large amounts of sugar in his daily diet will probably, as an adult, retain a taste for (or positive attitude toward) sweet foods.

cognitive learning contributions

Cognitive learning is also basic to the development and change of attitudes and tastes. As we have seen in this chapter, beliefs and knowledge are the building blocks of many types of attitudes. If we have learned to believe that fiber content and low sugar content are essential components of a good bread, and we believe that a certain brand has both high fiber content and low sugar content, these two learned beliefs should lead to a positive attitude toward that brand of bread. The more information an individual has about a product or service, the more likely he or she is to have an attitude toward it—either positive or negative.

classical conditioning

An originally neutral item, such as a brand name, can produce a favorable or unfavorable attitude if it is repeatedly followed by or associated with a reward or punishment. The idea of family branding is based on this form of attitude learning; by giving a new brand the same name as an old one, the marketer is counting on having the favorable attitude already associated with the brand name extend to the new product.

association

Closely tied to the cognitive learning and classical conditioning forms of attitude development is the approach taken by many marketers who associate positively evaluated product attributes or celebrities with their specific brands. This sort of association occurs when we positively evaluate a new product because of its similarity to a good existing product.

instrumental conditioning

A consumer can display behavior toward a product even without having an attitude toward it. She may buy a brand, for instance, because it is the only one available. If she finds satisfaction in the product, she may eventually develop favorable evaluations – attitudes – toward the brand.

INTERPERSONAL INFLUENCES

A person's attitudes are likely to be more similar to those of groups he or she is associated with than to those of other groups. The family, peers, social groups, and work groups can promote all the types of attitude learning and development mentioned above. For instance, the family is an important source of *early learning,* an individual is often *repetitively exposed* to certain types of products within a group, and the group can provide the rewards of *classical* and *instrumental conditioning* and the information necessary for *cognitive* attitude learning. Most important, perhaps, is the *associational* learning that occurs as a result of identification with the group. This becomes an important source of attitude change when group associations are made prominent to the consumer. (See the discussion of source credibility in Chapter 7.)

PERSONALITY EFFECTS

In the section on attitude learning, the words *rewards* and *rewarding* were used often. What any one particular consumer finds rewarding depends to some extent on his personality. The attitude a person has toward any given product, brand, or service is likely to be affected by his overall personality. Introverted individuals, for instance, are likely to express their introversion with negative attitudes toward flashy cars, dancing classes, group tours, and public activities. Similarly, attitudes of people with other personality and motivational configurations can also be predicted. Many attitudes toward new products and new consumption situations are formed and maintained on the basis of personality.

CONSISTENCY

One human need is so common that some theorists believe we are born with it. It is our need for consistency, or balance. We have a tendency to form new attitudes that are consistent with our old attitudes, values, and personality. And our need for consistency helps us maintain attitudes once they are formed. For instance, there is some evidence that the person who has just purchased a particular automobile is more likely to read and perceive ads for that automobile than ads for other cars.[15] Ads for the purchased car reinforce and develop the consumer's positive attitude. Because they serve to substantiate the appropriateness of his buying decision, those ads that support his purchase are read. But ads for other cars produce inconsistency and are somewhat threatening because they make the consumer question the wisdom of his choice. So there is a tendency to avoid those ads — thus maintaining the positive attitude toward the purchased car.

cognitive dissonance

When an individual receives new information concerning a fact, a belief or an attitude which does not agree with his original belief or attitude, he experiences a feeling of dissonance or inconsistency due to the two competing pieces of information.[16] This is called cognitive dissonance. In many cases, when a consumer buys a product, expecially an expensive one, such as a car, the alternative products or brands remind him that he may have made the wrong choice. This, too, creates dissonance. The feeling of cognitive dissonance which occurs *after* a purchase is made is very common, and is called *postpurchase dissonance*. In order to eliminate this dissonance and maintain his early favorable attitude toward his product choice, he avoids ads for other brands but pays attention to any information that supports his choice.

The tendency toward consistency can be used to change attitudes as well as to maintain them. For instance, if a consumer sees one of his favorite stars (positive attitude) promoting one of his least favorite brands (negative attitude), he experiences cognitive dissonance as a result of the inconsistency which he may resolve by changing his attitude toward the brand to a more favorable one or changing his attitude toward the star to an unfavorable one. In fact, the same processes that lead to development and maintenance of attitudes – learning, group influence, personality, and consistency – can lead to attitude change.

How to change attitudes

This chapter has already provided the basic tools for understanding attitude change:

1. We know that attitudes come from experience; therefore, experiences must be a means of implementing attitude change.

2. Attitude structure consists of perception, feeling, and intention components that are linked together in specific ways indicated by the tri-component model. If we can change one or more of these components, we should be able to change attitudes.

3. Attitudes are developed and maintained by learning, interpersonal and personality influences, and the need for consistency. If we can affect one of these influences, we can change attitudes in the same way that they are developed.

In fact, the five major methods of changing attitudes are based on the implications of what we have already learned about attitudes. They involve:

1. changing the importance of certain basic motivations,
2. associating the product with a specific group or event,
3. changing consumers' beliefs,
4. relating to conflicting attitudes, and
5. altering consumers' behavior patterns.

CHANGING THE BASIC MOTIVATION

We have seen that attitudes are a manifestation of general motivation. We have certain needs that make certain attitudes relevant. For instance, people buy cars and have attitudes toward those cars for a variety of motives, including status, security, utility, and pleasure. Some highly economical small cars are sold on the basis of utility alone, while others—with less impressive statistics in terms of mileage and costs—are sold primarily on the basis of status.

One way of changing attitudes toward brands is to make new needs prominent. One attitude-change theory that demonstrates how changing the basic motivation can change attitudes is known as the *functional approach*.[17] With this approach, we can classify attitudes in terms of four functions: the instrumental function, the ego-defensive function, the value-expressive function and the knowledge function.

the instrumental function

We hold certain brand attitudes partly because of the brand's utility. If a product has helped us in the past, even in a small way, our attitude toward it tends to be favorable. One way of changing attitudes in favor of a product is by showing people that it can solve a utilitarian goal that they may not have considered.

the ego-defensive function

We want to protect our self-concept from inner feelings of doubt. Cosmetics and personal-hygiene products, by acknowledging this need, make themselves seem much more relevant and heighten the possibility of a favorable attitude toward these products that offer reassurance to the consumer's self-concept.

the value-expressive function

Attitudes are one expression of our more general values. If there is a generally high evaluation of the leisure life, and a power boat is treated as a symbol of that life-style, attitudes toward the power boat will reflect the positive attitudes toward the values it represents. If a consumer segment holds a low valuation of the leisure life, however, the power boat will take on the negative attitudes which that segment bears toward the life-style the boat symbolizes.

the knowledge function

We need to know and understand an increasingly complex world. Most brand and product "positionings" are attempts to satisfy this need and increase attitudes toward the brand by clarifying how one brand differs from another. For instance, the Federal Express Airfreight Company pointed out in much of its advertising that it was the only such company that had its own airplanes.[18] The copy line "this is all you need to know about airfreight" invokes the knowledge function and should increase favorable overall attitude toward the brand. Family branding (discussed in Chapter 4) is another marketing approach that supports the knowledge function of attitudes.

It is important to realize that by highlighting a particular need or function, we promote particular beliefs, attitudes, and behaviors associated with it.

ASSOCIATING THE PRODUCT WITH A GROUP OR EVENT

Attitudes are related, at least in part, to certain groups or social events. It is possible to change attitudes toward products, services, and brands by pointing out their relationships to certain social groups and events. Examples include the attempts by certain cigarette and small-cigar manufacturers to relate their products to the women's movement. Other examples include serving butter instead of margarine to guests and serving wine at family meals to make a special event of a commonplace occasion.

Groups and events, like basic motive, evoke specific patterns of beliefs, attitudes, and behaviors and are fundamental to other attitude-influence approaches.

CHANGING RELEVANT BELIEFS

Two general types of beliefs or perceptions can affect attitudes: (1) beliefs about which product attributes are important, and (2) perceptions of the extent to which each brand has each attribute. Changing either category of these beliefs can change attitudes.

changing attribute importance beliefs

Among the "singles" segment in the early 1970s, Close-Up toothpaste probably had a higher brand rating than Crest, the overall market leader. This was primarily because the singles segment believed that cosmetic effectiveness (clean breath and whiter teeth) was much more important than decay prevention. There are two ways Crest marketing management could have dealt with this attribute-importance problem. One would have been to change the group association. For example, instead of highlighting interaction between members of opposite sexes, Crest advertising could have featured the dentist and the typical dental appointment.

The second counterattack that Crest advertising could have made would have been to try to directly change consumer' beliefs about the relative importance of decay prevention. Would Crest advertising's attempt to change these beliefs be successful?

There are two broad answers to this question.[19] One, which comes directly from a learning approach, says that the importance placed on a premise through advertising corresponds directly with the change in belief (and subsequent brand attitude) that will occur.[20] The other, which is called *assimilation-contrast* theory, warns that advertisers must be careful in trying to change attribute-importance beliefs. This theory suggests that a target segment will *assimilate* (or accept) only moderate changes. If the change suggested by the communication is too extreme, the *contrast* will result in the whole ad being rejected as too extreme. Assimilation-contrast theory suggests that Crest would not succeed in altering the relative importance of decay prevention and cosmetic effectiveness among the singles segment. The belief-changing message would be seen as too extreme (more so than it actually is); a contrast effect could be predicted.

The implication for changing attitudes by changing importance beliefs is that we should make the message position as extreme as possible without getting into the contrast area. Once the message is assimilated, subsequent campaigns could then effectively present somewhat more extreme positions.

If the importance-belief change strategy does not work, there are three other belief-related approaches that might: (1) adding an attribute, (2) changing brand perceptions, and (3) changing perceptions of the competing brand.

adding an attribute

A more difficult strategy to effect than changing importance beliefs is *adding* an attribute previously considered unimportant. The reason that this is so difficult is that the attributes considered for any product class have usually survived an extensive learning process, sometimes involving the equivalent of early basic learning (see Chapter 4). Most attributes have been considered by consumers at one time or another. If an attribute is not currently one of the relevant set, then it is likely that is has been carefully considered and eliminated in the past. To make it a part of the relevant set usually requires something more extreme than an advertising campaign. Typically, an actual product change or innovation is necessary.

Virtually all examples of adding attributes include either product change or severe environmental change. One example is the added attribute of an airfreight company owning its own planes, such as Federal Express, when it made that innovation.[21] Other examples are sportiness for small cars, introduced by the Mustang line; non-aerosols for spray toiletry products, introduced when environmental problems of aersols were discovered; and remote tuning, when this feature was made available for television sets.

In the toothpaste field, Crest was the beneficiary of an added attribute when it became the first toothpaste to receive the endorsement of the American Dental Association. It would have been difficult to add this attribute to those considered by the singles segment in 1971, however, because the endorsement was primarily an extension of the decay-prevention factor, which the singles segment had already taken into consideration and relegated to secondary importance.

changing brand perceptions

Another belief-oriented strategy for changing attitudes concentrates on changing beliefs or perceptions about the brand itself. This is by far the most common form of advertising appeal. Advertisers are constantly reminding us that their product has "more" or "better" of some important product attribute.

In the toothpaste example. Crest might improve its brand rating by changing beliefs on the extent to which the brand provides "taste fun" and "cosmetic effectiveness." If advertising could improve perceptions on these two attributes, young adult consumers might have a more favorable brand attitude toward Crest.

Several cautions are appropriate here. First, in the long run a brand attribute perception change will not work if the brand does not actually have the attribute in question. In Crest's case, the "taste-fun" appeal might work if Crest added an extra flavor. It would probably not work if Crest tried to use a "cosmetic effectiveness" appeal.

Second, the assimilation-contrast theory holds for attempts to change brand attribute beliefs, too. This means that only moderate changes in brand attribute beliefs should be attempted. Too extreme an advertising position would probably result in rejection of the whole message. Besides, there is some evidence that moderate appeals just at the border of rejection can create curiosity, which is often better than complete belief.[22] Curiosity can lead to trial after an initial reaction such as: "Can it be true? I'll have to try it and find out!"

The third caution about the brand perception change strategy is that by improving perceptions on one attribute, you may actually decrease positive perceptions on some other attribute. The classic example of this phenomenon is seen in price decreases or increases and their effects on brand quality perceptions. There is evidence that the greater the "low-price" attribute is, the lower the "high-quality" attribute tends to fall.[23] The creative challenge in advertising is to change beliefs on one attribute without adversely affecting the others.

changing perceptions of competitors

Still another belief-oriented strategy involves changing consumer perceptions toward the attributes of competitive brands. This became a more heavily utilized strategy in the mid-1970s with federal government encouragement of *comparative advertising,* in which the advertiser specifically mentions opposing brands. For instance, Total cereal mounted a campaign that showed the many bowls of natural cereals that had to be eaten to equal the vitamin content in one bowl of Total.

Once again, however, this approach must be used carefully. Some evidence suggests that this advertising approach can boomerang by giving support to competitive brands and claims.[24] Further evidence indicates that unless the audience is relatively sophisticated and highly involved with the product, it is unlikely to comprehend two-sided messages fully.[25] And if the audience is sophisticated and involved, its attitudes may be quite difficult to change with any kind of message. (Chapter 7 discusses comparative advertising and one-sided versus two-sided messages in more depth.)

RELATING TO CONFLICTING ATTITUDES

Thus far we have examined the following methods for changing attitudes: attempts to change basic motivations, to associate the attitude with particular groups and events, and to change the underlying beliefs. We will now consider an approach that relates directly to the attitudes themselves. Specifically, if the consumer can be made to see that his brand attitude is in conflict with some other more basic attitude, he might be "forced" to change his evaluation of the brand.

Two simple theoretical notions—*balance theory* and the *congruity principle*—show how this attitude change approach works.[26] These are *consistency* theories. As was mentioned earlier, they are based on the fact that individuals avoid inconsistency and seek consistency, balance, or congruity. Consistency theories make the assumption that we will take whatever is the easiest action (i.e., attitude change) in order to remain consistent.

These two approaches are valuable in understanding consumer attitude change because they consider the relationships between an individual and two of his attitudes that conflict.

Returning to the toothpaste example, the key relationships are between (1) the consumer and Crest, (2) the consumer and some other person, and (3) the other person and Crest. Assuming that the typical consumer in the singles segment does not like Crest, let us look at the four possible *balance* or *congruity* relationships that may exist:

1. *Admired friends dislike Crest.* If the consumer's friends dislike Crest, this kind of relationship would maintain his own negative feelings toward the brand. Since the friends are admired, their attitudes are likely to reinforce the consumer's.

2. *Disliked dentists like Crest.* If the consumer believes that dentists are overly concerned with the decay-prevention aspects of toothpaste, their endorsement of Crest may actually serve to maintain the consumer's negative feelings toward the brand.

3. *Disliked TV endorser rejects Crest.* Some commercials show a rather bumbling individual foolishly avoiding the advertised brand. If this depiction is accepted by the viewers, they may change their attitude in favor of the product in order to avoid identifying with the endorser. Unfortunately, however, this individual might merely be rejected as unrealistic, and no change would occur.

4. *Admired personality recommends Crest.* This situation probably presents the strongest one for change. If the consumer (in this case, the single person) is exposed to a strong endorsement by an idol who points out that the decay-prevention superiority of Crest is the best assurance of clean breath and white teeth, a negative attitude toward Crest is likely to be reevaluated and possibly changed.

The key to attitude change by relation to other attitudes is to choose other attitudes that are very strong and clearly conflicting with the one the marketer wishes to change. The approach with the bumbling TV character would probably not be effective because, although it produces conflict, the attitude toward the TV character is the least reliable. On the other hand, if the endorsement of an admired person is both strong and conflicting, it is likely to effect change.

It is not necessary that the conflicting attitude concern a person. In persuading consumers to change their negative attitudes about using automobile seat belts, for instance, it might be sufficient to point out that they almost always leave their seat belts on when they are in a plane, even though the danger is less than when they are in a car. Other examples include reminders that the consumer uses one brand in a company's line and therefore would undoubtedly like another. Johnson and Johnson used this approach by pointing out that favorable attitudes toward products used for babies are inconsistent with possibly negative attitudes toward use of the same products by adults. This strategy of using one attitude to change another led to the company's baby shampoo, powder, and oil becoming leading sellers in their respective adult markets.

CHANGING CONSUMER BEHAVIOR PATTERNS

The basis of the *changing attitudes by changing behavior* strategy is that attitudes are learned from experience. The most important experience is actual behavior and receiving rewards and punishments for that behavior. Thus, if we can get people to behave – to have experiences with a product—then it is possible to change their attitudes toward that product.

We have seen that one process of attitude development begins with behavior. More specifically, after buying a product, consumers often experience what is known as *postpurchase dissonance*. Since the choice between, say, two makes of automobiles is not always a clear one, the existence of the rejected choice and its advertising can produce an unpleasant feeling of *dissonance*. This can lead to seeking out supportive information and, as a result, developing a stronger attitude toward the chosen car.

A similar process is used when behavior is changed in order to change attitudes. By behaving in a certain way, people actually make a commitment, which can lead to attitude change. One explanation of this type of attitude change is called *self-perception theory*.[27]

In consumer behavior, there are several behavior patterns of varying strengths that can effect attitude change. The key aspect of these behaviors, which lead to attitude change, is the amount of *commitment* they imply. Trying a sample of a product that is received free in the mail does not imply a great deal of commitment; buying the product with a price-off coupon shows somewhat greater commitment; buying the product once, with no incentive, indicates somewhat greater commitment; and buying it repeatedly is evidence of even greater commitment.

Self-perception theory predicts that a consumer's own behavior infers to himself an attitude and the strength of that attitude. A person who merely tried a sample would probably assume that he had very little positive attitude toward it. A person who bought a product with a coupon, tried it once more without further inducement, or bought the brand repeatedly, could infer an increasingly positive attitude toward it.

Research has shown that almost any degree of commitment, even without actual induced behavior, can affect attitudes. One marketing study used *labeling*, a technique often used by salesmen, in which the prospective consumer is verbally labeled as being a person who has behaved favorably toward the product.[28] In the study on labeling, consumers were just *told* that they were "charitable" or helpful people. This statement to one group resulted in greater inclination to volunteer for the Red Cross, and in more advertising response, than by those individuals who did not receive the "charitable" label.

Any behavior that can be induced by marketing effort can have the effect of commitment or self-perception on attitude. The greater the real personal commitment or effort on the part of the consumer, the greater the impact on his attitude. Thus, at a minimum, getting a consumer to view a television commercial is inducing a behavior. But it is behavior of so little commitment that its effect on attitude change is likely to be negligible—unless the commercial is persuasive enough to change beliefs. Getting the consumer to write a statement supporting the product for a contest *does* involve substantial commitment and effort and therefore has the potential of changing attitudes.

Certain marketing stimuli, such as outstanding products or low-pressure selling, allow the consumer to conclude that his behavior was not forced and must therefore be due to a positive attitude. This positive attitude, in turn, has the potential of reinforcing favorable behavior in the future.[29]

Marketing applications

It has been said that attitude research is the major topic of social psychology. Attitude studies have achieved almost the same prominence in consumer research and in the applied field of marketing. The American Marketing Association has held a series of international conferences on attitude research in marketing since 1966. Attitudes are part of nearly every major model of consumer behavior that has been proposed. This chapter has offered a number of examples of the marketing use of attitudes; several additional applications are reviewed below.

NEW-PRODUCT DEVELOPMENT

Knowledge of consumer attitudes is extremely valuable in the development of new products. Attitude measures can indicate how consumers perceive and like the products presently available. Once this is known, it is possible to design new products that can *better* satisfy the salient need. The technique that is most often used for this purpose is perceptual mapping (see Chapter 3). The same type of approach can be used to develop the pricing and distribution strategy of a new product.

SETTING COMMUNICATION GOALS

The tri-component attitude model, consisting of the (1) perceptual-cognitive, (2) evaluative, and (3) action tendency components, can be used as benchmarks to determine communications goals in various situations. Since no single component of marketing communications—such as advertising, selling, or promotion—can be expected to achieve a sales goal on its own, communications goals are typically stated in terms of attitudes.[30] Percentage shifts in attitudes for some particular market segment over some given period of time become the goals of the promotional campaign.

EVALUATING RESULTS

As has been mentioned, attitudes have been used successfully as pre and post measures for evaluating the effectiveness of marketing programs. The overall-attitude type of measure can be used to give early warning of developing problems. Other types of attitude measures provide directions toward the solutions.

DETERMINING ADVERTISING APPEALS

The methods of attitude change detailed in this chapter are actually alternative strategies that might be used for advertising or other types of communication. In one review of the topic, the following five points were suggested as "an attitudinal framework for advertising strategy:"[31]

1. Affect product class linkages to goals and events;
2. Add a salient characteristic;
3. Alter the perception of existing product characteristics;
4. Change perceptions of advertiser's brand; and
5. Change perceptions of competing brands.

The reader will note the similarity between strategies in this list and some of the strategies mentioned earlier.

Summary

Attitudes have been defined as *learned tendencies to perceive and act in some consistently favorable or unfavorable manner with regard to a given object or idea, such as a product, service, brand, company, store, or spokesperson.* Each part of this definition is critical for understanding how attitudes are relevant in consumer behavior and marketing.

The tri-component model of attitude consists of three parts: (1) the *perceptual-cognitive* component, corresponding to knowledge, information, beliefs, comprehension, opinions, perceptions, and brand image; (2) the *evaluative* component, including feelings, emotions, and brand ratings; and (3) the *action-tendency* component, including intentions, preferences, tendencies, and brand loyalty. Measurement of the cognitive component is typically done through open-ended questions; the evaluative component is usually measured with brand-rating scales; and the action-tendency component is typically measured by questions regarding buying intentions.

The development and maintenance of attitudes are accomplished through the following learning processes: (1) exposure and repetition, (2) early basic learning, (3) cognitive learning, (4) classical conditioning, (5) association, and (6) instrumental conditioning. In addition to the learning processes, there are three other major ways in which attitudes can be developed and maintained: through interpersonal influence, through personality effects, and through consistency processes. Cognitive dissonance, and particularly postpurchase dissonance, are important concepts in the study and understanding of consumer behavior.

The methods for changing attitudes are very similar to the processes that develop and maintain them. They include (1) heightening the importance of certain basic motivations, (2) associating the attitude with a specific group or event, (3) changing beliefs, (4) relating to conflicting attitudes, and (5) getting people to behave first. Each of these approaches has major implications for marketing strategy, especially in the communications area.

Attitude research has important applications to the development of marketing strategy, including: (1) new-product development, (2) setting communications goals, (3) determining advertising strategy, and (4) evaluating results.

Endnotes

1. *Martin Fishbein and Icek Ajzen,* Belief, Attitude, Intention and Behavior: An Introduction to Theory and Research *(Reading, Mass.: Addison-Wesley, 1975), p. 6.*

2. *Michael Perry, "Discriminant Analysis of Relations between Consumers' Attitudes, Behavior, and Intentions,"* Journal of Advertising Research, 9 *(June 1969), 34–39.*

3. *These three parts are known respectively as the* cognitive, affective, *and* conative *in the research literature. See, for example, Michael L. Ray, "Attitudes as Communication Response," in* Attitude Research at Bay, *ed. Deborah Johnson and William D. Wells (Chicago: American Marketing Association, 1976).*

4. *This relationship, with beliefs about attribute importance and comprehension of brands' attributes leading to evaluation, is a rough statement of the "Fishbein" model—used often in marketing. See, for example, Fishbein and Ajzen,* Belief, Attitude, Intention and Behavior; *Edgar A. Pessemier and William L. Wilkie, "Multi-Attribute Choice Theory—A Review and Analysis," in* Buyer/Consumer Information Processing, *eds. G. David Hughes and Michael L. Ray (Chapel Hill: University of North Carolina Press, 1974), pp. 288–330; and Peter Sampson and Paul Harris, "A User's Guide to Fishbein,"* Journal of the Market Research Society, 12 (July 1970), 145–65.*

5. *Ray, "Attitudes as Communication Response."*

6. *Charles E. Osgood, George J. Suci, and Percy H. Tannenbaum,* The Measurement of Meaning *(Urbana: University of Illinois Press, 1957).*

7. *John C. Maloney, "Attitude Measurement and Formation" (Paper presented at the AMA Test Marketing Workshop, Chicago, 1966); Henry Assael and George S. Day, "Attitudes and Awareness as Predictors of Market Share,"* Journal of Advertising Research, 8 (December 1968), 3–10; and Alvin A. Achenbaum, "Knowledge Is a Thing Called Measurement," in* Attitude Research at Sea, *ed. Lee Adler and Irving Crespi (Chicago: American Marketing Association, 1966), 111–26.*

8. *Perry, "Discriminant Analysis."*

9. *Jan Stapel, "Predictive Attitudes," in* Attitude Research on the Rocks, *ed. Lee Adler and Irving Crespi (Chicago: American Marketing Association, 1968), 96–115.*

10. *Ibid.; Martin Fishbein, "The Search for Attitudinal-Behavioral Consistency," in* Conceptual Foundations of Consumer Behavior, *ed. Joel B. Cohen (New York: Free Press, 1972), 245–52.*

11. *Stephen A. Greyser,* Cases in Advertising and Communications Management *(Englewood Cliffs, N.J.: Prentice-Hall, Inc., 1972), 1–14.*

12. *Herbert E. Krugman, "Affective Response to Music as a Function of Familiarity,"* Journal of Abnormal and Social Psychology, *3 (1943), 388–92.*

13. *Robert B. Zajonc, "Attitudinal Effects of Mere Exposure,"* Journal of Personality and Social Psychology, Monograph Supplement, Vol. 9 (1968).

14. *Scott Ward, "Consumer Socialization,"* Journal of Consumer Research, *1 (September 1974), 1–14.*

15. *Danuta Ehrlich, Israel Guttman, Paul Schonback, and Judson Mills, "Post-Decision Exposure to Relevant Information,"* Journal of Abnormal and Social Psychology, *54 (January 1957), 98–102; James F. Engel, "Are Automobile Purchasers Dissonant Consumers?"* Journal of Marketing, *27 (April 1963), 55–58; and James H. Donnell, Jr., and John M. Ivancevich, "Post-Purchase Reinforcement and Back-Out Behavior,"* Journal of Marketing Research, *7 (August 1970), 339–400.*

16. *Leon Festinger,* A Theory of Cognitive Dissonance *(New York: Harper & Row, 1957); and Elliot Aronson, "The Rationalizing Animal,"* Psychology Today, *8 (May 1973), 46–52.*

17. *Daniel Katz, "The Functional Approach to the Study of Attitudes,"* Public Opinion Quarterly, *24 (Summer 1960), 163–91.*

18. *Christopher H. Lovelock, "Federal Express Company,"* Case *(Boston: Intercollegiate Case Clearinghouse, 1976).*

19. *Paul E. J. Gerhold and William J. McGuire, "Basic Research and Advertising Practice: A Dialogue," in* Psychology in Media Strategy, *ed. Lee Bogart (Chicago: American Marketing Association, 1966), 66–88.*

20. *Norman H. Anderson, "Linear Models for Responses Measured on a Continuous Scale,"* Journal of Mathematical Psychology, *1 (1964), 121–42; and Norman H. Anderson, "Integration Theory and Attitude Change,"* Psychological Review, *78 (March 1971), 171–206.*

21. *Lovelock, "Federal Express Company."*

22. *John C. Maloney, "Is Advertising Believability Really Important?"* Journal of Marketing, *27 (October 1963), 1–8.*

23. *Benson Shapiro, "The Psychology of Pricing,"* Harvard Business Review, *41 (1968), 14–16ff.; and Kent B. Monroe, "The Influence of Price Differences and Brand Familiarity on Brand Preferences,"* Journal of Consumer Research, *3 (June 1976), 42–49.*

24. *Alan G. Sawyer, "The Effects of Repetition of Refutational and Supportive Advertising Appeals,"* Journal of Marketing Research, *10 (February 1973), 23–33; and William L. Wilkie and Paul Farris, "Comparison Advertising: Problems and Potential,"* Journal of Marketing, *39 (October 1975), 7–15.*

25. *Sawyer, "Effects of Repetition of Refutational and Supportive Advertising Appeals;" and Wilkie and Farris, "Comparison Advertising."*

26. *George S. Day, "Theories of Attitude Structure and Change," in* Consumer Behavior: Theoretical Sources, *ed. Scott Ward and Thomas Robertson (Englewood Cliffs, N. J.: Prentice-Hall, Inc., 1973), 303–53, especially 331–33; and Fishbein and Ajzen,* Belief, Attitude, Intention and Behavior, *especially Chapter 2.*

27. *Daryl Bem, "Self Perception Theory," in* Advances in Experimental Social Psychology, *ed. Leonard Berkowitz, 6 (New York: Academic Press, 1972), 2–62.*

28. *William R. Swinyard and Michael L. Ray, "Advertising-Selling Interactions,"* Journal of Marketing Research, Vol. 14 (in press, 1977).

29. *Bem, "Self Perception Theory."*

30. *Colley,* Defining Advertising Goals; *and Ray, "Attitudes as Communication Response."*

31. *Harper W. Boyd, Jr., Michael L. Ray and Edward C. Strong, "An Attitudinal Framework for Advertising Strategy,"* Journal of Marketing, *36 (April 1972), 27–33.*

Discussion questions

1. How do attitudes differ from perceptions, motives, personality, actions, and values?

2. Under what research conditions is brand awareness the only cognitive measure necessary, and when are more complex belief and comprehension measures needed?

3. Using the tri-component attitude model, in what three ways could you affect buying *intentions*?

4. Under what conditions have brand-rating measures alone been useful?

5. A corporate marketing planner from ITT hears that you have just studied attitude change and he believes that for this brief period of time you probably know more about the area than anyone else does. Although you may assume that ITT has sophisticated attitude-monitoring systems for its products and services (ranging from Wonder Bread to telephone systems to hotels to aerospace to other industrial products), and although ITT understands what attitudes are, the company has had terrible problems changing attitudes. Outline for the corporate planner the major ways of changing attitudes. Show how each of the major methods might apply to attitude change problems that ITT might have.

6. Since attitudes are tendencies to behave, why don't marketers and consumer researchers just measure purchasing behavior and forget attitudes?

7. Select one product, service, candidate, or idea you "love" (positive attitude) and one you "hate" (negative attitude). Describe as thoroughly as you can, using the terms in this chapter, how you believe you developed and maintain each of these attitudes.

8. How can the following attitude theory ideas help to change attitudes: (a) the functional approach (b) the assimilation-contrast theory (c) cognitive dissonance and (d) self-perception theory?

9. Have you ever experienced postpurchase dissonance? How did you get over it? In what other ways do people reduce it? How can marketers help?

10. Evaluate this statement made by John C. Maloney: "Sometimes attitudes come first, sometimes behavior is first. It's a chicken-egg problem. The only sure thing is that marketing is the chicken feed."

7

communication and consumer behavior

Introduction

The preceding chapters focused on the individual consumer: what motivates him, how he perceives and learns, how his personality and attitudes influence his buying choices, and how these attitudes can sometimes be modified by persuasive marketing information. This chapter, which concludes Part II, explores the ways in which the consumer receives and is influenced by such marketing information. It discusses the structure and process of communication, the effects of communication sources on the consumer, and the types of marketing messages that he tends to find most persuasive.

Part III discusses the consumer, not as an individual, but in the context of his social-cultural involvement with others: his family, his friends, and other groups to which he may belong or aspire to belong. Because communications with and from such outside influences tend to have a major impact on each individual's consumption behavior, it is important for us to understand how communication operates to influence and persuade consumers to make buying choices. In effect, communication is the bridge between the individual consumer and his social-cultural world.

WHAT IS COMMUNICATION?

Everyone "knows" what communication is, yet textbooks often vary in their definitions. At a basic level, most writers agree that com-

Good communication is stimulating as black coffee, and just as hard to sleep after.
ANNE MORROW LINDBERGH:
"Argonauta," Gift from the Sea
(1955)

FIGURE 7-1

Basic Communication Model

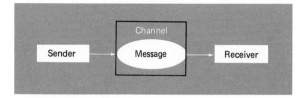

munication is *the transmission of a message from a sender to a receiver by means of a signal of some sort sent through a channel of some sort.* Figure 7-1 depicts this basic communication model.

However, the model leaves us with too many unknowns. What type of message does the sender wish to convey? Has he put it into a format that conveys his precise meaning? Through what medium (or what channel) is the message transmitted? Does his intended audience have access to this channel? Can the message surmount the psychological barriers that invariably surround all human receivers? Will the audience understand the message in the same way as the sender intended? And finally, how does the sender know if communication has taken place? Let us defer the answers to these questions till after we examine the structure and process of communication. In so doing, we will explore many of the questions posed above concerning the basic communication process.

The structure and process of communication

There are four basic components of all communication: a *source*, a *destination*, a *medium*, and a *message*. The source is the initiator of the message. She may wish to impart a feeling, an attitude, a belief, or a fact to another person or persons. To do so, she must first find some way to encode this message so that it will accurately convey her feelings to her intended destination. She may use words, or pictures, or a facial expression, or some other kind of signal or code, but she must use some means that is familiar to the receiver if she wishes him to understand her intended meaning.

The source must then find an appropriate channel through which to transmit her message. To facilitate its delivery, the channel must have direct access to the receiver and must be relatively free of distortion and static. The receiver must be willing and ready to accept the message. After receiving it, he decodes the message within the realm of his own experience. His acknowledgment of the message, in whatever form it may take, provides feedback to the sender that the message was received. In communications between two people, acknowledgment may

FIGURE 7-2

Communication Model

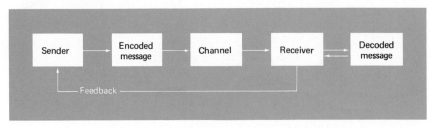

consist of a nod, a smile, a frown, or a signed contract. In an impersonal communication (e.g., an advertisement), acknowledgment may consist of a purchase, a vote, or a redeemed coupon. The basic communication model, then, should be somewhat modified, as depicted in Figure 7-2.

TYPES OF COMMUNICATION

There are basically two types of communication to which a consumer is exposed: *interpersonal communication* and *impersonal* (or *mass*) *communication*. Their impact and influence differ markedly.

interpersonal communication

Communication that occurs on a personal level between two or more people is called interpersonal communication. Such communication may take place between two people who meet on a face-to-face basis, who speak with each other on the telephone, or who correspond by mail. Interpersonal communication may be either formal or informal.

Informal communication concerning products or services is frequently called word-of-mouth communication. It differs from formal communication in that the sender does not speak in the capacity of a professional or commercial communicator (e.g., a sales representative). For example, two friends who discuss the merits of a specific product are engaging in informal communication. Alternately, each person may serve as the sender or the receiver of product information. *Formal interpersonal communication* is the kind of communication that takes place between a salesman and a prospect, in which the salesman serves as the sender and the prospect the receiver of product information.

Interpersonal communication tends to be effective because it enables the sender to detect almost at once the reaction of the receiver to his message. This is particularly true of face-to-face communication, and to a lesser extent it is true of telephone communication. Mail correspondence permits feedback also, but it is obviously slower. It depends on the willingness and ability of the receiver to answer, and the time required for mail transmission and delivery.

Face-to-face communication may be both *verbal* and *nonverbal*. A mother may express displeasure with her child through a frown; a customer may express her indifference to a sales pitch through a yawn. Other types of nonverbal communication include smiles, fear, quizzical expressions, finger drumming, fist clenching, and applause.[1]

INTERPERSONAL FEEDBACK. Both verbal and nonverbal feedback give the sender some indication of how the receiver has accepted his message and enable him to modify, repeat, or explain in greater detail the message he wishes to convey. An experienced communicator is very attentive to feedback and constantly modifies his messages in light of what he sees or hears from his audience.

Immediate feedback is the factor that makes personal selling so effective. It enables the salesman to tailor his sales pitch to the expressed needs and the observed reactions of each prospect. Similarly, it enables a political candidate to selectively stress specific aspects of his platform in response to questions posed by prospective voters in face-to-face meetings. Immediate feedback in terms of inattention serves to alert the college professor to the need to awaken the interest of a dozing class; thus, he may make a deliberately provocative statement, such as "This material will probably appear on your final exam."

Only through feedback can the sender know if and how well his message has been received. That is why, in our model of the communication process, feedback is shown to be an integral link.

impersonal communication

Communication directed to a large and diffused audience is called impersonal, or mass, communication. It operates in much the same way as interpersonal communication, even though there is no direct contact between source and receiver. The sources of mass communication are usually organizations that develop and transmit appropriate messages through specific departments or spokesmen. The destinations, or receivers, for such messages are usually a specific audience or several audiences that the organization is trying to inform, to influence, or persuade. For example, the American Cancer Society may wish to persuade teenagers not to smoke, or a bank may wish to convince businessmen to use its services, or a marketer may wish to persuade housewives to use his soap powder.

Impersonal communication is carried by such mass media channels as television, radio, newspapers, magazines, and billboards. Because mass communication sources are organizations, their messages are considered formal. When such organizations are marketing organizations, their mass communications usually have commercial objectives (e.g., to persuade consumers to buy their products). Obviously, however, not all mass communications have commercial objectives. A school board may wish to persuade townspeople to support the new school budget, or the government may wish to persuade taxpayers to file their tax returns early.

IMPERSONAL FEEDBACK. Feedback is just as important a concept in mass communication as it is in interpersonal communication. Indeed, because of the large sums of money required for mass communication, many people consider such feedback even more essential than interpersonal feedback.

The organization that initiates the communication must develop some method for determining whether its mass communications are, in fact, received by their intended audience, understood in the intended way, and successful in achieving their intended objectives. Unlike interpersonal communication feedback, mass communication feedback is rarely direct; indeed, it is usually inferential.[2] Receivers buy (or do not buy) the advertised product, renew (or do not renew) their magazine subscriptions, or vote (or do not vote) for the candidate. The sender infers how persuasive his message was from the resulting action (or inaction) taken by the audience.

Mass communication feedback does not have the timeliness of interpersonal feedback; instead, it is usually somewhat delayed. A marketer rarely has the opportunity to find out immediately how effective his consumer advertising is. Since the "pipeline" from factory to consumer is fairly extensive, he must usually wait some time for reorders to occur in order to judge the effects of a national campaign. Retail executives are more fortunate, in that they can usually assess the effectiveness of newspaper advertisements by midday on the basis of sales activity for the advertised product.

Mass communication sources often try to gauge the effectiveness of their messages by conducting audience research to find out which media are read, which television programs are watched, and which advertisements are remembered by their target audience. If he is able to obtain feedback relatively early, the source still has the opportunity to modify or revise his message so that his intended communication will, in fact, take place.

The audience

While marketers are primarily concerned with directing mass communications to multiple, or mass, audiences, such audiences must not be thought of as large, undifferentiated masses, but rather as hundreds or thousands or even millions of individual consumers. Since messages are received *by* individuals; they must be written and directed *to* individuals, albeit many of them. To do so successfully, the marketer must understand those personal characteristics of individuals that operate to help or hinder the acceptance of persuasive communications.

BARRIERS TO COMMUNICATION

There are many barriers to communication; some are physical, others are psychological. Among the psychological barriers that serve to filter receipt of mass communications are *selective attention, selective perception,* and *selective appeal*. These factors, discussed in detail in Chapter 3, will be briefly reviewed here.

selective attention

Since most individuals are bombarded daily with more messages than any one person could possibly comprehend, individuals tend to give their attention selectively to those messages that are in their realm of interest or experience. For example, a woman whose youngest child has gone off to college might look for announcements of women's vocational programs or employment opportunities, while ignoring ads for new furniture or for camping equipment. Expectant first-time parents or grandparents might eagerly look at advertisements for baby carriages and other infant equipment, but those not interested in babies would ignore such ads. It is because of selective attention that market segmentation is such an effective marketing strategy. Marketers segment their markets on the basis of some relevant product interest or need. Prospects who are homogeneous in relation to a product interest are likely to perceive advertisements which address that interest, while those who are not interested in the product category will simply ignore them.

In summary, people seek information about topics in which they are interested or which relate to their way of life, and they ignore information concerning matters in which they have no interest. For this reason, marketers must present their persuasive communications in a context with which their target audiences can identify or which will be of general interest to them.

NOISE. Related to selective attention is another communications barrier which is technically known as *noise*. In terms of communication reception, noise can be either mechanical or psychological. Static on a telephone or on a radio is mechanical noise, which may interfere with reception. No less a barrier to message reception is *psychological* noise, which may take the form of competing advertising messages or distracting thoughts. A consumer faced with the clutter of nine successive commercial messages during a television program break may actually receive and retain nothing of what she has seen. Similarly, a woman planning her dinner menu while driving to work may be too engrossed in her thoughts to hear a radio commercial. On a more familiar level, a student daydreaming about his Saturday night date may simply not "hear" a question directed to him by his professor. He is just as much a victim of "noise"—albeit psychological noise—as the student who literally cannot hear a question because of hammering in the next room.

In all of the instances mentioned, the best way for a sender to overcome noise is simply to repeat the message several times, much as the sailor does when sending an SOS over and over again to make sure it is received. (The effects of repetition on learning are discussed in Chapter 4.) Redundancy is constantly practiced by marketers who repeat the same advertisements over and over in the same medium and in supplementary media. For example, an advertising campaign usually consists of sev-

eral different commercials and/or advertisements that feature the same
advertising appeals presented in different contexts. The principle of redundancy is also seen in advertisements that use both illustrations and
copy to emphasize the same points. A major advantage of television is
that it enables the advertiser to repeat the same message both verbally
and visually. Redundancy frequently occurs in interpersonal communication—not only can the sender give examples and analogies to clarify
his message, but he can also reinforce them with his facial expressions
and body movements. Repeated exposure of an advertising message
(redundancy of the advertising appeal) helps surmount a very real barrier to message reception and thus facilitates communication.

selective perception

As our discussion on perception indicated, people actually see or
hear only those things in which they are specifically interested. Subconsciously, they filter out all messages in which they have no interest or
about which they have no expectations. A person riding in an automobile may pass fifty roadside restaurants without noticing them, but if he
gets hungry, he will be able to detect a small restaurant sign some sixty
yards off the road. The mother of a preschooler may note and carefully
read every sign and every advertisement she sees for tricycles, but once
her child outgrows tricycles, she literally will not perceive such ads, even
if they flood her local newspaper. A young married couple looking for a
new car will see and hear and read advertisements for all cars within
their relevant price range; however, they may not notice an ad for a
Rolls Royce. A similar couple, exposed to the same media but not interested in purchasing a car, would probably notice no automobile ads at
all. However, if the couple had just bought a new car, they would be likely to continue to note and read selected automobile advertisements in an
attempt to reassure themselves that they had made the right choice—i.e.,
they would try to alleviate their *postpurchase dissonance*.[3] (Cognitive dissonance and, more specifically, postpurchase dissonance, are discussed in
Chapter 6.)

In general, people tend to avoid dissonant or opposing information. They seek information that agrees with their beliefs, and they avoid
information that does not. Thus, Democrats tend to read Democratic
campaign literature, listen to Democratic political speeches, and attend
Democratic political rallies. Conversely, Republicans read Republican
campaign literature, listen to Republican political speeches, and attend
Republican political rallies. Each side carefully avoids information fur-
nished by the opposing party. Political campaign efforts to recruit votes
via mass communication efforts are often pointless, since such political
messages are received only by those who intend to vote for the party
anyway. The only campaign efforts that are truly worthwhile are those
directed at new voters and voters who have not yet made up their minds.
This latter group was especially relevant to both Ford and Carter during
the 1976 presidential race, since polls continually indicated that many
people remained uncommitted throughout most of the campaign.

selective appeal

A corollary of both selective attention and selective perception is the concept of selective appeal. Our discussion of motivation noted that individuals are motivated to satisfy their own needs, wants, and desires. Most of their shopping time and attention is focused on finding ways to fulfill their unique needs. Messages that address their specific problems or tell them how to fulfill their special needs generally receive their close attention; messages not related to their specific needs are usually ignored.

Thus the marketer must couch his advertising message to the consumer in such a way that it will clearly demonstrate that usage of his product or service will enable her to fulfill a specific objective. Advertisements that stress the benefits to be achieved and the needs which will be fulfilled by the product are much more effective than advertisements that stress the features of the product. The latter type of ad expects the consumer to mentally convert a product feature into a consumer benefit. However, not all consumers can readily see the connection between a product feature and its ability to fulfill an unsatisfied need. For this reason, the marketer must use care in selecting and depicting—in words and illustrations—appeals that clearly demonstrate that his product will satisfy the consumer's unmet need.

THE MASS AUDIENCE AS INDIVIDUAL RECEIVERS

We stressed earlier that all communications, whether interpersonal or impersonal, are received ultimately by individuals. A mass audience is simply a mass or number of individual receivers, each with his or her own interests, experiences, needs, wants, desires. It is unlikely that a marketer could develop a single communications campaign that would simultaneously appeal to the specific interests of great numbers of individuals in words they all understand via media they all see. For this reason, marketers who do try to reach their total audience with a single communications effort (i.e., those who do not segment their markets) are usually unsuccessful. Efforts to use "universal" appeals phrased in simple language that all can understand invariably result in advertisements to which few people will closely relate.

Clearly, all individuals are *not* unique, they have specific traits or interests or needs that are shared by many others. A market segmentation strategy enables the experienced marketer to exploit this fact by dividing his total audience into a number of smaller audiences, each of which is homogeneous in relation to some characteristic pertinent to his product. He can then design a specific advertising message for each market segment which will appeal directly to the common interests of all the people in the segment.[4] As a result, each individual in each market segment may feel that the advertising message he receives is specifically addressed to him, in that it focuses directly on his special interests or needs. Since individuals with similar interests and attitudes frequently expose themselves to the same media, the marketer can place such messages in the specific media each market segment prefers. Because it enables the marketer to tailor his appeal to the specific needs of like groups of people, market segmentation overcomes some of the problems inherent in trying to communicate with mass audiences.

MULTIPLE AUDIENCES

All organizations—and certainly marketing organizations—recognize that their ultimate success depends on their ability to persuade many different kinds of audiences of the worthwhile nature of their products and their other endeavors. Such audiences include selling intermediaries (distributors, wholesalers, and retailers), as well as other audiences that are important to the organization's ultimate well-being.

selling intermediaries

Most national manufacturers concern themselves primarily with transmitting persuasive communications to their ultimate consumers, but they must at the same time persuade the people through whom they sell their products—their "channels of distribution"—to buy and stock their products. It would be pointless to persuade final consumers to buy their products if the consumer could not find such products at her local store. Thus, in addition to advertising to the ultimate consumer (called national advertising), manufacturers usually direct advertising messages to each functional level of their distribution channels, utilizing appeals and media that are unique to that function (see Table 7 – 1).

For example, trade advertising is transmitted to product resellers (distributors, wholesalers, and retailers) through the relevant trade media by using appeals that are of specific interest to them, such as high profit, fast turnover, and increased store traffic. Industrial advertising is directed from one manufacturer to another manufacturer who can use the advertised product to make his own product (e.g., a thread manufacturer may advertise his product to a clothing manufacturer). The type of appeal used in industrial advertising stresses the fact that the advertised product will enhance the second manufacturer's product (or increase his profit, decrease his costs, etc.). Where appropriate, manufacturers also advertise to professionals in the field in order to persuade them to recommend or prescribe or otherwise specify the advertised product to patients or clients. For example, a drug manufacturer may advertise a new product to physicians, hoping that they in turn will prescribe the product for their patients.

Retailers monopolize the nation's newspapers with retail advertising directed to the ultimate consumer. Such ads often feature products, sale prices, store services, and facilities; their prime purpose is to bring the consumer into the store to do her shopping. Whether she actually buys the products or brands advertised is of little importance to the retailer, so long as she makes her purchases at his store.

The marketer also tries to reach other intermediaries (designers,

TABLE 7–1

Types of Mass Communication Efforts Initiated by Manufacturers and Selling Intermediaries

Source	Audience	Type of advertising	Typical appeals	Typical message
Manufacturer	Wholesalers Retailers	Trade	Assortment, profit, turnover, store traffic, etc.	Stock and display my product
Manufacturer	Consumers	National	Convenience, personal benefits	Buy my product anywhere
Manufacturer	Other manu- facturers	Industrial	Product improve- ment, cost, savings, etc.	Use my product to make your product
Manufacturer	Professionals	Professional	Satisfied clients, relieved patients	Recommend or prescribe my product
Wholesaler	Retailers	Trade	Large assortment, delivery, service	Buy your stock from me
Retailer	Consumers	Local or retail	Convenience, service, price	Shop and buy all your needs at my store

sales people, manufacturers, etc.) in the hope that each of these receivers will favorably affect the ultimate reception of the product by the end-user.

other audiences

Wise managers are very much aware of the influence that many outside publics have on the ultimate success of their organizations. Table 7 – 2 lists some of these publics and the reasons why their good favor is important. For example, suppliers who think well of a firm will advance it credit and give prompt delivery of materials in short supply. Stockholders who are impressed with a company and its prospects will buy and retain its stocks. Employees who are convinced they are working for a fine organization will be loyal, hardworking, and highly motivated. The financial community will readily advance short- and long-term funds for operations and expansion.

To maintain favorable communications with all of their publics, most large organizations employ public relations counselors or establish their own public relations departments to provide favorable information about the company or to suppress unfavorable information. A good public relations man will develop a close working relationship with editors of all the relevant media in order to facilitate editorial placement of desired messages. The greater credibility of editorial vehicles as compared with paid messages (advertisements) is discussed in greater detail in the next section.

TABLE 7-2

Audiences Outside the Channel of Distribution with Which Favorable Communications Must be Maintained

Audience	Communications Objectives
Suppliers	Obtain credit, prompt delivery
Customers	Encourage sales, profits
Government	Discourage unfavorable or restrictive legislation
Stockholders	Encourage stock purchases and reduce trading of company's stock
Community	Receive local support for building programs, attract labor pool, etc.
Employees	Motivate workers, improve product quality and production
Financial community	Raise short- and long-term capital at favorable rates when needed

The source

The source of a communication—the initiator of the message—is not only an integral component of the communication process itself but also a vital influence on the impact of the message.

CLASSIFICATION OF SOURCES OF CONSUMER COMMUNICATIONS

We have already noted that there are basically two types of communication: interpersonal and mass communication. Sources of *interpersonal* communication may be either formal or informal. Informal sources include friends, family, neighbors, fellow employees, and the like, who speak with the receiver regularly or irregularly and may, in the course of conversation, impart product or service information (Chapter 10 discusses the effects of such informal interpersonal influences.) Formal interpersonal sources include representatives of formal organizations, such as salesmen, company spokesmen, or political candidates, who are compensated in one form or another for influencing or persuading consumers to act in a prescribed way.

Impersonal sources of consumer communications are usually organizations—either commercial or noncommercial—such as manufacturers, service companies, institutions, and government and political groups, who want to promote an idea, a product, a service, or an organizational image to the consumer. Such organizations generally appoint a specific department or person to create and transmit approved messages to desired audiences. These communications are usually encoded in paid advertising messages and transmitted via impersonal or mass media such as television, radio, newspapers, magazines, and billboards. In addition, they sometimes use such personal media as direct mail or sales promotion techniques (e.g., coupon or sample distribution) to transmit intended messages.

Sometimes a medium itself will be the source or initiator of product-related messages. This is particularly true of media with independent editorial departments, which can take specific stands on issues, ideas, and products and impart their views to their audiences. Included among such media are specialized rating publications, such as *Consumer*

FIGURE 7-3

Sources of Consumer Communications and Related Message Vehicles

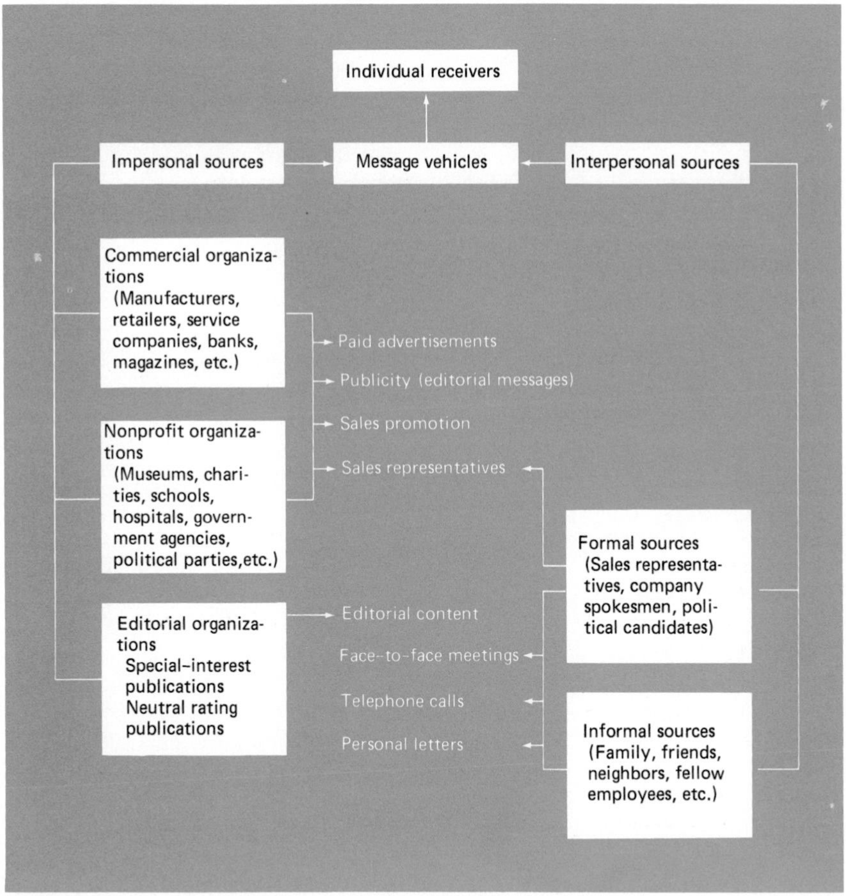

Reports. To avoid jeopardizing their reputation for impartial evaluations, these publications do not accept advertising.

Very often an organization's public relations department will encode a desired message within a newsworthy story format and transmit it via the editorial sections of mass media. The ensuing story is called *publicity* and differs from advertising only in that it appears in space or time that has not been bought by the sender. Since creation of the story events and subtle placement of the message may cost the sender considerably more in terms of money and trouble than a paid advertisement, cost savings are obviously not the basic motivation for publicity stories. The prime reason why companies prefer publicity is the increased credibility with which receivers regard editorial sources as compared with commercial sources of product communications.

Figure 7 – 3 depicts the various kinds of communication sources for consumer messages and the vehicles they use to transmit these messages. Among the most effective vehicles used by impersonal sources are formal interpersonal vehicles, such as sales representatives or other company spokesmen, who interact on a personal basis with individual receivers.

TABLE 7–3

Relative Importance of Message Sources in the Purchase Decision Process

SOURCE	Small appliances			Clothing			Food		
	First	Else	Most important	First	Else	Most important	First	Else	Most important
Commercial Sources									
Advertising	48%	23%	8%	35%	27%	16%	45%	25%	19%
Salesmen	1	1	1	4	1	6	0	0	0
Sales promotion*	9	7	9	19	14	32	26	16	27
Interpersonal Sources									
Friends, neighbors, relatives**	23	41	53	27	29	33	16	19	29
Immediate family	8	7	11	2	4	0	12	12	21
Professional advice	6	8	13	0	0	0	1	0	0
*Editorial and News Sources****	1	0	1	6	6	6	0	0	1
No Mentions	4	13	4	7	19	7	0	28	3
Total (N = 99)	100%	100%	100%	100%	100%	100%	100%	100%	100%

*Includes sampling, displays, in-store promotions, packaging.

**Includes actual discussions as well as noticing the item, or trying the item (e.g., in the home of a friend).

***Includes Consumer Reports.

Source: From Innovative Behavior and Communication, *by Thomas S. Robertson. Copyright © 1971 by Holt, Rinehart and Winston, Inc. Reprinted by permission of Holt, Rinehart and Winston.*

TABLE 7–4

Rank Order of Information Sources Influencing Selection of a Retail Outlet When Shopping for Men's Shirts and Television Sets

Information source	Men's shirts	Television sets
Previous Experience	1	2
Suggestion of Friends	2	5
Window Display	3	4
Newspaper Advertisements	4	1
Radio/TV Advertisements	5	3
Consumer Reports or other Services	6	6

Source: Ben M. Enis and Gordon W. Paul, "Store Loyalty as a Basis for Market Segmentation," Journal of Retailing, 46 (Fall 1970), 46.

Table 7–3 reports the findings of research undertaken to determine the relative importance of various communication sources in the purchase decision process. Women respondents were asked the following questions concerning purchases of small appliances, clothing, and food items: (1) Could you tell me how this product came to your attention for the *very first time?* (2) How *else* did you hear about this product before you bought it? (3) Which one of these ways was your *most important* source of information on your decision to buy this product?[5] As the table indicates, informal sources were most influential in the purchase decision process for each of the product categories under study. In the case of clothing purchases, sales promotion (such as displays) also played a very important part. For small appliances and food, neutral sources such as editorials and consumer rating services had surprisingly little influence.

Table 7–4 presents the results of a study in which women were asked to name the sources of information that influenced them to purchase (1) a man's shirt and (2) a television set in a specific retail store.[6] It is interesting to note that previous experience with the store ranked first and second, respectively, while information from *Consumer Reports* or other neutral rating sources ranked sixth. Impersonal sources such as advertisements were clearly more influential for a high priced technical product like a television set, while interpersonal sources such as friends were more influential for an inexpensive utilitarian item like a shirt.

THE CREDIBILITY OF COMMUNICATION SOURCES

The source of the communication, his perceived honesty and objectivity, has an enormous influence on whether or not the communication is accepted by the receiver. If the source is well respected and highly thought of by the intended audience, the message is much more likely to be believed. Conversely, a source who is considered unreliable or untrustworthy will have his messages received with skepticism and ultimately rejected.

Research shows that the credibility of the source is a vital element in the ultimate persuasibility of the message.[7] Credibility is built upon a number of factors, the most important of which is the perceived intention of the source. The receiver asks himself, "Just what does he stand to gain if I do what he suggests?" If the receiver perceives any type of personal gain for the sender as a result of the proposed action or advice, the message may become suspect: "He wants me to buy that product just so he'll earn a commission." Any prospect of personal gain for the sender immediately casts a veil of doubt upon his objectivity.

One of the major reasons why informal sources such as friends, neighbors, and relatives have such a strong influence on a receiver's behavior is simply that they are perceived as having no "ax to grind." Since they apparently have nothing to gain from a product transaction they recommend, their advice is considered totally objective, and their intentions are perceived to be in the best interests of the receiver.

Interestingly enough, such informal sources, called opinion leaders, often do profit—psychologically if not tangibly—by providing product information to others. A person may obtain a great deal of ego satisfaction by providing solicited as well as unsolicited information and advice to friends. As Chapter 10 points out, this ego gratification may actually improve the quality of the information provided, since the opinion leader will herself deliberately seek out impartial information in order to enhance her own position as "expert" on a particular product category.[8] The fact that the opinion leader does not receive material gain from the action she recommends increases her credibility with the receiver and improves the likelihood that her advice will be seriously considered.

Experienced marketers try to utilize the phenomenon of opinion leadership by targeting their mass communications to opinion leaders, hoping that they, in turn, will pass these communications on to the rest of the population.

Even with informal sources, intentions are not always what they appear to be. Individuals who experience postpurchase dissonance (see Chapter 6) often try to alleviate their uncertainty by convincing others to make a similar purchase choice. Each time they persuade a friend or an acquaintance to make the same brand selection, they are somewhat reassured that their own product choice was a wise one. The receiver, on the other hand, regards product advice from "the man who owns one" as totally objective, since the source had obviously conducted his own information search and is also able to speak from actual experience. Thus the increased credibility accorded the informal source may not really be warranted, despite his perceived objectivity.

Neutral or editorial sources have greater credibility than commercial sources because of the likelihood that they are more objective in their product assessments. That is why publicity is so valuable to a manufacturer; citations of his product in an editorial context, rather than in a paid advertisement, give the reader much more confidence in the message.

multiplicity of perceived sources

Where the intentions of the source are clearly profit-making, then reputation, expertise, and knowledge become important factors in message credibility. The credibility of commercial messages is often based on the composite evaluation of the reputations of (1) the initiator (the organization that approves and pays for the advertising message), (2) the retail outlet that carries the product. (3) the medium that carries the message, and (4) the company spokesman (the actor or sales representative who delivers the message).

THE MESSAGE INITIATOR. Initiators of commercial messages include manufacturers, service companies, commercial institutions, and retailers. Since their intentions are clearly to make a profit, their credibility is based on such factors as past performance, the kind and quality of service they are known to render, the quality and image of other products they manufacture, the type of retail outlets through which they sell, and their position in the community (e.g., their stand on such issues as social responsibility or equal employment).

The ability of a quality image to invoke credibility is one of the reasons for the growth of "family" brands. Manufacturers with favorable brand images prefer to give their new products the existing brand name in order to obtain ready acceptance from consumers. A study conducted among housewives in four cities across the nation concluded that a new product has a much better chance for acceptance if it comes in under an old name.[9] A manufacturer with a good reputation generally has high credibility among consumers. For this reason, many companies spend a sizable part of their advertising budget on *institutional* advertising, which is designed to promote a favorable company image rather than to promote specific products.

THE RETAILER AS A PERCEIVED SOURCE. The reputation of the retailer who sells the product also has a major influence on credibility. Products sold by well-known quality stores seem to carry the added endorsement (and implicit guarantee) of the store itself: "If Macy's carries it, it must be good." The aura of credibility generated by reputable retail advertising reinforces the manufacturer's message as well. A product carried in a quality store such as Saks Fifth Avenue is usually perceived as being of better quality than one carried by a mass merchandiser; therefore, a message concerning its attributes is more readily believed. That is why so many national advertisements (i. e., manufacturer-initiated ads) carry the line "Sold at better stores everywhere."

THE MEDIUM AS A PERCEIVED SOURCE. The reputation of the medium that carries the advertisement affects the credibility of the message. Marshall McLuhan underscored this fact in his book *The Medium Is the Message*.[10] The image of a prestige magazine like the *New Yorker* confers added status on the products whose advertisements it carries. The reputation of the medium in terms of honesty or objectivity also affects the credibility of the advertising. Consumers often think that a medium they respect would not accept advertising for products it did not "know" were good. For this reason, manufacturers are often happy to avail themselves of the merchandising services offered by some media, and purchase and distribute supplementary promotional material, such as counter cards and product hangtags that say, for example, "As advertised in *Vogue* Magazine."

THE SPOKESMAN AS A PERCEIVED SOURCE. People sometimes regard the person who gives the product message as the source (or initiator) of the message. Thus the "pitchman"—whether he appears personally or in an advertisement—has a major influence on message credibility. In interpersonal communication, a salesman who engenders confidence, and who gives the impression of honesty and integrity, is generally more successful in persuading a prospect than a salesman who does not have these characteristics. Such confidence or credibility is created in diverse ways. A salesman who "looks you in the eye" may appear more honest than one who evades direct eye contact. For many products, a salesman who dresses well and drives an expensive, late-model car may have more credibility than one without such outward signs of success (and inferred representation of a best-selling product). For some products, however, a salesman may achieve more credibility by dressing in the role of expert. For example, a man selling home improvements may achieve more credibility by looking like someone who just climbed off a roof or out of a basement than by looking like a stockbroker.

In impersonal communication, the reputation or expertise of the advertising spokesman may strongly influence the credibility of the message. That accounts for the popularity and effectiveness of testimonials as a promotional technique. If a known or reputed expert in a specific field endorses a related product, consumers are usually ready to follow his advice, even though his endorsement is clearly profit-motivated. This is true for testimonials given by recognized experts as well as for testimonials given by unknown but stereotyped actors with inferred or implied expertise. White-coated actors who look like doctors have been able to successfully persuade viewers to buy over-the-counter drugs, despite the fact that the audience was warned that the commercial was a staged presentation. Similarly, a commercial that depicts a garage mechanic endorsing a specific brand of automobile battery has great credibility among consumers because of the presumed knowledge and expertise of garage mechanics in general concerning automobile replacement parts.

Marketers who use a testimonial strategy should recognize that the potential success of their advertising rests on the credibility of the spokesmen they use. If a celebrity is used, he should be one who has some obvious knowledge about the product, or recognized expertise in the product category. The Federal Trade Commission has proposed guidelines governing the use of testimonials and endorsements (see Chapter 8). In brief, they require endorsers to have the experience, special competence, or expertise to form the judgment expressed by their endorsement. Persuasive endorsements by nonusers are considered deceptive advertising.

Advertisers who use testimonials must take care that the specific wording of the endorsement be within the recognized competence of the spokesman. A movie actress can believably endorse a face cream with comments about its overall skin coverage or smoothing effects; however, a recitation of its chemical properties is beyond her expected knowledge and expertise and thus reduces, not enhances, message credibility. A radio campaign by Pepperidge Farm bakery products featured Joan Fontaine endorsing a prepared poultry stuffing. Since few housewives can envision the cool and sophisticated Miss Fontaine stuffing a turkey, the commercials lacked credibility. Such testimonial strategy would have been more persuasive if it had featured a renowned cooking expert, and Joan Fontaine would have attained more credibility by endorsing beauty preparations.

experience affects message credibility

The consumer's own experience with the product or the retail channel acts to affirm or deny the credibility of the message. A product or a store that lives up to its advertised claims increases the credibility with which future claims are received. Research suggests that fulfilled product expectations tend to increase the credibility accorded future messages by the same advertiser, while unfulfilled product claims or disappointing products tend to reduce the credibility of future messages.[11]

the "sleeper effect"

A number of researchers have explored the effectiveness of persuasive messages given by high-credibility sources as opposed to persuasive messages given by low-credibility sources. In one experiment, a high-credibility source presented persuasive material to one group and a low-credibility source presented the same material to another group.[12] As might be expected, the group addressed by the high-credibility source was more persuaded than the one addressed by the low-credibility source. However, when the subjects were tested four weeks later, the percentage of those exposed to the high-credibility source who had been persuaded (i. e., who had changed their opinions) decreased, while the percentage of those exposed to the low-credibility source who had changed their opinions actually increased. In other words, both the positive and negative credibility effects of the source of the communication tended to disappear after several weeks. These findings were supported and extended by the results of a later experiment, which showed that a high-credibility source was initially more influential than a low-credibility source in persuading his audience.[13] However, remeasurement three weeks later revealed that effects of both persuasive messages were somewhat similar. This phenomenon has been termed the "sleeper effect."[14]

The medium

To receive a message, an individual must, at the very least, be exposed to the medium through which it is transmitted. If a marvelously persuasive commercial is shown on one television channel while a housewife is tuned to another channel, obviously there is no way for her to receive the message. If an advertisement runs in the *Reader's Digest,* only those people who read the magazine have any chance of seeing it and being persuaded by it. If an editorial endorsing longer hemlines appears in *Woman's Wear Daily,* only those people who see the paper have the opportunity of reading it.

There are so many different categories of media available today and so many media alternatives available within each category that individuals tend to develop their own special media habits. One cannot be exposed to all available media—there are simply too many. While it may be possible for a person to read all the newspapers in his hometown, the likelihood of his doing so tends to decrease as the number of newspapers available increases. Since an individual can reasonably watch only one TV channel or listen to only one radio station at a time, she can only expose herself to one of the numerous advertising messages that are broadcast simultaneously.

It is clear that only messages that are transmitted via media to which an individual is exposed have any chance of reaching her directly. However, as discussed earlier, such messages do have a chance of reaching her *indirectly* through opinion leaders.

MEDIA STRATEGY AFFECTS MESSAGE RECEPTION

Since individuals expose themselves selectively to various media, it is important that a mass communicator discover the specific media habits of those she wishes to reach. In this way she can be sure that her advertisements are run in media that are seen and read by the individuals who constitute her audience. For this reason, media strategy is one of the most critical components of advertising planning. The advertiser must determine the media habits of the buyers or (in the case of new products) the expected buyers of his product. He usually does this by segmenting his audience in terms of some relevant characteristic which enables him to develop a "consumer profile." He then tries to identify the specific media that individuals who fit this profile read or view. His search is facilitated by the media themselves, which carefully study their own audiences in order to develop descriptive "audience profiles." An efficient media choice is considered to be one that closely matches the advertiser's consumer profile to a medium's audience profile.

overlapping audiences

Since many media—especially those with similar editorial features and formats—have overlapping audiences, advertisers usually place their advertising messages simultaneously or sequentially in a number of similar media (media with similar audience profiles). This enables them to either reach a wider audience with the same relevant market characteristics, or to reach the same individuals in several media in order to give them repeated exposure to the same advertising message. For example, many women read one or more fashion magazines. A perfume manufacturer who wishes to reach fashion-conscious women may run the same advertisement simultaneously in *Vogue* and *Harper's Bazaar*. Each advertisement will reach a unique part of the desired market segment that reads only that magazine; in addition, however, each ad will reach women who read both magazines and thus see the ad twice. As Figure 7–4 illustrates, a *Vogue* ad will reach women in the desired market segment who read *Vogue* but not *Harper's Bazaar* (subset *A*); a *Harper's Bazaar* ad will reach women who read *Harper's Bazaar* but not *Vogue* (subset *B*); the overlapping area (subset *C*) reaches women who read both magazines and therefore see the advertisement twice. By using both media, the advertiser increases the size of the market segment exposed to his advertisement and, in instances of overlapping

Figure 7–4

Unique and Overlapping Readership of Magazines with Similar Audience Profiles

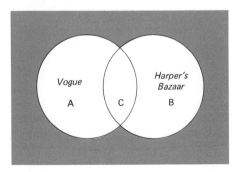

readership, increases the exposure (and therefore the redundancy and impact) of his advertising message.

media as product vehicles

Another aspect of media strategy focuses on the product and the intended message. The advertiser must select a general media category that will enhance the message he wishes to convey. Some media categories are more appropriate vehicles for certain products or messages than others. For example, a retailer who wants to advertise a clearance sale should advertise in his local newspaper, since that is where consumers are accustomed to looking for sale announcements. A manufacturer who wants to present a detailed argument in favor of his sewing machines should advertise in household magazines, where readers are accustomed to reading detailed articles and stories. A marketer who wants to promote a power mower with unique cutting features would be wise to use a medium like television, which enables him to demonstrate these features in action. Once the marketer has identified the appropriate media category, he can then choose the specific medium in that category that reaches his intended audience.

Some evidence indicates that the same advertisement will generate different communication effects when run in different media.[15] A study of the interaction of two types of magazine vehicles (a prestige magazine like the *New Yorker* and an "expert" or special-interest magazine like *Tennis World*) and two types of copy approaches ("reason-why" and "image" copy) found that, for nonusers of the product in question, prestige magazines were more persuasive in communicating product quality and image than expert magazines. Conversely, expert magazines were more effective in delivering factual information.[16] These results give support to the notion that a media vehicle induces a "mood" of receptivity that affects the impact of a persuasive communication.

Clearly, marketers must be familiar with the characteristics of their audiences and the characteristics of media if they are to make wise media choices. To implement the most effective media strategies, however, they must also be totally familiar with the characteristics of their products. That is a prime requisite for preparing a persuasive message.

The message

The message is often considered the most vital component of all in the communication process. The message is the thought, idea, attitude, image, or other information that the sender wishes to convey to his intended audience. In trying to encode the message in a form that will enable his audience to understand his precise meaning, the sender himself must clearly recognize exactly what he is trying to say and why he is saying it (what his objectives are and what he hopes the message will accomplish).

The marketer's objectives tend to vary with the audience. His objectives in communicating with the consumer, for example, may be one or all of the following: (1) informing her what is for sale, (2) creating brand awareness, (3) getting her to buy the product, (4) reducing her uneasiness after the purchase is made. His objective with intermediary customers is to get them to stock the product; with other manufacturers, to get them to buy the product and use it to make their own.

The sender must also know his audience well in terms of their education, interests, needs, and realms of experience. He must then endeavor to encode or phrase his message in such a way that it will fall within their zones of understanding and familiarity.

Suppose a manufacturer of expensive men's leather goods wishes to sell a new line of wallets in order to increase his firm's profits. He may identify his target audience as well-to-do business executives and their gift-giving wives. He will then select appropriate media through which to reach his audience. To develop effective advertising appeals, he must understand the needs or objectives of the target audience in regard to wallets. Conceivably, these needs may include the following: (a) a slim case that will not cause bulges in tailored suits, (b) an ample interior that will accommodate business cards, credit cards, and money, and (c) a handsome exterior that will signify status, wealth, and good taste. His copywriter will then create a suitable advertisement that will illustrate how well the wallet fulfills these needs. If the advertisement embodies a situation, a model, and copy with which the target audience can identify, it has a good chance of being successful. If it uses an inappropriate situation (such as a shoe salesman pulling out pictures of the kiddies), it will not work.

To attract the attention and interest of their target audiences, marketers should start their advertisements with an appeal to the needs and interests of the audience, and end their advertisements with an appeal relevant to their own needs (i. e., end with an effective sales closing). Marketers have found that the most effective ads conclude by telling the reader exactly what it is they want him to do: "Visit your Chevrolet showroom today;" "Ask for it at your favorite cosmetic counter;" "Send us your order by return mail." Advertisements that do not conclude with an "action" closing tend to provoke much *less* action on the part of the consumer than those that do.

METHOD OF PRESENTATION

We have already demonstrated that to be effective, a message must (1) be directed to the appropriate audience, (2) use appeals that are relevant to the interests and experience of the audience, and (3) be transmitted via media to which the audience is exposed. In addition, the *manner* in which a message is presented strongly influences its impact. The method of presentation affects the readiness with which the message is received, accepted, and acted upon. The following discussion examines some well-known principles concerning message presentation.

one-sided versus two-sided messages

Should an advertiser tell his audience only the good points about his product or should he also tell them the bad (or the commonplace)? Should he pretend his is the only product of its kind, or should he acknowledge competing products? These are very real strategy questions which marketers face every day, and the answers depend on the nature of the audience and the nature of the competition.

If the audience is friendly (e. g., if it uses the advertiser's products), if it initially favors the communicator's position, or if it is not likely to hear an opposing argument, then a one-sided (*supportive*) communication which stresses only favorable information is most effective.[17] However, if the audience is critical or unfriendly (e. g., if it uses competitive products), if it is well educated, or if it is likely to hear opposing claims, then a two-sided (*refutational*) message is most effective.[18]

These findings are especially relevant in today's marketing environment, in which many competing products claim superiority over others. Less sophisticated marketers continue to stress only positive factors about their products and pretend that competition does not exist. However, when competition does exist, and when it is likely to be vocal, such advertisers tend to lose credibility with the consumer. Some recent research suggests that claim credibility can be enhanced by actually *disclaiming* superiority in some product features in relation to a competing brand.[19]

Communication researchers not only have explored the problem of persuading audiences to take some prescribed action (e. g., to buy a product) but also have investigated ways to keep existing followers (e. g., customers) safe from outside persuasion.[20] Their findings suggest that two-sided appeals containing both pro and con arguments about the brand serve to *inoculate* consumers against arguments that may be raised by competitors. In effect, this strategy provides consumers with *counterarguments* with which to rationalize against future attacks by competing brands.

A practical illustration of two-sided advertising is seen in *comparison advertising,* a marketing strategy used by increasing numbers of marketers. Comparison advertising (also called *comparative advertising*) has been defined as advertising that explicitly names or identifies one or more competitors of the advertised brand for the purpose of claiming superiority, either on an overall basis or in selected product attributes (see Figure 7–5).[21] It is frequently useful for product positioning, for target market selection and for brand differentiation strategies (which stress the differential advantage of the "underdog" product over leading brands). To reinforce credibility, a clever marketer will use and cite an independent research organization as the supplier of data used for the comparison.[22]

Recent research findings indicate that the message-recall effectiveness of comparative advertisements is somewhat higher than that of advertisements that do not explicitly name the competition.[23] Although more empirical research is needed to document its effectiveness, com-

FIGURE 7–5

Comparative Advertising

parison advertising promises to be a very successful strategy in a highly competitive marketplace.

order effects

Is it best to present your commercial first or last? Should you give the bad news first or last? Communication researchers have found that the order in which a message is presented affects audience receptivity.[24] For this reason, politicians and other professional communicators often jockey for position when they address an audience sequentially; they are aware that the first and last speeches are more likely to be retained in the audience's memory than those in between.[25] The media recognizes the impact of order effects by according "preferred position" placement to front, back, and inside covers of magazines, which means they charge more for these positions than for inside magazine pages because of their greater visibility and recall.

When just two competing messages are presented one after the other, the evidence is somewhat conflicting as to which position is more effective. Some researchers have found that the material presented first produces a greater effect (the "primacy" effect), while others have found that the material presented last is more effective (the "recency" effect).[26] Further research is needed to see how audience characteristics and message characteristics influence primacy and recency effects.

When both favorable information and unfavorable information are to be presented (for example, in an annual stockholders report), placing the favorable material first often produces greater tolerance for the unfavorable news. It also produces greater acceptance and better understanding of the total message.[27]

COPY APPROACH

Sometimes rational or factual appeals are more effective; sometimes nonrational or emotional ones are. It depends on the kind of audience to be reached and the product itself. In general, logical, reason-why appeals are more effective in persuading high-IQ audiences, who tend to be "turned off" by unsupported generalities, irrelevant arguments, or emotional appeals. Conversely, emotional appeals tend to be more effective in persuading people of lower intellectual achievement.[28]

fear appeals

Fear is often used as an appeal in marketing communications. Early research findings reported a negative relationship between the intensity of fear appeals and their ability to persuade. That is, strong fear appeals were found to be less effective than mild fear appeals.[29] For example, after a brief decline in cigarette smoking following the *Attorney General's Report* in 1964 linking cigarette smoking to lung cancer, cigarette consumption actually increased. A number of explanations have been offered for this phenomenon. Strong fear appeals concerning a highly relevant topic (e.g., a smoking habit) cause the individual to experience cognitive dissonance, which he resolves either by rejecting the habit or by rejecting the unwelcome information. Since giving up a cherished habit is difficult, consumers more readily reject the threat. This they do by a variety of techniques, including denial of the validity of the fear claims ("There still is no real proof"), the belief that they are immune to personal disaster ("It can't happen to me"), and a diffusing process that robs the claim of its true significance and thereby renders it impotent ("I play it safe by smoking only filter cigarettes").[30]

Recent research has come up with diverse findings on the relationship between the intensity of fear appeals and persuasion.[31] An analysis of such research suggests that strong fear appeals are more persuasive than mild fear appeals when source credibility is high.[32] Characteristics of the audience may also influence the persuasive effects of fear appeals. For example, individuals who can cope well, and who are high in self-esteem or low in perceived vulnerability, appear to be most easily persuaded by fear.[33] Because of contradictory findings concerning the use of fear in persuasive communications, it seems apparent that more empirical research attention is needed before any firm principles can be formulated.

humor in advertising

Many advertisers use humor in their advertising in the implicit belief that humor will increase the acceptance and the persuasibility of their communications. Other advertisers avoid the use of humor because they fear that their product will become an object of ridicule, that consumers will laugh *at* them rather than *with* them. Reported studies on the use of humor in advertising do little to settle this controversy. Although several studies indicate that humor is persuasive, they do not show that humor is more effective than a serious version of the same appeal. The effects of humor in advertising have not been sufficiently explored to come to any definite conclusions; however, an analysis of existing research suggests some tentative generalizations:[34]

1. Humorous messages attract attention.
2. Humorous messages may impair comprehension.
3. Humor may distract the audience, thereby reducing counterargumentation and increasing persuasion.
4. Humorous appeals appear to be persuasive, but the persuasive effect at best is no greater than that of serious appeals.
5. Humor tends to enhance source credibility.
6. Audience characteristics may confound the effects of humor.
7. A humorous context may increase liking for the source and create a positive mood. This may increase the persuasive effect of the message.
8. To the extent that a humorous context functions as a positive reinforcer, a persuasive communication placed in such a context may be more effective than a serious appeal.

Clearly, additional research is needed before more definite conclusions can be reached concerning the effectiveness of humor in persuasive communications. In the meantime, advertisers who want to use humor should use it very selectively for products and audiences that seem to lend themselves to this approach.

"agony" advertising

All of us at one time or another have been repelled by the so-called agony commercials which depict in diagrammatic detail the internal and intestinal effects of heartburn, indigestion, clogged sinus cavities, and hammer-induced headaches. Nevertheless, pharmaceutical companies continue to run such commercials with great success because they appeal to a certain segment of the population that suffers ailments that are not visible, and which therefore evoke little symptathy from family and friends. Their complaints are suddenly legitimized by commercials with which they immediately identify. With the sponsor's credibility established ("They really understand the misery I'm going through"), the message itself is often highly persuasive in getting consumers to buy the advertised product.

abrasive advertising

Studies of the "sleeper effect," discussed earlier, suggest that an individual's agreement with a persuasive communication from a low-credibility source is greater a long time after exposure rather than immediately thereafter.[35] This has interesting implications for marketing—and helps explain the old public relations dictum: "It matters not whether they think well of you or ill of you so long as they remember your name." It suggests that the memory of an unpleasant commercial that saturates the media and antagonizes listeners or viewers may, in the end, dissipate, leaving only the brand name and the persuasive message in the minds of consumers. An example of this phenomenon was seen in the old Winston cigarette advertising campaign that "corrected" the grammar of an earlier campaign with the tag line "Winston tastes good *as* a cigarette should." Even though many people were irritated by this campaign, sales ultimately increased. Perhaps recollection of the details of the advertisements faded, leaving only the name of the product in the mind of the consumer.

audience participation

Earlier we spoke about the importance of feedback in the communication process. The provision of feedback changes the communication process from one-way to two-way communication. This is important to the sender, in that it enables him to determine whether and how well communication has taken place. But it is also important to the receiver, because it enables him to participate, to be involved, to actually experience in some way the message itself. Participation by the receiver reinforces the message. An experienced communicator will ask questions and opinions of his audience to draw them into the discussion. Many professors use the participative approach in classrooms rather than the more sterile lecture format because they recognize that student participation tends to facilitate internalization of the information discussed.

Although participation is easily accomplished in interpersonal situations, it takes a great deal of ingenuity in impersonal situations. Thus, it is a challenge for imaginative marketers to get consumers involved in their advertising. The counterargumentation provoked by two-sided messages may be one feasible way to do so. Two-way television, already an experimental reality, may be another.

Summary

This chapter has described how the consumer receives and is influenced by marketing communications. Communication is defined as *the transmission of a message from a sender to a receiver by a signal of some sort through a channel of some sort.*

There are four basic components of all communication: a source, a destination, a medium, and a message. The source is the initiator of the message; the destination is his audience. The audience can be a single individual or many individuals — collectively called a mass audience.

There are two types of communication: interpersonal and impersonal (or mass) communication. Interpersonal communication occurs on a personal level between two or more people and may be verbal or nonverbal. In mass communication, there is no direct communication between source and receiver. Interpersonal communication takes place in person, by telephone, or by mail; mass communication uses such impersonal media as television, radio, newspapers, and magazines. In both types of communication, feedback is an essential step because it provides the sender with some notion as to if and how well his message has been received.

Barriers to communication include selective attention, selective perception, and selective appeal. Repetition or redundancy of the message is used to surmount the barrier of psychological noise.

Informal sources of interpersonal communication include friends, family, neighbors, and fellow employees. Formal interpersonal sources include organizational representatives, such as salesmen or company spokesmen. Impersonal sources of consumer communications are organizations (both commercial and noncommercial) and the media (including neutral rating publications).

The credibility of the source, a vital element in the ultimate persuasibility of a message, is often based upon his perceived intentions. Informal sources and neutral or editorial sources are generally considered highly objective and, therefore, highly credible. The credibility of a commercial source is usually more problematic and is based on a composite evaluation of its reputation, expertise, and knowledge and that of the medium, the retail channel and the company spokesmen it uses.

Product endorsement by someone perceived to have experience or expertise with the product can be very persuasive if that person is also perceived as being highly credible. The consumer's own experience with the product also affects the credibility that she attributes to the source. The differential impact of high- and low-credibility sources tends to disappear over time, and the message alone remains. This has been termed the "sleeper effect."

The marketer cannot communicate effectively with a large, heterogeneous audience by using general appeals. Instead, he usually segments his market on the basis of some relevant product or market characteristic and transmits individually tailored messages to these segments via media to which they are exposed. In addition to his ultimate consumers, a marketer's audiences include selling intermediaries and other publics that are relevant to the organization's success.

The manner in which a message is presented influences its impact. For example, one-sided messages are more effective in some situations and with some audiences; two-sided messages are more effective with others. When three or more messages are given sequentially, the first and the last tend to be the best remembered. However, when just two messages are given, in some cases the first is more effective (primacy effect) and in others the last is more effective (recency effect).

It is apparent that conflicting research reports in some areas of message presentation and inadequate research studies in others make it very difficult to develop a firm set of "principles" to guide communication strategy. Future research studies will have to carefully identify the many situational variables that seem to mediate the effects of message order and message presentation in persuading consumers to buy.

Endnotes

1. *Starkey Duncan, Jr., "Nonverbal Communication,"* Psychological Bulletin, *72 (August 1969), 118 – 37.*

2. *Wilbur Schramm,* The Process and Effects of Mass Communication *(Urbana: University of Illinois Press, 1955), 639 – 51.*

3. *Shelby D. Hunt, "Post Transaction Communication and Dissonance Reduction,"* Journal of Marketing, *34 (July 1970), 46 – 51.*

4. *Charles W. King and John O. Summers, "Attitudes and Media Exposure,"* Journal of Advertising Research, *11 (February 1971), 26 – 32.*

5. *Thomas S. Robertson. "The Effect of the Informal Group Upon Member Innovative Behavior," in Robert L. King, ed.,* Marketing and the New Science of Planning *(Chicago: American Marketing Association, 1968), 334 – 40.*

199 *communication and consumer behavior*

6. *Ben M. Enis and Gordon W. Paul, "Store Loyalty as a Basis for Market Segmentation,"* Journal of Retailing, *46 (Fall 1970), 46.*

7. *Robert B. Settle and Linda L. Golden, "Attribution Theory and Advertiser Credibility,"* Journal of Marketing Research, *11, (May 1974) 181–85.*

8. *Elihu Katz and Paul F. Lazarsfeld,* Personal Influence *(New York: Free Press, 1955), 309–20.*

9. *Leo Bogart and Charles Lehmann, "What Makes a Brand Name Familiar?"* Journal of Marketing Research, *10 (February 1973), 17–22.*

10. *Marshall McLuhan,* The Medium Is the Message *(New York: Random House, 1967).*

11. *See, for example, Kurt Lewin, "Psychology of Success and Failure," in T. Costello and S. Zalkind, eds.* Psychology in Administration *(Englewood Cliffs, N. J.: Prentice-Hall, 1963), 67–72.*

12. *Carl I. Hovland and Walter Weiss, "The Influence of Source Credibility on Communication Effectiveness,"* Public Opinion Quarterly, *15 (Winter 1951–52), 635–50.*

13. *Herbert C. Kelman and Carl I. Hovland, "Reinstatement of the Communication in Delayed Measurement of Opinion Change,* Journal of Abnormal and Social Psychology, *48 (1953), 327–35.*

14. *Carl I. Hovland, Arthur A. Lumsdaine, and Fred D. Sheffield,* Experiments on Mass Communication *(New York: John Wiley, 1949), 182–200.*

15. *Charles Winick, "Three Measures of the Advertising Value of Media Context,"* Journal of Advertising Research, *2 (June 1962), 28–33.*

16. *David A. Aaker and Phillip K. Brown, "Evaluating Vehicle Source Effects,"* Journal of Advertising Research, *12 (August 1972), 11–16.*

17. *Hovland, Lumsdaine, and Sheffield,* Experiments on Mass Communication.

18. *Ibid.*

19. *Settle and Golden, "Attribution Theory."*

20. *William J. McGuire, "Inducing Resistance to Persuasion: Some Contemporary Approaches," in Leonard Berkowitz, ed.,* Advances in Experimental Social Psychology *(New York: Academic, 1964), I, 191–229; Peter L. Wright, "The Cognitive Processes Mediating Acceptance of Advertising,"* Journal of Marketing Research, *10 (February 1973), 53–62; Alan G. Sawyer, "The Effects of Repetition of Refutational and Supportive Advertising Appeals,"* Journal of Marketing Research, *10 (February 1973), 23–33; and George J. Szybillo and Richard Heslin, "Resistance to Persuasion: Inoculation Theory in a Marketing Concept,"* Journal of Marketing Research, *10 (November 1973), 396–403.*

21. *Kanti V. Prasad, "Communications Effectiveness of Comparative Advertising: A Laboratory Analysis,"* Journal of Marketing Research, *13 (May 1976), 128–37.*

22. *William L. Wilkie and Paul W. Farris, "Comparison Advertising: Problems and Potential,"* Journal of Marketing, *39 (November 1975), 7–15.*

23. *Prasad, "Communications Effectiveness."*

24. *For basic readings in this area, see Carl I. Hovland, ed.,* The Order of Presentation in Persuasion *(New Haven, Conn.: Yale University Press, 1957).*

25. *Frederick 'E. Webster, Jr.,* Marketing Communication *(New York: Ronald Press, 1971).*

26. *Ibid.*

27. *Scott M. Cutlip and Allen H. Center,* Effective Public Relations, *4th ed. (Englewood Cliffs, N.J.: Prentice-Hall, 1971), 151.*

28. *Donald F. Cox, "Clues for Advertising Strategists: Part I,"* Harvard Business Review, *September–October 1961, 160–76.*

29. *Irving L. Janis and Seymour Feshbach, "Effects of Fear-Arousing Communications,"* Journal of Abnormal and Social Psychology, *48 (January 1953), 78–92.*

30. *John R. Stuteville, "Psychic Defenses against High Fear Appeals: A Key Marketing Variable,"* Journal of Marketing, *34 (April 1970), 39–45.*

31. *Brian Sternthal and C. Samuel Craig, "Fear Appeals: Revisited and Revised,"* Journal of Consumer Research, *1 (December 1974), 22–34; and James C. McCrosky and David W. Wright, "A Comparison of the Effects of Punishment Oriented and Reward Oriented Messages in Persuasive Communication,"* Journal of Communication, *21 (March 1971), 83–93.*

32. *Gerald R. Miller and M. A. Hewgill, "Some Recent Research on Fear Arousing Message Appeals,"* Speech Monographs, *33 (1966), 377–91.*

33. *Michael Ray and William Wilkie, "Fear: The Potential of an Appeal Neglected by Marketing,"* Journal of Marketing, *34 (January 1970), 54–62.*

34. *Brian Sternthal and C. Samuel Craig, "Humor in Advertising,"* Journal of Marketing, *37 (October 1973), 12–18.*

35. *For a critical review of the "sleeper effect," see Noel Capon and James Hulbert, "The Sleeper Effect—An Awakening,"* Public Opinion Quarterly, *37 (Fall 1973), 322–58.*

Discussion questions

1. List and discuss the effects of psychological barriers on the communication process. How can a marketer overcome the communications barrier known as "noise"?

2. How may a consumer use an informal communications situation to reduce his post-purchase dissonance?

3. Select two advertisements with different advertising messages: one supportive and the other refutational. Explain why you believe each marketer chose to use his specific message strategy.

4. List and discuss the factors that influence the credibility of impersonal sources of product information.

5. Explain the differences between feedback from interpersonal messages and feedback from impersonal message sources. How does the marketer obtain and use each kind of feedback?

6. You are the marketing manager for a headache remedy. Your advertising agency has just presented two different promotional strategies, one using a humorous approach and one taking an "agony" approach. Which approach would you suggest they adopt? Why?

7. Why are publicity stories often more effective than advertisements for the same product?

8. What are the advantages and disadvantages of (a) interpersonal communication and (b) impersonal communication for the marketing of consumer products?

9. For what kind of audiences would you consider using comparative advertising? Why?

SOCIAL AND CULTURAL DIMENSIONS OF CONSUMER BEHAVIOR

III

The six chapters that follow are designed to provide the reader with a detailed picture of the social and cultural dimensions of consumer behavior. The objectives of Part III are (1) to explain how social and cultural concepts affect the attitudes and behavior of individuals, and (2) to show how these concepts can be employed by a marketing practitioner to achieve his organizational objectives.

group dynamics and consumer reference groups

8

With the exception of those very few people who can be classified as hermits, people tend to be involved with others on a rather constant basis. Like almost all behavior, an individual's social involvement is often motivated by the expectation that it will help in the satisfaction of specific needs. For example, a person might join a local political club to satisfy his need for community recognition. Another person might join a singles group in an effort to find compatible friends to satisfy his social needs. A third person might join a food cooperative to obtain the benefits of group buying power. These are just a few of the almost infinite number of reasons why people involve themselves with others.

This chapter discusses the basic concepts of social involvement and group dynamics. It gives particular emphasis to the role that reference groups play in both directly and indirectly influencing consumer behavior. The five chapters that follow discuss other social and societal groupings that influence consumer buying processes: the family, informal opinion leaders, socioeconomic classes, culture and subculture.

WHAT IS A GROUP?

A group may be defined as *two or more people who interact to accomplish either individual or mutual goals*. Within the broad scope of this

Every man with an idea has at least two or three followers.

BROOKS ATKINSON: *"January 2," Once Around the Sun* (1951)

203

definition are both an intimate "group" of two neighbors who informally decide to shop together for groceries, and a larger, more formal, group, such as a Parents Association, whose members are mutually concerned with the quality of education their children receive. Included in this definition, too, are more remote, one-sided, social involvements where an individual consumer looks to others for direction as to which products or services to buy, even though such others are largely unaware that they are serving as consumption models.

TYPES OF GROUPS

To simplify our discussion, we will consider four different types of group classification: (1) primary versus secondary groups, (2) formal versus informal groups, (3) large versus small groups, and (4) membership versus symbolic groups.

primary versus secondary groups

If a person interacts on a regular basis with other individuals (i.e., with members of his family, with neighbors, or with co-workers whose opinions he values), then these individuals can be considered a *primary* group for him. On the other hand, if a person interacts only occasionally with such others, or does not consider their opinions to be important, then these others constitute a *secondary* group for him. From this definition, it can be seen that the critical distinctions between primary and secondary groups are (1) the importance of the groups to the individual and (2) the frequency or consistency with which he interacts with them.

formal versus informal groups

Another useful way to classify groups is by the extent of their formality; that is, the extent to which the group structure, the members' roles, and the group's purpose are clearly defined. If a group has a highly defined structure (e.g., a formal membership list), specific roles and authority levels (e.g., a president, treasurer, and secretary), and specific goals (e.g., to support a political candidate, improve their children's education, or increase the knowledge or skills of members), then it would be classified as a *formal group*. On the other hand, if a group is more loosely defined—if it consists of several poker-playing cronies or three married couples who see each other frequently—then it is considered an *informal* group. The League of Women Voters, with elected officers and members who meet regularly to discuss topics of civic interest, would be classified as a formal group, while a group of friends who meet regularly for coffee and general conversation would be considered an informal group.

From the standpoint of consumer behavior, informal social or friendship groups are generally more important to the marketer, since their less clearly defined structures provide a more conducive environment for the exhange of information and influence about consumption-related topics.

large versus small groups

It is often desirable to distinguish between groups in terms of their size or complexity. However, it is difficult to offer a precise breaking point as to when a group is considered large or small. A *large* group might be thought of as one in which a single member is not likely to know more than a few of the group's members personally or be fully aware of the specific roles or activities of more than a limited number of other group members. Examples of large groups include such complex organizations as the American Telephone and Telegraph Company, with its numerous subordinate companies, or the Democratic party, with its many local clubs scattered throughout the nation.

In contrast, members of a *small* group are likely to know every member personally and to be aware of every member's specific role or activities in the group. For example, each member of a local college sorority is likely to know all the other members and be aware of their duties and interests within the group.

In the realm of consumer behavior, we are principally concerned with the study of small groups, since such groups are more likely to influence the consumption behavior of group members.

membership versus symbolic groups

Another useful way to classify groups is by membership versus symbolic groups. A *membership* group is a group to which a person either belongs or would qualify for membership. For example, the group of women with whom a young housewife bowls weekly or with whom she hopes to bowl when a team opening occurs would be considered, for her, a membership group.

In contrast, any group in which an individual is not likely to receive membership, despite his acting as if he were a member by adopting the group's values, attitudes, and behavior, is considered a *symbolic* group. For example, professional tennis players may constitute a symbolic group for an amateur tennis buff who identifies with certain players by imitating their behavior whenever possible (e.g., in the purchase of a specific brand of tennis racket or balls); however, the amateur does not and probably never will qualify for membership as a professional tennis player because he lacks the skill or opportunity to compete professionally. Both membership groups and symbolic groups influence consumer behavior; however, membership groups offer a more direct, and thus a more compelling, influence.

In summary, we can say that small, informal, primary membership groups are of greatest interest to the marketing manager, because they exert the greatest potential influence on consumer purchase decisions.

THE VOCABULARY OF GROUP DYNAMICS

To more fully comprehend the influence of groups on a consumer's behavior, we will now briefly examine a number of closely related behavioral concepts.

roles

A *role* is a pattern of behavior expected of an individual in a specific social position.[1] In analyzing roles, it is helpful to think in terms of ascribed roles and achieved roles.[2] *Ascribed* roles are those that are expected of an individual because of factors over which he has no control (birth, age, sex, family, race, or religion). For example, a teenage girl may be faced with two ascribed but opposing roles in terms of the clothing she wears: the implicit dress code of her teenage friends (a role ascribed by her age) and her parents' more conservative dress code (a role ascribed by her position as a family member or by her family's social position). Which of the two roles she adopts depends on which group influence is stronger.

Achieved roles are those roles that a person adopts as the result of personal attainment and growth (the level of education he has achieved, his income, his occupational status, or his marital status). For example, a salesman might have to choose between two competing achieved roles when selling to his brother-in-law: his role of salesman, with its implicit goal of maximizing the sale in order to maximize his commission, and his role as in-law; to give the best value for the lowest cost to his wife's brother. In this instance, his choice of role may be decided on the basis of which drive is stronger: his need for money (or his sales manager's esteem), or his need for family recognition, or love, or approval.

status

Status refers to the relative prestige accorded to an individual or the position he occupies within a specified group or social system. Status is frequently measured in terms of the degree of *influence* the individual exerts on the attitudes and behavior of others.[3] For example, a banker, by virtue of his profession, may be accorded a great deal of respect in his community and may influence the purchase decisions of many others either directly (e.g., through investment advice he gives) or indirectly (e.g., through the example he sets by driving a specific make of car). Conversely, a low-status person is one who has little or no influence on the attitudes and behavior of others. In the context of consumer behavior, factors that are likely to determine the amount of influence (i.e., status) that a person has over the purchase behavior of others include his general and product-specific knowledge, his experience, his interests, and his self-confidence. (These factors are discussed in greater detail in Chapter 10.)

group norms

The *norms* of a group can be thought of as the implicit rules of conduct or standards of behavior that are expected of its members. The degree to which a group member conforms to the group's norms determines both his acceptance and his relative status within the group.

Norms operate in a rather complex way. For example, a mother's involvement in the local Parents Association may influence the number and type of television programs she will allow her children to view, but it may have little influence on her choice of personal clothing. This is because the norms of the PTA to which she belongs may be more concerned with the upbringing of children than with the personal dress of members. In some communities, however, the PTA may play as strong a role in terms of dress and other social norms as it does in child rearing.

group cohesiveness

Group cohesiveness refers to the degree to which group members feel impelled to "stick together" and to follow the norms of the group. In a sense, it represents the attractiveness of the group to its members and the value they place on their interrelationships. A group is judged to be highly cohesive if all or most of its members perceive themselves to be members of the group, desire to continue their membership in the group, and regard the group as more attractive to belong to than other groups.[4] The more cohesive a group, the more effectively it can influence the attitudes and purchasing behavior of its members.

conformity

Conformity implies that members of a group have adopted attitudes and behavior that are consistent with the group's norms. In the context of consumer behavior, group conformity is measured by the percentage of group members who *knowingly* use the same brand or product. Group members who unknowingly or coincidentally use the same brand cannot be said to conform.

The lower a member's status within the group, the greater the pressure (both external and internal) for him to conform. Conversely, the higher a member's status within the group, the greater the freedom he has to deviate from group norms without fear of ostracism. Thus, high-status members are in a better position to innovate (i.e., to try a new product or service that is not consistent with group norms).

Even in situations of considerable conformity to group norms, there is usually some latitude for independence. One consumer researcher made the following observation:

> *Few individuals would care to be complete conformists in their consumption patterns. In many buying situations, an acceptable range of alternatives is avail-*

able within a given norm. We all know of cases where individuals conformed to the group norm by buying a product, but each individual purchased a different color, brand, etc., thus maintaining a feeling of independence.[5]

deviance

When a group member's behavior does not conform to the norms of the group, his behavior is considered "deviant." Groups usually attempt to curtail such behavior by pressuring deviant members to "fall into line." In some classrooms across the nation, excessive study may be considered deviant behavior, and the unfortunate practitioners of such behavior are "punished" by ridicule or outright ostracism.

Consumer-relevant groups

As the preceding discussion indicates, groups play an important role in influencing the consumption behavior of their members. To more fully comprehend the kind of impact that specific groups have on individuals, we will examine six basic consumer-relevant groups: (1) the family, (2) friendship groups, (3) formal social groups, (4) shopping groups, (5) consumer action groups, and (6) work groups.

THE FAMILY

An individual's family is often in the best position to influence his consumer decisions. The family's importance in this regard is based upon the frequency of contact that the individual has with other family members and the extent of influence that the family has had on the establishment of a wide range of values, attitudes, and behavior. (Chapter 9 examines the influence of the family on consumption behavior.)

FRIENDSHIP GROUPS

Friendship groups are typically classified as informal groups because they are usually unstructured and lack specific authority levels. In terms of relative influence, after an individual's family, it is his friends who are most likely to influence his purchase decisions.

Seeking and maintaining friendships is a basic drive of most people. Friends fulfill a wide range of needs for the individual: they provide companionship, security, and opportunities to discuss problems that one may be reluctant to discuss with members of one's own family. Friendships are also a sign of maturity and independence, for they represent a breaking away from one's family and the forming of social ties with the outside world.

Chapter 10 discusses the importance of friendship groups on the consumer decision process.

FORMAL SOCIAL GROUPS

In contrast to the relative intimacy of friendship groups, formal social groups are more remote and serve a different function for the individual. A person joins a formal social group to fulfill such specific goals as making new friends, meeting "important" people, broadening his perspectives, pursuing a special interest, or promoting a specific cause. Because members of a formal social group often consume certain products together, such groups are of interest to marketers. For example, the membership list of a ski club would be of explicit interest to tour operators, travel agents, resort hotel managers, and sporting goods retailers. The membership list of a woman's club would be of interest to beauty salon managers, clothing and home furnishings retailers, and special-interest publications.

Membership in a formal social group may influence a consumer's behavior in several ways. For example, members of such groups have frequent opportunity to informally discuss products, services, or shops. Some members may copy the consumption behavior of other members whom they admire.

Because Americans are active in so many different kinds of formal social groups, this country has been called a "nation of joiners." A major research study that examined membership in formal social organizations (e.g., veterans, civic, political, fraternal, church, economic, cultural, and social associations) found that active formal social group participants tended to be married, were better educated, earned higher incomes, and had higher-status occupations than inactive members or nonmembers.[6] Such information can be helpful to marketing managers concerned with segmenting their markets for new or existing products.

SHOPPING GROUPS

Two or more people who shop together—whether for food, for clothing, or simply to pass the time—can be called a "shopping group." Such groups are often offshoots of family or friendship groups. People like to shop with others who are pleasant company or who they feel have more experience with or knowledge about a desired product or service. Shopping with others also provides an element of social fun to an often boring but necessary task. In addition, it reduces the risk that a purchase decision will be unwise or socially unacceptable. In instances where none of the members have knowledge about the product being sought, a shopping group may form for defensive reasons; members may feel more confident with a collective decision.

Very few marketing or consumer behavior studies have examined the nature of shopping groups. However, one study of the in-store behavior of shoppers revealed some differences between group and individual shopping.[7] As Table 8–1 indicates, shopping parties of at least three persons deviated more from their original purchase plans (they bought either more or less than originally planned) than did either sin-

TABLE 8–1

A Comparison of Planned vs. Actual Purchases by Size of Shopping Group

	Size of the shopping group		
PURCHASES	One	Two	Three or more
No item planned or purchased	3.7%	2.9%	0.0%
Fewer purchases than planned	15.1	12.4	31.3
Purchases as planned	58.9	41.0	26.6
More purchases than planned	22.3	43.7	42.1
Total	100.0%	100.0%	100.0%

Adapted from Donald H. Granbois, "Improving the Study of Customer In-Store Behavior," Journal of Marketing, 32 (October 1968), 30.

gle shoppers or two-party groups. Furthermore, two or more people shopping together were almost twice as likely to buy more than planned than if they had shopped alone. The study also found that shopping groups tended to cover more territory in the store than individuals shopping alone, and thus they had more opportunity to see and examine merchandise and to make unplanned purchases.

A special type of shopping group is the in-home shopping group, which consists of a group of women who gather together in the home of a friend to attend a "party" devoted to the marketing of a specific line of products. The in-home party approach provides the marketer with an opportunity to demonstrate the features of his products simultaneously to a group of potential customers. Two related advantages are (1) some of the guests may feel obliged to buy because they are guests in the home of the sponsoring hostess, and (2) early purchasers tend to create a bandwagon effect in that undecided guests often overcome a reluctance to buy when they see their friends make positive purchase decisions.

CONSUMER ACTION GROUPS

A new kind of consumer group has emerged in recent years in response to the surging consumerist movement. This type of consumer group has become increasingly visible since the 1960s and has been able to influence product design and marketing practices of both manufacturers and retailers.

Consumer action groups can be divided into two broad categories: those that organize to correct a specific consumer abuse and then disband, and those that organize to address broader, more pervasive, problem areas and operate over an extended or indefinite period of time. A group of tenants who band together to dramatize their dissatisfaction with the quality of service provided by their landlord, or a group of irate community members who unite to block the entrance of a fast-food outlet into their middle-class neighborhood, are examples of temporary, cause-specific consumer action groups. An example of a more enduring consumer action group is Action for Children's Television (A.C.T.), which was organized in the 1960s by a group of Boston housewives who were distressed by the quality of children's television programs. Today, A.C.T. is involved in a wide range of related problem areas, including the content and timing of commercials concerned with toys, breakfast cereals, and other product categories directed primarily at children.

The overriding objective of many consumer interest groups is to bring sufficient pressure to bear on selected members of the business community to make them correct perceived consumer abuses. Through their collective action, a number of consumer interest groups have influenced the actions of the business community to a degree not possible by an individual consumer acting on his own behalf.

WORK GROUPS

The sheer amount of time that people spend at their jobs—frequently more than thirty-five hours per week—provides ample opportunity for work groups to serve as a major influence on the consumption behavior of members.

Both the formal work group and the informal friendship/work group have the potential for influencing consumer behavior. The formal work group consists of those individuals who work together as a team. Their direct and sustained work relationship offers substantial opportunity for one or more members to influence the consumer-related attitudes and activities of other team members. Informal friendship/work groups consist of people who have become friends as a result of working for the same firm, regardless of whether or not they work together as a team. Members of informal work groups may influence the consumption behavior of other members during coffee or lunch breaks or after-hours meetings.

While there is much intuitive appeal in the proposition that work groups are important sources of consumer information and influence, there is no empirical evidence to either support or reject this belief. However, it is likely that before long consumer researchers will turn their attention to examining the impact of the work group on consumption behavior.

Reference groups

Reference groups are groups that serve as a frame of reference for individuals in their purchase decisions. This basic concept provides a valuable perspective for understanding the impact of other people on an individual's consumption beliefs, attitudes and behavior. It also provides some insight into methods that can be used to effect desired changes in consumer behavior.

WHAT IS A REFERENCE GROUP?

A reference group is *any person or group that serves as a point of comparison (or reference) for an individual in the formation of either general or specific values, attitudes, or behavior.* The usefulness of this concept is enhanced by the fact that it does not place any restrictions on group size or membership, nor does it require that consumers identify with a tangible group (i.e., the group can be symbolic: prosperous businessmen, rock stars, or sport heroes).[8]

Reference groups that influence general values or behavior are called *normative* reference groups. An example of a child's normative reference group is his immediate family, which is likely to play an important role in molding his general consumer values and behavior (e.g., which foods to select for good nutrition, appropriate ways to dress for specific occasions, how and where to shop, and what constitutes "good" values for his money).

Reference groups that serve as benchmarks for specific or narrowly defined attitudes or behavior are called *comparative* reference groups. A comparative reference group might be a neighboring family whose life-style appears to be both admirable and worthy of imitation (the way they maintain their home, their choice of home furnishings and cars, the number and types of vacations they take).

Both normative and comparative reference groups are important. Normative reference groups can influence the development of a basic code of behavior; comparative reference groups can influence the expression of specific consumer attitudes and behavior. It is likely that the specific influences of comparative reference groups are to some measure dependent upon the basic values and behavior patterns established early in a person's development by normative reference groups.

broadening the reference group concept

Like many other concepts borrowed from the behavioral sciences, the meaning of "reference group" has changed over the years. As originally employed, reference groups were narrowly defined to include only those groups with which a person interacted on a direct basis (e.g., his family and close friends). However, the concept has gradually broadened to include both direct and indirect individual or group influences.

FIGURE 8–1

Major Consumer Reference Groups

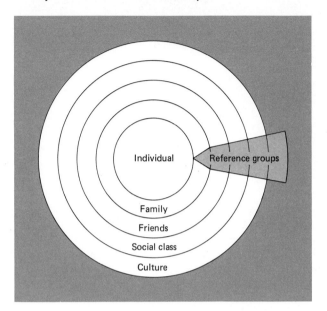

Indirect reference groups consist of those individuals or groups with whom a person does *not* have direct face-to-face contact, such as movie stars, sports heroes, political leaders, or TV personalities.

Referents that a person might use in evaluating his own general or specific attitudes or behavior vary from an individual to a small group of people, from his immediate family to a broader kinship, from a voluntary association to a social class, a profession, an ethnic group, a community, or even a nation.[9] As Figure 8–1 indicates, the major societal groupings that influence an individual's consumer behavior are, in order: his family, his friends, his social class, and his culture. (These important consumer reference groups are discussed more fully in Chapters 9, 10, 11, 12, and 13.)

types of reference groups

Reference groups can be classified in terms of a person's membership or degree of involvement with the group and in terms of the positive or negative influences they have on his values, attitudes, and behavior. Table 8–2 depicts four types of reference groups that emerge from a cross-classification of these factors: (1) contactual groups, (2) aspirational groups, (3) disclaimant groups, and (4) avoidance groups.

A contactual group is a group in which a person holds membership or with which he has regular face-to-face contact and of whose values,

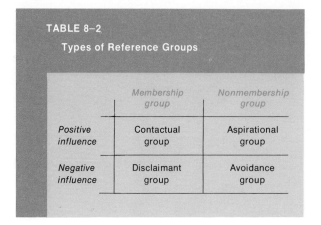

TABLE 8-2

Types of Reference Groups

	Membership group	Nonmembership group
Positive influence	Contactual group	Aspirational group
Negative influence	Disclaimant group	Avoidance group

attitudes, and standards he approves. Thus a contactual group has a positive influence on an individual's attitudes or behavior.

An aspirational group is a group in which a person does not hold membership or with which he does not have face-to-face contact, but of which he would like to be a member. Thus it serves as a positive influence on his attitudes or behavior.

A disclaimant group is a group in which a person holds membership or with which he has face-to-face contact, but of whose values, attitudes, and behavior he disapproves. Thus he intends to adopt attitudes and behavior that are in opposition to the norms of the group.

An avoidance group is a group in which a person does not hold membership or with which he does not have face-to-face contact and of whose values, attitudes, and behavior he disapproves. Thus he tends to adopt attitudes and behavior that are in opposition to those of the group.

FACTORS THAT AFFECT REFERENCE GROUP INFLUENCE

The degree of influence that a reference group exerts on an individual's behavior usually depends on the nature of the individual and on specific social or product factors. This section discusses how and why some of these factors operate to influence consumer behavior.

information and experience

If an individual has firsthand experience with a product or service, or can easily obtain full information about it, he is less likely to be influenced by the advice or example of others. On the other hand, if a person has little or no firsthand experience with a product or service, or if he does not expect to have access to objective information about it (i.e., he believes that relevant advertising may be misleading or deceptive), he is more likely to seek out the advice or example of others. Research on imitative behavior provides some interesting insights on how insufficient experience or information concerning a product makes consumers more susceptible to the influence—either positive or negative—of others.[10]

For example, if a college junior wants to impress his new girlfriend, he may take her to a restaurant that he knows from experience to be good or to one that has been highly recommended by the local newspaper's "Dining-Out Guide." If he has neither personal experience nor information that he regards as valid, he may seek the advice of friends, or imitate the behavior of others by taking her to a restaurant that he knows is frequented by seniors whom he admires.

group discussion and perceived risk

Group discussion is likely to influence the individual's and the group's willingness to accept risk in purchase decisions. A study of ten groups of housewives found that subjects were more willing to accept greater risk in a purchase decision during and after a group discussion than they were initially willing as individuals.[11] These findings are consistent with what researchers have called the "risky shift" phenomenon, the tendency for individuals and groups to accept *greater* risk after group discussion.[12]

However, a more detailed analysis, which examined each product purchase situation individually, suggested that for one high-risk product, the group discussion led to a *reduced* willingness to accept risk—i.e., a conservative shift.[13] This second analysis suggests that willingness to accept risk with group discussion depends to some extent on the product category and its inherent level of risk.

This finding is supported by a study conducted among female college students, in which three categories of products judged by prior research to be "low-risk products," "medium-risk products," and "high-risk products," were examined within the context of making a choice between an available but unknown brand and a hard-to-obtain but familiar brand.[14] The findings indicated a greater willingness to accept more risk for low-risk products (facial tissues and chewing gum) after group discussion, no meaningful shift in willingness to accept risk for medium-risk products (suntan lotion and eye shadow) after group discussion, and a movement to accept less risk after group discussion for products judged to be high in perceived risk (deodorants and cold remedies).

On the basis of these and similar studies, it would seem that a product's characteristics (its inherent perceived risk level) influence the direction of perceived risk produced by group discussion. For the marketer of a high-risk product, the results suggest that his advertising must provide sufficiently persuasive information to reduce perceived risk. Otherwise, any group discussion that may naturally occur is likely to persuade consumers *not* to buy the product.

conspicuousness of the product

The potential influence of a reference group varies according to how visually or verbally conspicuous a product is to others. A visually conspicuous product is one that can be seen and identified by others, and that will stand out and be noticed (e.g., a luxury item or novelty product). Even if a product is not visually conspicuous, it may be verbally conspicuous — it may be highly interesting or it may be easily described to others. Products that are both readily observable and easy to discuss with others (a new clothing fashion, a new house, a new automobile) are most likely to be purchased with some consideration given to the reaction of relevant others. Products that are less conspicuous (toothpaste, talcum powder) are less likely to be purchased with a reference group in mind.

credibility, attractiveness, and power of the reference group

A reference group which is perceived as credible, attractive or powerful can induce consumer attitude and behavior change. For example, when a consumer is concerned with obtaining accurate information about the performance or quality of a product or service, she is likely to be persuaded by those whom she considers to be trustworthy and knowledgeable. That is, she is more likely to be persuaded by sources with high credibility, as indicated in Chapter 7. When the consumer is primarily concerned with the acceptance or approval of others whom she likes, with whom she identifies, or who offer her status or other benefits, she is likely to adopt their product, brand, or other behavioral characteristics.

When a consumer is primarily concerned with the power that a person or group can exert over him, he might select products or services that conform to the norms of that person or group in order to avoid ridicule or punishment. However, unlike other reference groups which the consumer follows either because they are credible or because they are attractive, power groups are not likely to cause attitude change. The individual may conform to the behavior of a powerful person or group, but may not experience a change in his own attitudes.

Different reference groups may influence the beliefs, attitudes and behavior of an individual at different points in time or under different circumstances. For example, the dress habits of a young secretary may vary, depending on her place and role. She may conform to the dress code of her office when at work by wearing tailored clothing, and may drastically alter her mode of dress after work by wearing more conspicuous, revealing styles.

reference group impact on product and brand choice

In some cases, and for some products, reference groups may influence both a person's product category and brand (or type) choices. Such products are called "product-plus, brand-plus" items. In other cases, reference groups influence only the product category decision. Such products are called "product-plus, brand-minus" items. In still other cases, reference groups influence the brand (or type) decision. These products are called "product-minus, brand-plus" items. Finally, in some cases, reference groups influence neither the product category nor the brand decision, and these products are called "product-minus, brand-minus" items.[15] Table 8–3 classifies a variety of products in terms of reference group influence on product category and brand choices.

TABLE 8–3

Reference Group Influence on Product and Brand Choices

	Reference group influence on <u>product</u> *category*	
	Weak (−)	*Strong (+)*
Strong (+)	**Cell 1** clothing furniture magazines refrigerator (type) toilet soap	**Cell 2** automobiles cigarettes* beer (premium vs. regular)* drugs
Weak (−)	**Cell 3** canned peaches laundry soap refrigerator radios	**Cell 4** air conditioners* instant coffee* television sets

Reference group influence on <u>brand</u> *or* <u>type</u>

The classification of all starred products is based on actual experimental evidence. Other products in this table are classified speculatively on the basis of generalizations derived from the judgment of seminar participants.

Source: Bureau of Applied Social Research, Columbia University. Reprinted by permission.

REFERENCE GROUPS AND CONSUMER CONFORMITY

Marketers are particularly interested in the ability of reference groups to change consumer attitudes and behavior (i.e., to encourage conformity). To be capable of such influence, a reference group must:

1. Inform or make the individual aware of a specific product or brand;
2. Provide the individual with the opportunity to compare his own thinking with the attitudes and behavior of the group;
3. Influence the individual to adopt attitudes and behavior that are consistent with the norms of the group;
4. Legitimize an individual's decision to use the same products as the group.

The ability of reference groups to influence consumer conformity is demonstrated by the results of a classic experiment that was designed to compare the effects of lectures versus group discussions on family food consumption habits.[16] The purpose of this study was to find the most effective method for inducing housewives to serve such culturally undesirable cuts of meat as beef hearts, sweetbreads, and kidneys to their families during World War II. Findings indicated that group discussions were far more effective in inducing conformity than lectures in which group opinions were not aired (32 percent versus 3 percent).

A number of recent consumer research studies have also examined the impact of reference group influence on consumer conformity. For example, a study of male college students' responses to group pressure provides some insights on consumer conformity.[17] Three men's suits — labeled, respectively, *A, B, and C* — were described to groups of students as being of different quality and manufacture, though they were actually of identical quality and color and manufactured by the same firm. The experiment compared the evaluations of *control groups* (in which naive subjects selected a preferred suit in private) with the evaluations of *conformity groups* (in which naive subjects made their evaluations and choices publicly after three cooperating confederates in each group all chose the same suit). The results of the experiment indicated that the naive subjects in each of the conformity groups tended to conform to the product choices of the cooperating confederates, while the naive members of the control groups, who made their choices in private, made random choices. The marketing implication of this study is that, in the absence of objective quality standards, individual consumers tend to conform to group norms; that is, to the choices of the majority.

In another consumer study, ten informal friendship groups, each consisting of four or five housewives, were visited individually in their homes twice a week for eight weeks, and at each visit were requested to select one of four "brands" of bread.[18] Unknown to the subjects, all four brands (labelled *H, L, M,* and *P*) were identical loaves coming from the same bakery. Findings revealed that the more cohesive (close-knit) the group, the greater the likelihood that group members would select the same brand as their informal group leader. Furthermore, the greater the group leader's brand loyalty, the greater the likelihood that the other group members would be loyal to the same brand. These findings suggest that informal friendship groups positively influence member conformity.

A study of male college friendship groups offers some additional evidence on the relationship between group cohesiveness and brand choice conformity.[19] In this study, four low-cost consumer packaged goods (beer, after-shave lotion, deodorant, and cigarettes) were studied in an attempt to ascertain whether the purchase of different brands among various product categories depends on group influence. The results of the study indicated that for two of the products—beer and after-shave lotion—the more cohesive the group, the greater the brand choice conformity. No significant relationship between the extent of group cohesiveness and brand choice conformity was found in the initial analysis for either deodorants or cigarettes. However, when the share of market for each brand was accounted for, a significant relationship was found between group cohesiveness and brand choice conformity in the case of cigarettes, but not deodorants.[20] It is significant to note that for the three products where conformity was found to influence purchase choice (beer, after- shave lotion, cigarettes), the product categories tended to be more socially conspicuous than for the fourth category—deodorants. This study supports the proposition that consumer conformity is likely to vary, depending on the product category.

The research evidence reviewed underscores the fact that a consumer's selection of a product category, brand, style, or type of product is frequently influenced by the advice and information he obtains from others. We will complete our examination of the influence of reference groups by focusing on the applications of this concept to a firm's promotional policies.

Promotional applications of the reference group concept

Reference group appeals are used very effectively by some advertisers to segment their markets. Group situations or people with which a segment of the audience can identify are used to promote goods and services by subtly inducing the prospective consumer to identify with the illustrated user of the product. This identification may be based on admiration (e.g., of an athlete), on aspiration (e.g., of a celebrity or of a way of life), on empathy (e. g., with a person or situation), or on recognition (e.g., of a person—real or stereotypical—or of a situation). In some cases, the prospective consumer thinks, "If she uses it, it must be good. If I use it, I'll be like her." In other cases, the prospective consumer says to himself, "He's got problems I've got. What worked for him will work for me."

There are three types of reference group appeals in common marketing usage: (1) celebrities, (2) experts, and (3) the "common man." These appeals are often operationalized in the guise of testimonials or endorsements. In the case of the "common man," they may be presented as "slice of life" commercials (see Chapter 7).

CELEBRITIES

Celebrities, particularly movie stars, television personalities, and sports heroes, are a very popular type of reference group appeal. To their loyal followers and to much of the general public, celebrities represent an idealization of life which most people would like to live themselves. Advertisers spend enormous sums of money to have celebrities promote their products in the expectation that the reading or viewing audience will react positively to the celebrity's association with their product.

how celebrities are used

A firm that decides to employ a celebrity to promote its product has a choice of using the celebrity to give a testimonial, to give an endorsement, as an actor in a commercial, or as a company spokesman. These promotional roles differ as follows:[21]

1. *Testimonial* — If the celebrity has personally used the product or service and is in a position to attest to its quality, he may be asked to give a testimonial. An example would be a testimonial for a specific brand of golf ball given by a golf pro such as Arnold Palmer.

2. *Endorsement* — A celebrity who may or may not be an expert with regard to a product or service may be asked to lend his name and physical person to an advertisement for the product or service. Joe Namath's endorsement of panty hose is an example of an endorsement.

3. *Actor* — A celebrity may be asked to dramatically present the product or service as part of a character enactment, rather than as a personal testimonial or endorsement. An example of a celebrity used in this way is Jonathan Winters, the comedian.

4. *Spokesman* — A celebrity who represents a brand or company over an extended period of time, often in print, on television, and in personal appearances, can be called a company spokesman. Eventually, his appearance becomes closely associated with the brand or company. Robert Morley is a spokesman for British Airways and is closely identified with most of its advertising.

Table 8–4 gives a number of examples of each of these somewhat distinct uses of the celebrity as reference group appeals.

the credibility of the celebrity

Of all the positive characteristics that a celebrity might contribute to a firm's advertising program (his fame, talent, charisma), his credibility with the consumer audience is the most important. By *credibility* we mean both the audience's perception of the celebrity's *expertise* (how much he knows about the product area) and his *trustworthiness* (how honest he is about what he knows about the product).[22]

The importance of credibility in celebrity endorsements and testimonials cannot be overstated. The consumer must feel that the endorser knows what he or she is talking about.

credibility of sports celebrities

A large-scale study of sports celebrities was in part designed to identify the extent of association between three presumed celebrity characteristics (familiarity, talent, and likeability) and the celebrity's credi-

TABLE 8–4

How Celebrities Are Used in Reference Group Appeals

Types of use	Celebrity	Brand or company
1. Testimonial	Billie Jean King	Aztec Suncreams
	Mark Spitz	Schick Electric Shaver
	Farrah Fawcett-Majors	Fabergé
	Danny Thomas	Norelco Coffeemakers
2. Endorsement	Ted Williams	Sear's sporting goods
	Dorothy Hamill	Clairol Short & Sassy Shampoo
	Yogi Berra	Jockey underwear
	Bill Cosby	Ford Motor Company
	Dennis Weaver	National Bank Americard
	George Burns	Teacher's Scotch
	John Wayne	Datril 500
3. Actor	Jonathan Winters	Hefty bags
	Eve Arden	Imperial margarine
	Cecily Tyson	Crown Zellerbach
	Arte Johnson	Monsieur Henri Wines
	Nancy Walker	Bounty Paper Towels
4. Spokesman	Joe DiMaggio	The Bowery
	Don Rickles	National Car Rental
	O. J. Simpson	Hertz

Adapted from James M. Kamen et al., "What a Spokesman Does for a Sponsor," Journal of Advertising Research, 15 (April 1975), 17.

bility (would an endorsement or testimonial by the celebrity be trusted by the relevant public?)[23] Respondents were asked to rank two hundred sports personalities in terms of their familarity, talent, and likeability. Of all these attributes, "likeability" was found to be most closely associated with the individual's credibility as a product endorser. Table 8–5 presents the rankings on each dimension for the first twenty-five personalities in terms of how well they were known. The table indicates that visibility is not highly associated with confidence in that person's endorsements. For example, Joe Namath may rank second in terms of public awareness, but he ranks 143 out of 200 in terms of likeability and 156 in terms of credibility as an endorser. The evidence tends to correct the common misconception that it is the athlete's fame that contributes to his credibility.

The study also reported that consumers ". . . are a lot more receptive to the celebrity testimonials of sports figures than movie stars."[24] The findings further indicate that it is important that a product have a natural connection with sports if the sports celebrity endorsement is to be

TABLE 8–5

Selected Items from a Consumers' Ranking of 200 Sports Personalities

	Familarity	Talent	Likeability	Credibility
Willie Mays	1	5	3	31
Joe Namath	2	124	143	156
Muhammad Ali	3	189	192	190
Mickey Mantle	4	8	11	2
Arnold Palmer	5	33	17	4
Howard Cosell	6	186	176	131
Yogi Berra	7	11	4	3
Joe DiMaggio	8	34	20	30
Sandy Koufax	9	4	10	5
Johnny Unitas	10	22	24	29
Joe Garagiola	11	159	32	11
Hank Aaron	12	17	18	28
Johnny Bench	13	16	2	7
Jack Nicklaus	14	37	33	16
Sugar Ray Robinson	15	30	52	67
O. J. Simpson	16	1	27	32
Joe Frazier	17	158	164	145
Wilt Chamberlain	18	167	173	150
Dizzy Dean	19	86	55	82
Lee Trevino	20	107	57	63
Curt Gowdy	21	147	88	76
Mark Spitz	22	111	181	179
Ted Williams	23	15	29	14
A. J. Foyt	24	78	67	41
Stan Musial	25	3	1	1

effective. Four product categories were found to lend themselves to sports celebrity endorsements: sporting goods, athlete's foot remedies, sportswear, and electric shavers. Four other product categories were found to be very poor candidates for sports celebrity tie-ins: pet foods, home furnishings, wine, and house paint.[25]

These findings support the notion that source credibility of a company spokesman is based on both reputation and expertise in the product category, as discussed in Chapter 7.

THE EXPERT

A second reference group appeal used by marketers is the expert—a person who, because of his occupation, special training, skill, or extensive experience, is in a unique position to help the prospective consumer evaluate the product or service that the advertisement promotes. For example, an RCA Color Television advertising campaign featured endorsements by TV color engineers. AC Delco used a sterotypical service mechanic (an expert on automotive needs) in an advertisement designed to tell the audience about the special qualities of a Delco product (Figure 8–2).

THE "COMMON MAN"

Another frequently used type of reference group appeal employs the testimonials of satisfied customers. The advantage of this "common man" appeal is that it demonstrates to the prospective customer that someone just like him, or someone he would like to be, uses and is satisfied with the product or service advertised.

An advertisement for Blue Cross–Blue Shield health insurance programs (see Figure 8–3) depicts six stereotypical subscribers each giving their specific reasons for satisfaction with their health insurance. For the potential subscriber, the advertisement presents various reasons for having such medical coverage. For those who are already covered, it reassures them that they made the correct health coverage choice.

An advertisement for Manufacturers Hanover, a large New York City-based commercial bank, pictures over fifty recent high school graduates wearing the T-shirts of the colleges and universities they will be attending in the fall (see Figure 8–4). It suggests to students and their parents that Manufacturers Hanover has made educational loans to students who are now attending such schools. The advertisement also includes a number of young people wearing shirts that are not clearly legible. This makes it possible for the reader to assume that his proposed college, though not clearly depicted, might also be there.

The two advertisements differ in their use of the "common man" reference group appeal. The health insurance advertisement stresses the specific views of a number of subscribers, which are a testimonial for the service. The education loan advertisement presents numerous individuals with no indication of their attitudes or opinions; here the reader is free to project his own needs and to draw his own conclusions.

Many television commercials depict widely prevalent problem situations and show how a typical family or person has solved the problem by using the advertised product. These commercials are known as "slice of life" commercials because they depict situations "out of real life" with which the viewer can identify. For example, one commercial may show teenage members of a family squabbling over which television program to watch; another may show the man of the house "stealing" a light bulb from one lamp to replace one needed in another lamp. If viewers

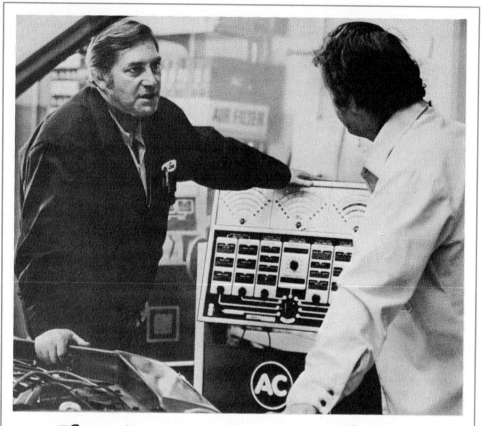

If you're getting poor mileage, perhaps your car needs a checkup.

If your gasoline mileage isn't what it used to be, AC-Delco suggests a diagnosis of your engine's vital signs from  your neighborhood AC-Delco serviceman.

If he prescribes a tune-up after the diagnosis, he'll probably recommend AC Fire-Ring Spark Plugs and Delco-Remy Points and Condenser as part of the remedy. There are matched AC-Delco parts engineered for your car and your kind of driving. That's important—especially with today's reduced speeds and shorter trips.

Keep an eye on your gasoline mileage. If it's poor, see your favorite AC-Delco serviceman for a checkup. Tune up with AC-Delco parts and help improve your car's performance and mileage.

AC-Delco
Division of General Motors Corporation

AC-DELCO DIVISION OF GENERAL MOTORS CORPORATION

FIGURE 8-3

Advertisement Employing "Common Man" Endorsement

"I had an accident at home last week and had to get into the hospital in a hurry. There was no delay, no red tape. All I said was, 'I Have Blue Cross and Blue Shield'."

"When you get sick 3,000 miles from home, there's one language everybody speaks. Blue Cross and Blue Shield."

"When you tell your employees you're giving them Blue Cross and Blue Shield, they know they're getting the best."

"Our family has used Blue Cross and Blue Shield so many times, I thought they'd cancel our membership. But they stick by you, no matter what."

"When you have Blue Cross and Blue Shield Family Membership, all your kids are covered at no extra cost. Even if you have a baseball team."

"Blue Cross and Blue Shield? You don't know what you've got until you use it."

More than 65 million Americans have Blue Cross and Blue Shield.
Maybe they know something you don't?

BLUE CROSS ® American Hospital Association ✚ **BLUE SHIELD** ® National Association of Blue Shield Plans

Courtesy of Eastern-Blue Cross and Blue Shield Plans.

225

FIGURE 8–4

Advertisement Portraying College Students in a "Common Man" Endorsement

Courtesy of Manufacturers Hanover Trust Co.

can identify with the situation, it is very likely that they will adopt the solution that worked for the family in the commercial.

In recent years, a number of advertisers have adopted the approach of "listening in" or showing a group interview in which, for example, young mothers are asked to discuss their laundry needs and evaluate the benefits of a new laundry soap. If the prospective consumer can identify with the laundry needs or other needs discussed by consumer-actors who are apparently just like her, it is likely that she will conform to the product wisdom expressed and buy the advertised product.

Still another "common man" approach is to use a model in an advertisement to represent the type of person the prospective consumer would like to be, or to represent a life-style to which the prospect may aspire. For example, the endorsement of an airline by an apparently prosperous and powerful businessman may induce a low- or middle-management executive to use that airline. The endorsement of a furniture polish by an attractive woman standing in the well-furnished living room of a beautiful home may influence an apartment dweller to buy the same polish.

BENEFITS OF THE REFERENCE GROUP APPEAL

Advertisers use celebrities, experts, and the "common man" to promote their products or services because they believe that such reference group appeals will give them a competitive advantage. Reference group appeals have two principal benefits for the advertiser: they increase brand awareness and they serve to reduce perceived risk.

increase brand awareness

The three types of reference group appeals described above provide the advertiser with the opportunity to gain and maintain the attention of prospective consumers with greater ease and effectiveness than is possible with many other types of promotional campaigns. This is particularly true of the celebrity form of reference group appeal, where the personality employed is generally well known to the relevant target segment. Celebrities tend to draw attention to the product through their own popularity. This gives the advertiser a competitive advantage in gaining the attention of the audience, particularly on television where there are so many brief and similar commercial announcements.

reduce perceived risk

The use of one or more reference group appeals may also serve to lower the consumer's perceived risk in purchasing a specific product. The example set by the endorser or testimonial-giver may demonstrate to the consumer that his uncertainty about the product purchase is unwarranted. Following are examples of how each type of reference group appeal serves to lower the consumer's perceived risk:

CELEBRITY. When consumers identify with a particular celebrity or consider the celebrity to be trustworthy, they often have the following reactions to the celebrity's endorsement or testimonial:

> "She wouldn't do a commercial for that product if she didn't believe it was really good."
> "An important person like him doesn't need the money, so he must be plugging the product because it really works."
> "If it's good enough for him, it's good enough for me."

EXPERT. When consumers are concerned about the technical aspects of a product, they are apt to be persuaded by the comments of an acknowledged or apparent expert and have the following reactions:

> "If he says it works, then it really must work."
> "If an expert uses the product, it must really be good."

COMMON MAN. When consumers are worried about how the product will affect them personally, they are apt to be positively influenced by a "common man" endorsement or testimonial and have the following reactions:

> "People just like me are using that new product."
> "If it can help her, it's just as likely to help me."
> "She has the same problem that I have; I wonder if that product will help me also?"

TABLE 8–6

Proposed Guidelines for Testimonials and Endorsements Issued by the Federal Trade Commission

1. An endorser who is represented as an expert must possess qualifications which in fact make him an expert.

2. An expert who endorses a product must employ his expertise in evaluating the product in a way which is relevant to the ordinary consumer.

3. When expert endorsement implies a comparison between the endorsed product and other products, such comparison must be undertaken by the endorser.

4. When an expert endorser claims that a product is at least equal or superior to other products, such claims must be as the result of his comparison.

5. Celebrity endorsers must use the product which they endorse and the endorsement must avoid distortions, reflecting only their honest views of the product.

6. If an endorsement or testimonial depicts an "actual consumer," it must use an actual consumer, or clearly disclose that an actor is being used.

7. If the actual consumer or actor used to endorse a product is being paid, the advertisement must clearly reveal that payment is being made.

8. Actual consumers (laymen endorsers) cannot be allowed to endorse any over-the-counter drug product.

Source: Federal Trade Commission, Guides Concerning Use of Endorsements and Testimonials in Advertising *(16 CFR, Part 255).*

GOVERNMENT GUIDELINES FOR THE USE OF TESTIMONIALS AND ENDORSEMENTS

Because reference group appeals have been used so successfully by some firms as part of their promotional strategy, they have recently come under the scrutiny of the Federal Trade Commission. The FTC has issued proposed guidelines for testimonial and endorsement advertising which have provoked a considerable amount of controversy among advertisers.[26] These guidelines are listed in Table 8–6. They are designed to protect consumers from the deceptive use of celebrities, experts, and the "common man" in advertising endorsements or testimonials. In fact, they serve to underscore the influence which reference groups have on consumer motivation.

Summary

Almost all individuals regularly interact with other people who directly or indirectly influence their purchase decisions. Thus the study of groups and their impact on the individual is of great importance to marketers concerned with influencing consumer behavior. Groups may be classified according to regularity of contact (primary or secondary groups), by their structure and hierarchy (formal or informal groups), by their size or complexity (large or small groups), and by membership or aspiration (membership or symbolic groups).

Six basic types of consumer-relevant groups influence the consumption behavior of individuals: family, friendship groups, formal social groups, shopping groups, consumer action groups, and work groups.

Reference groups are groups that serve as a frame of reference for individuals in their purchase decisions. Any or all of the groups listed above can serve as reference groups. Reference groups that influence general values in behavior are called *normative* reference groups; those that influence specific attitudes are called *comparative* reference groups. The concept of consumer reference groups has been broadened to include groups with which consumers have no direct face-to-face contact, such as celebrities, political figures, social classes, and cultures.

Reference groups which are classified in terms of a person's membership and the positive or negative influences they exert on him include: contactual groups, aspirational groups, disclaimant groups, and avoidance groups.

The credibility, attractiveness, and power of the reference group affect the degree of influence it has. In some cases, and for some products, reference groups may influence either the product category or brand choice purchase decisions, or both. Reference group appeals are used very effectively by some advertisers in promoting their goods and services because they subtly induce the prospective consumer to identify with the pictured user of the product.

The three types of reference groups most commonly used in marketing are celebrities, experts, and the "common man." *Celebrities* are used to give testimonials or endorsements, as actors, and as company spokesmen. *Experts* may be recognized experts in the product category or actors playing the part of experts (e.g., an automobile mechanic). The *common man* approach is designed to show that individuals "just like" the prospect are satisfied with the product advertised.

Reference group appeals are effective promotional strategies because they serve to increase brand awareness and reduce perceived risk among prospective consumers. Their usage may soon be regulated by the Federal Trade Commission, which is showing increased interest because of the apparent effectiveness with which such appeals influence the purchase decisions of consumers.

Endnotes

1. *Theodore Caplow,* Sociology, *2nd ed. (Englewood Cliffs, N.J.: Prentice-Hall, 1975), p. 14.*

2. *Ralph Linton,* The Cultural Background of Personality *(New York: Appleton-Century-Crofts, 1945).*

3. *Johan Arndt, "Role of Product-Related Conversations in the Diffusion of a New Product,"* Journal of Marketing Research, *4 (August 1967), 291–95; and Leon G. Schiffman, "Social Interaction Patterns of the Elderly Consumer," in Boris W. Becker and Helmut Becker, eds.* Combined Proceedings *(Chicago: American Marketing Association, 1972), 446.*

4. *Stanley E. Seashore,* Group Cohesiveness in the Industrial Work Group *(Ann Arbor: University of Michigan Press, 1954), 36–39.*

5. *M. Venkatesan, "Experimental Study of Consumer Behavior Conformity and Independence,"* Journal of Marketing Research, *3 (November 1966), 385.*

6. *Murray Hausknecht,* The Joiners *(New York: Bedminister Press, 1962).*

7. *Donald H. Granbois, "Improving the Study of Customer In-Store Behavior,"* Journal of Marketing, *32 (October 1968), 28–32.*

8. *T. Shibutani, "Reference Groups and Social Control," in Arnold Rose, ed.,* Human Behavior and Social Processes *(Boston: Houghton Mifflin, 1962), 132.*

9. *James E. Stafford, "Reference Theory as a Conceptual Framework for Consumer Decisions," in Robert L. King, ed.* Proceedings *(Chicago: American Marketing Association, 1968), 282.*

10. *Solomon E. Asch,* Social Psychology *(Englewood Cliffs, N.J.: Prentice-Hall, 1952).*

11. *Arch G. Woodside, "Informal Group Influence on Risk Taking,"* Journal of Marketing Research, *9 (May 1972), 223–25.*

12. *Dean G. Pruitt, "Conclusions: Towards an Understanding of Choice Shifts in Group Discussion,"* Journal of Personality and Social Psychology, *20 (August 1971), 495–510.*

13. *Arch G. Woodside, "Is There a Generalized Risky Shift Phenomenon in Consumer Behavior?"* Journal of Marketing Research, *11 (May 1974), 225–26.*

14. *Daniel L. Johnson and I. Robert Andrews, "Risky-Shift Phenomenon as Tested*

with Consumer Products as Stimuli," Journal of Personality and Social Psychology, 20 (August 1971), 328–85.

15. *Foundation for Research on Human Behavior,* Group Influence in Marketing and Public Relations *(Ann Arbor, Mich.: The Foundation, 1956), 8–9.*

16. *Kurt Lewin, "Group Decision and Social Change," in Theodore M. Newcomb and Eugene L. Hartley, eds.,* Readings in Social Psychology *(New York: Henry Holt, 1947), 330–44.*

17. *Venkatesan, "Experimental Study," 384–87.*

18. *James E. Stafford, "Effects of Group Influence on Consumer Brand Preferences,"* Journal of Marketing Research, 3 (February 1966), 68–75.

19. *Robert E. Witt, "Informal Social Group Influence on Consumer Brand Choice,"* Journal of Marketing Research, 6 (November 1969), 473–76.

20. *Robert E. Witt and Grady D. Bruce, "Purchase Decisions and Group Influence,"* Journal of Marketing Research, 7 (November 1970), 533–35.

21. *Joseph M. Kamen, Abdul C. Azhari, and Judith R. Kragh, "What a Spokesman Does for a Sponsor,"* Journal of Advertising Research, 15 (April 1975), 17.

22. *Patricia Niles Middleton,* Social Psychology and Modern Life *(New York: Knopf, 1974), 162.*

23. *Alan R. Nelson, "Can the Glamour and Excitement of Sports Really Carry the Ball for Your Product?"* Marketing Review, 29 (February 1974), 21–25.

24. *Ibid, p. 24.*

25. *Ibid.*

26. *Federal Trade Commission,* Guides concerning Use of Endorsements and Testimonials in Advertising *(16 CFR, Part 255).*

Discussion questions

1. In terms of influencing consumer behavior, what is the major difference between a primary and a secondary group?

2. Name and briefly describe three different types of groups that might influence an individual's consumer behavior. What is the importance of each of these groups for the marketer in planning his marketing strategy?

3. As a marketing consultant for a large retail chain, you have been asked to evaluate a new promotional campaign. The campaign strategy is aimed at increasing "group" shopping. What recommendations would you make to the retail executive you report to?

4. In terms of consumer behavior, discuss the differences between a normative and a comparative reference group.

5. How do the following factors influence the importance of a reference group in making a consumer purchase decision:
   a. prior experience with the product category
   b. conspicuousness of the product

6. Select two magazine advertisements that you feel reflect reference group appeals. One should be based on an aspirational group appeal, and the other on a contactual group appeal.

7. Imagine that you are the vice president of advertising for a large fur-

niture manufacturer. Your advertising agency is in the process of negotiating a contract to employ this year's most valuable baseball player to promote your products. Discuss.

8. Find a magazine advertisement for a consumer product that uses the *expert* as a reference group appeal. What impact do you feel this appeal has on consumers? Explain.

the family 9

Introduction

The family is a major influence and actor in the consumer behavior process. As the most basic group to which an individual belongs, the family provides the early childhood learning concerning products and product categories, provides the opportunity for product exposure and repetition, and sets the consumption norms for family members. As a major consumption unit, the family is a prime target for most products and product categories.

In order to understand how and why the family makes its purchase decisions, and how and why it affects the future consumption behavior of its young, it is useful to understand the prevailing types of families and the functions provided and roles enacted by family members to fulfill their consumption needs. By way of background, we will first examine some basic family terminology; then we will discuss family consumer decision making and the concept and marketing implications of the family life cycle.

WHAT IS A FAMILY?

Although the term *family* is a very basic concept, it is not easy to define because family structure and the roles fulfilled by family members vary considerably, depending on the particular society under study. However, to offer a simple and effective picture of what is meant by a family, we will define *family* as two or more persons re-

The family is the association established by nature for the supply of man's everyday wants.
ARISTOTLE: *Politics (4th Cent.* B.C.*)*

lated by blood, marriage, or adoption who reside together.[1] In a more dynamic sense, however, the individuals who constitute a family might be described as members of the most basic social group who "operate" together to satisfy their personal and joint needs.

While families are sometimes referred to as *households,* not all households are families. For example, a household might also include individuals who are *not* related by blood, marriage, or adoption, such as unmarried couples, family friends, roommates, or boarders. However, households and families are usually treated as synonymous within the context of consumer behavior, and we will continue this tradition.

In the United States, as in most of Western society, three types of families dominate: the married couple, the nuclear family, and the extended family. The simplest type of family, in terms of number of members, is the *married couple* — a husband and wife. As a basic household unit, the married couple is generally most representative of younger marrieds, who have not as yet started a family, and older couples, who have already raised their children.

A husband and wife and at least one offspring constitute a *nuclear family.* This type of family is the cornerstone of family life as it now exists in the United States. Since it is composed of parents and their children, the nuclear family can properly be thought of as consisting of two generations living in the same household.

When we have a husband, wife, children, and at least one grandparent living together, we have a three-generation family, commonly called an *extended family.* This type of family, which at one time was most representative of the American family, has been declining in number as increased mobility has separated parents and their married offspring. Table 9–1 summarizes the household composition of each of these three types of families.

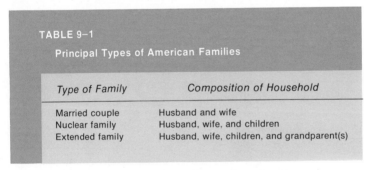

TABLE 9–1

Principal Types of American Families

Type of Family	Composition of Household
Married couple	Husband and wife
Nuclear family	Husband, wife, and children
Extended family	Husband, wife, children, and grandparent(s)

FUNCTIONS OF THE FAMILY

Four basic functions provided by the family are particularly relevant to a discussion of consumer behavior. These include the provision of (1) economic well-being, (2) emotional support, (3) childhood socialization, and (4) suitable life-styles.[2]

economic well-being

Although the family in an affluent society such as the United States is no longer formed primarily to provide economic security, the satisfaction of financial needs is unquestionably a basic function of the family. Indeed, there is evidence that economic wealth is strongly associated with happiness, despite the old adage that "the best things in life are free."[3]

How the family divides its responsibilities for economic well-being has changed considerably during the past twenty years. For example, while the traditional roles of the husband as economic provider and the wife as child rearer and homemaker are still valid, they are no longer so rigid. As more wives seek outside employment and more husbands share household responsibilities, the traditional economic roles are becoming blurred.

The economic role of children has also changed. Today, children are rarely expected to assist the family financially. Instead, they are expected to complete formal educational training and prepare themselves to be financially independent.

emotional support

The provision of emotional and therapeutic support to its members is an important basic function of the contemporary family.[4] In fulfilling this function, the family attempts to assist its members in coping with personal or social problems. Unemployment of a family member, death of a close family friend, or a child who is having trouble in school are just three illustrations of an almost unlimited number of potentially emotional or tension-producing problems that require family attention.

If the family cannot provide adequate assistance when it is needed, it may turn to a professional counselor or psychologist as a logical alternative. In general terms, the selection of such professional services is not very different from other types of consumption decisions made by the family.

childhood socialization

The socialization of young children is a central family function. In large part, this process consists of imparting to children the basic values and modes of behavior consistent with the culture, which may include (1) personality development, (2) interpersonal competence in dealing with others, (3) appropriate dress and grooming habits, (4) proper manners and speech patterns, and (5) the selection of appropriate occupational or career skills. Within a family setting, much of this socialization is accomplished either directly, through instruction or indirectly, as children imitate the behavior of their parents and older siblings.

Cutting across the various aspects of childhood socialization is the pertinent factor of *consumer socialization*. Consumer socialization is defined as the ". . . processes by which young people acquire skills, knowledge, and attitudes relevant to their functioning as consumers in the marketplace."[5] Consumer socialization has two distinct components: (1) those *directly* related to consumption, such as the acquisition of skills, knowledge, and attitudes concerned with budgeting, pricing, and brand attitudes; and (2) those *indirectly* related to consumption, such as the underlying motivations which spur a young man to purchase his first razor or a young girl to desire her first bra.[6] While both components of consumer socialization are significant, the indirect component, which emphasizes the underlying motivational factors, is of most interest to marketing executives who want to understand why people buy their products.

The socialization process is not confined to childhood, but is an ongoing process extending into adulthood. For example, when a newly married couple initially sets up a household, their adjustment to living and consuming together is part of a continuing socialization process.

suitable life-styles

Another important family function in terms of consumer behavior is the establishment of a suitable life-style (style of living) for the family. Although little is known about how families establish and alter their life-styles, it would seem that the personal and jointly determined goals of the spouses are prominent factors. For example, the importance placed on education, the family's interest in reading, the number and types of television programs viewed, the frequency of dining out, the selection of entertainment and recreational activities, are all examples of family decisions that set the tone for the family's life-style.

Family life-style commitments greatly influence consumption patterns. For this reason, marketers should be aware of trends concerning family allocation of time, for how time is spent reflects changing family life-styles.[7]

Family decision making

While many marketers believe the family is the basic decision making unit, they usually examine consumer behavior concerning their own products in terms of the one family member they believe to be the major decision maker. Although such a research approach can be justified as being simpler and less expensive than interviewing all members of the family, it may provide a distorted picture of the specific contributions of various family members to a purchase decision. For instance, men's formal wear might logically be thought of as a male-dominated decision, but the wife tends to strongly influence the purchase of such items. Similarly, men's underwear is often purchased by married women who independently select such items for their husbands and unmarried sons. Because the user is not always the sole decision maker or even the buyer, marketers should try to identify the decision making participants in the family and to direct a substantial portion of their advertising to family members who affect or select the final purchase.

As we can see, then, a very basic question for the marketer to answer is which family members are influential in making the relevant purchase decision. We will begin our discussion of this important question with an examination of family roles.

FAMILY ROLE SETTING

If a family is to function as a cohesive unit, roles or tasks—such as setting the dinner table, taking out the garbage, walking the dog, or dispersing family funds—must be carried out by one or more family members. Similarly, in the context of consumer purchase decisions, roles or tasks are carried out by one or more family members. To illustrate, a family's recent purchase of a motorboat might have been subject to the following role influences: the teenage son generated initial family interest in the purchase of a boat; information from friends and mass media was gathered by the husband; the amount to be spent on the boat was determined jointly by both spouses; the selection of appropriate product features was made by parents and their teenage children; and the selection of a retail outlet and the final purchase decision was undertaken jointly by the entire family.

Since family roles vary by product category, and since different families are apt to establish somewhat different family roles for the same product decision, it is not easy to develop a marketing strategy that reflects the specific roles of family members. Through carefully conceived consumer research, however, the marketer can usually uncover a pattern of decision making that describes the majority of families who are potential customers for his product.

In attempting to isolate the general consumer decision-making roles of family members, marketers seek answers to such questions as:

1. Which family members are most likely to *initiate interest* in the product category?
2. Which family members are most likely to *seek* out the required *information* about the product category?
3. Which family members are most likely to determine *how much will be spent* on the product?
4. Which family members are most likely to determine *specific product features* (color, size, style)?
5. Which family members are most likely to make the final decision regarding *which brand to purchase*?
6. Which family members are most likely to determine *when* the purchase will be made?

7. Which family members are most likely to determine *where* the product will be purchased?
8. Which family members are most likely to *actually purchase* the product?
9. Which family members are most likely to *use or consume* the product?

Answers to these questions provide a marketer with a sound basis upon which to develop products and design promotional strategies, and aid in the selection of retail outlets for his product.

six key consumption roles

The following classification system provides further insight into how family members interact in their various consumption-related roles:[8]

1. *Influencers*—those family members who provide information and advice, and thereby affect the selection of a product or service
2. *Gatekeepers*—those family members who control the flow of information about a product or service into the family, thereby influencing the decisions of other family members
3. *Deciders*—those family members who have the power to unilaterally or jointly determine whether or not to purchase a specific product or service.
4. *Buyers*—those family members who actually make the purchase of a particular product or service
5. *Preparers*—those family members who transform the product into a form in which it will be consumed by other family members
6. *Users*—those family members who use or consume a particular product or service

Quite naturally, the number and identity of the family members who fill these roles varies from product to product. In some cases, a single family member will independently assume a number of roles; in other cases, a single role will jointly be performed by two or more family members. In still other cases, one or more of these basic roles may not be required. For example, when a housewife is shopping in a supermarket and comes upon a new salad dressing which she thinks her family might enjoy, her decision to purchase it does not directly involve the *influence* of other family members. She is the *decider,* the *buyer,* and in a sense the *gatekeeper;* however, she may or may not be the *preparer* and will not be the sole *user.*

FAMILY DECISION MAKING AND PRODUCT USAGE

In considering family consumption behavior, it is often useful to distinguish between the *decision making* that leads to the purchase, and the eventual *consumption* or *use* of the product. Products might be consumed by a single family member (beer, lipstick) consumed or used *directly* by two or more family members (frozen vegetables, an automobile), or consumed *indirectly* by the entire family (paint, draperies, carpeting).[9]

determinants of family decision making

Seven factors which influence a family's decision-making style are social class, life-style, role orientation, stage in family life cycle, perceived risk, product importance, and time constraints.[10]

Social class. Both lower and upper class families tend to favor an autonomous or unilateral decision style, while middle class families tend toward egalitarianism or joint decision making (see Chapter 11).

Life style. A family's allocation of time, in terms of both work and leisure, its values and its interests, are likely to influence its decision making. Thus a family that frequently goes on vacation may make decisions differently than a family that does not.

Role orientation. The more specific the roles of family members (father takes out the garbage, mother shops for groceries, teenage daughter does the dinner dishes), the more likely are family members to make autonomous decisions related to their respective roles.

Family life cycle. The age and composition of a family tend to influence its decision-making style. Newly married and young families are more likely to make joint decisions; older families, who have had more chance to establish role specialization, are more likely to make independent or autonomous decisions.

Perceived risk. The more risk or uncertainty that family members perceive in a particular purchase decision, the more likely it is that the decision will be made jointly. Conversely, when a product purchase is not perceived to be especially risky, it is likely that an autonomous decision will be made.

Product importance. The more importance attached to a particular product's purchase, the greater the likelihood that the decision to purchase it will be jointly made.

Time constraints. The quicker a decision has to be made, the more likely that it will be an autonomous decision, since a joint decision generally requires more time.

An understanding of the relevance of these seven factors to his product and his target market can help the marketer develop an appropriate marketing strategy.

LOCUS OF HUSBAND/WIFE DECISIONS

Most husband/wife influence studies classify family consumption decisions as husband-dominated, wife-dominated, or joint decisions. To this typology, some consumer researchers have added a fourth category —the autonomous or unilateral decision. Let us consider each of these categories in turn:

Husband-dominated decisions—those in which a majority of the families interviewed in a study identify the *husband* as the most influential spouse in the decision to purchase a particular product.

Wife-dominated decisions—those in which a majority of the families interviewed identify the *wife* as the most influential spouse in the decision to purchase a particular product.

Joint decisions — those in which a majority of the families interviewed identify the *husband* and wife as equally influential in the decision to purchase a particular product.

Autonomous decisions — those in which either the *husband or* the *wife* — in somewhat equal proportions — has been identified as the sole decision maker for the purchase of a particular product.

dynamics of husband/wife decision making

Research that has examined both the extent and the nature of husband/wife influence in family decisions indicates that such influence is fluid and likely to shift, depending on the specific product or service, the specific stage in the decision-making process, and the specific product features being considered. Let us briefly review these factors and their effects on husband/wife decision making.

PRODUCT OR SERVICE VARIATIONS. Research on husband/wife decision making consistently indicates that the relative influence of a spouse depends in part on the product or service being studied. For instance, early studies revealed that the purchase of an automobile was strongly husband-dominated, while food and some financial decisions (weekly food expenditures and money management) were wife-dominated. For other products or services studied, husbands and wives tended to contribute equally (the selection of a house or apartment, vacations, and savings).[11]

A more recent large-scale study of some twenty-five hundred married men and women supports the notion that decision making varies in accordance with the specific product or service.[12] For example, husbands were found to dominate in certain areas (the purchase of automobiles and television sets), while wives were most influential in other areas (the selection of movies and television programs).

A replication of one of the pioneering studies cited above attempted to answer the basic question: Are husband/wife decision-making patterns changing? Some findings of this study are listed below:[13]

1. Life insurance has become a husband-dominated decision, while decisions concerning food and groceries have become more wife-dominated. These results represent an intensification of findings of the earlier study.

2. The selection of family housing and vacations are increasingly joint decisions, an intensification of the previously reported decision-making pattern.

3. Dramatic changes in the area of automobile decision making were reported. While the earlier study found that the husband strongly dominated the purchase decision, the later study showed a substantial shift toward joint decision making (45 percent of the cases in 1973 were joint decisions as compared with 25 percent in 1955). The automobile purchase decision remained a male-dominated decision in 52 percent of the households surveyed (a reduction, from 70 percent in the 1955 study). The change in influence over automobile purchases undoubtedly reflects the increased activities of the wife outside of the home and the move toward two-car or multi-car families.

Although this study suggests a generalized shift in the locus of family decision making, it is not clear whether the findings reflect a move toward greater *role specialization* (more husband or wife domination over specific decision categories) or greater *egalitarianism* (more joint and equal decision making). Future research might better identify role changes, particularly if a panel consisting of the same husbands and wives are interviewed annually over a five- or ten-year period.

To support the fruitfulness of panel data, additional insights into the dynamics of husband-wife decision making is provided by a study that focused on a single decision area—family financial management.[14] The research was specifically designed to identify which spouse in newly married couples undertook the principal responsibility for family money management (payment of bills and use of extra funds). The initial interview during the first year of marriage revealed that most couples shared equally in money management. However, follow-up interviews during the second year of marriage indicated a decline in joint financial decision making and a parellel increase in the money management responsibility of the wife. The results suggest that financially inexperienced newlyweds are likely to start out sharing the burdens of financial decision making; however, in a relatively short time, many young wives take the lead in this consumption-related area. For banking and other financial marketing executives, these results suggest that young married women are a particularly important target for their services.

VARIATIONS BY STAGE IN THE DECISION-MAKING PROCESS. The roles of husbands and wives often differ during the decision-making process. A study of Belgian households, for example, found that the roles of husbands and wives varied for a number of products in terms of a simple three-stage decision-making model: problem recognition, search for information, and final decision.[15] To illustrate, the recognition of a need for an automobile was unilaterally made (usually by the husband), the search for information concerning the potential purchase was husband-dominated, while the final decision was jointly made by both spouses.

VARIATIONS BY PRODUCT FEATURES. An exploratory study sponsored by *Time* magazine suggests that marketers should examine husband/wife decision making in terms of specific product features.[16] For example, the study found that in the determination of brand for a potential product purchase, the husband dominated for automobiles and television sets, the wife dominated for washing machines, while the brand of dress shirts was jointly determined. Table 9−2 presents these results and evidence pertinent to seven other purchase factors.

For the marketer, this study suggests that it is unwise to generalize about the relative influence of spouses from one product to another. Rather, the relative influence of husbands and wives should be determined uniquely for each product category.

Secondly, it would appear that a global measure of husband/wife influence is less insightful than an examination of their impact at specific

TABLE 9–2

Relative Influence of Husband and Wife on Selected Purchase Factors

Purchase factors	Automobiles	Dress shirts	Television sets	Washers
Brand (make)	H	=	H	W
Performance features	H	W	H	W
Style	W	H	W	W
Size	H	H	H	W
Warranty (guarantee)	=	–	H	H
Price	H	W	H	H
Store (dealer)	H	=	W	H
Service	H	–	H	H

Key:
H = Husband more influential than wife.
W = Wife more influential than husband.
= = Husband and wife equally influential.
– = Not applicable to product category.

Source: Adapted from Family Decision Making (New York: Time Magazine, Time Marketing Information Research Report 1428, 1967).

stages of the decision-making process or in terms of specific product features.

RELIABILITY OF HUSBAND/WIFE DECISION STUDIES

Studies of family decision making indicate that there can be substantial disagreement between spouses as to their relative influence on consumer purchases. An evaluation of these findings suggests that such differences should not be a source of major concern to the marketing manager, since these differences tend to cancel themselves out across the entire sample of respondents.[17] However, in carrying out a large-scale study of family decision making, it might be advisable for the marketer to undertake a pilot study to determine if this generalization is true for the product category under investigation.

CHILDREN

One has only to switch on a television set, especially on a weekend morning, or thumb through the pages of a magazine like *Boy's Life,* to come to the conclusion that many advertisers are interested in reaching children. This interest is not evident in the literature of consumer behavior or in the general field of family sociology, since relatively little data has been collected about the impact of children on family decision making.[18] It is likely, however, that greater attention will be paid to how children learn to make consumption decisions because of the surge of interest in the influence of mass media on child development.[19]

We will discuss the role of children in family decision making in terms of the family's impact on its children, and the children's impact on the family.

the family's impact on its children

As already noted, the socialization of children is a basic function of the family, and consumer socialization is an important component of this process. It is the vehicle through which the family imparts consumption-relevant knowledge, attitudes, and skills.

While the consumer socialization process is still largely unexplored, it is probable that preadolescent children tend to rely on their parents and older siblings as the major source of cues for their basic consumption learning. Adolescents and teenagers, on the other hand, are likely to shift much of their attention to the actions and behavior of friends.[20] Specifically, it might be expected that much of what preadolescents learn from their family is by way of imitation, such as imitating how an older child spends his money. In contrast, older children, who have already acquired the fundamentals of consumption behavior from their family, are likely to look to outside friends for models of socially acceptable consumption behavior, such as the "in" thing to wear.

Consumer socialization fulfills a unique function as a tool by which parents can influence other aspects of the socialization process. For instance, parents frequently use the promise or reward of material goods (e.g., a new toy) as a device to modify a child's behavior. These sanctions often become an important control mechanism for the parent; he may reward his child with a gift when the child does something to the parent's satisfaction, or withhold it or remove it if the child disobeys. In a sense, the use of material goods as a means of parental control over a child's behavior is intrinsic support for the importance of possessions and consumption in a society such as the United States. It also suggests that future research into various aspects of consumer socialization may provide significant insights for other behavioral science disciplines concerned with child development.

children as influentials

Children are not only influenced *by* their families, in turn they also influence family consumption decisions. Young children attempt to influence family decisions as soon as they possess the basic communication skills needed to interact with other family members. Most parents, even those of very young children, can recall frequent purchase-related requests, such as "Please buy me a Barbie Doll" or "let's eat at McDonalds." Of course, older children are likely to participate more directly in family consumption activities.

To illustrate the impact of children on parental decision making,

TABLE 9–3

Best Sources of Toy Ideas

Idea source	Parents* (N = 340)
Children themselves	40 %
Television	24
Store displays	13
Catalogs	10
Newspaper	4
Other adults	3
Other	1
No answer	5
	100 %

*Of children 12 years old or younger.

Source: Newspaper Advertising Bureau (formerly Bureau of Advertising, ANPA), The Adult Toy Buyer: A Further Exploration of How Parents and Non-Parents Buy Toys: 1967, New York, N.Y.

Table 9–3 shows that most parents surveyed by the American Newspaper Publishers Association in 1966 identified their children as their best source of toy ideas.

The parent-child relationship as it relates to consumer behavior can be viewed as an *influence versus yield* situation. Specifically, a child attempts to *influence* his parents to make a purchase (to *yield*). A few studies have examined the relationship between child influence and parent yielding. For example, in-store observations of purchase behavior in supermarkets indicate that children generally attempt to make their preferences known to their parents. Their efforts are strongest in areas of special interest to children (cereal, candy); however, they also occur with products of only remote interest to children (household or laundry detergents).[21]

Two other studies of the child-parent consumer relationship report conflicting results on the nature of influence and yielding. One study that focused exclusively on breakfast cereals found that the more involved the mother was with her child, the more likely she was *not* to yield, but to override the child's own choice of breakfast cereals and buy what she believed to be the best brand.[22] The researchers concluded that children's preferences for sugar-coated cereal were judged nutritionally unsound by their mothers who therefore did not yield.

The second study, which examined child-parent interaction across a number of products (including cereals), found a significant positive relationship between the number of children's influence attempts and their mothers' yielding.[23] The study also found that children's attempts to influence tend to *decrease* somewhat with age, whereas mothers' yielding requests were likely to *increase* with the child's age. These results seem to indicate that older children are more discriminating in their requests, and that parents are more willing to accede to older children's requests because they perceive them to be more mature in their judgments about purchase decisions.

There is also some evidence that teenage children significantly influence family decision making. A survey sponsored by *Co-ed* magazine (a magazine for teenage girls) indicates that an impressive number of high school girls plan or participate in the planning of family meals, and shop for their family's food needs. The study also suggests that girls with working mothers are somewhat more involved in homemaking activities than their counterparts with nonworking mothers.[24]

College students have also been shown to exert influence over the purchase decisions of their families. In one study, college students reported that they often attempted to influence their families' decisions to purchase television sets and automobiles, and that they perceived that they did influence these purchase decisions.[25]

While a number of studies indicate that children influence family decision making, the extent and specific nature of their influence (e.g., the range of products and the extent of their influence over such decisions) is still largely undocumented.

The family life cycle

Behavioral scientists, particularly rural and family sociologists, have utilized the concept of a *family life cycle* (FLC) to classify family units into meaningful groupings. More recently, classification by stage in the FLC has proved useful to researchers concerned with family consumption behavior and to marketers concerned with segmenting their markets. This section will describe the family life cycle and its relevance to the consumption activities of the family.

STAGES OF THE FLC

The FLC can be considered a progression of stages through which most families pass, starting with the bachelor or unmarried state. If the individual marries, his resulting family unit will move through a series of stages in which the size of his family first expands with the birth of children, and then contracts, as older children leave the household and, finally, as one of the original family members dies. Ultimately, the family comes to an end when the sole survivor dies or remarries.

For the researcher, FLC analyses are important because they enable her to classify families into one of a number of mutually exclusive developmental stages. The FLC is a *composite* variable because it is created by systematically combining such commonly used demographic variables as:

1. Marital status (single or married).
2. Age of family members (generally head-of-household and either oldest or youngest child).
3. Size of the family (number of children).
4. Work status of the head-of-household (working or retired).

By placing families into groups based on a combination of such demographic variables, a richer picture of the family is obtained than would be possible by using any single variable. Evidence supporting this contention will be examined later in this chapter.

Table 9–4 presents, in schematic fashion, several alternative FLC models. The models differ primarily in terms of the number of stages (or substages) utilized; these in turn reflect how finely the researcher cares to examine family development. Synthesizing the various FLC models depicted in Table 9–4, we will examine the following five stages in detail and show how they lend themselves to market segmentation strategies:

STAGE I: *Bachelorhood*—a young single adult not living with his parents
STAGE II: *Honeymooners*—a young married couple
STAGE III: *Parenthood*—a married couple with at least one child living at home
STAGE IV: *Postparenthood*—an older married couple with no children living at home
STAGE V: *Dissolution*—only one of the original spouses survives

stage i: bachelorhood

The first FLC stage consists of young single men and women who have set up their own households. Although most members of this FLC stage are fully employed, many are college students who live apart from their parents.

Young single adults are apt to spend their incomes on apartment rent, basic home furnishings, the purchase and maintenance of automobiles, travel and entertainment, and the acquisition of stylish clothing and accessories.

Members of the bachelor stage frequently have sufficient disposable income to pursue a kind of "hedonistic" spending pattern. In most large cities, one can find travel agents, housing developments, country clubs, sports clubs, etc., that find this FLC stage a lucrative target market for various products and services.

It is relatively easy to reach this audience, since a number of special-interest publications cater to the "single" life-style. For example, *Playboy* and *Penthouse* are directed to a young, sophisticated, single male audience; while *Cosmopolitan* and *Viva* are directed to young single females.

After the fling of bachelorhood wears off, singles often turn to the serious business of finding a spouse. Here again, the individual is likely

TABLE 9–4

Alternative Family Life Cycle Models

Broad categories	Lansing and Kish (1957)[a]	Blood and Wolfe (1958)[b]	Farber (1964)[c]	Wells and Gubar (1966)[d]
Stage I: Bachelorhood	Young single		Premarital stage	Bachelor stage, not living at home
Stage II: Honeymooners	Young married couple, no children	Honeymoon stage, childless and married less than four years	Couple stage	Newly married couple, young with no children
Stage III: Parenthood	Young married couple, with youngest child under 6	Preschool stage, oldest child under 6	Preschool phase	Full nest I, youngest child under 6
	Young married couple, with youngest child 6 or over	Preadolescent stage, oldest child 6 to 12	Elementary school phase	Full nest II, youngest child 6 or over
		Adolescent stage, oldest child 13 to 18	High school phase	Full nest III, older married couples with dependent children
		Unlaunched stage, oldest child 19 or older and still living at home	College phase — Postschool phase	
Stage IV: Postparenthood	Older married couple, no children	Postparental stage	In-law phase — Grandparent phase	Empty nest I, no children at home, head in labor force
				Empty nest II, head retired
Stage V: Dissolution	Older single	Retired stage, nonemployed husband 60 or over	Widowhood and remarriage — End of cycle	Solitary survivor, in labor force
				Solitary survivor, retired

Sources: [a]John B. Lansing and Leslie Kish, "Family Life Cycle as an Independent Variable," American Sociological Review, 22 (October 1957), 512–19.
[b]Robert O. Blood, Jr., and Donald M. Wolfe, Husbands and Wives (Glencoe, Ill.: Free Press, 1960).
[c]Bernard Farber, Family: Organization and Interaction (San Francisco: Chandler, 1964).
[d]William D. Wells and George Gubar, "Life Cycle Concept in Marketing Research," Journal of Marketing Research, (November 1966), 355–63.

to be offered numerous services (e.g., party and dating services) designed to provide the opportunity to meet the "perfect" mate.

When the right individual is found, there is usually a period of courtship, often followed by a formal engagement. In our society, the announcement of an engagement often triggers the onslaught of marketing efforts from specialized services eager to provide the betrothed couple and their parents with a full-blown wedding—a catered affair complete with music, photographs, bridal gown, men's formal wear, wedding rings, flowers, and a honeymoon vacation. Other marketers bombard the couple with communications concerning the numerous products that are likely to be required in the establishment of a household. This market is so fertile and so eager for information that the two leading bridal magazines, *Bride's* and *Modern Bride,* are made up primarily of product and service advertisements.[26]

stage ii: honeymooners

The honeymoon stage starts immediately after the marriage vows are taken, and generally continues up to the arrival of the couple's first child. This FLC stage serves as a period of adjustment to married life.

Since many young husbands and wives both work, they have available to them a combined income that often permits a pleasure-seeking life style similar to that enjoyed by many singles. The difference is that they are now spending together.

In addition to joint pleasure seeking, there are considerable "start-up" expenditures for their apartment or home (major and minor appliances, bedroom and living-room furniture, carpeting, drapes, dishes, and a host of utensils and accessory items). During this stage, the advice and experience of other married couples are likely to be important to the newlyweds. Also important as sources of new-product information are shelter magazines, such as *Better Homes and Gardens, Apartment Ideas,* and *House Beautiful.*

stage iii: parenthood

When young families have their first child, the honeymoon is considered over. The parenthood stage usually extends over more than a twenty-year period. Because of its long duration, it is useful to divide this stage into shorter phases: (1) the preschool phase, (2) the elementary school phase, (3) the high school phase, (4) the college phase, and (5) the postschool phase.

Throughout these parenthood phases, the interrelationships of family members and the structure of the family gradually changes. For example, the responsibilities of parenthood require a rather drastic recasting of the young couple's life style. Income previously spent on home decorating, dining out, and vacations is now redirected to baby foods, diapers, and baby furniture. Entertainment and social activities tend to center on the home and in the community.

As children get older and more independent, and as the family becomes financially better off (due to normal increments in the husband's earnings or the entrance of the wife into the work force), the family's life style gradually becomes less restrictive and more satisfying for all concerned.

There are many magazines that cater to the information and entertainment needs of parents and children. To illustrate, *Redbook* positions itself as the "Magazine for Young Mothers," *Ladies Home Journal* is directed to a broader age spectrum of homemakers, *Parents' Magazine* covers child rearing, health, and food topics. For children, there are many special-interest publications, such as *Humpty Dumpty,* designed for the young child just learning to read, *Scholastic Magazine,* for the elementary school pupil, *Boy's Life,* which is aimed at the young male and *American Girl, Seventeen, Glamour,* and *Mademoiselle,* which appeal to the fashion interest of teen and post-teen girls.

stage iv: postparenthood

Since parenthood extends over many years, it is only natural to find that postparenthood—the period when all the children have left home—is traumatic for many parents who suddenly feel unneeded and somewhat alone. However, there is a bright side to the postparenthood stage—the opportunity to start things over again as a husband-wife team. For this reason, after an initial adjustment, the postparenthood stage signifies the beginning of "doing things we've always wanted to do." For the wife, who has spent most of her time rearing children, it is a time to complete her education, to get a job, to seek new interests. For the husband, it is a time to indulge in new hobbies. For both, it is the time to travel, to entertain, perhaps to refurnish their home.

Thus the spending patterns of couples in the postparenthood FLC stage are apt to change quite dramatically, especially since there is likely to be more money available. In fact, it is during this stage that the married couple is often best off financially. For this reason, families in the postparenthood stage are an important market for expensive furniture, jewelry, new automobiles, and vacations to distant places for which they didn't have the time or money before.

If the older married couple are fortunate in terms of health, they will eventually retire together. If planned for adequately, retirement provides the opportunity to seek new interests and to fulfill previously less satisfied or unsatisfied needs. However, for older retired couples who do not have adequate savings or income, retirement is often very restrictive, and requires the management of a household on a minimal fixed income.

Available evidence suggests that older consumers tend to consider television an important source of information and entertainment. They favor programs that provide the opportunity to "keep up with things," especially news and public affairs programs.[27] As for magazines, one would expect older consumers to continue their existing reading patterns, with the possible addition of special-interest reading material like the publications of the American Association of Retired Persons and other retirement-oriented magazines.

stage v: dissolution

Just as the postparenthood stage of the FLC is initially a difficult time, so is the loss of one's spouse (most often the husband). The adjustment to such a loss is largely a function of how healthy and financially solvent the survivor is, and the extent to which emotional support from loved ones is available. If the surviving spouse is still in good health, is working or has adequate savings, and lives in close proximity to understanding friends or relatives, the adjustment tends to be easier.

In terms of spending patterns, the surviving spouse might sell the family home, which now may be too large and too filled with memories, and move into a smaller, more efficient apartment, possibly within a retirement community. At this point, there is often a need for goods and services that fill the vacuum of being alone. Pleasurable and time-consuming activities, such as trips, tours, vacations, and social events with peers, become very important.

As our society becomes more enlightened in regard to the special needs of the elderly, improved social and economic services should benefit them and enable them to lead more productive and satisfying lives.

LIMITATIONS OF THE FLC

Conventional FLC models (see Table 9–4) generally do not include all possible life cycle factors. This can create a classification problem for the researcher. Following is a list of family factors that are usually not included in traditional FLC models:

1. Childless couples
2. Families broken up by separation or divorce
3. Older families with children younger than six
4. Widowhood at an early stage of the FLC
5. Extended families (e.g., grandparents living with married children, or newly married couples living with in-laws)
6. Mature individuals who marry late in life (e.g., when they are in their forties or fifties)
7. Unmarried mothers
8. Unmarried couples

To deal with such cases, researchers tend to elect one of the following courses of action: (1) they eliminate such respondents, if they are few in number; (2) they add such respondents to the traditional life cycle stage to which they seem to most closely conform; or (3) they establish a separate FLC stage to accommodate such respondents, particularly if there are many of them.

These few limitations of the FLC models demonstrate that market-ers must not expect any single concept or variable, no matter how rich it may seem, to be perfectly applicable to all investigations of consumer behavior. Just as it is unrealistic to expect all consumers within a particu-lar market segment to react in the same way to a marketer's product, it is equally unrealistic to expect all consumers in an evolving society to fit neatly into the traditional categories of the FLC.

However, the FLC has demonstrated its value for market segmen-tation. It has provided insights into specific consumption activities that could not be obtained by using a single demographic variable. For exam-ple, evidence indicates a substantially greater decline in the proportion of home ownership for consumers in the dissolution stage (solitary survi-vors) than would be revealed by a census of consumers in the over sixty-five age category. The reason for this difference between FLC analysis and age categorization is that age does *not* distinguish between house-holds in which both the elderly husband and wife are living and those in which only one of the partners is alive.[28] Because of this, a firm renting or selling retirement housing might find that information gleaned from FLC analyses offers a more sensitive profile of its market than could be derived from age data alone.

APPLICATION OF FLC ANALYSIS BY PRODUCT CATEGORY

Marketers and researchers have found that FLC analysis can provide an indepth understanding of family consumption behavior for a variety of product categories.

residential telephone usage

The American Telephone and Telegraph Company (AT&T) has employed FLC variables in its efforts to better serve household tele-phone customers. Table 9-5 presents the specific FLC model that AT&T researchers have found most clearly accounts for family telephone usage. An examination of this model indicates that AT&T has redefined some of the FLC stages listed in the prototype models in Table 9-4. Most no-table among the differences are the division of (a) age of head-of-house-hold into younger or older than fifty-five years, and (b) families into those whose youngest child is over or under twelve years. These refine-ments reflect the nature of residential telephone usage. A finer division of age factors is unlikely to offer greater insight into customer telephone usage.[29]

Figure 9-1 shows the average monthly expenditures on long-dis-tance calls for each FLC stage. Note that young marrieds spend more than singles on long-distance calls, while both of these groups spend less than the average of all households studied. On the other hand, young families with and without teenage children spend more than the average, while those with teenagers spend more than those at any other stage.

TABLE 9–5

AT&T Family Life Cycle Status Categories

FLC stage	Variables employed	Description of stage
Younger No children	—Age of head-of-household	—Under 55 years of age
	—Size of family	—a. Single person b. Couple
Younger Young children	—Age of head of household	—Under 55 years of age
	—Size of family	—Three or more persons
	—Age of children	—Under 12 years of age
Younger Older children	—Age of head of household	—Under 55 years of age
	—Size of family	—Three or more persons
	—Age of children	—a. One child 12 years or older
		b. Two or more children 12 years or older
Older	—Age of head of household	—55 years or older
	—Employment status	—a. Employed b. Unemployed (Retired)

Source: Adapted from Richard B. Ellis, "Composite Population Descriptors: The Socio-Economic Life Cycle Grid," in Mary Jane Schlinger, ed., Advances in Consumer Research (Association for Consumer Research, 1974), Vol. II. Also, courtesy of the American Telephone and Telegraph Company.

Finally, older couples spend about the average, while older singles spend less than the overall average. While these results are limited to a sample of telephone users in the northeastern states, similar analyses are readily available for other geographic areas serviced by AT&T affiliate companies.[30] AT&T uses these life cycle analyses to better understand fluctuations in family telephone expenditure patterns and equipment usage, and thus is better able to plan future telephone products and services to satisfy its customers.

family food consumption

FLC analysis has been used in a study of food purchases and other consumption activities of over four thousand urban homemakers in seven southern states.[31] One of the dimensions of food consumption explored was the "goal satisfaction" of the homemaker. Goal satisfaction

FIGURE 9-1

**Average Monthly Long-Distance Telephone Expenditures by
Family Life Cycle Stages**

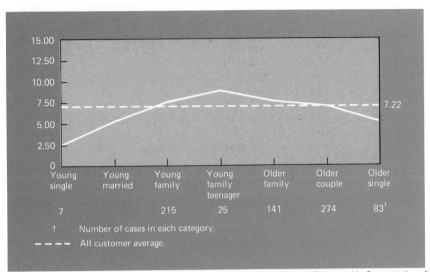

Source: A. Marvin Roscoe, Jr., and Jagdish N. Sheth, "Demographic Segmentation of
Long Distance Behavior: Data Analysis and Inductive Model Building," in M. Venkatesan,
ed., Third Annual Conference of the Association for Consumer Research 1972, 262.
Also, courtesy of the American Telephone and Telegraph Company.

was measured by asking each homemaker to evaluate such food-related
activities as time spent in meal preparation, foods served, and attention
given her own food preferences. On the basis of her responses, an overall food-consumption satisfaction score was determined. Respondents
were then categorized into one of the following six FLC stages based
upon the age of their youngest and oldest children:[32]

STAGE I: Childless young married (married less than ten years with no children)
STAGE II: Expanding (youngest child less than six years old and no child sixteen
or older)
STAGE III: Stable (youngest child six years or older and no child at home older
than age fifteen; or youngest child less than six and the oldest child older
than fifteen years of age)
STAGE IV: Contracting (at least one child aged sixteen years or older and no
child less than six years of age)
STAGE V: Postparental (childless couples with children who have all left home)
STAGE VI: Childless older married (childless couples married more than ten
years)

The results of this study indicated that homemakers in Stage I
(childless young married) were highly satisfied in terms of food consumption, those in Stage II (expanding) were least satisfied, while those
in Stage V (postparental) were most satisfied with their food consumption activities. The high degree of satisfaction expressed by the young

married and postparental homemaker groups is most likely related to their more leisurely life-styles and the relatively fewer financial pressures that exist prior to and after rearing a family. This is supported by evidence that respondents' satisfaction with food consumption is closely related to the amount of per capita income available, which was greatest for those in Stages I and V.[33] Another factor that may contribute to their satisfaction with food consumption may be that fewer compromises are required to satisfy the needs and desires of multiple family members.

Additional support for this study of homemakers' satisfaction with food consumption activities comes from a case history of an individual homemaker's perceptions of her meal preparation role over the stages of her FLC:[34]

1. As a young homemaker, she made a particular effort to intrigue her husband's appetite.
2. When she became a mother, she shifted her emphasis to the practicality of feeding a family.
3. After the children left home, she reverted to somewhat more imaginative cooking for her own pleasure and that of her husband.

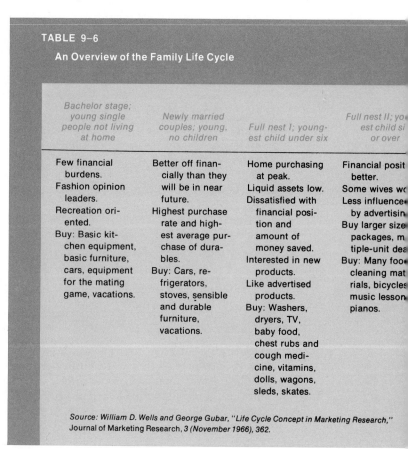

TABLE 9-6

An Overview of the Family Life Cycle

Bachelor stage; young single people not living at home	Newly married couples; young, no children	Full nest I; youngest child under six	Full nest II; youngest child six or over
Few financial burdens. Fashion opinion leaders. Recreation oriented. Buy: Basic kitchen equipment, basic furniture, cars, equipment for the mating game, vacations.	Better off financially than they will be in near future. Highest purchase rate and highest average purchase of durables. Buy: Cars, refrigerators, stoves, sensible and durable furniture, vacations.	Home purchasing at peak. Liquid assets low. Dissatisfied with financial position and amount of money saved. Interested in new products. Like advertised products. Buy: Washers, dryers, TV, baby food, chest rubs and cough medicine, vitamins, dolls, wagons, sleds, skates.	Financial position better. Some wives work. Less influenced by advertising. Buy larger size packages, multiple-unit deals. Buy: Many foods, cleaning materials, bicycles, music lessons, pianos.

Source: William D. Wells and George Gubar, "Life Cycle Concept in Marketing Research," *Journal of Marketing Research*, 3 (November 1966), 362.

These shifts in perception of food preparation activities over the FLC seem to coinside with the shifts in goal satisfaction discussed above.

entertainment activities

An exploratory study of family choice of leisure-time activities provided another opportunity to utilize the FLC concept.[35] Employing a rather simplified FLC model, families were placed into one of the following four stages: (1) under forty years of age without children, (2) under forty years of age with children, (3) forty years of age or older with children, and (4) forty years of age or older without children. The study found that bowling and expensive dining out were more frequently engaged in by those in later life cycle stages, whereas attending movies, nightclubs, and school-related athletic events were activities more frequently engaged in by those in earlier FLC stages.

Table 9–6 presents an overview of an FLC model which lists the

nest III; older rried couples th dependent children	Empty nest I; older married couples, no children living with them, head in labor force	Empty nest II; older married couples, no children living at home, head retired	Solitary survivor, in labor force	Solitary survivor, retired
ancial position till better. e wives work. me children et jobs. d to influence ith advertising. h average urchase of urables. y: New, more asteful furni- ure, auto avel, non- ecessary ap- liances, boats, ental services, nagazines.	Home ownership at peak. Most satisfied with financial position and money saved. Interested in travel, recrea- tion, self-edu- cation. Make gifts and contributions. Not interested in new products. Buy: Vacations, luxuries, home improvements.	Drastic cut in in- come. Keep home. Buy: Medical appliances, medical care, products which aid health, sleep, and di- gestion.	Income still good but likely to sell home.	Same medical and product needs as other retired group, drastic cut in income. Special need for attention, af- fection, and se- curity.

consumption activities that dominate the family at each stage of the life cycle.[36] A careful examination of this model reveals the potential usefulness of FLC analyses for strategic market planning.

MARKETING IMPLICATIONS OF THE FLC

FLC analysis permits marketers to segment the total universe of families into distinct, mutually exclusive markets composed of family units that are relatively homogeneous in terms of age, interests, needs, time utilization, proportionate disposable income, etc. Segmentation by stage in the FLC enables marketers to develop products and services to meet the very specific needs of families at each stage in their lives, and to design and implement promotional strategies with which their target audiences will identify.

TABLE 9–7

Factors Affecting the Future of the Family

Trend	Impact
More leisure time	A shorter work-week will mean increased emphasis on family recreation and entertainment. There should also be a greater demand for products that make the use of time more rewarding and enjoyable.
More formal education	Better education will mean a more aware consumer, which should increase the demand for more reliable products. There should also be increased interest in products and services that satisfy the need for individualism.
More working married women	A higher total family income should mean less economic pressure and more money available for the purchase of products previously out of reach for the family. There should also be increased joint husband-wife decision making, a greater sharing of domestic responsibilities, and a continued preference for smaller families.
Increased life expectancy	As people live longer, the demand for products and services designed to cater to the health, recreation, and entertainment needs of an older population will increase. There should also be a greater emphasis placed on proper nutrition and diet.
Smaller size families	Fewer children (zero population growth) will mean that parents will be able to spend more time and money on the development of each child's skills and capabilities. There will also be more discretionary income available for parents to spend on their own development, to pursue their own interests, and to improve the general standard of the family's life-style.
Women's movement	Husbands and wives will increasingly share household responsibilities, including joint decision making. Moreover, as an outgrowth of the women's movement, traditional sex-linked roles will continue to decline, and products that have generally been aimed at either males or females will increasingly be targeted to members of both sexes.

The future of the family

Despite widespread publicity about spiraling divorce rates and the emergence of unconventional alternatives to the traditional nuclear family (e.g., unmarried couples and open, group, or communal marriages), experts predict that the nuclear family will endure.[37] The survival of the family seems assured because of its capacity to continue to fulfill such basic functions as the provision of economic and emotional well-being to its members, child socialization and suitable life-styles. Moreover, as a dynamic institution, the family may become even more influential in the future as it serves to fortify its members against the strains of continued technological and social change.

Crystal ball gazing into the future of the family is not without its risks. However, consumer researchers must delve into the horizons; they must be able to predict change in order to predict how consumers will react to such change. In this spirit, Table 9–7 identifies six social-environmental trends that seem likely to influence the future of the family. It is our contention that marketers will benefit from periodic review of these and other evolving trends by asking themselves:

1. Which specific trends are most likely to influence my product or service?
2. Have there been any significant changes in the direction or intensity of the important trends, i.e., are they increasing or decreasing, and at what rate?
3. How will each important trend affect the marketing efforts for my product or service?

Summary

The family is a major influence on the consumption behavior of its members; in addition, it is the prime target market for most products and product categories. As the most basic membership group, families are defined as two or more persons related by blood, marriage, or adoption who reside together. There are three types of families: married couples, nuclear families, and extended families. The basic functions of the family are the provision of economic and emotional support, childhood socialization, and a suitable life style for its members.

The members of a family assume specific roles and tasks in their everyday functioning; such roles or tasks extend to the realm of consumer purchase decisions. Key consumer-related roles of family members include influencers, gatekeepers, deciders, buyers, preparers, and users. A family's decision-making style is often influenced by its social class, life style, role orientation, and stage in the family life cycle, and by the product importance, perceived risk, and time constraints of the purchase itself.

The majority of consumer studies classify family consumption decisions as husband-dominated, wife-dominated, joint, or autonomous decisions. The extent and nature of husband/wife influence in family decisions is dependent on the specific product or service, the stage in the decision-making process (i.e., problem recognition, information search, and final decision) and the specific product features under consideration.

Consumer socialization is an important component of the socialization process of children. It is the vehicle through which the family imparts consumer-relevant knowledge, attitudes, and skills. Children are not only influenced by their families; in turn, they also influence their family consumption decisions.

Classification of families by stage in the family life cycle provides valuable insights into family consumption behavior. These stages, which generally include bachelorhood, honeymooners, parenthood (children under 6), parenthood (children over 6), postparenthood, and dissolution, are an important basis of market segmentation for many products and services. Segmentation by stage in the family life cycle enables marketers to develop products and services that will meet the very specific needs of families at each stage in their lives, and to design and implement promotional strategies with which their target audiences will identify.

Endnotes

1. *F. Ivan Nye and Felix M. Berardo,* The Family: Its Structure and Interaction *(New York: Macmillan, 1973), 32.*

2. *For further elaboration of the functions of the family, see William F. Ogburn, "The Changing Family,"* The Family, *19 (July 1938), 139–43; and Carle C. Zimmerman,* Family and Civilization *(New York: Harper & Row, 1947).*

3. *Richard A. Easterlin, "Does Money Buy Happiness?"* Public Interest, *No. 30 (Winter 1973), 3–10.*

4. *F. Ivan Nye, "Emerging and Declining Family Roles,"* Journal of Marriage and the Family, *36 (May 1974), 238–45.*

5. *Scott Ward, "Consumer Socialization,"* Journal of Consumer Research, *1 (September 1974), 2.*

6. *Ibid., 2–3.*

7. *Michael Young and Peter Willmott,* The Symmetrical Family *(New York: Pantheon, 1973).*

8. *All but the "preparer" role have been identified as distinct roles of the buying center within the context of industrial buyer behavior. See Frederick E. Webster, Jr., and Yoram Wind,* Organizational Buying Behavior *(Englewood Cliffs, N.J.: Prentice-Hall, 1972), 78–80.*

9. *Jagdish N. Sheth, "A Theory of Family Buying Decisions," in Jagdish N. Sheth, ed.,* Models of Buyer Behavior: Conceptual, Quantitative and Empirical *(New York: Harper & Row, 1974), 24.*

10. *Ibid., 29–30.*

11. *Elizabeth H. Wolgast, "Do Husbands or Wives Make the Purchase Decisions?"* Journal of Marketing, *23 (October 1958), 151–158; and Harry Sharp and Paul Mott, "Consumer Decisions in the Metropolitan Family,"* Journal of Marketing, *21 (October 1956), 149–56.*

12. *"Who Really Makes the Decisions?"* The Bruskin Report: A Market Research Newsletter *(New Brunswick, N.J.: R. H. Bruskin Associates, September 1974), 1.*

13. *Isabella C. M. Cunningham and Robert T. Green, "Purchasing Roles in U.S. Family, 1955 and 1973,"* Journal of Marketing, *30 ·(October 1974), 61–64.*

14. *Robert Ferber and Lucy Chao Lee, "Husband-Wife Influence in Family Purchasing Behavior,"* Journal of Consumer Research, *1 (June 1974), 43–50.*

15. *Harry L. Davis and Benny P. Rigaux, "Perception of Marital Roles in Decision Processes,"* Journal of Consumer Research, *1 (June 1974), 51–62.*

16. Family Decision Making *(New York: Time Magazine, Time Marketing Information Research Report 1428, 1967).*

17. *Harry L. Davis, "Dimensions of Marital Roles in Consumer Decision Making,"* Journal of Marketing Research, *7 (May 1970), 168–77.*

18. *Constantina Safilios-Rothchild, "The Study of Family Power Structure: A Review 1960–1969,"* Journal of Marriage and the Family, *32 (November 1970), 549.*

19. *See Anees A. Sheikh, V. Kanti Prasad, and Tanniru R. Rao, "Children's TV Commercials: A Review of Research,"* Journal of Communication, *24 (Autumn 1974), 126–36.*

20. *Ward, "Consumer Socialization," 9.*

21. *William D. Wells and Leonard A. LoSciuto, "Direct Observation of Purchase Behavior,"* Journal of Marketing Research, *3 (August 1966), 227–33.*

22. *Lewis A. Berey and Richard W. Pollay, "The Influencing Role of the Child in Family Decision Making,"* Journal of Marketing Research, *5 (February 1968), 70–72.*

23. *Scott Ward and Daniel Wackman, "Purchase Influence Attempts and Parental Yielding,"* Journal of Marketing Research, *9 (August 1972), 316–19.*

24. Grocery Store Shopping Habits of the Young Consumer . . . for Her Family, *Research Report No. 2 (New York: Co-ed Magazine, published by Scholastic Magazines, Inc., 1974).*

25. *William D. Perreault, Jr., and Frederick A. Russ, "Student Influence on Family Purchase Decision,"* in Fred C. Allvine, ed., 1971 Combined Proceedings *(Chicago: American Marketing Association, 1971)*, 386–89.

26. *Stephen Grover, "The Bridal Magazines Prosper on a Formula of Advice and Optimism,"* Wall Street Journal, *January 29, 1974, 1 and 16.*

27. *Richard H. Davis, "Television and the Older Adult,"* Journal of Broadcasting, *15 (Spring 1971), 153–59.*

28. *John B. Lansing and Leslie Kish, "Family Life Cycle as an Independent Variable,"* American Sociological Review, *32 (October 1957), 514.*

29. *Richard B. Ellis, "Composite Population Descriptors: The Socio-Economic Life Cycle Grid,"* in Mary Jane Schlinger, ed., Advances in Consumer Research, *Vol. 2 (Association for Consumer Research, 1974).*

30. *A. Marvin Roscoe, Jr., and Jagdish N. Sheth, "Demographic Segmentation of Long Distance Behavior: Data Analysis and Inductive Model Building,"* in M. Venkatesan, ed., Third Annual Conference of the Association for Consumer Research, *1972, 258–78.*

31. *C. Milton Coughenour, "Functional Aspects of Food Consumption Activity and Family Life Cycle Stages,"* Journal of Marriage and the Family, *34 (November 1972), 656–64.*

32. *Ibid., 660.*

33. *Ibid., 662.*

34. *Wroe Alderson,* Dynamic Marketing Behavior *(Homewood, Ill.: Richard D. Irwin, 1965), 149.*

35. *Robert D. Hisrich and Michael P. Peters, "Selecting the Superior Segmentation Correlate,"* Journal of Marketing, *38 (July 1974), 60–63.*

36. *William D. Wells and George Gubar, "Life Cycle Concept in Marketing Resarch,"* Journal of Marketing Research, *3 (November 1966), 355–63.*

37. *See, for example, Betty Yorburg,* The Changing Family *(New York: Columbia University Press, 1973).*

Discussion questions

1. How does the family influence the consumer socialization of children?

2. Briefly describe a recent important purchase decision that your family made. Analyze the roles performed by various family members in terms of the following six consumption roles:
   a. influencers
   b. gatekeepers
   c. deciders
   d. buyers
   e. preparers
   f. users
   [Note: All of the consumption roles may not apply in a specific decision.]

3. Develop an FLC market segmentation strategy for each of the following four product categories:
   a. cosmetics
   b. food
   c. vacations
   d. housing

4. In purchasing a new TV set, how would you expect the following factors to influence the locus of decision making (i.e., husband-dominated, wife-dominated, joint, or autonomous):
   a. social class
   b. amount of perceived risk
   c. product importance
   d. time pressure

5. If you were the marketing executive in charge of convenience food products (such as frozen dinners) for a large food processor, would you spend a portion of your advertising budget to reach the teenage members of the family? Explain.

6. Select and discuss five newspaper or magazine advertisements, each of which is directed at families at a different stage of the family life cycle.

7. Suppose that you are a marketing manager for a local furniture retailer. How might a knowledge of the family life cycle help you identify
   appropriate market segments and establish suitable price and product
   lines? Explain.

8. How might the traditional family life cycle be revised so that it better
   accounts for changes in the structure and composition of families in
   the 1980s?

10

personal influence and the opinion leadership process

Introduction

Consumers are often influenced by advice they receive from other people, especially in choosing products to buy and services to use.

The preceding chapter described the influence of the family on an individual's consumption behavior. This chapter describes the influence that friends, neighbors, acquaintances, fellow workers, and so forth, have on the individual's consumption behavior. It examines the nature and dynamics of this influence, called the *opinion leadership* process, and the personality and motivations of those who influence (i.e., *opinion leaders*) and those who are influenced, called *opinion receivers*.

WHAT IS OPINION LEADERSHIP?

Opinion leadership is *the process by which one person (the opinion leader) informally influences the actions or attitudes of others, who may be opinion seekers or merely opinion recipients.* This influence is informal and usually verbal, though it may be visual as well. The informal flow of consumer-related influence between two people is sometimes referred to as product-related conversation, or word-of-mouth advertising. As Chapter 7 points out, this kind of influence takes place as informal, interpersonal communication.

The key characteristic of such informal communication is that it takes place between two or more people, none of whom represents a commercial selling source. Interpersonal communication implies personal communication, though it does not have to be face to face (i.e., it may take place in a telephone conversation between two friends).

One of the parties in an informal communications encounter is usually dominant in terms of offering advice or information about a specific product or product category, such as which of several brands is best, or how a particular product may be used. That person, the opinion leader, may become an opinion receiver when another product or product category is discussed.

Individuals who actively seek information and advice about products are sometimes called opinion seekers. For purposes of simplicity, the term *opinion receiver* will be used in the following discussion to identify those who actively seek product information from others and those who receive unsolicited information.

Simple examples of opinion leadership at work include the following:

1. While two neighbors enjoy a leisurely cup of coffee, one asks the other to recommend a plumber.
2. While two friends watch Sunday's football game, one suggests to the other that a new type of TV antenna might bring his set into sharper focus.

Most studies of opinion leadership are concerned with the identification and measurement of the behavioral impact that opinion leaders have on the consumption habits of others.

Dynamics of the opinion leadership process

The opinion leadership process is very dynamic. This section discusses those specific dimensions of opinion leadership which make it a powerful consumer force.

CREDIBILITY

The opinion leader is a highly credible source of product-related information because he is perceived as perfectly neutral (and thus objective) concerning the information or advice he dispenses. His intentions are perceived to be in the best interests of the opinion recipient, since he receives no compensation for his advice and apparently has no "ax to grind." Because the opinion leader often bases his product advice on firsthand experience, he reduces the perceived risk or anxiety inherent in new-product trial for the opinion receiver. Since the opinion leader is often unaware that he is influencing others, his product-related advice can be considered a "soft sell."

POSITIVE AND NEGATIVE PRODUCT INFORMATION

Information provided by commercial sources tends to invariably be favorable to the product; thus, the very fact that the opinion leader provides both favorable and unfavorable information adds to his credibility. An example of unfavorable, or negative, product information is "The problem with front-loading washers is that you can't add clothes to a wash already started."

INFORMATION AND ADVICE

The opinion leader is the source of both information and advice. He may simply talk about his experiences with a product, relate what he knows about a product, or, more aggressively, advise the person(s) to whom he is speaking to buy or avoid a product. Some examples of the kinds of product-related information that an opinion leader is likely to transmit during a conversation include the following:

1. *Which of several brands is best:* "I find that Brim tastes much better than Sanka and it doesn't keep me awake at night."
2. *How a person might best use a specific product:* "If you drain the gas out of your lawnmower in the fall, it starts up much more readily in the spring."
3. *Which is the best place to buy a product:* "You should shop at Gristedes; they have the best meat around."
4. *Who provides the best product-related service:* "If your vacuum is broken, why don't you take it to the L&S Repair Shop? They give very quick service."

OPINION LEADERSHIP IS A TWO-WAY STREET

A person who is an opinion receiver in one instance may subsequently become an opinion leader in another. Consider the following example. An individual contemplating the purchase of a new car may seek information and advice from other people to reduce his own indecision about which car to select. Once he buys a car, however, he may experience postpurchase dissonance and have a compelling need to talk favorably about his purchase to other people to confirm the fact that he made a wise choice.

An opinion leader may also be influenced by an opinion receiver as a result of their product-related conversation. For example, a man may tell a friend about his favorite seafood restaurant and, in response to questions from the opinion receiver, come to realize that the restaurant is really too large, too noisy, and somewhat overpriced.

OPINION LEADERSHIP IS CATEGORY-SPECIFIC

Opinion leadership tends to be category-specific; that is, opinion leaders often "specialize" in certain product categories about which they offer information and advice. When other product categories are discussed, they may reverse their roles and become opinion receivers. Thus a man who considers himself an expert gardener may be an opinion leader in terms of this subject to others; yet, when it comes to financial investments, he may seek advice from others — perhaps even from someone to whom he gives gardening advice.

THE MOTIVATIONS BEHIND OPINION LEADERSHIP

To understand opinion leadership, it is necessary to appreciate the motivations of those who participate in informal product-related conversations. To this end, we will review the underlying motivations of those who receive and those who provide product-related information and advice.

the needs of opinion receivers

The opinion leader fulfills a number of needs for the opinion receiver. First, he is a provider of new-product or new-usage information. Second, he reduces the perceived risk of the opinion seeker by endorsing — usually on the basis of firsthand knowledge — a specific product or brand. Third, he serves to reduce the search time entailed in the identification of a needed product or service. Moreover, the opinion receiver can be certain of receiving the approval of a person whose opinion he obviously respects when he follows that person's advice or product endorsement.

For all of these reasons, consumers often look to friends, neighbors, and other acquaintances for product information. One study reported:[1]

> the source of information most frequently consulted by durable goods buyers were friends and relatives . . . More than 50 percent of all buyers turned for advice to acquaintances and in most instances also looked at durable goods owned by them. Even more striking is the finding that a third of durable goods buyers bought a brand or model that they had seen at someone else's house . . .

the needs of opinion leaders

What motivates a person to talk about a product or service? Motivation theory suggests that people may provide information or advice to others in order to satisfy some basic need of their own (see Chapter 2). This notion is supported by a study of 255 consumers, which reported that "nobody will speak about products or services unless the talking itself, or the expected action of the listener, promises satisfaction of some kind — popularly speaking, unless he gets something out of it."[2]

However, the opinion leader may be unaware of his own underlying motives. As suggested earlier, the opinion leader may simply be trying to reduce her own postpurchase dissonance. If she buys a new oven and is then unsure of the wisdom of her choice, she may try to reassure herself by "talking up" the oven's virtues to others. In this way, she alleviates her own psychological discomfort; furthermore, if she can influence friends or neighbors to also buy the product, she confirms her own good judgment in selecting the product first. Thus the opinion leader's motivation may really be one of self-confirmation—what has been referred to as self-involvement.[3] Furthermore, the information or advice the opinion leader dispenses may serve to gain attention, help her to achieve status, assert her superiority, demonstrate her awareness and expertise, enable her to feel like an innovator, and give her the feeling of having inside information and of "converting" less adventurous souls.[4]

In addition to *self*-involvement, opinion leaders may also be motivated by *product*-involvement, *other*-involvement, and *message*-involvement.[5] The opinion leader who is motivated by *product*-involvement may find himself so enthused or so disappointed with a product that he simply must tell others about it. Those who are motivated by involvement with *others* have a need to share product-related experiences with those

---

TABLE 10–1

A Comparison of the Motivations of Opinion Receivers and Opinion Leaders

Opinion leaders	*Opinion receivers*
1. *Self-Involvement Motivations:* a. To clarify one's own thinking, or reduce post purchase uncertainty or dissonance b. To gain the attention or status one needs c. To assert superiority, awareness, and expertise d. To allow one to feel like an innovator e. To allow one to feel that he can "convert" others	1. *Self-Involvement Motivations* a. To reduce one's risk or uncertainty before making a purchase commitment b. To reduce search time; e.g., one will not have to shop around as much
2. *Product-Involvement Motivations:* To express one's satisfaction or dissatisfaction with a product or service	2. *Product-Involvement Motivations:* a. To learn how to use or consume a product b. To learn what is new
3. *Other-Involvement Motivations:* To express neighborliness and love by discussing products or services that will be appreciated by others	3. *Other-Involvement Motivations:* To do that which has the approval of others, therefore ensuring acceptance
4. *Message-Involvement Motivations:* To express one's reaction to a stimulating advertisement by telling others about it	

others. In this type of situation, the opinion leader uses his product-related conversation as an expression of friendship, neighborliness, and love.

The pervasiveness of advertising in our society encourages *message-involvement*, in that individuals who are bombarded with advertising messages and slogans tend to discuss them and the products they are designed to sell. Such word-of-mouth conversation is typified by the line "Try it, you'll like it" promoted by Alka-Seltzer in the early 1970s and widely repeated by consumers.

Table 10–1 compares the motivations of the opinion receiver with those of the opinion leader.

The measurement of opinion leadership

Consumer researchers are interested in identifying and measuring the impact of the opinion leadership process on consumption behavior. In measuring opinion leadership, the researcher has a choice of four basic measurement techniques: (1) the self-designating method, (2) the sociometric method, (3) the key-informant method, and (4) the objective method. We will briefly review each of these measurement methods in terms of its strengths, its weaknesses and its applications to consumer research.

SELF-DESIGNATING METHOD

In the self-designating method, respondents to a consumer survey are asked to evaluate the extent to which they have provided others with information about a product category or specific brand, or have otherwise influenced the purchase decisions of others.

Figure 10–1 shows three types of self-designating question formats, which are used to determine a respondent's opinion leadership activity. The first consists of a single question, while the other two consist of a series of questions. The use of multiple questions enables the researcher to more reliably determine a respondent's opinion leadership on the basis of a series of supporting statements.

In most cases where researchers use the self-designating method, they divide consumer respondents into two categories: those who influence others (opinion leaders), and those who do not influence others (non-opinion leaders). While this two-category classification scheme is simple and easy to accomplish, it does not realistically reflect the extent to which an individual might function as an opinion leader. Some people classified as nonleaders may truly have no influence on others, while other nonleaders may actually influence the consumption decisions of other people to some degree. Therefore, it would be more realistic to

FIGURE 10–1

Self-Designating Method of Measuring Opinion Leadership

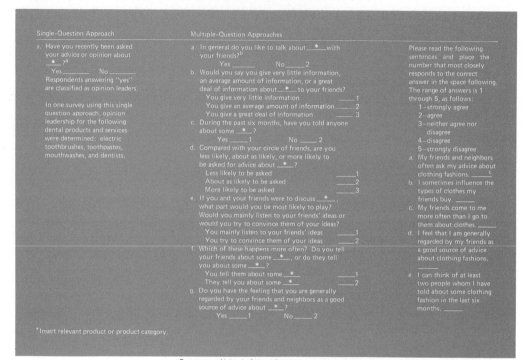

Single-Question Approach

a. Have you recently been asked your advice or opinion about ___*___ ?[a]
   Yes _____   No _____
   Respondents answering "yes" are classified as opinion leaders.

   In one survey using this single question approach, opinion leadership for the following dental products and services were determined: electric toothbrushes, toothpastes, mouthwashes, and dentists.

Multiple-Question Approaches

a. In general do you like to talk about ___*___ with your friends?[b]
   Yes _____   No _____ 2
b. Would you say you give very little information, an average amount of information, or a great deal of information about ___*___ to your friends?
   You give very little information _____1
   You give an average amount of information _____2
   You give a great deal of information _____3
c. During the past six months, have you told anyone about some ___*___ ?
   Yes _____1   No _____2
d. Compared with your circle of friends, are you less likely, about as likely, or more likely to be asked for advice about ___*___ ?
   Less likely to be asked _____1
   About as likely to be asked _____2
   More likely to be asked _____3
e. If you and your friends were to discuss ___*___, what part would you be most likely to play? Would you mainly listen to your friends' ideas or would you try to convince them of your ideas?
   You mainly listen to your friends' ideas _____1
   You try to convince them of your ideas _____2
f. Which of these happens more often? Do you tell your friends about some ___*___, or do they tell you about some ___*___ ?
   You tell them about some ___*___ _____1
   They tell you about some ___*___ _____2
g. Do you have the feeling that you are generally regarded by your friends and neighbors as a good source of advice about ___*___ ?
   Yes _____1   No _____2

Please read the following sentences and place the number that most closely responds to the correct answer in the space following. The range of answers is 1 through 5, as follows:
   1—strongly agree
   2—agree
   3—neither agree nor disagree
   4—disagree
   5—strongly disagree
a. My friends and neighbors often ask my advice about clothing fashions. _____[c]
b. I sometimes influence the types of clothes my friends buy. _____
c. My friends come to me more often than I go to them about clothes. _____
d. I feel that I am generally regarded by my friends as a good source of advice about clothing fashions. _____
e. I can think of at least two people whom I have told about some clothing fashion in the last six months. _____

*Insert relevant product or product category.

Sources: [a]Alvin J. Silk, "Overlap among Self-designated Opinion Leaders: A Study of Selected Dental Products and Services," Journal of Marketing Research, 3 (August 1966), 255–59.
[b]John O. Summers, "The Identity of Women's Clothing Fashion Opinion Leaders," Journal of Marketing Research, 7 (May 1970), 178–85.
[c]Fred D. Reynolds and William R. Darden, "Mutually Adaptive Effects of Interpersonal Communication," Journal of Marketing Research, 8 (November 1971), 449–54.

employ a classification scheme consisting of three or more categories, one that explicitly considers a *range* of opinion-leading activity—e.g., those who *never* or *infrequently* influence others, those who *more frequently* influence others, and, finally, those who are *highly influential* opinion leaders.

The self-designating technique is used more frequently than other methods for measuring opinion leadership because consumer researchers find it easy to include in market research studies. However, since this method relies on a consumer's self-evaluation of his opinion leadership activity, it may be open to bias should the respondent perceive "opinion leadership" (even though the term is not used) to be a desirable characteristic and thus overestimate his own role as an opinion leader.

SOCIOMETRIC METHOD

The sociometric method measures the person-to-person informal communication of consumers concerning products or product categories. In this method, each respondent is asked to identify (1) the specific individuals (if any) to whom he provided advice or information about the product or brand being studied, and (2) the specific individuals (if any) who provided *him* with advice or information about the product or brand being studied. In the first instance, if the respondent identifies one or more individuals whom he has provided with some form of product information, he is tentatively classified as an opinion leader. The researcher then seeks to validate this determination by interviewing the individual or individuals named by the primary respondent and asking him to recall whether or not he did, in fact, receive such product information.

In the second instance, respondents are asked to identify individuals who provided them with information about a product under investigation. Individuals so designated by the primary respondent are tentatively classified as opinion leaders. Again, the researcher attempts to validate this determination by asking the individuals so named whether or not they did, in fact, provide the relevant product information.

Thus, if Consumer A reports that he received information or advice concerning a specific product from Consumer B, then Consumer B must confirm that he provided such information or advice to Consumer A. In this way the sociometric method validly identifies the opinion leaders and opinion receivers in product-related conversations.

sociometric research designs

In using the sociometric method, the researcher has two options in terms of research design: he can study a self-contained community, or he can elect to study a more widespread respondent sample. If he studies a specific community that has definite physical boundaries (such as all the residents in a particular housing project), he will find it relatively simple to verify product-related conversations. If he chooses a more widespread respondent sample, he must be prepared to trace the web of word-of-mouth contacts by seeking out all individuals named by his primary respondent group, regardless of where they are located. The few consumer studies that have used the sociometric method have elected to study "intact" or self-contained communities, because such research is so much less costly and easier to manage.

consumer behavior applications

An early application of the sociometric approach to the study of consumer behavior examined opinion leadership among wives of graduate students living in university-sponsored housing.[6] The intact community provided the opportunity to measure the flow of word-of-mouth conversation concerning a new brand of coffee and the subsequent impact of such conversation on the trial of the new product. The researcher found that wives who received favorable comment or information concerning the product were more likely to try it than those who received either no information or negative information. This pioneering study concluded that positive informal communication promotes the acceptance of new products among members of a given community.

Figure 10–2 illustrates the type of questioning employed in the

FIGURE 10–2

Sociometric Questioning Approach to Assess Informal Communication about a New Product

A. *Providing Information to Others*
  1. Did you tell anyone, living here at Kissena I, about the "Brand X" salt substitute?

              yes _____   no _____

  2. If "yes"
     Which person did you first tell about the salt substitute?

         First Name   Family Name   Apt. or Floor

     _____   _____   _____

  3. Which other people, living here at Kissena I, did you tell about the "Brand X" salt substitute?

              (Space for three other names and locations)

  4. Did you suggest that they try or not try the "Brand X" salt substitute?

         Try _____   Not Try _____   Other _____

B. *Receiving Information from Others*
  1. What was the first thing you remember hearing about the "Brand X" salt substitute?

  2. Do you remember who made this first comment about "Brand X" salt substitute?

              yes _____   no _____

  3. If "yes," what was her name?

         First Name   Family Name   Apt. or Floor

     _____   _____   _____

  4. Does she live here at Kissena I?

              yes _____   no _____

  5. Did this person recommend that you *try* or *not try* the "Brand X" salt substitute?

         Try _____   Not Try _____   Other _____

  6. If the respondent bought "Brand X" salt substitute, then ask:

     "Did this conversation occur before or after you bought the "Brand X" salt substitute?

         Before _____   After _____   Do not remember _____

  7. Can you name any other persons, living at Kissena I, who have mentioned the "Brand X" salt substitute to you?

              (Space for three other names and locations)

sociometric research approach. It presents a series of questions used in a study of opinion leadership among elderly consumers residing in a retirement community.[7]

The objective of the study was to determine the impact of product-related informal communication among community members on their subsequent decisions to purchase or not to purchase a new salt substitute. The results of this study indicated that those community members who provided others with information or advice concerning the new product (the opinion leaders) and those who received positive information or advice from others concerning the new product (the opinion receivers) were both more likely to have purchased it than those who did not engage in any exchange of informal information about the product.[8]

KEY-INFORMANT METHOD

A third way to measure opinion leadership is through the use of a key informant—a person who is keenly aware or knowledgeable about the nature of social communication among members of a specific consumer group. This person, the key informant, is asked to identify those individuals in the group who are most likely to be opinion leaders.

The key informant does not have to be a member of the group under study (for example, a professor may serve as the key informant for a college class). This research method is relatively inexpensive, since it requires that only one individual—or at most several individuals—be intensively interviewed, while the self-designating and sociometric methods require that an entire consumer sample or community be interviewed. However, the key-informant method is generally not used by marketers because of the difficulties inherent in identifying an individual who can *objectively* identify opinion leaders in a relevant consumer group.

The key-informant method would seem to be of greatest potential use in the study of industrial or institutional opinion leadership. For example, a firm's salesmen might serve as key informants in the identification of specific customers who are most likely to influence the purchase decisions of other firms in their industry. Similarly, the purchasing agent of a specific firm might serve as a key informant by providing an outside salesman with the names of those persons in his organization who are most likely to influence the purchase decision.

In the study of consumers, possible key informants include influential community members such as the president of the local church or social group, the head of the local PTA, or a prominent local retailer.

OBJECTIVE METHOD

The objective method of determining opinion leadership is much like a controlled experiment. It involves the deliberate placement of new products or new-product information with selected individuals and then tracing the resultant web of interpersonal communication concerning the relevant product.

An intriguing study designed to measure the influence of opinion leaders in household matters provides a unique example of the objective method.[9] Fifteen friendship groups of women living in a self-contained community were individually interviewed via the sociometric method to assess their level of opinion leadership with regard to household management matters. The women who scored *highest* as opinion leaders in each of nine groups were chosen to serve as opinion-leader confederates (i.e., to cooperate with the researcher). In each of the other six groups, the women who scored *lowest* in opinion leadership were also chosen to serve as opinion-leader confederates. This research design enabled the researcher to compare the influence exerted by those identified as opinion leaders with the influence exerted by those identified as non-leaders, when all were placed in a controlled position to serve as opinion leaders.

All fifteen participants selected by the researcher to function as opinion leaders were provided with new freeze-dried food items and were asked to serve them to their families. They were also requested to give samples of the new food products to all other members of their friendship groups and to suggest that they, in turn, serve the items to their families.[10]

The results indicated that those individuals who received the new food items from "natural" opinion leaders tended to echo the leaders' opinions concerning the new product. Conversely, those individuals who received samples of the new food items from artificially created opinion leaders shifted away from the opinion leaders' sentiments. These findings suggest that true opinion leaders are capable of altering group members' opinions in the direction of their own opinions, whereas nonleaders (those who score low in opinion leadership studies) may adversely influence those whom they attempt to influence.

Table 10–2 presents an overview of each of the four methods of measuring opinion leadership.

A profile of the opinion leader

Just who is the opinion leader? Can he be recognized by any distinctive characteristics? Can she be reached through any specific media? Marketers have long sought answers to these questions, for if they are able to identify the relevant opinion leaders for their products, they can direct their promotional efforts to these leaders, confident that they in turn will influence the consumption behavior of others. For this reason, a number of consumer researchers have attempted to develop a realistic profile of the opinion leader. This has not been easy to do. It was pointed out earlier that opinion leadership tends to be category-specific; that

TABLE 10–2

Methods of Measuring Opinion Leadership—Advantages and Limitations

Opinion leadership measurement method	Description of method	Sample questions asked	Advantages	Limitations
1. Self-designating method	Each respondent is asked a series of questions to determine the degree to which he perceives himself to be an opinion leader.	Do you influence other people in their selection of products?	Measures the individual's own perceptions of his opinion leadership.	Dependent upon the objectivity with which respondents can identify and report their personal influence.
2. Sociometric method	Members of a social system are asked to whom they go for advice and information about a product category.	Whom do you ask? Who asks you for information about that product category?	Sociometric questions have the greatest degree of validity and are easy to administer.	Very costly analysis is often very complex. Requires a large number of respondents. Not suitable for sample designs where only a portion of the social system is interviewed.
3. Key-informant method	Carefully selected key informants in a social system are asked to designate opinion leaders.	Who are the most influential people in the group?	Relatively inexpensive and less time consuming than the sociometric method.	Informants who are not thoroughly familiar with the system would provide invalid information.
4. Objective method	Artificially places individuals in the position to act as opinion leaders and measures results of their efforts.	Have you tried the product?	Measures individual's ability to influence others under controlled circumstances.	Requires the establishment of an experimental design and the tracking of the resulting impact on the participants.

Reprinted with permission of Macmillan Publishing Co., Inc., from Communication of Innovations, by Everett M. Rogers and F. Floyd Shoemaker. Copyright © 1971 by The Free Press, a Division of The Macmillan Company.

is, an individual who is an opinion leader in one product category may be an opinion receiver in another product category. Thus the generalized profile of opinion leaders can only be considered in the context of specific product categories.

KNOWLEDGE AND INTEREST

It has been suggested that shared interest is the foundation upon which most informal communication is based.[11] However, some studies indicate that opinion leaders probably possess a keener level of interest in the product category than do opinion receivers.[12] Because of his interest, the opinion leader is likely to be better informed and because of his knowledge, others may turn to him for his relative expertise. This tends to be true regardless of whether the basic motivation of the opinion leader is self-involvement, product-involvement, or other-involvement.

A study designed to relate opinion leadership to perceived knowledge and degree of interest in the subject was conducted among four hundred members of a consumer buying panel in Los Angeles. The researchers found a moderate-to-strong relationship between opinion leadership and interest in household furnishings, and a strong relationship between opinion leadership and knowledge about cosmetics and personal care.[13] In another study, researchers reported that interest in fashion was a relatively stable predictor of opinion leadership in the area of male clothing fashions.[14]

Other research suggests that chief among the characteristics that distinguish opinion leaders from nonleaders is their unique *involvement* with the subject of interest.[15] Compared with nonleaders in a particular product category, opinion leaders read more about related consumer issues, are more knowledgeable about related new-product developments, participate more often in related consumer activities, and derive greater satisfaction from these product-related activities.

CONSUMER INNOVATORS

Consistent with his greater interest in a product category, the consumer opinion leader is more likely to try new products.[16] Thus opinion leaders tend to speak with some authority when providing advice to others who have not as yet tried the new product.

A study of consumer innovators found that about half of the individuals identified as innovators (the first 10 percent to adopt one or more of such consumer durable goods as color television or stereophonic equipment) claimed to have shown the purchased product to others, and that more than 60 percent of those to whom they showed the product later purchased it.[17] In another study, it was reported that innovators in the use of a new automotive diagnostic service (those who used it during its first two months of operation) claimed to have been asked their opinion more often about a variety of topics than did a comparable random sample.[18] Ninety percent of the innovators also reported telling at least one other person about the experience within a few days after using the automotive service; of this number, almost half reported telling two or more people. Another study found that 33 percent of the innovators in the adoption of Touch-Tone telephones claimed that they could name at least one other person who bought the innovation, in part or in whole, because of their influence.[19]

Clearly these few studies indicate that opinion leaders are also likely to be consumer innovators.

PERSONALITY TRAITS

Very few studies have explored the relationship between personality and opinion leadership. Of those that have, most have focused on the area of women's clothing fashions.

An obvious characteristic of the consumer opinion leader is her willingness to talk about a product-related topic. For example, women's fashion opinion leaders have been found to talk more about fashion, and to more often interpret fashion trends for friends, than do nonleaders.[20]

This characteristic of willingness to talk is supported by evidence that indicates that fashion opinion leaders possess greater *assertiveness* and *emotional stability,* which enable them to speak out more readily on topics in which they feel competent. Furthermore, their self perception as being *more likable* and *less depressive* may encourage their active participation in social conversations.[21]

One researcher reported that fashion opinion leaders tended to be more *progressive, outgoing* (less shy), and *susceptible to change* than nonleaders.[22] A second study found a significant relationship between *general self-confidence* and fashion opinion leadership.[23]

However, other researchers have reported finding no significant relationships between opinion leadership and such personality variables as *sociability, social presence, self acceptance, socialization, communality,* and *flexibility.*[24] Obviously, further research is needed to resolve these inconsistencies.

Several personality characteristics of opinion leaders would appear to bridge specific product-related contexts. Among these are *self confidence* and *gregariousness* (i.e., sociability). It may be that, to advise others, an individual must first have confidence in himself and his ideas. Several studies have reported that opinion leaders scored higher in terms of local friendships than did nonleaders.[25] This is not surprising, when one considers that opinion leaders must be involved in social interaction in order to function.

MEDIA HABITS

A number of interdisciplinary studies concerned with opinion leadership and the diffusion of information have concluded that opinion leaders make greater use of mass media—they tend to use "more impersonal and technically accurate" and more "cosmopolitan" (i.e., widespread) sources of information.[26] Few studies within the marketing literature have been able to confirm these findings. Rather, opinion leaders have been found to have much greater readership of special publications devoted to the specific product category in which the opinion leader "leads." For example, a study of automotive opinion leadership concluded that "opinion leaders will read media directly related to their consumer topics more often than nonleaders."[27] Other researchers have reported a significant relationship between women's fashion leadership and high exposure to fashion magazines.[28] Thus the opinion leader would appear to have greater exposure to media relevant to his area of interest than nonleaders, but not necessarily greater exposure to mass media in general. Much more research is needed to determine the usage of both mass and class (i.e., special-interest) media by opinion leaders.

SOCIAL CHARACTERISTICS

As with other characteristics of the opinion leader, social characteristics appear to depend upon the topic of interest. In most marketing studies, the opinion leader has been found to belong to the same socioeconomic group (social class) as the opinion receiver. This is not surprising; it would seem reasonable to expect an individual to turn to someone within his own social group for information or advice concerning a specific product category.[29] Similarly, an opinion leader would be most likely to give information or advice to those people with whom he regularly engages in informal communication, the people within his own social stratum.

A study of women's fashions found that opinion leaders tended

---

TABLE 10–3

Sociological Characteristics of Women's Clothing Fashion Opinion Leaders

Greater Physical Mobility
More Social Communication
More Organizational Memberships
More Organizational Participation
More Organizational Offices Held
Greater Organizational Affiliation
Greater Participation in Formal Social Activities
Greater Participation in Informal Social Activities
Greater Participation in Sporting Activities
More Total Social Activity Participation

Source: Adapted from John O. Summers, "The Identity of Women's Clothing Fashion Opinion Leaders," Journal of Marketing Research, 7 (May 1970), 180.

to have greater physical mobility and thus a greater opportunity for exposure to new and different fashion ideas.[30] This study also found opinion leaders to be higher in social communications, affiliations with organizations, and participation in social activities.[31] Table 10–3 summarizes these findings concerning the sociological characteristics of opinion leaders for women's fashions.

DEMOGRAPHIC CHARACTERISTICS

A number of studies indicate that informal communication generally flows between people of similar age. This characteristic is again category-specific. For example, one research study concerned with moviegoing found that opinion leaders and opinion receivers could be classified into three broad age categories.[32] It also found that 66 percent of all informal communications concerning movies occurred among people of the same age category. Another study found that individuals tend to seek advice from older people regarding physician selection.[33] Further analysis of this data revealed that parents tend to seek advice regarding physician selection from other parents with children of approximately the same age and number. A study of women's clothing fashions showed that opinion leaders tended to be younger and have more education, higher incomes, and higher occupational status.[34]

These studies suggest that for specific areas of interest, people may seek information and advice from those people whom they perceive to be more qualified informants. In the context of physician selection, older people may be perceived as having more information and experience. In the context of women's fashions, younger people, those with higher incomes, and/or those with higher occupational status may be perceived as being more qualified informants.

In summary, it is difficult to construct a generalized profile of the opinion leader outside of the context of a specific category of interest. However, on the basis of the limited evidence available, as shown in Table 10–4, opinion leaders, across categories, tend to be higher in the

TABLE 10–4

Profile of Opinion Leaders

Generalized attributes across product categories	Category-specific attributes
Innovativeness	Interest
Willingness to talk	Knowledge
Self-confidence	Special-interest media exposure
Gregariousness	Same age
	Same social status
	Social exposure outside group

following attributes: innovativeness, greater willingness to talk, self-confidence, and gregariousness. Within the context of specific subject areas, opinion leaders tend to have greater interest in and knowledge of the product category and more exposure to relevant special-interest media. They also tend to belong to the same socioeconomic and age groups as the opinion receivers.

Frequency and overlap of opinion leadership

Opinion leadership is not a rare phenomenon. Often more than one-third of the people studied in a consumer research project are classified as opinion leaders.[35] One researcher reported that almost half (47.5 percent) of his respondents identified themselves as opinion leaders in one or more of the product categories he investigated.[36] In another study, only 31 percent of the 976 respondents did not qualify as opinion leaders in at least one of six product areas examined.[37]

That consumer opinion leadership tends to be a frequently possessed characteristic suggests that people seem to be sufficiently interested in at least one product or product category to talk about it and give advice concerning it to others.

This leads to some interesting questions: Is opinion leadership generalized? Do opinion leaders in one product category tend to be opinion leaders in other product categories? Consumer researchers have concerned themselves with these questions in their search for a generalized profile of the opinion leader.

OVERLAP OF OPINION LEADERSHIP

A number of studies have investigated the overlap of opinion leadership across several product categories. A study of five dental product and service categories did not yield statistically significant evidence of overlap of opinion leadership and interest, although it did generate some evidence for this trend.[38]

A study that investigated whether opinion leaders tend to overlap more across certain combinations of interest areas than across other combinations of interest areas found that significant overlap did exist across all combinations of product categories studied. The researchers noted that opinion leadership overlap was highest between product categories that involved similar interests (large and small appliances, women's clothing fashions and cosmetics, personal grooming aids, household cleansers and detergents, and packaged food products).[39] Although the researchers did not measure product interest directly, they inferred it from the apparent similarity or dissimilarity of the product categories studied.

Self-designated female opinion leaders who were members of a national consumer panel were questioned about sixteen categories of consumer spending.[40] The findings of this study supported the hypothesis that opinion leadership overlaps product areas in which the opinion leaders' interests overlap (for example, in buying and preparing food, or in new clothing styles and furnishing a home).

The above evidence indicates that opinion leaders in one product area are often opinion leaders in related areas in which they are also interested.

The opinion leadership environment

Product-related discussions between two people do not take place in "thin air" or in a vacuum. Two people are not likely to meet and spontaneously break into a discussion in which product-related information is sought or offered. Rather, product discussions generally occur within relevant situational contexts—e.g., when a specific product or a similar product is being used or served, or as an outgrowth of a more general discussion which in some way touches upon the product category.[41] Thus, if two coeds are discussing the forthcoming Christmas dance and

TABLE 10–5

Situational Contexts of Interpersonal Influence with a New Coffee Product

	Information given	Information received	Total
Food related context			
Drinking coffee	25%	38%	30%
Drinking Maxim	9	–	6
Conversation concerning food	35	29	33
Shopping for food	5	8	6
Eating	5	–	3
Subtotals:	79%	75%	78%
Non-food context			
Spontaneously given	7%	17%	11%
Spontaneously received	–	4	1
Viewing/hearing Maxim ad	5	4	4
Unclear	9	–	6
Subtotals:	21%	25%	22%
Totals:	100%	100%	100%

Source: Russell W. Belk, "Occurence of Word-of-Mouth Buyer Behavior as a Function of Situation and Advertising Stimuli" Combined Proceedings (Chicago: American Marketing Association, 1971), 420.

one asks, "What are you going to wear?" their discussion might eventually lead to one student asking the other for advice on the appropriateness of a new style or fashion. In this situation, the opinion leader will provide information to the opinion receiver as an outgrowth of a conversation concerning a school dance which they both plan to attend.

A study of 134 randomly selected housewives concerning their awareness of a new coffee product (Maxim Freeze-Dried Coffee) revealed that discussions concerning the new product were most likely to come up in food-related contexts.[42] Table 10–5 presents data indicating that 79 percent of the respondents who *provided* information about Maxim to others did so in a food-related context, while 75 percent of the respondents who reported *receiving* such information did so in a food-related context.

OPINION LEADERS ARE FRIENDS OR NEIGHBORS

It is not surprising that opinion leaders and opinion receivers are often friends, neighbors, or work associates, since existing friendships provide numerous opportunities for conversation concerning product-related topics. It is also true that physical proximity is likely to increase the occurrences of product-related conversations.[43] A neighborhood center, for example, increases the opportunities for neighbors to meet and engage in informal communication concerning product-related topics.

The importance of physical proximity in the opinion leadership process was supported in a study concerning interpersonal influence in physician selection.[44] Analysis revealed that 11 percent of the participants in two-person discussions (i.e., dyads) were members of the same club, 15 percent belonged to the same church, 15 percent were employed by the same company, 27 percent lived within one block of each other, and 67 percent had visited the other person's home.

Additional support for the importance of physical proximity in informal product-related conversations comes from a study of word-of-mouth influence among elderly residents in a high-rise retirement community. The study found that 81 percent of the exchange of information and advice occurred between persons who lived on the same floor; the remaining 19 percent occurred between residents living one floor apart.[45]

The private home appears to be the most frequent setting for product discussions. A study of four different types of consumer products (see Table 10–6) revealed that such discussions are more likely to take place in the afternoon and are most likely to occur between two people rather than in a larger group.[46]

The foregoing studies demonstrate that product-related conversations generally occur between friends, neighbors, or work associates who have some physical proximity in a situational context relevant to the product under discussion.

TABLE 10–6

Social Settings for Interpersonal Communications

	Product Category				
	Durable press clothing	New type of nylon hose	New snack food	Electric toothbrush	Total
Physical location					
Private home	65%	50%	74%	77%	69%
Other	35	50	26	23	31
	100%	100%	100%	100%	100%
Time of day					
Morning	30%	28%	20%	26%	27%
Afternoon	44	44	35	38	40
Evening	26	28	45	36	33
	100%	100%	100%	100%	100%
Number of participants					
Two	72%	77%	54%	63%	66%
More than two	28	23	46	37	34
	100%	100%	100%	100%	100%
Number of respondents	(843)	(247)	(477)	(560)	(2,127)

Source: Adapted from John O. Summers, "New Product Interpersonal Communication," Combined Proceedings (Chicago: American Marketing Association, 1971., p. 432.

Theories of the interpersonal flow of communication

How does information provided by the mass media reach and influence the total population? Several theories suggest that the opinion leader is a vital link in the transmission of information and influence.

TWO-STEP FLOW OF COMMUNICATION THEORY

A study of voting behavior some thirty years ago concluded that ideas often flow from radio and print to opinion leaders and from them to the less-active sections of the population.[47] This so-called *two-step flow of communication* theory portrayed opinion leaders as direct receivers of information from impersonal mass-media sources, who in turn transmitted (and interpreted) this information to the masses. This theory views the opinion leader as a *middleman* between the impersonal mass media and the majority of society.

The major contribution of the two-step flow of communication theory was that it demonstrated that social interaction between people serves as the principal means by which information is transmitted, attitudes are developed, and behavior is stimulated. The theory rejected the notion that mass media alone influenced the sale of products, political candidates, and ideas to a mass audience.

Figure 10–3 presents a model of the two-step flow of communication theory. Information is depicted as flowing in a single direction (i.e., one-way) from the mass media to the opinion leaders (Step 1), and then from the opinion leaders (who interpret, legitimize, and transmit the information) to friends, neighbors, and acquaintances, who constitute the "masses" (Step 2).

FIGURE 10–3

Two-Step Flow of Communication Theory

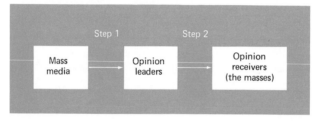

MULTISTEP FLOW OF COMMUNICATION THEORY

The two-step flow of communication theory is insightful in that it illustrates how people acquire information about issues of interest. However, we now realize that it is not an accurate portrayal of the flow of information and influence. The need for modification of this theory is in large part based upon more recent evidence, which suggests that:[48]

1. Mass media may inform both opinion leaders and opinion receivers; however, the opinion receiver is more likely to be influenced by the opinion leader than by the media.
2. Not all interpersonal communication is initiated by opinion leaders and directed to opinion receivers. Very often those who are receivers may initiate the interpersonal communication by requesting information or advice from the opinion leaders.
3. Those who receive information and advice *from* others (i.e., opinion receivers) are more likely to offer advice *to* others (including opinion leaders) than those who do not receive advice from others.
4. Opinion leaders are more likely than those who are nonleaders to both receive and seek advice from others.

It is apparent that the two-step flow of communication theory does not fully account for the complexity of interpersonal communications. A more recent model depicts the transmission of information from the media as a *multistep flow of communication.* The revised model takes into account the fact that information and influence are often two-way processes; that opinion leaders both influence and are influenced by opinion receivers.

Figure 10–4 presents a model of the multistep flow of communication theory. Steps 1a and 1b depict the flow of information from the mass media simultaneously to opinion leaders, opinion receivers, and information receivers (who neither influence nor are influenced by others.) Step 2 shows the transmission of information and influence from opinion leaders to opinion receivers. Step 3 reflects the transfer of information and influence from opinion receivers to opinion leaders.

FIGURE 10–4

Multistep Flow of Communication Theory

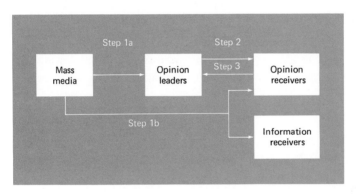

marketing implications of the multistep theory

Research evidence provides support for the multistep theory of communication.[49] It suggests that interpersonal communication cannot be neatly dichotomized into dominant, all-powerful opinion leaders and passive opinion receivers. For the marketing practitioner, the multistep flow of communication theory suggests that it is important to identify and reach opinion leaders because of the critical roles they play in transmitting information and influence about products to opinion receivers. However, the theory also suggests that it is equally important to identify and reach individuals who are the receivers or seekers of information and advice, for these individuals are likely to function eventually as opinion leaders themselves. As one astute observer remarked:[50] ". . . it appears that rather than distinguishing among opinion leaders and followers, one should distinguish among consumers engaging in more or [in] less personal communication about the product."

Marketers have long been aware of the powerful influence that opinion leadership exerts on consumer behavior. They try to encourage word-of-mouth communication and other favorable informal conversations concerning their products because they recognize that consumers place more credibility in such informal communication sources than in paid advertising. The seeking of product information and advice also tends to be the most widely used strategy for reducing perceived risk.

One marketing strategist suggested that new-product designers exploit the effectiveness of word-of-mouth communication by deliberately designing products to have word-of-mouth potential. He said the products "should give customers something to talk about, and to talk with—a powerful advantage idea that can be expressed in words."[51] Examples of new products that have had such word-of-mouth potential include the Polaroid camera, Diet-Rite Cola, the Sylvania flashcube, the Water Pik, Contac, Crest toothpaste, and the "pill." These revolutionary products "sold themselves," as consumers sold them to each other by word-of-mouth.

In some instances where informal word-of-mouth did not spontaneously emerge from the uniqueness of the product or its marketing strategy, marketers have deliberately attempted to stimulate or to simulate opinion leadership.

ADVERTISEMENTS THAT STIMULATE OPINION LEADERSHIP

Advertisements designed to get consumers to "tell your friends how much you like our product" are one way in which marketers have used advertising to increase product-related discussions. The objective of a promotional strategy of stimulation is to run advertisements that are sufficiently interesting and informative to provoke consumers into discussing the virtues of the product with others. For example, Inglenook Vineyards has sponsored a series of advertisements designed to increase the consumer's expertise in the selection and serving of fine wines. Figure 10–5 illustrates how such an advertisement can provide the consumer with sufficient knowledge and self-confidence to enable him to give advice on wines.

ADVERTISEMENTS THAT SIMULATE OPINION LEADERSHIP

A firm's advertisements can also be designed to simulate product discussion by portraying people in the act of informal communication. Such a promotional tactic has the characteristic of suggesting that it is appro-

FIGURE 10-5

Advertisement Designed to Stimulate Informal Communication

INGLENOOK VINEYARDS, RUTHERFORD, CALIFORNIA

WHAT TO DO WITH WINE BESIDES DRINK IT.

Unfortunately, wine doesn't come with instructions. And lots of people have never known much about its proper care.

We at Inglenook Vineyards would like to take this time to give you a few pointers on the subject.

We spend a lot of time and money in the making of our wine. And once it passes out of our hands, we'd like to feel that it's being given the best possible treatment.

DON'T MAKE THIS COMMON MISTAKE.

Wine should always be stored lying down on its side, never standing up. That's so the cork will

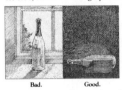

Bad.   **Good.**

always be moist. If the cork dries out, air will get to the wine and spoil it.

Keep wine in a cool, dark place. About 55–60 degrees is just right. But the most important thing is that the temperature be constant. It should vary no more than a few degrees year 'round.

DECANTING WINE.

If you have wines five years old and older, they may have a little sediment in them. In order to serve the wine without the sediment getting mixed up in the wine, you should decant it.

To do this, just pour the wine very slowly into another bottle or carafe. Place a candle behind the neck of the bottle and the second you see a little sediment coming across, stop.

THE ROOM TEMPERATURE MYTH.

White wines and sparkling wines such as Champagne and rosé should be served cold. How cold is cold? 45 degrees is just right. If you don't have a thermometer, put the wine in the refrigerator for 2½ hours before serving. Or in a bucket with ice cubes and water for 15 minutes.

Red wines should be served at room temperature. But this doesn't mean 72 degrees. The "room temperature" standard was established in Europe long before the invention of central heating. At that time, rooms in Europe were about 65 to 68 degrees, which is the perfect temperature for serving red wines. You can bring a wine's temperature down to that level by placing it in the

refrigerator five minutes before serving. But never heat a bottle of red wine in order to get it up to the proper temperature. There's no quicker way to destroy a bottle of wine than to heat it up.

AVOIDING THAT METALLIC TASTE.

Remove the metal capsule from the top of the wine bottle below the lip. With a napkin, clean off the top between the cork and the glass. This is done because it's impossible to pour wine from a bottle without spilling a little on the lip. And since the metal cap is sometimes corroded, the wine could pick up a metallic taste if it were to spill over the edge.

Now remove the cork, gently, so as not to disturb the wine. We recommend the wing-type corkscrew because you don't have to jerk it to get the cork out.

A FINAL WORD OF CAUTION.

Now that you know the basics of how to treat wine, you should also know there aren't many wines around that deserve this kind of treatment.

Because there's nothing you can do at home to save a wine if it's been mishandled at the winery.

Which brings us to Inglenook.

We take elaborate precautions to make sure our wine is handled properly.

For instance, the walls of our wine cellar are 3 feet thick limestone, which keeps the temperature constant.

Our wine casks rest upon a dirt foundation, instead of concrete, the usual practice. This promotes fresh air circulation, and it also stabilizes the humidity.

If you look on the label of our wine, you'll see the words, "Produced and Bottled by Inglenook Vineyards".

This means we produce the wine from start to finish, in order to make sure that our wine is never mishandled.

Naturally, this kind of extra care costs extra money.

And we pass the extra cost right on to you.

Inglenook is the most expensive wine made in America. So when you pick up a bottle of it, take good care of it.

And it'll take good care of you.

ESTATE BOTTLED
Inglenook
Napa Valley
JOHANNISBERG RIESLING

INGLENOOK
We make the most expensive wine in America.

This ad is one of a series. If you'd like copies of the other ads, send your name and address to The Cellarmaster, Box G, Inglenook Vineyards, Rutherford, CA 94573.

Courtesy of United Vintners, Inc.

priate to discuss a particular subject or product. For example, a simulated informal communication encounter between two women has been employed in the television advertising campaign for a feminine hygiene product to persuade women to discuss their use or contemplated use of this personal-care product. Such simulations also reduce the need for consumers to actually seek product advice from others.

An even more penetrating application of advertising designed to simulate informal communication is shown in Figure 10–6. This Hunt-Wesson Foods advertisement depicts a group of consumers in a "chain of communication" dispelling the false rumor that Hunt's products are owned by a rich Texan of the same name.

WORD OF MOUTH MAY BE UNCONTROLLABLE

Although most marketing managers believe that word-of-mouth communication is extremely effective, one problem they sometimes overlook is the fact that such informal communication is not easy to control. Negative comments—rumors that are untrue—can sometimes sweep through a population to the detriment of the product in question.

For example, for years DuPont was plagued by the rumor that Teflon (a resin used to coat cookware) gave off lethal fumes when heated. The rumor claimed that an unidentified machinist took one puff from a cigarette contaminated by a little Teflon and died within five minutes. At one point, DuPont's public relations department was answering twenty letters a day from worried stockholders and customers, but still the rumor persisted. Finally, Du Pont had one of its most distinguished scientists present a carefully documented paper at a technical meeting which detailed the exhaustive tests that Du Pont had conducted over the years to establish Teflon's safety. A booklet based on his speech was then distributed by the "tens of thousands" to the consuming public. After many years, the rumor finally died out. It is interesting to speculate about the number of lost sales which resulted from that unfortunate rumor.

THE CREATION OF OPINION LEADERS

Marketing strategists agree that promotional efforts would be most effective if they could segment their markets into opinion leaders and opinion receivers relevant to their product category. Then they could direct their promotional messages directly to the people most likely to "carry the word" to the masses. However, because of the difficulties inherent in identifying appropriate opinion leaders, some researchers have suggested that it might be more fruitful to "create" product-specific opinion leaders.

In one study, a group of socially influential high school students (class presidents, sports captains, etc.) were asked to become members of

FIGURE 10–6

Advertisement Depicting Word-of-Mouth Communication

Courtesy of Hunt-Wesson Foods, Inc.

a panel that would rate new rock-and-roll phonograph records. As part of his responsibility, each panel participant was encouraged to discuss his record choices with friends. Preliminary examination suggested that these influentials would not qualify as opinion leaders for records because of their relatively meager ownership of the product category.[52] However, by encouraging their interest, some of the records that the group evaluated made the top-ten charts in the cities where they lived, while these same records did not make the top-ten charts in any other city. This study suggests that product-specific opinion leaders can be created by taking socially involved or influential people and deliberately increasing their enthusiasm for a product category.

Summary

Opinion leadership is the process by which one person (the opinion leader) informally influences the actions or attitudes of others, who may be opinion seekers or merely opinion recipients. Opinion receivers perceive the opinion leader as a highly credible source of product information who, because of his presumed objectivity, can reduce their search time and their perceived risk. Opinion leaders, in turn, are motivated to give information or advice to others in part because it enhances their own status and self-image, and because such advice tends to reduce their own postpurchase dissonance. Other motives include product-involvement, other-involvement, and message-involvement.

Market researchers identify opinion leaders by the self-designated method, the key-informant method, the sociometric method, and the objective method. Studies of opinion leadership indicate that the phenomenon tends to be product-specific; that is, individuals "specialize" in a product or product category in which they are highly interested and involved. An opinion leader for one product category may become an opinion receiver for another.

Generally, opinion leaders are gregarious, self-confident, innovative people who like to talk. They acquire information about their areas of interest through avid readership of special-interest magazines and by new-product trial. Their interests often overlap adjacent product areas; thus their opinion leadership may extend into related areas.

The opinion leadership process usually takes place among friends, neighbors, and work associates who have frequent physical proximity and thus ample opportunity to hold informal product-related conversations. Such conversations usually occur naturally in the context of the product-category usage.

The two-step flow of communication theory, developed some thirty years ago, highlighted the role of interpersonal influence in the transmission of information from the mass media to the population at large. This theory provided the foundation for a revised multistep flow of communication model, which takes into account the fact that information and influence are often two-way processes, and that opinion leaders both influence and are influenced by opinion receivers.

Marketers recognize the strategic importance of segmenting their audiences into opinion leaders and opinion receivers for their product categories. In this way, they can direct their promotional efforts to the more influential segments of their markets, with some confidence that these individuals will in turn transmit this information to those who seek product advice. Marketers have found that they can also "create" opinion leaders for their products by taking socially involved or influential people and deliberately increasing their enthusiasm for a product category.

Endnotes

1. *George Katona and Eva Mueller, "A Study of Purchase Decisions," in Lincoln H. Clark, ed.,* Consumer Behavior *(New York: New York University Press, 1955), 45.*

2. *Ernest Dichter, "How Word-of-Mouth Advertising Works,"* Harvard Business Review, *44 (November-December 1966), 148.*

3. *Ibid., 149–51.*

4. *Ibid.*

5. *Ibid., 149–52.*

6. *Johan Arndt, "Role of Product-Related Conversations in the Diffusion of a New Product,"* Journal of Marketing Research, *4 (August 1967), 292–94.*

7. *Leon G. Schiffman, "Sources of Information for the Elderly,"* Journal of Advertising Research, *11 (October 1971), 33–37.*

8. *Ibid., 35.*

9. *John G. Myers, "Patterns of Interpersonal Influence in the Adoption of New Products," in Raymond M. Haas, ed.,* Proceedings *(Chicago: American Marketing Association, 1966), 750–57.*

10. *Ibid., 756–57.*

11. *Elihu Katz and Paul F. Lazarsfeld,* Personal Influence *(New Yrok: Free Press, 1955), 32.*

12. *For example, see David B. Montgomery and Alvin J. Silk, "Patterns of Overlap in Opinion Leadership and Interest for Categories of Purchase Activity," in Philip R. McDonald, ed.,* Proceedings *(Chicago: American Marketing Association, 1969), 377–86; and James H. Myers and Thomas S. Robertson, "Dimensions of Opinion Leadership,"* Journal of Marketing Research, *9 (February 1972), 41–46.*

13. *Myers and Robertson, "Dimensions of Opinion Leadership," 42–43.*

14. *William R. Darden and Fred D. Reynolds, "Predicting Opinion Leadership for Men's Apparel Fashions,"* Journal of Marketing Research, *9 (August 1972), 324–28.*

15. *Lawrence G. Corey, "People Who Claim to Be Opinion Leaders: Identifying Their Characteristics by Self-Report,"* Journal of Marketing, *35 (October 1971), 48–53.*

16. *For example, see John O. Summers, "The Identity of Women's Clothing Fashion Opinion Leaders,"* Journal of Marketing Research, *7 (May 1970), 178–85; and Steven A. Baumgarten, "The Innovative Communicator in the Diffusion Process,"* Journal of Marketing Research, *12 (February 1975), 12–18.*

17. *William Lazer and William E. Bell, "The Communication Process and Innovation,"* Journal of Advertising Research, *6 (September 1966), 7.*

18. *James F. Engel, Robert J. Kegerreis, and Roger D. Blackwell, "Word-of-Mouth Communication by the Innovator,"* Journal of Marketing, *33 (July 1969), 15–19.*

19. *Thomas S. Robertson, "Determinants of Innovative Behavior," in Reed Moyers, ed.,* Proceedings *(Chicago: American Marketing Association, 1967), 331.*

20. *Summers, "Identity of Women's Clothing," 183.*

21. *Ibid., 181.*

22. *Ibid.*

23. *Fred D. Reynolds and William R. Darden, "Mutually Adaptive Effects of Interpersonal Communication,"* Journal of Marketing Research, *8 (November 1971), 449–54.*

24. *Thomas S. Robertson and James H. Myers, "Personality Correlates of Opinion Leadership and Innovative Buying Behavior,"* Journal of Marketing Research, *6 (May 1969), 164–68.*

25. *For example, see Summers, "Identity of Women's Clothing," p. 181; and Leon G. Schiffman and Vincent Gaccione, "Opinion Leaders in Institutional Markets,"* Journal of Marketing, *38 (April 1974), 51.*

26. *For example, see Bruce Ryan and Neal C. Gross, "The Diffusion of Hybrid Seed Corn in Two Iowa Communities,"* Rural Sociology, *8 (March 1943), 15–24; and Verling C. Troldahl and Robert Van Dam, "Face-to-Face Communication about Major Topics in the News,"* Public Opinion Quarterly, *29 (Winter 1965), 626–32.*

27. *Corey, "People Who Claim to Be Opinion Leaders," 51.*

28. *Reynolds and Darden, "Mutually Adaptive Effects," 450; and Summers, "Identity of Women's Clothing," 185.*

29. *For example, see Sidney P. Feldman, "Some Dyadic Relationships Associated with Consumer Choice," in Raymond M. Haas, ed.,* Proceedings *(Chicago: American Marketing Association, 1966), 758–75; and Sidney P. Feldman and Merlin C. Spencer, "The Effect of Personal Influence in the Selection of Consumer Services," in Peter D. Bennett, ed.,* Proceedings *(Chicago: American Marketing Association, 1965), 440–52.*

30. *Summers, "Identity of Women's Clothing," 180.*

31. *Ibid.*

32. *Katz and Lazarsfeld, Personal Influence, 305–6.*

33. *Feldman and Spencer, "Effect of Personal Influence," 71.*

34. *Summers, "Identity of Women's Clothing," 179.*

35. *For example, see Corey, "People Who Claim to Be Opinion Leaders"; Charles W. King and John O. Summers, "Overlap of Opinion Leadership Across Consumer Product Categories,"* Journal of Marketing Research, *7 (February 1970), 43–50; and Alvin J. Silk, "Overlap across Self-designated Opinion Leaders: A Study of Selected Dental Products and Services,"* Journal of Marketing Research, *3 (August 1966), 253–59.*

36. *Silk, "Overlap across Self-designated Opinion Leaders," 257.*

37. *King and Summers, "Overlap of Opinion Leadership," 46.*

38. *Silk, "Overlap across Self-designated Opinion Leaders," 258.*

39. *King and Summers, "Overlap of Opinion Leadership," 48–50.*

40. *David B. Montgomery and Alvin J. Silk, "Clusters of Consumer Interests and*

Opinion Leaders' Spheres of Influence," Journal of Marketing Research, *8 (August 1971), 317–21.*

41. *Russell W. Belk, "Occurrence of Word-of-Mouth Buyer Behavior as a Function of Situation and Advertising Stimuli," in Fred C. Allvine, ed.,* Proceedings *(Chicago: American Marketing Association, 1971), 419–22.*

42. *Ibid.*

43. *For example, see William H. White, "The Web of Word of Mouth,"* Fortune, *November 1954, 140–43.*

44. *Feldman, "Some Dyadic Relationships," 768–71.*

45. *Leon G. Schiffman, "Social Interaction Patterns of the Elderly Consumer," in Boris W. Becker and Helmut Becker, eds.,* Combined Proceedings *(Chicago: American Marketing Association, 1972), 451.*

46. *John O. Summers, "New Product Interpersonal Communication," in Fred C. Allvine, ed.,* Combined Proceedings *(Chicago: American Marketing Association, 1971), 428–33.*

47. *Paul F. Lazarsfeld, Bernard Berelson, and Hazel Gaudet,* The People's Choice, *2nd ed. (New York: Columbia University Press, 1948), 151.*

48. *For example, see Thomas S. Robertson, "Purchase Sequence Response: Innovators vs. Non-Innovators,"* Journal of Advertising Research, *8 (February 1968), 47–52; Summers, "New Product Interpersonal Communication," 429–30; Reynolds and Darden, "Mutally Adaptive Effects," 451; Jagdish N. Sheth, "Word-of-Mouth in Low Risk Innovations,"* Journal of Advertising Research, *11 (June 1971), 15–18; and Schiffman and Gaccione, "Opinion Leaders," 51–52.*

49. *Robertson, "Purchase Sequence Response," 47–52; Summers, "New Product Interpersonal Communication, 429–30; Reynolds and Darden, "Mutually Adaptive Effects," 451; Sheth, "Word-of-Mouth in Low Risk Innovations, 15–18; and Schiffman and Gaccione, "Opinion Leaders," 51–52.*

50. *Flemming Hansen, "Backwards Segmentation Using Hierarchical Clustering and Q Factor Analysis," in M. Venkatesan, ed.,* Proceedings 3rd Annual Conference *(Association for Consumer Research, 1972), 226.*

51. *James J. Sheeran, " 'Me-Too' Marketing Mania,"* New Yrok Times, *March 11, 1973, 17.*

52. *Joseph R. Mancuso, "Why Not Create Opinion Leaders for New Product Introduction?"* Journal of Marketing, *33 (July 1969), 20–25.*

Discussion questions

1. Why is the opinion leader a more credible source of product information than a product advertisement?

2. As a marketing research consultant, you have been asked by a manufacturer of a new brand of instant coffee to identify the opinion leaders for this product category. Which one of the following four opinion leadership measurement techniques would you recommend: self-designating method, sociometric method, key-informant method, or objective method? Explain your selection.

3. Why would a consumer who has just made an important purchase attempt to influence the purchase behavior of others?

4. Is a person who is an opinion leader for stereo equipment likely to be an opinion leader for fashion clothing? Discuss.

5. A manufacturer of automobile parts is interested in adding a new product to his existing line of automobile products. Using Table 10–4 as a guide, identify and discuss those category-specific attributes of an opinion leader that you feel would be particularly useful in planning a marketing strategy.

6. The two-step flow of communication theory has been modified to portray more accurately the flow of information. Briefly describe this modification and explain its relevance to the marketing decision maker.

7. Assume that you have been asked by a major sporting goods retailer to prepare a promotional campaign that would *simulate* word-of-mouth conversation. What type of promotional story-line might you recommend? Explain why you think it would be effective.

8. Find an advertisement that attempts to *stimulate* word-of-mouth conversation. Explain why you believe the marketer used this appeal in his advertisement.

social class and consumer behavior

11

Introduction

Some form of class structure or social stratification has existed in all societies throughout the history of human existence. Therefore it is not surprising that even in America, the "land of equal opportunity," there is much evidence of social class groupings. As an indication of the presence of social classes in America, the people who are better educated or have more prestigious occupations generally have greater status than people with little education or less prestigious occupations. For example, the occupations of physician and lawyer are often more highly valued than those of truck driver and farmhand.[1] All four occupations, however, are necessary for our society's general well-being. Moreover, as will be discussed later, a wide range of differences in values, attitudes, and behavior has been shown to exist between members of different social classes.

The major questions we will explore in this chapter are: What is social class? What are its determinants? How is it measured? How do members of specific social classes behave? How do social class-linked attitudes and behavior influence consumer behavior?

All the people like us are We, and every one else is They.

RUDYARD KIPLING: *"We and They" (1926)*

WHAT IS SOCIAL CLASS?

While social class can be thought of as a range of social positions — a continuum — on which each member of society can be placed, researchers have preferred to divide the continuum into a small number of specific social classes, or *strata*. Within this framework, the concept of social class is used to assign individuals or families to a social class category. Consistent with this practice, social class is defined as *the division of members of a society into a hierarchy of distinct status classes, so that members of each class have relatively the same status and members of all other classes have either more or less status.*

To appreciate more fully the complexity of social class, we will briefly consider several underlying concepts pertinent to our definition.

social class and social status

Researchers often measure social class in terms of social status; that is, they define each social class by the amount of status the members of that class have in comparison with members of other social classes.

Status is frequently conceptualized as the relative rankings of members of each social class in terms of specific types of status factors. For example, relative *wealth* (amount of economic assets), *power* (the degree of personal choice or influence over others), and *prestige* (the degree of recognition received from others) are three popular status factors frequently employed in the estimation of social class.[2] As we will see later in our discussion of the measurement of social class, researchers often use selected aspects of wealth, power, and prestige to estimate social class standing.

social class is hierarchical

Social class categories are usually ranked in a hierarchy ranging from low status to high status. Thus, members of a specific social class perceive members of other social classes as having either more or less status than they do. To many people, therefore, social class categories suggest that others are either equal to them (about the same social class), superior to them (higher social class), or inferior to them (lower social class). The hierarchical nature of social class is encapsulated in the following quotation:[3]

The members of a social class are basically people who see others in their own class level as people they can accept as equals, and with whom they can participate socially without feeling that they are out of their social niche. At the same time, people in a superior social class level are looked on as being of greater importance and as moving in circles that are generally unobtainable, and people below are people of inferior positions and with whom they are not interested in participating.

This hierarchical aspect of social class is important to marketers. Consumers may purchase certain products because they are favored by members of their own or a higher social class, and they may avoid other products because they perceive them to be "lower-class" products.

social class and market segmentation

The various social class strata provide a natural basis for market segmentation for many products and services. In many instances, consumer researchers have been able to relate product usage to social class membership. Thus, a marketer can effectively tailor his product, his channels of distribution and his promotional message to the needs and the interests of a specific social stratum.

social class and behavioral factors

The assignment of society's members into a small number of social classes has enabled researchers to note the existence of shared values, attitudes, and behavioral patterns among members *within* each social class, and differing values, attitudes, and behavior *between* different social classes. Consumer researchers have been able to relate social class standing to consumer attitudes concerning specific products, and to examine social class influences on the actual consumption of products.

social class as a frame of reference

Social class membership serves as a frame of reference (i.e., a reference group) for the development of consumer attitudes and behavior. In the context of reference groups, we might expect members of a specific social class to turn to other members of the *same* social class for cues (or clues) as to appropriate behavior.

SOCIAL CLASS CATEGORIES

There is little agreement among sociologists on how many distinct class divisions are necessary to describe adequately the social class structure of the United States.[4] For example, most early studies divided the social class organizations of specific communities into five-class or six-class social structures. However, other researchers have found nine-class, four-class, three-class and even two-class schemes to be most suitable for their purposes. The choice of how many separate classes to use depends on the amount of detail the researcher believes is necessary to explain adequately the attitudes or behavior under study. Marketers are interested in the social class structures of communities that offer potential markets for their products and in the specific social class level of their potential customers. Table 11–1 illustrates the number and diversity of social class schemes.

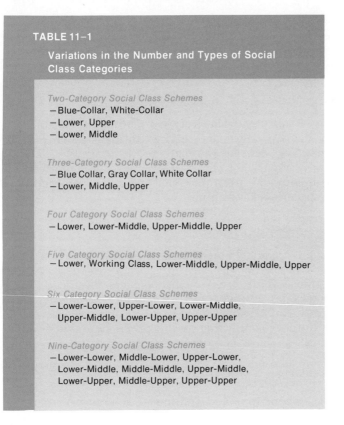

TABLE 11-1

Variations in the Number and Types of Social
Class Categories

Two-Category Social Class Schemes
—Blue-Collar, White-Collar
—Lower, Upper
—Lower, Middle

Three-Category Social Class Schemes
—Blue Collar, Gray Collar, White Collar
—Lower, Middle, Upper

Four Category Social Class Schemes
—Lower, Lower-Middle, Upper-Middle, Upper

Five Category Social Class Schemes
—Lower, Working Class, Lower-Middle, Upper-Middle, Upper

Six Category Social Class Schemes
—Lower-Lower, Upper-Lower, Lower-Middle,
Upper-Middle, Lower-Upper, Upper-Upper

Nine-Category Social Class Schemes
—Lower-Lower, Middle-Lower, Upper-Lower,
Lower-Middle, Middle-Middle, Upper-Middle,
Lower-Upper, Middle-Upper, Upper-Upper

The measurement of social class

Although most behavioral scientists tend to agree that social class is a valid and useful concept, there is no general agreement as to how to measure this complex social concept. To a great extent, researchers are
uncertain as to what constitutes the underlying dimensions of social class
structure. To attempt to resolve this dilemma, researchers have employed a wide range of measurement techniques which they feel capture
the spirit, if not the essence, of social class. Of course, no one can be certain that his particular approach does, in fact, fully measure the various
complexities of social class. In many cases, however, social class measures
are believed to give a "fair" approximation.

Systematic approaches for measuring social class fall into the following three broad categories: subjective measures, reputational measures, and objective measures. These measures are described below and
summarized in Table 11-2.

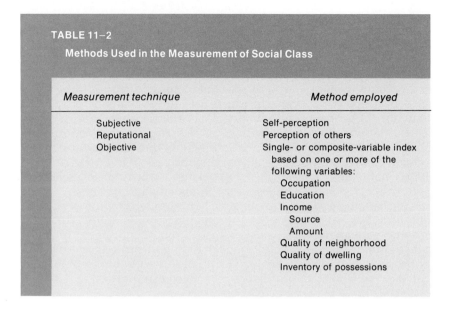

TABLE 11–2

Methods Used in the Measurement of Social Class

Measurement technique	Method employed
Subjective	Self-perception
Reputational	Perception of others

Objective	Single- or composite-variable index based on one or more of the following variables:
	Occupation
	Education
	Income
	  Source
	  Amount
	Quality of neighborhood
	Quality of dwelling
	Inventory of possessions

SUBJECTIVE MEASURES

In the subjective approach to measuring social class, individuals are asked to estimate their own social class positions. Typical of this approach is the following question:[5]

> *If you were asked to use one of these four names for your social class, which would you say you belong in: the middle class, lower class, working class, or upper class?*

The resulting classification of social class membership is based on the participants' self-perceptions or self images. Social class is treated as a "personal" phenomenon, one that reflects an individual's sense of belonging or identification with others.[6] This feeling of social group membership is often referred to as *class consciousness.*

Subjective measures of social class membership have been criticized because they tend to produce an overabundance of people who classify themselves as "middle class" (thereby understating the number of people — the "fringe" people — who would, perhaps, be more correctly classified as either "lower" or "upper" class), and because very few people elect to say "don't know" (thereby avoiding classification altogether).[7]

To date, subjective procedures have not been employed in consumer behavior studies. It is likely, however, that subjective perception of social class membership, as a reflection of self image, is related to product usage (see Chapter 3). Unfortunately, there is no available research that attempts to support this hypothesis.

REPUTATIONAL MEASURES

The reputational approach for measuring social class requires participants to make judgments concerning the social class membership of *others* within the community, rather than themselves.

Perhaps the best known of all reputational procedures is the "evaluated participation" approach, which uses the evaluations of selected community informants concerning the social class membership of others in the community to determine the social class structure of the community.[8] It is important to note that while this method requires informants to evaluate other community members, the final task of assigning community members to social class positions belongs to the trained researcher.

Sociologists have employed the reputational approach to social class measurement in order to obtain a better understanding of the specific social class structures of the communities under study. However, consumer researchers are concerned with the measurement of social class in order to obtain a better understanding of markets and marketing behavior, not of social structure. In keeping with this more focused goal, the reputational approach has proved to be impractical.

OBJECTIVE MEASURES

In contrast to the subjective and reputational measures of social class, which require people to evaluate their own class standing or that of other community members, *objective* measures (also called socioeconomic measures) require participants to answer several factual questions about themselves or their families. In selecting objective measures of social class, most researchers draw on the following variables:

1. Occupation
2. Income (amount or source)
3. Education
4. Quality of neighborhood
5. Value of residence
6. Inventory or quality of possessions

Such socioeconomic measures of social class appeal to marketers because they seem to capture the basic characteristics that provide status within our society. These measures are also relatively simple to obtain. By adding several factual questions to a consumer survey, the researcher is able to develop a measure of social class for the respondents.

Socioeconomic measures of social class are of considerable value to marketers for segmenting their markets. The requirements for efficient market segmentation, remember, are identification, size, and accessibility (see Chapter 1). The marketing manager who has developed a socioeconomic profile of his target market can locate (i.e., identify and measure) this market by studying the socioeconomic data periodically issued by the U.S. Bureau of the Census. In order to reach his desired target market, he simply has to match its socioeconomic profile to the audience profiles of selected advertising media. Socioeconomic audience profiles are regularly collected and routinely made available to potential advertisers by most of the mass media because of their ability to influence advertisers' media decisions. An example of such a profile can be seen in Table 11–3.

TABLE 11–3

Profile, *Smithsonian* Subscriber Families, June 1975

Income:		
Annual median income		$24,483
Annual average income		$33,793
Percent incomes over $25,000		48%
Percent incomes over $50,000		14%
Total college educated		85%
College grads	67%	
Attended college	18%	
Occupation:		
Total managerial, professional, technical		67%
Management	31%	
Professional/technical	36%	
Home Ownership:		
Median value of owned home		$47,422
Percent over $40,000 value		64%
Percent over $50,000 value		46%
Percent over $75,000 value		21%
Percent who own second home		20%
Investment Holdings:		
Own corporate stock		58%
Own real estate (other than homes)		36%
Own mutual funds		27%

Source: Smithsonian Magazine, *Washington, D.C.*

Objective measures of social class fall into two basic categories: single-variable indexes and composite-variable indexes.

single-variable indexes

A single-variable index does not combine socioeconomic factors; instead, just one socioeconomic variable is used to evaluate social class membership. Some of these variables are discussed below.

TABLE 11–4

Prestige Ratings of Occupational Titles in the United States, 1963

Occupations	Scores	Occupations	Scores	Occupations	Scores
U.S. Supreme Court Justice	94	Owner of a factory that employs about 100 people	80	Traveling salesman for a wholesale concern	66
Physician	93			Plumber	65
Nuclear physicist	92	Building contractor	80	Automobile repairman	64
Scientist	92	Artist who paints pictures that are exhibited in galleries	78	Playground director	63
Government scientist	91			Barber	63
State governor	91	Musician in a symphony orchestra	78	Machine operator in a factory	63
Cabinet member in federal government	90	Author of novels	78	Owner-operator of a lunch stand	63
College professor	90	Economist	78	Corporal in the regular army	62
U.S. representative in Congress	90	Official of international labor union	77	Garage mechanic	62
Chemist	89	Railroad engineer	76	Truck driver	59
Lawyer	89	Electrician	76	Fisherman who owns his own boat	58
Diplomat in the U.S. Foreign Service	89	County agricultural agent	76	Clerk in a store	56
Dentist	88	Owner-operator of a printing shop	75	Milk route man	56
Architect	88	Trained machinist	75	Streetcar motorman	56
County judge	88	Farm owner and operator	74	Lumberjack	55
Psychologist	87	Undertaker	74	Restaurant cook	55
Minister	87	Welfare worker for a city government	74	Singer in a nightclub	54
Member of the board of directors of a large corporation	87	Newspaper columnist	73	Filling station attendant	51
Mayor of a large city	87	Policeman	72	Dockworker	50
Priest	86	Reporter on a daily newspaper	71	Railroad section hand	50
Head of a department in a state government	86	Radio announcer	70	Night watchman	50
Civil engineer	86	Bookkeeper	70	Coal miner	50
Airline pilot	86	Tenant farmer—one who owns livestock and machinery and manages the farm	69	Restaurant waiter	49
Banker	85			Taxi driver	49
Biologist	85			Farm hand	48
Sociologist	83	Insurance agent	69	Janitor	48
Instructor in public schools	82	Carpenter	68	Bartender	48
Captain in the regular army	82	Manager of a small store in a city	67	Clothes presser in a laundry	45
Accountant for a large business	81	A local official of a labor union	67	Soda fountain clerk	44
Public school teacher	81	Mail carrier	66	Sharecropper—one who owns no livestock or equipment and does not manage farm	42
		Railroad conductor	66	Garbage collector	39
				Street sweeper	36
				Shoe shiner	34

Source: Robert W. Hodges, Paul M. Siegel, and Peter H. Rossi, "Occupational Prestige in the United States, 1925–1963," American Journal of Sociology, 70 (November 1964), 290–292, Copyright © 1964 by The University of Chicago. Reprinted by permission.

OCCUPATION. Occupation (i.e., inferred occupational status) is the most widely accepted and best documented measure of social class. The importance of occupation as a social class indicator is dramatized by the frequency with which people ask others whom they meet for the first time, "What do you do for a living?" Obviously, the response to such a question serves as a guide in evaluating and forming opinions of others.

Table 11–4 presents the results of a national study designed to estimate the relative prestige that people assign to some ninety basic occupational titles.[9] The findings of this study and similar studies are used by social class researchers to assign status scores to occupations encountered in their research.[10]

Most observers will agree that the occupations at the top of the list in Table 11–4 tend to earn the greatest incomes and require the most formal education. As we move down the list of occupational rankings, however, we find that the amount of income and the amount of required formal education tend to decrease. This suggests that there is a rather close association between occupational status, income, and education.[11]

INCOME. Individual or family income is another socioeconomic variable frequently used to approximate social class standing. Researchers who favor income as a measure of social class use either *amount* of income or *source* of income. Table 11–5 illustrates the types of categories used for each of these income variables.

TABLE 11–5

Typical Categories Used for Assessing Amount or Source of Income

Amount of Income	Source of Income
Under $5,000 per year	Public welfare
$5,000–$9,999	Private financial assistance
$10,000–$14,999	Wages (hourly)
$15,000–$19,999	Salary (yearly)
$20,000–$24,999	Profits or fees
$25,000–$29,999	Earned wealth
$30,000 and over	Inherited wealth

While income is a popular estimate of social class standing, not all consumer researchers agree that income is an appropriate index of social class.[12] They argue that a blue-collar truck driver and a white-collar schoolteacher may both earn $18,000 a year, yet each will spend his income in a different way. Therefore, though both earn the same income, how they decide to spend that income reflects different values. To such researchers, it is the difference in values that is an important discriminant of social class between people, not the amount of income they earn.

OTHER VARIABLES. Level of education, quality of neighborhood, and dollar value of residence are rarely used as sole measures of social class; however, they are frequently used informally to support or verify social class membership assigned on the basis of occupational status or income.

Finally, *possessions* have been used by sociologists as an index of social class. The best known and most elaborate social class rating scheme for evaluating possessions is Chapin's Social Status Scale, which focuses on the presence of certain items of furniture and accessories in the living

TABLE 11–6

Income, Occupation, and Education as They Relate to Use of Recycling Center (In Percentages)

Family Income Level	Uses Center	Does Not Use Center
0–$9,000	25	51
10,000–13,999	20	19
14,000–19,999	31	16
20,000 and over	24	14
	100%	100%
	(N = 84)	(N = 74)

Occupation Level Of Family Head	Uses Center	Does Not Use Center
Professional (Lawyer, M.D., professor, C.P.A., architect, etc.)	39	10
Manager, executive, self-employed manufacturer	11	11
Technical/engineer/artisan (Research asst., teacher, librarian, computer programmer, etc.)	22	27
Sales/clerical/owner of small retail store (white collar worker)	15	27
Craftsmen/service worker/farmer/ laborer (blue collar worker)	13	25
	100%	100%
	(N = 82)	(N = 67)

Educational Level Of Family Head	Uses Center	Does Not Use Center
Four years of high school or less	13	41
Some college	14	25
Four years of college or more	73	34
	100%	100%
	(N = 84)	(N = 75)

Source: William H. Peters, "Who Cooperates in Voluntary Recycling Efforts?" in Thomas V. Greer, ed., 1973 Combined Proceedings (Chicago: American Marketing Association, 1974), p. 507.

room (types of floor or floor covering, drapes, fireplace, library table, telephone, bookcases) and the condition of the room (cleanliness, organization, general atmosphere).[13] Conclusions are drawn about a family's social class position on the basis of such observations. Since the scale was developed over forty years ago, it is somewhat outdated, and a contemporary update is very much needed.

To conclude our examination of single-variable objective measures of social class, we will look at one example of how such variables are used in consumer behavior research. Table 11–6 presents the results of a study undertaken in a midwestern city of residents who used a local Coca-Cola bottler's can and bottle recycling center, and those who did not.[14] The findings revealed that users of the recycling center were most likely to have a family income in excess of $14,000 and a head-of-household who was a professional, with at least a college degree. In other words, the recycling center attracted a well-educated, professional, and higher-income family. When combined with other information (e.g., attitudes), such insights could help the bottler make strategic decisions as to how to attract additional users to the facility.

composite-variable indexes

Composite indexes strive to combine systematically a number of socioeconomic factors to form *one* overall measure of social class standing. Such indexes are receiving increased attention from consumer researchers because they better reflect the complexity of social class than do single-variable indexes. We will now briefly review several of the more important composite indexes.

INDEX OF STATUS CHARACTERISTICS. A classic composite measure of social class is Warner's Index of Status Characteristics (ISC).[15] The ISC is a weighted measure of the following socioeconomic variables: occupation, source of income (*not* amount of income), house type, and dwelling area (quality of neighborhood). Table 11–7 presents the specific seven-point rating scale used for each of the four variables and the weights by which they are adjusted.

SOCIOECONOMIC STATUS SCORES. Another important composite social class measure is the U.S. Bureau of the Census Socioeconomic Status Score (SES), which was developed for the 1960 census.[16] The SES combines three of the most basic socioeconomic variables: occupation, family income, and educational attainment. The appeal of the SES index to the consumer researcher is that it enables him to compare his findings with census data. For this reason, it is not surprising that a major corporation like the American Telephone and Telegraph Company has used the SES as a model in its research on the residence telephone market.[17]

OTHER COMPOSITE-VARIABLE INDEXES. There are many other composite social class measures available to the consumer researcher. Table

TABLE 11–7

Scores and Weights for Warner's Index of Status Characteristics

Occupation (weight of 4)	Source of income (weight of 3)	House type (weight of 3)	Dwelling area (weight of 2)
1. Professionals and proprietors of large businesses	1. Inherited wealth	1. Excellent houses	1. Very high: Gold Coast, North Shore, etc.
2. Semi-professionals and officials of large businesses	2. Earned wealth	2. Very good houses	2. High: the better suburbs and apartment house areas, houses with spacious yards, etc.
3. Clerks and kindred workers	3. Profits and fees	3. Good houses	3. Above average: areas all residential, larger than average space around houses; apartment areas in good condition, etc.
4. Skilled workers	4. Salary	4. Average houses	4. Average: residential neighborhoods, no deterioration in the area
5. Proprietors of small businesses	5. Wages	5. Fair houses	5. Below average: area not quite holding its own, beginning to deterio- rate, business entering, etc.
6. Semi-skilled workers	6. Private relief	6. Poor houses	6. Low: considerably deteriorated, rundown and semi-slum
7. Unskilled workers	7. Public relief and non- respectable income	7. Very poor houses	7. Very low: slum

Source: W. Lloyd Warner, Marchia Meeker, and Kenneth Eells, Social Class in America: A Manual of Procedure for the Measurement of Social Status (New York: Harper & Row, 1960), 123. Copyright © 1960 by Harper & Row, Publishers, Incorporated, Reprinted by permission.

11–8 identifies three of these indexes and the variables employed to establish their overall status scores.

an applied comparison of single and composite indexes of social class

The American Telephone and Telegraph Company has utilized a variety of single and composite indexes of social class in its efforts to more fully understand customer needs. The results it obtained from a study designed to provide information about long-distance calling be- havior are presented graphically in Figure 11–1.[18] Three single-variable

TABLE 11-8

Popular Composite Measures of Social Class

Composite index	Variables
Two-Factor Index of Social Position[a]	Occupation Education
Index of Urban Status (revised)[b]	Occupation (husband and wife) Education (husband and wife) Neighborhood of residence Quality of housing Church affiliation Community associations
Index of Cultural Classes[c]	Occupation Education Home value (or amount of rent)

Sources: [a]Marie Haug, "Social-Class Measurement: A Methodological Critique," in Gerald W. Thielbar and Saul D. Feldman, eds., Issues in Social Inequality (Boston: Little, Brown, 1972), 433–438.

[b]Richard P. Coleman and Bernice L. Neugarten, Social Status in the City (San Francisco: Jossey-Bass, 1971).

[c]James M. Carman, The Application of Social Class in Market Segmentation (Berkeley: Institute of Business and Economic Research, University of California Graduate School of Business Administration, 1965).

indexes — family income, education of the head-of-household, and occupation of the head-of-household — are compared with a composite Socioeconomic Status Scores Index modeled after the SES developed by the Bureau of the Census.

The single-variable studies found that families with incomes in excess of $10,000, those whose heads-of-household have more than a high school education, and those whose heads-of-household have mid-to-high occupational status tend to spend *more* on long-distance calls than the average amount spent by all customers. Families classified by the SES (a composite-variable index) as lower class (composite scores between 10 and 44) and lower-middle class (scores between 45 and 69) tend to spend *less* on long-distance calls than the average amount spent by all customers, while families classified as upper-middle class (scores between 70 and 89) and upper class (scores between 90 and 99) tend to spend *more* on long-distance calls than the average amount spent by all customers. These results demonstrate that the insights gained from several single-variable indexes and from a composite index tend to reinforce each other in terms of the information they provide concerning customer behavior.

FIGURE 11-1

Average Long-Distance Telephone Expenditures, by Socioeconomic Variables

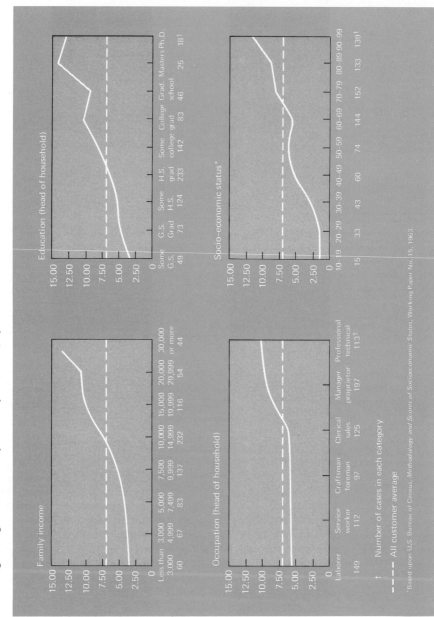

Source: A. Marvin Roscoe, Jr., and Jagdish N. Sheth, "Demographic Segmentation of Long Distance Behavior: Data Analysis and Inductive Model Building," in M. Venkatesan, ed., Third Annual Conference of the Association for Consumer Research, 1972, 262. Also, Courtesy of the American Telephone and Telegraph Company.

ISSUES IN THE MEASUREMENT OF SOCIAL CLASS

Before concluding our discussion of the measurement of social class, we will briefly consider two important issues: (1) the role of women in the measurement of social class, and (2) the relative efficiencies of social class and income to explain consumer behavior.

social class: the missing impact of women

Researchers have traditionally tended to evaluate a family's social class position exclusively in terms of the status of the *male* head-of-household. Although such an approach to measuring social class may have been adequate in previous decades, it is not appropriate today, when many women are actively pursuing higher education and are engaged in careers outside the home. Recent research has found that social class position would have been categorized higher for an important segment of blue-collar families if the wife's educational and occupational levels had been used to calculate social class instead of the husband's.[19] For example, based on a composite index of education and occupation, one researcher reported: "around a third of all dual-work families include a wife who has a higher social class level than her husband . . ."[20] A study concerned with the social class structure of a large urban metropolitan area (Kansas City) found that the wife's educational level was more closely related to the family's income and social class membership than the husband's educational level.[21]

These studies strongly suggest that the time is ripe to develop social class measurement schemes that either account for the educational and occupational levels of *both* spouses or use as a status indicator the spouse with the higher educational and occupational attainment. Some promising work on such broadened measures appears to be underway.[22] Eventually we may be able to determine just how much the social status of the *household* (as determined by a pooled husband-wife measure of social class) influences various aspects of consumer behavior.

composite versus single indexes

Considerable controversy exists regarding the relative merits of using a *single index* (e.g., income) versus a *composite index* of social class to explain consumer behavior. Two studies in particular have questioned the superiority of composite indexes as a determinant. The first study compared the efficiency with which income alone and a composite measure of social class accounted for the presence (or absence) of a relatively large number of common household products (toiletries, detergents, soft drinks, liquor, frozen and canned food).[23] With few exceptions, the evidence revealed that income was as good as or better than the composite measure of social class as a predictor of whether a family would have a specific product on hand. A follow-up study focused on the purchase of durable goods (furniture, appliances, family clothing) and selected consumer services (travel) during the previous year.[24] Again, for the overwhelming majority of products, income was found to be equal to or better than the composite measure as a determinant of whether a specific purchase was made during the preceding year.

Two studies have addressed themselves to demonstrating under what conditions composite indexes are better determinants of consumer behavior than income alone. The first study compared the ability of *income* and *social class* (as determined by a composite index) to account for the use or nonuse and the frequency of use of fourteen entertainment activities (e.g., movies, skiing, golf, and specific types of dining out).[25] Income was found to be a superior predictor of use or nonuse, while the composite measure of social class was found to be a better predictor of frequency of use. For example, income rather than social class was positively related to whether a family did or did not "dine at expensive restaurants," while the composite measure of social class rather than income was positively related to the frequency of such dining out. This study suggests that the research designs of the earlier studies were deficient in examining only one variable ("having or not having" a product on hand) and that a composite measure of social class may have been a more effective predictor of the frequency of such purchases.

The second study examined the relationship between *income, social class,* and numerous *life-style* (psychographic) items (see Chapter 5).[26] The objective of this study was to determine whether life-style characteristics (which are generally assumed to reflect social class) are in fact more closely associated with a composite social class index than with income alone. The findings support this hypothesis. Table 11–9 presents a sample of life-style items that were found to be strongly associated with social class.

While a debate about the relative merits of composite social class measures and income as predictors of consumer behavior may seem to be academic, it has served to provoke a careful evaluation of the relationships between consumer behavior and social class. Out of such an assessment will likely come a better understanding of consumer behavior. Although more research is needed on this issue, it appears that which variable is the better predictor may be a function of how consumption behavior (as a dependent variable) is defined. Income may be a more suitable predictor of consumer behavior for acquisitive types of behavior—"having" or "not having." On the other hand, composite social class indexes may be more predictive of expressive types of consumer behavior, such as which brands are purchased, the price which is paid, in what type of store the product is purchased, and how the product is used. It is also likely that composite social class indexes better reflect broad values such as the "inventory" or "bundle" of products that a family possesses, whereas income may better reflect the ownership of certain specific products.

A potentially interesting approach for circumventing the composite social class versus income issue comes from the findings of several research studies, which suggest that the members of each social class be

TABLE 11-9

Selected Life-Style Items That Were Found to Better Explain Social Class Than Income

Life-style items that are positively associated with social class	*Life-style items that are negatively associated with social class*
I enjoy going to concerts.	Somebody should stop all the protests that are going on.
I attend a bridge club regularly.	Long hair on boys should be banned.
I enjoy going through an art gallery.	I am a homebody.
I am usually an active member of more than one service organization.	If it was good enough for my mother, it is good enough for me.
I like ballet.	Any housewife who doesn't have a spring housecleaning is slovenly.
I think I'm a pretty nice looking person.	When I must choose between the two, I usually dress for comfort, not for fashion.

Source: Adapted from James H. Myers and Jonathan Gutman, "Life Styles: The Essence of Social Class," in William D. Wells, ed., Life Style and Psychographics *(Chicago: American Marketing Association, 1974), 250–51.*

divided into subgroups on the basis of their relative incomes. The resulting *social class/relative income* variable embodies the notion that within any social class there is a wide range of incomes; some members are clearly better off than others. More specifically, consumers who have incomes *above* the average of all members of their social class can be considered "overprivileged," while those who have incomes *below* the average can be considered "underprivledged," regardless of which level of social class they represent.

Two studies concerned with automobile purchase behavior before the gasoline crisis of 1974 serve to illustrate how a *social class/relative income* variable can contribute to our understanding of consumer behavior. In the first study, it was found that *overprivileged* members of each of three social classes (upper-lower, lower-middle, and upper-middle) were the primary market for Pontiacs, Buicks, Oldsmobiles, Chryslers, and Cadillacs. The members of each social class with *average* incomes (i.e., neither overprivileged nor underprivileged) were found to be the major users of full-size Fords and Chevrolets, while those who were classified as '*underprivileged*' within each of the three social classes constituted the prime market for compact automobiles.[27]

In the second study, which was restricted to the examination of *size* of automobiles, overprivileged members of each specific social class tended to own full-size cars, while underprivileged members of each specific social class owned more compacts and intermediate-sized automobiles.[28] These results seem to indicate that a status hierarchy, based on income, seems to exist *within* each social class. Thus, the blue-collar worker who is financially well off may make consumption decisions (at least for a conspicuous product like a car) which are more like affluent white-collar and professional workers than like other blue-collar workers who earn less money.

A general profile of the social classes

As indicated earlier, social science researchers have perceived social class structure as consisting of from two to nine categories. A fairly discriminating division of social class structure uses a six-class breakdown: upper-upper class, lower-upper class, upper-middle class, lower-middle class, upper-lower class, and lower-lower class. For purposes of discussion, it is easier to consider these classes as mutually exclusive categories; however, since we are classifying human beings—with their wide range of behavior and experience—it is important to remember that these classes are not really discrete, but actually overlap when individuals possess characteristics of two adjacent strata.

In this section we have pieced together from various sources a consolidated portrait of the members of each of the six social classes listed above.[29] It should be kept in mind that each of the six profiles is only a generalized picture of the class. There may be people in any class who possess values, attitudes, and behavioral patterns that are a hybrid of two or more classes. Table 11–10 illustrates the distribution of the population within a six-category social class scheme.

TABLE 11–10

Social Class Distribution in Population

Class	Percent of population
Upper-Upper Lower-Upper	.9
Upper-Middle	7.2
Lower-Middle	28.4
Upper-Lower	44.0
Lower-Lower	19.5
	100.0

Source: Adapted from Motivation in Advertising, by Pierre Martineau. Copyright 1957, McGraw-Hill Book Company. Used with permission of McGraw-Hill Book Company.

THE UPPER-UPPER CLASS

Members of the upper-upper social class are typified by the small number of well-established families that make up the "inner circle" or "Social

Register" of a community. The members of this highest status class are the nucleus of the membership of the best country clubs and the sponsors of the major charitable events. They provide the leadership and funds for community civic and cultural activities, and they serve as trustees for local universities, colleges, and hospitals. In terms of occupation, members of this class are likely to head the major local financial institutions, to own or manage the major long-established businesses, and to constitute the most prominent group of physicians, lawyers, and other key professionals within the community.

While such elite families have often accumulated money and property over the years, it is not the amount of their wealth, but the status and influence they have within the community, that sets them apart from others.

Since members of the upper-upper class are aware of the favorable position they occupy and over the years have become accustomed to their wealth, they are not likely to spend their money conspicuously. Indeed, though they have admirable life styles, they are unlikely to be ostentatious. Rather, they spend their money conservatively—e.g., they often wear tweeds and tailored clothing that whisper good taste and refinement rather than shout wealth.

THE LOWER-UPPER CLASS

The lower-upper class is primarily distinguishable from the upper-upper class by its members' family standing, which is not elite. Lower-upper class families are relatively new within the community, or, if resident for a long time, have never quite been accepted by the upper crust of society. They have a lot of "new money;" in fact, their incomes are often greater than those of the upper-uppers. This supports the notion that income alone is not enough to determine a family's social class position. Occupationally, lower-uppers are most likely to be successful business executives whose success is largely due to their own initiative. The members of the lower-upper class are also quite active in civic and philanthropic causes.

In contrast to the upper-upper class, members of the lower-upper class are likely to be conspicuous users of their new wealth. Their conspicuous consumption is an important symbol of their personal achievements. Lower-uppers are therefore most likely to be the major purchasers of large modern homes, to own luxury domestic and imported automobiles, to hold extravagant parties, to dress conspicuously and to otherwise consume extravagantly. Both the upper-upper and lower-upper classes together constitute less than 1 percent of the population.

THE UPPER-MIDDLE CLASS

The upper-middle class is comprised of families who possess neither family status nor unusual wealth. Their trademark, however, is that they are distinctly career-oriented. Occupationally, the upper-middle class consists of young successful professionals, independent businessmen, and corporate managers. Most members of this social class are college graduates, and many have professional or graduate degrees. Education and career advancement are therefore two very important ideals that members of this social class value, both for themselves and for their children. The upper-middle class are joiners; their professional, community, and social activities parallel their strong need to achieve and their interest in education.

Although they are financially comfortable (with incomes frequently in the $25,000 to $50,000 range), they are not wealthy. However, they share a keen interest in the "better things in life" with members of the two upper classes. They attend the ballet, opera, and theater and are active in a wide range of other cultural activities.

Upper-middle class families live in somewhat expensive, well-furnished modern homes, which serve as symbols of their achievement or as an indication that they are on the way up. They are therefore an important market for interior decorators and related home improvement services. Like the members of the lower-upper class, consumption is often conspicuous, though they do not possess enough money to satisfy all their consumption whims. They are highly interested in fashionable clothing and accessories and tend to buy expensive items like stereo equipment and cameras. Members of this class are very child-oriented in their consumption behavior. They tend to "purchase" art instruction, musical training, dance lessons, and other products or services designed to provide their children with the "tools" to get ahead. This social class represents about 7 percent of the population.

THE LOWER-MIDDLE CLASS

The lower-middle class is relatively large (approximately 30 percent of the population) and is composed primarily of nonmanagerial white-collar workers (office workers, small-business owners) and high-paid blue-collar workers (plumbers, factory foremen). Its members can be categorized as "typical" Americans, located as they are at the bottom of the white-collar group and at the top of the blue-collar group. Their primary concern is achieving respectability and acceptance as good citizens, and these values are reflected in their attitudes toward their children. They want their children to be well behaved, and they are anxious that their sons be manly and their daughters ladylike. Lower-middle class families are churchgoers and are often involved in church-sponsored activities and in fraternal organizations (Elks, Shriners, Masons, Odd Fellows).

Members of the lower-middle class frequently live in modest row houses in suburban neighborhoods. They tend to avoid extravagant home furnishings and prefer a comfortable, neat, clean, and "pretty" home. Lower-middle class families are a major market for do-it-yourself products, which they employ to keep their homes in good repair. Their tastes in clothing parallel their tastes in home furnishings: they prefer a neat and clean appearance and tend to avoid clothing that is faddish or high-style.

THE UPPER-LOWER CLASS

The upper-lower, or working, class is the largest social class segment (approximately 45 percent of the population). It is solidly blue collar—and consists of skilled or semiskilled factory workers. While members of the lower-middle class seek respectability and advancement, members of the upper-lower class strive for security and to protect what they already have. Upper-lower class members see work as a means to "buy" enjoyment rather than as an end unto itself, and they view union membership as the major way of attaining security. Although they are even more concerned than members of the lower-middle class that their children behave properly (like "little men" and "little ladies"), they are less likely to plan for their children's future in terms of a college education.

Upper-lower class families, who earn relatively high union wages, tend to spend impulsively, for today, rather than to save and plan for the future. They are less interested in their home and personal looks, and are more involved with purchasing items that make their leisure time enjoyable (TV sets, camping, sporting, hunting equipment). Working-class families are heavy TV watchers and were among the first to purchase television sets when they were introduced on the market.[30]

The working-class husband is likely to be active in local veterans, sporting, and hunting organizations. He has a strong "all-male" self-image; he is a sports enthusiast (baseball, boxing, and wrestling fan and a bowler), an outdoorsman (hunter and fisherman), and a heavy smoker and beer drinker. He also enjoys working around the house and relaxes by playing poker with the "boys." The working-class wife is primarily involved in her domestic role: with being a good mother and homemaker. She engages in limited social activity outside of the home, usually with a few friends who share her outlook on life. However, some recent evidence indicates that the horizon of the working-class woman may be expanding, and she may be acquiring greater interest in herself as a person and her place in the world outside her home.[31]

THE LOWER-LOWER CLASS

The lower-lower class is at the bottom of the social spectrum and consists of poorly educated, unskilled laborers (dishwashers, gas station attendants, domestics). Members of this class quite frequently find themselves out of work and on some form of public assistance. Their dwellings are generally substandard and are often located in slum areas.

Many lower-lower class women are "forced" to work (rather than desiring to work) because it is often easier for an unskilled woman to find employment than it is for an unskilled man. The life of the lower-lower class family is frequently consumed with frustration, anger, and indifference. In this kind of environment, children are often poorly treated and punished for acts that parents of other classes are more likely to tolerate or even encourage. If members of this class are at all optimistic, they hope that somehow tomorrow will be better.

Members of the lower-lower class are largely disorganized in their approach to life and tend to live a day-to-day existence, spending what they have with no real thought for the future. For this reason, their ownership of TV sets, automobiles, and even expensive stereo sets reflects their attempts to escape the hopelessness and despair of their lives and to taste, at least superficially, a more desirable style of life.

Consumer behavior applications of social class

Social class profiles provide a broad picture of the values, attitudes, and behavior that distinguish the members of various social classes. This information becomes much more useful to marketers, however, when it is related to consumption behavior. Therefore, in this section we change our focus and concentrate on specific consumer research that relates social class to the development of marketing strategy.

CLOTHING AND FASHION

A Greek philosopher said, "Know, first, who you are; and then adorn yourself accordingly."[32] This bit of wisdom is relevant to clothing marketers today, since most people dress to fit their self images, which include their perceptions of their own social class membership. A study that examined the fashion interests of women found that all women respondents, regardless of social class, considered fashionable clothing to be important; however, upper and middle class women were found to be somewhat more involved in fashion than their lower class counterparts. This was demonstrated by such factors as more active readership of fashion magazines, more frequent attendance at fashion shows, and more frequent discussions of fashion with others, particularly their friends and husbands.[33]

A study designed to compare working class (lower class) and middle class women found that working class women were more likely to consider "a dress for a special occasion" or "a trip to the beauty parlor" as a luxury than did middle class women.[34] However, a comparison of these findings with an earlier study indicates that the percentage of working class women who view such purchases as luxuries is declining, which suggests that fashion consciousness is becoming more important for lower class women.[35]

Still further evidence that there are social class differences regarding fashion is found in the usage of cosmetics. Research revealed that middle class women are more likely to be heavy users of cosmetics than lower class women.[36]

Differences in fashion interests between adjacent social classes are not strikingly evident because ". . . mass production and mass consumption have enabled most Americans to wear clothes, as well as to possess other artifacts, that are very much alike in *gross* appearance and quality."[37] More research is needed to examine the relationship between clothing purchase behavior and social class membership.

HOME DECORATION

To the extent that a family's home is its castle, the decor of the home should provide clues to the family's social class position. Of all the rooms in the home, the living room seems to best express how a family wants to be seen by those it entertains. Therefore, living-room furnishings are likely to be particularly sensitive to social class influences. It will be recalled that Chapin's Social Status Scale uses the presence and condition of living-room furnishings to measure a family's social class standing. The appropriateness of using living-room furnishings as a barometer of social class standing is underscored by a leading consumer researcher who noted: "The living-room of a home is essentially the face you present the world of your friends and acquaintances, and the average housewife is consciously or unconsciously concerned with the impression it makes."[38]

Figure 11–2 presents a typology of social class status based on the ownership of specific types of living-room furniture and accessories.[39] It classifies fifty-three living-room items or characteristics in terms of high or low social class status and modern or traditional decor. This classification scheme results in four distinct groupings: (1) low-status traditional (upper-left quadrant), (2) high-status traditional (upper-right quadrant), (3) high-status modern (lower-right quadrant), and (4) low-status modern (lower-left quadrant). This type of classification scheme is useful to marketers of home-furnishing products concerned with developing products or promotional campaigns for specific target segments. For example, the location of television sets in the lower-left quadrant indicates that a television set in the living room is more likely to occur in lower class households. Indeed, further analysis reveals that lower class families are likely to place their television sets in the living room, while middle and upper class families usually place their television sets in the bedroom or family room.[40] The marketing implications of these findings suggest that advertisements for television sets targeted at the lower class consumer should show the set in a living-room setting, while advertisements directed to middle or upper class consumers should show the set in either a bedroom or a family room.

A recent study undertaken by the American Telephone and Telegraph Company provides some additional insights into the relationship between style consciousness in home furnishings and social class.[41] Table 11–11 reveals that a significant difference in attitude exists among the four social classes studied concerning telephone design and basic style in home furnishings. An examination of the product-specific statements suggests that lower-middle class consumers feel that telephones should improve the style of a room and be available in a variety of patterns and designs. In contrast, lower class consumers simply express a desire for a

FIGURE 11–2

A Typology of Social Class Status Based on Ownership of Living-Room Objects

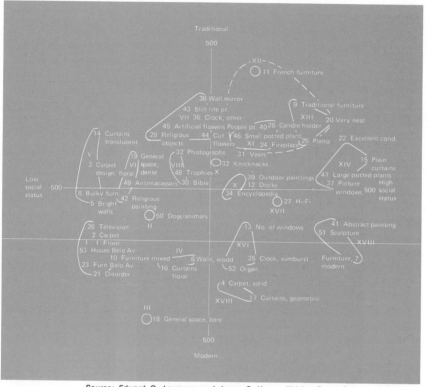

Source: Edward O. Laumann and James S. House, "Living Room Styles and Social
Attributes: The Patterning of Material Artifacts in a Modern Urban Community," Sociology
and Social Research, 54 (April 1970), 326. Reprinted by permission of the University of
Southern California.

telephone that works. Thus, lower-middle class consumers might be an
important market for new, stylish telephones. The results also indicate
that upper class consumers would be the best market for a variety of
telephone styles, particularly those that are modern in design. The three
general life-style statements tapped a broader aspect of home decorating
interests; findings suggest that upper-middle class consumers have a
greater preference for style than comfort in home decorations and that
they are also more likely than the other classes studied to buy colored
appliances.

THE PURSUIT OF LEISURE

For many products and services, social class membership is closely related to the choice of recreational and leisure-time activities. Research
suggests that upper class consumers are likely to attend the theater and

TABLE 11–11

A Psychographic Profile of Style Consciousness in Home Furnishings by Socioeconomic Status

Selected Style Consciousness Statements:	Lower class agreement	Lower middle class agreement	Upper-middle class agreement	Upper class agreement
Product-Specific Statements:				
Phones should come in patterns and designs as well as colors.	60%	80%	63%	58%
A telephone should improve the decorative style of a room.	47	82	73	77
Telephones should be modern in design.	58	85	83	89
A home should have a variety of telephone styles.	8	46	39	51
You can keep all those special phones, all I want is a phone that works.	83	67	68	56
The style of a telephone is unimportant to me.	86	54	58	51
General Life-Style Statements:				
Our home is furnished for comfort not style.	96	87	79	79
I have more modern appliances in my home than most people.	17	23	41	48
I prefer colored appliances.	57	73	87	92

Source: Adapted from A. Marvin Roscoe, Jr., Arthur LeClaire, Jr., and Leon G. Schiffman, "Theory and Management Applications of Demographics in Buyer Behavior," in Arch G. Woodside, Jagdish N. Sheth, and Peter D. Bennett, eds., Foundations of Consumer and Industrial Buying Behavior (New York: American Elsevier, 1977), 74–75.

concerts, to play bridge, and to attend college football games, while lower class consumers tend to be avid television watchers and fishing enthusiasts and enjoy attending drive-in movies and baseball games.[42] Furthermore, the lower class consumer spends more time on commercial types of activities (bowling, playing pool or billiards, visiting taverns) and craftsmanlike activities (model building, painting, woodworking projects).[43]

For the marketer of on-draft and bottled beers, the lower class consumer would appear to be a fruitful target market. This strategy implication is supported by the following description of the heavy in-tavern beer drinker, developed in a study undertaken for Schlitz Beer:[44]

> Demographically we saw that the heavy user. . . derives his income from primarily blue-collar occupations. He is young and has at least a high school education. The major life style patterns that emerged indicated that the heavy beer drinker was probably more hedonistic and pleasure-seeking toward life than the

FIGURE 11–3
Advertisement Targeted to the Heavy Beer Drinker

Courtesy of Jos. Schlitz Brewing Co.

318

non-drinker. He seemed to have less regard toward responsibilities of family and job. More than the non-drinker he tended to have a preference for a physical/ male-oriented existence and an inclination to fantasize. Finally we found, not surprisingly, a great enjoyment of drinking, especially beer which he saw as a real man's drink.

Figure 11–3 presents an example from the Schlitz "Gusto" advertising campaign designed to appeal to the heavy beer drinker.

SAVING, SPENDING, AND CREDIT

Saving, spending, and credit card usage all seem to be related to social class standing. For example, in response to a question that asked consumers what they would do if their income was doubled for the next ten years, upper class respondents were more likely to specify some type of saving, particularly more risky investments. In contrast, lower class respondents were more likely to spend their windfall income or save a portion of it in a non-risk savings account.[45] These findings suggest that upper class consumers are future-oriented and confident of their financial acumen, to the extent that they are more willing to invest in insurance, stocks, and real estate. In comparison, lower class consumers are more concerned with immediate gratification; however, when they do save, they are primarily interested in safety and security.

A research project designed to compare the attitudes of working class and middle class women provides some further insights on social class differences in this important area:[46]

Working-Class *women are relatively* anxious *about how they and other people handle money. They are uneasy about borrowing and thereby incurring financial obligations (which may not be paid back, at least not "on time," and thus lead to unpleasant recriminations—a "goof" indeed). They are fearful of the way men (husbands) handle money. And their feeling that young people should help their parents financially appears to indicate some willingness to become dependent in this area or perhaps a desire to continue being in control of the money earned by family members. The strong desire or need to* "control the purse strings" *suggests a primary anxiety about what (other) people will do when they have money in their hands. Impulsive Working-Class spending patterns make this anxiety understandable.*

Middle-Class *women manifest appreciably greater self-assurance in this area: they are willing to borrow money (after all, they are likely to have the savings to "dig into" if there were ever difficulties in repaying a loan), and they are more easygoing about the prospect of money being in the hands of others—husbands and offspring. All of this suggests a* more relaxed, carefree approach to money than typifies the Working-Class woman.

A study that focused on bank credit card usage also illustrates how social class influences consumer behavior.[47] Results indicated that members of the lower social classes tended to use their bank credit cards for installment purchases, while members of the upper social classes tended to be convenience users, paying their credit card bills in full each month. Furthermore, the lower class purchasers sought out stores that would honor their cards and used the card to buy appliances and other major purchases. In contrast, the upper class purchasers used their credit cards to buy gasoline or pay restaurant bills. In short, lower class purchasers tended to use their credit cards to "buy now and pay later" for things that they might not otherwise be able to afford, whereas upper class purchasers used their credit cards as a convenient substitute for cash.

SOCIAL CLASS AND COMMUNICATION

Social class groupings differ in terms of how they transmit and receive communications, and in their media habits. Knowledge of these differences is invaluable to marketers who segment their markets on the basis of social class. It enables them to develop promotional strategies specifically designed to "penetrate" their prospects' perceptual screens.

communication patterns

Evidence suggests that, in describing events, lower class members portray their world in rather personal and concrete terms, while middle class members are able to describe their experiences from a number of different perspectives.[48] The following responses to a question asking where the respondent usually purchased chewing gum illustrate how members of different social classes tend to see the world from different perspectives:[49]

UPPER-MIDDLE CLASS ANSWER: "At a cashier's counter or in a grocery store."
LOWER-MIDDLE CLASS ANSWER: "At the National or the corner drugstore."
LOWER CLASS ANSWER: "From Tony."

These variations in response indicate that middle class consumers have a broader or more general view of the world, while lower class consumers tend to see the world through their own immediate experience.

There also seem to be important social class differences in the *choice* of words used to describe things, people, and events. For example, one sociologist noted the following differences in word usage between lower and upper class members:[50]

Lower Class Usage	Upper Class Equivalent
evening	afternoon
dinner	lunch
supper	dinner

An awareness of such differences in language usage enables marketers to appeal more directly to their target markets in their advertising copy, their packaging, and in their labeling.

Researchers have also perceived real differences in the general speech patterns of different social classes.[51] This finding suggests that advertisers, when considering announcers for their radio and television commercials, should carefully select those who project a social class picture consistent with the target audience they are trying to reach.

Regional differences in terminology, choice of words and phrases, and patterns of usage tend to increase as we move down the social class ladder.[52] Therefore, in targeting appeals to the lower classes, marketers should try to make certain that the language in their advertisement reflects any regional differences that might exist.

media exposure

There is evidence that selective exposure to various types of mass media differs by social class. Higher class consumers tend to have greater exposure to magazines and newspapers than do their lower class counterparts. Lower class consumers are likely to have greater exposure to publications which dramatize romance and the life styles of movie and television celebrities. For example, magazines such as *True Story* and *Photoplay* appeal heavily to blue collar or working class women, who enjoy reading about the problems, fame, and fortunes of others. In the selection of specific television programs and program types, higher social class members tend to prefer current events and drama, while lower class individuals tend to prefer soap operas, quiz shows, and situation comedies.[53]

SOCIAL CLASS MOBILITY

Social class membership in this country is not as hard and fixed as it is in some other countries and cultures. The availability of free education to all citizens and opportunities for self-development and self-advancement make it possible for people to move up the social ladder into higher social classes than those to which their parents belonged. Indeed, the classic Horatio Alger tale of a penniless young man who managed to achieve great success in business and in life is depicted over and over again in popular novels, movies, and television shows. Because social mobility is possible in our society, the higher social classes often become reference groups for ambitious men and women of lower social status. The junior executive tries to dress like his boss; the middle manager aspires to belong to the president's club; the graduate of a free university wants to send his son to Princeton.

Some marketers, recognizing that individuals often aspire to membership in higher social classes, incorporate the symbols of higher class membership (both as products and props) in their advertisements addressed to lower social class audiences. For example, they might advertise an Oldsmobile to lower-middle class consumers, or golf clubs to lower management ranks.

Although studies of human levels of aspiration (see Chapter 2) indicate that individuals may reasonably aspire to the class immediately above their own, it appears that aspirations that skip social classes tend to be unrealistic and fade away into fantasy. Therefore, marketers must be careful not to incorporate symbols in their advertisements that are too far above the social class status of their intended audience. Some years ago, a leading marketer of watches in the popular price range ran a campaign that featured such props as a man's top hat, beautiful crystal champagne glasses, and opera tickets, in advertisements directed to a lower-middle class market. This intended audience, however, could not identify with the situations depicted and did not respond; and higher class audiences who noted his ads could not identify with an inexpensive watch. Thus the advertising campaign failed dismally.

Many advertisers make the same mistake. For example, advertisements for economy cars often show them parked in front of elaborate country homes. The viewer who identifies with the background is unlikely to identify with the car, and vice versa. Marketers should therefore pay closer attention to the relevance of their advertising symbols to the social class of their target audiences. Symbols that either represent the same social class or the class immediately above that of the target market are usually appropriate; symbols that skip to a higher social class or represent a lower social class are usually not effective.

RETAIL SHOPPING

Consumers' shopping values, attitudes, and behavior are also influenced by their social class. For example, although most women tend to enjoy shopping, their reasons vary by social class. A study of the shopping behavior of Cleveland women found that the *acquisition* of new clothing and household products was the principal enjoyment received by lower class shoppers. In contrast, upper-middle class and upper class shoppers tended to enjoy the *act* of shopping itself (store atmosphere and displays) and tended to shop more frequently than lower class women.[54]

Furthermore, while department stores attract a large portion of shoppers from all social classes, there is a definite tendency for higher class women to favor traditional department stores, and lower class women to patronize mass merchandisers and "downtown" stores.[55] A detailed analysis of the type of department store preferred by women from different social classes is presented in Table 11–12. The evidence indicates that price appeal stores draw lower class shoppers, broad appeal stores attract middle class shoppers, and stores that feature a high-fashion image are preferred by upper class shoppers.[56]

A study that investigated the retail preferences of different social classes found that upper class consumers prefer department and specialty stores for items that they perceive to be socially risky, but are willing to use discount stores for items that are not perceived to be socially risky.[57] On the other hand, lower class consumers are willing to patronize discounters for products of both high and low social risk.

The study indicates that discounters have successfully developed acceptance across social class boundaries for a wide range of products

TABLE 11–12

Types of Department Store Favored, by Social Class

TYPES OF DEPARTMENT STORE	Social class		
	Lower class	Middle class	Upper class
Price Appeal Store	65%	33%	19%
Broad Appeal Store	28	42	12
High Fashion Store	7	25	69
Total	100%	100%	100%
Number of Respondents	(275)	(275)	(42)

Source: Adapted from Stuart U. Rich and Subhash C. Jain, "Social Class and Life Cycle as Predictors of Shopping Behavior," *Journal of Marketing Research*, 5 (February 1968), 48.

with low social risk. However, they have not attracted large numbers of upper class consumers for products that can be classified as *socially risky* (such as clothing or conspicuous home furnishings). In terms of marketing, it would probably be a gross error for discounters to trade up their merchandise in an attempt to capture the upper class consumer. Such a strategy would also run the risk of providing an atmosphere that might alienate the lower class consumers who are their established customers.

Finally, there is evidence that in-home consumers—those who purchase from a catalog, by mail, or by telephone—are socioeconomically different from those consumers who rely solely on retail stores.[58] The results indicate that in-home consumers tend to have high family incomes, white-collar occupations, and more formal education than consumers who do not shop at home. These findings suggest that middle and upper class consumers are a fertile market for direct mail and telephone marketing.

CONSUMERISM

Marketers, public policy makers, and private consumer advocates are becoming increasingly interested in the nature of consumer dissatisfaction. For this reason, consumer behavior studies are now beginning to receive attention from consumer policy researchers.

A recent study of the types of consumers who take advantage of a publicly sponsored consumer "hot line" found that lower class callers reported considerably more service or repair problems; both middle and upper class callers complained about purchase and delivery problems; and upper class callers were more likely to complain about deceptive or offensive advertisements.[59] Table 11–13 categorize the callers by social class and type of problem.

TABLE 11–13

Problem Categories of Hot Line Callers by Social Class

PROBLEM CATEGORY	Social Class			
	Low (N = 39)	Middle (N = 66)	High (N = 45)	Total (N = 150)
Prepurchase	13%	11%	20%	14%
Purchase transaction/ delivery	10	31%	31	27
Product performance	13	18	18	17
Guarantee/warranty/ contract	15	11	9	11
Service/repair	39	25	18	26
Deposits/credit/ collections	8	1	4	4
Other	2	3	0	1
	100%	100%	100%	100%

Source: Steven L. Diamond, Scott Ward, and Ronald Faber, "Consumer Problems and Consumerism: Analysis of Calls to a Consumer Hot Line," Journal of Marketing, 40 (January 1976), 60.

These findings reveal significant social class differences in the frequency and type of consumer complaints. They suggest that social class analysis might be fruitful within the context of other consumer problem areas.

Summary

Social stratification—the division of members of a society into a hierarchy of distinct social classes—exists in all societies and cultures. *Social class* is usually defined by the amount of status that members of a specific class possess in relation to members of other classes. Social class membership often serves as a frame of reference (i.e., a reference group) for the development of consumer attitudes and behavior.

The measurement of social class is concerned with classifying individuals into social class groupings. These groupings are of particular value to marketers, who use social classification as an effective means to identify and segment target markets.

There are three basic methods for measuring social class: subjective measurement, reputational measurement, and objective measurement. Subjective measures rely on an individual's self perception, reputational measures rely on his perceptions of others, and objective measures use specific socioeconomic measures, either alone (as a single-variable index) or in combination with others (as a composite-variable index). Composite-variable indexes combine a number of socioeconomic factors to form one overall measure of social class standing.

Social class structures range from two-class systems to nine-class systems. A frequently used classification system consists of six classes: upper-upper, lower-upper, upper-middle, lower-middle, upper-lower, and lower-lower. Profiles of each of these classes indicate that the socio-economic differences between classes are reflected in differences in attitudes, in leisure-time activities, and in consumption habits. That is why segmentation by social class is of special interest to marketers.

Research has revealed social class differences in clothing habits, home decoration, telephone usage, leisure-time activities, retail patronage, and saving, spending, and credit habits. Thus the astute marketer will differentiate product and promotional strategies for each social class target segment.

Studies of consumer dissatisfaction reveal a relationship between social class and the types of problems consumers complain about. In summary, it would appear that social class analysis holds enormous promise for marketers, public policy makers, and consumer advocates in terms of understanding, influencing, and improving the conditions for consumer behavior.

Endnotes

1. Robert W. Hodges, Paul M. Siegel, and Peter H. Rossi, "Occupational Prestige in the United States, 1925–1963," American Journal of Sociology, 70 (November 1964), 286–302.

2. David Popenoe, Sociology, 2nd ed. (Englewood Cliffs, N.J.: Prentice-Hall, 1974), 251–58.

3. Burleigh B. Gardner, "Social Status and Consumer Behavior," in Lincoln H. Clark, ed., The Life Cycle and Consumer Behavior (New York: New York University Press, 1955), 58.

4. Marcus Felson, "A Modern Sociological Approach to the Stratification of Material Life Styles," in Mary Jane Schlinger, ed., Advances in Consumer Research, 2 (Association for Consumer Research, 1975), 34.

5. Richard Centers, The Psychology of Social Class (New York: Russell and Russell, 1961), 233.

6. Ibid., p. 27.

7. Hadley Cantril, "Identification with Social and Economic Class," Journal of Abnormal and Social Psychology, 38 (January 1943), 75–79.

8. W. Llody Warner, Marchia Meeker, and Kenneth Eells, Social Class in America: Manual of Procedure for the Measurement of Social Status (New York: Harper & Brothers, 1960).

9. Hodges, Siegel, and Rossi, "Occupational Prestige."

10. *Albert J. Reiss, Jr., Otis Dudley Duncan, Paul K. Hatt, and Cecil C. North*, Occupational and Social Status *(New York: Free Press, 1961)*.

11. *Felson, "Modern Sociological Approach," 34.*

12. *Chester R. Wasson, "Is It Time to Quit Thinking of Income Classes?"* Journal of Marketing, *33 (April 1969), 54–57.*

13. *F. Stuart Chapin*, Contemporary American Institutions *(New York: Harper, 1935), 373–97.*

14. *William H. Peters, "Who Cooperates in Voluntary Recycling Efforts?" in Thomas V. Greer, ed., 1973* Combined Proceedings *(Chicago: American Marketing Association, 1974), 505–8.*

15. *Warner, Meeker, and Eells*, Social Class in America.

16. Methodology and Scores of Socioeconomic Status, *Working Paper No. 15 (Washington, D.C.: U.S. Bureau of the Census, 1963).*

17. *Richard B. Ellis, "Composite Population Descriptors: The Socio-Economic/Life Cycle Grid," in Mary Jane Schlinger, ed.,* Advances in Consumer Research, 2 *(Association for Consumer Research, 1975), 481–93.*

18. *A. Marvin Roscoe, Jr., and Jagdish H. Sheth, "Demographic Segmentation of Long Distance Behavior: Data Analysis and Inductive Model Building," in M. Venkatesan, ed.,* Third Annual Conference of the Association for Consumer Research, *1972, 258–78.*

19. *Alvin B. Coleman, "Class Structure: A Comparison of Lower-Working and Upper-Middle Family Characteristics,"* Clearing House, *42 (April 1968), 470.*

20. *Marie R. Hang, "Social Class Measurement and Women's Occupational Roles,"* Social Forces, *52 (September 1973), 92.*

21. *Richard P. Coleman and Bernice L. Neugarten*, Social Status in the City *(San Francisco: Jossey Bass, 1971), ix.*

22. *See Arun K. Jain, "A Method for Investigating and Representing Implicit Social Class Theory,"* Journal of Consumer Research, *2 (June 1975), 53–59; and Peter H. Rossi, William A. Sampson, Christine E. Bose, Guillermina Jasso, and Jeff Passel, "Measuring Household Social Standing,"* Social Science Research, *3 (1974), 169–90.*

23. *James H. Myers, Roger R. Stanton, and Arne F. Haug, "Correlates of Buying Behavior: Social Class vs. Income,"* Journal of Marketing, *35 (October 1971), 8–15.*

24. *James H. Myers and John F. Mount, "More on Social Class vs. Income as Correlates of Buying Behavior,"* Journal of Marketing, *37 (April 1973), 71–73.*

25. *Robert D. Hisrich and Michael P. Peters, "Selecting the Superior Segmentation Correlate,"* Journal of Marketing, *38 (July 1974), 60–63.*

26. *James H. Myers and Jonathan Gutman, "Life Style: The Essence of Social Class," in William D. Wells, ed.,* Life Style and Psychographics *(Chicago: American Marketing Association, 1974), 235–56.*

27. *Richard P. Coleman, "The Significance of Social Stratification in Selling," in Martin L. Bell, ed.,* Marketing: A Mature Discipline *(Chicago: American Marketing Association, 1961), 171–84.*

28. *William H. Peters, "Relative Occupational Class Income: A Significant Variable in the Marketing of Automobiles,"* Journal of Marketing, *34 (April 1970), 74–77.*

29. *The social class profiles in this section are drawn from a variety of sources, including Coleman and Neugarten,* Social Status; *and Harold M. Hodges, Jr., "Peninsula People: Social Stratification in a Metropolitan Complex," in Clayton Lane, ed.,* Permanence and Change *(Cambridge, Mass.: Schenkman, 1969), 5–36.*

30. *Saxon Graham, "Class and Conservatism in the Adoption of Innovations,"* Human Relations, *9 (February 1956), 91–100.*

31. A Study of Working-Class Women in a Changing World *(prepared for Macfadden-Bartell Corporation by Social Science Research, Inc., May 1973).*

32. *Epictetus,* Discourses *(2nd cent.), 31, trans. Thomas Higginson.*

33. *Stuart U. Rich and Subhash C. Jain, "Social Class and Life Cycle as Predictors of Shopping Behavior,"* Journal of Marketing Research, *5 (February 1968), 43–44.*

34. Study of Working-Class Women, *154–55.*

35. *Ibid.*

36. *William D. Wells, "Seven Questions about Life Style and Psychographics," in Boris W. Bunker and Helmut Becker, eds., 1972* Combined Proceedings *(Chicago: American Marketing Association, 1973), 464.*

37. *Thomas E. Lasswell,* Class and Stratum *(Boston: Houghton Mifflin, 1965), p. 231.*

38. *Gardner, "Social Status," 60.*

39. *Edward O. Laumann and James S. House, "Living Room Styles and Social Attributes: The Patterning of Material Artifacts in a Modern Urban Community,"* Sociology and Social Research, *54 (April 170), 324–27.*

40. *Ibid.*

41. *A. Marvin Roscoe, Jr., Arthur LeClaire, Jr., and Leon G. Schiffman, "Theory and Management Applications of Demographics in Buyer Behavior," in Arch G. Woodside, Jagdish N. Sheth, and Peter D. Bennett, eds.,* Foundations of Consumer and Industrial Buying Behavior *(New York: American Elsevier, 1977), 67–76.*

42. *William R. Cotton, Jr., "Leisure and Social Stratification," in Gerald W. Thielbar and Saul D. Feldman, eds.,* Issues in Social Inequality *(Boston: Little, Brown, 1972), 520–38.*

43. *Alfred C. Clarke, "Leisure and Occupational Prestige,"* American Sociological Review, *21 (June 1956), 305–6.*

44. *Joseph T. Plummer, "Life Style and Case Studies," in Fred C. Allvine, ed., 1971* Combined Proceedings *(Chicago: American Marketing Association, 1972), 292.*

45. *Pierre Martineau, "Social Classes and Shopping Behavior,"* Journal of Marketing, *23 (October 1958), 128.*

46. Study of Working Class Women, *151.*

47. *H. Lee Mathews and John W. Slocum, Jr., "Social Class and Commercial Bank Credit Usage,* Journal of Marketing, *33 (January 1969), 71–78.*

48. *Leonard Schatzman and Anselm Strauss, "Social Class and Modes of Communication,"* American Journal of Sociology, *60 (January 1955), 329–38.*

49. *Ibid., 337.*

50. *John Kenneth Morland,* Millways of Kent *(Chapel Hill: University of North Carolina Press, 1958), 192, 277.*

51. *Lasswell,* Class and Stratum, *223–24.*

52. *Ibid., 221–22.*

53. *Sidney J. Levy, "Social Class and Consumer Behavior," in Joseph W. Newman, ed.,* On Knowing the Consumer *(New York: John Wiley, 1966), 155.*

54. *Rich and Jain, "Social Class," 44.*

55. *Ibid., 45–46.*

56. *Ibid., 46.*

57. *V. Kanti Prasad, "Socioeconomic Product Risk and Patronage Preferences of Retail Shoppers,"* Journal of Marketing, *39 (July 1975), 42–7.*

58. *Peter L. Gillett, "A Profile of Urban In-Home Shoppers,"* Journal of Marketing, *34 (July 1970), 40–5.*

59. *Steven L. Diamond, Scott Ward, and Ronald Faber, "Consumer Problems and Consumerism: Analysis of Calls to a Consumer Hot Line,"* Journal of Marketing, *40 (January 1976), 58–62.*

Discussion questions

1. Give an example from your own experience of how social class may serve as a frame of reference for an individual's consumption behavior.

2. Marketing researchers have generally used the objective method to measure social class, rather than the subjective or reputational methods. Why has the objective method been preferred by researchers?

3. What is the principal drawback of evaluating a family's social class position exclusively in terms of the male head-of-household?

4. Under what circumstances would you expect income to be a better predictor of consumer behavior than a composite measure of social class (based on income, education, and occupation)? On the other hand, when would you expect the composite social class measure to be superior?

5. Identify either a men's or women's clothing retailer in your local community that you feel appeals primarily to upper-middle class shoppers. What is there about the store that makes you feel that it attracts this particular social class? How does this store differ from other stores that cater to lower social class shoppers?

6. If you were invited to a family's home for the first time, what factors might you consider in making an estimate of their social class standing? Explain.

7. Assume that you were a marketing consultant for a small savings bank. What advice would you give the management of the bank about the use of social class as a variable for segmenting its market?

8. If you were asked by a local consumer protection agency to provide them with guidelines on how lower and middle class consumers differ in terms of consumer protection needs, what advice would you give them?

the influence of culture on consumer behavior

12

Introduction

The study of culture is a challenging undertaking because its primary focus is on the broadest component of social behavior — an entire society. Thus, in contrast to the psychologist, who is principally concerned with the study of individual behavior, or the sociologist, who is concerned with the study of groups, the anthropologist is primarily interested in identifying the very fabric of society itself.

This chapter explores the basic concepts of culture, with particular emphasis on the role culture plays in influencing consumer behavior in the American society. We will first consider the specific dimensions of culture that make it such a powerful force in regulating human behavior. Then we will review several measurement approaches that researchers employ in their efforts to understand the impact of culture on consumption behavior. Finally, we will show how a variety of core American cultural values influence consumer behavior.

This chapter is concerned with the more general aspects of culture; the following chapter focuses on smaller subcultures and on foreign cultures and will show how marketers can use such knowledge to shape and to modify their marketing strategies.

Culture is not an exotic notion studied by a select group of anthropologists in the South Seas. It is a mold in which we are all cast, and it controls our daily lives in many unsuspected ways.

EDWARD T. HALL
The Silent
Language *(1959)*

WHAT IS CULTURE?

Given the broad and pervasive nature of culture, its study generally requires a global examination of the character of the total society, including such factors as its language, knowledge, laws, religion, food customs, music, art, technology, work patterns, products and other artifacts which give the society its distinctive flavor. In a sense, culture is a society's "personality." For this reason, it is not easy to define its boundaries.

Since our specific objective is to understand the influence of culture on consumer behavior, we will define culture as the *sum total of learned beliefs, values, and customs which serve to regulate the consumer behavior of members of a particular society.*[1]

The *belief* and *value* components of our definition refer to the accumulated feelings and priorities that individuals have about "things." More precisely, *beliefs* consist of the very large number of mental or verbal statements (i.e., "I believe that . . .") which reflect a person's particular knowledge and assessment of *something* (another person, a store, perhaps a product, a brand). *Values* are also beliefs. However, values differ from other beliefs in that they meet the following criteria: (1) they are relatively few in number; (2) they serve as a guide for "culturally appropriate" behavior; (3) they are enduring or difficult to change; and (4) they are widely accepted by the members of a society.[2]

Therefore, in a broad sense, both beliefs and values are "mental images" that affect a wide range of specific attitudes, which in turn influence the way a person is likely to respond in a specific situation (see Chapter 6). For example, the criteria that a person employs in evaluating alternative brands and his eventual conclusion concerning these brands are influenced by his beliefs and values.

In comparison with beliefs and values, *customs* are overt modes of behavior that constitute culturally approved or acceptable ways of behaving in specific situations. Customs have been called ". . . behavior at its most commonplace."[3] For example, a consumer's routine behavior, such as reading the comics on Sunday morning, or serving cream with coffee, involves customs. Thus, while beliefs and values are *guides* for behavior, customs are *usual* and *acceptable ways of behaving*.

Within the context of our definition, it is easy to see how an understanding of the beliefs, values, and customs of a society will enable the marketer to accurately anticipate consumer acceptance of his products.

Characteristics of culture

To more fully comprehend the scope and complexity of culture, we will now examine a number of its underlying characteristics.

THE INVISIBLE HAND OF CULTURE

The impact of culture is so natural and so automatic that its influence on behavior is usually taken for granted. For example, when consumer researchers ask people why they do certain things, they frequently answer, "Because it's the right thing to do." This seemingly superficial response partially reflects the ingrained influence of culture on our behavior. Frequently, it is only when a person is exposed to people with different cultural values or customs (e.g., when visiting a different region or a different country) that he becomes aware of how culture has molded his own behavior. The following statement dramatically illustrates the invisible nature of culture and the difficulties of objectively studying its impact on human behavior:[4]

> It has been said that the last thing which a dweller in the deep sea would be likely to discover would be water. He would become conscious of its existence only if some accident brought him to the surface and introduced him to air. Man, throughout most of his history, has been only vaguely conscious of the existence of culture and has owed even this consciousness to contrasts between the customs of his own society and those of some other with which he happened to be brought into contact.

Thus, a true appreciation of the influence that culture has on our daily life requires some knowledge of at least one other society with different cultural characteristics. For example, to understand that brushing our teeth twice a day with flavored toothpaste is a cultural phenomenon requires some awareness that members of another society either do not brush their teeth at all or do so in a manner distinctly different from our own.

CULTURE SATISFIES NEEDS

Culture exists to satisfy the needs of the people within a society. It offers order, direction, and guidance in all phases of human problem solving by providing "tried and true" methods of satisfying physiological, personal, and social needs. For example, culture provides standards and "rules" regarding when to eat and what is appropriate to eat for breakfast, lunch, dinner, and snacks, and what to serve to guests at a dinner party, a picnic, or a wedding.

Cultural beliefs, values, and customs continue to be followed so long as they yield satisfaction. However, when a specific standard no longer fully satisfies the members of a society, it is modified or replaced, so that the resulting standard is more in line with the current needs and desires of the society. Thus, culture gradually but continually evolves to meet the needs of society.

Within a cultural context, a firm's products and services can be viewed as offering appropriate or acceptable solutions for individual or social needs. If a product is no longer acceptable because a value or custom related to its use does not adequately satisfy human needs, then the firm producing it must be ready to adjust or revise its product offerings. For example, as Americans have become more informal and relaxed in their style of living, there has been a strong movement away from formal dress customs. Astute clothing manufacturers responded by offering more informal clothing (such as leisure suits for men and pant suits for women) and thus were able to maintain or even improve their market position. Marketers who were not perceptive enough to note these changing life-styles were likely to find themselves squeezed out of the market.

CULTURE IS LEARNED

Unlike our biological characteristics (e.g., sex, skin, hair color, and innate intelligence), we are not born "knowing" our culture. At an early age, however, we begin to acquire from our social environment a set of beliefs, values, and customs which constitute our culture. Culture is thus *learned* as part of social experience.

how is culture learned?

In answering this question, anthropologists have identified three distinct types of cultural learning: (1) *formal learning,* in which adults and older siblings teach a young family member "how to behave;" (2) *informal learning,* in which a child learns primarily by imitating the behavior of selected others (family, friends, TV heroes); and (3) *technical learning,* in which teachers instruct the child in an educational environment as to *what* should be done, *how* it should be done, and *why* it should be done.[5]

A little girl who is told by her mother to stop climbing trees because "little girls don't do that" is *formally* learning a value that her mother feels is right. In contrast, if she "dresses up" by copying her mother or older sister, she is *informally* learning certain dress habits. Finally, if she is given ballet lessons, she is experiencing *technical* learning.

Although a firm's advertising can influence all three types of cultural learning, it is likely that many product advertisements enhance *informal* cultural learning by providing the audience with a model of behavior to imitate. Figure 12-1 indicates how informal learning can be utilized as part of a firm's marketing efforts. The headline of the ad contains a strong cultural message, "Like Father, Like Son," which is reinforced with a picture of a father and son dressed alike. It suggests that it is appropriate for a little boy to be dressed like his father (i.e., in Wrangler products). At a more subtle level, however, the advertisement suggests that dressing a little boy like his father helps him to grow up to be a man.

The repetition of advertising messages also creates or reinforces cultural beliefs and values. For example, many advertisers continually

FIGURE 12–1

Advertisement That Reinforces Informal Cultural Learning

Courtesy of Blue Bell, Inc.

stress the same selected benefits as integral features of their products or brands. To illustrate, ads for toothpaste often stress one or more of the following benefits: prevents cavities, whitens teeth, makes the mouth feel better or taste fresher. After decades of cumulative exposure to such potent advertising appeals, it is difficult to say with any degree of certainty whether people *inherently* desire these benefits from toothpaste or whether they have been *taught* by marketers to desire them. In a sense, while specific product advertising may reinforce the benefits that consumers want from the product (as determined by consumer behavior research), such advertising also "teaches" future generations of consumers to expect the same benefits from the specific product category.

enculturation and acculturation

In discussing the acquisition of culture, anthropologists often distinguish between the learning of one's own or "native" culture and the learning of some other culture. The learning of one's own culture is known as *enculturation*. In contrast, the learning of a new or foreign culture is known as *acculturation*. In the next chapter, we will see that acculturation is an important concept for marketers who plan to sell their products to consumers with distinctly different cultures in foreign or multinational markets. In such cases, the marketer must study the specific cultures of his potential target markets in order to determine whether his product will be acceptable to its members, and how he can best communicate the characteristics of his products to persuade them to buy.

language and symbols

To acquire a common culture, the members of a society must be able to communicate with each other through a common language. Without a common language, shared meaning could not exist and true communication would not take place (see Chapter 7).

In order to communicate effectively with their audiences, marketers must use appropriate symbols to convey desired product images or characteristics. These symbols can be *verbal* or *nonverbal*. Verbal symbols may include a television announcement, or an advertisement in a magazine. Nonverbal communication includes the use of such symbols as figures, colors, shapes, even textures to provide additional meaning to print or broadcast advertisements, to trademarks, and to packaging or product designs.

Basically, it is the symbolic nature of human language that sets it apart from all other animal communication. A *symbol* is anything that stands for something else.[6] Any word is symbol. The word *table* calls forth a specific image related to an individual's own knowledge and experience. The word *fire* not only calls forth the notion of burning but also has the power to stir us emotionally, arousing feelings of warmth, danger, and fascination. Similarly, the word *Cadillac* has symbolic mean-

FIGURE 12–2

Advertisement Incorporating Symbolic Learning

ing—to some it suggests a fine luxury automobile, to others it implies wealth and status, to still others it may suggest a brand of dog food.

Because the human mind has a substantial capacity to process symbols, it is possible for a person to read an advertisement for a product such as a rechargeable battery (see Figure 12–2) and understand its purpose and how it works, even though he has never before seen or used such a product. The capacity to learn symbolically is primarily a human phenomenon; most other animals learn by direct experience. Clearly, the ability of humans to understand symbolically how a product or an idea may satisfy their needs makes it easier for marketers to sell the features and benefits of their products.

Inasmuch as a symbol may have several meanings, even contradictory ones, it is important that the advertiser ascertain exactly what his symbols are communicating to his intended audience. For example, the advertiser who uses a trademark depicting an old craftsman to symbolize careful workmanship may instead be communicating an image of old age, outmoded methods, and lack of style. The marketer who uses slang in his copy to attract a teenage audience must do so with great care. Slang that is misused or outdated will symbolically outdate his firm and his product.

Price and channels of distribution are also significant symbols of the marketer and his product. For example, price often implies quality to potential buyers (see Chapter 3). For certain products, the type of store in which the product is sold is also an important symbol of quality. Thus, all of the elements of the marketing mix—the product, its promotion, its price, and the stores at which it is available—are symbols that communicate ranges of quality to potential buyers.[7]

CULTURE IS SHARED

To be considered a characteristic of a culture, a particular belief, value, or practice should not be the sole province of a few individuals; rather, it must be shared by a significant portion of the society. Accordingly, culture is frequently viewed as group customs that link together the members of a society.[8] And, of course, common language is the critical component of a culture which makes it possible for people to share values, experiences, and customs.

Various social institutions within a society transmit the elements of culture and make the sharing of culture a reality. Chief among such institutions is the family, which serves as the primary agent for enculturation—the passing along of basic cultural beliefs, values, and customs to society's newest members. A vital part of the enculturation role of the family is the consumer socialization of the young (see Chapter 9). This includes the teaching of such basic consumer-related values and skills as the meaning of money, the relationship between price and quality, the establishment of product tastes, preferences, and habits, and appropriate methods of response to various promotional messages.

In addition to the family, two other institutions traditionally share much of the responsibility for the transfer of selected aspects of culture — the school and the church. Educational institutions are specifically charged with imparting basic learning skills, history, patriotism, citizenship, and the technical training needed to prepare people for significant roles within society. Religious institutions provide and perpetuate religious consciousness, spiritual guidance, and moral training. Although it is in the family environment that the young receive much of their consumer training, the educational and religious systems reinforce such training through the teaching of economic and ethical concepts.

A fourth, frequently overlooked, social institution that plays a major role in the transfer of culture throughout society is the mass media. Given the extensive exposure of the American population to both print and broadcast media, and the easily ingested, entertaining format in which the contents of such media are usually presented, it is not surprising that the mass media are a powerful vehicle for imparting a wide range of cultural values.

Advertising is an important component of most mass media to which we are exposed daily. It not only underwrites or makes economically feasible the editorial or programming contents of the media, but it also transmits much about our culture. Without advertising, it would be almost impossible to disseminate information about products, ideas, and causes. A leading historian noted: ". . . advertising now compares with such long-standing institutions as the schools and the church in the magnitude of its social influence."[9]

Thus, while the scope of advertising is often considered to be limited to stimulating or altering the demand for specific products or services, in a cultural context advertising has the expanded mission of reinforcing established cultural values and aiding in the spread of new tastes, habits, and customs. In planning his advertising, the marketer should therefore recognize that advertising is an important agent of social change in our society.

CULTURE IS DYNAMIC

In our discussion of the need-gratifying role of culture, we have noted that culture must change if it is to continue to function in the best interests of a society. We have also suggested that to effectively market an existing product, or develop promising new products, the marketer must carefully monitor the social-cultural environment.

This is not an easy task, since many factors are likely to produce cultural changes within a given society (new technology, population shifts, wars, changing values, customs borrowed from other cultures). For example, a major cultural change in our society is the expanded role choices of American females. A number of factors have been cited in connection with this change, including increased educational opportunities, the availability of labor-saving devices which make homemaking less restrictive, the increased number of women in the labor force, the availability of new birth-control techniques, the efforts of female acti-

FIGURE 12–3

Advertisement Pointing Up the Changing Nature of Culture

Courtesy of Yamaha International Corp.

vist groups, and the enactment and enforcement of equal employment laws. Just which of these factors are basic forces in the shifting role of women in American society, and which are outgrowths that have their own impact on other areas of life, is difficult to say.

However, it is clear that the role choices of American women have definitely changed. More women are working outside the home, often in careers that once were considered exclusively male, and more women are active in social and athletic activities outside of the home. All this adds up to an increased blurring of traditional male-female sex roles. These changes mean that marketers must reconsider *who* are the purchasers and the users of their products (males only, females only, or both), *when* they do their shopping, *how* and *where* they can be reached by the media, and *what* new product and service needs have been created.

Marketers who monitor cultural changes often find new opportunities to increase corporate profitability. For example, Yamaha is now targeting its motorcycles to young women (see Fig 12–3). The headline asks the important question, "Why not?" A few years ago such an advertisement might have been inappropriate, but today such a product is within the scope of female interests.

Marketers of life insurance, leisure wear, electric trains, and small cigars, among others, have attempted to take advantage of the dramatically shifting definition of what is "feminine." This sex-role shift has also had its impact on traditional male roles. For instance, today toy manufacturers are successfully marketing dolls to parents of little boys (Action Joe, Bionic Man), and men's toiletry manufacturers are busily selling cologne and cosmetics to men.

Other aspects of the changing roles of women and their effect on consumer behavior patterns will be discussed in the next chapter as part of our examination of subculture.

The measurement of culture

A wide range of measurement techniques have been employed to study culture. Some of these techniques have already been described in earlier chapters. For example, the projective tests used by psychologists to study motivation and personality (discussed in Chapters 2 and 5), and the attitude measurement techniques employed by social psychologists and sociologists (Chapter 6) are relatively popular tools in the study of culture.

In addition, observational fieldwork, content analysis, and value measurement instruments are three data collection techniques that are frequently associated with the examination of culture. We will briefly discuss each of these techniques.

OBSERVATIONAL FIELDWORK

In studying a specific society, anthropologists frequently immerse themselves in the environment they wish to explore. As trained observers, they often select a small sample of people from a particular society and observe their behavior. Based upon their observations, they draw conclusions about the values, beliefs, and customs of the society under investigation.

To illustrate, if a researcher were interested in how women shop for detergents, he might position himself in the detergent section of a supermarket and note the specific types of detergents selected (cold water versus hot water, liquid versus powdered) and the size and price of specific brands selected. The researcher might also be interested in the degree of indecision that accompanies the choice; that is, how frequently shoppers tend to hesitate (e.g., take packages off the shelf, read the labels, place them back again) before selecting the brand they purchase.

The distinct characteristics of field observation are: (1) it is performed within a natural environment, (2) it is sometimes performed without the subjects' awareness, and (3) it focuses only on observation of behavior. Thus, since the emphasis is on a natural environment and observable behavior, field observation concerned with consumer behavior is usually limited to in-store behavior, and only rarely to in-home preparation and consumption.

In some cases, instead of just observing behavior, researchers become *participant-observers*. Such researchers actually become an active member of the environment they are studying. For example, if a researcher were interested in examining how men select a new shirt, she might take a sales position in a men's clothing store in order to observe directly and even interact with customers in the transaction process.

Both field observation and participant-observer research require highly skilled researchers who can separate out their own emotions from what they actually observe in their roles as researchers. Such techniques, however, can provide valuable insights which might not easily be obtained through survey research that simply asks consumers to answer questions about their behavior.

CONTENT ANALYSIS

Conclusions about a society, or some specific aspect of a society, can sometimes be drawn from an examination of the content of its messages. The *content analysis* approach, as its name implies, focuses on the content of verbal and pictorial communication (e.g., the copy and art components of an ad).[10]

Content analysis can be used as an objective means of determining whether social and cultural changes have occurred within a specific society. For instance, in the next chapter, we discuss the results of several content analysis studies that were designed to determine how the roles of blacks and females, as depicted in magazine ads, have changed with the passage of time. Content analysis is equally useful to marketers and to public policy makers who are interested in comparing the advertising claims of competitors and other firms within a specific industry.

VALUE MEASUREMENT SURVEY
INSTRUMENTS

Anthropologists have traditionally observed the behavior of members of a specific society and *inferred* from such behavior the dominant or underlying values of the society. In recent years, however, there has been a gradual shift to measuring values *directly* by means of survey (or questionnaire) research. Researchers use data collection instruments called "value instruments" to ask people how they feel about such basic personal and social concepts as freedom, comfort, national security, and peace.

Research involving the relationship between people's values and their actions as consumers is still in its infancy. However, it is an area that is destined to receive increased attention, for it taps a broad dimension of human behavior that could not be effectively explored before the availability of standardized value instruments.

A promising instrument which has been employed in several consumer behavior studies is the Rokeach Value Survey.[11] This self-administered value inventory is divided into two parts, with each part measuring different, but complementary, types of personal values. The first part consists of eighteen "terminal" value items, which are designed to measure the relative importance of "end-states of existence" (i.e., personal goals). The second part consists of eighteen "instrumental" value items, which measure basic approaches an individual might follow to reach end-state values. Thus the first half of the measurement instrument deals with "ends," while the second half considers "means."

The first consumer study to employ the Rokeach Value Survey examined the relationship between the thirty-six values and subjects' evaluations of automobile attributes (style, amount of service required, amount of pollution produced, economy of operation, and quality of warranty).[12] The findings revealed that specific values were associated with specific automobile attributes. For instance, the attribute *style* was found to be related to such terminal values as "a comfortable life," "an exciting life," and "pleasure." The attribute *amount of pollution produced* was found to be related to the terminal value "a world at peace," and the instrumental values "helpful" and "loving."

In a second study of automobile attributes, the values of college students and their parents were compared by means of the Rokeach Value Survey.[13] Not surprisingly, the results revealed that students and parents had different instrumental and terminal values concerning automobiles.

Specifically, the study found that students evaluated "an exciting life" and "pleasure" as particularly important values; whereas their parents gave higher ratings to values that reflected standards of social and individual responsibility — "national security," "a world of beauty," and "obedience." In terms of automobile attributes, students considered styling and speed to be important attributes and preferred compact cars; their parents rated such features as comfort, handling, service, and warranty as most important and preferred standard-sized cars.

The results of these two studies suggest that the Rokeach Value Survey can be used by marketers to segment their markets by specific values and perceptions of specific product attributes. Such information would be useful in developing new products for specific market segments.

Based upon the results of these and other studies, it appears that consumer values may prove to be an important new consumer behavior variable.[14] When combined with other behavioral variables examined in this book, values can be employed to predict shifts in consumption patterns. Such insights would be particularly useful in developing new product concepts, repositioning existing products, and adjusting the firm's general marketing efforts.

American core values

What is the American culture? In this section we shall try to identify a few core values that both affect and reflect the character of American society. This is a difficult undertaking for several reasons. First, the United States is a diverse country, consisting of a number of subcultures (religious, ethnic, regional, racial, and economic groups), each of which interprets and responds to society's basic beliefs and values in its own specific way. Second, America is a dynamic society, one that has undergone almost constant change in response to its leadership role in the development of new technology. This element of rapid change makes it especially difficult to monitor changes in cultural values. Finally, the existence of contradictory values in American society is often somewhat confusing. For instance, Americans traditionally embrace freedom of choice and individualism, yet simultaneously they show great tendencies to conform (in dress, in furnishings, in fads, etc.) to the rest of society. In the context of consumer behavior, Americans like to have a wide choice of products, and prefer those which uniquely express their personal lifestyles. Yet there is often a considerable amount of implicit pressure to conform to the values of family members, friends, or other socially important groups. It is difficult to reconcile such seemingly inconsistent values; however, their existence demonstrates that America is a complex society with numerous paradoxes and contradictions.[15]

In selecting the specific core values to be examined here, we were guided by three criteria:

1. *The value must be pervasive.* A significant portion of the American people must accept the value and employ it as a guide for their attitudes and actions.
2. *The value must be enduring.* The specific value must have influenced the actions of the American people over an extended period of time (as distinguished from a short-run "trend").
3. *The value must be consumer related.* The specific value must provide insights that help us understand the consumption actions of the American people.

Utilizing these criteria, we will now discuss a number of basic values that expert observers of the American scene consider the "building blocks" of that rather elusive concept we call the American Character.[16]

ACHIEVEMENT AND SUCCESS

In our discussion of human needs and motives (Chapter 2), we pointed out that the need for achievement is often a propellant for individual behavior. In a broader cultural context, achievement is a central American value, with historical roots that can be traced to the traditional religious belief—the Protestant ethic—that hard work is wholesome, spiritually rewarding, and an appropriate end in itself. Indeed, substantial research evidence shows that the achievement orientation is closely associated with the technological development and general economic growth of the American society.[17]

Success is a closely related American cultural theme. However, achievement and success do differ. Specifically, achievement is its own direct reward (it is implicitly satisfying to the achiever), while success implies an extrinsic reward (such as financial or status improvements).

Both achievement and success influence consumption. They often serve as social and moral justification for the acquisition of goods and services. For example, "You owe it to yourself," "You worked for it," and "You deserve it" are popular achievement themes used by advertisers to coax consumers into purchasing their products. Figure 12–4 depicts an ad from an ongoing advertising campaign which closes with the question, "And you're still drinking ordinary scotch?" This campaign says, in effect, that the reader has worked hard to achieve the "good life" for others close to him, and he should no longer deny himself his just rewards. Thus the campaign appeals to both achievement and success values.

ACTIVITY

Americans attach an extraordinary amount of importance to being "active" or "involved." Keeping busy is widely accepted as a healthy and even necessary part of the American life-style. The hectic nature of American life is attested to by foreign visitors who frequently comment that they cannot understand why Americans are always "on the run" and seemingly are unable to relax.

The premium placed on activity has had both a positive and a negative effect on the popularity of various products. For example, the main reason for the enormous growth of fast-food chains, such as McDonald's and Kentucky Fried Chicken, is that so many people want quick, prepared meals when they are out of the house and on the run. In contrast, one of the reasons for the decline in the consumption of eggs is that Americans are usually too rushed in the morning to prepare and to eat a traditional breakfast. According to an egg industry executive, "There's

FIGURE 12–4

Advertisement Incorporating Achievement and Success Appeals

Look at it this way:
Your wife's idea of a vacuum cleaner
costs $317.46.
And you're still drinking ordinary scotch?

Pinch 12 year old Scotch
About $10

86 PROOF BLENDED SCOTCH WHISKY – RENFIELD IMPORTERS, LTD. N.Y.

Courtesy of Renfield Importers, Ltd.

nothing that could make most people sit down and eat a 25-minute breakfast ever again."[18]

leisure pursuits

From the point of view of consumer behavior, an important category of American activity is commonly referred to as "leisure-time activities." Leisure time can be defined as *choice or discretionary time during which a person pursues recreational and self-fulfilling non-work related activities.*[19] This definition excludes all required time, such as time on the job, sleep time, and personal work time (housekeeping, clothes maintenance, required home repairs).

A recent consumer behavior study addressed itself to the question: How do Americans spend their leisure time? The researchers asked a national sample of male and female respondents to identify their three most favorite activities from a list of fifty leisure-time endeavors. Table 12–1 presents the ten most popular leisure-time pursuits for males and for females by rank and by percentage. The results revealed that the ten most popular leisure-time activities do not involve physical exertion. Additional rankings (not shown in Table 12–1) also indicated that relatively strenuous participative sports received relatively low rankings.[20]

TABLE 12–1
The Ten Most Popular Leisure-Time Activities,
(Rank Ordered by Frequency of Pursuit)

LEISURE-TIME ACTIVITY	Female Rank	Female %	Male Rank	Male %
Listening to music	1	89.9	3	83.2
Visiting with friends, partying	2	89.2	1	85.4
Reading a book for pleasure	3	88.7	9	62.9
Writing letters, doing crossword puzzles	4	85.9		
Playing with the children	5	84.4	5	77.1
Attending movies	6	84.2	4	82.4
Driving around for pleasure	7	84.1	2	85.2
Creative crafts (e.g., painting, drawing, and knitting)	8	83.9		
Picnicking	9	81.6	6	75.0
Bingo, bridge, or similar card or board games	10	80.6	*7	67.2
Attending spectator sporting events			8	64.8
Visiting a bar or club			10	61.9

Note: "Fixing up the house, remodeling, and making repairs" was actually ranked seventh. However, since these activities could be considered "personal work" we have excluded them and shifted the rankings.

Source: Adapted from Douglass K. Hawes, W. Wayne Talarzyk, and Roger D. Blackwell, "Consumer Satisfactions from Leisure Time Pursuits," in Mary Jane Schlinger, ed., Advances in Consumer Research, 2 *(Association for Consumer Research, 1975), 821.*

Table 12–1 also reveals that female respondents are somewhat more likely than their male counterparts to favor activities centered on the home. A comparison of the percentage of respondents pursuing each activity indicates that females are somewhat more homogeneous, that is, less diffused in their leisure-time involvements than males. For example, 80 percent of the women actively pursued their top ten interests, whereas only 60 percent of the men did.

For the marketer, these results suggest that (1) Americans' leisure-time activities are primarily focused on non-physically-exerting pursuits; (2) women are more likely than men to favor home-centered interests; and (3) men tend to have more diverse leisure interests than women. This type of information should prove useful to the marketer interested in reaching a specific segment of the estimated $80 billion – $150 billion leisure and recreational market.[21]

EFFICIENCY AND PRACTICALITY

With a basic philosophy of down-to-earth pragmatism, Americans pride themselves on being efficient and practical. When it comes to efficiency, they admire anything that saves time and saves effort. In terms of practicality, they are generally receptive to any new product that can make tasks easier and can help solve problems. For example, Americans wholeheartedly accepted such a labor-saving institution as the sawmill, which was outlawed in England (where it was developed) for fear that it would create unemployment.[22]

Here in America, where mass production has been so ingeniously refined, it is now possible for a manufacturer of almost any product category to offer the public a wide range of interchangeable components. For example, a consumer can design his own "customized" wall treatment from standard components of compatible base, sides, color, front panels, and special-function shelves, at a cost not much greater than a completely standardized unit. The capacity of American manufacturers to create mass-produced components that offer the consumer a customized product has in some instances taken two basically contradictory concepts, "mass produced" and "customized," and blurred their differences.

Another illustration of Americans' attentiveness to efficiency and practicality is the extreme importance attached to *time*. Americans seem to be convinced that "time waits for no man," which is reflected in their habitual attention to being prompt. The frequency with which Americans look at their watches, and the importance attached to having an accurate timepiece, tend to support the American value of punctuality. Figure 12–5 presents one of a series of advertisements for the Bulova Accutron tuning fork watch which stresses the importance of punctuality. Similarly, the Hertz advertisement in Figure 12–6 presents the agile superstar O. J. Simpson claiming: "On business trips these days, you've got to make every minute, every dollar count!" This advertisement combines the values of activity (he is in a rush) and efficiency (the belief that "time is money").

FIGURE 12–5

Advertisement Stressing Punctuality

FIGURE 12–6

Advertisement Appealing to Activity and Efficiency

"On business trips these days, you've got to make every minute, every dollar count!

That's why you need Hertz more than ever."

O.J. Simpson

You can depend on Hertz. Hertz has more good people to take care of you, so you can get away fast into a clean, reliable car. More locations. More cars. More kinds of cars. And with Super Saver Rates, you save money, too. With all this, wouldn't you rather rent from Hertz?

Hertz

The Superstar in rent-a-car.
HERTZ RENTS FORDS AND OTHER FINE CARS.

Courtesy of The Hertz Corporation

PROGRESS

Belief in progress is another watchword of American society. Indeed, America has been labeled a "cult of progress."[23] Its receptivity to progress appears to be closely linked to other core values already examined (achievement and success, efficiency and practicality) and to the central belief that man can always improve himself, that tomorrow should be better than today.

In a consumption-oriented society such as the United States, progress often means the acceptance of change—new products or services designed to fulfill previously undersatisfied or unsatisfied needs. In the name of progress, Americans appear to be receptive to product claims that stress "new," "improved," "longer lasting," "speedier," "quicker," "smoother and closer," and "increased strength." Figure 12–7 depicts an advertisement for a "tougher" floor wax which appeals to the core value of progress. It is not surprising that marketers often stress progress in promoting their products. Unfortunately, they may have overdone it, for available research indicates that such product claims seem to have lost their potency.[24]

MATERIAL COMFORT

For most Americans, material comfort signifies the attainment of "the good life"—a life that may include a self-defrosting refrigerator, a self-cleaning oven, an air conditioner, a trash compactor, and an almost infinite variety of other convenience-oriented goods and services.

General acceptance of such time- and labor-saving products is a rather new phenomenon for most Americans. In fact, for many Americans, the acceptance of convenience products has not been an emotionally easy task. People tend to have mixed feelings about the benefits of convenience products.[25] On the one hand, these products provide material comfort, which is symbolic of achievement and success. On the other hand, they produce anxiety and guilt, for they run counter to the notion of "hard work" as a symbol of self worth.

A landmark consumer behavior study supports the contention that convenience products initially produce feelings of uncertainty and guilt. This study, reported in 1950 when instant coffee was still in its infancy, found that homemakers perceived women who used instant coffee as lazy housekeepers and poor wives. In contrast, users of regular grind coffee were perceived as thrifty and good wives.[26] This research suggests that convenience foods may sometimes be viewed with skepticism, and that people tend to judge others by the cultural acceptability of the products they own or use.

In response to our dynamic culture, Americans' values with regard to convenience products, particularly instant coffee, have shifted toward general acceptance during the last 25 years. Indeed, a replication of the original study described above indicates that, by 1968, the stigma attached to the use of instant coffee had disappeared.[27]

FIGURE 12–7

Advertisement Incorporating a Progress Appeal

Although the use of convenience products by American households is now almost entirely culturally acceptable, many marketers are still reluctant to stress convenience in promoting their products. For example, in promoting Pampers (a disposable baby diaper), Procter and Gamble makes almost no reference to how easy or convenient the product is for mothers. Instead, it stresses how much softer, drier, and more comfortable the product is for baby. This copy approach avoids possible guilt feelings that she is selfishly using the product to satisfy her own needs rather than those of her baby.

america's response to shortages

Until the early 1970s, many Americans felt that abundance and material comfort were inalienable "rights." However, the combined impact of actual and rumored shortages in such product categories as oil, natural gas, antifreeze, sugar, grain, and coffee has altered this blind optimism and made Americans realize that their personal comfort could be in danger.

Americans were shocked and frightened by the rationing, long lines, and curtailment of service station hours that occurred during the gasoline shortage of 1974. According to one consumer psychologist, the gasoline shortage was perceived as ". . . a loss of freedom of mobility as well as a direct threat to Americans' life-style and even economic existence."[28] He identified the following five stages of "trauma" produced by the reality of scarcities:[29]

STAGE 1: Consumers convince themselves that shortages cannot occur or are only temporary.
STAGE 2: Consumers bargain or search for solutions.
STAGE 3: Consumers became hostile—blaming government, business, ecologists, and other organizations or institutions.
STAGE 4: Consumers realize that they are relatively helpless to deal with the shortages and become psychologically depressed.
STAGE 5: Consumers begin to accept the reality of the shortages and reshape their attitudes and goals.

A resistance to full-sized "gas-eating" automobiles (which forced Detroit to offer a greater variety of compact and subcompact cars) and taking vacations closer to home are two ways in which consumers attempted to deal constructively with the impact of higher gasoline prices and the realization that such shortages could occur again in the future.

When events such as the gasoline shortage occur—when companies find that raw materials and other supplies are no longer available in sufficient quantities to adequately satisfy existing demand—they must consider how they can responsibly deal with the problem of excess demand. The marketing task that exists when there is greater demand than supply has been characterized as *demarketing*.[30] The marketer's objective in demarketing is to discourage demand. When shortages are likely to be temporary, this task may be a short-run goal. When shortages are likely to be permanent, demarketing becomes a long-run goal. The scope of the demarketing effort may be the reduction of demand across all customers (general demarketing), or it may be targeted toward a specific segment of customers (selective demarketing).

In terms of consumer behavior, demarketing is not easily accomplished. It means that marketers must change existing consumption customs by encouraging people to alter their life styles. This is particularly difficult for a society such as ours, where consumers have acquired a strong appetite for material goods designed to make their lives more comfortable. To change these customs, marketers have to be extremely creative in designing marketing programs that motivates a historically affluent people to limit their consumption behavior.

However, given that shortages are not going to disappear, and are symptomatic of a larger ecological problem, consumers will have to learn to conserve scarce natural resources for the benefit of their own physical and environmental well-being. Consumers must be persuaded to undertake more "responsible" consumption.[31] For example, Americans will have to learn to turn lights off in rooms that are vacant, refrain from doing less than full loads of laundry, and avoid many other forms of excessive or wasteful consumption.

Responsible consumption is likely to require public policies that stimulate selected forms of *deconsumption*. We can think of deconsumption as consumers' selective curtailment or elimination of purchase activities. The appeals that are likely to be effective in gaining consumer cooperation in deconsuming include personal, environmental, political or even nationalistic themes.

INDIVIDUALISM

Americans place a strong value on "being themselves." Self-reliance, self-interest, self-confidence, self-esteem, and self-fulfillment are all exceedingly popular expressions of individualism. The striving for such individualism seems to be linked to the rejection of dependency.[32] That is, it is better to rely on one's self than on others.

In terms of consumer behavior, an appeal to individualism frequently takes the form of reinforcing one's own sense of identity with products or services which both reflect and emphasize that identity. Marketers with effective segmentation strategies often design their entire marketing mix — product, price, promotion, and retail channels — with the view of enhancing the feeling of individuality of selected audience segments. For example, advertisements for high-style clothing and cosmetics usually "promise" the reader that their products will emphasize her exclusive or distinctive character, and will set her apart from others. An advertisement for cologne in Figure 12–8 states "Cachet. As individual as you are." The body copy supports this individualistic theme with such statements as "It's different on every girl who wears it."

FIGURE 12–8

Advertisement Stressing Individuality

What makes Cachet different on Nancy and Melissa and Pat? Nancy and Melissa and Pat.

We know you don't want to look like the next girl. Or wear a fragrance like the next girl's either. That's why we created Cachet. It's different on every girl who wears it. You see, aside from being fresh and fascinating on everyone, Cachet was designed to pick up your own chemistry. So Cachet can be as individual as Nancy or Melissa or Pat. But on you it's only you. Cachet. You'll feel like you're the only girl wearing it.

Cachet by Prince Matchabelli.

Pat Sanna raises and trains Spaniels for show. "These dogs are high-strung. If you're not sure of yourself, they sense it and won't obey." Pat is sure of herself. She knows exactly who she is. So does Cachet.

Cachet. As individual as you are.

Melissa Huffman and her husband don't worry about who brings home the bacon and who cooks it. Melissa works as a designer 9 to 5 so Jim can study 9 to 5. It's not having rules or roles that gives Melissa a strong sense of her own individuality.

Nancy Benedict's way of getting her head straight is to stand on it. "Yoga's terrific for limbering up. But ultimately, what I find in yoga is me. The same me I find in Cachet."

Courtesy of Prince Matchabelli Inc.

FREEDOM

Freedom is another very strong American value, one that has historical roots in such democratic ideals as "freedom of speech," "freedom of the press," and "freedom of worship."

As an outgrowth of these democratic beliefs in freedom, Americans have a strong preference for *freedom of choice*—the opportunity to choose from a wide range of alternatives. This preference is reflected in the large number of competitive brands and product variations that can be found on the shelves of the modern supermarket. For many products, consumers can select from a wide variety of sizes, colors, flavors, even special ingredients (e.g., toothpaste with stannous fluoride or special whiteners, or toothpaste designed for sensitive gums). The advertisement depicted in Figure 12–9 offers the consumer a choice of three "mood" fragrances: "Sharing," "Caring," and "Embracing." These three product variations are designed to provide the consumer with the perceived "freedom of choice" to try and wear different fragrances.

Given all this choice, it may just be possible that American consumers are beginning to feel they have too much choice; making a selection from many competing brands can be difficult. A recent study found that consumers believed that "overchoice" existed for such product categories as facial tissue, margarine, breakfast cereal, cake mix, and laundry detergent.[33]

EXTERNAL CONFORMITY

Although Americans deeply embrace freedom of choice and individualism, they nevertheless accept the reality of conformity. External conformity is a necessary process by which the individual adapts to his society. It has been said that "no social organization, no culture, no form of institutionalized relationship whatever could exist without the process of interaction we call conformity."[34]

In the realm of consumer behavior, conformity (or uniformity) takes the form of standardized goods and services. Standardized products have been made possible by mass production. The availability of a wide choice of standardized products places the consumer in the unique position of being individualistic (by selecting specific products that his close friends do not have) or conforming (by purchasing a similar product). It is within this context that individualism and conformity exist side by side as choices for the American consumer.

Consumer dress behavior would seem to be a particularly potent and observable area of external conformity. A study that explored the relationship between male college students' dress patterns and their social-cultural attitudes found that students categorized as "radical" dressers (e.g., unkempt hair, unpressed or dirty clothing) were politically more liberal, had more permissive sexual attitudes, were more conscious of youth as a distinct social grouping, and were more likely to play down conventional male-female sex role differences than were members of

FIGURE 12–9

Advertisement Offering Freedom of Choice

the "traditionally" dressed student group.[35] This research suggests that dress behavior functions as a visible symbol of people's attitudes, which in turn may foster external conformity among those who wish to be associated with a specific point of view.

HUMANITARIANISM

Americans are a generous people when it comes to those in need. They support with a passion many humane and charitable causes, and they sympathize with the "underdog" who must overcome adversity or get ahead by working hard.[36] This humanitarian spirit seems to extend to decisions concerning products and services. A classic illustration is the Avis promotional campaign that stressed that because Avis was only "number two" in the automobile rental business (behind Hertz), it had to "try harder" to satisfy its customers. (See Figure 12–10 for an early Avis advertisement.) This campaign and others like it often successfully enlist the empathy of a sufficient number of consumers to have a very favorable impact on sales.

YOUTHFULNESS

Americans place an almost sacred value on youthfulness. This emphasis is a reflection of America's rapid technological development. In an atmosphere where "new" is so constantly stressed, being "old" is often equated with being "outdated." This is in contrast to traditional European, African, and Asian societies, where the elderly are revered for possessing the wisdom of experience, which comes with age.

"Youthfulness" should not be confused with "youth," which describes an age grouping. While there is obviously some relationship between age and youthfulness, we are really concerned with Americans' preoccupation with *looking* and *acting* young, regardless of their actual age. For Americans, youthfulness is a state of mind and a state of being, sometimes expressed as being "young at heart," "young in spirit," or "young in appearance."[37]

A great deal of advertising is directed to people's sense of urgency about retaining their youth and to their fear of aging. Hand cream ads talk about "young hands," skin treatment ads state "I dreaded turning 30 . . .," fragrance and cosmetic ads stress looking "sexy and young," and detergent ads ask the reader "Can you match their hands with their ages?" (see Figure 12–11). Such advertising themes reflect the American premium placed on youthfulness as they promise the consumer the benefits of youth.

CORE VALUES NOT AN AMERICAN PHENOMENON

The cultural values just examined are not all uniquely or originally American. Some of these values have been borrowed, particularly from

FIGURE 12–10
   Advertisement Appealing for Support for the Underdog

When you're only No.2, you try harder. Or else.

Avis can't afford to relax.

Little fish have to keep moving all of the time. The big ones never stop picking on them.

Avis knows all about the problems of little fish.

We're only No.2 in rent a cars. We'd be swallowed up if we didn't try harder. There's no rest for us.

We're always emptying ashtrays. Making sure gas tanks are full before we rent our cars. Seeing that the batteries are full of life. Checking our windshield wipers.

And the cars we rent out can't be anything less than spanking new Plymouths.

And since we're not the big fish, you won't feel like a sardine when you come to our counter.

We're not jammed with customers.

Courtesy of Avis Rent A Car System, Inc.

FIGURE 12–11

Advertisement Underscoring the Value of Youthfulness

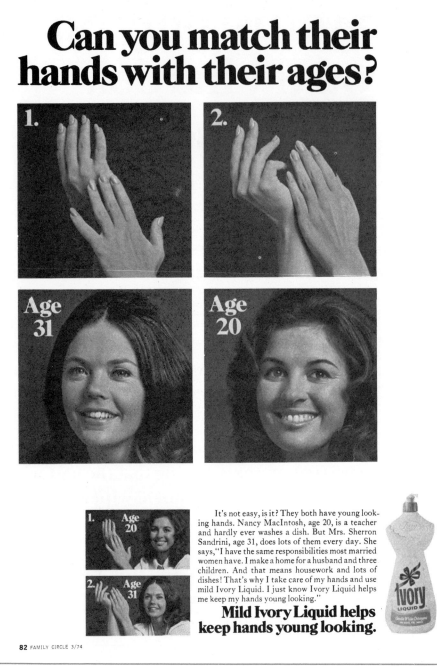

European society, as people emigrated to the United States. Some values which originated in America are now part of the fabric of other societies. Furthermore, all Americans do not necessarily accept each of these values. We do suggest, however, that these values, when taken as a whole, do account for much of the American character. Table 12–2 presents the highlights of our discussion of American core values and their relevance to consumer behavior.

TABLE 12–2

Summary of American Core Values

Value	General features	Relevance to consumer behavior
Achievement and success	Hard work is good; success flows from hard work	Acts as a justification for acquisition of goods ("You deserve it")
Activity	Keeping busy is healthy and natural	Stimulates interest in products that save time and enhance leisure-time activities
Efficiency and practicality	Admiration of things that solve problems (e.g., save time and effort)	Stimulates purchase of products that function well and save time
Progress	People can improve themselves; tomorrow should be better	Stimulates desire for new products that fulfill unsatisfied needs; acceptance of products that claim to be "new" or "improved"
Material comfort	"The good life"	Fosters acceptance of convenience and luxury products that make life more enjoyable
Individualism	Being one's self (e.g., self-reliance, self-interest, and self-esteem)	Stimulates acceptance of customized or unique products that enable a person to "express his own personality"
Freedom	Freedom of choice	Fosters interest in wide product lines and differentiated products
External conformity	Uniformity of observable behavior; desire to be accepted	Stimulates interest in products that are used or owned by others in the same social group
Humanitarianism	Caring for others, particularly the underdog	Stimulates patronage of firms that compete with market leaders.
Youthfulness	A state of mind that stresses being young at heart or appearing young	Stimulates acceptance of products that provide the illusion of maintaining or fostering youth

Summary

The study of culture is the study of all aspects of a society — its language, knowledge, laws, customs, etc. — which give that society its distinctive character and personality. In the context of consumer behavior, *culture* is defined as the sum total of learned beliefs, values, and customs which serve to regulate the consumer behavior of members of a particular society. Beliefs and values are *guides* for consumer behavior; customs are usual and acceptable *ways of behaving*.

The impact of culture on society is so natural and so ingrained that its influence on our behavior is rarely noted. Yet culture offers order, direction, and guidance to members of society in all phases of their human problem solving. Culture is dynamic and gradually and continually evolves to meet the needs of society.

Culture is learned as part of social experience. As children, we acquire from our environment a set of beliefs, values, and customs which constitute our culture (i.e., we are "encultured"). These are acquired through formal learning, informal learning, and technical learning. Advertising enhances formal learning by reinforcing desired modes of behavior and expectations; it enhances informal learning by providing models for our behavior.

Culture is communicated to members of the society through a common language and through commonly shared symbols. Because the human mind has the ability to absorb and to process symbolic communication, marketers can successfully promote both tangible and intangible products and product concepts to consumers through mass media.

All the elements in the marketing mix serve to communicate symbolically with the audience. Products project images of their own; so does promotion (e.g., through the format of the advertisement and the media used); both price and retail outlets symbolically convey images concerning the quality of the product.

The elements of culture are transmitted by three pervasive social institutions: the family, the church, and the school. A fourth social institution that plays a major role in the transmission of culture is the mass media — both through editorial content and through advertising.

A wide range of measurement techniques have been employed to study culture. These include projective techniques, attitude measurement methods, field observation, participant observation, content analysis, and value measurement survey techniques.

A small number of core values of the American people appear to be relevant to the study of consumer behavior. These include achievement and success, activity, efficiency and practicality, progress, material comfort, individualism, freedom, conformity, humanitarianism, and youthfulness.

Since each of these values varies in importance to the members of our society, they provide an effective basis for segmenting consumer markets.

Endnotes

1. *This definition is similar to the one suggested in Mary Ellen Goodman,* The Individual and Culture *(Homewood, III.: Dorsey, 1967), 32.*

2. *Milton Rokeach,* The Nature of Human Values *(New York: Free Press, 1973), 5; and Francesco M. Nicosia and Robert N. Myer, "Toward a Sociology of Consumption,"* Journal of Consumer Research, *3 (September 1976), 67.*

3. *Ruth Benedict, "The Science of Custom,"* Century Magazine, *117 (1929), 641.*

4. *Ralph Linton,* The Cultural Background of Personality *(New York: Appleton-Century-Crofts, 1945), 125.*

5. *Edward T. Hall,* The Silent Language *(Greenwich, Conn.: Fawcett, 1959), 69–72.*

6. *Raymond Firth,* Symbols: Public and Private *(Ithaca, N.Y.: Cornell University Press, 1973), 47.*

7. *M. Wayne DeLozier,* The Marketing Communications Process *(New York: McGraw-Hill, 1976), 163.*

8. *George Peter Murdock,* Culture and Society *(Pittsburgh: University of Pittsburgh Press, 1965), 81.*

9. *David M. Potter,* People of Plenty *(Chicago: University of Chicago Press, 1954), 167.*

10. *For a comprehensive discussion of content analysis, see Harold H. Kassarjian, "Content Analysis in Consumer Research,"* Journal of Consumer Research, *4 (June 1977), 8–18; and Fred N. Kerlinger,* Foundations of Behavioral Research, *2nd ed. (New York: Holt, Rinehart and Winston, 1973), 525–34.*

11. *Rokeach,* Nature of Human Values; *and Milton Rokeach, "Change and Stability in American Value Systems, 1968–1971,"* Public Opinion Quarterly, *38 (Summer 1974), 222–38.*

12. *Jerome E. Scott and Lawrence M. Lamont, "Relating Consumer Values to Consumer Behavior: A Model and Method for Investigation," in Thomas V. Greer, ed.,* 1973 Combined Proceedings *(Chicago: American Marketing Association, 1974), 283–88.*

13. *Donald E. Vinson and J. Michael Munson, "Personal Values: An Approach to Market Segmentation," in Kenneth L. Bernhardt, ed.,* Marketing: 1776–1976 and Beyond *(Chicago: American Marketing Association, 1976), 313–17.*

14. *For example, see Walter A. Henry, "Cultural Values Do Correlate with Consumer Behavior,"* Journal of Marketing Research, *13 (May 1976), 121–27.*

    Lowell D. Holmes, Anthropology *(New York: Ronald Press, 1965), 121.*

16. *Many of the ideas for the value concepts examined in this section were inspired by the comprehensive treatment in "Major Value Orientations in America," appearing in Robin M. Williams, Jr.,* American Society: A Sociological Interpretation *(New York: Knopf, 1970), 438–504.*

17. *David C. McClelland,* The Achieving Society *(New York: Free Press, 1961), 150–51.*

18. *Steve Lohr, "Hens Are Willing but People Aren't,"* New York Times, *July 11, 1976, Sec. 3, 1.*

19. *Justin Voss, "The Definition of Leisure,"* Journal of Economic Issues, *1 (June 1967), 91–106.*

20. *Douglass K. Hawes, W. Wayne Talarzyk, and Roger D. Blackwell, "Consumer Satisfactions from Leisure Time Pursuits," in Mary Jane Schlinger, ed.,* Advances in Consumer Research *(Association for Consumer Research, 1975), 2, 817–36.*

21. Geoffrey H. Moore, "*Measuring Leisure Time,*" Conference Board Record, *July 1971, 53–54.*

22. Henry Fairlie, The Spoiled Child of the Western World *(New York: Doubleday, 1976), 79.*

23. Williams, American Society, *p. 468.*

24. Michael L. Dean, James F. Engel, and W. Wayne Talarzyk, "*The Influence of Package Copy Claims on Consumer Product Evaluations,*" Journal of Marketing, *36 (April 1972), 34–39.*

25. Edward M. Tauber, "*How Market Research Discourages Major Innovation,*" Business Horizons, *17 (July 1974), 24.*

26. Mason Haire, "*Projective Techniques in Marketing Research,*" Journal of Marketing, *14 (April 1950), 649–56.*

27. Frederick E. Webster, Jr., and Frederick Von Pechmann, "*A Replication of the 'Shopping List' Study,*" Journal of Marketing, *34 (April 1970), 61–63. Also see Johan Arndt, "Haire's Shopping List Revisited,"* Journal of Advertising Research, *13 (October 1973), 57–61.*

28. Joseph M. Kamen, "*Learning of Scarcities May Depress Consumers,*" Marketing News, *August 1, 1973, 3.*

29. *Ibid.*

30. Philip Kotler and Sidney J. Levy, "*Demarketing, Yes Demarketing,*" Harvard Business Review, *November-December 1971, 74–80; Philip Kotler, "The Major Tasks of Marketing Management,"* Journal of Marketing, *37 (October 1974), 42–49; and David Cullwick, "Positioning Demarketing Strategy,"* Journal of Marketing, *39 (April 1975), 51–57.*

31. George Fisk, "*Criteria for a Theory of Responsible Consumption,*" Journal of Marketing, *37 (April 1973), 24–31.*

32. Holmes, Anthropology, *136.*

33. Robert B. Settle and Linda L. Golden, "*Consumer Perceptions: Overchoice in the Market Place,*" in Scott Ward and Peter Wright, eds., Advances in Consumer Behavior, *1 (Association for Consumer Research, 1974), 29–37.*

34. Robert A. Nisbet, The Social Bond *(New York: Knopf, 1970), 69.*

35. L. Eugene Thomas, "*Clothing and Counterculture: An Empirical Study,*" Adolescence, *8 (Spring 1973), 93–112.*

36. Williams, American Society, *462.*

37. "*Why 'Youth' Needs a New Definition,*" Business Week, *December 12, 1970, 34–35.*

Discussion questions

1. Distinguish between beliefs, values, and customs. Illustrate how the clothing a person wears, at different times or for different occasions, is influenced by custom.

2. Give an example from your own experience of each of the following types of cultural learning:
   a. formal learning
   b. informal learning
   c. technical learning

3. Describe how mass media participates in the transmission of cultural beliefs, values, and customs.

4. As the media planner for a large advertising agency, you have been asked by top management to identify recent cultural changes that affect your selection of the media in which to place clients' advertising. List five cultural changes that you believe have bearing on the selection of television shows for different types of products.

5. How do achievement and success differ? Discuss the implication of these differences for marketing strategy.

6. Find advertisements which illustrate three of the cultural values summarized in Table 12–2. Describe your choices.

7. As a marketing consultant to one of the major oil companies, you have been asked to create a *demarketing* campaign. Outline your recommendations for a campaign to discourage wasteful use of oil products. Which American cultural values are effected?

8. Which basic American cultural values would you expect to influence the various types of automobiles that Americans buy? Explain.

13

subcultural and cross-cultural aspects of consumer behavior

Introduction

Culture has a potent influence on all consumer behavior. Individuals are brought up to follow the beliefs, values, and customs of their society and to avoid behavior that is frowned upon or considered taboo. Marketers who incorporate an understanding of culture into their marketing strategies are likely to satisfy consumers more fully by providing them with added, though intangible, product benefits. However, culture, as a concept, has a very broad beamed focus in that it embraces total societies. To even better satisfy consumers, marketers have learned to segment society into smaller subgroups, or "subcultures," that are homogeneous in relation to certain customs and ways of behaving. These subcultures provide important marketing opportunities for astute marketing strategists.

Our discussion of subcultures, thus, will *narrow* its focus. Instead of examining the dominant beliefs, values, and customs that exist within an entire society, it will explore the marketing opportunities created by the existence of certain beliefs, values, and customs among specific subcultural groups *within* a society. Subcultural divisions based on nationality, religion, geographic locality, race, age, and sex often enable the marketer to segment his market in terms of the specific beliefs, values, and customs shared by members of a specific subcultural group.

In the second section of this chapter, we will *broaden* our scope of analysis and consider the marketing implications of cultural

Different men seek after happiness in different ways and by different means. . .
ARISTOTLE:
Politics *(4th cent.* B.C.)

differences and similarities that exist between the people of two or more nations. Recognition of cross-cultural differences can provide expanded sales and profit opportunities for the multinational marketer, who can tailor his marketing mix to the specific customs of each target nation.

Subcultures

In the world of primitive tribal society, the same set of cultural values and customs prevails throughout the group; there are no subgroups with distinctive cultural traits. A society with such a highly unified culture is ruled by "commonness." All of its people worship the same god, all have a common racial background, and all eat the same kinds of food. Social organizations and institutions are extremely simple. In contrast, in a complex society like the United States, there is considerable diversity in religious beliefs, in racial backgrounds, in food customs, and in other social practices and institutions. Indeed, the members of a complex society belong to many different kinds of subcultural groups. It is such diversity that makes subculture a useful segmentation variable.

WHAT IS SUBCULTURE?

A subculture can be thought of as *a distinct cultural group which exists as an identifiable segment within a larger, more complex society.*[1] The members of a specific subculture tend to possess beliefs, values, and customs that set them apart from other members of the same society. In addition, they also adhere to most of the *dominant* cultural beliefs, values, and behavioral patterns of the overall society.

Thus the cultural profile of a society or nation can be viewed as a composite of two distinct elements: (1) the unique beliefs, values, and customs subscribed to by members of specific subcultures, and (2) the central core cultural themes that are shared by most of the population, regardless of specific subcultural memberships. Figure 13–1 presents a model of the relationship between two subcultural groups (easterners and westerners) and the larger culture. As the figure depicts, each subculture has its own unique traits, yet both groups share the dominant traits of the overall American culture.

Let us look at it another way. Each American is in large part a product of the "American Way of Life." However, each American is at the same time a member of a variety of subcultures. For example, a fifteen year old girl may simultaneously be an Irish-Catholic, a teenager, and a southerner. We would expect that membership in each different subculture would provide its own set of specific beliefs, values, attitudes, and customs. Table 13–1 lists the typical subcultural categories and gives corresponding examples of specific subcultural groups. This list is by no means exhaustive. For example, Boy Scouts, college students, "jet-setters," feminists, and intellectuals—in fact, any group that shares common beliefs and customs—may be classified as a subculture.

FIGURE 13–1

Relationship between Culture and Subculture

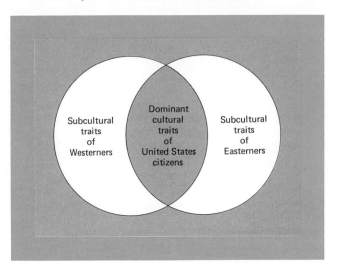

TABLE 13–1

Subcultural Categories

Subcultural category	Illustrative subculture
Nationality (i.e., birthplace of ancestors)	Italian, Puerto Rican, Mexican
Religion	Mormon, Protestant, Jew
Region	Midwestern, Northern, Southern
Race	Black, White, Oriental
Age	Elderly, Teenage, Middle-age
Sex	Female, Male
Occupation	Carpenter, Lawyer, Schoolteacher
Social class	Lower, Middle, Upper

Subcultures as market segments

Subcultural analysis enables the marketing manager to focus on rather large and "natural" market segments. In carrying out such analyses, the marketer must determine whether the beliefs, values, and customs shared by members of a specific subgroup make them strong candidates for special marketing attention. According to one marketing expert,

"Subcultures are the relevant units of analysis for market research. *They represent definable target groups for specific products and logical units for segmenting of larger markets.*"[2]

We will now examine the marketing implications of the following subcultural categories: (1) nationality, (2) religion, (3) geographic location, (4) race, (5) age, and (6) sex. (Occupational and social class subgroups are discussed in detail in Chapter 11.)

NATIONALITY SUBCULTURES

With the exception of the American Indian, most United States citizens have their roots in European, African, South American, and Asian countries. In terms of numbers, most of these Americans can trace their family ancestry to Europe. During the period 1820 to 1975, over two-thirds of all the immigrants to the United States came from seven European countries: Germany, Great Britain, Ireland, Italy, Austria, Russia, and Sweden.[3]

While most Americans, especially those born in the United States, see themselves as "Americans," they frequently retain a sense of identification and pride in the language and customs of their forefathers.

When it comes to consumption behavior, this ancestral pride is manifested most strongly in the consumption of ethnic foods, in travel to the "homeland" country, and in the purchase of numerous cultural artifacts (ethnic clothing, art, music, foreign-language newspapers). It is through such purchase behavior that members of specific nationality subcultures attempt to maintain some contact with their cultural heritage. Figure 13 – 2 presents the storyboard for a Pan American Airlines commercial that appeals to the consumer's identity with his cultural heritage.

Unfortunately, with the exception of the Hispanic subculture, there is little information available about the consumption behavior of the many nationality subcultural groups found in the United States.

hispanic subcultures

There is no single Hispanic subculture; rather, there are a number of distinct subcultures. In terms of country of origin, the three largest Hispanic subcultural groups consist of Mexican-Americans, Puerto Ricans, and Cubans. These subcultures are heavily concentrated geographically, with over 75 percent of their members living in the top thirty United States metropolitan areas. For example, about 40 percent live in New York and Los Angeles alone.[4]

According to available evidence. Hispanic-Americans are consumption-oriented and have a strong preference for major name-brand products.[5] Table 13 – 2 shows data on brand preferences for both Hispanic and Anglo consumers. The data reveal that Hispanic consumers' preferences among the leading brands in several major consumer packaged goods categories differ considerably from those of the general

FIGURE 13-2

An Appeal to Ancestral Pride

Carl Ally Inc.
437 MADISON AVENUE, NEW YORK, N.Y. 10022
MURRAY HILL 8-5300

Client: PAN AMERICAN WORLD AIRWAYS, INC.
Product: CORPORATE
Title: "HERITAGE"
Commercial No.: PNST6354 - 30 SECONDS
Date Approved: 11/16/76

1. (MUSIC THROUGHOUT) ANNCR: (VO) In America, there are millions of Italians
2. who've never seen Italy.
3. And Poles who've never seen Poland.
4. And Japanese who've never seen Japan.
5. And Englishmen ...
6. And Latins ...
7. And Scandinavians who've never seen those places.
8. And that's kind of a shame.
9. Every American has two heritages.
10. Pan Am would like to help you discover the other one. (MUSIC OUT)

market. These results reflect not only subcultural differences, but the explicit efforts of marketers like Procter and Gamble, Colgate, Bristol-Myers, Carnation, Chrysler, Chevrolet, Pepsi-Cola and Coca-Cola to penetrate the Hispanic markets via Spanish language mass media.[6]

The Spanish language is the bridge that links the various Hispanic subcultures. However, though they share a common language, each of the major Hispanic subcultures do have their own distinct beliefs, values, and customs. It has been suggested that ". . . what may be popular in New York, [i.e., among Puerto Ricans] might fail in Miami [i.e., among Cubans]. . ."[7] Thus, a marketer may wish to segment the Hispanic market even further by appealing to the distinct cultural values of a specific nationality.

TABLE 13-2

Estimated Brand Share Studies for Selected Products

Product	Anglo	Hispanic
Soaps (powdered or flakes)		
Tide	30.2	15.3
Cheer	15.0	42.3
Lipstick		
Revlon	26.5	21.0
Avon	23.9	50.7
Indigestion remedies		
Alka Seltzer	31.6	7.7
Pepto Bismol	31.3	65.4
Cold remedies		
Contac	54.1	45.5
Coricidin	20.3	9.1
Coldene	2.7	13.6
Dristan	10.8	0.0
Soft drinks		
Pepsi-Cola	25.0	52.4
Coca-Cola	25.0	33.0
Seven-Up	9.0	5.1
Cigarets		
Winston	31.1	7.0
Marlboro	7.3	21.6
Viceroy	2.2	12.5

Source: Reprinted with permission from the November 27, 1967, issue of Marketing Insights. *Copyright 1967 by Crain Communications, Inc.*

RELIGIOUS SUBCULTURES

Over 220 different organized religious groups reportedly flourish in the United States.[8] Of this number, the major Protestant denominations, Roman Catholicism, and Judaism are the principal organized religious faiths. The members of all these religious groups are at times likely to make purchase decisions that are influenced by their religious identity. However, as American life becomes increasingly secularized (i.e., as religion plays less of a central role in determining basic beliefs and values), adherence to traditional religious rules tends to diminish. Therefore, it is likely that consumer behavior is most directly affected by religion in terms of products that are *symbolically* associated with the celebration of various religious holidays. For example, as the major gift-purchasing season of the year, Christmas is important to most marketers of consumer goods.

Although members of most major religions can be reached through religious publications, marketers are reluctant to do so because they feel uncomfortable about mixing religion and business.[9] Those firms that do advertise in religious media tend to advertise in all major religious publications in order to avoid alienating the members of any one faith.

GEOGRAPHIC OR REGIONAL SUBCULTURES

The United States is a large country, one that enjoys a wide range of climatic and geographic conditions. Given the country's size and physical diversity, it is only natural that the American people have a sense of regional identification and use this identification as a way of describing others (e.g., he's a big Texan). Such labels often assist us in developing a mental picture—a stereotype—of the person in question.

Anyone who has traveled across the United States has probably noted many regional differences in consumption behavior. For example, the term *regular coffee* means different things in different parts of the country (e.g., with or without milk or sugar). There are also geographic differences in the consumption of a staple food like bread. Specifically, in the south and midwest soft bread (white bread) is preferred, while on the east and west coasts firmer breads (rye, whole wheat, and French and Italian breads) are favored.[10]

Fashion fads and preferences also seem to be regional. For instance, relaxed modes of dress such as men's leisure suits were first accepted on the west coast, especially in California. Gradually, however, such fashions were adopted on the east coast, and then in other sections of the country.

There are few research studies available to document such differences in consumption patterns. Most academic consumer research focuses on single geographic areas (usually the locale of the researcher's university). However, the findings of a large-scale study of consumer life-styles and buying preferences suggest that commercially sponsored studies can provide rich insights into the regional variations of consumer behavior. This study, which questioned two thousand male and two thousand female consumers, reported the following specific geographic differences:[11]

1. Southern men were more likely to use mouthwash or deodorants than eastern men.
2. Southern men were more likely to listen to western music than any other regional group, and least likely to read a Sunday newspaper. Also, a southern household was more likely to own a freezer than other regional households.
3. Western men tend to consume more cottage cheese, vitamins, and regular coffee than either easterners or southerners. A western family is also more likely to own a garbage-disposal unit.

Such regional differences tend to dispel the myth sometimes held that American consumers are one big "mass" market, and reinforce the need for market segmentation for a variety of goods and services.

RACIAL SUBCULTURES

The major racial subcultures in the United States are white, black, Oriental, and American Indian. Although there are differences in lifestyles and consumer spending patterns among all of these groups, the vast majority of racial consumer research has focused on black-white consumer differences.

the black consumer

Black consumers constitute the largest racial minority segment of the United States population (approximately 12 percent). This group of over 24 million consumers has too frequently been portrayed as a single, undifferentiated "black market," consisting of economically deprived consumers who have a uniform set of consumer needs. However, though a substantial portion of the black population is economically less well off than the white majority, there does exist an important and growing black middle class.[12] Therefore, just as the white majority has been divided into a variety of submarket segments, each with its own distinctive needs and tastes, so too can the black market be segmented. Unfortunately, there is not sufficient research data available concerning market segments within the total black market to examine them in detail. Instead, the following sections deal with more general consumer dimensions of the black subculture.

REACHING THE BLACK AUDIENCE. A question of central importance to marketers is: What is the best way to reach the black consumer? Traditionally, marketers have subscribed to one of two distinct marketing strategies. Some have followed the policy of running all their advertising in the general mass media in the belief that blacks have the same media habits as whites; others have followed the policy of running additional advertising in selected media directed exclusively to blacks.

Both of these strategies may be appropriate in specific situations and for specific product categories. For certain products of very broad appeal (e.g., aspirin, cold remedies, toothpaste), it is quite possible that the mass media (primarily television) may effectively reach all relevant consumers, black and white alike. However, for other products (e.g., food products), an advertiser may find that the general mass media do *not* communicate effectively with the relevant black market.

If a marketer feels that his product is not realizing its potential among black consumers, he may supplement his general advertising with black-targeted advertisements in magazines, newspapers, and other media directed specifically to blacks. If a marketer is offering a product exclusively for the black market (e.g., a line of black cosmetics), he should probably spend the major part of his advertising budget in socalled black media, where it will most effectively reach his target audience.

Recent research that compares the media exposure habits of a national sample of black and white consumers found substantial differences in exposure to weekly and monthly magazines, and in TV viewing.[13] However, when the data were further analyzed in terms of income categories, some distinctly different conclusions emerged. Specifically, lower-income (under $10,000) and higher-income (over $15,000) black consumers displayed media exposure patterns similar to whites with comparable income levels. This finding initially suggests that black and white upper- and lower-income groups may be effectively reached through the same media. However, this does not take into account any differences in advertising appeals that may be appropriate between the two markets. The greatest number of black-white differences was found to exist among the middle-income classes ($10,000 to $15,000). This suggests that marketers who wish to reach the middle-income black market should consider the use of black media such as *Jet* and *Ebony* magazines. Thus, income seems to be a reasonable variable to use in segmenting the black market.

Several studies have compared the responses of black and white consumers to advertising and point-of-purchase promotions that feature all black models, all white models, or both black and white models ("integrated" promotions).[14] Not surprisingly, the majority of these studies indicate that black consumers tend to be more strongly in favor of ads that feature black models than white consumers. White consumers tend to respond either neutrally or positively to ads that feature black models. This research suggests that, while black consumers welcome ads that include black models, white consumers are unlikely to respond adversely to such ads.

In part, this conclusion is supported by a recent experiment that measured the sales response of southern black and white consumers to supermarket displays that featured black only, white only, and black and white models.[15] Both black and white consumers were found to respond *equally* well to all three types of displays. It may be that black consumers do prefer to see more blacks in advertisements but are really indifferent to the model's race when it comes to the actual purchase situation.

A number of studies that employ content analysis (described in Chapter 12) have examined the frequency of use and the status roles of black models in general mass-media magazines. The findings indicate that during the twenty-year period from 1946 to 1965, blacks increasingly have been portrayed in higher-status occupations, and that the number of ads containing black models more than doubled in the five-year period 1965–69.[16] Finally, a study that examined the portrayal of blacks in a black-oriented magazine, *Ebony*, for the period 1950–70, found an increased emphasis on "black pride" (more self actualization and self confidence) and increased usage of selective middle class symbols.[17]

DO BLACKS PAY MORE? This question is of prime interest to leaders of local black communities and government public policy makers concerned with the quality of life in such communities.

Most of the evidence on the question has focused on poor blacks living in central-city communities. A review of the topic suggests that supermarket chain stores charge the same prices in their stores located in black communities as they do in their stores located in predominantly white urban or suburban communities.[18] However, the research also indicates that small independent groceries located in black communities do charge more than the major supermarket chains, and therefore blacks who shop at these stores are likely to pay more.

Since almost all of these studies examined the "price asked" by retailers located inside and outside of black communities rather than the "price paid," it is difficult to determine whether black consumers actually do pay more. One study found that blacks tend to avoid the higher prices charged by small independent stores in their communities by shopping outside of their immediate community.[19] Another study, more rigorously designed, examined the actual prices paid by inner-city blacks, inner-city whites, and suburban whites for food and related items.[20] It found that inner-city blacks paid more than inner-city whites, and that both these groups paid more than suburban whites. However, the evidence failed to reveal whether the higher prices paid by blacks was due to discriminatory pricing practices. Instead, the researcher suggested that the additional amount paid by blacks (which averaged about 1 percent) was likely to have been a function of the fact that blacks more often bought the relatively higher-priced smaller sizes of the products studied.[21] These results indicate the need for effective consumer education for lower-income blacks.

PURCHASE MOTIVES AND BEHAVIOR. In terms of their basic drive as consumers, blacks have been characterized in terms of their motivation to strive (or not to strive) for middle-class values, as such values are reflected in the consumption of material goods.[22] According to this "striving" framework, the black consumer faces the dilemma of ". . . whether to strive against odds for middle-class values as reflected in material goods, or to give in and live more for the moment."[23] Strivers were identified as those black consumers who perceive that it is possible for them, in terms of present or expected incomes, to attain a middle-class lifestyle. Nonstrivers are described as those black consumers who feel financially blocked from such goals and who therefore do not seek the material goods associated with being "middle class."

A comparison of two groups of black students—one that strongly subscribed to basic American values and one that did not—provides some support for the "striver" notion.[24] The findings indicated that those black students who identified strongly with basic American values were more likely to be "strivers" (i.e., aspire to attain higher social class status) than those who did not.

Segmentation of the black market on the basis of motivation suggests that the nonstrivers may constitute a distinct market segment. They have to be reached through copy appeals that differ from the traditional values stressed in most mass-media advertising. The striver-nonstriver framework also suggests that as more blacks acquire middle-class economic status, the striver segment of the black market will increase.

Other research studies that have explored the product preferences and brand purchase patterns of black consumers have found the following:

1. Black consumers usually favor popular brands, often the leading brand within a product category.[25] It has been proposed that this purchase pattern is due to two factors: (a) black consumers have a strong desire to impress others, and (b) buying the "best" is their strategy for coping with perceived risk.

2. Black consumers are loyal consumers; that is, they tend to establish definite brand preferences.[26] Brand loyalty may also be a strategy for avoiding perceived risk. Furthermore, it is a simple decision strategy which frees up time that would otherwise be spent searching for product information.

3. Research suggests that blacks are more likely than whites to be clothing innovators (i.e., to purchase new styles).[27] Other evidence indicates that within each income category, blacks are more likely than whites to own higher-priced automobiles.[28] It has been suggested that the purchase of socially conspicuous products serves to enhance the black consumer's self-image or self-worth.

Research that compared basic black/white values in terms of the Rokeach Value Survey (see Chapter 12) found that differences in values that exist between blacks and whites are primarily due to socioeconomic differences.[29] When the analysis controlled for income, only minor differences appeared between blacks and whites at the same socioeconomic levels.

AGE SUBCULTURES

All major age subgroupings of the population might broadly be thought of as separate subcultures. Within the context of the family life cycle, Chapter 9 examined the major age segments of the adult population. Each stage of the life cycle (bachelorhood, honeymooners, parenthood, postparenthood, and dissolution) could be considered a separate subculture, since important shifts occur in the demand for specific types of products and services.

In this section we will limit our examination of age subcultures to just two groups: the *young adult* and the *elderly*. These two age groups have been singled out because they are on opposite ends of the age spectrum of the adult population, and because their distinctive life-styles qualify them for consideration as subcultural groups.

the young adult market

Many marketers perceive young adults to be a particularly desirable target audience because (1) they are on the threshold of adult life, (2) they are often anxious to spend the discretionary money at their disposal, and (3) they are still forming their purchase patterns and brand loyalties for many product categories.

WHO ARE THE YOUNG ADULTS? When we speak of young adults, we are referring to the segment of the population that is between eighteen and twenty-four years of age. According to United States Census Bureau figures, in 1977 there were approximately 29 million young adults, which constituted 13 percent of the total population.[30] It is expected that the size of this segment will increase slightly through the early 1980s and then begin to decline, so that by the year 2000 there should be approximately 23 million young adults, constituting about 9 percent of the population. This expected shrinkage in the size of the young adult market reflects the decline in birthrate which began in the early 1960s.[31]

It is helpful to think of the young adult market as consisting of three somewhat overlapping subgroups: (1) college students, (2) young singles, and (3) young marrieds. Following is a brief profile of each of these major subdivisions of the young adult market:

1. *College students.* Approximately 37 percent of the members of the young adult market are enrolled in post-high-school educational programs.[32] The majority of these students live at home or consider their parents' homes to be their permanent address. Many of them have part-time jobs to meet their expenses and to provide them with spending money.

2. *Young singles.* Most of the members of the young adult segment are single (70 percent of the males and 51 percent of the females).[33] Moreover, available evidence indicates that members of this age segment tend to stay single longer than the same age group of a decade ago. Among the major reasons why they remain single longer are: (1) the increased accessibility of college and graduate education, (2) the growing preference among young adults for extensive travel, (3) the desire among women to achieve an independent identity and career recognition, (4) changing attitudes toward the acceptability of premarital sexual behavior, and (5) the rising divorce rate, which tarnished the romantic image of marriage as an institution of never-ending love and fidelity.[34]

3. *Young marrieds.* This is a relatively small segment of the young adult market (about 4.2 million families are headed by a person under twenty-five).[35] At this early stage in the formation of their family units, the overwhelming majority of young marrieds live in rented dwellings and are just beginning to establish family-oriented consumption patterns. It is estimated that young women who were in the eighteen to twenty-four year age bracket in 1974 will give birth to an average of 2.2 children during their child-bearing years, a decline from 1967, when it was estimated that young women would average 2.9 births.[36] For marketers, this trend toward fewer children per family is likely to mean that more money will be spent on each child, and that more discretionary money may be available for parents to spend on themselves. It also suggests that today's young parents will complete their parenthood roles at an earlier age than their parents did.

YOUNG ADULTS AND THE ACHIEVEMENT-SUCCESS ORIENTATION. The period between the mid-1960s and the early 1970s was one of considerable unrest and uncertainty on many college campuses. This social-political upheaval was characterized by such events as protests against the Vietnam War, demonstrations to minimize the importance of grades and encourage student participation in the running of college affairs, and a general downgrading of traditional achievement and success-related values.

Many observers of this so-called youth movement prophesized that these changes in values and behavior were likely to have a permanent impact on the youth of America. Table 13–3 summarizes a study conducted prior to 1971, which compared the values of Boston area college graduates who had been out of school for ten years with those of graduating seniors. The comparison indicates rather marked differences with regard to such achievement- and success-related values as competition, the importance of work, material status and wealth, and personal self-fulfillment. The researchers concluded that many of these differences were indicative of a long-range decline in the importance placed on achievement-related values, and that these changes were likely to alter traditional consumption patterns, especially conspicuous consumption.[37]

TABLE 13–3

Contrasting Achievement Values of Different Generations

College graduates Ten years out of school	College seniors
The system works, with reservations.	The system does not work, but used to.
Competition is a positive element.	Competition is negative, "anti-humanist."
Hard work brings society's rewards.	Hard work isn't worth the rewards it brings.
Work itself is an important value.	Work is a questionable value.
Material success is desirable and attainable.	Material success is questionable and no longer attainable for everyone.
Success means accumulation.	Conventionally-defined success means accumulation.
Material success and status go together.	Material success and conventionally-defined status are questionable values.
Personal self-fulfillment comes with material success.	Personal self-fulfillment may have no relation to material success.
Freedom comes with money—the more money, the more freedom.	Freedom is a state of mind; it requires only minimum money. Hunting after money and success curtails freedom.
Whatever cuts the incentive to work hard is dangerous for the system and its values.	Working too hard and devoting too much attention to work is dangerous for the individual.

Source: Scott, Ward, Thomas S. Robertson, and William Capitman, "What Will Be Different About Tomorrow's Consumers?" in Fred C. Allvine, ed., 1971 Combined Proceedings (Chicago: American Marketing Association, 1972), 373.

By the year 1973, however, an ongoing study of the values of college students indicated that the earlier de-emphasis on achievement and success might really have been a short-run phenomenon.[38] As Table 13–4 shows, there has been a movement back to more traditional beliefs. While it is still difficult to determine just how much the values and behavior of young adults have changed in recent years, we tend to agree with the following appraisal of the youth market: ". . . when the young

TABLE 13–4

Belief in Traditional American Achievement Values

	1973 %	1971 %	1969 %	1968 %
Commitment to a meaningful career is very important**	81	79	*	*
People should save money regularly and not have to lean on family and friends the minute they run into financial problems**	71	67	76	59
Private property is sacred	67	69	75	*
Depending on how much strength and character a person has, he can pretty well control what happens to him**	65	60	62	51
Competition encourages excellence	62	62	72	*
Duty comes before pleasure	54	63	*	*
Hard work always pays off**	44	39	56	69

*Question was not asked.

**Indicates return to more traditional values.

Adapted from The New Morality: A Profile of American Youth in the 70's, *by Daniel Yankelovich. Copyright 1974, McGraw-Hill Book Company. Used with permission of McGraw-Hill Book Company.*

reach thirty-five they will act, think, and have values more like present thirty-five-year olds than like twenty-year olds."[39]

CONSUMER CHARACTERISTICS OF THE YOUNG ADULT. Most young adults are in a transitional stage between adolescence, and "full" adulthood, where they will assume responsibility for a wide range of individual and family purchase behavior.

In terms of consumer behavior, young adulthood is a unique stage because most young adults still live at home, or temporarily at college, and rely on their parents for their primary support. Thus the money they have (either earned through part-time jobs or provided by their parents) is almost completely *discretionary.* This means that they are relatively free to spend their money on "luxury-type" items. For instance, young adults are heavy purchasers of books, records, stereo equipment, cameras, fashion clothing, hair driers, and a host of other personal-care and grooming products.[40]

The young adult market has been characterized as low in brand loyalties and high in new-product interests.[41] For marketers, these traits are extremely inviting, for they suggest that young people are a very receptive market.

A study that compared unmarried coeds from a large midwestern university with nearby housewives provides a unique opportunity to evaluate these two distinct market segments in terms of a number of important consumer behavior factors.[42] The coeds were found to have a higher level of perceived fashion opinion leadership than the housewives, were more likely to have received fashion advice from others, were more interested in fashion, and were more likely to be fashion innovators. The coeds also had read more news and fashion magazines, and fewer romance magazines, and watched less television.[43]

Additional research to identify the unique consumption patterns of the young adult market segment would enable marketers to more directly target their marketing efforts to this group.

the elderly consumer

Unlike the young adults, who are such a desired market segment, the elderly are frequently misunderstood and avoided. The distorted image that some marketers have of the elderly has been aptly summed up as follows: "The tendency of marketers is either to treat the elderly, over-65, consumers as a more or less homogeneous group, or to pay virtually no attention to them at all."[44]

WHO IS THE ELDERLY CONSUMER? In the United States, "old age" is officially assumed to begin with a person's sixty-fifth birthday (i.e., when the individual qualifies for full Social Security insurance and Medicare). However, research suggests that Americans who are seventy years old still tend to view themselves as "middle aged," and that it is only when a person reaches his seventy-fifth birthday that he begins to consider himself to be "elderly."[45]

The elderly are among the fastest-growing age segment in the American population. According to United States Census Bureau data, in 1977 there were over 23 million people sixty-five years of age and older, or about 11 percent of the population.[46] This age segment is expected to grow to approximately 31 million, or 12 percent of the population, by the year 2000. This expected growth means that the total elderly market will increase by about 32 percent in the 1977–2000 period, in contrast to only a 20 percent increase in all younger age segments. This disproportionate growth in the elderly segment of the population can be explained by the declining birthrate, improved medical diagnoses and treatment, and the resultant increase in general life expectancy.

A MISUNDERSTOOD MARKET. Some marketers have an extremely narrow and inaccurate picture of the elderly consumer, which causes them to overlook the potential profit to be derived from catering to the needs of this special market segment. For example, marketers are often reluctant to research the elderly market in order to identify unsatisfied needs because they believe that, in general, the elderly cannot afford to buy new products or services. This stereotyped view of the elderly fails to recognize that today many older people do have sufficient funds available for products that could improve the quality of their lives. Indeed, available evidence suggests that the elderly are very willing to try new products, especially those designed to promote or maintain good health.[47] Furthermore, with more and more elderly consumers receiving the benefits of private pension funds in addition to Social Security and Medicare, this age segment is even more likely to be able to afford new products and services in the future.

It has been the retailer, rather than the manufacturer, who has been most atuned to the needs of the elderly and quickest to realize their value as customers. For instance, Kroger, the large midwestern supermarket chain, promotes a "Senior Citizens Club," which offers anyone who is over fifty-nine years of age and on a fixed income a special shopping program designed to cut food costs.[48] Other retailers across the nation have introduced senior citizen sale days and other discount privileges for the elderly.[49]

Retailers have recognized the elderly as a special market segment for the following reasons: (1) they are price sensitive, (2) they have comparatively more time and interest in shopping, and (3) they often view shopping as a social activity to be undertaken with friends or relatives.[50]

THE NEEDS AND MOTIVATIONS OF ELDERLY CONSUMERS. The elderly are by no means a homogeneous subcultural group. Available research suggests that, in terms of how they approach life, the elderly can be divided into three major subgroups: (1) *the reorganizers*—those who substitute new involvements for lost ones (e.g., shifting attention after retirement to family, church, social groups, and community activities); (2) *the focused*—those who become active in a selective or narrowed range of activities; and (3) *the disengaged*—those who become uninvolved or withdrawn.[51]

In order to develop special products and special promotional programs to meet the needs of these market segments, marketers must not only recognize their different approaches to life, but they must also conduct research into their specific needs. Table 13–5 presents the find-

---

TABLE 13–5

A Ranking of Sources of Satisfaction and Dissatisfaction with Life in Old Age

Satisfactions	Rank	Dissatisfactions
Entertainment and diversions	1	Dependency—financial or physical
Socialization	2	Physical discomfort or sensory loss
Productive activity	3	Loneliness, bereavement
Physical comfort	4	Boredom, inactivity, confinement
Financial security	5	Mental discomfort or loss
Mobility and movement	6	Loss of prestige or respect
Good health and stamina	7	Fear of dying

Adapted from Margaret Clark and Barbara G. Anderson, Culture and Aging: An Anthropological Study of Older Americans, *1967. Courtesy Charles C. Thomas, Publishers, Springfield, Illinois.*

ings of a study that asked a sample of elderly consumers to rank sources of satisfaction and dissatisfaction with life in old age. The results revealed that the elderly derive most satisfaction from meaningful social involvement and purposeful activity. On the other hand, they are most fearful of financial and physical dependency and of loneliness. These findings suggest that the elderly need products and services that help them feel that their lives are useful and socially enjoyable, and which reduce their fears of financial and physical dependency. Builders of retirement communities for the elderly have successfully recognized these needs by promoting the organized activities and the security measures their communities offer.

In aiming products at the elderly, marketers must be careful not to embarrass them and make them feel uneasy about their age. When Heinz found that many elderly people were buying baby food because of the small sizes and easy chewing consistency, it introduced a line of "senior foods." The new product failed because elderly consumers were ashamed to admit that they required strained foods; instead, they preferred to buy baby food which they could always pretend they were buying for a grandchild.[52]

REACHING THE ELDERLY CONSUMER. Relatively little is known about the specific media habits of the elderly consumer. However, it would seem that television should be a particularly good medium through which to reach the elderly. Television would appear to fulfill a number of distinct functions. It provides an escape from loneliness and boredom, a substitute for social interaction, and a means of maintaining a sense of participation in society.[53] For these reasons, perhaps, the elderly tend to prefer TV programs that provide information, news, and current events (a way of keeping in touch with society).

SEX AS A SUBCULTURE

It may seem surprising to see sex (i.e., gender) included in a discussion of subcultures. Sex-related characteristics are not usually treated as subcultural differences. However, as one marketing expert has pointed out, this is a "notable omission."[54] Indeed, since sex roles are largely culturally determined, it is quite fitting to examine gender as a subcultural category. Moreover, given the extensive amount of attention that changing sex roles and sex discrimination have received in recent years, this is a timely issue.

sex roles and consumer behavior

All known societies assign certain traits and roles to males ("masculine" traits and roles) and others to females ("feminine" traits and roles). In the American society, for instance, aggressiveness, competitiveness, independence, and self-confidence are considered to be traditional masculine traits; while neatness, tactfulness, gentleness, and talkativeness are considered to be traditional feminine traits.[55] Similarly, in terms of role differences, women have historically been cast as home-makers with responsibility for child care, and men have been considered the providers or breadwinners.

While such traits and roles are no longer strongly associated with members of a specific sex, they are nevertheless still prevalent. Many advertisers still appeal to such sex-linked roles, and consumer tastes are frequently influenced by such sex-role factors.

CONSUMER PRODUCTS AND SEX ROLES. Within every society, it is quite common to find products that are either exclusively or strongly associated with the members of one sex. In the United States, for example, shaving equipment, cigars, pants, ties, and work clothing were historically male products; whereas bracelets, hair spray, hair driers, and sweet-smelling colognes were generally considered to be feminine products. For most of these products, the sex-link has either diminished or disappeared; while for others, the prohibition still lingers.

On the basis of a study that examined male acceptance of a tradi-tionally feminine product (hair spray), it appears that males with a strong masculine self concept and those who are less anxiety-prone may be good prospects for products that initially had a feminine image.[56]

MASS MEDIA AND SEX ROLES. A series of investigations have em-ployed content analysis to examine the portrayal of women in mass me-dia advertising.[57] Generally, these studies indicate that women have not been depicted accurately in terms of the range and scope of their cur-rent roles. For instance, general audience magazine advertisements have tended to stereotype women into four restrictive feminine roles:

1. *A woman's place is in the home.* Advertisements do not adequately represent the fact that about half of all American women work outside of the home.
2. *Women do not make important decisions or do important things.* Advertisements rarely depict women making non-household decisions, nor do they show them engaged in meaningful activities outside of the home.
3. *Women are dependent and need men's protection.* Advertisements portray women as dependent rather than independent or interdependent beings.
4. *Men regard women primarily as sexual objects.* Advertisements show women being treated by men not as equal human beings, but rather as subordinate, "decorative" and/or sexual objects.[58]

Table 13–6 compares the roles portrayed by women in advertise-ments in 1958, 1970, and 1972. It reveals some modest improvement in the proportion of magazine ads that portray women in a working en-vironment. The 1972 analysis found that some advertisements portrayed women in professional positions, and an increase in the proportion of ads that depicted women in middle-management positions.

An experiment that required female subjects to create print ads for a variety of product categories provides some additional insights into the prevalence of traditional sex roles in advertising.[59] Each subject was sup-

TABLE 13–6

A Comparison of Working and Nonworking Roles of Women Portrayed in Advertisements

	1958 Percent[a]	1970 Percent[b]	1972 Percent[c]
a. Working Roles			
Percent shown in a working environment	13.0	9.0	21.0
Occupational categories:			
High-level business	0.0	0.0	0.0
Professional	0.0	0.0	4.0
Entertainment, sports	11.1	58.0	23.0
Middle-level business	5.6	8.0	15.0
Secretarial, clerical	74.4	17.0	46.0
Blue collar	8.9	17.0	12.0
Total	100.0	100.0	100.0
b. Nonworking Roles			
Percent shown in a nonworking environment	87.0	91.0	79.0
Family	24.2	23.0	8.0
Recreational	28.3	46.0	36.0
Decorative	47.5	31.0	56.0
Total	100.0	100.0	100.0

Sources: Adapted from [a]Ahmed Belkaoui and Janice M. Belkaoui, "A Comparative Analysis of the Roles Portrayed by Women in Print Advertisements: 1958, 1970, 1972," Journal of Marketing Research, 13 (May 1976), 170–71.

[b]Alice E. Courtney and Sarah Wernick Lockeretz, "A Woman's Place: An Analysis of the Roles Portrayed by Women in Magazine Advertisements," Journal of Marketing Research, 8 (February 1971), 93–94.

[c]Louis C. Wagner and Janis B. Banos, "A Woman's Place: A Follow-Up Analysis of the Roles Portrayed by Women in Magazine Advertisements," Journal of Marketing Research, 10 (May 1973), 214.

plied with a portfolio of pictures depicting women in five roles (neutral, family, career, sex-object, fashion-object) and was asked to match product pictures to female role pictures. The findings indicated no uniform selection of a single female role for all product categories. Instead, female subjects tended to select different role/product combinations, depending on the nature of the specific product. For instance, the *neutral* and *career* roles were preferred for personal and grooming products, while the *family* role was preferred for household and food products. However, there was no product category for which a *sex-object* role was considered the most appropriate role portrayal. For the advertiser, these results tend to confirm that there is no universal female role; rather, women should be portrayed in roles that are consistent with the environment in which the product is likely to be consumed.

Advertisers who have creatively appealed to the expanded role of contemporary women are likely to have their efforts rewarded. For example, Figure 13–3 presents an ad for Fram Air Filters which encourages women to change the air filter in their automobiles themselves. The ad, which initially appeared in the *Ladies' Home Journal,* has reportedly been highly successful in stimulating awareness of the company and generating interest in the product.[60]

feminism and consumer behavior

What impact does the feminist movement have on the locus of family decision-making? According to one study, a wife who has a "liberal" view of the female role (e.g., strongly favors sexual equality) is more likely to participate with her husband in family decision making.[61] In fact, for selected product categories, the equality-minded woman often played a *dominant* role in the decision-making process (e.g., she was more likely to influence the amount to be spent). In those households where the wife had either a "moderate" or a "conservative" view of the female role, husbands were more likely to dominate in a wide range of family purchase decisions.

The research also indicated that age and family income affect sex-role differences in family decision making. Specifically, younger "liberal" women from higher-income families were less likely to report husband-dominated decisions than those who were older and from lower-income families. In general terms, the results suggest that sex-role perceptions of married women reflect the amount of influence that either spouse has in family decision making.

The relationship between various measures of feminist involvement and opinion leadership has also been examined.[62] Studies indicate that feminists may be an important force in the marketplace. For instance, one study found that women who were members of a feminist group (the National Organization of Women) were more likely to be opinion leaders than women who belong to nonfeminist women's organizations (Women's Democratic Club, Young Women's Christian Association, and League of Women Voters). Since opinion leaders influence the consumer attitudes and behavior of others, these findings suggest that marketers should explicitly consider feminist values and attitudes in developing promotional campaigns. Failure to do so may significantly impede the acceptance of new products and services for this growing market segment.

the working woman

In recent years, marketers and consumer researchers have been increasingly interested in the working woman, especially the *married* working woman. They recognize that working wives are a large and growing market segment whose needs differ from those of women who do not work outside the home.

According to government sources, nearly half (47 percent) of all American women are now employed outside the home.[63] Moreover,

Figure 13–3

Advertisement Appealing to an Expanded Female Role

Linda Jean Jernigan Fram/Autolite Car Care Counselor and Professional Truck Driver.

"If you can change the filter in your coffee machine, you can change the air filter in your car."

"Believe me, it isn't hard. All you have to do is:
1. Take off the filter holder lid. That's the cover of the big round thing that sits right on top of the engine. (Just undo one nut. Or two or three clips.) 2. Lift out the old filter. 3. Put in the new filter. And 4. Put back the lid.

It's a good idea to do it at least once a year, because a dirty air filter can play some very dirty tricks on you.

It can make your car cough and hesitate. Which isn't a pleasant thing to have happen when you're overtaking a truck.

A dirty air filter can also make your car hard to start. That can be very upsetting when you're rushing off to the supermarket. Or trying to get the kids to school.

You can buy a new Fram air filter from anyone who sells auto parts.

It isn't expensive. And it really is as easy as changing a coffee filter. But it's much more important."

Automotive Division
Fram Corporation, Providence, R.I.

Courtesy of Fram Corporation — Automotive Division.

about 45 percent of all *married* women have jobs. Still more revealing, about 37 percent of all married women with *preschool children* are working. In fact, young married working women with young children are the fastest growing segment in the female work force.[64]

These married working women have become an important market segment. However, marketers still know relatively little about how the dual demands of job and family influence consumer behavior.

WHY DO MARRIED WOMEN WORK? Many social-cultural factors are responsible for why so many married women now work. Some of the chief factors are: (1) the increased level of female educational attainment, (2) a need to supplement the husband's income, (3) the high divorce rate, (4) the growing conviction that women can simultaneously be mothers and have careers, (5) growth in the number of service jobs that appeal to women, (6) the trend toward fewer children, and (7) the availability of products that make homemaking easier and less time consuming.[65]

consumer behavior and working women

A study based on a large sample of women living in a major southwestern metropolitan area compared the consumption behavior of working women and nonworking women.[66] The results indicated that working women were more likely than nonworking women to shop just once a week for their food needs and were more likely to do so either during evening hours or on Saturday. Working women were also found to spend less money at the supermarket; however, this may be explained by the greater likelihood that they eat out one or more times a week.

When it came to clothing shopping, working women were found to prefer self-service stores and evening shopping and to be store loyal; nonworking women were more likely to use newspapers to select clothing stores and other retailers and were more price conscious. Finally, working women were somewhat less likely than nonworking women to read a daily newspaper and tended to watch less television. Table 13–7 summarizes these and other differences found to exist between working women and nonworking women.

Another study that compared working and nonworking women found that working women averaged fewer food shopping trips in a given week than nonworking women.[67] In addition, working women were found to be more brand loyal. Because brand loyalty is a way of reducing shopping time, this finding is consistent with the finding that working women make fewer food shopping trips each week.

For marketers, these studies suggest that working women make shopping a less time-consuming activity. They accomplish this "time economy" by shopping less often, and by being brand and store loyal. Not surprisingly, the working woman is also likely to do her shopping during evening hours or on the weekend.

TABLE 13-7

Consumer Behavior Differences between Working Women and Nonworking Women

Consumer area	The working woman is more likely to:	The nonworking woman is more likely to:
Food shopping	Shop once a week or less. Shop evenings or Saturdays. Spend $11-$25 per week.	Shop several times a week. Shop Monday to Thursday. Spend $26-$50 per week. Find newspaper food ads helpful.
Clothing shopping	Prefer self-service. Shop evenings. Shop same store.	Use newspaper to select store. Be price conscious. Be concerned with how flattering clothing is.
Services	Not use a maid. Not shop by mail-order catalog. Make more frequent use of vending machines. Eat out one or more times a week.	Use a maid once a week. Shop by mail-order catalog and by phone. Use cents-off coupons from newspapers.
Media exposure	Watch less than three hours of TV per day.	Read a newspaper daily.

Source: Adapted from Suzanne McCall, "Analytical Projections of Lifestyle Identification in Consumer Behavior," in Kenneth L. Bernhardt, ed., Marketing: 1776–1976 and Beyond (Chicago: American Marketing Association, 1976), 355.

SUBCULTURAL INTERACTION

We have just examined six important subcultural categories. It should be remembered that all consumers are simultaneously members of two or more subcultural segments (for example, a consumer may be a young, Hispanic, Catholic, working wife living in the northeastern section of the country). For this reason, marketers should strive to understand how multiple subcultural memberships *interact* to influence their target consumers' relevant consumption behavior. Promotional strategy should not be limited to a single subcultural membership.

Cross-cultural consumer analysis

In our examination of psychological, social, and cultural concepts, we have continuously pointed out how various segments of the American consuming public differ. If such diversity exists between segments of a *single* society, then even more diversity should exist among the members of two or more societies. The international marketer must understand the differences inherent in different societies (i.e., cross-culturally) so that he can develop appropriate marketing strategies to effectively penetrate each of his foreign markets.

WHAT IS CROSS-CULTURAL CONSUMER ANALYSIS?

In deciding whether to enter a foreign market, and how to approach that market, it is appropriate for the marketer to engage in cross-cultural consumer analysis. Within the scope of this discussion, we will define cross-cultural consumer analysis as the effort to determine *to what extent the consumers of two or more nations are similar or different.* Such analyses are designed to provide the marketer with sufficient understanding of the differences in psychological, social, cultural, and environmental characteristics to enable him to design effective marketing strategies for each of the specific countries involved.

similarities and differences among people

A major objective of cross-cultural consumer analysis is the determination of how consumers in two or more societies are similar, and how they are different. An understanding of the similarities and differences that exist between nations is critical to the multinational marketer, who must devise appropriate marketing strategies to reach the consumers in specific foreign markets. The greater the similarity between nations, the more feasible it is to employ similar marketing strategies in each nation. On the other hand, if the cultural beliefs, values, and customs of specific target countries are found to differ widely, then a highly *individualized* marketing strategy is indicated for each country.

Some marketers have argued that the world is becoming more and more similar, and therefore standardized marketing strategies are increasingly feasible.[68] Indeed, such companies as Philip Morris, Coca-Cola, and Volkswagen have frequently used the same marketing themes on a global basis.[69] However, other marketers have argued that differences between countries are sufficiently glaring to make "localized" marketing a more effective approach. A recent survey of multinational business executives found that individualized marketing efforts are becoming more common.[70] One marketing authority has aptly summed up the arguments as follows: "The only ultimate truth possible is that humans are both deeply the same and obviously different. . . ."[71]

This book is based upon the very same thesis. Earlier chapters have attempted to point up the underlying similarities that exist between people, and the external influences that, at the same time, serve to differentiate them into distinct market segments. If we believe in tailoring marketing strategies to specific segments in the American market, it follows that we also believe in tailoring marketing strategies to the needs — psychological, social, cultural, and functional — of specific foreign segments.

acculturation is a needed marketing viewpoint

Many American marketers make the strategic error of believing that "if Americans like it, then everyone will." Such a biased viewpoint increases the likelihood of marketing failures abroad. It reflects a complete lack of understanding of the unique psychological, social, cultural, and environmental characteristics of distinctly different cultures.

To overcome such a narrow and culturally myopic view, marketers must become *acculturated;* that is, they must learn everything that is relevant to the foreign cultures in which they plan to operate.

In a sense, acculturation is a dual process for the marketer who is entering a foreign market with which he is not familiar. First, he must thoroughly orient himself to the values, beliefs, and customs of the new society if he hopes to be successful in marketing his products. Second, to gain acceptance of a culturally new product in a foreign society, he must persuade the members of that society to break with their own traditions. For example, a social marketing effort designed to encourage consumers in developing nations to employ artificial birth-control devices would require a dual acculturation process. First, the marketer must acquire an in-depth picture of the society's present attitudes and customs with regard to birth control; then he has to devise promotional strategies that will persuade his target market to adopt the new practice in place of its traditional customs.

It stands to reason that the more similar the target society is to our own, the easier the process of acculturation. A study that focused on consumer acculturation found that foreign students who came from *developed* countries, with cultural heritages similar to the United States, were most likely to become acculturated; while those who came from *developing* nations were significantly less likely to adopt American consumption values and behavior.[72]

distinctive characteristics of cross-cultural analysis

The same research techniques used to study the American consumer are used to study consumers in foreign lands. In cross-cultural analysis, however, there is the additional burden that language and word usage often differs from nation to nation.

To illustrate how important proper wording is in cross-cultural analysis, and the necessity of designing questionnaires that reflect a country's specific beliefs, values, and customs, consider the following:[73]

1. A six-nation study indicated that consumption of spaghetti and macaroni was substantially greater in France and West Germany than in Italy. Upon further consideration, however, the researchers realized that their question had asked about the purchase of "packaged and branded spaghetti" rather than about level of consumption. Since many Italians purchase their spaghetti loose, their responses in no way reflected their actual purchase or consumption of spaghetti. Thus the finding that Italians were lighter spaghetti consumers than the French and West Germans had no basis in fact.

2. A pretest of a seven-country study designed to discover whether married or engaged women had received an engagement ring identified the following prob-

lems with the wording of the original questionnaire: (a) the word "engaged" did not mean the same thing in all nations (e.g., for a young Italian or Spanish woman, it refers to a relationship with any man who has taken her out more than once); (b) the question "Do you own an engagement ring?" is not appropriate for all countries (e.g., in Germany it is a common practice for a young woman to receive a gold wedding band upon her engagement). These and other aspects of the questionnaire were modified to meet the specific cultural traits of each country studied.

To avoid such research design problems, a marketer or consumer researcher must familiarize himself with the culture and availability of research facilities in the countries that are being evaluated as potential markets. Table 13–8 lists eight basic factors that the multinational marketer must consider in planning cross-cultural consumer research.

TABLE 13–8

Eight Basic Factors Influencing Cross-Cultural Analysis

Factors	Examples
Language differences	The words or concepts of a promotional theme may not translate adequately, and the meaning might be lost.
Differences in consumption patterns	Two countries may differ substantially in the level of consumption of a product.
Differences in potential market segments	The income or social class, age, and sex of consumers may differ dramatically in different countries.
Differences in the way that products or services are used	Two nations may use the same product or service in very different ways.
Differences in the criteria for evaluating products and services	The benefits that consumers seek from a product or service may differ from country to country.
Differences in economic and social conditions	The locus of family decision making may vary significantly from country to country.
Differences in marketing conditions	The types and quality of retail outlets may vary greatly between countries.
Differences in marketing research opportunities	High illiteracy rates or lack of telephones may inhibit data collection in certain countries.

Source: Adapted from Paul Howard Berent, "International Research Is Different," in Edward M. Mazze, ed., 1975 Combined Proceedings (Chicago: American Marketing Association, 1975), 295.

MARKETING MISTAKES: A FAILURE TO UNDERSTAND DIFFERENCES

In most cases, the "gamble" in international marketing is not knowing if the product, the promotional appeal, the pricing policy, or the retail channels that are effective in America will also work in other countries and what specific changes should be made to ensure acceptance in each foreign market. To provide the reader with a vivid picture of the problems inherent to international marketing, we will briefly examine some international marketing blunders. These examples illustrate that a failure to tailor marketing strategy to the target market's distinctive cultural traits can lead to costly mistakes.

product problems

International marketers frequently neglect to modify their products to meet local customs and tastes. For example, one American marketer learned the hard way (through poor sales performance) that English homemakers were not interested in American-style cake mixes but preferred instead ". . . a tough, rather spongy item which was traditional for tea."[74] To avoid such problems, marketers must ascertain whether the physical characteristics of their products are acceptable to the new market. For instance, Nestlé learned that it was necessary to market more than sixty different formulations of Nescafé in order to meet local foreign coffee preferences.[75]

Products brought from Europe to the United States also have had problems. For example, the *Delacre* line of luxury biscuits proved too rich for American tastes, and its ingredients and promotional appeal have since been revised to make it more acceptable to Americans.[76]

Color is an extremely critical variable in international marketing because the same color frequently has different meanings in different cultures. To illustrate, a yellow cologne failed to sell in Africa because consumers believed that it was animal urine; however, it sold successfully when its color was changed to green.[77] Similarly, General Foods, which markets its Instant Maxwell House coffee worldwide in a red can, found that red was inappropriate in Japan, where it means "fire sale."[78]

promotional problems

When communicating with consumers in different parts of the world, it is imperative that the promotional message be consistent with the language and customs of the specific society. Following are the kinds of problems that international marketers have faced in communicating with widely different customer groups.

The Seven-Up Company's highly successful "Uncola" theme, which was developed for the United States market, was considered inappropriate for many foreign markets because it does not translate well into other languages.[79] In its place, 7 UP uses a theme that features a pair of white-gloved hands coming out of a green box (see Figure 13–4). It was determined that this theme could be easily translated into the respective languages of some eighty countries.

In Japan, Seiko employed the headline "Like a Wind, I am the Color of a Bird" to introduce a new line of colored dial watches. To a Japanese consumer, this headline might mean "This watch is light and

Figure 13–4

The Seven-UP Company's Foreign Alternative to Its American "Uncola" Promotional Theme

Seven-Up International, Inc.

"Table"

Length: :60 & :30   Code #: US-42-60 & US-43-30

(MUSIC: 7UP THEME)

ANNCR. (VO): People have discovered something about 7UP.

It's not only different, it's delicious. Light, clean, and fresh.

And, after all, ...

only 7UP tastes like 7UP.

Courtesy of Seven-Up International, Inc.

delicate. It perhaps floats on your hand like a seedpod on the wind. Or a bird. A hummingbird with its jewel-like colors, the colors of the watch itself."[80] Yet to most Americans, the headline would be meaningless.

Product names also cause considerable problems for international marketers. For instance, Pledge, the Johnson wax product, translated inappropriately in several European languages.[81] To avoid product name difficulties, marketers must often use different names in different countries. To this end, General Foods' Dream Whip in the United States is called Dream Topping in England and Copo Imperial in Venezuela.[82]

pricing and distribution problems

An international marketer must also adjust his pricing and distribution policies to meet local economic conditions and customs. For instance, in many developing nations where the average income is quite low, small-sized packages of products are often a necessity, because consumers cannot afford the cash outlay required for the larger sizes popular in the United States and other affluent countries. Even in developed nations, however, there are important differences. To illustrate, supermarkets are very popular in Switzerland, but in France, which is just across the border, consumers prefer smaller and more intimate stores for their grocery shopping.[83] Thus marketers must vary their distribution channels by nation.

THE NEED FOR SYSTEMATIC CROSS-CULTURAL CONSUMER RESEARCH

The striking aspect of cross-cultural consumer behavior is how little is actually known about the consumption behavior of people outside the United States. Until quite recently, the systematic study of marketing and of consumer behavior has been dominated by Americans, and therefore it was only natural that most marketing and consumer behavior research would focus on the United States. The following comment reflects the "state of the art" of cross-cultural consumer research: "With few exceptions, most of the current information on consumption patterns of people outside the United States is strictly observational and often emphasizes colorful idiosyncrasies rather than systematic behavioral modes."[84]

In response to the growing interest in multinational marketing, it is likely that academic consumer researchers, especially American and European scholars, will increasingly undertake systematic and conceptual research investigations designed to identify the psychological, social, and cultural characteristics of consumers in different societies.

a comparison of american and french consumers

A study that compares selected characteristics of American and French consumers provides some useful insights into cross-cultural consumer behavior.[85] The investigation found that American consumers are more willing to try new grocery products and new types of retail establishments than French consumers. Americans reported more word-of-mouth conversations with friends concerning grocery products than did French consumers, while French consumers were more likely to have discussed new types of retail outlets.

These results support the image of Americans as quick to respond to new products and eager to talk about them. That French consumers talked more about new types of retail outlets (e.g., discount furniture stores and delicatessen departments in supermarkets) may reflect the fact that these new retail services have only recently become highly visible in France, while they are already fairly commonplace in the United States.

Summary

Subcultural analysis enables the marketer to segment his market to meet the specific needs, motivations, perceptions, and attitudes that are shared by members of a specific subcultural group. A *subculture* is a distinct cultural group which exists as an identifiable segment within a larger, more complex society. Its members possess beliefs, values, and customs that set them apart from other members of the same society; at the same time, they hold to the dominant beliefs of the overall society. Major subcultural categories in this country include nationality, religion, geographic location, race, age, sex, and occupation. Each of these can be broken down into smaller segments which can best be reached through special copy appeals and selective media choices. In some cases (e.g., the elderly consumer), product characteristics can be tailored to the specialized needs of the market segment. Since all consumers are simultaneously members of several subcultural groups (e.g., a young, married, northern, Catholic working woman of Italian parentage), the marketer should try to determine how specific subcultural memberships interact to influence the consumer's overall purchase decisions.

With such diversity among the members of just one nation, it is easy to understand that numerous larger differences exist between members of different nations. If the international marketer is to effectively penetrate selected foreign markets, he must understand the relevant similarities and differences that exist among the peoples of these countries. Such cross-cultural analyses will provide the marketer with sufficient understanding of the psychological, social, cultural, and environmental characteristics of the countries in which he is interested to develop appropriate marketing strategies.

For some international marketers, *acculturation* may be a dual process: first, they must learn everything that is relevant to the society in which they plan to market; then they must persuade the members of that society to break with their own traditional ways of doing things to adopt the new product. The more similar the target society is to our own, the easier the process of acculturation. Conversely, the more different the target society, the more difficult the process of acculturation.

Some of the problems involved in cross-cultural analysis include differences in language, consumption patterns, needs, product usage, economic and social conditions, marketing conditions, and market research opportunities. There is an urgent need for more systematic and conceptual cross-cultural analyses concerning the consumption habits of foreign consumers. Such analyses will serve to identify increased marketing opportunities that will benefit both international marketers and the consumers they seek to serve.

Endnotes

1. *Robin M. Williams, Jr.,* American Society: A Sociological Interpretation, *3rd ed. (New York: Knopf, 1970), 415.*

2. *Gerald Zaltman,* Marketing: Contributions from the Behavioral Sciences *(New York: Harcourt, Brace & World, 1965), 8.*

3. Annual Report *(Washington, D.C.: United States Immigration and Naturalization Service, 1976).*

4. *"Spanish Speaking Are $20 Billion U.S. Market,"* Advertising Age, *November 21, 1973, 56.*

5. *Ibid.*

6. *Richard P. Jones, "Spanish Ethnic Market Second Largest in U.S.,"* Marketing Insights, *November 27, 1967, 10; and "Spanish Speaking Are $20 Billion U.S. Market," 56.*

7. *Chuck Wingis, "Spanish TV Net Grows, Looks to East,"* Advertising Age, *August 18, 1975, 214.*

8. Yearbook of American Churches *(Nashville, Tenn: Abingdon, 1976), p. 232*

9. *Arthur W. VanDyke, "Stop Killing Us with Kindness,"* Journal of Marketing, *40 (July 1976), 90–91.*

10. *Subhash C. Jain, "Life Cycle Revisited: Applications in Consumer Research," in Mary Jane Schlinger, ed.,* Advances in Consumer Research, *2 (Association for Consumer Research, 1975), 42.*

11. *Philip H. Dougherty, "Matching Products to Lifestyle,"* New York Times, *April 21, 1976, 58.*

12. *Kevin A. Wall, "New Market: Among Blacks, the Haves Are Now Overtaking the Have-Nots,"* Advertising Age, *February 11, 1974, 35–36.*

13. *Parvat K. Choudhury, Francis J. Connelly, and Ronald Kahlow, "The Effect of Income on Black Media Behavior," in Kenneth L. Bernhardt, ed.,* Marketing: 1776–1976 and Beyond *(Chicago: American Marketing Association, 1976), 422–25.*

14. *Mary Jane Schlinger and Joseph T. Plummer, "Advertising in Black and White,"* Journal of Marketing Research, *9 (May 1972), 149–53; John W. Gould, Norman B. Sigband, and Cyril E. Zoerner, Jr., "Black Consumer Reactions to 'Integrated' Advertising: An Exploratory Study,"* Journal of Marketing, *34 (July 1970), 20–26; and Arnold M. Barban and Edward W. Cundiff, "Negro and White Response to Advertising Stimuli,"* Journal of Marketing Research, *1 (November 1964), 53–56.*

15. *Paul J. Solomon, Ronald F. Bush, and Joseph F. Hair, Jr., "White and Black Consumer Sales Response to Black Models,"* Journal of Marketing Research, *13 (November 1976), 431–34.*

16. *Harold H. Kassarjian, "The Negro and American Advertising, 1946–1965,"* Journal of Marketing Research, *6 (February 1969), 29–39; and Harold H. Kassarjian, "Blacks in Advertising: A Further Comment,"* Journal of Marketing Research, *8 (August 1971), 392–93.*

17. *Jacob M. Duker, "Value Orientation of Middle-Class Blacks," in Boris W. Becker and Helmut Becker, eds.,* 1972 Combined Proceedings *(Chicago: American Marketing Association, 1973), 429–33.*

18. *Donald E. Sexton, Jr., "Comparing the Cost of Food to Blacks and to Whites—A Survey,"* Journal of Marketing, *35 (July 1971), 40–46.*

19. *Charles S. Goodman, "Do the Poor Pay More?"* Journal of Marketing, *32 (January 1968), 18–24.*

20. *Donald E. Sexton, Jr., "Do Blacks Pay More?"* Journal of Marketing Research, *8 (November 1971), 420–26.*

21. *Ibid., 425–26.*

22. *Raymond A. Bauer, Scott M. Cunningham, and Lawrence H. Wortzel, "The Marketing Dilemma of Negroes,"* Journal of Marketing, *29 (July 1965), 1–6.*

23. *Ibid., 3.*

24. *Joseph F. Hair, Jr., Ronald F. Bush, and Paul S. Busch, "Acculturation and Black Buyer Behavior," in Edward M. Mazze, ed.,* 1975 Combined Proceedings *(Chicago: American Marketing Association, 1975), 253–56.*

25. *Kelvin A. Wall, "Positioning Your Brand in the Balck Market,"* Advertising Age, *June 18, 1973, 71; and Robert B. Settle, John H. Faricy, and Richard W. Mizerski, "Racial Differences in Consumer Locus of Control," in Fred C. Allvine, ed.,* 1971 Combined Proceedings *(Chicago: American Marketing Association) 1972., 629–33.*

26. *Bauer, Cunningham, and Wortzel, "Marketing Dilemma," 4; and Carl M. Larson, "Racial Brand Usage and Media Exposure Differentials," in Keith Cox and Ben M. Enis, eds.,* New Measure of Responsibility for Marketing *(Chicago: American Marketing Association, 1968), 208–15.*

27. *Thomas S. Robertson, Douglas J. Dalrymple, and Michael Y. Yoshino, "Cultural Compatibility in New Product Adoption," in Philip R. McDonald, ed.,* Marketing Involvement in Society and the Economy *(Chicago: American Marketing Association, 1969), 70–75.*

28. *Fred C. Akers, "Negro and White Automobile-Buying Behavior: New Evidence,"* Journal of Marketing Research, *5 (August 1968), 283–90.*

29. *Milton Rokeach and Seymour Parker, "Values as Social Indicators of Poverty and Race Relations in America,"* Annals of the American Academy of Political and Social Science, *388 (March 1970), 97–111.*

30. *U.S. Bureau of the Census,* Current Population Reports, *Series p-25, No. 601, "Projections of the Population of United States 1975 to 2050" (Washington, D.C.: Government Printing Office, 1975).*

31. *Fabian Linden, "Consumer Markets: The Young Family,"* Conference Board Record, *12 (November 1975), 61.*

32. *U.S. Bureau of the Census,* Current Population Reports, *Series p-20, No. 281, "Income and Expenses of Students Enrolled in Postsecondary Schools: October 1973" (Washington, D.C.: Government Printing Office, 1975).*

33. *U.S. Bureau of the Census,* Current Population Reports, *Series p-20, No. 287, "Marital Status and Living Arrangements: March 1975" (Washington, D.C.: Government Printing Office, 1975).*

34. The Life Cycle, *Trend Report No. 8 (New York: Institute of Life Insurance, February 1974), 11.*

35. Current Population Reports, *Series p-20, No. 287.*

36. *U.S. Bureau of the Census,* Current Population Reports, *Special Studies p-23, No. 51, "Characteristics of American Youth; 1974" (Washington, D.C.: Government Printing Office, 1975).*

37. *Scott Ward, Thomas S. Robertson, and William Capitman, "What Will Be Different About Tomorrow's Consumers?" in Fred C. Allvine, ed.,* 1971 Combined Proceedings *(Chicago: American Marketing Association, 1972), 374.*

38. *Daniel Yankelovich,* The New Morality: A Profile of American Youth in the 70's *(New York: McGraw-Hill, 1974).*

39. *William Lazer et al., "Consumer Environments and Life Styles of the Seventies,"* MSU Business Topics, *20 (Spring 1972), 6.*

40. *Melvin Helitzer and Carl Heyel,* The Youth Market *(New York: Media Books, 1970), 58.*

41. *Ibid., 18.*

42. *Stephen A. Baumgarten and John O. Summers, "A Comparison of the Predictors of Fashion Opinion Leadership across Two Populations," in Edward M. Mazze, ed.,* 1975 Combined Proceedings *(Chicago: American Marketing Association, 1975), 429 – 32.*

43. *Ibid., 431.*

44. *Jeffrey G. Towle and Claude R. Martin, Jr., "The Elderly Consumer: One Segment or Many?" in Beverlee B. Anderson, ed.,* Advances in Consumer Research, *3 (Association for Consumer Research, 1976), 463.*

45. *Ethel Shanas, "What's New in Old Age?"* American Behavioral Scientist, *14 (September-October 1970), 5.*

46. Current Population Reports, *Series p-25, No. 601.*

47. *Leon G. Schiffman, "Perceived Risk in New Product Trial by Elderly Consumers,"* Journal of Marketing Research, *9 (February 1972), 106 – 8.*

48. *"Kroger Testing Promotion for Senior Citizens,"* Advertising Age, *July 28, 1975, 8.*

49. *Ibid.*

50. *Joseph Barry Mason and Brooks E. Smith, "An Exploratory Note on the Shopping Behavior of Low Income Senior Citizens,"* Journal of Consumer Affairs, *Winter 1974, 204 – 9.*

51. *B. Neugarten, R. J. Havighurst, and S. S. Tobin, "Personality and Patterns of Aging," in B. Neugarten, ed.,* Middle Age and Aging *(Chicago: University of Chicago Press, 1968), 173 – 77.*

52. *"The Power of the Aging in the Marketplace,"* Business Week, *November 20, 1971, 52 – 58.*

53. *Lawrence Wenner, "Functional Analysis of TV Viewing for Older Adults,"* Journal of Broadcasting, *20 (Winter 1976), 77 – 88.*

54. *Frederick D. Sturdivant, "Subculture Theory: Poverty, Minorities and Marketing," in Scott Ward and Thomas S. Robertson, eds.,* Consumer Behavior: Theoretical Sources *(Englewood Cliffs, N. J.: Prentice-Hall, 1973) 476.*

55. *Inge K. Broverman, Susan Raymond Vogel, Donald M. Broverman, Frank E. Clarkson, and Paul S. Rosenkrantz, "Sex Role Stereotypes: A Current Appraisal,"* Journal of Social Issues, *28 (1972), 63.*

56. *George P. Morris and Edward W. Cundiff, "Acceptance by Males of Feminine Products,"* Journal of Marketing Research, *8 (August 1971), 372 – 74.*

57. *Alice E. Courtney and Sarah Wernick Lockeretz, "A Woman's Place: An Analysis of the Roles Portrayed by Women in Magazine Advertisements,"* Journal of Marketing Research, *8 (February 1971), 92–95; Louis C. Wagner and Janis B. Banos, "A Woman's Place: A Follow-up Analysis of the Roles Portrayed by Women in Magazine Advertisements,"* Journal of Marketing Research, *10 (May 1973), 213–14; and Ahmed Belkaoui and Janice M. Belkaoui, "A Comparative Analysis of the Roles Portrayed by Women in Print Advertisements: 1958, 1970, 1972,"* Journal of Marketing Research, *13 (May 1976), 168–72.*

58. *Courtney and Lockeretz, "A Woman's Place," 94–95.*

59. *Lawrence H. Wortzel and John M. Frisbie, "Women's Role Portrayal Preferences in Advertisements: An Empirical Study,"* Journal of Marketing, *38 (October 1974), 41–46.*

60. *"Fram Presents Its Install-It-Yourself Ad Story to Women,* Advertising Age, *March 15, 1976, 78.*

61. *Robert T. Green and Isabella C. M. Cunningham, "Feminine Role Perception and Family Purchasing Decisions,"* Journal of Marketing Research, *12 (August 1975), 325–32.*

62. *Maureen Daly,* Feminism and Opinion Leadership *(New York: Baruch College of the City University of New York, Honors Paper, 1976).*

63. *Barbara Lee,* Working Women *(New York: CBS, Inc., Office of Social Research, July 1976).*

64. *Ibid., 4.*

65. *Ibid.; and Suzanne McCall, "Analytical Projections of Lifestyle Identification in Consumer Behavior," in Kenneth L. Bernhardt, ed.,* Marketing: 1776–1976 and Beyond *(Chicago: American Marketing Association, 1976), 354–59.*

66. *McCall, "Analytical Projections."*

67. *Beverlee B. Anderson, "Working Women versus Non-Working Women: A Comparison of Shopping Behavior," in Boris W. Becker and Helmut Becker, eds.,* 1972 Combined Proceedings *(Chicago: American Marketing Association, 1973), 355–59. Also see Susan P. Douglas, "Working Wife vs. Non-Working Wife Families: A Basis for Segmenting Grocery Markets?" in Beverlee B. Anderson, ed.,* Advances in Consumer Research, *3 (Chicago: Association for Consumer Research, 1976), 191–98.*

68. *For example, see Arthur C. Fatt, "The Danger of 'Local' International Advertising,"* Journal of Marketing, *31 (January 1967), 60–62.*

69. *S. Watson Dunn, "Effect of National Identity on Multinational Promotional Strategy in Europe,"* Journal of Marketing, *40 (October 1976), 55.*

70. *Ibid., 54.*

71. *Sidney J. Levy, "Myth and Meaning in Marketing," in Ronald C. Curhan, ed.,* 1974 Combined Proceedings *(Chicago: American Marketing Association, 1975), 555–56.*

72. *Joseph Franklin Hair, Jr., and Rolph E. Anderson, "Culture, Acculturation and Consumer Behavior: An Empirical Study," in Boris W. Becker and Helmut Becker, eds.,* 1972 Combined Proceedings *(Chicago: American Marketing Association, 1973), 426.*

73. *Paul Howard Berent, "International Research Is Different," in Edward M. Mazze, ed.,* 1975 Combined Proceedings *(Chicago: American Marketing Association, 1975), 294.*

74. *Albert Stridberg, "U.S. Advertisers Win Some, Lose Some in Foreign Market,"* Advertising Age, *May 6, 1974, 18.*

75. *J. Douglas McConnell, "The Economics of Behavioral Factors on the Multi-National Corporation," in Fred C. Allvine, ed.,* 1971 Combined Proceedings

(Chicago: American Marketing Association, 1972), 263; and H. T. Parker, "International Markets Look Bright," Advertising Age, May 13, 1974, 53.

76. *Stridberg, "U.S. Advertisers," 40.*
77. *Eliyahu Tal, "Advertising in Developing Countries," Journal of Advertising, 3 (Spring 1974), 21.*
78. *"GF International Moves to Centralized Policies," Advertising Age, February 25, 1974, 148.*
79. *Ramona Bechtos, "Man in the Green Box Sells 7UP in World Markets," Advertising Age, May 19, 1975, 25, 43, and 45.*
80. *Larry O'Neill, "How to Cope with 'Tokyo Trauma,'" Advertising Age, May 28, 1974, 32.*
81. *Stridberg, "U.S. Advertisers," 18.*
82. *"GF International Moves to Centralized Policies," 148.*
83. *Walter Weir, "What Americans Can Learn from Europe—Market Segmentation," Advertising Age, February 16, 1976, 41.*
84. *Robert T. Green and Eric Langeard, "A Cross-National Comparison of Consumer Habits and Innovator Characteristics," Journal of Marketing, 39 (July 1975), 34.*
85. *Ibid., 34–37.*

Discussion questions

1. Discuss the importance of subcultures in segmenting the market for food products.
2. What specific recommendations would you offer the management of a firm that produces household detergents on how they might more effectively reach (a) the Hispanic market and (b) the black market?
3. Describe two ways in which the changing life styles of young adults has influenced their behavior as consumers.
4. Illustrate how changes in traditional sex roles have provided opportunities to reposition products that formerly have been marketed exclusively to either males or females.
5. Describe two ways in which the changing roles of women have affected their decision making or purchasing behavior.
6. How can a multinational company use cross-cultural consumer analysis to design each factor in its marketing mix? Discuss.
7. If you wanted to name a new product so that it would be acceptable throughout the world, what cultural factors would you consider?
8. List four reasons why a product that is successful in one society might fail in another society.

CONSUMER DECISION MAKING

IV

Part IV uses the concepts discussed throughout the book to construct a conceptual framework for the consumer decision-making process. Chapter 14, "Diffusion of Innovations," focuses on how consumers make decisions about new products and services. The final chapter, "Consumer Decision Making," takes a broader perspective and demonstrates by means of a simple model how the contributions of psychological, sociological, and cultural theory influence the consumer's consumption-related decisions.

diffusion of innovations

Introduction

This chapter examines a major aspect of consumer behavior—the acceptance of *new* products and services. The introduction of new products is vital to both the consumer and the marketer. For the consumer, new products represent an increased opportunity for better satisfaction of personal, social and environmental needs. For the marketer, new products provide an important mechanism for keeping the firm competitive and profitable.

Our framework for exploring consumers' acceptance of new products is drawn from the area of research known as the *diffusion of innovations*. Actually, the study of the diffusion of innovations is interdisciplinary in scope, and has its earliest roots in anthropology and rural sociology. Other disciplines, such as communications, education, medical sociology, and marketing, have recently investigated selected aspects of diffusion. Table 14–1 lists the kind of topics and units of analyses examined by these various behavioral disciplines.

The central interests of consumer researchers who have specialized in the diffusion of innovations have been to better understand: (1) how the acceptance of a new product spreads within a market, and (2) the individual consumer decision-making process which led up to the acceptance or rejection of a new product. Therefore, this chapter, with its focus on *new* product decision making, and the next chapter, with its broader focus on the general dimensions of consumer decision making, are complementary.

TABLE 14–1

Type of Diffusion of Innovation Studies Undertaken, By Discipline

Discipline	Typical innovations studied	Main unit of analysis
Anthropology	Technological ideas (e.g., steel ax)	Tribal or peasant villages
Early sociology	City manager government, postage stamps, "ham" radios	Communities or individuals
Rural sociology	Agricultural ideas (e.g., weed sprays, hybrid seed, fertilizers) and health ideas (e.g., vaccinations, latrines)	Individual farmers in rural communities
Education	Kindergartens, driver training, modern math, programmed instruction	School systems or teachers
Medical sociology	Medical drugs, vaccinations, family-planning methods	Individuals
Communications	News events, agricultural innovations	Individuals
Marketing	New products (e.g., a coffee brand, the touch telephone, clothing fashions)	Individual consumers

Within the scope of our discussion of the diffusion of innovations, we will concentrate on two closely related processes: (1) the diffusion process, and (2) the adoption process. In the broadest sense, the diffusion process is a *macro* process which is concerned with the spread of a new product (an innovation) from its source to the consuming public. In contrast, the adoption process is a *micro* process which focuses on the stages through which an individual consumer passes in making a decision to accept or reject a new product. In addition to these two interrelated processes, we will present a profile of *consumer innovators*—those consumers who are the first to purchase a new product. A marketer's ability to identify and reach this important group of consumers plays a major role in the success or failure of his new product marketing efforts.

The diffusion process

The diffusion process is concerned with the general dimension of how innovations spread—how they are assimilated—within a market. More precisely, the diffusion process is the *process by which the acceptance of an innovation* (a new product, new service, new idea, new practice) *is spread by communication* (mass media, salesmen, informal conversations) *to mem-

bers of a social system (a target market) *over a period of time.* This definition includes the four basic elements of the diffusion process, namely: (1) the innovation, (2) channels of communication, (3) the social system, and (4) time. Each of these elements will be considered in turn.

THE INNOVATION

Defining a "product innovation" or a "new product" is not an easy task. The various approaches that have been used to define a *new product* can be classified as product-oriented, market-oriented, and consumer-oriented.

A *product-oriented* approach focuses on the features inherent in the product itself, and the effects these features are likely to have on consumers' established usage patterns. One product-oriented framework is based upon the extent to which a new product is likely to be disruptive to the consumer's already established behavioral patterns. It defines three types of product innovations: continuous, dynamically continuous, and discontinuous.

1. A *continuous* innovation has the least disrupting influence on established patterns. It involves the introduction of a *modified* product, rather than a totally new product . Examples: fluoride toothpaste, new automobile models, menthol cigarettes.

2. A *dynamically continuous* innovation is somewhat more disruptive than a continuous innovation, but it still does not alter established behavioral patterns. It may involve the creation of a new product or the modification of an existing product. Examples: the electric toothbrush, the correcting selectric typewriter, Touch-Tone telephones.

3. A *discontinuous* innovation requires the establishment of new behavioral patterns. Examples: television, pocket calculators, computers.[1]

In another product-oriented approach, the extent of "newness" of a product is defined in terms of how much impact its physical features or attributes are likely to have on user satisfaction.[2] Thus, the more satisfaction a consumer derives from a new product, the higher it ranks on the scale of "newness." This concept leads to the classification of products as *artificially new, marginally new,* or *genuinely new.* A genuinely new product would have features that satisfy the user in a manner that differs significantly (better, quicker, or more convenient) from that of an older product. New products that have been judged to possess enough "newness" to qualify as genuinely new products include nonrefrigerated prepared salad spreads, frozen breakfasts, canned puddings, and instant omelet mixes.

A *market-oriented* approach judges the newness of a product in terms of how much potential exposure consumers have to the new product. Two market-oriented definitions of product innovation have been used quite extensively in consumer studies:

1. A product is considered new if it has not been purchased by more than a relatively small (fixed) percentage of the potential market.

2. A product is considered new if it has only been available on the market for a relatively short (specified) period of time.

Both of these market-oriented definitions are basically subjective because they leave to the researcher the task of establishing the degree of sales penetration within which it is appropriate to call the product an innovation (such as the first 5 percent to use the new product) or how long a product can be on the market and still be considered "new" (such as the first three months the product is available). These approaches have been useful to consumer researchers in their attempts to study the diffusion of innovations. Table 14–2 gives some examples of how products have been defined as innovations in terms of these two market-oriented schemes.

TABLE 14–2

Examples of Market-Oriented Definitions of Innovation

Scheme	Innovation	Definition
Percent of target market to purchase	Various durable goods (e.g., color TV)[a]	The first 10% to purchase
	Touch-Tone telephones[b]	The first 10% to purchase
Extent of time on the market	Automobile diagnostic center[c]	The first three-months after the opening of the center
	Ladies' fashion hats[d]	The five-and-one-half month period from August through mid-January

Sources: [a]William E. Bell, "Consumer Innovators: A Unique Market for Newness," in Stephen A. Greyser, ed., Toward Scientific Marketing (Chicago: American Marketing Association, 1963), 85–87.
[b]Thomas S. Robertson, "Determinants of Innovative Behavior," in Reed Moyer, ed., Changing Marketing Systems (Chicago: American Marketing Association, 1967), 328–32.
[c]James F. Engle, Roger D. Blackwell, and Robert J. Kegerreis, "Consumer Use of Information in the Adoption of an Innovation," Journal of Advertising Research, 9 (December 1969), 3–8.
[d]Charles W. King, "Fashion Adoption: A Rebuttal to the 'Trickle Down' Theory," in Greyser, Toward Scientific Marketing, 108–25.

Some researchers have suggested that a *consumer-oriented* approach is the most appropriate way to define an innovation.[3] Within the context of this approach, a new product is any product that a potential consumer judges to be new. In other words, newness is based on the consumer's *perception* of the product, rather than on physical features or market realities. Although the consumer-oriented approach has been accepted by some advertising practitioners and marketing strategists, it has not as yet received any systematic attention from consumer researchers.

product characteristics that influence diffusion

All new products are not equally susceptible to consumer acceptance. For example, some products seem to catch on almost overnight (e.g., skateboards), whereas other innovations take a very long time to gain acceptance (e.g., organizational blood donor programs). Some new products never seem to achieve widespread consumer acceptance (e.g., light whiskeys and the leather substitute Corfam).

It would reduce the uncertainties of product marketing if a marketer could anticipate how consumers will react to his product. For example, if a marketer knew that his product contained features that were likely to retard its acceptance, he would be able to either develop a marketing strategy that would compensate for these features or decide not to market the product at all. While there are no precise formulas by which a marketer can evaluate a new product's acceptance, diffusion researchers have identified five product characteristics that seem to influence consumers' acceptance of new products: (1) relative advantage, (2) compatibility, (3) complexity, (4) trialability, and (5) observability.[4]

Relative advantage is the degree to which potential customers *perceive* a new product as superior to existing substitutes. For example, the seal of approval awarded to Crest toothpaste in 1966 by the American Dental Association was a strong relative advantage. Mothers of young children concerned with tooth decay were impressed by this first-time endorsement, as evidenced by a dramatic increase in sales within a relatively short time. However, since product perception is highly selective, it is likely that young, single adults, who are primarily interested in toothpastes that whiten their teeth and freshen their breath, did not perceive the ADA approval as a relative advantage.

In addition to unique product features, promotional programs that include cents-off coupons, two-for-one sales, and a variety of special services (such as American Motors' "Buyer Protection Plan" or Burger King's "Have it your way!") also have the potential of being perceived by consumers as a relative advantage and may led to increased acceptance.

Compatibility is the degree to which potential consumers feel that a new product is consistent with their present needs, values, and practices. For example, male university students who shave daily took a shorter period of time to decide to try stainless steel blades than did less frequent shavers.[5] These results suggest that when a new product is compatible with existing needs and experience, it is likely to enjoy increased acceptance. A new cream designed to remove facial hair might be simpler to use than a razor, but it is less likely to receive mass acceptance because (1) it would require a major adjustment in behavior, and (2) it would not be consistent with the values most males possess with regard to the ritual of shaving.

Complexity is the degree to which a new product is difficult to comprehend or use. Clearly, the easier it is to understand and use a new product, the greater the likelihood that it will be accepted. For example, the acceptance of such convenience products as TV dinners, premixed alcoholic drinks, and instant mashed potatoes generally is due to their appeal to consumers' desires for ease of preparation and use. Card games like poker and gin rummy are played by a greater segment of the population than bridge and canasta because they are less complex.

Trialability is the degree to which a new product is capable of being tried by consumers on a limited basis. The greater the opportunity to try a new product, the easier it will be for consumers to evaluate it. The inherent quality and low cost of a new chewing gum like Freshen-up (the first gum with a liquid center) made it relatively easy to try on a limited basis, since it involved such a minor purchase commitment. On the other hand, durable items such as major appliances are difficult, if not impossible, to try without making a major commitment. This may explain why publications like *Consumer Reports* are so widely used for their ratings of infrequently purchased durable goods.

As a general rule, it would seem that frequently purchased household products tend to have qualities that make trial relatively easy.[6] Figure 14–1 indicates that 63 percent of the consumers studied made a trial purchase of a new brand in a smaller quantity than they usually pur-

Figure 14–1

Classification of Households by Type of Change in Trial Purchase

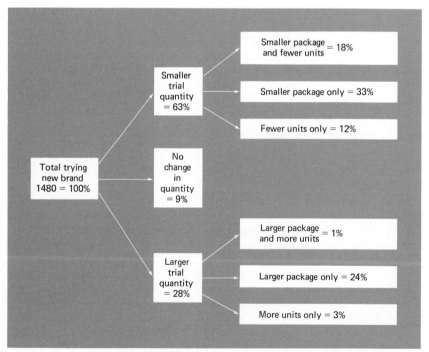

Source: Robert W. Shoemaker and F. Robert Shoaf, "Behavioral Changes in the Trial of New Products," Journal of Consumer Research, 2 (September 1975), 107.

chased (33 percent bought a smaller package and 18 percent purchased both a smaller size and fewer units). For the marketer of household products, these findings suggest that it may be wise to offer a new product initially in smaller-than-typical sizes to stimulate trial.

Because it recognized the importance of trialability, Gillette undertook a massive promotional campaign to introduce the Trac II razor blade. It mailed a free razor handle and a single Trac II blade to a large segment of the adult male population. By supplying the free, reusable razor handle, Gillette was able to establish an almost instantaneous replacement market for its new Trac II blades. Test drives for automobiles, money-back guarantees, and free samples also enhance the acceptance of products by making consumer trial easy.

Observability (or communicability) is the ease with which a product's benefits or attributes can be observed, imagined, or described to potential consumers. Products that have a high degree of social visibility, such as fashion items, are more easily diffused than products that are used in private, such as new brands of toothpaste. Similarly, a tangible product is more easily promoted than an intangible product (i.e., a service).

To date, only a few studies have examined the influence of these five innovation characteristics on consumers' trial of new products. The first consumer study to examine these five characteristics found that relative advantage, compatibility, trialability, and observability were positively associated with consumers' intentions to buy a variety of new product concepts.[7] This study did not examine actual purchase behavior. However, its findings were supported by a subsequent study that used actual purchase data.[8]

It must be recognized that each of these product attributes is dependent on consumer perception. A product that is *perceived* as having a strong relative advantage, as fulfilling present needs and values, as easy to try on a limited basis, and as simple to understand and to see (and/or examine), is more likely to be purchased than a product that is not so perceived.

THE CHANNELS OF COMMUNICATION

How quickly a product innovation spreads through a market depends to a great extent on communication between the marketer and the consumer, and communication between consumers. For this reason, researchers interested in diffusion have paid particular attention to the transmission of product-related information through various channels of communication, and to the impact of the messages and the channels on the adoption or rejection of new products. Of central concern has been the influence of both impersonal sources (e.g., advertising and editorial matter) and interpersonal sources (e.g., salespeople and informal opinion leaders). In fact, most of our discussion of personal influence and the opinion leadership process (see Chapter 10) is based on evidence that is part of the general tradition of diffusion research.

One major stream of communication research has focused on the relative importance of certain *types* of information sources on early-versus-later adoption of new products. Specifically, the following generalizations gleaned from the general diffusion literature are important to marketers:[9]

1. Early adopters have more change-agent contact (e.g., with salesmen) than later adopters.
2. Early adopters have greater exposure to mass media communication channels than later adopters.
3. Early adopters seek information about innovations more frequently than later adopters.
4. Early adopters have greater knowledge of innovations than later adopters.
5. Early adopters have a higher degree of opinion leadership than later adopters.

We will discuss these generalizations in greater detail in our examination of the consumer innovator.

THE SOCIAL SYSTEM

The diffusion of a new product usually takes place in a social setting—frequently referred to as a *social system*. Within the framework of consumer behavior, the terms *market segment* or *target market* are equivalent to the term *social system* used in diffusion research. Regardless of what it is called, however, a social system is a physical, social, or cultural environment to which people belong and within which they function. For example, for a new hybrid seed corn, the social system might be all farmers in a number of local communities; for a new drug, the social system might consist of all physicians within several specified cities; for a new special-diet product, the social system might include all residents of a geriatric community.[10] As these examples indicate, the social system serves as the boundary within which the diffusion of a new product is examined.

The orientation of a social system, with its own special values or norms, is likely to influence the acceptance or rejection of new products. If the social system is "modern" in orientation, the acceptance of innovations is likely to be high. In contrast, if the orientation of a social system is "traditional," innovations that are perceived as radical or as infringements on established custom are likely to be avoided. According to one authority, the following characteristics typify a "modern" social system:[11]

1. A positive attitude toward change.
2. An advanced technology and skilled labor force.
3. A general respect for education and science.
4. An emphasis on rational and ordered social relationships rather than on emotional ones.
5. An outreaching perspective, in which members of the system frequently interact with outsiders, thus facilitating the entrance of new ideas into the social system.
6. The system's members can readily see themselves in roles quite different from their own.

Of course, the opposite of these characteristics would describe a traditionally oriented social system.

These orientations (modern or traditional) may be national in scope and influence members of an entire society, or they may exist at the local level and influence only those who live in a specific community. The critical issue is that a social system's orientation is the "climate" in which marketers have to operate in attempting to gain acceptance for their new products. For example, the United States is now experiencing a rapid increase in the introduction of new food products that stress natural ingredients (i.e., which contain no artificial ingredients or preservatives, such as natural ice cream, health breads, and natural cereals). If these new products are to be successful, the prevailing values of a sufficient number of consumers must agree with the concept of natural ingredients.

TIME

Time is the backbone of the diffusion process. It pervades the study of diffusion in three distinct but interrelated ways: (1) in *purchase time,* (2) in the identification of *adopter categories,* and (3) in the *rate of adoption.*

purchase time

Purchase time is concerned with the amount of time that elapses between the consumer's initial awareness of a new product and the point at which he purchases it or rejects it. The purchase of an expensive camera will serve to illustrate how a consumer's decision might progress over time.[12] Figure 14-2 shows an average purchase time frame and pinpoints the influence of various communications sources on the first-time purchaser of an expensive camera. An examination of the overall

Figure 14-2

Time Frame for First-Time Purchasers of Expensive Cameras

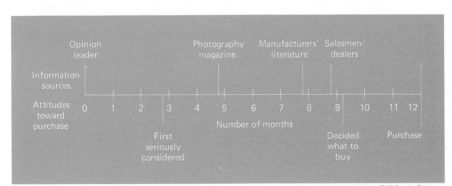

time frame reveals that it takes about twelve months from contact with an opinion leader (a friend or relative who is perceived to be knowledgeable about photography and who introduces the idea of the purchase of an expensive camera) to the actual purchase.

The figure illustrates how long and complex a process consumer decision making can be, and how different information sources become important at successive stages in the process. Purchase time is an important concept, because the average time a consumer takes to adopt a new product is a predictor of the overall length of time that will be required for the new product to be diffused throughout the market. For example, when the individual purchase time is short, a marketer has reason to expect that the overall rate of diffusion will be faster than when the individual purchase time is long, as in the purchase of a new camera. Thus, individual purchase time influences the total amount of time necessary for a product to achieve widespread adoption.

adopter categories

The concept of adopter categories involves the determination of a classification scheme that indicates where a consumer stands in relation to other consumers in terms of when he adopted a new product. Five adopter categories are frequently cited in the diffusion literature: (1) innovators, (2) early adopters, (3) early majority, (4) late majority, and (5) laggards.[13] Table 14–3 describes each of these adopter categories and estimates their relative proportions within the total population which eventually adopts the new product.

As Figure 14–3 indicates, the adopter categories take on the characteristics of a normal distribution (i.e., a bell shaped curve). It is based

TABLE 14-3

Adopter Categories

Adopter category	Description	Relative percentage within the population which eventually adopts
Innovators	"Venturesome"—willing to accept risks	2.5
Early adopters	"Respectable"—regarded by many others in the social system as a role model	13.5
Early majority	"Deliberate"—willing to consider innovation only after peers have adopted	34.0
Late majority	"Skeptical"—overwhelming pressure from peers needed before adoption occurs	34.0
Laggards	"Traditional"—oriented to the past	16.0
		100.0

Reprinted with permission of Macmillan Publishing Co., Inc. from Diffusion of Innovations, *by Everett M. Rogers. Copyright © The Free Press, 1962.*

FIGURE 14–3

The Sequence and Proportion of Adopter Categories Among the Population that Eventually Adopts

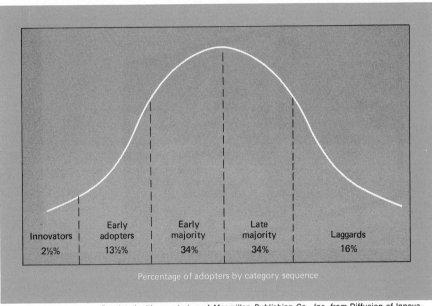

Reprinted with permission of Macmillan Publishing Co., Inc. from Diffusion of Innovations, by Everett M. Rogers. Copyright © The Free Press, 1962.

on the sociologists' assumption that 100 percent of the members of the social system under study (the target market) will eventually accept the product innovation.[14] This assumption is *not* in keeping with marketers' experiences, since very few, if any, products fit the needs of all potential consumers. For example, theoretically all American women could be expected to color their hair. In reality, however, a relatively small proportion of adult females use hair coloring, and it would be unrealistic for the hair-coloring industry to expect that all women eventually will. For this reason, it is important to think of an additional category, that of *nonadopters*. A "nonconsumer" category is in accord with marketplace reality, in that not *all* potential consumers do adopt a product innovation.

For these reasons, consumer behavior studies usually avoid using the classic five-category adopter scheme. However, there is not as yet any generally accepted alternative procedure for defining adopter categories.[15] Instead, as Table 14–4 indicates, consumer researchers have employed a variety of adopter schemes, most of which consist of two or three categories which compare innovators or *early triers* with *later triers* or *nontriers*. As we will see, this focus on the innovator or early trier has produced some important generalizations which have practi-

TABLE 14–4

Types of Adopter Categories Used in Marketing Diffusion Studies

Innovation	Adopter categories	Researchers' definitions of categories
New brand of regular coffee[a]	Pioneers	The first 12% (or first two days)
	Early adopters	The next 18% (or third to ninth day)
	Late adopters	The next 12% (or tenth to sixteenth day)
New movie *(In Cold Blood)*[b]	Innovators	Those who attended opening night
	Early adopters	Those who attended the fourth night
	Late adopters	Those who attended the sixth night
Automobile diagnostic center[c]	Innovators	Those who used the center during its first three months of operation
	Nonadopters	A random sample drawn from the same city
A new health food (a salt substitute)[d]	Innovators	Those who tried the product during a two-week trial period
	Non-innovators	Those who did not try the product during the trial period

Sources: [a]*Johan Arndt, "Role of Product-Related Conversations in the Diffusion of a New Product,"* Journal of Marketing Research, *4 (August 1967), 291–95.*

[b]*Johan Arndt, "A Cold Blooded Analysis of Movie-Going as a Diffusion Process,"* Markedsokonomic, *March 1969, 90.*

[c]*James F. Engel, Roger D. Blackwell, and Robert J. Kegerreis, "Consumer Use of Information in the Adoption of an Innovation,"* Journal of Advertising Research, *9 (December 1969), 3–8.*

[d]*Leon G. Schiffman, "Perceived Risk in New Product Trial by Elderly Consumers,"* Journal of Marketing Research, *9 (February 1972), 106–8.*

cal significance for marketers planning the introduction of new products.

rate of adoption

The rate of adoption is concerned with how long it takes for a new product to be adopted by members of a special social system; that is, how quickly a new product is accepted by those who will adopt it.

The diffusion of television sets provides an illustration of this concept. Figure 14–4 compares the growth in the total number of United States households with the growth in television-owning households for the twenty-five year period 1950–74. Note the very.rapid rate of adoption of television sets between 1950 and 1958, and the emergence of multiset homes as an important market segment since 1958. The ownership of color television sets is shown as having a very low rate of adoption within the ten-year period 1955–64, probably due to their high sales price, the lack of color programming, and consumers' perceived func-

FIGURE 14–4

25 Years of Television Growth

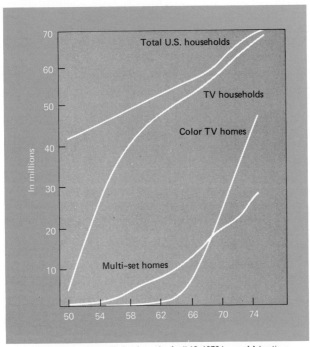

Source: Reprinted with permission from the April 19, 1976 issue of Advertising Age. Copyright 1976 by Crain Communications Inc. Also, courtesy of Television Bureau of Advertising and McCann Erickson, Inc.

tional risk (see Chapter 3). Since 1965, however, there has been a dramatic acceleration in the acceptance of color television sets.

In the marketing of new products, the objective is usually to gain very wide acceptance of the product as quickly as possible. The reasons why marketers desire a rapid rate of product adoption include the following:

1. To penetrate the market and establish market leadership (obtain the largest share of the market) before competition takes hold. A penetration policy is usually accompanied by a relatively low introductory price designed to discourage competition from entering the market.

2. To demonstrate to the channels of distribution (wholesalers and retailers) that the product is worthy of their full and continued support.

Under certain circumstances, a marketer might prefer to avoid a rapid rate of adoption for a new product. For example, a marketer who wishes to employ a pricing strategy that will enable him to recoup his development costs quickly might follow a *skimming* policy—he first makes the product available at a very high price to consumers who are willing to pay "top dollar," and then gradually lowers the price in a series of steps designed to attract additional market segments at each price reduction.

The adoption process

The second major process within the overall scope of the diffusion of innovations is the *adoption process*. The focus of this process is on the stages through which an individual consumer passes in arriving at a decision *to try* or *not to try, to continue using* or *to discontinue using* a new product.

STAGES IN THE ADOPTION PROCESS

It is often assumed that the consumer moves through five stages in arriving at a decision to purchase or reject a new product: (1) awareness, (2) interest, (3) evaluation, (4) trial, and (5) adoption (or rejection).[16]

AWARENESS. During this first stage, the consumer is exposed to the product innovation. This exposure is somewhat neutral, since the individual is not yet sufficiently interested in the product to search for additional product information.

INTEREST. When the consumer develops interest in the product or product category, he searches for information about how the innovation can benefit him.

EVALUATION. Based upon his stock of information, the consumer draws conclusions about the innovation or determines whether further information is necessary. The evaluation stage thus represents a kind of "mental trial" of the product innovation. If the evaluation is satisfactory, the consumer will actually try the product innovation; if the mental trial is unsatisfactory, the product will be rejected.

TRIAL. At this stage, the consumer actually uses the product innovation on a limited basis. His experience with the product provides him with the critical information he needs to adopt or reject.

ADOPTION. Based upon his trial and/or favorable evaluation, the consumer decides to use the product on a full rather than limited basis or he decides to reject it.

The adoption process provides a framework for determining which types of information sources consumers find most important at specific decision stages. For example, a study of early users of the first automobile diagnostic center in a midwestern city found that *mass media sources* (magazines and radio publicity) were most important for disseminating general knowledge about such services and awareness of the specific service offered in the city. However, early users' final pretrial information was drawn primarily from informal discussions with *personal sources.*[17]

A study concerned with the acceptance of stainless steel blades among university students found that the mass media were the principal sources of initial product awareness, while informal sources (friends and relatives) were influential in the final decision to try the new type of blade.[18] As a final example, a study designed to examine the influence of various information sources on the *rejection* of a new clothing style found that mass media served as the main source of awareness for women concerning the style, while informal sources were most influential at the evaluation stage.[19]

These and other studies support the notion that impersonal mass media sources tend to be most valuable for creating initial product awareness; however as the purchase decision progresses, the relative importance of these sources declines, and the relative importance of interpersonal sources (friends, salesmen, and others) increases. Figure 14–5 depicts this relationship.

FIGURE 14–5

The Relative Importance of Different Types of Information Sources, by Adoption Process Stages

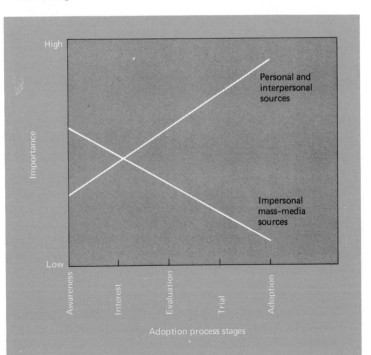

CRITICISMS OF THE ADOPTION PROCESS

Although the adoption process model has been instructive for consumer researchers, it has been criticized because of the following limitations:

1. It does not adequately acknowledge that a need or problem recognition stage may precede the awareness stage.
2. It does not adequately provide a rejection alternative (i.e., a consumer may never advance from the trial stage to the adoption stage, but may reject the product after trial, or never use the product on a continuous basis).
3. It does not adequately recognize that evaluation occurs throughout the decision making process and not only at the "evaluation" stage.
4. It does not adequately account for the possibility that the five stages may not always occur in the specific order suggested (e.g., trial may occur before there is any evaluation); nor does it consider that some of the stages may, in fact, be skipped (e.g., in the case of consumer durables, like a refrigerator, there may be no opportunity for a trial).
5. Finally, it does not explicitly acknowledge that after trial or adoption there is a *post-purchase evaluation.* This evaluation may lead to a strengthened commitmit or it may lead to a decision to discontinue use of the product.[20]

THE INNOVATION DECISION PROCESS

To overcome these limitations, the traditional adoption process model has been updated into a more general decision-making model — the *innovation decision process.* The four stages of the revised adoption process model are:

1. *Knowledge.* The individual is exposed to the innovation's existence and gains some understanding of how it functions.
2. *Persuasion.* The individual forms a favorable or unfavorable attitude toward the innovation.
3. *Decision.* The individual engages in activities which lead to a choice to adopt or reject the innovation.
4. *Confirmation.* The individual seeks reinforcement for the innovation decision he has made, but he may reverse this decision if exposed to conflicting messages about the innovation.[21]

Figure 14-6 depicts in diagrammatic form the operation of the innovation decision process. Very briefly, the model suggests that a number of individual consumer (receiver) and environmental (i.e., social system) variables influence his reception of information about the product innovation during the *knowledge* stage. At the *persuasion* stage, the consumer is further influenced by communications sources, and by his perceptions of the characteristics of the innovation (its relative advantage, compatibility, complexity, trialability, and observability). Additional information received by the consumer during the *decision* stage, enables him to assess the innovation and decide whether to adopt or reject. The final stage, *confirmation,* is also influenced by communication sources; it is at this stage that the consumer evaluates his purchase expe-

FIGURE 14–6

The Innovation Decision Process

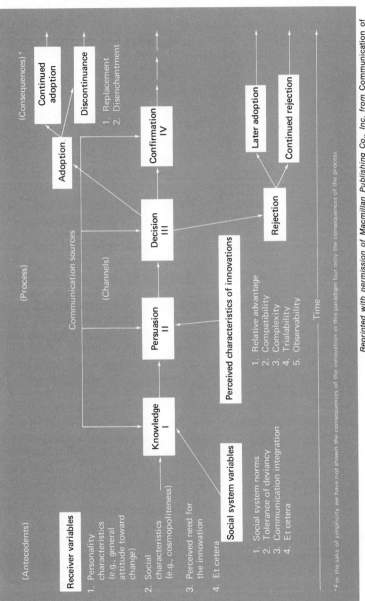

Reprinted with permission of Macmillan Publishing Co., Inc. from Communication of Innovations, by Everett M. Rogers and Floyd Shoemaker. Copyright © 1971 by The Free Press, a Division of The Macmillan Company.

*For the sake of simplicity we have not shown the consequences of the innovation in this paradigm but only the consequences of the process.

rience, looks for support for his behavior, and decides to continue or discontinue using the product.

To sum up, the innovation decision process model is more comprehensive than the earlier adoption process model and eliminates many of its basic limitations. It is also much more atuned to the realities faced by the marketer who is launching a new product.

A profile of the consumer innovator

Who is the consumer innovator? What characteristics set the innovator apart from later adopters and those who never purchase? How can the marketer reach and influence the innovator? These are key questions that are of interest to the marketing practitioner about to introduce a new product or service.

DEFINING THE CONSUMER INNOVATOR

The consumer innovator can be defined as one of the relatively small group of consumers who are the earliest purchasers of a new product. The problem with the definition, however, centers on the concept "earliest," which is, after all, a relative term. Sociologists have treated this issue by sometimes defining innovators as the first 2.5 percent of the social system to adopt an innovation. In a good number of marketing diffusion studies, however, consumer researchers have *derived* the definition of the consumer innovator from the status of the new product under investigation. For example, if the researcher assesses the new product as an innovation for the first three months of its availability, then he defines the consumers who purchase it during this period as consumer innovators.

Other researchers have defined the innovator in terms of his *innovativeness,* that is, his purchase of some minimum number of new products from a selected group of new products. In a study of the adoption of new fashion items, innovators were defined as those consumers who purchased more than one fashion product from a group of ten new fashion products; non-innovators were defined as those consumers who purchased only one or none of the new fashion products.[22] In other instances, researchers have defined innovators as those falling within an arbitrary proportion of the total market (e.g., the first 10 percent of the population in a specified geographic area to buy the new product).

INTEREST IN THE PRODUCT CATEGORY

Not surprisingly, researchers have found that consumer innovators are much more interested than either later adopters or non-adopters in the product category that they are among the first to purchase. For example, the earliest purchasers of the rotary-engined Mazda automobile were found to have a substantially greater interest in automobiles (they enjoyed looking at auto magazines and were interested in the performance and functioning of automobiles) than those who purchased different small cars during the same period, or those who purchased the Mazda during a later period.[23]

Furthermore, consumer innovators are more likely than non-innovators to seek out information concerning their specific interests from a variety of informal and mass media sources.[24] Contrary to what might be expected, the consumer innovator does not seem to be an impulsive purchaser; rather, he seems to give greater deliberation to the purchase of a new product than non-innovators.[25]

THE INNOVATOR IS AN OPINION LEADER

In discussing the characteristics of the opinion leader (see Chapter 10), we indicated a strong tendency for consumer opinion leaders to be innovators. Within our present context, it is worthwhile to note that an impressive number of studies on the diffusion of innovations have found that consumer innovators are likely to provide other potential consumers with information and advice about new products, and that those who receive such advice frequently follow it. Thus, in the role of opinion leader, the consumer innovator often influences the acceptance or rejection of new products.[26] If the innovator is enthusiastic about a new product and encourages others to try it, the product is likely to receive broader and quicker acceptance. On the other hand, if consumer innovators are dissatisfied with a new product and discourage others from trying it, its acceptance will be severely handicapped and it may even die a quick death. With products that do not generate much excitement (either positive or negative), consumer innovators may not be sufficiently motivated to provide advice; thus the marketer has to rely almost entirely on the mass media and personal selling to influence future purchasers. In such cases, the absence of *informal* influence is likely to result in a somewhat slower rate of acceptance (or rejection) for the new product. Since a motivated consumer innovator can evidently speed up acceptance or rejection of a new product, he can thereby influence its eventual success or failure.

PERSONALITY TRAITS

In Chapter 5 we examined the personality traits that distinguish the consumer innovator from the non-innovator. In this section we will briefly highlight what researchers have learned about the personality of the consumer innovator.

First, the consumer innovator has been found to be *less dogmatic* than the non-innovaotr.[27] He tends to approach a new or unfamiliar product with considerable openness and little anxiety. In contrast, the non-innovator seems to find new products threatening, to the point where he prefers to delay purchase until a product's success has been clearly established.

Consistent with his open-mindedness, the consumer innovator has also been found to be *inner-directed;* that is, he relies on his own values or standards in making a decision about a new product.[28] In comparison, the non-innovator is *other-directed,* tending to rely on others for guidance on how to respond, rather than trusting his own personal values or standards. There is some research evidence that the initial purchasers of a new model automobile were inner-directed, and that later purchasers of the same model tended to be other-directed.[29] This suggests that as acceptance of a product progresses from early to later adopters, there is a gradual shift in the personality type of adopters from inner- to other-directedness.

Finally, in terms of *category width,* which purports to measure an individual's risk-handling orientation (see Chapter 3), the consumer innovator has been found to be a broad categorizer, while the non-innovator tends to be a narrow categorizer.[30] Broad categorizers tend to try many new products, even though, by doing so, they subject themselves to the risk of trying unsatisfactory products. On the other hand, narrow categorizers are so afraid of making poor product choices that they limit their trial of new products, even though this means they may forego the benefits of desirable new products. However, for trivial or "artificially" new products (such as a new-flavored dessert), the narrow categorizer may adopt more quickly than the broad categorizer.[31] This suggests that the consumer innovator does not respond to superficially different products, but tends to single out substantially different products.

To sum up, the consumer innovator seems to be more receptive to the unfamiliar; she is more willing to rely on her own values or standards than on the judgments of others. She is also willing to run the risk of a poor product choice in order to increase her exposure to new products. For the marketer, the personality traits that distinguish innovators from non-innovators suggest the need for separate promotional campaigns for innovators and for later adopters. The consumer innovator is more likely to react favorably to informative or fact-oriented advertising which appeals to his increased interest in the product category, and to readily evaluate the merits of a new product on the basis of his own personal standards. To reach the non-innovator, it would seem appropriate to feature reference group settings and to use a recognized and trusted expert or celebrity to appeal to his other-directed responsiveness to those with authority.

VENTURESOMENESS

Venturesomeness is a broad-based measure of a consumer's willingness to accept the risk of purchasing new products. Measures of venturesomeness have been used to evaluate a person's general values or attitudes toward trying new products. Typical questions include:

Do you prefer to: (1) try a new food product when it first comes out, or (2) wait and learn how good it is before trying it?

How do you feel about buying new things that come out for the home?

When I am shopping and see a brand of heavy duty detergent I know of but have never used, I am very anxious or willing to try it, hesitant about trying it, or very unwilling to try it.[32]

Research designed to measure venturesomeness has uniformly found that consumers who indicate a willingness to try new products tend to be consumer innovators (as measured by their actual purchase of new products). On the other hand, consumers who express a reluctance to try new products are in fact less likely to purchase new products. Therefore, venturesomeness seems to be an effective barometer of actual innovative behavior.

PERCEIVED RISK

Perceived risk, discussed in detail in Chapter 3, is another measure of a consumer's tendency to try new brands or products. Specifically, perceived risk can be thought of as the degree of uncertainty or fear as to the consequences of her purchase that a consumer feels when considering the purchase of a new product. For example, a consumer experiences uncertainty when she is concerned that a new product will not work properly or will not be as good as other alternatives. Research on perceived risk and the trial of new products overwhelmingly indicates that the consumer innovator is a low risk perceiver.[34] Consumers who perceive that little or no risk is associated with the purchase of a new product are much more likely to purchase it than consumers who perceive a great deal of risk. In other words, high risk perception limits innovativeness.

Consistent with his greater venturesomeness and lowered perception of risk, the consumer innovator is also likely to believe that he learns about innovations earlier than others. He also tends to be more intrigued with the prospect of "newness" than are non-innovators.[35]

PURCHASE AND CONSUMPTION CHARACTERISTICS

Consumer innovators have purchase and usage traits that set them apart from non-innovators. Studies have shown consumer innovators are *less* brand loyal (*more* apt to switch brands) than non-innovators. For example, with regard to a new brand of regular coffee, consumer innovators were found to be less loyal to established brands of coffee than non-innovators.[36] Similarly, in a study of the diffusion of a series of new grocery products, innovators were found to be less loyal to established brands than later adopters.[37] It is not surprising that innovators tend to be less brand loyal, for brand loyalty would seriously impede their willingness to try new products.

Consumer innovators are also more likely to be *deal-prone* (i.e., to take advantage of special promotional offers such as free samples and cents-off coupons).[38] Not surprisingly, consumers who are deal-prone have generally been found to be less brand loyal.[39] The consumer innovator is also likely to be a heavy user of the product category in which she innovates. For example, two different studies of the diffusion of new brands of coffee found that consumer innovators either purchase larger quantities of coffee or consume more cups of coffee daily than non-innovators.[40] The study of the diffusion of stainless steel blades (described earlier) found that respondents who were heavy shavers (i.e., daily shavers) and more experienced at shaving were more likely to be innovators (i.e., to take less time to make a decision to try the new product) than either occasional or less-experienced shavers.[41]

These studies indicate a positive relationship between innovative behavior and heavy usage. They suggest that consumer innovators not only are an important market segment from the standpoint of being the first to use a new product, but also represent a substantial market in terms of the quantity of the product used. However, their propensity to switch brands and to buy promotional "deals" also suggests that they will continue to use a specific brand only so long as they do not perceive that a new and potentially better alternative is available.

ARE THERE GENERALIZED CONSUMER INNOVATORS?

Do consumer innovators in one product category tend to be consumer innovators in other product categories? The answer to this strategically important question is a guarded "no." The few studies that have specifically attempted to measure the overlap of innovativeness across product categories have noted some degree of overlap, particularly between product categories that seem to be related to the same basic interest area. The overlap, however, does not seem to be sufficiently strong to warrant a marketing strategy that would treat innovators of diverse product categories as members of the same basic market segment.[42]

There seems to be much stronger evidence that consumers who are innovators in regard to one new food product or one new appliance are more likely to be innovators for other new products within the same product category.[43] In other words, although no single or generalized consumer-innovativeness trait seems to operate *across* broadly different product categories, evidence suggests that consumers who innovate *within* a specific product category will innovate again within the same product category. For the marketer, these findings indicate that it may be good marketing strategy to target a new product to those consumers who were the first to try other products within the same basic product category.

MEDIA HABITS

In launching a new product, it is desirable that the marketer be able to identify specific mass media that will reach the consumer innovator. To accomplish this task, the marketer has to determine whether consumer innovators selectively expose themselves to any specific types of media that could be used to reach them more effectively.

Research studies that have compared the media habits of innovators and non-innovators suggest that innovators have somewhat greater total exposure to magazines. For example, in a study of the earliest users of a new automobile diagnostic center, innovators were found more likely than non-innovators to subscribe to more than five magazines.[44] In a study that compared early and later adopters of women's fashion hats, it was also found that early adopters had greater total magazine exposure than later adopters.[45]

Certain evidence indicates that consumer innovators are likely to have greater exposure to *special interest* magazines devoted to the product category in which they innovate. For example, a study of female fashion innovators found that innovators had greater exposure to women's fashion magazines such as *Glamour* and *Vogue* than non-innovators.[46] Similarly, two studies of male fashion innovators found that innovators had greater exposure to male special interest publications such as *Playboy* and *Penthouse*.[47] Studies outside the realm of fashion innovativeness have also found that innovators are more likely to read special interest magazines. For example, women who were early adopters of household cleansers and detergents had greater exposure to magazines devoted to the home (e.g., *Better Homes and Gardens* and *Good Housekeeping*).[48] Though innovators tend to have greater total magazine exposure than non-innovators, it would be more efficient for the marketer to attempt to reach them through appropriate *special interest* magazines relevant to their specific product category rather than through general interest magazines.

A number of studies reveal that consumer innovators are likely to have *less* exposure to television than non-innovators.[49] However, a study of male fashion innovators revealed that the innovators were somewhat more interested in watching TV sports programs than non-innovators. A study that examined the media exposure patterns of innovators in six product categories found that the large appliance innovator watched less television than the non-innovator; however, no difference was found in television viewing for any of the other five product categories examined.[50] These studies suggest that the mass appeal of television does not make it a particularly effective medium for reaching the consumer innovator for all product categories.

Studies concerning the relationship between innovative behavior and exposure to other mass media, such as radio and newspapers, have been too few in number and too varied in results to provide any useful conclusions. Definitive research in this area would provide marketers with more comprehensive guidelines as to where to reach the consumer innovator.

SOCIAL CHARACTERISTICS

Available evidence indicates that consumer innovators are more socially accepted and socially involved than noninnovators. For example, a number of studies reveal that consumer innovators are more socially integrated within the community than non-innovators. Specifically, push-button telephone innovators were found to be better accepted by others and to have more social involvement with other members of the community than non-innovators.[51] A diffusion study that examined the acceptance of a new brand of regular coffee found that residents who were well integrated into the community (i.e., those who received more sociometric citations as a "relatively close friend") were quicker to adopt the new product than residents who were less integrated (see Figure 14–7).[52] Evidence also indicates that consumer innovators are *social strivers*—that is, they are more socially mobile (aspire to move up the social class ladder), they are more physically mobile (have relocated more often), and they are more occupationally mobile (have changed jobs more often) than non-innovators.[53]

FIGURE 14–7

Relationship between Time of First Purchase and Number of Citations Received as "Relatively Close Friend"

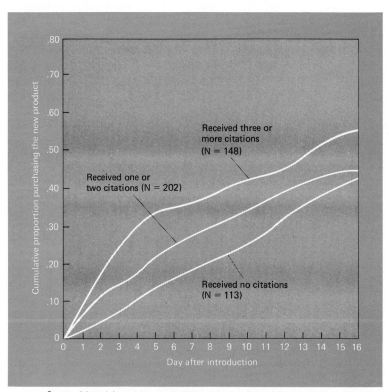

Source: *Adapted from Johan Arndt, "Role of Product-Related Conversations in the Diffusion of a New Product,"* Journal of Marketing Research, 4 (August 1967), 293.

Innovators are likely to belong to more social groups and organizations than non-innovators. For example, in two separate studies, female fashion innovators were found to belong to more formal organizations than later adopters or non-innovators.[54] Innovators in the acceptance of a community antenna television system (CATV) were found to hold more memberships and to be more involved in social and civic clubs, professional associations, and organized church groups than later adopters.[55]

The greater social acceptance and involvement of the consumer innovator may in part explain why he functions as an effective opinion leader.

DEMOGRAPHIC CHARACTERISTICS

It is reasonable to assume that the age of the consumer innovator is related to the specific product category in which he innovates; however,

TABLE 14–5

Comparative Profiles of the Consumer Innovator and the Non-innovator or Later Adopter

Characteristic	Innovator	Non-innovator (or later adopter)
Product Interest	More	Less
Opinion Leadership	More	Less
Personality:		
Dogmatism	Open-minded	Closed-minded
Social character	Inner-directed	Other-directed
Category width	Broad categorizer	Narrow categorizer
Venturesomeness	More	Less
Perceived Risk	Less	More
Purchase and Consumption Traits:		
Brand loyalty	Less	More
Deal proneness	More	Less
Usage	More	Less
Media Habits:		
Total magazine exposure	More	Less
Special interest magazines	More	Less
Television	Less	More
Social Characteristics:		
Social integration	More	Less
Social striving (e.g., social, physical, and occupational mobility)	More	Less
Group memberships	More	Less
Demographic Characteristics:		
Age	Younger	Older
Income	More	Less
Education	More	Less
Occupational status	More	Less

many studies have found consumer innovators to be younger than either later adopters or non-innovators.[56] The inconsistency between our expectations and recent evidence is no doubt a function of the fact that many of the products selected for examination (fashion, convenience grocery products, new automobiles) are particularly attractive to younger consumers.

Available evidence indicates that the consumer innovator has more formal education, has a higher personal or family income, and is more likely to have a higher occupational status (i.e., to be a member of a profession or have a managerial position) than later adopters or non-innovators.[57] In other words, innovators tend to be more up-scale than other consumer segments.

The profile in Table 14–5 summarizes the major differences between the consumer innovator and the later adopter or non-innovator.

Summary

The diffusion process and the adoption process are two closely related concepts concerned with the acceptance of new products by consumers. The diffusion process is a *macro* process, which focuses on the spread of an innovation (a new product, a new service, a new idea) from its source to the consuming public. The adoption process is a *micro* process, which examines the stages through which an individual consumer passes in making a decision to accept or reject a new product.

The term *innovation* can be defined in a product-oriented sense (as a continuous innovation, a dynamically continuous innovation, and a discontinuous innovation), in a market-oriented sense (by how long the product has been on the market and by the percentage of the potential target market that has purchased it) and in a consumer-oriented sense. Market-oriented definitions of innovation are most useful to the study of the diffusion and adoption of new products.

Five product characteristics influence a consumer's acceptance of a new product: (1) its *relative advantage* over existing products, (2) its *compatibility* with the consumer's present needs, values, and practices, (3) its *complexity*, (4) its *trialability* (how easy it is to try on a limited basis), and (5) its *observability* or *communicability* (the ease with which it can be viewed by or described to potential consumers).

Diffusion researchers are concerned with two aspects of communication: the channels through which word of a new product is spread to the consuming public, and the types of messages which influence the adoption or rejection of new products. Diffusion is always examined within the context of a specific social system, such as a target market, a community, a region, or even a nation.

Time is an integral consideration in the diffusion process. Researchers are concerned with the amount of time required for an individual consumer to adopt or reject a specific new product *(purchase time)*, with the percentage of the target market who have adopted the new product by a given time period (the *rate of adoption*), and with the identification of sequential adopter categories. The five adopter categories are innovators, early adopters, early majority, late majority, and laggards.

Marketing strategists try to control the rate of adoption in accordance with their new product pricing policies. Marketers who wish to penetrate the market in order to achieve market leadership try to achieve wide adoption in as short a period as possible; those who choose a skimming pricing policy deliberately plan a longer adoption process.

The traditional adoption process model describes five stages through which an individual consumer passes in arriving at her decision to adopt or reject a new product: awareness, interest, evaluation, trial, and adoption. The newer *innovation decision process* model is a more general decision making model which focuses on four stages of adoption: knowledge, persuasion, decision, and confirmation. Both models offer a framework for determining the importance of various information sources on consumers at the various decision stages.

Marketers are vitally concerned with identifying the consumer innovator so that they may initially direct their new product promotional campaigns to the people who are most likely to try new products, to adopt them, and to influence others in the target market. Consumer research has identified a number of consumer-related characteristics and personality traits that distinguish consumer innovators from later adopters. These serve as useful variables for the segmentation of markets for new product introductions.

Endnotes

1. Thomas S. Robertson, "The Process of Innovation and the Diffusion of Innovation," Journal of Marketing, 31 (January 1967), 14–19.

2. James H. Donnelly, Jr., and Michael J. Etzel, "Degrees of Product Newness and Early Trial," Journal of Marketing Research, 10 (August 1973), 295–300.

3. Everett M. Rogers and F. Floyd Shoemaker, Communication of Innovations, 2nd ed. (New York: Free Press, 1971); and Gerald Zaltman and Ronald Stiff, "Theories of Diffusion," in Scott Ward and Thomas S. Robertson, eds., Consumer Behavior: Theoretical Sources (Englewood Cliffs, N.J.: Prentice-Hall, 1973), 416–68.

4. Rogers and Shoemaker, Communication of Innovations, 138–55.

5. Jagdish N. Sheth, "Perceived Risk and Diffusion of Innovation," in Johan Arndt, ed., Insights into Consumer Behavior (Boston: Allyn & Bacon, 1968), 173–88.

6. Robert W. Shoemaker and F. Robert Shoaf, "Behavioral Changes in the Trial of New Products," Journal of Consumer Research, 21 (September 1975), 104–9.

7. Lyman E. Ostlund, "The Role of Product Perceptions in Innovative Behavior," in Philip R. McDonald, ed., Marketing Involvement in Society and the Economy (Chicago: American Marketing Association, 1969), 259–66.

8. *Lyman E. Ostlund, "Perceived Innovation Attributes as Predictors of Innovativeness," Journal of Consumer Research, 1 (September 1974), 23–29.*

9. *Rogers and Shoemaker,* Communication of Innovations, *371–75.*

10. *Bruce Ryan and Neal C. Groas, "The Diffusion of Hybrid Seed Corn in Two Iowa Communities," Rural Sociology, 8 (March 1943), 15–24; James Coleman, Elihu Katz, and Herbert Menzel, "The Diffusion of an Innovation among Physicians," Sociometry, 20 (December 1957), 253–70; and Leon G. Schiffman, "Perceived Risk in New Product Trial by Elderly Consumers," Journal of Marketing Research, 9 (February 1972), 106–8.*

11. *Rogers and Shoemaker,* Communication of Innovations, *32–33.*

12. *Based upon* The Decision-Making Process in Purchasing Expensive Photographic Equipment *(a study conducted for* Popular Photography *by MPI Marketing Research, Inc., 1974).*

13. *Evertt M. Rogers,* Diffusion of Innovations *(New York: Free Press, 1962), 185.*

14. *Ibid., 152–59.*

15. *Robert A. Peterson, "A Note on Optional Adopter Category Determination," Journal of Marketing Research, 10, No. 3 (August 1973), 325–29.*

16. *Rogers,* Diffusion of Innovation, *81–86.*

17. *James F. Engel, Roger D. Blackwell, and Robert J. Kegerreis, "Consumer Use of Information in the Adoption of an Innovation," Journal of Advertising Research, 9 (December 1969), 3–8.*

18. *Sheth, "Perceived Risk and Diffusion," 185; and Jagdish N. Sheth, "Word-of-Mouth in Low Risk Innovations," Journal of Advertising Research, 11 (June 1971), 15–18.*

19. *Fred D. Reynolds and William R. Darden, "Why the Midi Failed," Journal of Advertising Research, 12 (August 1972), 39–44.*

20. *Rogers and Shoemaker,* Communication of Innovations, *104–5.*

21. *Ibid., 103.*

22. *John Jay Painter and Max L. Pinegar, "Post-High Teens and Fashion Innovation," Journal of Marketing Research, 8 (August 1971), 368–69.*

23. *Lawrence P. Feldman and Gary M. Armstrong, "Identifying Buyers of a Major Automotive Innovation," Journal of Marketing, 39 (January 1975), 47–53.*

24. *James F. Engel, Robert J. Kegerreis, and Roger D. Blackwell, "Word-of-Mouth Communication by Innovator," Journal of Marketing, 3 (July 1969), 15–19; and Thomas S. Robertson, "Purchase Sequence Responses: Innovators vs. Non-Innovators," Journal of Advertising Research, 8 (March 1968), 47–52.*

25. *Engel, Blackwell, and Kegerreis, "Consumer Use of Information," 5.*

26. *For example, see Johan Arndt, "Role of Product-Related Conversations in the Diffusion of a New Product," Journal of Marketing Research, 4 (August 1967), 291–95; and Thomas S. Robertson, "Determinants of Innovative Behavior," in Reed Moyer, ed.,* Changing Marketing Systems *(Chicago: American Marketing Association 1968), 328–32.*

27. *Jacob Jacoby, "Personality and Innovativeness Proneness," Journal of Marketing Research, 8 (May 1971), 244–47; Kenneth A. Coney, "Dogmatism and Innovation: A Replication," Journal of Marketing Research, 9 (November 1972), 453–55; and J. M. McClurg and I. R. Andrews, "A Consumer Profile Analysis of the Self-Service Gasoline Customer," Journal of Applied Psychology, 59 (February 1974), 119–21.*

28. *James H. Donnelly, Jr., "Social Character and Acceptance of New Products," Journal of Marketing Research, 7 (February 1970), 111–13; and Painter and Pinegar, "Post-High Teens," 369.*

29. James H. Donnelly, Jr., and John M. Ivancevich, "A Methodology for Identifying Innovator Characteristics of New Brand Purchasers," Journal of Marketing Research, 11 (August 1974), 331–34.

30. Donald T. Popielarz, "An Exploration of Perceived Risk and Willingness to Try New Products," Journal of Marketing Research, 4 (November 1967), 368–72; Donnelly and Etzel, "Degrees of Product Newness," 299; and James H. Donnelly, Jr., Michael J. Etzel, and Scott Roeth, "The Relationship between Consumers' Category and Trial of New Products," Journal of Applied Psychology, 57 (May 1973), 335–38.

31. Donnelly and Etzel, "Degrees of Product Newness," 299.

32. Schiffman, "Perceived Risk," 107; Thomas S. Robertson, "Consumer Innovators: The Key to New Product Success," California Management Review, 10 (Winter 1967), 28; and Edgar A. Pessemier, Philip C. Burger, and Douglas J. Tigert, "Can New Product Buyers Be Identified?" Journal of Marketing Research, 4 (November 1967), 352.

33. Schiffman, "Perceived Risk," 107; Robertson, "Consumer Innovators," 28; and Pessemier, Burger, and Tigert, "Can New Product Buyers Be Identified?" 352.

34. For example, see Arndt, "Role of Product-Related Conversations," 294; and Schiffman, "Perceived Risk," 107–8.

35. Engel, Blackwell, and Kegerreis, "Consumer Use of Information," 5; and McClurg and Andrews, "Consumer Profile Analysis," 120.

36. Johan Arndt, "Profiling Consumer Innovators," in Johan Arndt, ed., Insights into Consumer Behavior (Boston: Allyn & Bacon, 1968), 79.

37. Kenneth Uhl, Roman Andrus, and Lance Poulsen, "How Are Laggards Different? An Empirical Inquiry," Journal of Marketing Research, 7 (February 1970), 52.

38. Arndt, "Profiling Consumer Innovations," 79.

39. David B. Montgomerey, "Consumer Characteristics Associated with Dealing: An Empirical Example," Journal of Marketing Research, 8 (February 1971), 118–20; and Leon G. Schiffman and Clifford J. Neiverth, "Measuring the Impact of Promotional Offers: An Analytic Approach," in Thomas V. Greer, ed., 1973 Combined Proceedings (Chicago: American Marketing Association, 1974), 256–60.

40. Ronald E. Frunk and William F. Massy, "Innovation and Brand Choice: The Folger's Invasion," in Stephen A. Greyser, ed., Toward Scientific Marketing (Chicago: American Marketing Association, 1964), 106; and Arndt, "Profiling Consumer Innovators," 79.

41. Sheth, "Perceived Risk and Diffusion," 188.

42. John O. Summers, "Generalized Change Agents and Innovativeness," Journal of Marketing Research, 8 (August 1971), 313–16; and Thomas S. Robertson and James H. Myers, "Personality Correlates of Opinion Leadership and Innovative Buying Behavior," Journal of Marketing Research, 6 (May 1969), 164–68.

43. Schiffman, "Perceived Risk," 107; and Robertson, "Consumer Innovators," 28.

44. Engel, Blackwell, and Kegerreis, "Consumer Use of Information," 4.

45. Charles W. King, "Communicating with the Innovator in the Fashion Adoption Process," in Peter D. Bennett, ed., Marketing and Economic Development (Chicago: American Marketing Association, 1965), 429.

46. John O. Summers, "Media Exposure Patterns of Consumer Innovators," Journal of Marketing, 36 (January 1972), 43–49.

47. John J. Painter and Kent L. Granzin, "Profiling the Male Fashion Innovator— Another Step," in Beverlee B. Anderson, Advances in Consumer Research,

3 (Association for Consumer Research, 1976), 43; and William R. Darden and Fred D. Reynolds, "Backward Profiling of Male Innovators," Journal of Marketing Research, *9 (February 1974), 79–85.*

48. *Summers, "Media Exposure Patterns," 47–48.*

49. *King, "Communicating with the Innovator," 428; Painter and Granzin, "Profiling the Male Fashion Innovator," 43; and Painter and Pinegar, "Post-High Teens," 369.*

50. *Summers, "Media Exposure Patterns," 45–47.*

51. *Robertson, "Purchase Sequence Responses," 49.*

52. *Arndt, "Role of Product-Related Conversations," 293.*

53. *Robertson, "Consumer Innovators," 29; Painter and Granzin, "Profiling the Male Fashion Innovator," 42; and Louis E. Boone, "The Search for the Consumer Innovator,"* Journal of Business, *43 (April 1970), 138.*

54. *King, "Communicating with the Innovator," 430; and Painter and Pinegar, "Post-High Teens," 369.*

55. *Boone, "Search for the Consumer Innovator," 138.*

56. *For example, see Feldman and Armstrong, "Identifying Buyers," 50; McClurg and Andrews, "Consumer Profile Analysis," 120; and William E. Bell, "Consumer Innovators: A Unique Market for Newness," in Stephen A. Greyser, ed.,* Toward Scientific Marketing *(Chicago: American Marketing Association, 1963), 90–93.*

57. *For example, see Robert J. Kegerreis and James F. Engel, "The Innovative Consumer: Characteristics of the Earliest Adopters of a New Automotive Service," in Philip R. McDonald, ed.,* Marketing Involvement in Society and the Economy *(Chicago: American Marketing Association, 1969), 357–61; Feldman and Armstrong, "Identifying Buyers," 50; Bell, "Consumer Innovators," 90–93; and Boone, "Search for the Consumer Innovator," 138.*

Discussion questions

1. What are the essential differences between "product," "market," and "consumer" oriented definitions of a *new* product? Which definition do you feel is most suitable for the marketer? Why?

2. Describe how the manufacturer of a new type of cosmetic remover might use knowledge of the following five product characteristics to speed up the acceptance of the new product:
   a. relative advantage
   b. compatibility
   c. complexity
   d. trialability
   e. observability

3. An appliance manufacturer is considering the introduction of a new microwave oven that cooks food three times as fast as competitive ovens, while selling at about the same price. Identify those product characteristics that will influence the new oven's rate of acceptance.

4. Describe three dimensions of *time* that make it a particularly important factor in the diffusion of a product.

5. How might a firm alter its promotional appeal to effectively reach members of each of the following adopter categories:
   a. innovators
   b. early adopters
   c. early majority
   d. late majority
   e. laggards

6. Compare and contrast the basic nature of the *adoption* and *diffusion* processes. How are these two processes interrelated?

7. How would a profile of the *consumer innovator* assist a marketer planning a mass media advertising campaign for a new line of male cosmetics? Be specific in your recommendations.

8. Select three characteristics of the consumer innovator summarized in Table 14–5. For each of these consumer characteristics, indicate how a marketer might effectively use the profile information to positively influence the adoption process.

15

consumer decision making

Introduction

This final chapter ties together the relevant psychological, social, and cultural concepts developed throughout the book into a framework for understanding how consumers make decisions. Unlike Chapter 14, which examined the dynamics of *new* product adoption, this chapter takes a broader perspective, and examines consumer decision making within the context of *all* types of purchase choices, ranging from the purchase of new products to the selection of old and established products.

WHAT IS A DECISION?

Nothing is more difficult, and therefore more precious, than to be able to decide.

NAPOLEON I:
Maxims (1804–15)

Each of us makes numerous decisions every day concerning every aspect of our everyday lives. However, we generally make these decisions without stopping to think about *how* we make them, about what is involved in the decision making itself. In the most general terms, a decision is *the selection of an action from two or more alternative choices.*[1] In other words, in order for a person to make a decision, there must be more than one alternative available to him. To illustrate, if a person has a choice of purchasing Brand *X* or Brand *Y* or making no purchase at all, he is in a position to make a decision. On the other hand, if he has no alternative courses of action open to him, and he must act, then his single "non-choice" action does not constitute a decision. For example, if a person must make a purchase within a specific product category (say, milk) and only one brand and size are available (e.g., Borden's homogenized milk in quart containers), then this purchase does not involve a decision.

Table 15–1 summarizes various types of purchase-related decisions. While this list is not exhaustive, it does serve to demonstrate that the scope of consumer decision making is much broader than the mere selection of one brand from a number of brands.

TABLE 15–1

Types of Consumer Decisions

Decision category	Alternatives	
Basic purchase decision	To purchase a product (or service)	Not to purchase a product (or service)
Brand purchase decisions	To purchase a specific brand	To purchase another brand
	To purchase one's usual brand	To purchase another established brand (possibly with special features)
	To purchase a new brand	To purchase one's usual brand or some other established brand
	To purchase a standard quantity	To purchase more or less than a standard quantity
	To purchase an on-sale brand	To purchase a non-sale brand
	To buy a national brand	To buy a store brand
Channel purchase decisions	To purchase from a specific type of store (e.g., a department store)	To purchase from some other type of store (e.g., a discount store)
	To purchase from one's usual store	To purchase from some other store
	To purchase in-home (by phone or catalog)	To purchase in-store
	To purchase from a local store	To purchase from a store requiring some travel (out-shopping)

Three views of consumer decision making

Before presenting a simple model of how consumers make decisions, we will pause to consider several models of man that depict consumer decision making in distinctly different ways. The term *model of man* refers to a general perspective held by a significant number of people concerning how (and why) individuals behave as they do. Specifically, we will examine the following consumer-related models of man: (1) economic man, (2) passive man, and (3) problem-solving man.

ECONOMIC MAN

In the field of theoretical economics, which portrays a world of perfect competition, the consumer is often characterized as an "economic man" — that is, one who makes *rational decisions*. This model has been attacked by consumer researchers for a number of reasons. To behave rationally in the economic sense, a consumer would have to be aware of all available product alternatives, would have to be capable of correctly ranking each alternative in terms of its benefits and its disadvantages, and would have to be able to identify the one best alternative. However, consumers do *not* generally have enough information, or sufficiently accurate information, about the available brands in the product category under consideration to make perfect decisions.

According to a leading social scientist, the *economic man* model is unrealistic for the following reasons: (1) man is limited by his existing skills, habits, and reflexes, (2) man is limited by his existing values and goals, and (3) man is limited by the extent of his knowledge.[2] Thus, the consumer operates in an imperfect world, one in which he does not maximize his decisions in terms of such economic considerations as price-quantity relationships, marginal utility, or indifference curves. Instead, he usually settles for a "satisfactory" decision, one that is "good enough."[3] For this reason, the economic model of man is rejected as too idealistic and too simplistic.

PASSIVE MAN

Quite opposite to the economic man model is the *passive man* model, which depicts the consumer as basically submissive to the self-serving interests and promotional efforts of marketers. The following statement captures the flavor of the passive model of man:[4]

> *The image of man implied in advertising and in modern sales methods is one of a passive person, open and vulnerable to external and internal stimuli leading to spending. The unconscious becomes a vehicle for directing economic behavior. The prototype is the dissatisfied, restless housewife who, after husband and children have left for the day, visits the department store, lets herself be titillated by the exhibited goods, and spontaneously, without clear-cut wants and purpose, succumbs to the lure of salesmanship and buys something she does not "really" need and will later regret having bought.*

As this quotation implies, consumers are sometimes perceived as impulsive and irrational purchasers, ready to yield to the arms and aims of marketers. At least to some degree, the passive model of the consumer was subscribed to by the hard-driving supersalesman of old, who was trained to regard the consumer as an object to be manipulated. The following excerpt from a 1917 salesmanship text dramatically illustrates the long held belief in the dominance of the salesman over the unresisting, somewhat passive consumer:[5]

> In the development of the selling process, there are four distinct stages. First, the salesman must secure the prospect's undivided attention. Secondly, this attention must be sustained and developed into interest. Thirdly, this interest must be ripened into desire. And fourthly, all lingering doubts must be removed from the prospect's mind, and there must be implanted there a firm resolution to buy; in other words, the sale must be closed.

This view of the prospective consumer implies that if he does not buy, it is only because the salesman has failed to handle him properly.

The principal limitation of the *passive model of man* is that it fails to recognize that the consumer plays an equal, if not dominant, role in most buying situations by seeking out information about product alternatives and selecting the product that appears to offer the greatest satisfaction. All that we know about motivation (Chapter 2), selective perception (Chapter 3), learning (Chapter 4), attitudes (Chapter 6), communication (Chapter 7), and opinion leadership (Chapter 10) serves to support the proposition that consumers are *not* objects of manipulation. Therefore, this simple and single-minded view must also be rejected as an unrealistic model of consumer behavior.

PROBLEM-SOLVING MAN

The third model of man portrays consumers as *problem solvers*. Within this framework, consumers are pictured as entering the marketplace in search of products and services to fulfill their needs and enrich their lives. This model of man treats consumers as active seekers of information about available brands and retail outlets which enable them to make satisfactory choices.

Because *choice* is an inherent factor in all consumer decisions, risk (or uncertainty) also is an integral component of the problem-solving model. Chapter 3 discusses several types of consumer perceived risk (functional risk, economic risk, social risk, psychological risk) and the strategies consumers adopt for handling risk (e.g., collecting information about alternatives, patronizing specific retailers, brand loyalty). Such strategies depict the consumer as a problem-solver, attempting to effectively dispel the risk she perceives in making product choices.[6]

In contrast to the economic man model, the problem-solving model of man more realistically portrays the consumer as unlikely to obtain perfect product information about all available alternatives. Instead, his information-seeking efforts are likely to cease when he obtains what he perceives to be sufficient information concerning some of the alternatives to enable him to make an "adequate" decision.

In contrast to the passive man model, the problem-solving model portrays the consumer as an active pursuer and *user* of product-related information that will enable him to make a product decision. In a sense, the problem-solving model depicts a consumer who is somewhere between the extremes of the economic man and passive man models—a consumer who does not possess complete knowledge and therefore cannot make *perfect* decisions, but one who nevertheless actively seeks information and attempts to make *satisfactory* decisions.

The problem-solving model seems to capture the essence of a well educated and involved consumer who seeks information upon which to base consumption decisions. Our discussions of specific aspects of consumer decision making throughout the book have generally depicted a consumer who is consistent with the problem-solving model.

A simple model of consumer decision making

In this section, we will present a simple model of consumer decision making, one that reflects the picture of the general problem-solving consumer we have just considered. Our primary purpose in offering this model is to tie together many of the ideas discussed throughout this book on consumer decision making. The model is not designed to provide an exhaustive picture of the complexities of a consumer decision; rather, it is designed to synthesize and coordinate relevant concepts into a meaningful whole. We will conclude this final chapter with a brief review of several more comprehensive models of consumer decision making.

Figure 15–1 presents in schematic form our simple model of consumer decision making. The model has three major components: *input, process,* and *output.*

INPUT

The input component of our consumer decision making model consists of external influences that serve as sources of information about a particular product and which influence a consumer's product-related values, attitudes, and behavior. Chief among these input factors are the marketing-mix activities of organizations who are trying to communicate the benefits of their products to potential consumers, and nonmarketing social-cultural influences which affect the consumer's purchase decisions.

marketing inputs

The firm's marketing activities constitute a direct attempt to reach, inform, and persuade consumers to buy and use its products. These inputs to the consumer's decision making process take the form of specific marketing-mix strategies, which consist of: (1) the product itself (including its package, warranties, and guarantees), (2) mass-media advertising, personal selling, and other promotional efforts, (3) pricing policy, and (4) the selection of distribution channels to move the product from the manufacturer to the consumer.

social-cultural inputs

The second type of input, the social-cultural environment, also exerts a major influence on the consumer. Social-cultural inputs (examined in Part III) consist of a wide range of noncommercial influences. For example, the comments of a friend, usage by a family member, an editorial in the paper, or an article in *Consumer Reports* are all specific, and direct noncommercial sources of information. The influences of one's social class, culture, or subculture, though less tangible, are nevertheless important input factors that affect how consumers judge products and which products they eventually buy. Indeed, the unwritten codes of conduct communicated by culture indicate which purchases are considered "right" or "wrong." For example, until the mid-1950s, most men would not be seen wearing a red sweater; today, males wear clothing of every imaginable hue. Until the mid-1960s, few women would wear slacks to the office; today, pant suits are quite often the rule.

Unlike the firm's marketing efforts, social-cultural inputs do not necessarily *support* the purchase of a specific product. Instead, they may influence consumers to *avoid* the product by underscoring its negative features. For example, when fashion designers tried to introduce a longer hemline style some years ago, they were unable to do so because of widespread informal negative discussions among women.[7]

The cumulative impact of each firm's marketing efforts, the influence of family, friends, and neighbors, and society's existing code of behavior, are all inputs that are likely to affect what a consumer purchases and how he uses what he buys. Since these influences may be directed *to* the individual or actively sought *by* the individual, a two-headed arrow is used to link the input and process segments of our model (Figure 15–1).

PROCESS

The process component of our model is concerned with how consumers make decisions. To understand this process, we must consider the influences of many of the psychological concepts that were examined in Part II. In our model, the *psychological field* represents the internal influences that affect the consumer's decision making process (what the consumer feels she needs or wants, her awareness of various product choices, her information-gathering activities, and her evaluation of alternatives). As pictured in the process component, the act of making a consumer decision consists of three stages: (1) need recognition, (2) prepurchase search, and (3) evaluation of alternatives.

need recognition

The recognition of a need is likely to occur when a consumer perceives a problem that she desires to solve, such as a refrigerator that breaks down and has to be repaired or replaced. Within this context, the

FIGURE 15–1

A Simple Model of Consumer Decision Making

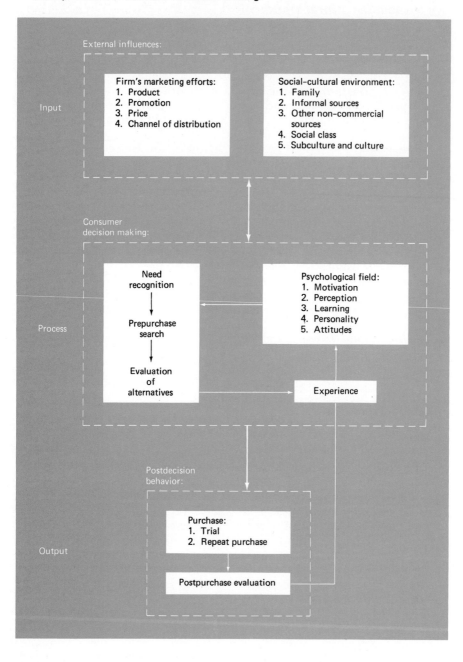

recognition of a need is the realization by the consumer that there is a difference between "what is" (e.g., a nonfunctioning refrigerator) and "what should be" (a refrigerator that keeps foods cold). Thus a consumer who is confronted with the reality that her present refrigerator is not working must quickly make plans to either repair it or replace it. If her refrigerator is relatively new or the estimated repair cost is low, she will probably have it repaired. If it is old or estimated repair costs are excessive, its malfunction will serve to trigger a search for information about various brands, types, styles, and sizes of refrigerators; an estimate of how much she can afford to spend on a new refrigerator; and a mental listing of retail outlets from which she might make the purchase.

prepurchase search

The prepurchase search state begins with the consumer's perception of a need that she feels may be satisfied by the purchase and consumption of a product. A sign that the consumer is at this stage is her active seeking out of information upon which to base a decision. The prepurchase information a consumer gathers is designed primarily to provide her with knowledge in two areas: (1) the identification of those brands from which she will make her selection, and (2) the criteria she will use to evaluate each brand. In our discussion of product perception (Chapter 3), we noted that those brands from which a person will make a choice are called her *evoked set*. The evoked set is generally only a part—a subset—of all the brands of which the consumer is aware; the brands she is aware of are, in turn, frequently only a segment of all the brands available on the market.[8] Making a selection from a *sample* of all possible brands is a human characteristic that helps simplify the decision making process.

The criteria a consumer employs in evaluating the brands that comprise her evoked set are usually product attributes that she feels are important to her. Examples of product attributes that consumers have employed as criteria in evaluating six product categories are presented in Table 15–2.

How much information a consumer will gather about alternative products (or brands) depends on the consumer and on the situation. For example, the consumer with a malfunctioning refrigerator may need to replace it immediately; thus, her search will be limited. She may rely primarily on past experience if she was satisfied with the performance of her old refrigerator. In this case, she would probably attempt to identify the retailers in her area that carry "her" brand. She might turn to the *Yellow Pages* for a listing of authorized appliance dealers who sell the brand she wants. If the refrigerator happens to be a store brand, such as Sear's Cold Spot, her search will be even simpler: she has only to visit the store to examine the current models and make her choice. If she has the time to consider a variety of brands, she might also turn to the *Yellow Pages,* this time to make a list of local appliance stores in which to look.

TABLE 15–2

Product Attributes Used as Purchase Criteria for
Six Product Categories

Brassieres	Lipstick	Mouthwash
Comfort	Color	Color
Fit	Container	Effectiveness
Life	Creaminess	Kills germs
Price	Prestige factor	Price
Style	Taste/flavor	Taste/flavor

Orange juice (frozen)	Toilet tissue	Toothpaste
Nutritional value	Color	Decay prevention
Packaging	Package size	Freshens mouth
Price	Price	Price
Taste/flavor	Strength	Taste/flavor
Texture	Texture	Whitens teeth

Source: Frank M. Bass and William L. Wilkie, *"A Comparative Analysis of Attitudinal Pre-dictions of Brand Preference,"* Journal of Marketing Research, *10 (August 1973), 263.*

She might even visit the library to determine which makes and models are rated highest by *Consumer Reports.*

The consumer's own prior experience is an important source of his prepurchase information. The consumer usually searches his memory (the "psychological field" depicted in the model) before seeking out external sources of information regarding a given consumer-related need. In this sense, past experience is an *internal* source of information. The greater the relevant past experience an individual possesses, the fewer the external sources of information he is likely to need in order to reach a decision. However, it is likely that, for many consumer decisions, a combination of both past experience (internal sources) and marketing and noncommercial information (external sources) is used before a decision is reached.

The amount of relevant prior experience is therefore an important determinant of the extent of external search that a consumer undertakes before making a product decision. Table 15–3 presents a comprehensive list of product, situational, and personal factors that are likely to *increase* the amount of information search a consumer will undertake as part of his decision making process.

evaluation of alternatives

After gathering what is felt to be a sufficient amount of prepurchase information, the consumer begins the evaluation process by ap-

TABLE 15–3

Factors That Are Likely to Increase Prepurchase Search

Product Factors

Long interpurchase time (a long lasting or infrequently used product)
Frequent changes in product styling
Frequent price changes
"Volume" purchasing (large number of units)
High price

Situational Factors

Experience:
   First time purchase
   No past experience because the product is new
   Past experience within the product category has been unsatisfactory
Social Acceptability:
   The purchase is for a gift
   The product is socially visible
Value-related Considerations:
   Purchase is discretionary rather than necessary
   All alternatives have both desirable and undesirable consequences
   Family members disagree on product requirements or evaluation of alternatives
   Product usage deviates from important reference group
   The purchase involves ecological considerations

Personal Factors

Demographic Characteristics of Consumer:
   Well educated
   High income
   White-collar occupation
   Under 35 years of age
Personality:
   Low dogmatic (open-minded)
   Low risk perceiver (broad categorizer)
Others Personal Factors:
   High product involvement
   Enjoyment of shopping and search

Adapted from Donald H. Granbois, "The Role of Communication in the Family Decision Making Process," in Stephen A. Greyser, ed., Toward Scientific Marketing *(Chicago: American Marketing Association, 1964), 50–56.*

praising the benefits to be derived from the various alternatives, and narrowing down her choices.

This process is accomplished by evaluating the brands in her evoked set in terms of the criteria that she feels reflect what she seeks in the product she will purchase. For example, the evoked set of our consumer in need of a new refrigerator might consist of the following three brands: General Electric, Frigidaire, and Sear's Cold Spot. She may consider the following five criteria most important in evaluating the three alternatives: color, brand name (trustworthiness), size (interior and exterior), special features (e.g., an automatic ice maker), and style. By some mental trade-off process or decision strategy (to be discussed later), she will come to a decision as to which brand to buy. Of course, she may also conclude that *none* of the alternatives offer sufficient benefits to warrant their purchase. If this were to occur with a necessity like a refrigerator, the consumer would probably either lower her standards and settle for the best of the available alternatives, or seek additional information about other brands, hoping to find one that more closely meets her criteria. If the purchase is more discretionary in terms of time (such as an oil painting for the living room), the consumer would probably postpone the purchase.

To sum up, the evaluation process is a kind of mental trial of the alternative choices in the consumer's evoked set, a process that ends in a decision. If the decision is to make a purchase, then the consumer advances to the output segment of our model. On the other hand, if the decision is *not* to purchase, the decision-making exercise becomes part of the individual's experience, and ends up as part of her *psychological field*, possibly to be used in the future.

OUTPUT

The output portion of the model is concerned with two closely associated kinds of postdecision activity: (1) purchase behavior and (2) postpurchase evaluation. The objective of both of these activities is to increase the consumer's satisfaction with his purchase.

purchase behavior

Consumers make two types of purchases: trial purchases and repeat purchases. If a consumer purchases a product (or brand) for the first time, and buys a smaller quantity than is usual for him, such a purchase would be considered a trial. Thus, trial is the exploratory phase of purchase behavior in which consumers attempt to evaluate a product through direct use. Research evidence indicates that when a consumer purchases a new brand about which he may be uncertain, he tends to purchase a smaller quantity than he would if it were a familiar brand.[9] Trial, of course, is not always feasible. For example, with most durable goods (dishwashers, air conditioners, refrigerators), a consumer usually moves directly from evaluation to a long-term commitment through purchase, without the opportunity for an actual trial.

If the consumer evaluates the trial of a product in a product category that she purchases on a regular basis (food products, cigarettes, beauty and health aids) as satisfactory or better than her previous brand, she is likely to repeat the purchase. Repeat purchase behavior is closely related to the concept of *brand loyalty*, which most firms try to encourage because it ensures them of stability in the marketplace. Therefore, unlike trial, in which the consumer uses the product on a small scale, a repeat purchase signifies that the product meets with the consumer's approval and that she is willing to use it in larger quantities.

postpurchase evaluation

As the consumer uses a product, particularly during a trial purchase, he evaluates its performance in light of his own expectations. For this reason, it is difficult to separate the trial of a product from the postpurchase evaluation of the product. The two go hand in hand.

An important component of postpurchase evaluation is the reduction of any lingering uncertainty or doubt that the consumer might have about his selection. The consumer, as part of his postpurchase analysis, tries to convince himself that his choice was a wise one; that is, he attempts to reduce *postpurchase cognitive dissonance* (see Chapter 6). He does this by adopting any one of the following strategies: (1) he may rationalize the decision as being wise, (2) he may seek out advertisements that support his choice and avoid those of competitive brands, (3) he may attempt to persuade his friends or neighbors to buy the same brand (and thereby confirm his own beliefs), and (4) he may turn to other satisfied owners for reassurance.

The degree of postpurchase analysis a consumer undertakes is likely to depend on the importance of the product decision and the experience he acquires in using the product. If the product lives up to his expectations, he will probably buy it again. However, if the product's performance is disappointing, he will undoubtedly discontinue its use, and the next time a similar need arises he will search for a more suitable alternative. Thus, the consumer's postpurchase evaluation "feeds back" as *experience* to the consumer's psychological field, and serves to influence future related decisions.

SOME ADDITIONAL POINTS ABOUT CONSUMER DECISION MAKING

To put our model of consumer decision making into proper perspective, we will briefly consider three additional aspects of purchase choice behavior: (1) levels of consumer decision making, (2) consumer decision strategies, and (3) group decision making.

levels of consumer decision making

Not all purchase decisions encompass the same level of problem solving; that is, not all consumer decisions require the same degree of mental or physical effort. This is fortunate—if all purchase decisions required extensive effort, consumer decision making would be an exhausting process that left little time for anything else. On the other hand, if all purchases were routine, they would tend to be monotonous and would provide little pleasure or novelty. On a continuum of effort ranging from very high to very low, we can distinguish three specific levels of consumer decision making: (1) extensive problem solving, (2) limited problem solving, and (3) routinized response behavior.[10]

EXTENSIVE PROBLEM SOLVING. When a consumer has no established criteria for evaluating a product category or specific brands within the category, or has not narrowed down the number of brands he will consider to some small manageable subset (the evoked set), his decision making process can be classified as *extensive problem solving*. At this level, the consumer needs a great deal of information in order to establish a set of criteria on which to judge specific brands, and a correspondingly large amount of information concerning each of the brands to be considered.

LIMITED PROBLEM SOLVING. At this level of problem solving, the consumer has already established his basic criteria for evaluating the product category and the various brands within the category. However, he has no fully established preferences concerning a select group of brands. His search for additional information is more like "fine tuning;" he has to gather additional brand information in order to discriminate among the various brands.

ROUTINIZED RESPONSE BEHAVIOR. At this level, the consumer has some experience with the product category and a well established set of criteria with which to evaluate the brands in his evoked set. In some situations, he may search for a small amount of additional information; in others, he simply reviews what he already knows.

Just how extensive a consumer's problem-solving task is depends on how well established his criteria are for selection, how much information he has about each brand he is considering, and how narrow is the set of brands (the evoked set) from which he will choose. Clearly, extensive problem solving implies that the consumer must seek a greater amount of information in order to make a choice, while routinized response behavior implies a minimum need for additional information.

consumer decision strategies

Consumer decision strategies have been broadly categorized as either optimizing or simplifying procedures.[11] With an *optimizing* decision strategy, the consumer evaluates each brand option in terms of all nontrivial criteria (e.g., product features or attributes). For example, if a consumer were contemplating the purchase of one of three headache remedies and had four relevant product criteria in mind—speed of relief, total amount of relief, safety, and cost—he would evaluate each brand in terms of each of the four relevant criteria, then select the brand that he believed would provide the greatest potential satisfaction. In contrast, a consumer following a *simplifying* decision strategy might choose a brand on the basis of only one relevant criterion. For example, he may select one of the three brands of headache remedies solely because of its reputation as "the fastest-acting brand." We have illustrated only two decision strategies; in reality, there are many variations of both optimizing and simplifying decision strategies that a consumer might employ.[12] Which strategy is used often depends on a variety of factors, such as the product category (e.g., frequently purchased grocery products versus durable goods), the consumer's personality, and the specific need he hopes to satisfy.

Since the marketer's objective is to convince consumers to purchase *his* brand from among all possible alternatives, an understanding of which decision strategies consumers are likely to choose is useful in formulating the marketing effort.[13] For example, a marketer familiar with the consumer's likely decision strategy could prepare promotional messages in a format that would facilitate the process, or he might even suggest how the consumer should make a decision. Figure 15–2 presents an advertisement for a quality camera which asks the readers to "Compare the advantages." The body copy provides the interested reader with eight specific criteria on which to compare various alternative brands. The second line of the headline, "FTb is the obvious choice," suggests that after a comparative evaluation, the Canon FTb camera will be selected. Thus this advertisement not only provides information about the camera, it also suggests the criteria the decision maker should use in arriving at his choice.

group decision making

Our discussion of consumer decision making has focused on the individual decision maker and the commercial and noncommercial information sources that influence his consumption decisions. However, not all purchases reflect individual decisions. As indicated in our discussion of family decision making, very often family purchase decisions are a group or joint process that actively and directly involves two or more family members (see Chapter 9). In such situations, the marketer must determine the relevant decision-making roles of all concerned family members so that he may direct appropriate advertising messages to the influential family members.

Comprehensive models of consumer behavior

It is fitting to end this final chapter with a discussion of earlier comprehensive models of consumer buying behavior that examine consumer decision making from several different perspectives. Some of these complex models have been designed primarily to tie together or to

FIGURE 15–2

Advertisement Suggesting Criteria for Decision Making

Compare the advantages. FTb is the obvious choice.

We think that the FTb is the best camera in its class in the world. It earned this distinction. It has solid value. Meticulous construction and quality. It has the kind of refined performance features, versatility and human engineering you'd expect from Canon. But don't take our word for it. Decide for yourself.

● Exposure Metering
Any photographer serious about precision in exposure knows that it's vital to understand the exact area of the subject that the camera's metering. The spot metering system of the FTb measures only the central 12% of the viewfinder area. In difficult exposure situations, you never have to doubt that your exposures will be perfect.

● Breech Lock Mount
The lens mount of the FTb and all Canon SLR's is the exclusive Breech Lock system. When you push a lens, the breech lock ring automatically turns slightly. All you have to do for a secure fit is turn the ring a little more. And because there's no turning between lens mount and body, there's no wear to affect sharpness.

● The Viewfinder
The FTb's viewfinder has everything you need to stay in complete control. It shows shutter speeds, over- and under-exposure warning marks, a stopped-down metering index and meter needle and aperture indicator ring. The bright focusing screen has a microprism focusing aid, and the metering area is shaded, so you never have to guess what you're measuring.

● Versatility
The unique FTb Booster lets the FTb read down to an exposure level of f/1.2 at 15 seconds with ASA 100 film (EV-3.5)! This coupled with the host of Canon accessories for every job from photomicrography to astro-photography makes the FTb a camera a novice can grow with—or a pro can stick with.

● Flash Photography
The exclusive CAT (Canon Auto Tuning) system for automatic electronic flash couples both to selected FD lenses *and* the camera's metering system. To use it, just focus and align meter needles as usual. Whatever you've focused on will be precisely exposed. Period.

● Film Loading
The FTb incorporates Canon's exclusive QL quick film loading system. All you do is position the film leader, close the back and start winding. It saves time and prevents film waste.

● Lenses
The FTb accepts all of the nearly forty superb Canon lenses, from 7.5mm Fish Eye to 1,200mm Super-Telephoto. These lenses are tops in sharpness, contrast and mechanical quality. They incorporate all of the latest optical refinements, including Spectra and Super Spectra Coating, the Canon Floating System and the most modern optical glasses.

● Control Flexibility
The FTb's Stopped-Down/Self-Timer lever activates the self-timer *and* stops the lens down for checking depth-of-field. Adjacent controls can lock the aperture and lock up the mirror.

Canon® FTb

Canon USA, Inc., 10 Nevada Drive, Lake Success, New York 11040. Canon USA, Inc., 140 Industrial Drive, Elmhurst, Illinois 60126. Canon USA, Inc., 123 Paularino Avenue East, Costa Mesa, California 92626. Canon USA, Inc., Bldg. B-2, 1050 Ala Moana Blvd., Honolulu, Hawaii 96814. Canon Optics & Business Machines Canada, Ltd., Ontario.

Courtesy of Canon USA, Inc.

summarize the contents of a specific consumer behavior book. Taken together, they provide insights for the design of future research which might more fully explain or predict consumer behavior.

Interest in comprehensive models of consumer behavior is a rather recent phenomenon. Within a relatively short time (since the mid-fifties), a variety of models have been proposed by consumer researchers. We have selected for examination three models of *individual* decision making and one model of *joint* or *group* decision making.[14] These specific models were selected because we believe them to be good illustrations of the "state of the art" of integrative models of consumer behavior. We have attempted to keep our discussion of the components, variables, and interrelationships of the various parts of each model as simple as possible, even at the risk of understating the uniqueness or richness of the models. The reader who desires a complete description of any of these models is encouraged to consult the original sources.

NICOSIA MODEL

The Nicosia model focuses on the relationship between the firm and its potential consumers.[15] In the broadest terms, the firm communicates with consumers through its marketing messages (its advertising), and consumers communicate with the firm by their purchase responses. Thus the Nicosia model is *interactive* or circular in design: the firm tries to influence the consumers, and the consumers—by their actions (or inaction)—influence the firm.

In its full-blown form, the Nicosia model is an elaborate computer flowchart of the consumer decision making process. For our purposes, it is sufficient to examine a *summary* flowchart which highlights the full model. As depicted in Figure 15–3, the Nicosia model is divided into four major fields: (1) the span between the source of a message to the consumer's attitude, (2) search and evaluation, (3) the act of purchase, and (4) feedback. A brief discussion of each of these four fields and related subfields follows.

field 1: the source of a message to the consumer's attitude

The first field of the Nicosia model is divided into two subfields. Subfield One includes aspects of the firm's marketing environment and communications effort which affect consumer attitudes, such as product attributes, competitive environment, characteristics of relevant mass media, the choice of a message appeal or theme, and characteristics of the target market.

Subfield Two specifies various dimensions of the consumer's predispositions (e.g., personality and experience) which mediate her reception of the firm's messages. The output of the first field is an *attitude* toward the product based on the consumer's interpretation of the message.

FIGURE 15–3

Summary Flowchart of the Nicosia Model of Consumer Decision Processes

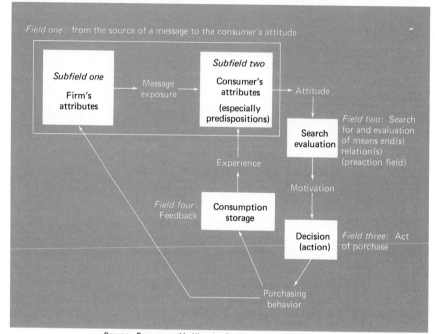

Source: Francesco M. Nicosia, Consumer Decision Processes *(Englewood Cliffs, N.J. Prentice-Hall, 1966), 156.*

field 2: search and evaluation

The second field of the Nicosia model deals with the search for relevant information and the evaluation of the firm's brand in comparison to other alternatives. The output of this stage is motivation to purchase the firm's brand. (Of course, evaluation could also lead to rejection of the firm's brand; however, the model illustrates a positive response.)

field 3: the act of purchase

In the third field, the consumer's motivation toward the firm's brand results in actual purchase of the brand from a specific retailer.

field 4: feedback

The final field consists of two important types of feedback from the purchase experience; one to the firm in the form of sales data, and the second to the consumer in the form of experience (satisfaction or dissatisfaction). The consumer's experience with the product affects her attitudes and predispositions concerning future messages from the firm.

HOWARD-SHETH MODEL

The Howard-Sheth model is a major revision of an earlier systematic effort to develop a comprehensive theory of consumer decision making.[16] Among its important features, the Howard-Sheth model explicitly distinguishes between three levels or stages of decision making: (1) extensive problem solving, (2) limited problem solving, and (3) routinized problem solving (see our discussion earlier in this chapter). A simplified version of the Howard-Sheth model is presented in Figure 15-4. The model consists of four major sets of variables: (1) inputs, (2) perceptual and learning constructs, (3) outputs, and (4) exogenous (i.e., external) variables (not depicted in Figure 15-4). A brief description of each of these sets of variables follows.

inputs

The input variables consist of three distinct types of stimuli or information sources in the consumer's environment. Physical brand characteristics (*significative* stimuli) and verbal or visual product characteristics (*symbolic* stimuli) are stimuli supplied by the marketer in the form of product or brand information. The third type of stimulus is provided by the consumer's social environment (his family, reference groups, and social class). All three types of stimuli provide inputs concerning the product class or specific brands to the prospective consumer.

perceptual and learning constructs

The central component of the Howard-Sheth model consists of psychological variables which are assumed to operate when the consumer is contemplating a decision. While these constructs are the "heart" of the model, Howard and Sheth treat them as abstractions which are not operationally defined or directly measured. Some of the variables are perceptual, and are concerned with how the consumer receives and processes information acquired from the input stimuli and other parts of the model. For example, "stimulus ambiguity" occurs if a consumer is unclear about the meaning of information received from the environment, and "perceptual bias" occurs if the consumer distorts the information that is received so that it fits his established needs or experiences.[17]

There are also learning constructs, which include the consumer's goals, information about brands in his evoked set, criteria for evaluating alternatives, preferences, and buying intentions. The proposed interaction (linkages) between the various perceptual and learning variables and the variables in the other segments of the model give the Howard-Sheth model its distinctive character.

outputs

The model indicates a series of outputs that correspond in name to some of the perceptual and learning construct variables (attention,

FIGURE 15–4

Simplified Version of the Howard-Sheth Model of Buyer Behavior

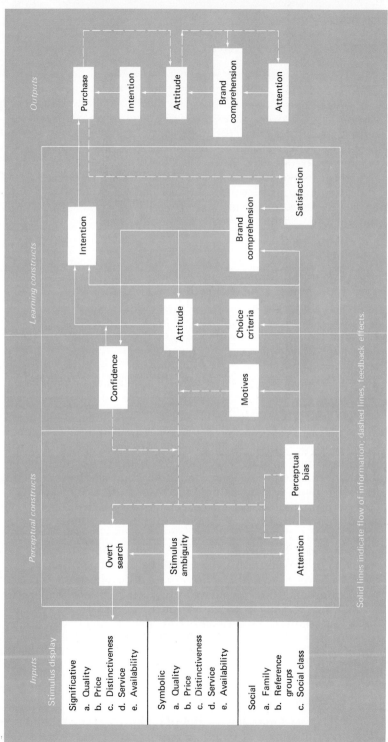

Source: John A. Howard and Jagdish N. Sheth, The Theory of Buyer Behavior (New York: John Wiley, 1969), 30.

brand comprehension, attitudes, intention) in addition to the actual purchase.

Exogenous variables are not directly part of the decision making process and are not shown in the model presented here. However, because external variables influence the consumer, they should concern the marketer in his segmentation efforts. Some of the important exogenous variables include: importance of the purchase, consumer personality traits, time pressure, and financial status.

In an effort to understand the underlying relationships among the variables, Howard and Sheth have tested the model with actual data on consumer decision making.[18] The first test, undertaken with the cooperation of the General Foods Corporation, focused on the instant breakfast market.[19] It found that consumers are quite systematic in their use of information and in their establishment of attitudes about brands.

A more recent test of the model examined consumers' decisions to purchase a Vega automobile.[20] From their analysis of the data, the researchers concluded that informal influence (particularly information acquired from friends) was more critical than information gained from advertisements for the Vega.[21] However, while advertising was found to be a relatively ineffective information source, exposure to a Vega advertising message did have some impact on comprehension of the Vega's features and on the intention to purchase. Future research on a wider range of products and services is needed to obtain a better picture of the strengths and limitations of commercial and noncommercial information sources on various aspects of the consumer decision making process.

ENGEL-KOLLAT-BLACKWELL MODEL

The Engel-Kollat-Blackwell model of consumer behavior was originally designed to serve as a framework for organizing the fast-growing body of knowledge called consumer behavior.[22] Like the Howard-Sheth model, it has gone through a number of revisions aimed at improving its descriptive ability and clarifying basic relationships between components and subcomponents.[23] Figure 15–5 presents the latest version of this comprehensive model, which consists of four basic components: (1) a central control unit, (2) information processing, (3) the decision process, and (4) environmental influences. A brief description of each of these components follows.

central control unit

The central control unit is a kind of "brain center," which uses four basic psychological characteristics as *filters* through which stimuli concerning a consumer decision must pass. The four subcomponents of the central control unit are: (1) stored information and past experience, which serve as a memory (an internal reference for considering product or brand alternatives), (2) evaluative criteria or attributes which an individual consumer employs in judging likely alternatives, (3) general and specific attitudes which influence purchase choice, and (4) basic or enduring personality traits which influence how the consumer is likely to respond to purchase alternatives.

information processing

The information processing component consists of the consumer's *selective* exposure, attention, comprehension, and retention of product or brand information (stimuli) from marketing and nonmarketing sources. According to the model, in order for a product or brand message to be filtered into the central control unit, the consumer must be exposed to it, must attend to it, must comprehend it, and must retain it. Thus, as depicted in Figure 15–5, these four perceptual dimensions provide information which the central control unit filters or selectively processes.

decision process

The decision process component of the model consists of five basic stages: (1) problem recognition, (2) internal search and evaluation, (3) external search and evaluation, (4) purchase processes, and (5) decision outcomes. How many of these stages actually figure into a specific purchase decision depends on how extensive is the problem-solving task. For example, in "extended decision process behavior," the consumer is assumed to pass through all five stages; in "habitual decision process behavior," the consumer is assumed to advance directly from internal search to actual purchase.

environmental influences

The fourth and final component of the model consists of the environmental influences that may affect the consumer at various stages in the decision making process. The specific environmental factors noted are income, culture, family, social class, and physical situations. It is suggested that any of these factors may block or alter the consumer's decision making process; thus they serve as intervening variables.

A COMPREHENSIVE MODEL OF FAMILY DECISION MAKING

Earlier in this chapter we indicated that very often family consumption decisions are more appropriately described as *group* or *joint* decisions rather than as individual decisions.

FIGURE 15–5

The Engel-Kollat-Blackwell Model of Consumer Behavior

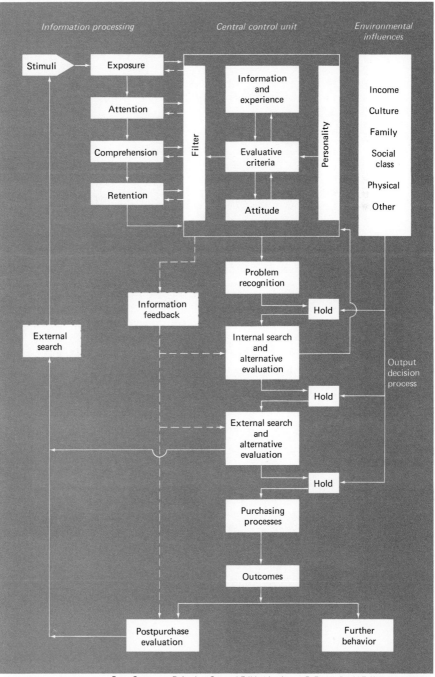

From Consumer Behavior, *Second Edition by James F. Engel, David T. Kollat, and Roger D. Blackwell. Copyright © 1968, 1973 by Holt, Rinehart and Winston, Inc. Reprinted by permission of Holt, Rinehart and Winston.*

FIGURE 15-6

A Model of Family Decision Making

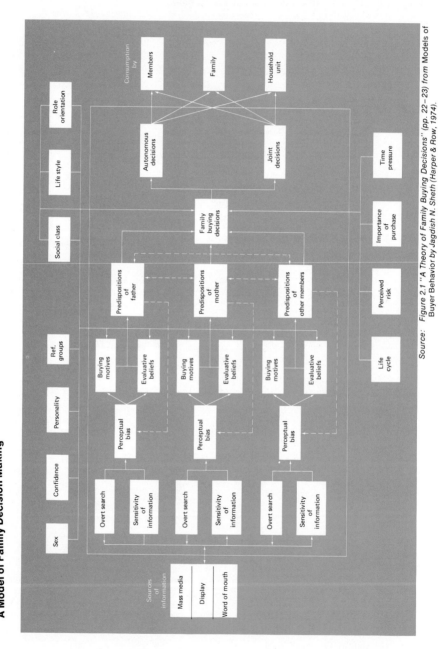

Source: *Figure 2.1 "A Theory of Family Buying Decisions" (pp. 22–23) from Models of Buyer Behavior by Jagdish N. Sheth (Harper & Row, 1974).*

Figure 15–6 presents a model of the family decision making process.[24] The left side of the model depicts separate psychological systems, which represent the distinct predispositions of the father, the mother, and other family members. These separate predispositions lead into "family buying decisions," which may be either individually or jointly determined.

The right side of the model lists seven family and product factors that influence whether a specific purchase decision will be autonomous or joint: (1) social class, (2) life-style, (3) role orientation, (4) family life cycle stage, (5) perceived risk, (6) product importance, and (7) time pressure. The model suggests that joint decision making tends to prevail in families that are middle class, closely knit, with few prescribed family roles, and newly married. In terms of product-specific factors, it suggests that joint decision making is more prevalent when there is a great deal of perceived risk or uncertainty, when the purchase decision is considered to be important, and when there is ample time to make a decision. (For a discussion of how these seven factors influence joint and individual decision making, see Chapter 9.)

Of all the consumer decision models presented here, only the Howard-Sheth model has been subjected to systematic testing. To the best of our knowledge, the Nicosia model has not been tested since its original development to the time of this writing, the Engel-Kollat-Blackwell model has received only modest small-scale testing, and the family model has not been tested. Given the still rather primitive "state of the art" for testing complex decision making models, it may be some time before comprehensive decision making models are adequately tested.[25]

Nevertheless, the future of comprehensive models of consumer behavior seems promising because of the opportunity these models provide to tie together what is known about consumers, and because they are useful as a framework for undertaking new research. For the marketing manager and the public policy maker, such "grand" models may eventually provide a clearer and more accurate picture of what makes people buy, and thus will produce a stronger foundation for the design and regulation of marketing strategy.

Summary

The consumer's decision to purchase or reject a product is the moment of final truth for the marketer. It signifies whether his marketing strategy has been wise, insightful and effective, or whether it was poorly planned and missed the mark. Thus, marketers are particularly interested in the consumer decision making process. In order for a consumer to make a decision, there must be more than one alternative available to him. (The decision *not* to buy is also an alternative.)

Theories of consumer decision making vary, depending on the

researcher's own assumptions about the nature of man. The various "models of man" (economic man, passive man, and problem-solving man) depict the consumer and his decision making process in distinctly different ways.

A simple consumer decision making model was presented which ties together the psychological, social, and cultural concepts examined in Parts II and III into an easily understood framework. This decision model has three distinct sets of variables: input variables, process variables, and output variables.

Input variables that affect the consumer's decision making process include commercial marketing efforts as well as noncommercial influences from the consumer's social-cultural environment. The decision *process* variables are influenced by the consumer's own psychological field, which affects his recognition of a need, his prepurchase search for information, and his evaluation of alternatives. The *output* phase of the model includes the actual purchase (either trial purchase or repeat purchase) and postpurchase evaluation. Both prepurchase and postpurchase evaluation feed back in the form of *experience* into the consumer's psychological field, and serve to modify his future decision processing.

The various levels of consumer decision making include extensive problem solving, limited problem solving, and routinized response behavior. Consumers employ a variety of decision strategies in making brand choice decisions, ranging from complex optimizing strategies to simplifying strategies.

Most consumer behavior models describe the decision making processes of individual consumers; however, there is increasing interest in the joint or group decision making processes often undertaken by families. Several comprehensive models of consumer behavior were briefly examined, including the Nicosia model, the Howard-Sheth model, the Engel-Kollat-Blackwell model, and the Sheth family buying model.

As the study of consumer behavior progresses into a mature, scientific discipline, it is likely that consumer researchers will increasingly consider the development and testing of these and other comprehensive models of consumer behavior in order to better understand the decision process. Knowledge of how individuals make consumption decisions is important to students of human behavior, to students of marketing behavior, and to the public policy planners who shape the environment in which we all must function.

Endnotes

1. *This definition is similar to the one suggested in Irwin D. J. Bross,* Design for Decision *(New York: Free Press, 1953), 1.*

2. Herbert A. Simon, Administrative Behavior, 2nd ed. *(New York, Free Press, 1965), 40.*

3. James G. March and Herbert A. Simon, Organizations *(New York: John Wiley, 1958), 140–41.*

4. Walter A. Weisskopf, "The Image of Man in Economics," Social Research, *40 (Autumn 1973), 560.*

5. John G. Jones, Salesmanship and Sales Management *(New York: Alexander Hamilton Institute, 1917), 29.*

6. *For interesting ideas on consumer decision strategies, see Lawrence X. Tarpey, Sr., and J. Paul Peter, "A Comparative Analysis of Three Consumer Decision Strategies,"* Journal of Consumer Research, *2 (July 1975), 29–37.*

7. Fred D. Reynolds and William R. Darden, "Why the Midi Failed," Journal of Advertising Research, *12 (August 1972), 39–44.*

8. John A. Howard and Jagdish N. Sheth, The Theory of Buyer Behavior *(New York: John Wiley, 1969), 26.*

9. Robert W. Shoemaker and F. Robert Shoaf, "Behavioral Changes in the Trial of New Products," Journal of Consumer Research, *2 (September 1975), 104–9.*

10. Howard and Sheth, Theory of Buyer Behavior, *27 and 46–47.*

11. Peter Wright, "Consumer Choice Strategies: Simplifying vs. Optimizing," *Journal of Marketing Research, 12 (February 1975), 60–67.*

12. *Ibid., 61.*

13. Peter L. Wright, "Use of Consumer Judgment Models in Promotional Planning," Journal of Marketing, *37 (October 1973), 32.*

14. *Several other particularly noteworthy comprehensive models not reviewed here are: Alan R. Andreason, "Attitudes and Customer Behavior: A Decision Model," in Lee Preston, ed.,* New Research in Marketing *(Berkeley: Institute of Business and Economic Research, University of California, 1965), 1–16; Flemming Hansen,* Consumer Choice Behavior *(New York: Free Press, 1972); and Frederick E. Webster, Jr., and Yoram Wind, "A General Model for Understanding Organizational Buying Behavior,"* Journal of Marketing, *36 (April 1972), 12–19.*

15. Francesco M. Nicosia, Consumer Decision Processes *(Englewood Cliffs, N.J.: Prentice-Hall, 1966), especially 156–88.*

16. Howard and Sheth, Theory of Buyer Behavior, *especially 24–49.*

17. *Ibid., 36–37.*

18. *For example, see John U. Farley, John A. Howard, and L. Winston Ring,* Consumer Behavior: Theory and Applications *(Boston: Allyn & Bacon, 1974); and Donald R. Lehmann et al., "Some Empirical Contributions to Buyer Behavior Theory,"* Journal of Consumer Research, *1 (December 1974), 43–55.*

19. Stanley E. Cohen, "Ads a 'Weak Signal' in Most Buying Decisions: Howard," Advertising Age, *June 12, 1972, 3 and 78.*

20. *Ibid., 78.*

21. *Ibid.*

22. James F. Engel, David T. Kollat, and Roger D. Blackwell, Consumer Behavior *(New York: Holt, Rinehart & Winston, 1968), 40.*

23. James F. Engel, David T. Kollat, and Roger D. Blackwell, Consumer Behavior, *2nd ed. (Holt, Rinehart & Winston, 1973), 49.*

24. Jagdish N. Sheth, "A Theory of Family Buying Decisions," in Jagdish N. Sheth, *ed.,* Models of Buyer Behavior *(New York: Harper & Row, 1974) 17–33.*

25. *For a discussion of the problems of testing consumer behavior models, see Gerald Zaltman, Christian R. A. Pinson, and Reinhard Angelman,* Metatheory and Consumer Behavior *(New York: Holt, Rinehart & Winston, 1973); and Shelby D. Hunt,* Marketing Theory *(Columbus, Ohio: Grid, 1976).*

Discussion questions

1. Briefly describe how a consumer is assumed to make a decision in terms of the economic, passive, and problem-solving models of man.

2. Give an example (not mentioned in the text) of a product which you believe is influenced, either positively or negatively, by the social-cultural environment. Explain.

3. Identify three different products that you believe require reasonably intensive prepurchase search by a consumer. Then, using Table 15-3 as a guide, identify the characteristics of these products that make intensive prepurchase search likely.

4. Discuss the role of a consumer's evoked set in evaluating brand alternatives.

5. Describe a recent purchase you have made in terms of the model of consumer behavior presented in Figure 15-1.

6. Describe the general characteristics of extensive, limited, and routinized decision making.

7. Using a product that you are familiar with, distinguish between optimizing and simplifying decision strategies.

8. Select a newspaper or magazine advertisement that attempts to provide the consumer with a decision strategy to be followed in making a purchase decision. Explain the decision strategy.

EPILOGUE

Consumer behavior is a young, fast growing discipline built upon the theoretical foundations of more mature sciences. Principles from the fields of psychology, sociology, and cultural anthropology are used to shed light on the behaviors of individuals in their consumption-related roles. As interest in *why* and *how* individuals make their consumer decisions has grown among marketers, policy planners, and academicians, consumer researchers have delved more and more deeply into the study of consumer behavior. Their findings have provided meaningful insights into this most prevasive human activity. We believe future studies will help to strengthen the conceptual framework we have tried to build, so that consumer behavior can develop into a mature and more predictable science, and a more consistently rewarding activity for all of us.

glossary

Absolute Threshold. The lowest level at which an individual can experience a sensation.

Acculturation. The learning of a new or "foreign" culture.

Achieved Role. A role expected of an individual as the result of some factor concerned with his or her personal attainment, such as level of education, income, occupational status, or marital status.

Achievement Need. The need for personal accomplishment as an end in itself.

Acquired Needs. Needs that are learned in response to one's culture or environment (such as the need for esteem, prestige, affection, or power). Also called secondary needs.

Action Tendency Component. An element of the tri-component model of attitude. The relation between attitudes and actual buying behavior is typically made through the action tendency component.

Activities, Interest, and Opinions (AIO's). See psychographic characteristics.

Actual Self Concept. The image that an individual has of himself as a certain kind of person, with certain characteristic traits, habits, possessions, relationships, and behavior.

Adaptation. Becoming accustomed to a sensation or a specific stimulation (such as a hot bath), so that it no longer produces a sharp sensation.

Adopter Categories. A sequence of categories which describes how early (or late) a consumer adopts a new product in relation to other adopters. The five typical adopter categories are: innovators, early adopters, early majority, late majority and laggards.

Adoption. See adoption process.

Adoption Process. The stages through which an individual consumer passes in arriving at a decision to try (or not to try), to continue using (or to discontinue using) a new product. The five stages of the traditional adoption process are: awareness, interest, evaluation, trial, and adoption.

Affiliation Need. The need for friendship, for acceptance, and for belonging.

Aggressive individual. One of three personality types identified by Karen Horney. The aggressive person is one who moves *against* others (e.g., who competes with others).

Aided Recall Measures. A technique frequently used to measure advertising awareness, in which a respondent may be told the product class or given some other cue concerning the advertisement to be recalled.

Ascribed Role. A role expected of an individual as the result of factors over which he has no control, such as age, sex, family, race, or religion.

Aspirational Group. A group to which a nonmember would like to belong.

460

Assimilation-Contrast Theory. A theory of attitude change which suggests that consumers are likely to accept only moderate attitude changes. If the change suggested is too extreme, the contrast with presently held attitudes will cause total rejection of the entire advertisement. An extreme belief-changing message is likely to be perceived as more extreme than it actually is; and contrast (and thus rejection) can be predicted.

Attitudes. Learning tendencies to perceive and act in some consistently favorable or unfavorable manner with regard to a given social object or idea, such as a product, service, brand, company, store, or spokesperson.

Autonomous Decisions. Family purchase decisions in which either the husband or the wife makes the final decision.

Avoidance Group. A group with which a non-member does not identify and does not wish to be identified, and of whose values, attitudes, or behavior he disapproves.

Awareness. The first stage of the traditional adoption process.

Bachelorhood. The first stage of the family life cycle, in which young single adults do not live with their parents.

Beliefs. Mental or verbal statements that reflect a person's particular knowledge and assessment about some idea or thing.

Brand Loyalty. Consistent purchasing of one brand or service in a specific product category.

Category Width. The range or number of choices a person tends to consider when making product decisions. Broad categorizers are more likely to risk a poor product choice in order to maximize their opportunity to make good choices; narrow categorizers prefer to limit their purchase decisions to known and safe choices.

Classical Conditioning. A learning process in which behavior is stimulated by a cue that has been associated with a stimulus to the resultant behavior, but that does not, itself, normally cause that behavior.

Closure. A principle of Gestalt psychology that stresses the individual's need for completion. This need is reflected in the individual's subconscious reorganization and perception of incomplete stimuli as complete or whole pictures.

Cognitive Component. See perceptual component.

Cognitive Dissonance. A theory that predicts that when a new fact, belief, or attitude is inconsistent with an existing belief or attitude, a feeling of dissonance occurs which the individual resolves by changing the more weakly held attitude in the direction of the stronger attitude.

Communication. The transmission of a message through selected channels by a sender to a receiver, designed to influence the receiver in a way that the sender intends.

Comparative Reference Group. A group whose norms serve as a benchmark for highly specific or narrowly defined types of behavior. (See normative reference group.)

Comparison Advertising. Advertising that explicitly names or identifies one or more competitors of the advertised brand for the purpose of claiming superiority, either on an overall basis or on selected product attributes.

Compatibility. The degree to which potential consumers feel that a new product is consistent with their present needs, values, and practices.

Complexity. The degree to which a new product is difficult to comprehend and/or to use.

Compliant Individual. One of three personality types identified by Karen Horney. The compliant person is one who moves *toward* others (e.g., one who desires to be loved, wanted, and appreciated by others).

Composite-Variable Index. An index that combines a number of socioeconomic variables (such as education, income, occupation) to form one overall measure of social class standing. (Also see single-variable index.)

Concept. A mental image of an intangible trait, characteristic, or idea.

Conformity. The extent to which an individual adopts attitudes and/or behavior that are consistent with the norms of a group to which he belongs or would like to belong.

Construct. A term that represents or symbolizes an abstract trait or characteristic, such as motivation or aggression.

Consumer Behavior. The behavior consumers display in searching for, purchasing, using, and evaluating products, services, and ideas that they expect will satisfy their needs.

Consumer Innovator. A consumer who is one of the earliest purchasers of a new product.

Consumer Socialization. The process by which an individual first learns the skills and attitudes relevant to functioning as a consumer.

Contactual Group. A formal or informal group with which a person has regular face-to-face contact and with whose values, attitudes, and standards he tends to agree.

Content Analysis. A method for systematically

and quantitatively analyzing the content of verbal and/or pictorial communication. The method is frequently used to determine prevailing social values of a society.

Continuous Innovation. A "new" product entry which is an improved or modified version of an existing product rather than a totally new product. A continuous innovation has the least disrupting influence on established consumption patterns.

Cross-Cultural Consumer Analysis. Research designed to determine to what extent the consumers of two or more nations are similar or different in relation to specific consumption behavior.

Culture. The sum total of learned beliefs, values, and customs that serve to guide the behavior of members of a particular society.

Customs. Overt modes of behavior that constitute culturally approved or acceptable ways of behaving in a specific situation.

Decision. A choice made from among several possible alternatives.

Decision Time. Within the context of the diffusion process, the amount of time required for an individual consumer to accept or reject a specific new product.

Deconsumption. The promotion of selective curtailment or elimination of specific purchase activities by consumers.

Demarketing. The marketing task of discouraging consumers or consumer segments from purchasing selected goods.

Demographic Segmentation. The division of a total potential market into smaller subgroups on the basis of such objective characteristics as age, sex, marital status, income, occupation, or education.

Dependent Variable. A variable whose value will change as a result of a change in another (that is, independent) variable. For example, consumer purchases are a dependent variable subject to level and quality of advertising (the independent variable).

Depth Interview. A research technique designed to uncover consumers' underlying attitudes and/or motivations through lengthy and relatively unstructured interviews.

Detached Individual. One of three personality types identified by Karen Horney. The detached person is one who moves away from others (for instance, one who desires independence, self-sufficiency, and freedom from obligations).

Differential Threshold. The minimal difference (that is, the "just noticeable difference") that can be detected between two stimuli. See also Weber's Law.

Diffusion Process. The process by which an innovation is accepted over time by the members of a social system.

Disclaimant Group. A group with which a member prefers not to identify (for instance, those of whose values, attitudes, or behavior he disapproves).

Discontinuous Innovation. A dramatically new product entry that requires the establishment of new consumer behavior patterns.

Dissolution. The final stage of the family life cycle, which consists of only *one* of the original spouses.

Dogmatism. A personality trait that measures the amount of rigidity a person displays towards information that is contrary to his own established beliefs.

Drive. An internal force that impels a person to engage in an action designed to satisfy a specific need.

Dynamically Continuous Innovation. A new product entry that is sufficiently innovative to have some disruptive effects on established consumer patterns.

Economic Man Model. A model of man that depicts the consumer as a perfectly rational being who is able to objectively evaluate and rank each product alternative and select the alternative that gives him the most value for his money.

Ego. In Freudian theory, the part of the personality that serves as the individual's conscious control. It functions as an internal monitor that balances the impulsive demands of the *id* and the social-cultural constraints of the *superego*.

Emotional Motives. Motives or goals based on subjective criteria, such as love, pride, fear, affection, or self-esteem.

Enculturation. The learning of the culture of one's own society.

Engel-Kollat-Blackwell Model. One of several comprehensive models of consumer behavior.

Evaluation. The third stage of the traditional adoption process, in which the consumer either draws conclusions about the product innovation or determines if he needs further information.

Evaluation of Alternatives. A stage in the consumer decision making process in which the consumer appraises the benefits to be derived from each of the product alternatives he or she is considering so that the choice may be narrowed down.

Evaluative Component. An element of the tri-component attitude model.

Evoked Set. The specific brands a consumer considers in making a purchase choice in a particular product category.

Extended Family. A household consisting of a husband, wife, offspring, and at least one other blood relative.

Extensive Problem Solving. A search by the consumer to establish the necessary product criteria to enable him to knowledgeably evaluate and select the most suitable product to fulfill his needs.

Extrinsic Cues. Cues, external to the product (such as price, image of the store that carries it, and image of the manufacturer who produces it), which serve to influence the consumer's perception of a product's quality.

Family. Two or more persons related by blood, marriage, or adoption who reside together.

Family Branding. The assignment of the same brand or "family" name to two or more products on the theory that if one brand is successful, another product with the same brand name will be more rapidly accepted. See also Stimulus Generalization.

Family Gatekeeper. A family member who controls the flow of information about a product or service into the family, thereby regulating the related consumption decisions of other family members.

Family Influencer. A family member who provides product-related information and advice to other members of the family, thereby influencing the related consumption decisions.

Family Life Cycle. The classification of family units into meaningful stages through which most families pass, such as bachelorhood, honeymooners, parenthood, postparenthood, and dissolution.

Fatigue. See Habituation, Wear-Out.

Formal Group. A group that has a clearly defined structure, specific roles and authority levels, and specific goals, such as a political party.

Formal Interpersonal Communication. Direct communication between a person who speaks to one or more other people on behalf of a profit or non-profit organization, (e.g., a discussion between a salesman and a prospect).

Freudian Theory. A theory of personality and motivation developed by the psychoanalyst Sigmund Freud. (See psychoanalytic theory.)

Geographic Segmentation. The division of a total potential market into smaller subgroups on the basis of geographic variables. (e.g. region, state, or city).

Goals. The sought-after results of motivated behavior. One fulfills a need through achievement of a goal.

Group. Two or more people who interact on either a regular or irregular basis in their pursuit of individual or common goals.

Group Cohesiveness. The extent to which group members tend to "stick together" and follow the norms of the group.

Group Norms. The implicit rules of conduct or standards of behavior which members of a group are expected to observe.

Habit. A consistent pattern of behavior performed without considered thought. Consistent repetition is the hallmark of habit.

Habituation. The mechanism by which an individual systematically ignores those stimuli (e.g., products or advertising messages) that are predictable or readily recognizable because of prior repeated exposure. See also Wear-Out.

Honeymooners. A stage of the family life cycle consisting of young married couples with no children.

Howard-Sheth Model. One of several comprehensive models of consumer behavior.

Hypothesis. A tentative statement of a relationship between two or more variables.

Hypothetical Construct. See Construct.

Id. In Freudian theory, the part of the personality that consists of primitive and impulsive drives that the individual strives to satisfy.

Ideal Self Concept. The way an individual would like to perceive himself (as opposed to actual Self-Concept—the way he actually perceives himself).

Impersonal Communication. Communication directed through mass media channels to a large and diffused audience (also called *mass communication*).

Independent Variable. A variable that can be manipulated to effect a change in the value of a second (that is, dependent) variable. For example, price is an independent variable that often affects sales (the dependent variable).

Index of Status Characteristics (ISC). A measure of social class that weights the following four socioeconomic variables into one single index of social class standing: occupation, source of income (*not* amount), house type, and dwelling area. (Also called *Warner's ISC.*)

Informal Group. A group of people who see each other frequently on an informal basis, such as weekly poker-players or friends who take turns entertaining each other on a monthly basis.

Informal Interpersonal Communication. Direct communication between two or more people who are friends, neighbors, relatives, or coworkers.

Innate Needs. Basic physiological needs such as hunger, thirst, sex. Also called *primary needs,* or biogenic needs.

Innovation-Decision Process. An update of the traditional adoption process model. The model consists of the following four stages: knowledge, persuasion, decision, and confirmation.

Innovativeness. A measure of a consumer's willingness to try new products.

Innovator. See Consumer Innovator.

Institutional Advertising. Advertising designed to promote a favorable company image rather than to promote specific products.

Instrumental Conditioning. A form of learning based on rewarding of the desired response. To the subject, the response becomes "instrumental" in causing the reward.

Interest. The second stage of the traditional adoption process. During this stage the consumer actively seeks out information upon which to form an opinion of the product innovation's possible benefits.

Interpersonal Communication. Communication that occurs directly between two or more people by mail, by telephone or in person.

Intrinsic Cues. Physical characteristics of the product (such as size, color, flavor, and aroma) which serve to influence the consumer's perceptions of product quality.

Joint Decisions. Family purchase decisions in which the husband and wife are equally influential.

Just Noticeable Difference (J.N.D.). The minimal difference that can be detected between two stimuli. See also Differential Threshold and Weber's Law.

Key Informant Method. A method of measuring various aspects of consumer behavior (such as opinion leadership or social class) whereby a knowledgeable person is asked to classify individuals with whom he is familiar into specific categories.

Learning. The effect of experience on tendencies to behave in a particular way in response to given stimuli or situations.

Life-style. See psychographic characteristics.

Limited Problem Solving. A search by a con-

sumer for a product that will satisfy his basic criteria from among a selected group of brands.

Manufacturer's Image. The way in which consumers view (i.e., perceive) the "personality" of the firm that produces a specific product.

Marketing. Activities designed to enhance the flow of goods, services, and ideas from producers to consumers in order to satisfy consumer needs and wants.

Marketing Concept. A consumer-oriented philosophy which suggests that satisfaction of consumer needs and wants should provide the focus for product development and marketing strategy in order for the firm to meet its own organizational goals.

Marketing Mix. The unique configuration of the four basic marketing variables (product, promotion, price, and channels of distribution) over which a marketing organization has control.

Market Segmentation. The division of a large heterogeneous market into smaller segments, homogeneous in relation to some characteristic relevant to a target product, in order to develop a distinct marketing mix for one or more segments.

Maslow's Need Hierarchy. A theory of motivation which postulates that individuals strive to satisfy their needs according to a basic hierarchical structure, starting with physiological needs, then moving on to safety needs, then social needs, ego needs, and self-actualization needs.

Mass Communication. See Impersonal Communication.

Membership Group. A group to which a person either belongs or qualifies for membership.

Model. A simplified representation of reality designed to show the relationships between the various elements of a system or process under investigation.

Motivation. The driving force within an individual which impels him to action. This driving force is produced by a state of tension that exists as the result of an unfilled need.

Motivational Research. A type of consumer research designed to uncover consumers' subconscious or hidden motivations. The basic premise of motivational research is that the consumer is not always aware of the basic reasons underlying her actions.

Need Hierarchy. See Maslow's need hierarchy.

Need Recognition. The realization by the consumer that there is a difference between "what is" and "what should be."

Neo-Freudian Personality Theory. A school of psychology that stresses the fundamental role of social relationships in the formation and development of personality.

Nicosia Model. One of several comprehensive models of consumer behavior.

Normative Reference Group. A group that influences the general values or behavior of an individual. (See comparative reference group.)

Nuclear Family. A household consisting of a husband and wife and at least one offspring.

Objective Measurement of Social Class. A method of measuring social class whereby individuals are asked specific socioeconomic questions concerning themselves or their families. On the basis of their answers, people are placed within specific social class groupings.

Observability. The ease with which a product's benefits or attributes can be observed, visualized, or described to potential customers.

Observational Research. Research procedures designed to study the actual behavior of consumers. The objective of such research is to draw inferences or conclusions about consumers' needs, motivations and attitudes from their actual shopping-related behavior.

Opinion Leader. A person who informally influences the attitudes or behavior of others.

Opinion Leadership. A social communication process by which one person influences the attitudes and behavior of others, who may be opinion seekers or merely opinion recipients. This influence is informal and usually verbal.

Opinion Leadership Overlap. The degree to which people who are opinion leaders in one product category are also opinion leaders in one or more other categories.

Opinion Recipient. One who informally receives the advice or opinions of another (the opinion leader).

Opinion Seeker. One who informally seeks the advice or opinion of another.

Optimizing Decision Strategy. A strategy whereby a consumer evaluates each brand in terms of significant product criteria. (Also see simplifying decision strategy.)

Organizational Consumer. A purchasing agent (or group) who buys the goods, services, or equipment necessary for the organization (which may be a business, government agency, or other institution, profit or nonprofit) to function.

Parenthood. A stage of the family life cycle consisting of married couples with at least one child living at home.

Partial Reinforcement A partial or inconsistent reward for a particular kind of behavior (e.g., a type of purchase). Although learning research indicates that experimental subjects who are not rewarded on every trial generally continue to perform longer and harder than subjects who are rewarded consistently, inconsistent rewards such as occasional poor product quality do not encourage repeat purchase behavior.

Participant Observer. A researcher who becomes an active member of the environment he is studying.

Passive Man Model. A theory of man that depicts the consumer as basically submissive to the promotional efforts of marketers.

Perceived Quality. The quality attributed to a product by the consumer on the basis of various informational cues associated with the product. (See intrinsic and extrinsic cues.)

Perceived Risk. The degree of uncertainty perceived by the consumer as to the consequences or outcomes of a specific purchase decision. Generally, the greater the perceived risk, the less likely the individual is to make the purchase.

Perception. The process by which an individual selects, organizes, and interprets stimuli into a meaningful and coherent picture of the world.

Perceptual Blocking. The subconscious screening out or blocking of stimuli that are threatening or inconsistent with one's needs, values, beliefs, or attitudes.

Perceptual Component. The informational element of the tri-component model of attitude.

Perceptual Defense. The process of subconsciously distorting stimuli that are threatening or inconsistent with one's needs, values, beliefs, or attitudes.

Perceptual Mapping. A research technique that enables marketers to plot consumers' perceptions concerning product attributes of competing brands.

Perceptual Organization. The subconscious ordering and perception of stimuli in groups or configurations, according to certain principles of Gestalt psychology.

Personal Consumer. The individual who buys goods and services for his or her own use, for household use, for the use of a family member, or for a friend. (Sometimes referred to as the *ultimate consumer* or *end user*.)

Personality. The inner psychological characteristics that determine and reflect how a person will respond to his or her environment.

Personality Scale. A series of questions or statements designed to measure a single personality trait.

Personality Test. A pencil-and-paper test designed to measure an individual's personality in terms of one or more traits or inner characteristics.

Positioning. Establishing a clear discriminative position for a specific brand in the consumer's mind. See also Product Positioning.

Postparenthood. A stage of the family life cycle consisting of older married couples whose children live permanently apart from them.

Postpurchase Dissonance. Cognitive dissonance which occurs after a consumer has made a purchase commitment. The consumer resolves this dissonance through a variety of strategies designed to convince him of the wisdom of his choice.

Postpurchase Evaluation. An assessment of a product, based on actual trial, as to whether the product fulfills expectations.

Power Need. The need to exercise control over one's environment, including other persons or various objects.

Prepotent Need. An overriding need, from among several needs, that serves to initiate goal-directed behavior.

Prepurchase Search. A stage in the consumer decision making process in which the consumer perceives a need and actively seeks out information concerning products that will help satisfy that need.

Price-Quality Relationship. The perception of price as an indicator of product quality (e.g., the higher the price, the higher the perceived quality of the product).

Primary Group. A group of people who interact (e.g., meet and talk) on a regular basis, such as members of a family, neighbors, or co-workers.

Primary Needs. See innate needs.

Problem Solving Man Model. A model of man which portrays the consumer as an active seeker of information that will enable him to make satisfactory purchase decisions.

Product Image. The "personality" that consumers attribute to a product or brand.

Product Positioning. A marketing strategy designed to project a specific image for a product, either by itself or in relation to competitive products (such as Mercedes as the dependable luxury car).

Projective Techniques. Research procedures designed to identify consumers' subconscious feelings and motivations. These tests are often based on the presentation of ambiguous stimuli such as incomplete sentences, word association

tests, cartoons, and inkblots to consumers for interpretation.

Psychoanalytic Theory. A theory of motivation and personality which postulates that unconscious needs and drives, especially sexual and other biological drives, are the basis of all human motivation and personality.

Psychographic Characteristics. Intrinsic psychological, social-cultural and behavioral characteristics that reflect how an individual is likely to act in relation to consumption decisions. (Also, frequently referred to as *life-style* or *activities, interests, and opinion (AIO)* characteristics.)

Psychographic Segmentation. The division of a total potential market into smaller subgroups on the basis of intrinsic characteristics of the individual, such as personality, buying motives, lifestyle, attitudes, or interests.

Rate of Adoption. The percentage of adopters within a specific social system who have adopted a new product by a given time period.

Rational Motives. Motives or goals based on economic or objective criteria, such as price, size, weight, or miles per gallon.

Recognition Measures. A research technique in which the consumer is shown a specific advertisement and is asked whether he or she has seen it.

Reference Group. A group that serves as a frame of reference for an individual making a consumption decision.

Relative Advantage. The degree to which potential customers perceive a new product as superior to existing substitutes.

Reliability. The degree to which a measurement instrument is consistent in what it measures.

Repeat Purchase. The act of repurchasing the same product or brand after an earlier usage.

Reputational Measurement of Social Class. A method of measuring social class whereby knowledgeable community members are asked to judge the social class position of other members of their community. (See key informant method.)

Role. A pattern of behavior expected of an individual in a specific social position, such as the role of mother, daughter, teacher, or lawyer. One person may have a number of different roles, each of which is relevant in the context of a specific social situation.

Routinized Response Behavior. A habitual purchase response from a small group of product alternatives based on predetermined criteria.

Secondary Group. A group of people who interact infrequently or irregularly, such as two women who meet for the first time since high school days.

Secondary Needs.   See Acquired Needs.

Selective Attention.   The heightened awareness of stimuli relevant to one's needs or interests, and the depressed awareness of stimuli irrelevant to one's needs.

Selective Exposure.   Conscious or subconscious exposure of the consumer to certain media or messages, and the subconscious or active avoidance of others.

Self-Designated Method.   A method of measuring some aspect of consumer behavior (such as opinion leadership) in which a person is asked to evaluate or describe his own attitudes or actions.

Self-Image.   The image a person has of himself as a certain kind of person, with certain characteristic traits, habits, possessions, relationships, and behavior.

Self Perception Theory.   A theory whose main assumption is that a person knows that he has an attitude only by observing himself behaving in an attitude-consistent way.

Sensation.   The immediate and direct response of the sensory organs to simple stimuli (for example, color, brightness, loudness, smoothness).

Sensory Receptors.   The human organs which receive sensory inputs (eyes, ears, nose, mouth, skin). Their sensory functions are to see, hear, smell, taste, and feel.

Simplifying Decision Strategy.   A strategy whereby the consumer evaluates alternative brands in terms of one relevant criterion. (Also see optimizing decision strategy.)

Single-Variable Index.   The use of a single socioeconomic variable (such as income) to estimate an individual's relative social class. (Also see composite-variable index.)

Sleeper Effect.   The tendency for persuasive communication to lose the impact of source credibility over time (i.e., the influence of a message from a high credibility source will tend to decrease over time, while the influence of a message from a low credibility source will tend to increase over time).

Social Character.   In the context of consumer behavior, a personality trait that ranges on a continuum from *inner-directedness* (reliance on one's own "inner" values or standards) to *other-directedness* (reliance on others for direction).

Social Class.   The division of members of a society into a small number of distinct status classes, so that members of each class have relatively the same status and members of all other classes possess either less or more status.

Social-Cultural Segmentation.   The division of a total potential market into smaller subgroups on the basis of sociological or cultural variables, such as social class, stage in the family life cycle, religion, race, nationality, values, beliefs, or customs.

Socioeconomic Status Scores (SES).   A social class measure used by the United States Bureau of the Census which combines the following three socioeconomic variables into one measure of social class standing: occupational status, family income, and educational attainment.

Sociometric Method.   A method of measuring opinion leadership whereby the actual pattern of person-to-person informal communication is traced.

Status.   The relative prestige accorded to an individual or the position he or she occupies within a specific group or social system.

Stimulus.   Any unit of input to any of the senses. Examples of consumer stimuli include products, packages, brand names, advertisements, and commercials.

Stimulus Discrimination.   The ability to differentiate between alternative stimuli because of perceived differences between them.

Stimulus Generalization.   The extension of a response to a given stimulus to stimuli with somewhat similar characteristics.

Store Image.   The way in which consumers perceive the "personality" of a store and the products it carries.

Subculture.   A distinct cultural group that exists as an identifiable segment within a larger, more complex society.

Subjective Measurement of Social Class.   A method of measuring social class whereby people are asked to estimate their *own* social class position.

Subliminal Perception.   Perception of very weak or rapid stimuli received beneath the level of conscious awareness.

Superego.   In Freudian theory, the part of the personality that represents the individual's internal expression of society's moral and ethical codes of conduct. It serves to insure that the individual satisfies his needs in a socially acceptable fashion.

Supraliminal Perception.   Perception of stimuli at or above the level of conscious awareness.

Symbolic Group.   A group in which an individual is not likely to receive membership, despite the fact that he identifies with the group by adopting its values, attitudes, or behavior (for instance, the Baseball Hall of Fame may be a symbolic group for a 12 year old Little Leaguer).

Theory.   A hypothesis or group of hypotheses that offers an explanation of behavior.

Trait.   A distinguishing and relatively enduring personality characteristic of an individual.

Trait Theory.   A theory of personality that focuses on the measurement of personality in terms of specific psychological characteristics or constructs called *traits*.

Trial.   The fourth stage of the traditional adoption process in which the consumer tries the product innovation on a limited basis.

Trialability.   The degree to which a new product is capable of being tried by consumers on a limited basis (for instance, through free samples and small quantities).

Trial Purchase.   A type of purchase behavior in which the consumer purchases a product for the first time, frequently in a smaller quantity than is usual, in order to evaluate it.

Tri-Component Model.   A theory of attitude structure that views attitudes as consisting of three components: perceptions, evaluations, and action tendencies. The relationships between each component influences the nature of consumer behavior in any given situation.

Two-Step Flow of Communication Theory.   A communication model that portrays opinion leaders as direct receivers of information from mass media sources who in turn interpret and transmit this information to the masses.

Unaided Recall Measures.   An approach frequently used to measure advertising awareness, in which a respondent is provided with no cues as to the identity or product class of the advertisement to be recalled.

User Behavior Segmentation.   The division of a total potential market into smaller subgroups on the basis of product and brand usage (e.g., by rate of usage or brand loyalty).

Validity.   The degree to which a measurement instrument accurately reflects what it is designed to measure.

Value Instruments.   Data collection instruments used to ask people how they feel about basic personal and social concepts such as freedom, comfort, national security, and peace.

Values.   Beliefs, relatively few in number, that serve as guides for what is considered to be "appropriate" behavior, that are relatively enduring or stable over time, and that are widely accepted by the members of society.

Variable.   A thing or idea that may vary (that is, assume a succession of values).

Venturesomeness.   A personality trait that measures a consumer's willingness to accept the risk of purchasing new products.

Warner's Index of Status Characteristics.   See index of status characteristics (ISC).

Wear-Out.   The point at which repeated exposure to a stimulus, such as an advertising message, no longer has a positive or reinforcing influence on attitudes or behavior.

Weber's Law.   Used to compare similar stimuli of different intensities. It states that the stronger the initial stimulus, the greater the additional intensity needed for the second stimulus to be perceived as different.

Index